A

AMERICAN PANORAMA

Portraits of 50 States
By Distinguished Authors

A **HOLIDAY** MAGAZINE BOOK

DOUBLEDAY & COMPANY, INC.

Garden City, New York

The illustrations in this book are the work of the photographers listed:

John Lewis Stage — Massachusetts, Connecticut, Rhode Island, Delaware, Texas

Pinto Studios — New Jersey
Laurence Lowry — New York, Illinois, Florida
Elliott Erwitt — Washington, D.C., Iowa
Tom Hollyman — Virginia, Georgia, California, Missouri
David E. Scherman — Mississippi
Ewing Krainin — Hawaii
Walt Dyke — Oregon
Ray Atkeson — Utah
Emil Schulthess — Idaho
George Leavens — Colorado
Josef Muench — Arizona
Thomas Peter Lake — Louisiana
George Leavens — Nebraska

AMERICAN PANORAMA

EAST OF THE MISSISSIPPI

A HOLIDAY MAGAZINE BOOK

DOUBLEDAY & COMPANY, INC.

Garden City, New York

Contents

Part II   *The Mid Atlantic States*

Part III   *The East Central States*

Contents

Introduction

The twenty-six states east of the Mississippi are the older half of the Republic, a series of regions within a region whose boundary lines are a great ocean and our greatest river. When we use the expression "Eastern United States," we are knowingly imprecise, for this land mass with its patchwork of history and manners and folklore is an arbitration of geography. New England, the industrial Middle Atlantic states, the sensitive South, the Middle West: to the Westerner, with his feeling of living in a growing-up land, all this is the East. Yet the difference between Boston and Miami, between Kentucky and the Pennsylvania Dutch country, is as deep-seated as it is dramatic. The climate varies sharply, so does the topography, even more do the people.

Besides a common purpose, the people of this region share a consciousness of living in the crucible of American history. Here are the landmarks, the monuments, the scars of a noble experiment. Here the past envelops, as in the West the future beckons. Another past is here, too, the past of Europe, for this is the region watered by the streams of immigration, in which hundreds of thousands from old countries found promise and fulfillment in the new, as did the original settlers before them. These ties to Europe, financial, cultural, emotional, remain strong and persistent. Finally, the East is the seat of our government, the center of commerce and industry, the marketplace where much of our money is made and many of our goods manufactured and dispersed.

This book is a gallery of portraits of the Eastern states, including Washington, D.C., and is part of Holiday's continuing coverage of the United States. They were drawn by some of the country's most distinguished writers. Together with its companion volume, *American Panorama: West of the Mississippi*, it provides a quilted pattern of this country—its people, its character, its beauty, its hope.

The Editors

American Panorama

East of the Mississippi

PART I *New England*

Maine

by ARTHUR BARTLETT

When the District of Maine was separated from the Commonwealth of Massachusetts in 1820, a Maine man under the spell of
the mother state's ponderous phraseology proposed that it set itself
up as the Commonwealth of Maine. A more typical Maine man,
serving as a delegate to the convention, promptly objected. "It'll be
called a state, wun't it?" he demanded. "What's the sense in naming
it Jonathan if it's alluz going to be called just plain John?" This
realism prevailed, and Maine became the State of Maine. Moreover,
the decision so won the approval of a people to whom pretentiousness
is at once the most amusing and the most unforgivable of foibles, and
whose pride in the lack of it sometimes seems pretentious, that, to
this day, State of Maine is the common usage. It is spoken almost
as if it were one word, and a Maine man is invariably a State-of-
Mainer.

In these days, when an average summer finds more than a million
paying guests swarming into Maine, whose year-round population
is something less than a million, the stubborn insistence of the typical
State-of-Mainer on being himself, and his amused disdain for people
who talk big, often tend to conflict with his pecuniary instincts. Some
years ago, for instance, some publicity-minded individuals hit upon
an idea for getting Maine's tourist and resort business some free advertising, and persuaded the legislature to decree that all the state's

automobile registration plates, except those issued for hearses, should have the word Vacationland on them. This boosterism offends the natural conservatism and sense of dignity of many State-of-Mainers, and a determined attempt was made in the legislature to put an end to it.

One prominent legislator, noted for his dry, down-East manner of speech, declared that he had formed the instinctively defensive habit of approaching his car from the front, where there is no plate. "Seeing that thing," he announced solemnly, "always induces a mild attack of nausea."

The principal argument of those opposing the tag line on the plates was that it created the impression that Maine is *nothing but* a vacationland. The naïveté of the occasional outlander who thinks that moose roam constantly on the streets of Maine cities and that everything north of Portland (actually near the southern tip of the state) is uncharted wilderness produces the same combination of amusement and irritation in many State-of-Mainers that many Midwesterners feel from hearing of Europeans who think that Indians and cowboys still ride wild just west of Jersey City.

The question, "What on earth do you do here after the summer people leave?" is another frequent irritant; and the late Shavy Noyes, the town of Norway's favorite sidewalk philosopher for many years, gave a lady summer visitor the classic answer: "Oh, we jest fumigate." The summer visitors are an important source of income for the state, however, and the anti-Vacationlanders lost their fight to purge the registration plates of the boosterism. Indeed, so thriving is the business of accommodating tourists and vacationers, particularly during July and August, that one somewhat sour motorist who had driven into the state on U. S. Route 1, expecting to house his family for the night in one of the many tourist-cabin establishments along the road, stopped finally at the headquarters of the State of Maine Publicity Bureau, on the outskirts of Portland, and suggested an additional phrase for the registration plates: making them read: Vacationland—No Vacancies.

Maine is nearly as large as the five other New England states combined, and can suit almost any topographical taste, whether for seacoast, woods, lakes, streams or mountains. Its mountains, admittedly, are less grandiose and concentrated than the White Mountains of neighboring New Hampshire; but it is nevertheless a definitely bumpy state, with hundreds of protuberances ranging from good-sized hills to the 5267-foot Mount Katahdin, which compilers of Maine's triumphs claim as the first spot in the United States to feel the morning sun. More than four fifths of the state is still wooded; and—to dispose immediately of as many statistics as possible—it has 2465 lakes and ponds, ranging from millponds to forty-mile-long Moosehead, one of the largest lakes completely within one state; five large rivers and 5147 smaller rivers and streams; and a direct coast line of nearly 250 miles, so notched with bays and inlets that its tidal line is nearly ten times that long, and equal in length to one half the whole Atlantic coast line of the United States.

With all this to offer, plus a northern climate which assures moderate summer days and cool summer nights, Maine has been in the vacation business for more than a hundred years, ever since a group of rich New Yorkers discovered Mount Desert Island before the Civil War, and started the Bar Harbor summer colony. The father of Mrs. J. Pierpont Morgan, Sr., was one of the original summer settlers, and Bar Harbor has thrived, through the years, on the patronage of such wealthy families as the Rockefellers, Vanderbilts, Whitneys, Stotesburys, Pulitzers and McCormicks. It was, however, the late Henry Ford, who put cars within reach of families of moderate income, who made recreation Big Business for Maine. The state today has perhaps half a dozen big summer hotels where the rates tend to limit the clientele to the wealthier classes, and Bar Harbor has branches of the New York shops; but it is the thousands of smaller hotels, overnight cabins, sports camps, tourist homes, roadside lunches, and all the service-of-supply businesses dependent on them which bring in the bulk of the $250,000,000 or more which is Maine's recreational income in a good year.

Joe Doakes, on a two-weeks vacation with his family, or on a fishing or hunting trip with some cronies, is the man who supports these institutions, and who eventually often buys a cottage or an old farmhouse where his family can spend the whole summer. A superhighway, built at great cost with private capital and running from Portsmouth, New Hampshire, to Portland and on up to Augusta, makes it easier for him to get into the state.

Yet the tourists and vacationers are not quite so important to the state's economy as they seem during the brief summer season when they outnumber the natives. Industry still puts more money into

Maine pockets than summer visitors. Agriculture ranks second to industry. The recreation business comes in third, ahead only of commercial fishing among Maine's four major ways of making a living.

Maine's two major attractions for vacationers, the seacoast and the woods, were the mainstays of the state's earliest economy. Into the many harbors formed by the undulating coast line, ships began sailing as early as 1497, when the Cabots explored the coast. In 1607, the first ship ever built by Europeans on this continent, the "Virginia," took shape under the hands of the ill-fated Popham colonists at the mouth of the Kennebec River; and by 1642, when Sir Ferdinando Gorges converted, at least on paper, the little fishing hamlet of Agamenticus (now York) into the first chartered city in this country, both fishing and trading vessels were plying the Maine coast in substantial numbers. The Maine woods provided cargoes of furs for the earliest trading ships. They soon provided, too, the raw material for more ships; and dozens of little coastal villages, with lumber from the back country, built and manned ships that sailed all over the world. Lumber became the principal cargo that they hauled out of Maine, and lumbering the state's principal industry.

Sailors, fishermen, woodsmen and, as some of the woods were cleared, farmers were Maine's founders and builders. Most of them came down from Massachusetts. (Maine is always down, no matter how it looks on the map, because the prevailing winds along the coast made it usually a down-wind sail from Boston.) They were virtually all of English stock, of course. With the exception of a few landed proprietors—and most of those preferred to stay in Boston or, even better, in England, and administer their settlements at long distance—they had no claims to aristocracy and no backlog of wealth. They were isolated and on their own, and acutely aware of it. If their cousins of Massachusetts Bay thought of them as rough backwoodsmen, they thought of those cousins as inflated characters whom it was prudent and not unenjoyable to remind, from time to time, that hard-working and self-respecting backwoodsmen had the same rights as anybody else.

They insisted on having not only elementary schools but a college of their own, and got Bowdoin, which was chartered by the Massachusetts General Court in 1796 and opened in 1802; and after they got it, they bedeviled the legislature for being too generous toward Harvard and slighting Bowdoin. Sometimes their Yankee wariness of being victimized led them into ingenious arguments, as when the General Court imposed an excise tax on rum. The people of Cumberland and Lincoln counties demanded special consideration because they lacked good orchards for cider, they said, and were, therefore, "under the necessity of using more rum than their brethren to the westward."

Early Maine, as a matter of fact, was a notoriously hard-drinking area, as might have been expected of a place where nearly everybody was a sailor or a woodsman. As the farm population increased, however, a strong temperance reaction set in, and in 1846 the state passed one of the earliest prohibition laws in our history. It was officially dry, with only minor interruptions, from then until it voted wet again after the repeal of national prohibition. Authorities differ as to how dry Maine actually was during the three quarters of a century when the law forbade the sale of liquor—"not including cider," according to the terms of its constitutional amendment. Most State-of-Mainers, however, live in small communities where sinning in secret is difficult, go to church as a matter of course, and tend to conform to a moral code which, though somewhat liberalized now, still bars excesses. "Even if you aren't worried about going to hell," a Maine judge recently admonished a young man brought before him for continued drunkenness, "you'd better begin to worry about how much it's costing you to do it. I'll give you thirty days to think it over."

With only about as many people as live in the city of Boston scattered over the state's spacious area, Maine has only twenty-one communities which call themselves cities, and several of them seem to be stretching a point to do it. On the other hand, there are over 400 incorporated towns, which govern themselves at town meetings, sixty so-called plantations, too sparsely populated to maintain a town government, and 395 completely unorganized townships which are just lines on the map, and in most of which nobody at all lives. Many of these are in the Big Woods, which cover the northwestern corner of the state, but some are in other areas, and serve, as Maine people like to say, "to hold up the road" from one place to another.

Ever since the early part of the last century, when so many people left Maine for the newly opened lands of the West that the contagious restlessness became known as the Ohio fever, the rate of desertion has been high, and Maine has supplied so many citizens for other states that its own population growth has been in driblets. Many of those who left at the time of the Ohio fever were farmers, who sold their farms and goods at public auctions—and even auctioned off the care of elderly relatives and other dependents unequal to the migration by taking bids on their room and board for the rest of their lives and turning them over to the low bidders. Since then, however, the migrants from Maine have been largely young people, looking for wider occupational opportunities, and the tendency has been for those with family farms, businesses or other property interests to remain. This selective process has no doubt accentuated the already strong sense of property of the average Maine Yankee and his personal and political conservatism. A lobsterman of the town of Friendship was admittedly expressing an extreme view, yet one indicative of the average State-of-Mainer's attitude toward governmental interference with what he considers his rights, when he cussed out a state official not long ago, and insisted that all regulations about lobster fishing ought to be repealed.

"If God wanted them lobsters protected," he declared, "He'd send somebody to do it. So long's He don't, a man ought to be allowed to sell any of 'em he catches."

The present population of Maine is preponderantly of the old Yankee stock—at least sixty per cent, by most estimates. Most of the non-Yankees are Canadian, by birth or ancestry, and a large proportion of them French Canadian. The representation of other races and nationalities in the state is fragmentary. Only about one tenth of one per cent of the population, for instance, is Negro—a proportion equaled by the Indians still surviving on the Penobscot and Passamaquoddy tribal lands at Old Town, Eastport and Princeton. In the 1920's, when the Ku Klux Klan was driving hard for members, its greatest successes in Maine were in rural areas where the organizers' scare stories about Catholics and Jews were the more readily accepted because their prospects had never had any firsthand acquaintance with either. The French Canadians, or, as many of them prefer to be known, Acadians, are Catholic, of course, but most of them live in industrial cities, like Lewiston or Biddeford, or along the St. John River, which forms part of the northern boundary line with Canada. Maine industry relies heavily on them for labor, and since the pulp-and-paper industry is by far Maine's greatest, and is based on the continuing exploitation of the forests, the proficiency of French Canadians as lumberjacks is one of the state's major human assets.

With so much of the state's land surface still in timber and wood lots, including ten million acres in the Big Woods, the largest area of unbroken wild land in private ownership in any state in the country, the cutting of trees for lumber remains an important industry. Many factories around the state, mostly small plants, also use State-of-Maine wood for a multiplicity of products: clothespins, spools, bobbins, tool handles, skewers, heels, toothpicks, tongue depressors, stoppers, bungs, barrels, boxes, casks, hoops, ladders, sleds, paddles, pickle crocks, meat blocks, coat hangers and lollipop sticks, to name just a few at random. One factory uses 40,000 cords of wood a year solely for clothespins. Much the greatest part of the wood cut in Maine, however, is reduced to pulp for the manufacture of paper, and the big paper companies employ more labor and turn out more dollars' worth of product than any other single industry. Modern mechanical contrivances have taken some of the Paul Bunyan flavor out of logging. Lumberjacks, their axes on their shoulders, used to go into the logging camps and stay all winter; they now use automobiles and come out to town at least once a week. The ax and saw remain essential tools of the trade, and while trucks haul out a considerable amount of lumber, millions of logs are still driven down the rivers and lakes, with lumberjacks deftly hopping the booms to keep them going. One lumberman with a long-log mill at the mouth of the Saco River, is of the fourth generation of his family in the business. He still drives logs down the river under rights granted his family in colonial days.

The manufacture of textiles, a business which came into the state in the middle and latter part of the last century, primarily because of the water power generated by the many rivers and streams, ranks second among Maine industries. The cotton mills are mostly large plants, around which typical small mill cities have grown up; but most of the more numerous woolen mills are smaller enterprises, more typical of Maine, operating in semirural villages.

The manufacture of machinery and other metal products and of boots and shoes follow, in that order of importance, the textile industry, and also make use of the water power of the rivers. Auburn, on the Androscoggin, is the principal shoe-manufacturing center, while Waterville and Augusta, on the Kennebec, make a considerable part of the machinery. Maine's other important industry, canning, is closely related to its agriculture and its fishing, though several big canners now reach far beyond the borders of the state for their raw products. California pea beans, for instance, come to Maine in huge quantities to become New England baked beans, and State-of-Mainers take great delight in the fact that many of them then go all the way back to California to be eaten. For the most part, however, Maine canneries are situated in small towns near their source of supply, whether sweet corn, the most important single canning crop, blueberries, fish, or something else; and they play an important part in the economy of those areas, both as markets for farmers and fishermen and as employers of labor. Many of them operate only seasonally, relying largely on farm and small-town women who take time out from their household duties to add their bit to the family incomes.

It is typical of the Maine pattern of life for people to turn their hands to different kinds of work as varying opportunities arise. Many winter sawmill workers, for instance, are farmers in the summer; many men who act as guides in the summer, work in the woods or go trapping in the winter. During World War II, as during the previous one, when the normally small shipbuilding industry had to be tremendously expanded almost overnight, thousands of Maine farm people and others who knew nothing of ships but did know how to handle tools were quickly converted into skilled shipyard workers. A large proportion of factory workers live on small farms, and have their own gardens, and, perhaps, a cow. So do many fishermen, and one of them recently described his technique of shearing a sheep this way: "I grab him by the starboard aft leg and work for'ard." Chamber-of-commerce people and others concerned with trying to attract new industry to Maine make a big point of the versatility and stability of Maine workers. The executive secretary of the Associated Industries of Maine, put it this way: "Suppose John Jones works in a woolen mill. He owns his own house, and pays his bills. He is a good mechanic, and has always made a good living, whether in the mill or some other way. He can walk down the street in his town, and people speak to him with respect. He is a successful man. He can call the banker Fred, the lawyer Bill, and the owner of the mill where he works Charlie, and he probably plays whist and goes fishing with them. He has his vote in the town meeting, and may be elected selectman. He may join a union, but he isn't going to be pushed around by agitators. We haven't had a serious, crippling strike in Maine in a long time."

One of the weaknesses of this small-town economy is that the loss of a single small industry on which a town depends can be critical; and scattered about Maine are dozens of towns with beautiful and impressive old houses, evidence of an earlier prosperity, which have fallen into disuse, been sold to summer residents, or converted into tourist accommodations. The town of Cherryfield, on the Narraguagus River, once had fourteen sawmills in operation, but as the near-by timber on which they depended became less plentiful the town's reason for existence all but disappeared; hunters, fishermen and summer visitors are now a major factor in keeping it alive. Industry has been growing, however, rather than declining in recent years, as the national trend toward decentralization has strengthened; and many small communities which seemed in danger, during the depression, of becoming ghost towns, have come to life again as new industries have supplanted old ones. The little village of Mechanic Falls is an example: the paper mill and the shoe factory which used to support it had both become vacant before the war, and the mechanics of Mechanic Falls became farmers; today a big national cosmetic company is using the paper mill for the manufacture of facial tissue, the shoe factory has become a wooden-box factory, a machine shop is making precision machines, and the mechanics are all busy being mechanics again.

If a man has three acres or more of land and gets as much as $250 of agricultural income from it, the Census Bureau counts him as a farmer, no matter what else he may do. Under this definition, Maine has some 43,000 farms, but less than half of them are full-time commercial farms in the Midwestern sense. Most of the rest are pieces of land on which people live and do a little farming while also turning a penny by other means.

The fisherman-farmer previously quoted on the subject of shearing sheep, who stoutly maintains that the island where he keeps his sheep is so rocky that he has to go out and file down their noses so they can get at the grass, has a whole fleet of lobster boats and an interest in a shipyard. The fact that many Maine farm owners have a similar eye to other business, as well as an ingrained thriftiness, may be part of the reason why Maine farms are less burdened by mortgage debts than those of any other Northern state. Many a Maine farm has been passed down free and clear by previous generations. So long as it provides enough cash income to pay the taxes and to buy the few essentials of life that it does not grow, its owner is satisfied. It was the late Ed Allen, a philosophic farmer of the town of Stoneham, who stopped his Model T one day in 1930 to talk with a friend about the stockmarket crash, and said, "I feel awful sorry for all those city folks. They got used to thinking they had a lot of money, and now it's gone, and they don't know what to do. I figure I'm pretty lucky. I never had any money, and things are just the same as they always were."

However, up in Aroostook County, which produces more potatoes than any single state except its own, the attitude toward money is different. About half of the state's farm income comes from potatoes, and Aroostook grows over eighty per cent of them. Many farmers grow more than 100 acres, some more than 500, and a few more than 1000. This is big business, and the average Aroostook potato farmer is as acutely market-conscious as any stock speculator. During the war, the Government supported the potato market, to assure adequate supplies, and most growers were assured of reasonable profits; but in other years, the fluctuations of prices have been so violent that Aroostook farmers were commonly said to ride in Rolls Royces one year and go barefoot the next. A big national crop would send prices down, often to disastrous levels. In 1934, for instance, when potatoes sold at an average of fifty-five cents a barrel, Aroostook growers lost heavily. On the other hand, in 1925, when Aroostook had a good crop but the crops over the rest of the country were very poor, Aroostook had the wildest boom year it ever knew. Potatoes went to ten dollars a barrel, and everybody got rich. One farmer, with about 100 acres in potatoes, sold just enough of them at the early-season prices to pay his bills, and held the rest for the killing. He still had 10,000 barrels when the price hit ten dollars, making a clear profit of $100,-000. He built a new house with six baths, and a big barn, and began planting more potatoes. A few years later he lost everything and had to go to work as a hired hand. It is a story that has been repeated, with varying details, many times in Aroostook; though many shrewder men are able to hang on to their fortunes, making it one of the wealthiest farming counties in the country.

Unlike farmers of the philosophic Ed Allen school, who try to make the soil provide directly for as many of their wants as possible, most Aroostook farmers stand or fall on their potatoes. The county grows some grain, has recently grown enough peas to keep a freezing plant supplied, and some farmers vary their farm programs by raising livestock; but the more typical Aroostook farmer likes to be free to go to Florida in the winter if he feels like it—and if it is one of the years when he can afford it. Aroostook is the northernmost county in the state, jutting well up into Canada, so this craving for warmer climes in winter is, perhaps, understandable. Temperatures of twenty below are commonplace, and snow that fails to reach second-story windows is considered trifling by Aroostook veterans. Two thirds of Aroostook is still in the Big Woods, and logging and pulp operations along the St. John River constitute an important industry, but otherwise even the industry of the county is based on the potato: canning plants, starch mills and a distillery making potato alcohol, which has recently started producing gin and, of all things, a State-of-Maine vodka.

Elsewhere in Maine, dairying, poultry raising and apple orchards account for a large part of the farm income. These are types of farming which require little extensive cultivation of the soil. The Maine landscape is checkered with picturesque stone walls built by earlier generations of farmers who laboriously dug the rocks out of the earth to make cultivation possible, but modern Maine farmers find it more practical to do their farming on a sod basis, and let the cultivated crops be grown somewhere else. Ed Allen used to like to pick up odd-shaped rocks in his fields, and he had one, shaped like a human heart, which he called Pharaoh's heart, and which he showed visitors as proof that his farm was "the original Eden Spot." Such romanticizing of the rocks on Maine hill farms is hardly usual, however, and the more common attitude is one of resignation, as expressed by another Maine farmer, possibly apocryphal, who was asked by a summer visitor how there happened to be so many rocks on his farm. "Glacier brought 'em," he said. What was he going to do about it? the summer visitor asked. "Wait for another glacier to take 'em away again," he said.

Maine soil is by no means all rocky, but some of it is worse, and the thrifty stubbornness of State-of-Mainers keeps some of the most unlikely soil producing. Years ago, great fires swept some of the coastal counties, in the wake of lumbering operations, reducing large areas to barrens. The only thing edible the thin, acid soil would grow with any success was blueberries, which came in wild, and the picking of blueberries became a major means of livelihood for people in the area. Every few years they would burn part of the barrens over again, as the simplest way to prune the bushes and get rid of other growth, and the blueberries would come back as thick as ever. Presently a Yankee entrepreneur built a blueberry-canning plant, and others followed. Today there are seventeen, and Washington County leads the world in blueberry production, and, with two or three other Maine coastal counties, supplies the country with virtually all its canned blueberries and a large proportion of its fresh and frozen ones.

In a good year, the barrens may produce over three million dollars' worth of blueberries. The blueberry farmers still burn over portions of the land every three years, and, at harvest time, rake in the berries, literally, with specially designed wooden rakes. The canners admit that, until they perfected their machinery and equipment in recent years, the popularity of their product was considerably affected by the inclusion in the cans of leaves and sticks that had been raked in with the berries—everything, according to a common saying, "from cordwood to Christmas trees." This hardly constitutes full-time work, and since general agriculture is still unrewarding on the barrens, the blueberry growers have plenty of time, during the year, to exercise other talents. That may be one reason why sometimes more deer are shot in Washington County than in any other county in the state. Summer visitors help to provide seasonal work and income, and one blueberry grower in Columbia Falls, who also runs a summer hotel, rounds out his year as principal and (half the faculty) of the local high school. Obviously such opportunities are limited, but what with wood to be cut, boats to be built, and other odd jobs, State-of-Mainers are seldom idle, even on the barrens.

Most Maine farms, having been carved out of the woods in the first place, are still more or less wooded. About half the total farm acreage of the state is in woodlots; and cutting wood in winter is a conventional farm operation. Many farms and many rural villages off the main lines of transportation rely on wood for fuel, and a big pile of wood beside a one-room schoolhouse is still a common sight on country roads (to the chagrin, it may be said, of state educational officials, whose efforts to persuade Maine communities to consolidate their schools make little headway against the Yankee determination to hold on to what they already have, even if it is a poor thing). Most of the farm-cut wood, however, is sold for lumber or pulp, and provides a substantial part of farm income. Maine farmers also harvest a considerable quantity of maple sap for syrup and sugar, though some is suspected of finding its way to Vermont, which has a bigger reputation for this product, and whose labels accordingly command a better market.

If Maine contributes its bit to the Vermont maple-syrup output, it can be safely assumed, though it is a very hush-hush matter in Maine, that Canada similarly contributes to the volume of Maine lobsters supplied to the nation. Such Canadian lobsters as go to market through Maine shippers, and thus masquerade as Maine lobsters, are, in any case, the same kind of lobsters, *Homarus americanus.* The unforgivable sin, as Maine lobstermen see it, is to sell crawfish as lobster, as is done in Florida and California. The sale of crawfish from Africa in the state, in fact, has been forbidden by law, and may be punished by a fine of as much as $1000.

Even without benefit of Canadian assistance, Maine lobstermen catch eight of every ten lobsters taken in this country (always bearing in mind that the only real lobster is *Homarus americanus*), and this does not include any of illegal size that may get eaten without passing through the regular channels of trade. Under Maine law, only lobsters measuring no less than $3\frac{1}{16}$ and no more than 5 inches from the rear of the eye socket to the end of the body shell may be kept, on the theory that the short ones should be left to mature and the big ones to breed, and the restrictions are reasonably well respected. It requires considerable strength of will, however, for a State-of-Mainer to part with a perfectly good lobster merely because it happens to be a fraction of an inch too short or too long. The story is told of two Bailey Island lobstermen who worked their traps together, one hauling, the other measuring, with a firm understanding that whenever the one who was measuring found an illegal lobster, he automatically forfeited his whole share for the day. The story illustrates the reluctance of many lobstermen to take their measuring sticks too literally, and it is no secret that many of their families and neighbors find short lobsters both succulent and nourishing.

The lobstermen tend to be extremely independent-minded citizens, even for the State of Maine. Efforts to organize them into cooperatives have invariably failed. "I guess I'll sell my own lobsters," one man told an organizer, "and sell 'em to anybody I please, or give 'em away if I have a mind to." When prices dropped one fall, however, so many of them took their guns and went hunting that it had the effect of an organized strike—an action which, by that name, they would never have considered. During the war, when prices soared, some lobstermen made as much as $20,000 a year, though poor seasons may find them barely making a living. "I always guess wrong," moaned one lobsterman who quit just before the war and took a job in a sea-moss plant. "I've done it ever since I was twenty-one, and decided to be a Democrat."

The pride of State-of-Mainers in their possessions is seldom expressed in direct boasts, but nevertheless displays itself unmistakably, and the state's pre-eminence in the lobster business provides a good example of this quirk of character. Most Maine people like to believe that the Maine lobster is the best in the world, but they instinctively shy away from the extravagance of such a bald statement. Instead, they talk at great length about whether Maine lobster is better boiled, broiled or in a stew, just how it is best prepared in each case, and how to eat it. The Brunswick *Record* recently recommended lobster stew for breakfast, asserting, "we can think of nothing tastier on a subzero morning," while dismissing lobster Newburg, thermidor and even broiled-live as "effete and tasteless versions." Directions for eating lobsters (boiled-live) have been given as follows:

1. Twist off the claws.
2. Crack each claw with a rock, or what have you.
3. Separate the tailpiece and break off the flippers.
4. Insert a fork where the flippers broke off, and push.
5. Unhinge the back from the body, and eat the green parts.
6. Suck the small claws, drawing out the meat like sipping cider with a straw.

Clam chowder is another dish which gives State-of-Mainers an opportunity to boast, by indirection, about their sea-food resources. Maine clam chowder is made invariably with milk, and the watery Manhattan version, using tomatoes, is universally scorned as a glorified vegetable soup, probably so made because of the inferiority of non-Maine clams. Some years ago a member of the State Legislature drew up a bill forbidding the manufacture or sale, as clam chowder, of any concoction with tomatoes or other vegetables in it, and specifying as a penalty that the offender should be forced to dig a barrel of clams at high tide. The bill, though never formally introduced, was given wide publicity, which the author of the bill, with Yankee cunning, no doubt anticipated. Several canners, just at that time, had an oversupply of Maine clam chowder which they were anxious to move.

Maine clam diggers are as characterful as its lobstermen, and have shared with them the prosperity of peak prices. A good clam digger can get from two and a half to three barrels of clams a day, and the prices have fluctuated from a low of about a dollar and a quarter a barrel to sixteen and, at one time, even twenty dollars.

Nearly half of all the fish landed by Maine fishermen are herring, which are canned as sardines. Eastport (incidentally, the eastern-most city in the United States) is the center of this industry, and has been periodically rich and poor for many years, as Maine sardines have had good and poor markets. During the war the Maine canners both increased their output and took the opportunity to move into a higher-quality field previously more or less monopolized by the foreign packers. The bulk of the Maine output used to be a cheaper product, usually packed in cottonseed oil, tomato sauce or mustard; and one of the lowest points in the industry's history came when National Prohibition cut off a major market by putting an end to free-lunch counters at bars. It was at a meeting of the packers during this period that the late Chief Justice William R. Pattangall, a man whose dry, sarcastic wit so pleased State-of-Mainers that he has taken rank with their favorite legendary characters, indirectly offered the advice which the packers have since taken. After listening to much moaning about the way Prohibition had ruined their business, and to many expressions of helplessness in meeting the situation, the judge arose and remarked, modestly, that he had little knowledge of the business, but that one question had occurred to him. "I have just been wondering," he said, "if any of you gentlemen ever thought of packing a sardine a man could eat when he was sober."

Whoever eats sardines, State-of-Mainers eat a lot of fish chowder, and are as didactic about it as they are about clam chowder or lobsters. Most connoisseurs specify haddock as the proper fish to use, and Maine fishermen take large quantities of this fish from the ocean, as well as even more cod and substantial quantities of other varieties. Yet the fish that ranks next to herring in total poundage taken, and even exceeds herring in dollar value to the fishermen, is one that State-of-Mainers practically never eat: rosefish. Just as most Maine inlanders refuse to eat the common yellow perch, which insists on getting caught in most of the lakes and which summer visitors usually eat with relish, Maine coastal people have long been prejudiced against the redfish, as they prefer to call it, and fishermen always used to throw it out with skates and other trash fish until it was discovered that the fish had a ready market in other parts of the country. It is, in fact, one of the five leading fish in national sales, and the only one of the five that is taken in New England waters; but the Maine coast attitude is still as expressed recently by a Portland fisherman: "I'll catch them and take the money, but you couldn't pay me to eat one of those things."

The largest fish commonly taken off the Maine coast, tuna, are of minor importance among the state's commercial fish, but many fishermen have discovered that by fitting out their boats for the accommodation of summer visitors eager for big game, they can make more money than by taking the tuna themselves. Accordingly, a number of fishing skippers at Bailey Island, Boothbay Harbor, Portland, Ogunquit, York Harbor and Kennebunkport have embraced the Vacationland idea, and equipped their boats, as the state's official publicity puts it, "with every convenience for the comfort and enjoyment of their patrons." This includes a fishing chair and tackle for sportsmen who want to try for quarter-ton fish with rod and reel, a procedure which seems slightly insane to the average commercial fisherman.

This big-game fishing is a development of the last few years in Maine waters, and few State-of-Mainers have yet become addicted to it, yet fishing and hunting are the state's favorite sports. One year, for instance, the resident fishing and hunting licenses issued amounted to one for approximately every five men, women and children in the state, despite the fact that veterans got permits free and no license was required for anybody under sixteen. Without counting the veterans or the youngsters, this adds up to more than three times as many State-of-Maine hunters and fishermen as those coming in from other states, and would seem to indicate that most adult males went fishing, hunting or both sometime during the season. They usually do.

Fishing along the coast is mostly a matter of dangling a line from a dock for cunners and flounders or deep-sea fishing with a hand line for cod and haddock, though some fishermen go after pollack and mackerel with rod and reel, and striped bass are taken in some Maine waters. The seagoing fish that most stimulates Maine's pride of possession, however, is the Atlantic salmon, a great game fish which visited many rivers on the eastern seaboard to spawn a half century ago, but which has been so discouraged by obstructions and pollution elsewhere that Maine now has the only rivers in the country where it can be caught. One of these is the Narraguagus, which is a boon to the old town of Cherryfield; another is the Dennys, way down East; but it is the Penobscot, one of the state's largest rivers, which provides the occasion for a typical Maine indirect boast every year about its pre-eminence in this respect. A pool at the head of tidewater in the Penobscot, lying within the city limits of Bangor, has been designated the Bangor Salmon Pool, and the first fish taken out of it every spring is sent ceremoniously to the President.

There are fish of some kind in virtually all of the state's many lakes and streams; and fishing, both by natives and by visitors, runs the gamut from the bamboo-pole variety to the highest rites of the fly rod. The Big Woods still have waters that have never been fished at all, because of their inaccessibility, though a few ardent sportsmen have flown in, with pontoons on their planes, in recent years, and come out with tall tales of the big ones to be caught there. Most of the state's other waters have been fished, some of them intensively, for years; but the Inland Fisheries and Game Department restocks them every year with more fish than are taken out. Landlocked salmon in the lakes and square-tailed brook trout in the streams are the favorites of most serious anglers, but black bass, lake trout (usually called togue in Maine) and white perch are also widely distributed, while pickerel and the ubiquitous yellow perch usually assure the smallest and most inexpert fisherman something to catch. The state has also introduced a number of non-Maine fish to its waters, such as chinook salmon, brown trout and rainbow trout, though the average State-of-Maine fisherman finds it difficult to grant them equality with Maine's own landlocked salmon and squaretails.

Approximately four out-of-state visitors get fishing licenses in Maine in an average year to every one who gets a hunting license, probably because the fishing season runs through the summer vacation period, but more resident State-of-Mainers go hunting than go fishing—or, at least, take out licenses for the purpose. They start in October, shooting partridge, woodcock and ducks; hunt deer during the open season, which starts on October twenty-first in some counties, on November first in others; go coon hunting until the middle of

December, fox hunting until the middle of February, and shoot bears and bobcats whenever they can find any to shoot. Deer hunting is a major preoccupation throughout the state. One year recently deer were shot in nearly every town in the state—though it is *not* true moose roam constantly in the streets of Maine cities—even within the geographical limits of most of the cities: seven in Lewiston, for example, twenty-eight in Bangor, and 248 in Ellsworth, which has more woods than city proper. The total for the state was 32,000 deer.

Incidentally, there is some slight justification for the moose stories. Moose have been increasing in numbers in the state for several years, and they do occasionally stumble into a town or city, but, this is usually because they are sick and know no better. Few realize this, however, and the appearance of a moose always creates excitement, and usually gets into the newspapers. State-of-Mainers nevertheless pooh-pooh all stories of moose attacking human beings.

There is no open season on moose in Maine, though several are killed every year by being struck at night by automobiles and, more particularly, trains, in the headlights of which they stand transfixed. Experts know approximately where the moose herds are at any given time of year, and when they will change from one feeding ground to another. Signs are put up to protect them, like one on U. S. Route 1, near Waldoboro: CAREFUL—MOOSE CROSSING. Bears have also been increasing in recent years, and the state now pays a bounty of ten dollars on every bear killed in municipal or state-sponsored territory, such as cities, towns, townships, and plantations. Bears kill some sheep and game, break down apple trees in trying to get at the apples, and are general nuisances.

The typical Maine sports camp, at which many visiting fishermen and hunters stay, is a rustic hotel with a central dining hall and detached cabins for parties. Camps of this sort are scattered over the state, in the various regions where fishing and hunting are major attractions. Usually available are guides who will act as boat-rowers, camp-pitchers, outdoor cooks, storytellers and, if desired, instructors or coaches, but who, like most State-of-Mainers, take their own equality for granted, and are unlikely to engage themselves a second time to anyone who takes an employer-servant attitude toward them. Many a Maine guide has rowed clients back to shore and left them when he found them trying to order him around too loftily. They know their own superiority in their own field and way of life, and see no reason to be awed by a client's superiority in some other.

Many sportsmen become so attached to particular guides, once the man-to-man basis is established, and so addicted to their conversation, that they go on hiring them year after year, even if they do not particularly need their professional help. Old Man Farnham, for many years a famous Belgrade Lakes guide, used to have a regular client with whom he almost invariably got into a shouting argument as soon as they began to fish, either as to the lure to be used or some other fishing technicality. After some mutual bellowing, they usually settled down and fished all day without speaking to each other again; and when they came in at night, they both usually vowed they would never go out together again. The next day they would start all over again, and the next season.

Supplying sportsmen is a major Maine business in itself, and hardware stores and general stores all over the state, and even some drugstores and grocery stores stock sportsmen's supplies. There are also many specialized sporting-goods stores, and it is not at all unusual for a log cabin in a town of two thousand population or less to have a stock of rods, reels, rifles and gear rivaling the big-city stores. The log cabins are modern, and therefore somewhat phony, but the proprietor is usually so genuine an expert and enthusiast that he spends a considerable amount of time practicing what he preaches, and can stand storekeeping only because it gives him an opportunity to be surrounded by his favorite articles. L. L. Bean, the mail-order sporting-goods tycoon of Freeport, has made a fortune out of his ability to communicate his enthusiasm for the things he sells; and several others, in recent years, have moved into the mail-order field. Some, like the D. T. Sanders & Son Company of Greenville, on Moosehead Lake, which started as a general store in 1857, make a point of supplying not only sporting equipment, in the narrower sense, but everything people might need on a fishing, hunting or camping expedition. They engage guides, rent cottages, plan trips, and see that the cottages of their regular customers are stocked with wood during the winter, and cleaned up for occupancy in the spring.

One authoritative estimate places the annual volume of sporting-goods sales in Maine at $10,000,000. In addition, Maine manufactures many of the goods sold. Old Town canoes and Bass moccasins, for instance, are well-known trade names. An example of the way the interests, aptitudes and opportunities of State-of-Mainers have coincided to develop this field is the town of Norway, which turns out, in a factory, more snowshoes than any other town in the world. What modern industrialists like to call the know-how came from hand craftsmen to whom the knack of making snowshoes had been passed down by earlier generations to whom snowshoes were a necessity. One such Norway craftsman of a generation ago was Mellie Dunham, a white-whiskered old State-of-Mainer who made snowshoes during the long winter months on his farm on Crockett Ridge. During the course of a lifetime of snowshoe making, Mellie's talents became so well recognized by explorers like Peary that they had him make the snowshoes for their expeditions. Incidentally, Mellie was also a fiddler, and toward the end of his life was proclaimed by the late Henry Ford, after a contest, as the champion old-fashioned fiddler of the country. This brought him much publicity and a brief vaudeville contract. It also brought a comment, not too inaccurate, on the vagaries of modern publicity from one of his neighbors: "Mellie's the best damn snowshoe maker in the world, and there don't hardly anybody know it; but now the newspapers have made him famous as a fiddler, and he can't fiddle for sour apples."

Artists and writers have been discovering Maine for years, and it is a poor literary season when less than a couple of dozen books glorify the woods, the coast and the rocky hills. To the average State-of-Mainer, these gifts are just part of the everyday scene, like the Empire State Building to a New Yorker, yet they have their effect on the naturally philosophical, and most Maine towns have their village characters who roam the woods or beaches communing with Nature. One such character once startled a summer visitor, whom he met on a hillside clearing, by opening and closing a conversation with the following words: "That mountain over there don't give a damn for you or me."

A somewhat more orthodox State-of-Mainer who has been deeply impressed by the state's natural grandeur is former Governor Percival P. Baxter of Portland, who has devoted most of his life, since retiring from the governorship in 1925, to buying up, with his personal fortune, the whole wild area of Mount Katahdin and its surrounding mountains—an area of some 150 square miles—in order to present it to the state, to "forever be left," as his deed of gift specifies, "in its natural wild state, forever be kept as a sanctuary for wild beasts and birds, and forever be used for public forest, public park and public recreational purposes." Mr. Baxter is a thrifty Yankee, who is proud of the fact that he put a gift of eighty dollars in the bank at the age of seven and watched it grow to $583 in fifty years. He is also a bachelor, with no immediate family to inherit a fortune which has similarly grown since it was left to him; and he conceived the Katahdin project as a way to save for the state a legacy which he was afraid might be squandered.

Climbing Katahdin is a rigorous sport, but many do it every year. The wildness of the terrain is indicated by the fact that when an eleven-year-old Rye, New York, lad, Donn Fendler, got separated from a mountain-climbing party near the summit, several years ago, searching parties were unable to find him, and it was only because he made use of his Boy Scout training, lived on berries, and kept moving for eight days, following a stream, until he finally came to a sports camp, that he survived.

More than 200 boys' and girls' camps in Maine initiate youngsters into the wilderness life, but most of them are in the tamer wildernesses. Many of the older boys and girls are taken on canoe trips down the Allagash, a rugged, 150-mile excursion through the Big Woods, or are otherwise given a sampling of the real wilds; while younger ones may, as in one Maine camp, be safely supervised in an outdoor "Pooh Corner." Very few State-of-Maine boys and girls are deemed by their parents to need such organized camping experience.

The gratifying income from the summer recreational business has whetted the appetite for more, and some efforts have been made, in recent years, to add winter sports to the state's attractions. The distance and the lack of direct transportation from principal out-of-state cities to the points most favorable for such development have kept the number of winter resorts limited, but the promotional agencies of the state are now urging people to come to Maine for winter vacations. To travel from Boston, say, all the way into the interior of Maine just for a day, or even a week end, of skiing, would seem an unreasonable extravagance to the average State-of-Mainer, and he would much prefer to deal with people who planned to stay long enough to get their money's worth.

State-of-Mainers tend to disapprove of people who seem to them, in the Yankee phrase, to have more money than brains, and some people get the impression that they dislike all outsiders. This is erroneous, except for the occasional misanthrope who appears in any society. What makes it difficult for a State-of-Mainer to judge the common sense of a visitor fairly, however, is the weight he subconsciously gives to the obvious fact that the visitor chooses to live, during a large part of the year, somewhere else than in the State of Maine. "How did you like the city?" a friend asked a Maine outdoorsman, just back from the Sportsmen's Show in Boston. The traveler shook his head disparagingly. "You can't see nothing but houses," he said. "Beats me how anybody can live in a place like that."

New Hampshire

by DONALD WAYNE

Some people insist you can tell the difference as soon as you cross the state line. This—and people say it about other states—is purely a mystical notion, because the country looks at first exactly the same as that you left in Vermont or Maine or Northern Massachusetts, but before long you know you're in New Hampshire, and you know that it's different.

It isn't simply that you've seen the "Old Man of the Mountains" in Franconia Notch, or the colonial houses of Portsmouth, or smelled the Berlin pulp mills. There's something else. New Hampshire is a sort of effulgence. There's a reason why more poetry has been inspired by this little Yankee state than any other: why New Hampshire can't always be counted on to vote Republican; why the devil was afraid to come back after Daniel Webster kicked him out. Don't ask me what it is; it's partly scrutable, partly something in the air.

Think of New Hampshire as a slab of northern granite shaped like a sitting bunny, its ears pointed into Canada a little way, about 180 miles long and half as wide across the paunch. It is nearly landlocked, but it clings to a small pucker of seacoast in the southeast corner—the place where it was born. Yet New Hampshire is the highland "mother" of at least five important Yankee rivers, has 1300 lakes and fishing ponds, and its White Mountains bulking across the upper part of the state are the tallest, loveliest and most storied mountains of the U.S. Northeast.

All this plus superb summer climate foreordained New Hampshire's pre-eminence as a resort state. At Wolfeboro they show you the site where the colonial governor John Wentworth built the first summer home in America, in 1768. The modern tourist was born when F. O. Stanley, inventor of the Stanley Steamer, drove one of his contraptions up the carriage road to the top of Mt. Washington in 1899. Today summer visitors, counted in the millions, add up to New Hampshire's second industry, smaller in dollar volume than the industries making shoes, textiles and wood products, but bigger than farming. In human volume recreation is biggest, for the visitors, at the season's end, have outnumbered New Hampshire's 590,000 population by something like four to one.

When you cross from Massachusetts into New Hampshire you're in the New England "upcountry," a significant word, for its implications are as social as they are geographical. Locally, a New Hampshire Yankee goes "upcountry" for the good hunting and fishing, and when he says "downcountry" he may mean New England as far south as Boston. But New Hampshire itself is all "upcountry"—closer, that is, to its Yankee origins. It has the look of the frontier as the frontier must have been in colonial days. Of course the Indians and forts are gone, and descendants of the French have trickled back from Canada to work in the northern logging camps and the factories of Manchester, Nashua and Laconia. (These cities, as a matter of fact, have an average 50 per cent French-Canadian population.) There is also nothing frontierlike about Wilder Dam on the Connecticut River below Hanover, or the Rockingham Park race track. But the New Hampshire countryside is raw; it looks untamed. It looks old—not only in the colonial-looking Yankee towns but in the thickly wooded hills and vales where the green is a lush, fast-growing green. You tramp through the woods and come upon some small, forgotten graveyard among the trees, or stub your toe on some chimney remnant near the traces of an obliterated wagon path, and you wonder about these people and how long it took for the earth to wipe them out.

You part the weeds to read the names on the weathered stones, and the chances are a hundred to one you'll find the same names on nearby rural mailboxes. Yankees are a stubborn, imperishable people.

Concord, the state capital, is the crossroad of New Hampshire's paunch, lying spang in the Merrimack Valley, about as central to things as a capital can be. It is a gray little city of granite government buildings and elm-shaded streets, austere and bleak even in the August sun. The first thing to be cleared up about Concord, for the edification of muddled tourists, is that it hasn't any "rude bridge" where minutemen fired the opening shots of the Revolution. That Concord is in Massachusetts. "But," a member of the State Planning Commission told me, "it was here that the United States was technically created. New Hampshire was the ninth state to ratify the Constitution, and that was the deciding vote." The date was 1788.

Spending the day in New Hampshire's capital I had a ramble through the Statehouse, which drowsed in echoes and summer torpor. The Statehouse, a bleak pile of Concord granite with a green dome, has been classed with America's ugliest state capitols, an effect of mood, I think, rather than architecture. It has seen a lot of Yankee weather and maybe a surfeit of governors and legislatures. It is a tired-looking Statehouse, not an ugly one. This fatigue may also be due to gross weight, for New Hampshire has the largest state legislature in the United States—a General Court, as it is called, of about 400 lawmakers, or roughly one for every 1300 people.

If New Hampshire has progressive ideas about the world—and they tell you it has—it hates to make internal changes. (Not until 1950, for example, did the voters get around to changing the official legal tender from pounds and shillings to dollars and cents, and scrapping its militia—that is, its minutemen. And don't get the idea the vote was unanimous!) The way representatives are chosen is by towns, according to a population denominator. This system was smooth and ultrademocratic back in 1784 when it was adopted, but New Hampshire has since had to remodel the Statehouse twice to accommodate the growing legislature.

A lot of New Hampshire's history centered on Concord, which has been the capital since 1782. The character of this history is reflected in the four bronze statues on the Statehouse green: there's the Revolutionary soldier-blacksmith, General John Stark, who beat the Hessians at Bennington; there's Daniel Webster; and Franklin Pierce, who was New Hampshire's only President (and a Democrat); and John P. Hale, whose main distinction was that he was the first U. S. Senator to oppose slavery. If they suggest a theme, it is a Yankee single-mindedness.

"Just don't say John Stark was an 'obscure Revolutionary patriot,'" I was warned. "A writer used that phrase in a national magazine once, and if he is ever caught in New Hampshire some uncontrollable elements will give him the ducking stool. You can't say that about John Stark."

You learn before you leave Concord that this is where Mary Baker Eddy, who was born at nearby Bow, founded Christian Science, though in the mode of the times she established the Mother Church at Boston. You also see the name Rumford around town, a name fancied by business establishments. (The Rumford Press, for instance, is one of New England's biggest printing houses.) Rumford was an early name for Concord when it belonged to Massachusetts— and it tells the famous story of a Yankee count.

Benjamin Thompson was a farmer's son who came up from Massachusetts as Concord's schoolteacher. He was a dashing, brilliant young man with aristocratic fancies. In a short time he wooed and won Concord's wealthiest lady, the widow of Colonel Benjamin Rolfe, and plunged into the high life of Tory society. When the Revolution broke out he left his wife and hied himself with his royalist friends to England, where George III gave him a knighthood. He became a celebrity of European courts, a famous inventor and physicist, the Bavarian minister of war, and finally a count in the Holy Roman Empire.

"What title do you choose?" he was asked.

Thompson thought back to his beginnings, his Concord days. "Count Rumford," he replied.

And Count Rumford it was. Thompson never came back to America, though he founded a Rumford professorship at Harvard. His daughter Sarah rode the streets of Concord a bona fide New Hampshire countess, and when she died a Yankee stonecutter carved the title on her tombstone. For many years the Rolfe-Rumford house on Hall Street has been used as an orphan home for girls.

North of Concord on the Daniel Webster Highway, as Route 3 is called, you soon emerge into open resort country, the so-called lakes region, and directly north of that are the White Mountains. A good starting point for touring either area is the town of Plymouth, which I reached on a rainy Sunday afternoon, only a couple of hours from Concord. Plymouth's hotel, perched on a hilly street above the business section, is the Pemigewasset House, a rather grandiose reminder of a bygone tourist era.

New Hampshire has a bevy of famous old hotels that find it tough competing these days with motels and auto courts; but they manage somehow to maintain an air of pedigree. I was moderately disillusioned to learn that this "Pemi" House is not the original where Nathaniel Hawthorne, that inveterate New Hampshire tourist, died, but a later edition, the old one having burned down about sixty years ago. The room clerk was almost apologetic about it; but from the pictures I decided this second "Pemi" House to be much more attractive and comfortable. The morning was clear and lovely, and before nine o'clock I was headed north into the White Mountain National Forest.

Touring the White Mountains is largely a tour of the White Mountain National Forest, a 700,000-acre scenic and recreational demesne that spreads over the greater part of the mountains, spilling briefly into Maine. You follow a serpentine route roughly in the shape of the letter *N*, passing in turn through the three popular notches—Franconia, Crawford and Pinkham—then looping up through the North Country where the hills fall away toward Canada.

I timed myself to get to Franconia Notch in the afternoon. In Yankee mountains a notch is simply a pass or gap, and here jutting from the steep cliffside of Profile (i.e., Cannon) Mountain is New Hampshire's famous landmark—the "Old Man of the Mountains." The afternoon sun, dipping behind the mountain, throws the face into perfect relief, and from the little clearing on the shore of Profile Lake you look up and remember Hawthorne's schoolbook classic *The Great Stone Face*. This is it. I looked up and made a discovery. The Old Man has an Adam's apple. Now, I don't claim to be the first to see such a self-evident detail, but nobody, as far as I know, has bothered to mention it before. The Adam's apple simply gives the Profile its startling verisimilitude, and just to be sure I wasn't imagining things I checked it with a man standing next to me. "Looks a little low," he said. "Could be a goiter."

The face, 1200 feet high above Profile Lake (referred to as the "Old Man's Washbowl"), is a miniature cameo to the naked eye, but I dropped a coin into one of the binocular machines in the arena, which blew him up to postcard size. The Adam's apple was still there.

The Profile was discovered in 1805 when a pair of road surveyors washing in the lake looked up toward the setting sun and thought they saw the image of Thomas Jefferson, who was then President. Since that time the Old Man has been identified with an interesting genealogy of resemblances, most persistent of which are Uncle Sam, Ernest (the hero of Hawthorne's story), and of course Jesus Christ.

The religious note, always strong in New England, inspired the majority of fancies. When Daniel Webster, with his flair for dedicating whatever he laid his eyes on, saw the Profile he called it God's shingle hung out in the hills of New Hampshire to show that His trade is making men.

In Franconia Notch, which is run as a 6000-acre park, you visit the Flume, an incredibly lovely gorge in the woods near the base of Mt. Liberty; or ride to the top of Cannon Mountain via the aerial tramway—one of the numerous ski lifts doing double duty for summer tourists. In this neighborhood there's an interesting side trip to Lost River, where I spent a morning going through caverns and rocky slots with such fanciful names as the Judgment Hall of Pluto, the Cave of Lost Souls, the Human Sandwich and the Guillotine. Lost River lies in beautiful mountain scenery between Mt. Moosilauke and Kinsman Notch, and after the gorge tour the head guide, and the director of the reservation, told me about the Society for the Protection of New Hampshire Forests, which owns and operates the place.

The SPNHF saved the White Mountains. Fifty years ago, when it was founded, private owners were lumbering the hills to death, and it was mainly through the fight led by the Society that the land was bought and set up as a National Forest in 1911. Not all the hills could be included in the purchase, however (the White Mountains are still a hotchpotch of private and public properties), and in 1925 the Society waged a "buy a tree" campaign to save Franconia Notch from being reduced to slash.

The policy of the SPNHF has been to aid, not to keep. It bought, developed and then turned over to the state such valuable and scenic areas as Crawford Notch, Mt. Sunapee and Mt. Kearsarge—all parks now—and will probably in time turn over Lost River and the piece it owns today of Grand Monadnock, a mountain in the southern part of the state.

The day was lovely and I paused for a look northward at Kinsman Notch. A party of "goofers" (as tourists are called) shambled in bright shirts and summer prints along the gravel path toward the Bear Crawl, the Elysian Land, the Center of the Earth. "Before we start down the gorge," the green-shirted guide said, "it might be a good idea to check your cameras, loose change, car keys, or anything that might fall out of your pockets. This is an absolutely safe tour, but . . ."

The Willey Slide is a famous bit of mountain history you come across in Crawford Notch. Landslides are occasional commotions of the White Mountains—you see old scars and fresh scars in every range in the hills—but you have to imagine the one on Mt. Willey.

A landslide is usually caused by a heavy, soaking rain after a long dry spell. Rocks, soil and trees tumble down with the rushing noise of an express train. The Willey family heard such a noise on a stormy August night in 1826. A huge hunk of mountain roared down toward their flimsy cabin. They rushed out—nine of them, including the children and two hired men—heading for a shelter down the Notch, but none of them made it. Some of the bodies were never found. The tragic irony was that a huge boulder above the cabin parted the slide into two streams and the cabin was untouched.

The irony so intrigued Hawthorne, who heard the story one night at the old Crawford House, that he used the Willey Slide as the basis for *The Ambitious Guest*, a story in *Twice-Told Tales*. A state park has been created around the site.

Crawford Notch is part of Hart's Location, a town that has an odd tradition. On election day, Hart's Location is the first U.S. town to announce its returns. "Hart's Location, First in the Nation" is almost a political motto.

"It started accidentally about fifteen years ago," a local innkeeper explained. "We had only a dozen voters in the town. Most of them worked for the railroad (the Maine Central) and were afraid of losing pay if they took time out to vote. So I said, why not meet at my house for a six o'clock breakfast and cast our ballots at the same time? Well, we did, and the newspapers picked it up and made a thing out of it." Hart's Location has been first ever since.

I stopped at Bretton Woods to drop in at the Mount Washington Hotel, a modern Xanadu impressively set against a backdrop of the Presidential Range. This is where the international money conference met in 1944 with Henry Morgenthau, Jr., representing the United States. The hotel, easily the most sumptuous and expensive summer caravansary in New England, struck me as rather flashy. "You'll see more mink and diamonds here on a Saturday night," said the manager, "than on opening night at the Met." I didn't stay for that. The scenery was really terrific, and from the porch, I contemplated the Presidential peaks with Mt. Washington's monarchial bulk rising above them all. It looked like a perfect day to visit the sum-

mit, and a half hour later I was buying a ticket at the base station of
Colonel Teague's cog railway east of Fabyan.

Mt. Washington, with an altitude of 6288 feet, is the highest peak
east of the Rockies and north of the Carolinas. To the Abnakis it was
the sacred mountain of Agiochook, the dwelling place of the Great
Spirit. One of their legends told how the great Chief Passaconaway
rose to heaven from its windy summit like Elijah, on a fiery sledge
drawn by wolves. They said the mountain twinkled from a "great
carbuncle." A man named Darby Field of Portsmouth thought this
might be diamonds, and in 1642 became the first man to climb the
White Mountains, a feat that has been called the beginning of outdoor recreation in America.

Today the mountains are threaded with over 1500 miles of climbing trails and shelters, huts and camps maintained by the U. S.
Forestry Service in collaboration with private organizations like the
Dartmouth Outing Club and the oldest and best known of all, the
Appalachian Mountain Club. The great Appalachian Trail, which
comes up from Georgia, crosses the White Mountains from Dartmouth's Mt. Moosilauke over into Maine; but that is a mere artery in
this large intricate pattern. You can visit National Forest camps like
the Dolly Copp, Campton Pond or Zealand—there are maybe a
dozen all together—and see where summer visitors pitch tents and
rough it in the great outdoors.

These Great White Hills are mountain climbers' mountains. You
see the hiking fraternity all over the place, along the roads, in the
inns and taverns, and of course at favorite rendezvous like Gorham,
Franconia, and Pinkham Notch, headquarters of the Appalachian
Mountain Club.

What was the carbuncle? Hawthorne—bless the fellow—got out a
story about *that*, too, without explaining it. The phenomenon is supposed to be a trick of light (though I've yet to nail down an actual
eyewitness), the way the sunlight hits the snow or, more likely, the
sun glistening on the tumbling rivulets of Tuckerman Ravine.

You can drive to the summit of Mt. Washington on the auto toll
road from Glen House in Pinkham Notch, an eight-mile spiral of
successively wonderful mountain views, or go up, as I did, on the cog
railway. You are nudged three and a half miles up the steep slope
of the mountain and nudged down again, a round trip of about two
hours. I got rather used to it part way up the mountain and found it

created a certain lugubrious camaraderie in the car; something like being trapped in a fun house. The amusement-park effect is heightened by the toylike appearance of the locomotive, a pusher type with a slanted boiler (tilted so as to be horizontal on the mountainside); but the grime it threw in the windows was the real McCoy.

I was curious about the cog railway and later, talking to its vice-president and general manager, learned that it is one of the oldest and shortest and safest railroads in the world. (Also the most expensive, at something like sixty cents a mile.) It was invented by Sylvester Marsh, who let Swiss engineers copy it free of charge for the Alps. Old Peppersass, the original engine, made the first ascent to the summit in 1869, and the cog railway, except for intermissions during the two world wars, has been carrying passengers ever since. The railway's only serious accident involved Old Peppersass. In 1929, at the age of sixty, she was taken out of moth balls for a big celebration; she climbed the trestle in fine style. But on the way back something broke. The antiquated engine started down the trestle like a bat out of hell, jumping the track at the steepest grade, Jacob's Ladder, and killing the only man who failed to jump, a publicity photographer named Rossiter. Rossiter had his revenge. Old Peppersass was reassembled and is on display at the base station, evidently under a photographic curse. All day long tourists use it as a background for snapshots.

The summit of Mt. Washington was blanketed in fog, so I missed seeing the panorama that Barnum called the "second-greatest show on earth." On a clear day you look off, I am told, at a vista 130 miles in any direction. But you're on surer ground picking winners at Rockingham Park than gambling on Mt. Washington weather.

This is one of the world's stormiest mountains, and you hear about climbers who froze to death in the middle of summer or wandered lost in fogs and gales; you hear about the wind that blew 231 miles an hour in April, 1934—the biggest wind ever recorded. Mt. Washington has a weather of its own, which explains why I ran into fog. All the way up, the day was clear and lovely. On the rocky plateau of the mountaintop the wind blew the fog in swirls; and it was cold. Mt. Washington has a few buildings: a summer hotel called the Summit House or Mount Washington Club run by the cog-railway people, an Air Force icing-research station, and a weather observatory. The men in the observatory work for Harvard and the U. S. Weather Bureau and live on Mt. Washington all year round, which isn't so dull or lonely as it sounds. The boys tuned in their TV set and we watched half an inning of a Red Sox ball game. When I left, the Red Sox were up, one out and none on. They won, I heard later.

The North Country, as you leave the mountains, is New Hampshire's forest primeval. For long stretches in this lonely rolling country yours is the only car on the road. Occasionally a loaded lumber truck goes by headed south, and you pass log-cabin homes with the day's wash hanging out on the porch and the woodpile in the yard and the inevitable flower garden—I've never seen such flower-loving people as the New Hampshire Yankees—and all around is the great silent wilderness. Once I stopped to look across a valley at the rolling meadows backed by a great forest of hemlock and spruce and gleaming white birch. And across the valley from one of the farms drifted the clear, casual tones of a man's voice. I'm sure it came a good half mile. It doesn't seem the place for a man who wants to keep things to himself.

There aren't many places to visit here in upper Coos County unless you're a serious sportsman or an apprentice hermit. The Connecticut Lakes—First and Second in particular—are the finest fishing waters in the state, and if you're curious to see the source of New England's great river, the Connecticut, you climb to a small beaver-dammed tarn, called Fourth Connecticut Lake, almost touching the Canadian border, where the mighty stream that journeys all the way to Long Island Sound begins as a trickle in the reeds. You pause at Pittsburg, New Hampshire's northernmost settlement, a rugged frontier village where practically everyone in town is a guide and kids cut their teeth on venison and bear meat.

I stopped at the Balsams in Dixville Notch, a town-size luxury hotel where rumba lessons start right after breakfast and you play golf on top of a mountain. I will always love this hotel because the breakfast I had of steamed finnan haddie with eggs was a gustatory revelation I have since rejoiced in at home on alternate Sundays.

Coming down the Androscoggin, a river of floating logs, you hit Berlin (accent on the first syllable, to distinguish it from all other Berlins in the world). This is New Hampshire's wood-pulp metropolis where the Brown Paper Company each year transmutes hundreds of thousands of cords of wood into things like paper towels, playing cards, and wood fibers that go into a variety of industrial products. This is done in part by boiling, and when you boil trees you produce a stink that, on dank days, is strong enough to fell Paul Bunyan's blue ox.

"It's better than it used to be," natives say cheerfully, and at the Brown Company—which for a hundred years has meant Berlin—they wage unremitting chemical warfare against the whiff.

Coming back south through the mountains, this time down the Eastern Slope, you visit North Conway. The town is so full of summer people that if you see a native you're allowed to make a wish—a custom that used to apply to maidens gazing up at White Horse Cliff. A century ago North Conway supported a summer art colony that turned out some famous canvases—one hangs in Windsor Castle —but North Conway today is, in a manner of speaking, the town that Harvey Gibson built.

Gibson was a local boy who became a famous New York banker and came back to his old home town to end his days. But Gibson was a hard man to retire. Instead, he promoted North Conway into a bigtime skiing and summer-resort center.

You come down to the Ossipees, where the mountain country peters out and the lakes country begins to spread itself in a great belt across the state, but as long as you can see Chocorua it commands your attention. Chocorua, they say, was an Indian chief who, pursued to the top of the mountain, pronounced a curse on the white man before he leaped to his death. After that the cattle of surrounding farms mysteriously sickened and died and for generations people said it was Chocorua's curse—till scientists found it was a noxious element in the water, muriate of lime, that poisoned the cows. It still makes them sick, but farmers cure them today with a home remedy of soapsuds.

According to a precise friend of mine who used to teach Arthurian legend at Harvard and had been a summer resident of Chocorua since the '90's, the curse itself is a bald piece of fiction.

"Then there's no curse?" I said.

"My boy," he said, "do not despise legend. It is often a way of revealing truth. You know the story of the Holy Grail." He sat back and gazed thoughtfully at his favorite mountain. "Chocorua's curse is simply a demonstration of due respect."

New Hampshire has, incidentally, a kind of grail legend of its own that grew out of a notorious historical episode. In 1759 Rogers' Rangers went up to wipe out the St. Francis Indians in Canada—you may remember the episode in Kenneth Robert's *Northwest Passage* or the movie version with Spencer Tracy—to stop raids on the Vermont settlements (Vermont being then the divided property of New York and New Hampshire). Caught by surprise, the Indians were massacred, their village sacked, plundered and left a smoking ruin. Part of the loot the Rangers carried off was a pair of golden candlesticks and a silver statue of the Holy Mother, stripped from the Indian chapel.

The expedition, pursued and broken up into wandering parties, was one of the most ill-fated of the French and Indian Wars. Only a pitiful number, including the indomitable Major Rogers himself, survived the escape down the Connecticut Valley, and for years the people of upper Coos would come across skeletons of the lost men with wampum and silver buckles and other telltale evidences of their swag. Legend says the Rangers were so starved they ate their moccasins, powder horns and even their own dead—which one may reasonably doubt. Good woodsmen don't die of starvation; it was probably the cold and exhaustion that did them in.

In 1815 the golden candlesticks were found near Lake Memphremagog, but the silver statue vanished into the White Mountains. The nine men who had it in their possession were last heard of around Crawford Notch. Years afterward a hunter related a strange experience. He was caught in a storm on Mt. Adams. Suddenly, as if in a Bible tale, the storm parted and a vision rolled out of the mists. He saw a stone church and a candlelit chapel with Indians kneeling in prayer. Then, as the church faded, the Indians filed down the mountainside in a solemn procession led by the silver statue, which vanished into a ledge of rock. People say this ledge is where the miraculous statue (it is said to weigh about eight pounds) will probably be found some day—by a Parsifal, of course.

Lake Winnipesaukee, translated as the "Smile of the Great Spirit," has a mainland shore line of 183 miles. It has 274 islands that are big enough to hold summer estates, boating colonies and children's camps, and it is, as any local booster will tell you at the drop of a popcorn ball, one of the largest intrastate lakes in the United States.

You take the sixty-mile drive that circumscribes the lake, passing through relatively peaceful lakeside hamlets like Moultonborough and Alton Bay and Center Harbor with their sunny little docks and fishing cottages and summer inns; through Wolfeboro (named for the general who took Quebec from the French), the town that started as America's first summer resort—and finally you arrive at The Weirs. The Weirs, where the Indians of pre-tourist days laid their salmon nets, is a Sunday driver's heaven of cruise boats, outboard races, water carnivals, casino dances, parachute jumps, fishing contests and a bathing-beauty pageant whose winner is crowned Miss Winnipesaukee. Shutting my eyes to the honky-tonk (though I unbent to gorge myself on lobster rolls and taffy candy), I found the lake really very nice.

Endicott Rock, close to The Weirs on the channel leading into Paugus Bay, is a state park built around the marker of the old Massachusetts boundary. I found Winnipesaukee to have other interesting historic high lights. Guernsey Island, for instance, now shrill with the voices of boy campers, is where Guernsey cows were introduced into America in 1831, and where Harvard and Yale held their first crew race in 1852. Harvard won.

Speaking of Guernseys, you'll find the American Guernsey Club at Peterborough, organized, the man there told me, in 1877 and keeping file on 550,000 registered contemporary Guernseys. Oddly enough, Guernseys are not the favorites of New Hampshire farmers, who prefer Brown Swiss and Durham. Milk is New Hampshire's biggest farm product, and practically all of it goes to Boston.

Yankee soil never made anybody rich—it was the shipbuilders and rum sellers and slave traders and millowners and land-grabbing politicians who got rich—and you'll find many a New Hampshire farmer these days who gets up with the sun to milk his cows, drives to a factory for the seven o'clock shift and gets back around four-thirty to milk again and do the rest of his chores.

They don't get rich that way either, of course, and don't particularly care about it, because Yankees place a high premium on their independence and self-assertiveness. If you do run across a well-to-do New Hampshireman you'll rarely know it by the way he lives. He'll run his old car till the wheels wobble off and drop his fifteen cents (maybe a quarter nowadays) in the collection plate on Sundays, whittle his own fence posts and collect rusty nails in an old tobacco can; but he might have enough credit at the town bank to float a small war loan. They tell a fable about a frostbitten old native who lost all his friends. A stranger inquired why everybody had stopped talking to the old boy. "He dipped into his capital," was the indignant answer.

Newfound is often said to be a "picture-postcard" lake but I don't think it has anything on Squam and Winnisquam, which seemed to me livelier and more interesting. There are snooty summer colonies hidden among the trees, and the inevitable moppet charivari of the children's camps. Back in 1888 an avuncular genius named Ernest Balch, whose smile evidently emulated that of Winnipesaukee's Great Spirit, opened what many aver to be America's first children's camp on Squam's Chocorua Island. Today the lakes region abounds in more than 200 of them.

The Ossipee hills entertain the whiskered ghost of John Greenleaf Whittier, the Quaker poet who eulogized the Bear Camp country, though he traveled over and wrote much about the state. Like Hawthorne, Whittier died as a summer tourist—at Hampton Falls near the seacoast, in 1892. A town and a mountain in the Ossipees are called Whittier, New Hampshire's way, and a rare one it is among states, of returning a writer's compliment.

At Sunapee State Park, newest but one of New Hampshire's twenty-four state parks, I took the chairlift ride to a festive lobster-clambake on top of Mt. Sunapee.

Sunapee is a typical New Hampshire park, which is to say it amounts to a complete summer resort. There's an annex on the lake shore with a beach and boathouses, but the main part of the park sprawls at the foot of the gentle wooded mountain in a dell that used to be a rendezvous for Rogers' Rangers in the bloody Indian raids on the Connecticut Valley forts.

The park is beautifully kept, and the State Forestry and Recreation Department wisely lets park managers do things without interference.

Portsmouth, New Hampshire's once-great seaport and provincial capital, lives on two things: "The Yard" and memories of its opulent past. It is still a bustling little city and has such a compelling 18th Century atmosphere that I half expected along the neat, winding, lane-like streets to run into Wyseman Claggett, the King's Attorney, or the pretty barmaid Martha Hilton who scandalized society by snagging Governor Benning Wentworth for a husband.

Benning (whose name lives in a couple of Benningtons) was an amiable guy. He handed out grants till his plump arm ached, but always kept a little piece for himself—just in case the woods turned into real estate. You won't find many New Hampshire towns that don't bear some mark of the Wentworths (there were three of them governors), but Benning was an ardent patron of Dartmouth and cut the famous College Road up to Hanover to attend the first commencement. Sections of this road are now tourist highway.

Portsmouth hasn't worked seriously at being a seaport since the whaling industry petered out and Boston copped most of the maritime trade. But it's still a sea town. Bridges span the Piscataqua to the Portsmouth Navy Yard—which is actually in Kittery, Maine. The river mouth broadens out to sea, and you stroll along the harbor where fish-market smells pay court to the onetime mansions of merchant princes, shipbuilders and governors.

Portsmouth, whose Navy Yard now builds submarines, was building fighting ships during the Revolution. On Badger's Island in the river, Tobias Lear built the *Ranger* which John Paul Jones—flying a flag made of the gowns of Portsmouth's belles—sailed to France in 1777 with the news of Burgoyne's surrender. The Yard was the scene in 1905 of the historic Treaty of Portsmouth by which Teddy Roosevelt put an end to the Russo-Japanese War. The delegates, and the toothy Trustbuster himself, stayed at the huge genteel summer hotel at New Castle, the Wentworth-by-the-Sea, where I stayed myself as I toured the seacoast. The hotel is huger now and genteel enough to have entertained a recent Governors' Conference.

A ramble around Portsmouth is an 18th Century stroll (though the town goes much farther back—it was New Hampshire's first settlement in 1623) along streets with original cracked flagstones and narrow brick sidewalks and colonial doorways flush with the lane. Television antennas seem incongruous. The streets are dead quiet except for the sounds of boat horns in the morning fog. All the Historic Houses are in the general area of the harbor save for a couple that are over in Kittery.

These were the homes of early famous men, and I'm told that architects and designers come here to study them as examples of Georgian elegance. Today they are mostly kept up by such ministering guardians as the Colonial Dames and the Society for the Preservation of New England Antiquities.

You visit St. John's Church in Chapel Street, which claims to have one of the four American copies of the Vinegar Bible, and where "it is impossible," wrote Thomas Bailey Aldrich, "to walk anywhere (in the graveyard) without stepping on a governor." Aldrich, incidentally, was raised in his grandfather's house on Court Street—the

Nutter House of his *Story of a Bad Boy*—which is included among the Historic Houses. Aldrich is Portsmouth's literary figure. He came back in the 1880's and wrote his nostalgic ramble, *An Old Town by the Sea*, which ought to be required reading if you want to enjoy Portsmouth.

Bad weather killed my trip out to the Isles of Shoals, which are a group of tiny barren islands ten miles offshore and part of which belongs to Maine.

But I did hear some of the Shoalers' tales—about the pirate Philip Babb whose ghost walks at Babb's Cove (guarding a treasure, they say), and the famous murder at Smuttynose which the late Edmund Pearson, that eminent scholar of homicide, saw as a study in violence brought on by the sea.

Captain John Smith, browsing around the Yankee coast in 1614, discovered the reeflike islands and they were first called Smith's Isles. They have lent themselves to holy and devilish purposes. Successors to the pirates were the rumrunners of the '20's who hid out in the rocky and often fogbound coves. Today Star Island is the scene of Congregational and Unitarian-Universalist religious conferences. It is the only occupied island, the only one with a dock for the daily tourist steamers from Portsmouth.

New Hampshire's coastline is only eighteen miles long. From Portsmouth to Seabrook it extends in a stretch of rocky sea-sprayed coves and jetties and curving beaches, and dispenses as much social rank as it does sunshine and sea air.

From the snooty beach colonies of Rye and Jenness and Little Boar's Head with their wealthy estates and fancy clubs you drive down to Hampton Beach, which, during Carnival Week in August, is New Hampshire's answer to Coney Island. Hampton Beach, which has a little boardwalk and a big state park right on the ocean and a kind of midway of hot-dog stands and incessant music, draws heavily on the working classes of Boston and Lowell, especially week ends. Then there are the independent souls who picnic on the rocks by their own spot of beach and let the rest of the world go by.

A historic spot on the Rye coast is Odiorne's Point, which is the New Hampshire equivalent of Plymouth Rock. Settlers landed here in 1623, three years after the *Mayflower* dumped its Pilgrims farther south. New Hampshire had the bad luck of playing stepchild to Massachusetts on other counts. Paul Revere galloped in a mad dash up to Portsmouth on a cold December day of 1774. He streaked into the New Hampshire capital announcing—exactly as he did later on when the historians were listening—that the British were coming. A Portsmouth mob swarmed over to New Castle and stormed Fort William and Mary (now Fort Constitution), where it carried off the gunpowder supply and some spare muskets.

This should have been the opening gun of the Revolution, but the garrison surrendered without firing a shot. The gods were waiting to give the nod to Massachusetts, and Paul Revere had another try the following April.

Traveling over the state I kept casual score on the number of artists I observed sketching and painting covered bridges, old mills, pastorals, seascapes, barns and hills. I counted forty-six (including a water-color class near Center Sandwich). Of course there must be hundreds.

Lincoln's two most conspicuous memorials have a New Hampshire connection. Daniel Chester French, the state's outstanding sculptor, made the statue for the Lincoln Memorial in Washington. The other is the standing Lincoln of Augustus Saint-Gaudens in Chicago's Lincoln Park.

Saint-Gaudens was looking for a model, the story goes, when a friend told him that in New Hampshire he would find "plenty of Lincoln-looking men." He came up to Cornish, a little town on the Connecticut River below Hanover, and stayed there the rest of his life.

Today his studio is run as a memorial, and every summer the curator and his wife put on a few art shows. You might walk in on an exhibit of Charles Platt, or Paul Sample, or Maxfield Parrish.

The Cornish colony never had any motive. The MacDowell Colony at Peterborough has. It's a retreat for writers, artists and composers who want to work without distractions.

Edward MacDowell, the composer, found creative inspiration among the cool birches and water lilies under the benign eye of Mt. Monadnock, and after his death Mrs. MacDowell, who really founded the Colony, developed it into something. Over the years it has helped writers like Willa Cather, Thornton Wilder, Edward Arlington Robinson, composers like Aaron Copland and Lukas Foss.

From late September through October, when the town fairs are over, when Old Home Week is over, when driving along a New

Hampshire road is that sheer experience of flaming fall colors labeled a "foliage tour"—when the turning leaves reach a high mark of brilliance and there are baked-bean suppers and real barn dances by the natives (now that most of the summer folks are gone) and bird hunters in red caps tramping in the woods, the smell of wood smoke and fallen apples and the grass with early-morning frost, and over the rivers the first geese coming down from Canada—why it's enough to bring out the artist in any man.

You can understand then why New Hampshire has a growing crop of fall tourists.

Vermont

by DOROTHY CANFIELD

When you pass the state-line marker, you may hear someone in your car say, "Oh, can't you just *feel* that now you are in Vermont? What a difference!" If it is your first trip, most likely you look out on the mild, home-like landscape and think that there is nothing in sight to get excited about. Agreeable, yes, and varied. Certainly not spectacular. Even disappointing. Compared with the Alps or the Rockies, these tree-covered, rounded Green Mountains would hardly rate as foothills.

Yet if you stay a while, and later come again, you may be surprised to hear your own voice murmuring, "There certainly is a difference, as soon as you cross the state line." Something about the country has a quality of its own. You can't put it into words. If you have a traveled person in the back seat, he may give you a clew. "It's like the Westmorland lake country in England," he says, or, "You'd think you were in the Vosges, in France."

He may be stretching a slim resemblance to show off his tourist experiences, but he is right. The resemblance is there. That is what makes Vermont look different from the wilder parts of Canada, or the Adirondack country or our own West. Odd that one of the most intensely American corners of our country should bring Europe faintly to mind. Probably it is because the countryside has been mellowed and visibly molded by the humanizing influences of the men,

women and children who have lived, are still living, close to those
hills, those slanting fields, those tumbling streams. Not many people.
Never more than enough to make up one fair-sized modern city, and
spread thin over some six million acres, but fairly evenly distributed,
and (most important of all) with the sort of character needed to
put their special mark on the background.

So when we say "Vermont is different," part of what we mean is
that a distinctive way of life has been worked out there. Like most
generalizations, this is debatable. It makes many of our young folks
impatient. "Oh, that's the bunk," they say. "We're just like anybody
else."

I see their point. They go to schools neither better nor worse than
the U.S. average. They read national magazines. They pore over
mail-order catalogues. They share all the rest of fashion-regulated
modern life. Just the same, no generation can throw off the past like
a suit of old clothes.

Just the same, there is such a thing as Vermont personality. One
of the first visible marks noticed by visitors is orderliness. Henry L.
Mencken, of Baltimore, some years ago motored down the length
of our shoestring-narrow territory, perhaps two hundred miles as the
north-south roads wind. Writing about it afterward, he spoke of the
"old-maidish neatness" of Vermont villages. We knew very well that
he did not mean it as a compliment. But we took it that way. We
figured that what a man from Maryland called old-maidish neatness
was just about what we could call decent-looking.

Another thing you'll notice at once is that these clean-raked, lawn-
mowered, syringa-and-lilac-and-elm-adorned villages rarely have big
handsome houses. Few Vermont homes look (as many older American houses look, elsewhere) as though they had been planned for a
sizable staff of servants to take care of. Some of them are roomy
enough, evidently built to shelter a lot of people. But those people
were the children of the family and their parents, maybe some step-
children, too, and grandparents and spinster aunts and invalided
uncles and assorted cousins. Ask to see the "servants' room" in such
a house, and you will more than likely get a queer look from a
Vermonter.

A tall man can touch the ceilings in any of those older houses, a six-
footer can put the flat of his hand against them. Like much of what
you see in Vermont, this building habit did not just happen. It is
functional. It tells of long winters and people who do not expect

to run away to Florida when the first snow flies. Like other functional elements in life, it also shapes the character of its background, for it is practically impossible to put on style and "live handsomely" in a house with very low ceilings.

It is only little by little that you realize how the Vermont landscape with its homes, barns, shops, churches, fields, is a vessel for human life as carefully, minutely, purposefully shaped to hold exactly what it does hold, as any receptacle modeled by a creative hand in porcelain, silver or pottery. It is folk stuff, not mass produced.

The first look at the landscape and buildings of a new region reveals the material background. Most travelers next turn their eyes to the inhabitants. And of course the quality most apparent to the newcomer is the "general attitude" of the people with whom he comes in contact. According to some, Vermonters are sharp-spoken, unaccommodating, with a remarkably well-developed gift for being disagreeable. Yet other visitors are touched that, in the hurly-burly of the modern world, there are still Americans with time to be kind, to be aware in the old neighborly way of the existence of other human beings in the same world with them. Both these impressions are accurate. I've taken both "attitudes" myself in the same half hour, moved by impulses far too deeply rooted for me to resist.

Probably the explanation lies far back in our history. Vermont alone, among the older states settled before the Revolution, never had two kinds of inhabitants—gentry and plain folks. Even New Hampshire and Maine had, in their colonial days, a few who were gentry of a sort, people in prosperous seaports, whose money came from trade. They wore good clothes all the week around, their wives did not wash their own dishes, their children had nursemaids. Between them and the rough inland farm and forest folk, there was a relationship not at all mutually admiring or friendly.

Nathaniel Hawthorne, describing the students of Bowdoin College in his day, makes a distinction between the well-dressed, sophisticated young men from the seaports, and the "inland rustics," who yet were, he mentions casually, remarkably vigorous intellectually. Massachusetts always had the same division between the well-to-do tradesmen's families in Boston, and the farmers and small handworkers of the western end of the state. Connecticut had its bookish Yale academic world as well as prosperous merchants on the seacoast, in contrast to its rustics. Just look back at elegant tidewater Virginia, set against its primitive hill people; at the white-pillared bluegrass Kentucky big house, so different from the ignorant hill-billy's shelter; at the patroons of the Hudson Valley, detested generation after generation by the farmers.

Of course, even in Vermont, there were born a certain proportion with a taste for being gentry. But they went somewhere else to live, if they possibly could. And, at the other end of the social scale, there never were any slaves in our history. Vermont had the first constitution on the continent which forbade holding human beings, black or white, as chattels.

The state has always belonged to all of us. There has been nobody to condescend to anybody else—except to the shiftless, on whom we all look down with un-Christian intolerance. But they are not helpless, and they don't look up to the thrifty. That's a vital point. The mark of a caste system is not that some individuals look down on others. What, in our Vermont opinion, makes caste deadly, is that it creates a class that looks up to another, just because they themselves are looked down on.

Neither of these two attitudes ever marked any class in Vermont. The reason is historical. Vermont was settled soon after 1763, at the time when the younger generation all over the western world was rising in hot rebellion against fixed old social and economic lines—the rebellion which made the success of both the American and the French Revolutions. The first Vermonters *were* young generationers. Our first census showed an astonishing proportion under thirty-five. Our ancestors were the flaming youth of their period. They detested the idea of any ruling class, whether clerical, aristocratic or economic.

Consequently they were much disapproved of by the clerical powers in the older colonies which they had left behind. Timothy Dwight, of Yale, said of our first Vermont forefathers, "A considerable number of those who have influence in the State of Vermont are men of loose principles. We cannot expect to find the public measures of Vermont distinguished by any proofs of integrity."

Some of the "loose principles" reprobated by the 18th Century gentry, we especially glory in upholding. One that meets with our whole approval is lack of deference for social rank. As evidence, let me tell you one of the old-time stories, which constantly reappear in our casual talk.

During the Colonial days and immediately after them, governors were grand officials. They and everybody else felt that to uphold their social status they must live in state. You've seen pictures of them in American history textbooks—velvet coats, satin breeches, coaches with footmen, their wives with serving maids, and all the rest.

The first governor of Vermont was Thomas Chittenden. He was a farmer who worked his own farm. The Chittendens lived for a while in Arlington, my own home town, which lies near the New York State line. One day Mrs. Chittenden had visitors from Albany, elegant ladies, wives of York State officialdom. They were surprised to see their hostess bustling about, cooking dinner, with the help of a neighbor's daughter. Still more surprised to see her, when the meal was ready, step to the door and ring the big bell to call in the hired men. In response to their look of astonishment, Mrs. Chittenden said (her words have come down to us verbatim, in oral tradition, and you will notice the typically dry turn of her ironic phrase), "Yes, I know it must seem queer to you, for us to eat at the same table with the haymakers. They've been working hard mowing out in the hot sun, while we've been comfortably in the house. By rights, of course, they ought to eat first and we ought to wait for a second table. But I thought since you're company, we'd make an exception and all eat together."

I present that to you as a distilled drop of the tradition which is the essence of our "attitude."

The Vermont farmer of whom, leaning from your car, you ask road directions, is saturated in that distilled essence. An autoist recently said to a neighbor of mine, who was raking stones from the road, "My man, we want to go to Rutland." My neighbor replied with gentle, slow precision, "I haven't a mite of objection." Naturally some people think that Vermonters are cussedly cranky. They are.

On the other hand, it is seldom that anybody is refused who asks for help. That is, if it is asked as you'd appeal to somebody who lives next door to you, not as you'd ask somebody who lives in a shanty across the tracks. Not long ago a motorist from Illinois, driving through Vermont, told me that he had slid into a deep mudhole on a solitary and very muddy road, and asked for help from a farmer passing by in an old buggy. The Vermonter gave up his own business for over an hour to contrive and heave and finally to cut young tree trunks for levers (on somebody else's land, but he said nobody

would mind under the circumstances). When the Illinois car stood
once more in the middle of the road, the Vermonter said quietly,
as he wiped his muddy hands on his worn overalls, "No, I don't cal'-
late to charge you anything. Might have happened to me," got into
his buggy, clucked to his horse and went on his rattling way.

Now it is all very well in theory to feel that you are anybody's
social equal, and that anybody who is decently clean and self-respecting is your social equal. But in actual practice this theory is
closely tied to your economic security. If you absolutely depend for
your livelihood on another man, it is hard to feel yourself his equal.
Here is a theme—let's call it economic life—which profoundly influences the Vermont attitude towards our summer and our winter
visitors. You probably think of Vermonters as poor people. Up here,
we don't call any man poor who is pretty sure that he can always
get his bills paid, without being forced to take orders from somebody
else. The key word in that sentence is *forced.*

In my youth, when a Vermont man or woman was asked to work
for somebody else, the answer was always, "Well, I'll do it to accommodate you." Nowadays we have become aware that this formula
is considered rustic and queer, not to say infuriating, by people from
the outside. They have back of them the industrial idea, a century
and a half old now, that there is no difference between buying a
human being's time and buying a pound of butter. So the old phrase,
worn as smooth by usage as a pebble in a brook, is now not often
heard. But for the Vermonter, it is still the tacit basis of his working
for somebody else. He doesn't need money to bet on the races, his
wife can get along without a fur coat; but both of them are silently
willing to buy, at no matter how high a price, the absence of compulsion in their daily life.

It's true this complicates the economic life in Vermont. For example, our game laws permit the hunting of deer for a week or ten
days in the early winter. During part of that time factories might
as well close, farm work is cut to the barest minimum, offices and
stores are undermanned, senior classes in high schools are thinned,
the streets of towns and villages look as though the able-bodied
men were off in a war. There are plenty of Vermonters, of course,
who don't care for hunting, but they stand up as firmly as those who
do for a man's right to decide whether he wants to work or to amuse
himself. "Deer week" is an affirmation of that right.

There have been times, naturally, when one of our factories had a rush order to be filled, and the men gave up their cherished week in the woods, to sweat long hours at lathe, press or saw. But when that happened it was "to accommodate" the management, and so understood all around.

Vermonters are not more courageous than other folks who need to make their livings. They are just not so hard put to it—even though they may look to you like poor people. There is nearly always, for any family not made up of half-wits, some money in the savings bank, some potatoes in the cellar of the self-owned house, firewood available to anybody with an ax. Many observers have said of Vermonters that they know nothing, nothing whatever, about the black hopelessness of the average modern urban wage earner, who, when his job is lost, can only sit in his tenement-house flat and wait for the rent collector to come around.

In other words, when a Vermonter feels himself "economically secure," as he generally does, he does not at all mean that he has money enough out at interest so that he can be sure he will never have to work again. We see economic security, not as a cushioned armchair into which we can sink with all our weight, once and for all, but rather as sufficient skill in balancing on a tightrope so that we are not in much danger of falling off.

Do you ask how young widows, left with little children to support, balance on that economic tightrope? Or the sick, or infirm old people? The sad answer is that they can't. The Vermont scheme of life is fine for able-bodied, hard-working people sound in wind and limb, and with good headpieces; but it is very hard on the sick, the old, the helplessly dependent, and tragically hard on the mentally subnormal. Vermonters know that, and regret it. We've made a start at social welfare service. But we have not been able, as yet, to do as much as is needed. Perhaps a community can't have things both ways at once, any more than an individual can.

What is surprising is how many of us do manage. Talking the other day with a venerable teamster who was hauling firewood to accommodate me, I was surprised to have him speak of a great-uncle of mine. I said, "Why, Mr. West, can you remember my Uncle Niram? He died so long ago—when I was a little girl." Mr. West said, "Yes, I remember him. We were neighbors. You see, I'm eighty-three years old." I exclaimed in surprise, "Really? I'd no idea of it. Why, it's wonderful that you can still drive a big pair of workhorses into the woods, and handle logs." Mr. West took up the reins to go on, dropping over the wheel to me, "I may be eighty-three years old, but I don't aim to do no settin' down on the Old-Age Pension Act."

Along with such self-dependence necessarily goes a certain hardness in judging others who are not so enduring, also a practiced and skillful sharpness in expressing such hard judgments. A farmer I know, living in the next town to ours, has considerable skill as a carpenter. He has been working at that trade, lately, for a city man, who took his silent employee for just an employee, not for a fellow human being. When the "employee" came into our general store, a group of neighbors asked him, "What kind of man *is* the fellow that's bought the old Perkins place?" To which the Vermonter, who had been good at mathematics in high school, answered gently, "Well, I should say he's kind of an imaginary line drawn through a suit of clothes."

In general, though, Vermonters keep their opinions to themselves. But sometimes silence is impossible. The big automobile draws up to a farmhouse and honks a loud imperative horn to summon somebody to a parley. It sounds several times before the door opens, showing a farmer in overalls and shirtsleeves. With no courteous preliminaries of salutation, the man behind the wheel calls out, "I understand you take orders here for fireplace-length firewood." The answer is, "Well, yes, I do have some wood cut the right length for fireplaces. And I do sometimes sell it. But," as the door quietly narrows its opening, "I don't take orders from nobody." The period at the end of that sentence is the click of the latch as the door shuts.

There is a common misapprehension about Vermonters. They haven't much money, and they are very careful with what they have. Often their thrift is mistaken for something else—for sharp, grasping ability to bargain. The usual Vermonter does not enjoy either buying or selling, though he is entertained sometimes by swapping. In general, he is a poor businessman.

One of the innumerable stories about this trait tells of a Vermont grocer, playing checkers with a friend in the back room of the store. His friend says, "A customer has just come in." The storekeeper answers, "Sh! If we keep quiet, maybe he'll go away." And with my own ears I heard the elderly proprietor of a grocery in our town (he was a relative of ours) say impatiently over the counter, "No, I have *not* got that kind of crackers. I'm not going to carry that brand any more. People buy it so fast I can't keep it in stock."

A French friend of mine, spending a vacation up here, told me rather casually, "Vermont is rather like France; it is the only place in the United States where I ever hear thrift spoken of with respect." But I have never heard anybody admire Vermont ability to run a business. Indeed most Americans when they hear how we do run the finances of our farms, towns, villages and state, marvel that we are solvent at all. A man from Iowa, looking around him at the small stony fields and thin pastures, said wonderingly to a Vermonter, "I shouldn't think it would pay to try to farm such land. I'm surprised that anybody tries to." To which the Vermonter patiently answered, "Does seem queer, don't it, that we can make a living out of it, and save enough to invest in mortgages on Iowa farms."

Of course, the normal number of people must be born in Vermont who like gambling better than hard work, and have a hankering for diamonds and drink and flashy ladies. Jim Fisk, that gaudy, successful confidence man, was a Vermonter born. But he didn't stay here. You know where he went to live.

Another aspect of Vermont tradition is the fact—maybe it is important enough to call a phenomenon—of nonviolence in the state's past and present. The rifles and shotguns you see in every house up here are not for shooting people but for hunting. Vermont has, and always has had, one of the lowest homicide rates in the country (in the world for that matter). Yet the state was settled at almost exactly the same date, and by almost exactly the same kind of "old-American-stock" people as the Kentucky and Tennessee mountains, where the homicide rate has always been extremely high. Vermonters aren't pacifists. The state has taken a little more than its full share of every war our country has been in. One of Vermont's most prized inheritances is a saying that, by tradition, comes from a big battle in the Civil War, when a general, directing the order of men being sent into the fight, said, "Put the Vermonters in the front line." And few outsiders know the quaint item that Vermont declared war on Germany and Japan before the Federal Government did. Fact. What was at issue was paying the State Guard, called out for duty, but (since they could be legally paid only in wartime) not getting any pay checks. So the Vermont Legislature very sensibly and realistically voted that "since a state of war really existed" those men should be put on a wartime basis. Vermonters fight in wartimes; but there are no personal shooting feuds in our mountains.

We like to think our nonmurderous tendencies are due to the fact that Vermont is the only state which never had any trouble with Indians. Never have I seen in print any adequate recognition of this prodigious stroke of good luck for our ancestors. We can't claim that it was more than good luck. It was not a blessing earned, like the Quakers' steady, purposefully friendly relations with the Indians. It just happened that way here. The deeply forested, well-watered, tumbled mountainous country which became Vermont had been for Indians since time immemorial a hunting field, not a staked-out, fought-over place of habitation. Several different tribes had the habit of roaming around in that region; but the game was of such prodigious abundance there was little need for any one tribe to try to keep others out. There was enough for everybody.

Our Vermont forefathers displaced nobody, burned nobody's tepee, had nobody's wrathful resentment to fear. They could and did live in peace with the land to which they were wedding themselves. Not fearing the Indians, they did not hate them, and not hating them, neither killed nor were killed by them. From old-time Vermont talk, no hideous axiom has come down about the only good Indian being a dead Indian. Probably those long-legged, good-natured, lively young folks from way down south in Connecticut, who came up here after 1764, would have killed Indians to avoid being killed by them, like other white settlers elsewhere. But not one recorded instance is in our history of an unprovoked Indian attack on white settlers in Vermont. There have been raids, yes, and scalpings and prisoners taken—but every such incident was part of a white man's war, was a regular military maneuver, and every such expedition was led by white officers in one or another army.

Our forefathers no more thought of shooting Indians than we think of shooting gypsies. It took white settlers in other parts of our continent more than a hundred years after the settling of Vermont to reach this state of mind.

And after Indians? I know you have heard about the Green Mountain Rangers and Ethan Allen and their fight for our land against grasping York State. (Give me credit that till now I haven't mentioned Ethan Allen.) No matter where you studied history, I am sure you have some notions about that fight. Probably when you think of it, you see fierce, powerful, unruly, buckskin-clad guerrilla fighters, every one a sharpshooter, every one armed with his own rifle, with Ethan Allen swaggering and cursing as he led them into the fight. Right. But did you ever hear that not one of those rifles ever killed a human being in battle? The only actual physical violence done any man during those guerrilla years was some floggings— a taken-for-granted procedure in those days—and that one man's thumb was put out of joint. They didn't like York State officials, but they didn't shoot any of them.

And after the Green Mountain Boys? No record of any mob violence in our history. No building ever burned by angry crowds. Feeling ran high in the U.S.A., you may remember, in the early '40's when nobody knew whether our country would enter the war. Some isolationist propagandists came into the state then. (Maybe they were communists; this was when Russia was still an ally of Germany.) We never did know exactly what they were up to. They had a little puppet theater, with which they gave a play attacking President Roosevelt for what they called "warmongering." (You wouldn't think that criticism of President Roosevelt would be much disapproved of in Vermont. Yet I never heard F.D.R. spoken of here with the ugly resentful hate of many rich people elsewhere.) In addition, there was a distinctly pro-Russian communist slant to the play. It was shown a couple of times, greatly to the distaste of the audience.

Then a small mountain town prepared to resist. The people who gathered to see the play in the little wooden theater set up on the village green consisted only of men and boys. They listened to every word in that profound attentive silence which is one of our Vermont social gifts, and very intimidating to outsiders. At the end, without a word, they slowly walked forward in a mass. Those who had been giving the show probably thought that they were to be lynched, or physically attacked, and took to their heels, leaving the marionettes and their little theater behind them. They barricaded themselves in a house. But the "mob" did not go near them. It carried the little theater out to a vacant lot, burned it to ashes and went home.

Sober, responsible people all over the state were shocked by "mob violence" appearing within our boundaries. Property had been destroyed illegally. (As I remember the amount, it was between thirty and forty dollars.) Restitution must be made. A collection was taken up, every county in the state being represented in the sum raised. It was forwarded to the puppeteers, with a letter which read about like this: "We do not like your ideas. We are sorry you came to Vermont. We hope you won't come again. But we regret that your property was destroyed here, and we are sending you enough money to pay for the damage done." Traditions are lasting in Vermont.

But why *should* anybody go to Vermont for his vacation, or be interested in a state where the people are so standoffish and taciturn and so crabbedly independent; where living conditions are pretty plain, where a newcomer is likely to stub his toe any minute on a granite ledge of an unsuspected "tradition"? Well, to tell a truth seldom mentioned, Vermonters themselves sometimes wonder why people who, as the phrase goes, "have everything," leave their comforts and come up to a land where everybody gets along with mighty little.

We are in this matter rather like the family who have in their living room an old chair, come down from a great grandfather. They sink down into it after a hard day's work for an evening's look at the newspaper. They are genuinely astonished (although they would not show this for the world) to have a visitor exclaim about it as a fine antique, point out its "good lines," admire the "sturdy workmanship" which stands up to more than a century's hard use. After the visitor goes, the family look hard and wonderingly at the old chair, which they had always taken for granted.

We do know several reasons why you might like to come to our plain old state for your vacations. One is that Vermont is beautiful. The word "beautiful" is in itself a superlative, and Vermont tradition is against superlatives in speech. But I not only let it stand, I add to it "lovely," "harmonious," "exquisite," "graceful." Please note I do not say "sublime," "magnificent" nor above all "gorgeous" or "spectacular." When you feel like looking at landscapes to which such adjectives can be applied, turn your automobile towards the West and the Rockies, where, as you gaze, your ears ring with the resounding brass of Wagner and Berlioz.

When you climb to the ridge of a Vermont hill pasture and find yourself before the spaciousness of what we call "a four-town view," your inner ear doesn't hear anything loud at all, at first only a gentle inner quiet. From your seat on such a pasture rock, continue to look at the flowing lines of the blue mountains, rhythmically meeting, crossing, parting, carrying your spirit far into the still sunlit distance. Presently you become aware of the shapely, symmetrical (but discreetly unobtrusive) pattern of the green or tawny rectangles of the fields, drawn in with gray-golden stone walls, or with feather-light, green, wild hedgerows. And when, as all this and the blue radiance of the summer sky move together in a perfect composition, your vision centers slowly on a noble ancient maple thrusting its great roots into the earth with such power that it strengthens you to see it— it's not Wagner's percussion bangs and trumpet shrieks you hear, it is perhaps one of those persuasive, mild-seeming Mozart passages which, as you listen to them, sink deeper and deeper into your heart; or maybe one of Beethoven's later quartets, purified of all but heart-shaking emotion.

You probably think that a very purple passage? It's nothing to what I could do, to what I am moved to, as I lift my eyes to what I see all around me, as I move here and there about my daily work. For instance, an incredible miracle of color sometimes blooms on the mountain range on the other side of our valley, on a clear midwinter afternoon. For about twenty minutes, just as the sun sinks behind the mountains back of us to the west, some heavenly quirk of slanting light rays casts a great transparent cloak of glowing color over the eastern slopes.

When it comes, we stop our work for the brief time it lasts, pull the kitchen curtains to one side, or stand knee-deep in the snowy woods to watch it slowly come to life, and then as slowly, as imperceptibly, subside through a million shades of stained-glass mauve to the cold, ringing blue of the winter twilight, with the first star showing.

And the warm, mellow, deep blue and gold of a summer night, as you walk back over the short upland grass, after a picnic on Gravel Pit Hill. And the flooding electrifying splendor of a July morning when you look out from your bedroom window to see what the weather is. And a zero night when the Northern Lights flicker and burn in long rays over the mountains.

Every place has weather, landscapes and light effects, and many places lots more than Vermont. There is the thundering magnificence of Niagara, and the epic glory of the Grand Canyon, and the slam-bang melodrama of the rocks at Bar Harbor where the sea surges up with sullen, terrifying force and breaks into tall geysers of white foam; the great forests of the Western Coast, and the illimita-

ble spacious ground swell of the Wyoming plains, and the jagged
snow-topped peaks of the Sierras.

To such gorgeousness, a Vermont landscape with its intricately interlaced lines of mountain slopes, tilted fields, brooks, roads, with its
hundreds of transparent colors, every one of them gently tempered
to a harmony with the others by the gentle light—it is like a little
plain rustic Greek temple, compared to a Gothic cathedral. But
there, that's enough about Vermont's looks. I must remember the
austere adage on which we are all brought up:

> *Praise to the face*
> *Is open disgrace.*

I meant only to suggest that one reason why people do come to Vermont may be the serene, unobtrusive, harmoniously composed Vermont landscape.

Another reason may be Vermont standoffishness. This is a trait of
great value to newcomers who have a lot of work to do, such as
painters and writers. Vermonters don't know much about what an
artist or a writer does, but it seems natural to them that he should
work very hard at it for long hours, and be tired when he gets
through. They put on him no spoken or unspoken social pressure to
more liveliness than comes natural to him.

And they do not pry into his affairs. They detest anybody's prying
into their own affairs—this is part of the "tradition" of stubborn
independence and not depending on others. Shortly after Sinclair
Lewis had gone to live in a Vermont town, he said that he had known
all kinds of American communities, but never a place where folks
were so little nosy about their neighbor's business as in Vermont.
Perhaps this, in addition to the calm classic beauty of the landscape,
is one reason why Norman Rockwell, John Atherton, Mead Shaeffer,
Luigi Lucioni, Dorothy Thompson, Vincent Sheean, Robert Frost
and ever so many other such working people are drawn to live in
Vermont.

Perhaps another reason is that Vermonters came away from the
Puritanism of older New England, intending to enjoy life, as their
elders did not. They have kept on enjoying life. They have always
danced with abandon and zest. Vermont is one of the few places
where the old square dances never went out of fashion. Now one

special feature of square dances is that everybody dances in them. Many's the time I have sashayed to the left and swung my partner in a set where two grandparents were dancing with their grandchildren.

And we are sociable. Not in the summer when outsiders mostly see us. Too much to do then. We take four months off from sociability for the exciting crescendo and the peaceable decrescendo of farming and gardening and canning or summer-boarder operations. Nobody expects to see anybody else, except in passing, in the summer. "How have you all been?" we ask a neighbor we happen to meet, almost as though he or we had been away.

But come November, every Vermont group has a common meeting place, a Grange Hall, a plain old community house, church parlors, some big room with a kitchen attached which your group pays no fee for. You meet and you eat, and you talk about everything—family affairs, town affairs, state offices, national and international relations; you dance, you play cards (those who like to), you sew. Even the people who come from the outside to live in Vermont share in this group life. When they want to come they're welcome. They're let alone if they don't feel like it. Since every party is everybody's party, there is no obligation to "return the hospitality." Take it or leave it is the lighthearted Vermont way of managing sociability. But the weightiest, deepest reason for your coming up to visit Vermont and share in our "traditions" is that *they are your traditions too.* You find here (with all kinds of individual exceptions, of course) life lived according to the basic ideas of the pre-industrial, pre-big-capitalistic-business, revolutionary young men who wrote the Declaration of Independence and the Bill of Rights.

Are you wondering why I have said nothing so far about Vermont cities? One reason is that their downtown business-center Main Streets look strikingly like those dotted all over the U.S.A., along every touring highway. Another reason, more important, is that, except for this standardized veneer, generally no deeper than a plate-glass show window, the people in them are not very different from Vermonters anywhere. There aren't enough cities in the state, and there aren't enough people in any one of them, to establish any noticeable big-town folkways in politics, customs, ideals.

Vermont has just three centers of population with more than ten thousand people. These three, lumped together (and actually they

are miles apart), come to about 65,000 people. Their total is equal
only to one moderate-sized U.S. human beehive such as Johnstown,
Pennsylvania or Decatur, Illinois. Adding all other centers (whatever
you want to call them—small cities, incorporated villages, towns,
hamlets) from just below 10,000 down to 2500, we get another block
of some 64,000 people. This means that of our total population, about
a third live close enough to their neighbors to have somebody hear
them when they shout out of a window.

Be that as it may, we Vermonters consider our "cities" big enough
for our purposes. For the other two thirds of us, these clusters of
buildings provide post offices, stores, churches, high schools, music
teachers, courthouses and lawyers' offices, banks, newspapers, radio
stations, business blocks (a few) which house insurance agents, dentists and doctors, and state, county and town officials.

It is, naturally, in these towns that our Vermont institutions of
learning are located. There are quite a lot of them, for such a rustic state—colleges at Middlebury, Poultney, Rutland, Bennington,
Northfield, Plainfield, Montpelier, Winooski, a good practical state
agricultural school at Randolph Center and a State Agricultural Department with extension service at Burlington. There are normal colleges for training our teachers, business colleges, not to speak of a
sure-enough university, with graduate schools, at Burlington.

Naturally, given the way the U.S.A. has developed, it is in our
cities and towns, such as they are, that our industrial production is
mostly centered. For there are factories in Vermont, many more than
you might guess from the small number and low population of cities.
They are widely scattered up and down the state, providing jobs
which take care of many of those who don't find work on the farms or
in the professions.

Our industrial production is varied, as it is in most Northern states,
ranging from an output of woolen and cotton textiles, to woodwork-
ing establishments, to miscellaneous manufacturing, to lumber, paper and paper products, and knit goods. Of course lots more, too
long a list to set down. You can see that serving ski and summer
tourists (although we are very glad of the chance to do it) is not the
only way Vermonters have of making a living. Yet, driving through
the state in your car, you hardly ever see a traditional "factory town"
recognizable as such. As like as not, elms and lawns and old lilac

bushes and green shutters characterize houses lived in by factory workers.

Lifelong acquaintance with the state makes me guess that a good number of these industrial establishments are factories which demand much more skill, character, intelligence than just the ability to stand on an assembly line.

Springfield, Vermont, is a notable example of this kind of manufacturing. The factories there, clustered around the river, produce finely accurate steel instruments of precision and the like. Springfield needs accurately skilled workers, and continually encourages the high-school boys and girls of the region to learn those skills. For many miles around, every village, hamlet and many a farm sends workers daily to the Springfield manufacturing plants. These men and women bring back good industrial wages to their own communities, where they often own their own homes, not infrequently because they were born there and inherited the house. So little has industrialization disturbed Vermont personal and communal stability. My own town has two factories in it, plastics and chairs, to which cars stream every morning, bringing workers from thirty miles around.

In my list of the life elements of our more-or-less cities, I should mention those Vermonters whose families came from overseas more recently than the original 18th Century settlers. We have plenty of "foreign" blood in Vermont, most of it in the larger settlements. In Burlington, our biggest city, you hear French spoken familiarly on the streets. They have churches where the sermon is in French, and names over shops are often Gallic. Why not? It is only three hours by train to Montreal. Burlington people, Perkinses and Gallipeaux together, occasionally go to Montreal for concerts or to buy sweaters.

There are also plenty of Irish names among the city government officials. That goes without saying in New England. They all work together to make Burlington what it is, a city of factories, a shopping, banking and business center and, because of the rapid growth of the University of Vermont, an increasingly gracious college town.

Barre's prosperity has been a slow-motion Vermont kind of affair, based on the high-grade granite which underlies all that region. Vermonters are by tradition woodworkers, not stonecutters. Hence Barre was the magnet for many non-Vermont-stock families. Scots came in by the hundreds. There is an elaborate statue in honor of Robert

Burns in Barre. Is there in any other American city of the size of
Barre a monument commemorating not a rich man who gave the
money for the local hospital or library, nor yet anybody in a military
uniform, but a poet? I wonder. Nobody but the Barre Scots would
have achieved it in Vermont. They even have bagpipers up there.

Polish people came to Barre, too, and the Italians, natural-born
stoneworkers. Poletti, the former lieutenant-governor of New York
State, was born and brought up in Barre. He is a Vermont Italian
of the kind brought to Vermont by granite and marble, just as our
slate industry has brought choral-singing Welsh people. Of them it
is said, "Did you ever hear Poultney people sing a hymn? They take
the roof right off the church."

In the business city of Rutland, also, there are plenty of Italians
and Poles and Finns and French. So many of the inhabitants of
nearby Proctor, the marble town, are from Carrara, marble-quarry
center of Italy, that the saying goes, "Everybody in Proctor knows
Carrara gossip, and everybody in Carrara knows what's going on in
Proctor and Rutland."

My godfather was one kind of Vermonter, often seen, one who
went elsewhere and made a fortune. He was a highly paid big-city
corporation lawyer. But he never could keep away from Vermont.
He used to say, "Vermont is a hundred years ago. It ought to be
kept as a national park where modern Americans could come to see
how their great-grandfathers lived."

He died years ago. I often wish he were alive, so that I could
talk over with him a dimly glimmering idea I have that tourists who
now come to Vermont may not only see people living as their great-
grandparents lived but also, perhaps, in some respects, as their great-
grandchildren may live.

Modern society, everywhere, is undoubtedly bowing out the very
rich man, as the 19th Century bowed out the birthright aristocrat.
Social fibers which had clung around him will be bruised for a while.
Vermont never depended on, or crystallized around, great wealth.
There will be no empty place here. You can see here what ordinary
American life is like, without rich people.

What I have been describing is a classless society. Nowadays that
phrase carries a formidable political connotation. Not here. Through
a century and a half Vermont has remained classless and also pas-

sionately, fanatically anti-totalitarian. Perhaps because it never had any aristocrats or capitalists to liquidate.

Then there is the size of population. Till very recently Vermont had been laughed at because its population stood still. All my life long, my own home town (Arlington, population 1418) has stayed very close to the number shown in the census taken shortly after the American Revolution. Here is an aspect of life in which Vermont, with its small, stable, stationary and solvent population, unexpectedly looks more like the future than the past. The sight of it may provide you with some reassurance that Americanism will survive without constantly increasing numbers of Americans.

Much of what we call "Vermontism" is nothing but "old-Americanism" surviving in an out-of-the-main-current community, which has not been so beaten upon as communities elsewhere by the storms of modern life. For good and for not so good, it has kept its old personality, just because it has not been driven to become different by industrial prosperity. Maybe this is the reason why, as you drive over the state line, somebody in your car is apt to murmur, "There seems, somehow, to be a difference in the air."

You have come to a place not remarkable, pretty bare compared to what you are used to, but with something of the tension-relaxing old-shoe comfort of getting back home.

Massachusetts

by HENRY MORTON ROBINSON

Among persons who have heard of Massachusetts, there exists almost no agreement as to its geographical location, mode of support or reason for being. Americans living south of the Mason-Dixon line will tell you that the Bay State lies somewhere between Ipswich and Labrador. Lending-library readers claim that Massachusetts—far from being a sovereign state—is a proprietary fief hewn out of Mr. J. P. Marquand's imagination. Others regard it as a historic shrine, or a kind of National Park, maintained at public expense for the benefit of tourists. My post-card invitation to a hand-picked group of executives, "Define Massachusetts in any terms that you care to dictate," drew a mixed bag of replies: "Hallowed ground," "Appendix to Yesterday," "Cradle of Christian Science," and "A Body of Culture surrounded by Antique Shops."

Taken singly or together these viewpoints fail to convey even a pallid idea of the Bay State's unique charm or abiding mystery. No writer, living or dead, has ever succeeded in fusing all the elements of the Massachusetts story into a luminous, coherent whole. Not that attempts haven't been made. Seldom has a citizenry leaped so eagerly to the challenge of authorship, or recorded in such loving detail their native state. Every nook and cranberry, every brook and cornice in the 8000 square miles of Massachusetts has been immortalized—or at least photographed—in such works as *We Chose Co-*

hasset, Yours Truro, Sandwich Now and Then, and *Buyways of Old Byfield.* Collectors of old pewter will be delighted by the *fabulae* of Mr. Cleveland Amory; visiting gourmets will relish the optimistic forecasts of Mr. Duncan Hines. Microfilm copies of the *Boston Transcript* may be inspected at the Boston Public Library, and back numbers of the *Atlantic Monthly* are available the moment they hit the newsstands.

The warning, ALL RIGHTS RESERVED, on the title pages of these publications unfortunately places them beyond my poor power to pad or extract. My only recourse, then, is to resurrect the sheaf of moist-with-feeling notes collected during my travels up and down, around and about the Commonwealth at various intervals during the past fifty-six years.

I should warn you in advance that these personalized impressions are not intended to be a definitive treatment of Massachusetts. We must wait for Mr. John Gunther's brisk wrap-up before striking a final balance here. Call this, then, an interim report, and watch out for the tremolo in my voice as I begin by summoning up remembrance of things past.

My preparations for writing this eye-on-the-object, I-as-the-subject memoir began on September 7, 1898, when I was born scarcely an anchor chain's distance from the gilded dome of the Capitol on the "water side"—that is, the Charles River slope—of Beacon Hill. Two weeks later I was baptized by a rubicund curate named Father William O'Connell, who went on to become a wearer of the Red Hat and a fairly recognizable character in my novel *The Cardinal.* At the age of six months, mewling in my mother's arms, I was kissed by John L. Sullivan, the Boston Strong-Breath, and immediately sank into a profound slumber from which I awoke to find myself searching for Indian arrowheads on the outskirts of Malden, a suburb five miles north of Boston.

With no more conscious awareness than a tadpole in a pleasant pond, I began to feel quite early that Massachusetts was a special act of creation, set apart and above all others. History was something built into the bricks of Faneuil Hall, Bunker Hill Monument and the Old North Church; the very air was a laureate ozone breathed by benevolent poets. I grew up on level terms of intimacy with such neighbors as Miles Standish, Paul Revere, Lydia Pinkham, Lucius Beebe, Noah and Daniel Webster (for a long time I thought they were brothers), Oliver Wendell Holmes, Frank Merriwell, Henry David Thoreau and Bill Carrigan—the latter being a Red Sox catcher who had sworn a mighty oath to block Ty Cobb at the plate. Carrigan's heroism left indelible scars on his shins—and my nervous system. To this day my first after-coffee question is: "How did the Red Sox come out?" If they've won, the thorn's dew-pearled; if they lose, I fall upon the thorns of life and bleed with Carrigan once more.

I wouldn't swap a single hour of my boyhood in Massachusetts for the combined adventures of Tom Sawyer, Penrod Schofield and J. Alfred Prufrock, a trio of insufferable prigs who have bewrayed American youth these many years. How beggarly, how provincial, their experiences compared with mine. While they scrounged around for catfish and hominy grits, I was hooking fat cod in Massachusetts Bay and demolishing steaks at Locke-Ober's—then, as now, one of the finest restaurants on the continent. To them, *Walden* was merely the name of a book; to me, it was a swimming hole fringed with checkerberries. Where Tom Sawyer had nothing better to admire than a whitewashed fence, I could feast my eyes on Abbey's gold-and-scarlet murals in the Boston Public Library. Prufrock's overwhelming question: "Dare I disturb the Universe?" never troubled my days. I joyously accepted the Universe and assumed that it would return the compliment by accepting me.

Throbbing with political ambitions, I heard John F. ("Honey-Boy") Fitzgerald, perennial Mayor of Boston, sway the electorate with baritone renditions of *Sweet Adeline*. (We're going to hear more about Johnny Fitz later, so keep his name in mind.) Another vocalist of the period was Geraldine Farrar, a neighboring Melrose girl, whose *Carmen* shook more than the chandeliers in the new Boston Opera House. Somewhere about this time, I was permitted to give a public performance on my Oliver Ditson "Strad" at the New England Conservatory of Music. After the concert, Professor Winternitz, in charge of the violin section, gently advised me to become a prodigy in some other branch of the arts.

On my tenth birthday—memorable because my father presented me with a silver Waltham watch—I fell in with fast company. It was considered fashionable in those days to keep a rig at the Victoria Stables in Allston and go for a spin along the Fenway three or four afternoons a week. On the afternoon in question I helped my father hitch our pretty mare, Helen W., to a rubber-tired buggy, and half an hour later we were warming her up along the measured mile reserved for gentleman riders. A roan gelding drew alongside; its owner held up five fingers. My father upped the challenge another five, and the race was on. Helen W. laid back her ears and won going away. I could scarcely believe my Waltham! She did that mile in 2.39—considerably faster than an automobile can travel over that same traffic-congested mile today. Helen W. got an extra quart of oats that evening and I polished off another steak at Locke-Ober's. *Ah, le temps retrouvé!*

In winter I played hockey on Spot Pond; in summer I dug clams on the Duxbury flats, poled rafts across the salt marshes to Plymouth, and ventured on the first of those dory voyages across Massachusetts Bay which later took me to Provincetown, Marblehead and Glouces-ter, bailing for dear life as white water broke over my dory's prow. The nameless inventor of the dory, doubtless a Bay State fisherman, should have a monument erected to his memory; in my biased opin-ion, it is the most seaworthy small boat ever constructed by man. Or put it this way: A dory will take you any place that you dare to go, and instruct you meanwhile in the art of dead reckoning, the science of meteorology and the tricks of self-preservation—all of which are parts of a Massachusetts education.

The key word here is "meteorology," which brings us by supple transition to the subject of Massachusetts weather. Ill-conditioned strangers emphasize its worst features: the bone-chilling gales whirl-ing inland from the North Atlantic, the Ides-of-March slush, and August's sweltering heat. Viewed at short range, the climate of Mas-sachusetts *can* be disagreeable, but over the long pull one comes to regard it as the paradigm for all other climates. By comparison, the weather elsewhere seems monotonous—tepid and unchallenging or, at the other extreme, too brutal.

In Massachusetts as nowhere else, the seasons fall into place with measured precision. Snow usually falls shortly after Thanksgiving and is accompanied by an electric cold which brings an invigorating rush of adrenalin to the bloodstream. On a December night, the stars over Massachusetts don't glow—they *glitter* with a hard crystalline ray which has its earthly counterpart in the diamond snow. This snow of which I speak so lyrically remains on the ground until a late March sun converts it first to slush and afterward to mud. (Need I point out here the reason for Massachusetts' leadership in the manu-facture of rubber footgear?) The slush is finally sluiced away by spring rains; April laughs its vernal laughter, and May enters coolly across a carpet of arbutus.

But wait, the best is yet in store. It was a Massachusetts poet who asked: "What is so rare as a day in June?" then capped his own quotation with lines that can be found in any good anthology. In July one can hear the timothy growing; a month later it is cut down for hay. On perhaps a dozen summer days the thermometer may register in the high 90's, but relief is always nearby in numberless inland ponds and coastal beaches.

The fine weather continues throughout September and, save for red chevrons on the maple bough, one might fancy that June were coming in. In October the year's last aster waits the year's first frost, and it is during this waiting period that the North Temperate Zone displays its finest product: football weather. Six or seven weekend games culminate in the annual classic between Harvard and Yale. Then, flurries of snow appear again, and the quartet of seasons repeats itself *da capo al fine*.

When coal, iron, oil—and even good farm dirt—were being handed around, Massachusetts was hiding under a glacier, which probably accounts for the poverty of its soil and the inexhaustible wealth of its scenery. There is grander topography, of course; Mt. Greylock, the loftiest peak in Massachusetts, could scarcely gain a foothold among the foothills of the Rockies, and Chicopee Falls is somewhat less impressive than Niagara. But nowhere in the United States does the eye encounter a landscape more various and contrasting than in the postage-stamp cosmos of Massachusetts.

The shore line, nearly two thousand miles long, is traditionally stern and rockbound in places—Cape Ann, for instance; yet for the most part, it is jigsawed into tiny coves and inlets which alternate with marshy estuaries and long stretches of fine-sanded beaches sloping so gently seaward that one can bathe at any tide of day without fear of undertow.

Motoring inland, the scenery unfolds in an ever-changing pattern of weathered loveliness. Surprise lurks around every corner in the road, which not only curves but also dips and climbs as if determined to avoid the flat tedium of Iowa or the monotony of Texas. There are thirteen hundred lakes and ponds in Massachusetts, each fringed with birch, willow, lily pads, and often enough tourist cabins. No one has ever bothered to count the numberless brooks, or trace their meandering courses through meadows and under wooden bridges; these brooks will accompany you for a mile or so in a purling roadside *obbligato*, then are seen and heard no more. Meanwhile you have passed a boulder-strewn field, an orchard laden with russet apples, or entered a chancel of aromatic pines. Resisting temptations to picnic in a fern-carpeted glade, you push on to the Connecticut Valley where the terrain levels off into tobacco fields and prosperous farms. West of Springfield, the altitude steadily rises and the incomparable scenery of the Berkshires begins.

At any point in your passage across the state, you are likely to encounter the cool white spire of a Congregational meetinghouse with its tiny plot of lichened burial stones. If your parents were American-born, some of your ancestors may be sleeping under these stones, for no matter what license plates your car bears, the chances are that your family got its New World start in Massachusetts.

A word, please, about the original settlers of the Bay State. By one of the luckiest coincidences in history, they were equipped by character (and purpose) to match, then master, an environment that would have broken the spirit of a softer race. Merely to survive they had to be ingenious, and their ingenuity swung like a pendulum between catchpenny opportunism and theological hairsplitting. They were skillful in the use of edged tools—whether that tool were a jack-knife (whittling, like American history, began in Massachusetts), a quill pen pared down for "close figuring," or a mind sharpened upon the whetstone of Calvinism.

These settlers, and their descendants, lived in small houses, went to sea in small boats, worshiped in small churches, founded small colleges, worked in small factories, and made small articles of commerce—shoes, clocks, glassware, locks—each superior to anything else on the market. Emerson's maxim concerning "the better mousetrap" was based on first-hand observation of his neighbors; and when Thoreau needed a couple of dollars (enough to keep him through the winter) he turned his craftsman hand to the making of fine pencils.

The present inhabitants of the state—slightly more than five million in number—bear certain marked resemblances to the hardy Massachusetts originals. They still engage in the manufacture of small articles, dwell in small homes, worship in small churches, send their children to small colleges and have an intense love of local self-government. Inevitably, however, both the racial make-up and population pattern of the state have altered greatly. Strong admixtures of Irish, French-Canadian, Italian and Polish elements have now cross-fertilized, and enriched thereby, the native stock. Half of these people are concentrated within a twenty-five-mile radius of Boston.

You must not expect me to become ecstatic about our cities; some of them are fairly ugly. Yet others—I think particularly of Northampton on the Connecticut River, and Pittsfield near the western border of the state—combine the authentic New England flavor with a liberal gloss of industrial prosperity. I'm always refreshed by a visit to Northampton, where my two daughters attended Smith College; but because of Pittsfield's elm-shaded streets, broad lawns, substantial homes, the bustle of its business center (and more particularly because I've paid premiums for years to one of its leading insurance companies) I'm inclined to rank it first among the municipal "proud spots" of Massachusetts.

Any attempt to "do" Massachusetts—in the sense that one "does" the Norman cathedrals—would bring on an aggravated case of diplopia *cum* vertigo. The course of wisdom lies in selecting a limited number of objectives—each rewarding in itself and representing a typical aspect of the Bay State. But since it would be easier to catch the east wind with a butterfly net than snare Massachusetts in a few paragraphs, I phoned the Boston *Herald* and asked my old friend, Bill Cunningham, for advice as to where the deadfalls should be set.

For many years Bill has conducted the best column in New England and knows everything that can be known about the Bay State. Without even glancing into the bag, he can tell you the winner of the next fight in the Boston Garden, what the boys in Research Row are cooking up in electronics, and who's knifing who in City Hall. To give you a sample of Bill's quality: one summer I asked him where the Red Sox would finish in the pennant race. "Fourth," said Bill—and that's the way it came out. (O, that everything in life were as certain as Bill Cunningham's predictions!)

As we sat in the Ritz bar, I tested him with more difficult material. "For a light once-over of Massachusetts," I asked, "what points of interest, other than Plymouth Rock and Longfellow's Home, would you recommend to a well-heeled, reasonably literate and highly mobile audience?"

Quicker than you could say S. S. Pierce (pronounced "Perce" up here), Bill batted out twenty suggestions, which I promptly inserted into my portable electronic computer, moved the decimal point over a couple of notches, compared the results with my own findings, and came up with a card punched as follows: Old Sturbridge, Provincetown, the Arnold Arboretum, Tanglewood and (wouldn't you know?) Boston & Environs. Neither Mr. Cunningham nor myself are prepared to shoulder responsibility for these choices. Disgruntled letters from Old Grads of Andover, Groton, Deerfield, and other handsomely situated academies; curators of twenty-seven splendid museums; press agents for the Brockton Fair and Berkshire dance colonies; female poets who weave votive offerings around Emily Dickinson's shrine at Amherst; photographers with perfectly stunning shots of the Quabbin Reservoir and wee salt-box houses in Nantucket —all this correspondence should be addressed to the Dead Letter Office.

No one (and this means residents of Massachusetts as well as summer visitors) can visualize just what a Colonial village looked like until he has seen Old Sturbridge, approximately halfway between Springfield and Worcester just off Route 20. Old Sturbridge is the Yankee equivalent of Virginia's Williamsburg—but with this difference: Williamsburg represents a splendid reconstruction of an actual town, while Old Sturbridge is a piece of pure invention, a re-creation of a rural community as it might have appeared say, in the year 1790, built to actual scale with a fidelity unequaled, I think, elsewhere in the world.

Here are some fifty-one buildings—homes, shops, mills, barns and a general store—moved piecemeal from all parts of New England and carefully re-erected around an oblong village green. At one end of the Common stands the crisp white Meeting House (Baptist in this case); at the opposite end is the Mansion House, built in 1796 by General Salem Towne, the most substantial citizen of Charlton. Commoner folk dwelt in unpainted houses, the front doors flush with the ground and the simple furnishings—blackened pots, hand-hewn settles, rush-bottomed chairs and pewter porringers—visible through tiny-paned windows.

There is a tavern, of course, a replica of those hospitable inns which offered bodily comfort to the traveler and a rum-flavored forum for local oracles. In front of the tavern stand the pillory and stocks—instruments of public atonement so important in Colonial literature and penology. Although guiltless of any crime, scarlet or even mauve, I thrust my head into the wooden collar of the pillory and felt, at the distance of two centuries, its shaming ignominy. When my transgressions are discovered, please put me in a quiet cell far removed from the jeers of my neighbors.

A whole civilization came alive as I stepped inside the Sturbridge General Store. By comparison, today's supermarket offers a meager line of goods. From wooden pegs hung the intricate gear of leather and brass (generically known as harness) that transmitted Colonial horsepower *via* collar, hames and breeching to the wagon or plough. There on the shelves were the percales, ginghams and calicoes that fascinated my distaff ancestry, and an array of buggy whips, ax helves, sledges, wooden jacks and horseshoes. I bought horehound drops that didn't taste quite as I had remembered them, and a rope of twist tobacco which proved why snuff—also on sale—was so popular among the gentry.

Some notion of the moral qualities expected of a rising young man of the period may be gained from an ad, dated 1793, tacked to the door.

> Wanted: An apprentice to attend store—a lad about 15 years old —honest, healthy, obliging and naturally diligent; who can write and cypher and is full willing not to assume the Buck or Man of Pleasure till he is out of his apprenticeship, as the person that wants him expects he will attend to business. For terms &c enquire of the printers.

For three centuries a feud has existed between Provincetown and Plymouth; both claim the honor of being the original landing place of the Pilgrims, and although I'm a Plymouth partisan myself it's only fair to admit that Provincetown has marshaled an impressive array of documents and memorials. The most imposing of these is the Pilgrim Monument, 252 feet in height, bearing an inscription written by the late Charles W. Eliot, president emeritus of Harvard University.

I happened to be present at the dedication of the Pilgrim Monument on August 5, 1910, and a more unscheduled presence would be hard to imagine. Accompanied by two other twelve-year-old Vikings I had shoved out of Green Harbor on a predawn tide for the express purpose of robbing some choice lobster pots about three miles off-shore. Now hauling up a lobster pot is a winch-sized job; in the process of boating a heavy trap we snapped off the centerboard of our dory, a catastrophe comparable to the *Queen Mary's* loss of her keel. A stiff offshore breeze drove us twenty-two miles straight into the fishhook pocket of Provincetown harbor; seeing the crowd at the base of the Monument, I thought that a committee had gathered to hail our safe passage. Not until I saw President Taft among the crowd did I realize that a landing more historic than mine was being commemorated.

In 1910, Provincetown was a sparsely populated village of rickety wharves and "Portygee" fishermen. Eugene O'Neill and Edna St. Vincent Millay hadn't yet added the luster of their names; and Harry Kemp, now the accredited laureate of the dunes, was scribbling verses in Greenwich Village. At that time one couldn't buy a post card or souvenir ash tray; the only merchandise on sale was cordage and fish nets, and the only mode of approach (other than by dory) was a narrow-gauge railroad that puffed interminably from Harwichport. The isolation of the place is illustrated by the case of the man who elected lifelong exile in Provincetown rather than live with his wife in Truro, some eight miles distant.

Today, although Provincetown struggles to maintain the fish-net simplicity of that earlier epoch, it has been taken over by "trippers" who arrive at noon by excursion boat from Boston and motorcars from every part of the United States. This daily influx is augmented by phalanges of Bohemians representing the seven moribund arts, and reaches a high-water mark during the summer months. When I was last there I found myself in a tide rip of tourists heavy with brummagem booty—hand-painted clamshells, periwinkle beads, glassware of dubious origin and pastels signed by the artist himself. The village of rickety wharves has become a neon-lighted midway flanked by motels, hamburger stands and gas stations.

Nothing in the foregoing paragraph should be interpreted as a slander against the natural beauties of Cape Cod or the unspoiled charm of such villages as Nauset, Eastham and other oceanside settlements which have managed to avoid the blight of summer mobs. Some of the finest smallboat harbors in the world are to be found on the southern coast of the Cape; among these, my personal choice is little-known Osterville. Approaching this snug anchorage by a winding road, I found myself crossing the Great Marshes, melancholy, though not somber, through a veil of gray rain. So Massasoit or any other pre-Colonial Indian must have seen these marshes and grieved at the prospect of losing them to the invaders, who first arrived in sailing ships but now come in twin-screw diesel yachts bringing plenty of wampum in their mahogany holds.

This wampum from all tourist sources now amounts to nearly a half-billion dollars annually. The care and feeding of out-of-state visitors ranks third among Massachusetts sources of revenue.

The Arnold Arboretum, controlled by Harvard University, is a 265-acre tract situated in Jamaica Plain and open to visitors throughout the year. Don't miss this nonstop show played by an everchanging cast of six thousand different specimens of flowers, shrubs and trees. The flowering season begins in late March with the blooming of exotic witch hazels, soon followed by alder and birch catkins heavy with pollen. Around the third week in April, Oriental cherry trees take over with a display of deep-pink blossoms, while Crabapple Sunday and Lilac Sunday, like ecclesiastic festivals, follow each other in blossomy procession. These weekend performances attract audiences of fifty thousand or more, and easily outdraw the attendance at a Red Sox double-header, which is about as high as one can go in estimating a Massachusetts crowd. On their appointed date in the horticultural calendar the torch azaleas flame into a red so brilliant that the air above them seems to be on fire. Mid-June sees the collection of shrub roses take the center of the stage, followed by the fragrant mock orange. As summer deepens into July, the viburnum is berried over with red fruit which ripens throughout August. Birds migrating to warmer climes pause in their passage for a day of feasting.

My personal interest reaches its peak when the mountain laurel (*Kalmia latifolia*) lies massed, pink-blossomed and glossy-leaved, at the base of Hemlock Hill. I have a special fondness for laurel, traceable in part to sentiment, yet mixed, unsentimentally enough, with bread-and-butter considerations. *Kalmia latifolia* gave my father his start in business; as a young man of eighteen, he plunged into the woods of Northern Massachusetts, gathered a wagonful of wild laurel, sold it in the Boston flower market, and thus founded the business which still bears his name. When I was old enough to enter the woods, I spent whole summers gathering this hardy growth in the most inaccessible parts of my native state. During my travels, sometimes on horseback but mostly on shank's mare, I climbed the slopes of Mt. Greylock, followed the Appalachian Trail in Western Massachusetts, and found not only laurel but, infinitely more valuable, the taproots of an inner tranquillity to which I often return, in memory at least, for renewal and courage.

Tanglewood is located between Lenox and Stockbridge in Western Massachusetts. More formally known as The Berkshire Music Center, it attracts hundreds of students and thousands of music lovers to its annual summer sessions. Tanglewood was established in 1937 by the Boston Symphony Orchestra as a training ground for promising young musicians; under the distinguished leadership of the late Serge Koussevitzky and Charles Münch it has become the American equivalent of Bayreuth.

For six midsummer weeks the Berkshire glade vibrates like a harp string. Merely to identify the sounds made by the various instruments —bassoons, oboes, horns, trumpets, trombones, bass fiddles, violas, flutes and timpani—as they rise singly or in unison from every part of the forest, is in itself a musical education. Public Open Rehearsals, held every Saturday morning, enable the lay visitor to watch and hear a Stravinsky *divertimento* or a Bach suite being whipped or cajoled (according to the maestro's temperament) into presentable form.

Anyone who presumes to write about Boston runs the risk of being branded a literary poacher. You see, the city has been sequestrated as a kind of game preserve by the author of *H. M. Pulham, Esq.* Anecdotal rights are fiefed out (in a manor of speaking) to Mr. Cleveland Amory, and thus Boston has become a strictly posted property with seignorial dues payable at the end of every royalty period. I have no wish to disturb this highly profitable arrangement between two fellow authors—but look, I saw the place first. May I not be permitted (just this once) to mention Beacon Street, Commonwealth Avenue and Scollay Square without risking a plagiarism suit? I'll take the chance anyway. To paraphrase Van Wyck Brooks' remark about Bronson Alcott: "Who can expel a man from the Garden of Eden that exists behind his own brow?"

My favorite view of this personal Eden is the 180-degree panorama of Boston as seen from a twelfth-story window in the Ritz Carlton Hotel. The foreground of this nostalgic scene hasn't changed for fifty years. Directly below my eyes is a willow-fringed lake, its waters cloven by the prow of that enchanted vessel, the Swan Boat, familiar to good little boys and girls whose parents take them holidaying in the Public Gardens—as mine took me, and as I, in turn, took my own children. To the left are the Versailles-like flower beds; from their midst rises the equestrian statue of George Washington, heroic bronze gathering a patina of ever-deepening green. At the extreme left, Beacon Street climbs upward past a façade of fine Bulfinch houses, some of them jeweled with occasional panes of amethystine glass. My gaze, continuing to rise, encounters the dome of the State House, originally coppered by the ubiquitous Paul Revere.

In summer the foliage of specimen trees on the Common obscures the battlefield where young Henry Adams and his Brahmin schoolmates clashed with the "muckers" (sons of Irish immigrants) in snowball fights. When winter turns these trees into bare ruined choirs, the discerning eye can pick out the spire of the Park Street Church where Henry Ward Beecher preached hell-and-damnation sermons that still reek of brimstone every time you open their printed versions. Opposite the Boylston Street exit of the subway—the first to be built in the United States—the eye encounters two almost equally ancient landmarks: the once exclusive Touraine, and the Colonial Theatre.

All this, or something very much like it, has been going on forever. The changeless prospect gives one a sense of permanence—character, if you will—not to be found in any other American city. This sense of permanence will be undisturbed so long as you remain in your Ritz eyrie; the real test occurs when you descend, Leica in one hand, guidebook in the other, to the level of sidewalk mortals and start off jauntily for a tour of the city.

The late, greatly lamented Bernard DeVoto once advised: "The best way to see Boston is on foot." Excellent advice, I'd say; the only danger being that most people get lost. Boston is a model city—modeled that is, after the Cretan labyrinth with cowpath complications. As one who has trod this maze of narrow streets and still narrower alleys until they are as familiar as his own signature, let me lead you to a few well-remembered, and worth-remembering, scenes.

Stand with me on the steps of the Boston Public Library and gaze eastward across the wide, comparatively uncluttered plaza of Copley Square. You are looking at Trinity Church, a massive cruciform structure of Dedham granite, symbolizing (for me at least) the unbroken continuity between Renaissance architecture and its noble adaptation by Henry Hobson Richardson to a plot of New England real estate. On our right is the Sheraton Plaza . . .

But no, forgive me, I cannot wear the uniform of a Blue Line

Guide. I must wander off by myself, secretly grieving at the shabby blight that has fallen upon buildings once fresh with promise. The old Georgian Café, where Vernon and Irene Castle introduced the Castle Walk, is now a sea-food restaurant. The closed doors of the Opera House are plastered with ancient cinema posters. The mean streets in the North End become more desolate with the passing years; the long-ago fashionable Faubourg of the West End has deteriorated into a jungle of rooming houses, and not even Commonwealth Avenue has escaped the spreading rash of TO LET placards.

These symptoms of decay are more than offset by a terrific expansion in the suburban area. Successive migrations, first to Dorchester and Brookline, later to Milton, Winchester, Dover and Lexington, have created a flourishing metropolitan area outside of Boston proper. If these cities and a half-hundred like them could be induced to merge into a single municipality, Boston with a population of 2,500,000 would be the fourth largest city in the United States. (At present it's tenth.) Well, *tempers fidgit*, as James Joyce says, and who knows; a quarter of a century hence Boston may regain its former high rank in the census tabulation.

Meanwhile, I like the place just as it is. I like the benches beside the placid Charles, where I can watch one of the oldest rivers on the continent flow seaward past the oldest university in the United States. I like the sauerbraten in Jake Wirth's, and the bargain-stalls in Goodspeed's Book Store. I like the bustle of the Italian district; the fine shops along Marlboro Street and the seemly hush of the Boston Athenaeum. I like Paul Brooks to invite me to lunch at the Botolph Club, where I can hear urbane conversation and enjoy clam chowder uncontaminated by tomatoes. I like the purple haze of the Blue Hills as seen from my brother Charles' lawn in Milton; and I like to bake under a July sun along the first-base line in Fenway Park with my boyhood friend Lieutenant Governor Robert F. Murphy. Most particularly I like Louisburg Square with its prim-fronted bowwindowed houses facing each other across a central green enclosed by an iron fence with no gate. I do not, however, like Scollay Square, and the next few lines should tell you why.

Few remember more vividly than I the events which took place in Scollay Square on the evening of September 10, 1919, when the Boston Police Force went on strike. Within an hour after the police laid down their badges, the life and property of some half million persons were threatened by a reign of terror. Hordes of bullying rascals swarmed up from the North and South Ends; flying squadrons of petty thieves pilfered small shops, assaulted pedestrians and played dice in the middle of Court Square.

Shocked by these indignities, I immediately tendered my services to the mayor as a volunteer policeman. In the Joy Street station a grizzled police captain named Goff handed me a loaded .32-caliber revolver and asked me if I knew how to use it. As a former Navy instructor in small arms, I said "Yes." "Don't let them get behind you," he warned, then dispatched me to Scollay Square, the vortex of the riot.

Here I met the People, 20,000 of them, milling about in their raw unbolted state, throwing their nightcaps in the air, and acting like all mobs since and before Caesar. I had been directed to keep the trolley tracks clear; with some faint notion that my orders should be followed, I managed to get one trolley car through that human puddle; then the tidal wave of mob-rage broke. A cobblestone whizzed out of the crowd and traveled in a lethal arc toward my head; the cobblestone was intercepted by the cheekbone of a hunchback who was flailing me with his huge fists. The hunchback slumped unconscious, and the mob leaped for vengeance upon the Volunteer.

"Kill the bastard," they cried, stripping me of my coat and shirt. They knocked me down upon the cobblestones; they covered me with a filth of mud and language. As I lay on the stones, being kicked to death, I drew my revolver, and in language I'd rather not repeat—

Well, why not repeat it?

My exact words were: "I'll kill the next son of a bitch that touches me." And I meant it. The crowd opened like a fan and I stood with my back to a subway kiosk for sixteen mortal hours. I saw another volunteer make the fatal mistake of running away. The mob trampled him like a roach, and no bronze plaque marks the spot of the second Boston Massacre.

Violence, whether physical or intellectual, has always been the norm in Massachusetts; Henry Adams, most thoughtful of her sons, failed in his lifelong effort to discover harmony (education, he called it) in the scuffle of opposites—political, economic, religious and racial —which gives the state its dynamic character. Properly read, the *Book of Massachusetts* is a saga of fierce contradictions, loud on every page with the voices of tea spillers and Tories, patriots and six-per-centers, poet-idealists and bigot-reformers. Yes, the schism in the soul of Massachusetts is deep, but her tissues like those of Leviathan are mysteriously self-repairing. If the Bay State provides a study in contrasts, it may also be regarded as a triumph of adaptation.

Striking evidence of this adaptive process may be found in the personalities of the state's two U. S. Senators. Glance briefly at their lineage and achievements, then ask, "What hath evolution wrought?"

For three centuries the name Saltonstall has been a synonym for all that betokens tradition, social leadership and strongly entrenched wealth. The senior Senator from Massachusetts is a descendant of Sir Richard Saltonstall, who in 1630 sailed into Boston Harbor on the *Arbella* and proceeded to found Watertown, the first inland settlement of Massachusetts. The senior Senator is a former governor of Massachusetts, a Republican, a Unitarian, a member of the Somerset Club, a graduate of Harvard College and, if I may permit myself the luxury of a *non sequitur,* an outstanding public servant.

John F. Kennedy, Democrat, Roman Catholic, and also a Harvard graduate, is a grandson of that "Honey-Boy" Fitzgerald, whose repertory began and ended with *Sweet Adeline.* Johnny Fitz, as he was called by his loyal American-Irish constituents, could be mayor of Boston any time at all, at all, but higher he could not go. The Somerset Club, arbiter of who is or isn't a proper Bostonian, rolled out the wicked blackballs whenever his name came up for admission, and the close-packed phalanx of State Street investment brokers, "hard-shelled Protestants" and Republicans west of Boston seconded the motion by rebuffing "Honey-Boy's" gubernatorial aspirations.

The Fitzgerald story might have ended with Johnny Fitz's retirement to Hull, where I frequently saw him wandering rather aimlessly about his modest estate. But just about this time, one of "Honey-Boy's" daughters married a brilliant young man, Joseph Patrick Kennedy by name, and this J. P. Kennedy went on to become very rich—richer, probably, than any Saltonstall. Kennedy became in the space of two decades a bank president, an investment broker, Chairman of the S.E.C., and wound up—much to the consternation of the Somerset Club—as Ambassador to the Court of St. James's.

A phenomenal one-generation climb, as you'll agree. But his son, John F. Kennedy, has outstripped both his father and grandfather in a career of distinguished public service.

The moral of my tale—if indeed there be a moral—is this: in two generations the people of Massachusetts have closed the gulf that formerly yawned, deep as the Continental Abyss, between the Brahmin few and the immigrant-sprung many. The *rapprochement* existing between two such highly civilized human beings as Senators Saltonstall and Kennedy does not mean, of course, that the millennium has arrived in Massachusetts. Conflicts still rend the state; many barnacles must yet be scraped from her hull. But the collective impulse is definitely forward. My own feelings, which happily agree with those of less biased observers, tell me that Massachusetts is entering upon a second flowering more vigorous than its first.

The state may never again generate cultural energies exactly similar to those which emanated a century ago from Boston, Concord and Cambridge. Yet something deeper than personal optimism causes me to believe that this sixth-smallest, sixth-richest, much-visited state will continue to be "learning's altar," a magnet for capital, the Log, Ledger and Pentateuch of North Temperate Civilization—and, not too incidentally, one of the loveliest scenic cameos ever carved by Nature's hand.

Rhode Island

by CHRISTOPHER LAFARGE

I found myself talking about Providence, Rhode Island, with a man from Kansas City, Missouri.

Armed with considerable curiosity and a letter of introduction, he had lunched with me, and afterwards I had taken him to the cabin I use as a workshop, on the shore of Buckey Pond, in South County, Rhode Island. This man, whom I shall call the Stranger, had the intention of settling in Providence, moving his jewelry business and his family there from Kansas City; and he had asked me to tell him about Providence.

I inquired how much he knew about the city.

"I've just spent three days there," he said, "and I don't understand it. It doesn't add up according to my standards. From a business point of view I figure I can do well there, but what I want to know is, what's the city like to live in?"

"If you're prepared to conform rigidly to the doctrines of tolerance, individualism and conservatism—in other words, to follow strictly a pattern of nonconformity—you ought to be able to be happy in Providence," I said.

"That sounds pretty contradictory," said the Stranger.

"Maybe it is," I said. "But that's Providence. The city is full of inconsistencies and contradictions. That's part of its particular quality and charm."

"Is it?" he said. "For instance?"

Instead of answering his question, I asked what sort of impression the city had made on him.

"It didn't make a very good first impression," he answered. "But what struck me most was the wild country before you get to the city. Looked so deserted."

"That's one of the odd things about it," I said. "There's Providence, the second largest New England city, and the capital of the smallest state in the Union—with, incidentally, the longest name. . . ."

"Longest?" he interrupted.

"The State of Rhode Island and Providence Plantations," I said. "Almost 90 per cent of the state's population lives within a fifteen-mile radius of the downtown area of the city. So you have the curious fact that Rhode Island has huge areas so wild and sparsely settled that they look almost as they did a hundred and fifty years ago—and this in a state with the densest population in the Union; 712 people per square mile."

"Well," he said, "you land right in the middle of the population when you get off the train!"

"Did you see the State Capitol?" I asked.

"I got a good look at that from the train. That's a mighty handsome building. I can't say as much for the depot you land in, that Union Station."

"No," I said. "It's old and plain—though they used to serve the best clam chowder you ever sat down to. One of the sad things is the way the station and its elevated tracks block off the view of the capitol. One of America's most famous architects, Charles McKim, designed the capitol. A curious thing about it is the figure on top of its dome. It's not a statue of a famous Rhode Islander like Roger Williams, or General Nathanael Greene, or Canonicus, the Indian chief, or Benedict Arnold, or . . ."

"Benedict Arnold?" the Stranger said. "Why should anyone put his statue on a dome?"

"He was the excellent first Governor of Rhode Island," I said. "A different man; 17th Century. It's a tough break for him that his name was worn so differently later on."

"Who's the statue of?"

"The Independent Man," I said. "But he's more often referred to—and more accurately—as 'The Individual Man.' That's what you always come back to in Providence. Individualism. It costs a lot."

"It always does," said the Stranger. "Particularly nowadays. You wonder if it's worth it sometimes."

"It's worth it if you think it is," I said. "Providence thinks so. It began with it and it hangs on to it. It hangs on to a great many things that other cities have discarded. Some are good and some are bad."

"I don't get the picture, then," said the Stranger. "I came here because I was told Providence was an industrial city. I'm in the jewelry business, and it's the most important jewelry-manufacturing city in the country. It didn't get to be that by lack of progress, did it? Because I was interested, I asked questions and I found that there's nearly every kind of manufacture and industry you can think of. It's been rich and I guess it still is. What I don't understand is how a city can get to be like that and yet have a main street like Westminster Street."

"What struck you about it?"

"It's the contrasts that are so sudden," he went on. "When you get out of the Union Station you land in Exchange Place. There you see the only skyscraper in the city, the Industrial Trust Building. It's big and it's modern, but it's alone in its glory, and it certainly doesn't go very well with that ugly old City Hall at the other end. And right back of the Industrial Trust is that funny little tunnel they call The Arcade. It looks old."

"It is," I said. "It was built in 1828."

"You wouldn't think it could have survived in the middle of a business district," he said. "It may be good to look at but I can't see how it can claim enough usefulness to warrant survival."

"They like it," I said. "That's the reason."

"Anyway, after I got settled in at the Biltmore Hotel—that's a fine hotel, too—I took a walk through the shopping district. It seems to center on Westminster Street. Boy! I was brought up on the theory that the quickest way you could size up a town was to case its shopping district and see what sort of shops you found. Well, the busiest block on Westminster Street held three five-and-dime stores—and the streets of the shopping district are so narrow that the traffic can hardly move in them."

"That's true," I said. "But there's another shopping district, with good shops, small ones, up on Wayland Square, on the hill of the East Side."

"That may be," he said, "but I didn't find it. And another thing. I walked along South Main Street looking for an address, and the building there that's numbered 50 stands between those numbered 72 and 86."

"That's right," I said. "That's the office of John Nicholas Brown. You've probably heard of him. When he was little the papers used to call him the richest baby in the world. Even with that handicap he has become a fine citizen. His office was numbered 50 before the other buildings were put up and the state passed a special law giving it the right to keep its old number."

"Are there many more things like that?"

"Everything's like that," I said, "including the whole Brown family that John Nicholas comes from. There's little about Providence that hasn't a contradiction attached to it except the fact that the city isn't like any other city—not even like any other in New England. I mean in all ways—history, industry, wealth, social life, customs and manners, architecture and even politics."

"Can you give me some examples?"

I took a deep breath. "Make yourself comfortable," I said. "I love to talk about Providence."

The Stranger lit a cigar.

"Begin with the history," he said.

"All right," I said. "There were five people who really founded the state between 1636 and 1645, and all of them were kicked out of Massachusetts. Individualists, too early in the game for the Bay State. The first was Roger Williams. He got thrown out of Massachusetts in 1635 because they thought his religious preaching was seditious. He settled in Providence and he gave the place that name in commemoration of 'God's providence to him in his distress.' But what was unusual about Williams was that he instituted the doctrine of religious tolerance so effectively that it continues with vitality today. When the earliest settlers drew up a covenant to live under, it stated specifically that it bound its subscribers 'only in civil things.'"

"Who were the other four?"

"John Clarke and William Coddington, Anne Hutchinson and Samuel Gorton. These people had been pushed around so much that they set up a government that was against pushing around. They let in a Jewish congregation in 1658. They let in the Quakers in 1657—over the howls of protest of Massachusetts. Even as late as 1842, Rhode Island had to refuse to co-operate with other states in expelling Quakerism."

"Were these people particularly religious?" the Stranger asked.

"Yes. Williams and a man called Ezekiel Holyman founded the Baptist Church soon after, and later Williams became what he called a Seeker."

"I don't know what a Seeker is," he said.

"Someone who accepted no organized doctrine but continued to search for the good in all doctrines."

"But do you class that as an inconsistency?"

"Only in the sense that it helped to set the pattern—still strong—of the ability of man to be a nonconformist there," I said. "All the inconsistencies followed—they still follow—that pattern. For instance, Rhode Island got rid of all religious bars to suffrage by 1783, but it didn't begin to remove the restriction of property ownership until Thomas Wilson Dorr staged his rebellion in 1842. It was abortive as a rebellion, but it was ultimately effective."

"Rebellion?" he asked. "Anyone get hurt?"

"The casualties were one cow and the wounding of the usual innocent bystander," I said. "But here is some more of the same sort of thing. The state eliminated slavery in 1784—you can still see the old slaves' graveyards in the state—yet it continued to make money by running slaves to the South. It had enough patriotic privateers turned pirate to hang twenty-six of them in 1723. It passed its own Act of Independence on May 4, 1776—two full months before the more famous July 4, so it can justly claim to be the oldest independent state in the union. Yet it nearly didn't join the union afterwards. It was little and it had been pushed around so much by its two bigger neighbors, Massachusetts and Connecticut, that it distrusted the whole idea of a federal union. It did finally join in May, 1790—but by a vote of only 34 to 32."

"Rhode Islanders sound as if they were tough people to push around," the Stranger said.

"They still are," I said. "We talked of the Capitol building in Providence. It was finished in 1900, and in that year this tiny state finally settled on Providence as its only capital. Before that it had five capitals, so that no district could push any other around."

"Five capitals!" he exclaimed. "Where were they?"

"Newport, South Kingstown, Bristol, East Greenwich and Providence," I said. "They were used in rotation. But I remember that my father told me most nostalgically of the final session of the legislature at Newport, quite as though something valuable had been lost. Centralization to him, as well as to masses of other Rhode Islanders, living and dead, must have seemed to make more difficult the free growth of the individual—the Individual Man who stands on the dome, as it were—and to limit his opportunities to practice nonconformity."

"You say they don't like change," said the Stranger, "but Providence couldn't always have been an industrial city."

"No," I said. "It made itself into a prosperous city with a remarkably large group of wealthy citizens by agriculture, with slaves, to begin with. And they raised horses—the famous Narragansett pacers. When all that declined, they took to commerce on the high seas, with profitable side lines in slaves and rum. Although it's thirty miles from city to ocean, Providence is a natural harbor, well sheltered, lying at the head of Narragansett Bay. Then when wars and railroads made shipping less than highly profitable, the city began a successful industrial growth, starting with the milling of textiles and going on to that great diversity of industry and manufacture you mentioned yourself. At that point, like every other city, it enlarged and changed its population."

"You see a lot of different sorts," he said. "I kept meeting people with Irish and French and Italian names."

"Yes," I said. "The foreign-born and their first-generation children are about 65 per cent of the population now. You mentioned the three largest groups, but there are also English, Germans, Swedes, Hungarians, Syrians, Greeks, Poles, Czechs, Portuguese, and Yugoslavs."

"How have they assimilated?" he asked.

"Very well," I said. "The Italians perhaps the best of the lot. They've produced many fine citizens. They've even fallen in with the doctrine of individualism. And in spite of a mixed population, Providence hasn't got a corrupt government, really. But it has some funny quirks to it. The state government is Republican in control and the city is unchangeably Democratic. In fact, it is said of city politics that to be backed by the G.O.P. is to receive the kiss of death."

"But they get Democratic governors and senators," he said.

"Yes," I said. "But look. There's the perennial deadlock on representational reform in government and, in particular, in the state senate. The Democrats, who have been in the ascendant for many years, keep trying to call a constitutional convention. It's the only way by which they can ever get control of the senate. The senate remains firmly Republican because senators are elected by an antiquated system which gives each town, regardless of size, equal representation.

A Republican town like Exeter, with only a few hundred voters, thereby elects a Republican senator—but Newport, for instance, also can elect only one. As there are a great many rural Republican towns you get what is in effect a 'rotten borough' system. A constitutional convention requires the sanction of the Senate which of course refuses. This long deadlock was almost broken in 1923, but the explosion of a stink bomb—an odd weapon for a conservative opposition—knocked out five senators, and the subsequent self-exile to Massachusetts—of all places—of twenty-one Republican senators prevented a quorum from assembling and neatly blocked the reform. It failed again in 1950. Perhaps it will require another Thomas Dorr to break the deadlock at the expense of another innocent bystander and cow."

The Stranger laughed and he said, "Well, you get funny business in politics everywhere. I'll take it easy till I get it all figured out."

"In the meantime," I said, "you've got to find a place to live with your family."

"What are the choices?" he asked.

"Depends on how you like to live and how much you want to spend. There are pretty violent contrasts. You have the sort of crowded sections you find on Federal Hill to the west of the Capitol, where the Italians congregate. Except for the physical appearance of the architecture—mostly shabby and wooden—the place is more foreign than American in atmosphere. The inhabitants call it 'The Hill'—which has its humor because the East Side, the social side of Providence, also refers to itself as 'The Hill.' Just depends on which hill you're climbing up to—or coming down from.

"If you want to live in Providence, you'll probably live in a house. There are very few apartments. The house will probably sit on a small plot of ground with a garden for flowers. Or you can live in the country and commute."

"I don't like commuting," he said. "I'd like to live in a really pleasant section of the city."

"That narrows your choice, then," I said. "It probably means the East Side—the other 'Hill.' That's the part that has so many of the beautiful old houses—and the streets with the delightful names, such as Benevolent, Hope, Benefit, Faith, and Friendship."

"Do the inhabitants live up to those names?"

I laughed and said, "About as well as any community. Have you seen that part of the city?"

"No," he said.

"You should go," I said, "and take your wife. Do it simply as tourists, it's well worth it. The famous houses are well listed in the WPA Guide for Rhode Island, but I'll tell you a few of my favorites that you shouldn't miss. Visit the First Baptist Meeting House, built in 1775, and the John Brown House on Power Street, which houses the magnificent collection of local material of the Rhode Island Historical Society. President John Quincy Adams said of the John Brown House that it was the most magnificent and elegant mansion he had seen in this country. From my own observation I'm inclined to agree with him. Both these buildings were designed by an extraordinary man named Joseph Brown, who was accomplished as an astronomer, merchant, philosopher and architect, and was one of four astonishing brothers who founded a fortune and a precedent so well that, in Providence to this day, there are members of the family who are still wealthy, intelligent and useful citizens. I spoke before of his descendant, John Nicholas Brown.

"You should also see the Nightingale house on Benefit Street, built about 1792, and the Crawford Allen house of 1820 on Benevolent Street. There are plenty of beautiful old buildings in the East of the United States, but there are none more lovely, or built with greater grace or sophistication than those in Providence."

"Does anyone still live in these houses?" the Stranger asked me.

"Oh, yes," I said. "In some of them. Lots of the houses are still lived in by descendants of their builders. If you could work it, you'd be interested to get inside some of those East Side houses. They might surprise you too. Mrs. Bruce Merriman's house, for example, is famous for the superb Chinese decorations in its unique ballroom by the late Harry Sleeper, in particular the ancient Chinese wallpaper. Then there's the lovely Edward Carrington House which belonged to a prominent shipping family and is now owned by the Rhode Island School of Design. About the only thing these houses have in common is excellence of taste—and that's traditional to Providence. Add the fact that in Providence there is absolutely no one 'fashionable' church, and you see what I mean by individualism and diversity."

"Your East Side, then," said the Stranger, "doesn't have the inconsistency you spoke of."

"Yes, it does," I said. "It consists in this: walk from the center of its grace and charm and, no matter which direction you choose, it declines architecturally into dreary wooden slums, or geographically into the open sewer of the Providence River. The contrast is striking and depressing, and I'm afraid it's quite as typical of Providence as any other single characteristic. Sometimes the act of preservation of what you have leads to atrophy."

"What causes that, in so rich a city?" he asked.

"Maybe it's because Providence is a city where the bulk of the wealth, which is very considerable, is held by an infinitesimal minority of the citizens—who have struck a cool and workable bargain with the politically dominant majority; where intelligent planning and reform, for roads, airports, housing developments (Providence is successfully busy at all of these), can coexist with the fact that the city did not inaugurate its own rubbish-collection service until 1950.

"Tolerance, the freedom of the individual to be nonconformist— indeed the necessity to be so—these remain. But they have bred over the years a splitting off of wealth from the responsibilities and the risks of government.

"This is not to say that there is no vitality left in Providence. There is plenty of it. But no city group can flourish where most of its money is tied up in the sterility of the custodian account—the 'it's-so-safe-I-don't-have-to-think-or-take-any-responsibility' attitude. People like Mr. Royal Little keep fighting against this, and they're now being listened to."

"Well," said the Stranger, "that's all very interesting, but I don't think you're talking about my kind of person. What do people like me and my family do for recreation?"

"Again, it depends on what you're looking for," I said. "You can go sailing and fishing in the waters of Narragansett Bay. You can occupy your spare time pleasantly at Roger Williams Park, which is an uncommonly good one, with so many trees that there's hardly room for any more.

"Providence has a mild climate—except when hurricanes lambaste it the way they did in 1938 and 1944—and it's neither very cold in winter nor very hot in summer. But it can be hot enough so that you will want to take your family somewhere for a swim in salt water. That presents somewhat of a problem unless you are sufficiently well off to afford a summer place in the southern part of the state. Those who have money enough own or rent houses near Newport or Narragansett, and some of them, of course, belong to the very expensive clubs like Bailey's Beach or the Dunes Club. But it's a sad fact that the upper reaches of Narragansett Bay—that is to say, about the first twenty miles south of Providence—are polluted enough to make bathing disagreeable. The average inhabitant of Providence, therefore, must either buck the tremendous week-end traffic in his own car, or take a bus down to the magnificent beaches of Narragansett and Scarborough, almost thirty miles away—and there are no finer beaches, nor better salt-water bathing in the world.

"There's a good deal of music. The Boston Symphony Orchestra plays a series of Tuesday evening concerts and is supported and attended slightly more religiously than any of the churches. I think that orchestra has been playing in Providence for close to sixty years. The Rhode Island Philharmonic, under Francis Madeira, is particularly interesting because it is a full symphony orchestra using both professionals and amateurs. There are various groups of string quartettes that do chamber music, the Monday Morning Musical Club (which doesn't meet on Monday mornings), and the Chaminade Club.

"The Providence Public Library is a really first-class institution. Or you might be able to buy one of the 1009 membership shares in the Providence Athenaeum. This charming little library was founded in 1800 but it merged with an older one which had been founded in the 18th Century, and thus the contents of the library go back almost 200 years. It contains an interesting collection of books on travel, voyages, history, and a very complete line of detective stories."

"That sounds like a pretty complete cultural layout," said the Stranger.

"Yes," I said, "but maybe I should repeat to you Albert Jay Nock's observation about Providence. He said that he had never seen a city endowed with so superb a machinery of culture and without any visible, general effect of it through the city itself."

"But I understand Providence has its own colleges," the Stranger said. "How about them?"

"It's well supplied," I said. "It has Brown University, which is the seventh-oldest college in the United States and was chartered first in 1764 as Rhode Island College. It moved to Providence in 1770 and took the name of the Brown family in 1804. It's an excellent university with a lovely campus and some fine old buildings. An enormous proportion of those who can be called influential in Providence are graduates of Brown; yet it's a curious fact that the university as such has very little connection with the life of the city—even though it is situated in the middle of it. Pembroke College is the female counterpart of Brown. There are also the Rhode Island College of Education, a normal school, Providence College, which is Dominican-Catholic, and the Rhode Island School of Design. This last was helped by many gifts, notably from the Metcalf family, and began literally as a school of design, but is now an active and fully accredited college. If you have a son of college age, you should be able to satisfy his needs without his leaving Providence."

"I read a little about that in the papers," said the Stranger. "I can't remember whether it was in the Providence *Journal* or the *Evening Bulletin*. And speaking of that, how is it that a city the size of Providence has only those two papers?"

"I don't know," I said. "But what's even more extraordinary is that both of them are the property of the same Metcalf family I just spoke of. Both of them are really excellent in their reportage of local and foreign news, and both are notable for their editorials—but what beats me is that, although both are Republican and are thus, in Providence, on the conservative side of the fence, they can excoriate a Republican senator for isolationism and praise a Democratic mayor for his outstanding eleven-year record in the restoration of a sound financial system. Maybe this is one of the things that made you feel Providence didn't add up?"

"I hadn't thought of that specifically," said the Stranger. "It was just that the whole place sort of baffled me. I'm beginning to think it's because of these inconsistencies and contradictions you tell about."

"I've told you almost enough," I said. "But I'll add just one or two more observations. Maybe they will help you to understand Providence.

"First, I'll tell you about a brilliant individual of the older generation, whom I shall call Mr. X. Mr. X has a mind thoroughly educated in the best sense of the word. He retains, in the fashion of Macaulay, practically anything which he has ever read in the course of his long life—and he is a constant reader of catholic taste. He comes from one of the old Providence families and he has been (until recently) head of an old, established, and once very prosperous Providence concern. He owns one of the fine houses of Providence and he has another outside of the city. He subscribes, for himself, his friends, and in particular for his employees, to the doctrine of punctuality and hard work.

"This gentleman—I am using the term advisedly—almost wrecked the business he owned, by refusing to modernize his methods. This business has been heavily indebted for years, but it has been kept alive by its creditors because there was always hope that a younger relative, a man of ability and imagination, would ultimately be able to wrest control from Mr. X. During this prolonged process, before the relative *did* succeed, Mr. X continued to live as handsomely as he had always lived and to withdraw from the business, regardless of its condition, such sums as he needed to continue his pleasant process of living. And all that time, he remained one of the most interesting and distinguished minds of his city.

"Yet even when the concern, by sheer necessity, had passed into the management of the younger man, Mr. X continued to arrive with punctuality at the office—a blessing of dubious value, since he was likely to send out to buy expensive cigars with the concern's petty cash.

"I know of almost no other American community where such an individual, operating openly and with a sort of rugged acerbity and contempt for opinion, could continue to be tolerated and even somewhat admired.

"The last observation I shall make is this one. There are lots of charitable enterprises in Providence, but there's one that's really unique. It's called the Providence Female Charitable Society, and it was founded during the Civil War to sew for the wives and widows of soldiers. From this not unusual beginning it developed into a society where each member made it her personal concern to help privately, with comfort, or with money, some woman who needed help but was of a class that could not—or because of pride, would not—be helped by public charities. Aid from their funds is never accounted for except to the Directress or the Treasurer. What's done is done by the individual for the individual, in such a fashion that no regimentation is possible nor can interfere with the graciousness of its method.

"I have told you these stories because they sum up for me much of the quality of Providence: its stiffly maintained individuality; its civilized, tolerant, flexible backwardness; its juxtapositions of opposites in beauty and ugliness, progress and reaction, intelligence and mediocrity.

"If you decide to live in Providence, it may take five or even ten years before they really accept you. Once you have been accepted you will find many things and places and people to respect, to admire, and to love. But don't try to conform—be yourself if it kills you. You may even become enough of a Providencian to look down your nose at the rest of New England."

"All right," said the Stranger. "I think I'll give it a whack. Sounds as if the place was full of quality."

"It is," I said. "It's stiff with it."

Connecticut

by ARTHUR BARTLETT

The Indian word *Quinnehtukqut* meant: "Beside the long tidal river." The state of Connecticut, as now constituted, is well served by rivers—7600 miles of them; but the one from which it takes its name, along which it was originally settled, and which is still its central axis, is the Connecticut. "The Great River," the early settlers called it. Perhaps this was partly because the Indian word was too much of a mouthful, but it was also an honest evaluation. After the New England hurricane of 1938, a descendant of those early settlers expressed a like view. Surveying his fishing boat securely wedged between two trees in his back yard, where the wind and the gigantic tidal wave had deposited it, he remarked in melancholy admiration: "Ain't many rivers could do that."

It is indeed a Great River, the longest in New England. Up at the Canadian border, where it rises, it is just a trickle, but it picks up force and volume all the way down its 360-mile course between New Hampshire and Vermont, through Massachusetts, and then through Connecticut to Long Island Sound. Dropping some 1600 feet en route, it provides the water power on which are based many of New England's cities—Bellows Falls, Brattleboro, Turners Falls, Greenfield, Holyoke, Springfield, Windsor Locks, Hartford, Middletown. These are important cities in the economic life of New England, and the Great River made them so.

Yet by the time the river crosses the Connecticut state line—and it is with the river and its valley from that point on that this writer is primarily concerned—it is, for the most part, a practical Yankee river, little given to the exhibitionism of swirls and rapids. For some five miles, above Hartford, it does churn up what the settlers called the "white water" of Enfield Rapids, but for the rest of its course through the state it offers no more serious menace to navigation than currents and tides and an occasional sand bar through which a channel must be kept dredged. Ever since Adriaen Block, a Dutch seafarer, discovered it in 1614, and sailed up as far as the "white water," the river has been a busy waterway.

For well over two centuries, sailing ships came in and out, and as towns grew up in the river valley, sailors from these towns went all over the world in ships built along its banks. After the steamboat era came, every town from the mouth of the river up to Hartford had its dock; and such vessels as the *Oliver Ellsworth,* the *Water Witch* and the *City of Hartford* successively cut down the length of time it took to make the run to and from New York—only a few of them bursting their boilers in the attempt. Today the commercial vessels moving up and down the river are mostly barges and tankers; but in summer white sails again stand out against the green shores, and little skiffs with outboard motors share the water with ocean-going power yachts, as a generation of pleasure sailors makes the river a playground.

The broad central valley through which the river flows for two thirds of its course through Connecticut is the heart of the state, a rich, busy, self-sufficient middle ground between an extended New York suburbia to the west and a hilly hinterland to the east. Some of the state's greatest industrial cities are here—though one hardly thinks of them as river towns; and the center of population of the state is only slightly to the southwest of the valley. Here, too, are the state's richest agricultural lands. The valley is the most important tobacco-growing area in the North, and the tobacco raised in half a dozen of its towns is the state's third greatest crop in cash value; while in total value of all farm products sold, Hartford County, which is the upper half of the valley, is the twenty-fourth ranking county in the nation. Even culture seems to flourish along what is sometimes called the River of Colleges, though at least four of the institutions which justify the name are above the Connecticut state line—Dartmouth in New Hampshire and Amherst, Smith and Mt. Holyoke in

Massachusetts—and the famous College Highway veers westward from the river at Northampton to emerge, eventually, at New Haven, the seat of Yale. Yet Yale itself was originally founded in the valley, at Saybrook, and Trinity at Hartford and Wesleyan at Middletown still have their being in the valley.

At Middletown the river takes an eastward swing, cutting through hill country to Long Island Sound. Thus its shoreline varies from green fields and meadows to wooded slopes, sandy beaches and sheer ledges, and brought from Timothy Dwight over a century ago the boastful opinion: "No other tract within the United States can be compared to it with respect to those objects which arrest the eye of painter and poet."

Mr. Dwight could hardly have seen, at that time, all that the United States has to offer, and, as a Connecticut Yankee, he may have been prejudiced; but in recent years this valley has arrested so many eyes—of painters, poets and many more—that country towns have been changed into suburban communities, farms into country estates, barns into summer theaters, lodge halls into art museums, hayfields into airports, and steamboat docks into yacht stations. Pratt's Village Smithy in Essex, which, until old Jim Pratt died a few years ago, had been a blacksmith shop for more than 250 years and was said to have been handed down from father to son longer than any other business in the United States, has since been converted, first into headquarters for a group of industrial-product planners, transplanted from New York, then into an antique shop. An old cranberry bog in Deep River has been dredged out to make a private harbor in front of the home of a wealthy new resident. So it goes.

Old Yankee families, with their roots in an earlier civilization of farming, shipbuilding and going to sea, still dominate the town meetings of most of the smaller towns, and much of the business and industry of the valley, but their control is being increasingly challenged by the newcomers. Two or three years ago the legislature held a hearing on a bill to permit certain zoning restrictions in one area where many newcomers had established homes. "Artists, writers and retired rich people," an old-timer scornfully called them, in opposing the bill, which was subsequently defeated. This is a very incomplete cataloguing, however, of the many new kinds of people who have moved into the valley in recent years, and whose ideas often tend to conflict with those of conservative Connecticut Yankees. "We're glad to have them buy property and improve it," said the opponent of change. "That's good for the tax list. But we don't like to have new people telling us how we can use our own property."

All this is in the pattern of the valley's history. In 1633, some Dutchmen from Manhattan Island tacked a sign on a tree at the mouth of the river. It bore the Dutch coat of arms, signifying, in modern terms: "Private Property. No Trespassing." A couple of years later, a party of English settlers pitched camp in the very shadow of the tree, tearing the sign down unceremoniously. Where it had been, one of the Englishmen carved a crude comment on Dutch pretensions to exclusive possession: a grinning face with the tongue stuck out derisively.

Ever since the Indians watched Adriaen Block sailing up the river in 1614, old-timers have been learning that when new people discover this covetable valley it is likely to mean a change in the way of life within it. The Indians were delighted to sell land to the white men for red calico and rum. They thought—not unlike some of their successors of more recent date—that it was a fine thing to have new neighbors move in to trade with them. By the time it had dawned on them that their own institutions were being overwhelmed, all they could do was to move to extinction as bloodily as possible.

The Dutch were quicker—but not quick enough—to realize the consequences of sharing the valley with new people. At first, thinking English help would be valuable to them in developing it, they had sent word to the Pilgrims at Plymouth that it was "a fine place for both plantation and trade." Their "No Trespassing" sign retracted this invitation when they concluded that the English might try to squeeze them out. The English moved in anyway, and did just that. The Dutch held on for a few years with a fortified trading post at Hartford, but finally gave up. The English, by that time, had well-established settlements at Windsor, Wethersfield, Hartford and Saybrook, and were spreading out all through the valley.

Even the Plymouth Pilgrims, the first Englishmen to start a settlement in the valley—or anywhere in Connecticut, for that matter—had to learn the lesson the hard way. Having explored the valley and been impressed by it, the Pilgrims invited the Puritans of Massachusetts Bay to join them in sending settlers. The Bay people, not having seen the place, declined, and the Pilgrims went ahead with their own expedition. Settling at Windsor, their party erected a house which had been built in sections and brought along on their boat—undoubtedly the first prefabricated house ever built in America. In the meantime, however, the Bay people had done some exploring of their own, and had changed their minds about the desirability of the valley. The Pilgrim settlers had hardly expanded beyond their one prefabricated house when an outnumbering detachment of Puritans arrived and insisted on taking over Windsor and running it their way. The Pilgrims argued their prior rights, but it finally became obvious that they were wasting their breath, and they sold out to their Bay brethren, bemoaning their "unkindness."

The Old Yankees of the valley today are therefore mostly descendants of Massachusetts Puritans, who kept things firmly in their own hands and remained overwhelmingly in the majority for two hundred years or so. Back in the early 1800's, Elbridge Gerry, Jr., son of the Massachusetts statesman, crossed the valley on horseback, on his way to Washington, and left in his diary a pen picture of Connecticut Yankees which has never found its way into chamber of commerce literature. "With a very few exceptions," wrote Gerry, "they are rude and surly, and partake of the manner of bears. Always unwilling to oblige, when at any trouble, and the most inquisitive and officious of any people I know." Of course all this was many years ago, and no doubt young Gerry was a captious youth. It seems highly unlikely that Connecticut Yankees ever differed very much from other Yankees in the characteristics of which countless writers have sung—some singing sweet, some sour. Nevertheless, they have always been unmistakably Yankee, and they are today.

Just before World War I, an old gentleman named Mather—a name prominent in valley towns ever since divines of that formidable breed came with the early settlers—delivered a sort of valedictory address to his neighbors in the town of Deep River. He recalled that in his youth he had never seen anyone in the village who was not native born, that the "hired help" sat in complete equality at the family table, that the village store was the country club, and that everybody went to prayer meeting on Saturday night to get in the proper mood for observance of the Sabbath. "My years are about numbered," he concluded, "and my solicitude is that this town shall retain the tone the founders gave it."

It was a pious but futile hope. During his very lifetime, the valley had felt the inevitable effects of another influx of new people, European immigrants, mostly, who came during the era of industrialization. The first to come in any considerable numbers were Irish, but in the years just before and after the turn of the century even larger contingents of Italians and Poles moved in, along with occasional groups of others. Their threat to the previous way of life was not so much in any militant determination to take things over as in the evolutionary forces of economic and social change which they represented. Hartford, a town of only about 5000 in the early 19th Century, grew rapidly into a great industrial city. Middletown underwent a similar though less expansive metamorphosis.

To the west of the river, but still in the broad valley belt, in places where there had been little but farms and woodland, such new industrial cities as Meriden and New Britain grew up. Many of the smaller towns, like Mr. Mather's Deep River, also acquired new industries—and new people to man them. Today the families of these later arrivals from Europe outnumber the Old Yankees even in many of the small towns, while in the cities they are heavily in the majority. Though most of them came originally to work in factories, they have branched out into many other lines of activity. The change in the pattern of community life is never more apparent than on Sunday mornings, when the white-steepled Congregational meetinghouses, which dominate most of the valley towns architecturally, hold services for mere handfuls by comparison with the newer, cross-crowned Catholic churches.

Yet the small towns retain a definite Yankee flavor, which gives the valley its main character. The beautiful old colonial houses of Windsor and Wethersfield, for instance, face typical New England village greens; and Wethersfield takes a chuckling pride in the sagacity of an earlier generation which equipped the meetinghouse with a three-faced clock, saving the cost of a fourth face because it would serve only the burying ground. "All the old characters are gone," one Old Yankee mourned recently, as he braced himself against the counter of a general store in one of the valley's crossroads villages. The other loungers in the store looked at each other and grinned. The old relic, with his drooping mustache, his rubber boots, his wool shirt and his critical outlook on a changing civilization, was apparently unaware that he was a living refutation of his complaint. At the Chester and Hamburg fairs, yokes of oxen still engage in pulling contests, and, though tractors have long since become the major source of farm power, a few Old Yankees still hitch up the oxen for plowing.

In the spring, shad nets appear all along the river, from Higganum (from an Indian word for fishing place) to Saybrook, as they have for nearly three centuries, and Yankee fishermen peddle by day the fish they have taken by night. Connecticut River shad have long been hailed by many connoisseurs—and by astute Connecticut Yankees with an eye to markets—as the best in the world. Admittedly, the shad that goes up the Connecticut to spawn is the same shad—*Alosa sapidissima*—that goes up the Hudson, the Chesapeake and various other rivers, but some magic of Nature assumedly favors the Connecticut branch of the family with a superior flavor and texture—a superiority, many Old Yankee shad addicts insist, that is wasted on those finicky moderns who have their shad boned before cooking it. Old-timers can remember when shad were so plentiful in the spring that they sold at ten cents each, and eating places like the Pease House at Saybrook—still a famous shore-dinner resort—made a specialty of shad dinners which included all the shad a customer could eat. The shad run is smaller nowadays, but everybody still eats shad in season, and hundreds of thousands of pounds are shipped every year to New York and other markets. If the run is comparatively heavy, some surplus buck shad, even in these days of locker plants and home freezers, are still thriftily "put down" in brine, while smoked shad is one of the valley's notable delicacies.

A business directory of Essex, which is fairly typical, would include such names as Ferranti, Czepiel, Kelly, Greenberg, MacWhinney and Alexaitis along with such others as Doane, Lord, Burdick, Bushnell, Pratt and Prann, but the bankers are still likely to be named Bailey or Barnes, and such families as the Comstocks and the Wrights still live in the big Victorian houses and own the principal factories.

It is frequently said in the Connecticut Valley, as in many other parts of New England, that it takes at least twenty-five years for a newcomer to be accepted. This is an arbitrary and inexact rule of thumb. The actual length of time varies, depending on the newcomer's background, personality, manners and way of life. Most of the foreign families that moved into the valley during the era of industrialization won acceptance, or at least toleration, remarkably fast, considering their strangeness. As one veteran Yankee merchant explains: "They worked hard, paid their bills and minded their own business." Nothing could have commended them more to Yankee favor. By now most of these families have grown up with the Yankees, have been to school with them, and in some cases have intermarried with them, and they are no longer considered foreigners, except in the rarefied sense that only an Old Yankee is a bona-fide native.

Many of the more recent immigrants into the valley, though of old American stock, fit less readily into a simple, workaday pattern of life, and tend to set up new societies of their own. Their acceptance by the old society is accordingly less readily achieved. Artists are an obvious example. In the 1890's, an artist named Clark G. Voorhees, bicycling through Connecticut, made his own personal discovery of the valley and was so pleased with it that he bought an old house by the river and settled down. A year or so later, another artist, Henry W. Ranger, came along, was similarly impressed, and prevailed upon an Old Yankee maiden lady, Miss Florence Griswold, to take him and some of his friends into her ancient colonial house in Old Lyme as boarders.

This was the beginning of Old Lyme as an artists' colony: it soon became the largest in the East. Artists began buying old houses and farms, and today they own much of Old Lyme. Many of the most famous artists of the century have lived and worked there, and their work has made Old Lyme itself famous.

Only a moderate proportion of the valley's newer residents are "artists, writers and retired rich people." Other kinds of people, following other interests, have also settled here, and they have worked changes in the old communities. Essex, for instance, with its fine harbor just a few miles up the river from the Sound, was a famous shipbuilding port in the old days. In recent years it has become one of the most popular yachting centers along the North Atlantic coast, and a considerable number of its newer residents are yachtsmen. One of them, Chester Bowles, who built his house on Hayden's Point some years ago—partly, at least, because it gave him anchorage at his very front door—later went into politics.

Elsewhere in the valley towns, businesses and small industries have been started by new people, most of whom, like the artists, have been attracted by the rusticism and the Old Yankee character of the valley—which, of course, they are somewhat diluting by their presence.

Many of the younger and more modern-minded Yankees fraternize with them, and welcome them into the Rotary Clubs, the chambers of commerce and even into politics; but the more unreconstructed Old Yankees find it difficult to give their full approval to the kind of people who value a farm primarily on the basis of its view, the number of Dutch ovens and the width of the floor boards.

The Yankee ideal was left on record in the Mather valedictory address to Deep River. Captain Al Pratt, a schooner captain, had decided to quit the sea, Mr. Mather related, and had therefore bought a place to live. After much discussion around the potbellied stove in the store, one of his neighbors gave the final verdict:

"It's just the place Captain Al wants—four or five acres of ground, a stunwall around it, a story-and-a-half house, can keep a cow and a pig and what on airth more does a man want?"

Most valley towns have summer residents, though only a few are full-fledged resort towns. East Haddam, where Nathan Hale taught school, and where occasional subterranean rumblings known as the "Moodus Noises" have mystified people since Indian days, has a dozen or more big camps, hotels and boardinghouses, which cater to vacationists. Along the shore of the Sound, on either side of the mouth of the river, are beach colonies. One is Fenwick, named for George Fenwick, a leader of the early colonists, whose wife lies buried nearby. (Also nearby is the original site of Yale College, now marked only by a boulder in a field.) Katharine Hepburn has a summer home at Fenwick. As a Hartford girl, Miss Hepburn is, of course, an Old Yankee, and most of her Fenwick neighbors are well-to-do Hartfordians; but the majority of summer residents through the rest of the valley are New Yorkers, who may be considered a seasonal reinforcement of the other new people.

One summer recently, the *New Era,* a weekly newspaper circulating in the lower valley towns, published a gracious little editorial welcoming the summer folks back for the season. Being engaged, at the time, in a series of post-card opinion polls, the paper queried a sampling of its readers as to whether they enjoyed the valley more in the summer, when the summer residents were there, or in the winter, when they were not. A majority promptly voted for the winter. The editor was frankly surprised.

"Oh, well," said one Old Yankee, "he's only been around these parts himself a dozen years or so, or he wouldn't have asked the question. He said a lot of nice things about the summer folks, and he took it for granted that everybody would agree with him. Well, I expect most people did. Most of the summer folks are fine people—and what's more, they put money in our pockets by coming here. We wouldn't have 'em *not* come. But—well, when they come, the place is different, that's all."

It was ever so along the Great River.

PART II *The Mid Atlantic States*

New York

by CARL CARMER

The happiest entry into New York State, my grandfather used to say, is to be born there. The only disadvantage, he would add, is that you will not realize your enviable lot until you have grown old enough to travel and see how much less fortunate the natives of other regions are. Since he wore the long white beard of a patriarch and unfailingly served buckwheat pancakes and maple sirup for breakfast, I received his every word as gospel. Indeed, my boyish pride in New York was fortified on each of my frequent visits to his home in Dryden, in the center of the state, especially when he reminded me, as he did invariably, that my very birth might have occurred uncomfortably, high on a Tomkins County hill, had not his team of white-faced, York-State-bred Morgans made a record dash to the Cortland hospital.

If a life is begun by a hopscotch jump into a state's middle, it is natural that the early years of it be spent in concentric circles. The Genesee Valley, my mother's former home, was the first perimeter. My earliest memory is of a cobblestone inn beside the waters of Conesus, a minor digit of the Finger Lakes about twenty-five miles south of the city of Rochester. I was wakened in a second-floor bedroom and carried to a balcony outside a window. Below me, horses switched nervously under blue-jacketed riders, and long-eared dogs, brown-spotted on white, padded about eagerly snuffling the ground.

Such images lie far back in an adult's life; clouds surround them, then open for only a split second of sun. I would be a man before I knew that these riders of the Genesee Valley Hunt had 18th Century prototypes, that the Wadsworth family, who organized the Hunt in post-Revolutionary times, had chosen the blue-and-buff of Continental uniforms for their jackets rather than the conventional "hunting pink," which former riflemen of Washington's army might mistake for the garb of a British lobster-back. It was upon a latter-day unit of this same hunt that I looked down from the inn balcony.

My State is bright with glinting waters. That first glimpse of Conesus Lake was only a happy sample. Before too long I discovered that the winding Genesee River, pastoral in most of its reaches, raced so far below high bluffs at Mount Morris and at Letchworth Park that few dared stand at the edge of the Palisades to watch its white-water rapids and foaming cascades. At Rochester, the river was roofed over and went boiling under Main Street stores to make its long drop to the jagged rocks below. The waves of Ontario welcomed it a few miles farther north, making a wide blue ribbon border for the land.

I also discovered Niagara Falls, from the high wet spot where the Niagara thundered down past the Cave of the Winds and raced into the whirlpool beyond. My father and I once embarked on the little steamer *Maid-of-the-Mist*, whence we could see ahead of us the rushing mass of water leap from the high, sharp ledges and crash into the pool below, lifting clouds of spray which glittered into rainbows under the bright sun. "Why did you come here for your honeymoon?" my father asked of a couple standing beside us. "Because," said the bride, "it's the most wonderful place in all the world for a honeymoon," and I wondered why my dignified parent chuckled occasionally throughout the rest of the day. The mid-century elegance of the Cataract House impressed me, and I was awed when the desk clerk took an old register from the safe behind him and showed me the signature, "A. Lincoln."

And I discovered the bubbling springs that dot the countryside—springs that burn with a blue flame when ignited, like those in the Bristol Hills and in the little town of Cuba; waters that spurt hot from the depths of the earth and bring healing to men, like those at Sharon and Clifton and Lebanon; and others containing yellow sulphur of such repellent taste and smell that God-fearing folk agree it *must* be good for what ails them. Rambling, many-verandaed hotels grew up where people "took the waters"—not only at the famous spas in Saratoga and Ballston but even in little towns like Dryden where the taste of the springs was peculiarly abhorrent. My grandfather could recall when there was a cotillion almost every Saturday night in Dryden, and folks dressed fit-to-kill "promenaded" while the orchestra rested on the high balcony above the shining ballroom floor. Most of the guests were ladies, so there was always a need for extra gentlemen, and many a farm boy, if he had a clean shirt and a blue suit, received a little flowered card from the hotel management inviting him to foot it with the smart set.

In the red and gold of mid-October, 1825, came the opening of the great Erie Canal, with a boat parade that began at Buffalo and ended in New York Harbor. Governor Clinton's man-made river proved its worth by paying for itself promptly. It also scattered along its length the quick-grown settlements with the nautical names—Lockport, Middleport, Eagle Harbor, Brockport, Adams Basin, Spencerport, Weedsport, Port Byron—to compete with the older towns, those that had been given scholarly names years before by a lover of the classics—Syracuse, Ilion, Rome, Utica, Pompey, Homer, Marathon.

When I was seven we moved from the Genesee Valley to a canal town first named Newport but rechristened Albion, between Rochester and Niagara Falls. First I mourned the high hills we had left behind, then blessed the day we did. I learned to swim in a swift-running culvert that tapped the Erie to run a gristmill. I practiced jumping to the decks of the slow canal boats at one bridge and climbing back at the next. In the town's grimy newspaper office, whence a man of authority could spit through an open window into mid-channel, I heard tell of a day when a break in the canal bank left the water level so low that an Albion housewife, scooping out a washtubful, grounded all boats west of Rochester. And a certain carpenter, nearly seven foot tall and bearded like God—or Moses—sometimes came by to tell how he carried the Stars and Stripes through battle after battle in the Civil War and was never hit.

There was always work for a boy in Western New York State in the days that followed the turn of the century. Farmers had retired after a lucky run of five good harvests, industrialists had invested in the Suspension Bridge at Niagara Falls, speculators had risked a few hundred on Eastman Kodak stock at ten dollars a share, against the advice of their elders. ("It's only a passing fad.")

With their new wealth they had built big, rectangular, cupola-crowned houses far back from the wooden sidewalks, and hired boys to mow the level green lawns on Saturdays.

North toward the lake was more work, in the apple country—Baldwins, they keep well in the cellar; Greenings, nothing can beat 'em for pies; Pound Sweets, if you like 'em that way; Maiden Blush, pretty as they sound; Seek-no-furthers, they mean what they say; Northern Spies, best flavor in the world. Through the autumn days, pickers rode the swaying ladders, and when they emptied their pickbags into the barrels there was a hollow thundering against the staves. All night long the pickers tossed restlessly, as if their ladders were still bouncing on the resilient boughs.

Sometimes we bicycled nine miles to Oak Orchard, on Ontario's sandy shore. Our object was swimming and sunburn, but there were rewards en route. The road led through the "Land of the Cobblestone Houses," dwellings with local fieldstones, rounded and smoothed by the waves of Ontario, set into the mortar walls. Some are reddish because their walls hold only disks of a local rust-colored sandstone; others are striped in alternate red and white rows or have the stones slanted in herringbone patterns or set alternately deep and shallow to give a dappled shadow effect. Finding enough stones took as long as three years, even with neighborhood "gathering bees" which ended in feasting and dancing.

Oak Orchard today holds a more solemn mood than when I pedaled the country miles to its refreshing beach. The covered bridge that sang echoing welcome when a team trotted through and also offered deep shade to canoeing couples—("Paddle from under quick when a wagon comes, those floorboards don't sprinkle talcum powder")—has now been replaced by sullen steel and concrete. The Victorian dwellings no longer look upon green lawns. Wind-blown whitecaps have dug under the banks on which they were founded, and the gabled structures seem to waver in precarious balance as if they were about to dive into the rolling surf.

Other communities on the southern shore of Ontario have a gayer and more lasting look. Follow the coastline east to Sodus Bay and you will see stable, commodious summer residences sporting whimsical labels ("Our Social Security"), and boathouses sheltering fast sleep-in cruisers and faster speedboats. And westward, in the neighborhood of Buffalo, lakeside communities are numerous and crowded, and there are still others on the southern shores of smaller, more treacherous Lake Erie. And inland, along the slim streaks of blue water called the Finger Lakes, towns that until recently took their water-vacation advantages as personal blessings, have realized that people will travel long distances to enjoy cool breezes, fishing, sailing, water skiing, swimming, yacht-club life.

The most irresistible of all lures to vacationing Yorkers is culture. In summer months the whole area teems with it. New Englanders were the chief settlers, and an inherited Yankee conscience makes their descendants so uneasy over idling during their vacations that they demand intellectual "improvement." How strongly this attitude persists can be seen on the shores of one of the state's westernmost small lakes, Chautauqua, where the famous Chautauqua Institution has been functioning since Victorian times.

Life changes somewhat once you have entered the gates of the Chautauqua Institution. Its taboos are simple—no automobiles, no cats, no alcoholic beverages. You may live in one of the old cottages that shoulder each other along the brick-paved, leaf-shadowed streets—which were built long before the first horseless buggy and are too narrow for two-way motor traffic—or in a hotel, possibly in the dignified Athenaeum, the last American tavern, so far as I know, to abandon the custom of serving cornmeal mush and milk for supper every Sunday night.

You soon discover that the taboos at Chautauqua are balanced by intellectual and spiritual blessings. The loud-speaker in the sunken Amphitheatre, center of the most important activities, carries morning hymns and the sermon of a distinguished prelate. In the intervals between events the bells of the carillon down by the lake tumble appropriate tunes into the quiet air, and the morning program continues with an economist, a sociologist or an explorer at the Amphitheatre microphone. Comes then the cacophony of an orchestra (made up mostly of artists from the New York Philharmonic) tuning up to run through the evening's concert.

In the meantime, the distinguished artist who is head of the Art Center has sought a dell where light streams from the north upon the canvases of his elderly pupils; the Chautauqua Repertory Theatre rehearses a comedy (there are few demands for heavier fare); the writers giving courses in the Writers' Workshop strive mightily

to tell the ambitious amateurs ("I've always thought I could write")
how to compose and sell their works.

To facilitate adult improvement, the clubs of Chautauqua are remarkably active. The Bird and Tree (it exiled the cats) now works
continuously at beautifying the grounds. The Woman's Club is active
in good works. The W.C.T.U. (it has tried, not always with success,
to keep the liquor out) still wields a powerful influence. One Amphitheatre speaker, according to local folklore, tried to recommend
an occasional cocktail to his white-haired audience and was ushered
from the platform to the gate, where his suitcase awaited him,
packed by an efficient member of the W.C.T.U. The Literary and
Scientific Circle, oldest book club in the United States, has been pre-
scribing reading to its thousands of members for more than three
quarters of a century. Those who complete its four-year course are
graduated at Chautauqua each year on Recognition Day with ceremonies that are impressive if somewhat sentimental and dated by
now.

Far to the east of Chautauqua, a little over an hour's ride southwest of Albany and inaccessible except by automobile, lovely old
Cooperstown curves about the southern end of Otsego Lake, known
as Glimmerglass in the *Leatherstocking* novels of James Fenimore
Cooper, whose father founded the town. No gate or fence guards
the treasures of this cluster of historic houses, quiet and luxurious
hotels and three museums, but the small population is used to seeing
automobiles from all over the Union pour into Main Street, park for
an hour or two, and move on.

The Baseball Museum, a modest red-brick building, is not easily
identifiable, but a Cooperstonian can spot a pilgrim unfailingly and
issue directions almost before he is asked. The cars are crowded,
and they have baggage tied on top, and there's pretty sure to be a
boy inside. Once past the ticket office, the family scatters. Mother
and the girls look at the paintings and the old programs, and soon
tire. Grandpa finds a photograph of Christy Mathewson, who
pitched a game he saw in the old days. Father sentimentalizes over
Lou Gehrig's uniform, and sonny dashes from the cleated shoes of
Babe Ruth to the ball Mickey Mantle socked over the center-field
fence in Washington.

Not all the baseball enthusiasts visit the other two educational
showplaces of Cooperstown. One is the Farmers' Museum, which

houses fascinating relics of rural New York before the Civil War and also serves as the last resting place of the Cardiff Giant. Yorkers love the story of this stone man who was carved in Iowa and buried in 1869 behind Stub Newell's barn in Cardiff, a midstate village not far from Syracuse. The figure's "discovery" led to controversy and controversy to fortune for Stub and for David Hannum and the rest of the conspirators who plotted the magnificent hoax. Many a noted scientist lost his reputation by claiming the "grand old sleeper" to be the petrified body of a man who lived when giants walked the earth. Even today the curious wait in long queues to look upon his passive form, and since an admission is charged, he is still making money for his custodians.

Most rewarding of Cooperstown treasures is Fenimore House, once an elaborate private residence, now a treasure house of Americana. Here you will see early paintings, both skilled and primitive, that show the nation as it looked long ago; the remarkable life masks, made by J. H. I. Browere, of the great men of America's beginnings (some of them the only true likenesses we have); furniture made by Shakers, whose prohibitions of ornament led to clean lines and exquisite curves. For two weeks each summer, in the auditorium of this building and in make-do assembly rooms nearby, large groups attend the New York State Historical Association's Seminars on American Culture. One titled The Frugal American Housewife, in which they baked bread in "beehive" ovens, made butter in wooden churns and wove homespun on ancient looms has proved so popular it has been often repeated.

Yorkers approve all this so strongly that the state is fairly peppered with exhibitions of their pioneering past, yet they squirm a little when reminded of all their ancestors who were stricken with moon madness. Consider the Shakers, who whirled, danced, marched in the "square order" or the "quick manner," and spoke strange gibberish when endowed with "the gift of tongues." Their sturdy dwellings had two doors—one leading to the men's dormitory and the other to the women's—because they believed that only when all sexual practices ceased would the Kingdom of the Lord arrive. They increased their numbers only by conversion and by adoption of orphans. They believed all adornments wicked, wore plain costumes, and made furniture and utensils so beautiful in functional simplicity that they are cherished by a grateful posterity. "Hands to work and hearts to God" was their creed—and through the streets of their villages, neat and quiet, drifted the odors of their herb gardens.

Eventually the Shakers moved into Ohio, where a section of Cleveland still remembers them with its name, Shaker Heights. The last of those who remained in New York died only a few years ago, held in warm affection by other Yorkers, who hope that in Shaker heaven the Sisters are wearing the promised gowns "of twelve different colours," with colored handkerchiefs about their necks, blue silk gloves, silver shoes and bonnets "of silver colour trimmed with white ribbon," and that they are marching in the square order and the quick manner with Shaker gentlemen dressed in sky-blue jackets with gold buttons, "beautiful fine trousers, as white as snow" and adorned with shining stars and sky-blue glass buttons, neck scarves of white silk bordered with gold, flawlessly white shoes and fine fur hats of a silver color.

While the Shakers were moving toward Ohio, a ten-year-old boy named Joseph Smith left Vermont with his mother and came to the bustling York State town of Palmyra. Twelve years later, on a September midnight, he climbed to the summit of a nearby drumlin and found, or claimed he found, a book of golden pages. This was the Book of Mormon, which he translated with the aid of diamond-lensed spectacles that were lying beside it. Then he organized the Church of Jesus Christ of the Latter Day Saints, which considers the words of Mormon an authentic complement of the Christian Bible. While Shakerism died because it denounced propagation of the race, the Mormon faith succeeded, aided partly by an early tenet (discontinued in the 1890's) which encouraged polygamy. Today the disciples of Joseph Smith and his successor, Brigham Young, number more than a million and a half.

In 1847 another prophet came out of Vermont, this time to Oneida and with another idea regarding human continuance. Exiled by his Yankee neighbors, John Humphrey Noyes, Dartmouth graduate, arrived with his disciples to put into practice his theories on Perfect Living. Noyes believed that spiritual and physical love were parts of a unified quality, and that all Perfectionists must love one another equally well. Monogamous love he denounced as wickedness and sin.

If any man or any woman in the colony desired to mate, it was necessary only to ask the Central Committee's permission—usually granted if the prospective partner agreed; and thanks to a contraceptive technique called "male continence," only four out of fifty-eight births at Oneida were unintended. When the object of mating was parenthood, the Central Committee held a solemn meeting to discuss the health, background and temperaments of both parties. The children were raised in a separate house as wards of the entire community, and parents were advised to show no preference for their own offspring. Pierrepont Noyes, one of the founder's nine children, each by a different mother, has delightfully described the life of the youngsters in his book *My Father's House, an Oneida Boyhood*.

The Oneida Community's eugenic theories died out in 1880. One reason was that the younger people objected to the sexual proposals they received from their elders. Another was the disapproval of many neighbors, who proclaimed the colony a hotbed of sin. But not to this day has there been so meticulous an experiment in breeding humans. Researches indicate that the Oneida Community's children had physical and mental endowments far above the average in their vicinity, though fifty-four examples of planned births would seem to be too few to justify grand generalizations.

Now that the boy remembered in earlier paragraphs has long been a man, I am glad to live no farther from the surroundings of my youth than the width of the state. Here in eastern New York, the towns that are nearest me are older than the towns of my boyhood, and the land more thickly settled. Crowds flow daily back and forth in this area, as inevitably as the tidal waters of the Hudson River. Morning takes them southward to New York City, the many-towered metropolis that most of them regard as alien territory. Evening brings them back to the river-town stations, where queues of automobiles await them, each piloted by a pitying wife bent on reacclimating her husband to restful greenery and the contentments of family life.

There is, however, a wavering boundary beyond which the crowds move north to their work. The line falls across the Hudson at a point where the Catskill Mountains lift blue summits into the sky of its western banks. North and west of this line lies a cherished land called upstate.

The Catskills are the most gregarious and hospitable of American mountains. Neither high nor steep, they suggest no climbing ropes, no spiked shoes. Each spring they welcome thousands of happy companions to the almost countless hostelries hidden within their comfortable folds. A cheerful uproar prevails, provided partly by the hotel guests, who are mostly from New York City, and partly by the hotel managements, which offer lavish entertainments. Professional entertainers, theatrical troupes, dance orchestras, famous basketball teams, tennis players, golfers travel the profitable trail known as the Borscht Circuit. Once happily described by Arthur Kober's comedy, *Having Wonderful Time,* this vacationland is crowded with people who are openly enthusiastic about people. An air of carnival rises from these hills that were named for squalling wildcats. Rip Van Winkle would find a long sleep difficult here today!

Ride north along the Hudson, beside the Catskills, then leave its shores at Rip Van Winkle Bridge and make west for Cairo, a country town proclaimed cosmopolitan by its pizzerias, cafés, beer halls, delicatessens. Roads join in a star here. One goes north to more Catskill caravansaries. Another, branching south, leads to the hill-circled hamlet of Purling, where the Old Heidelberg and the Bavarian Manor invite to dark elegance and darker beer. Take the northwest route numbered 145, the Sharon Road, to the old village of Leeds, and at midtown you will see a building labeled Jerry Shea's Irish Center. Roll on a few miles and suddenly Ireland has confiscated the hillsides. Here, in fittingly named Greene County, stand the Emerald Isle, the Shannon View, the Shamrock House. Here the O'Neills, the Weldons, the Hagans, the Kearneys, the Mooneys, the Donellys are hosts to families whose old-country names are their best references. Turn in for an Irish stew at Erin's Melody, caper a bit at Blarney's Star Casino and go to early Mass next morning at the tiny chapel of St. Mary's.

"New York State has everything" is a familiar boast among New Yorkers, and sometimes they add, "even two kinds of mountains." North of the Catskills lie rolling hills and the river plain of the east-flowing Mohawk, and beyond that lies rising land again—the foothills of the Adirondacks. Steeper and higher than the Catskills, the tree-lined slopes of the Adirondacks offer silence, the companionship of nature, the shade of balsam, spruce and hemlock, and hidden lakes where the only sounds are those of fish jumping and the whisper of wind riffling the water.

While the Adirondacks are not high compared with Western mountains, more than two score of their countless peaks rise above the four-thousand-foot level. The highest, to which the Adirondack

Indians gave the name of Tahawus (the cloud splitter), is over five thousand feet and provides on its steep sides not only a level nook for Lake Tear-of-the-Clouds, where the Hudson rises, but also an iron mine.

The "uphisted lands," as lumberjacks call this country, fill most of the northeast corner of the state. The towns of Lake Placid and Saranac Lake are in the busiest vacation areas, with palacelike clubs and inns and sophisticated shops where people can spend money when they are bored with other diversions. But such places are far from characteristic. Simple log dwellings, even log inns, are not infrequent in the Adirondacks. In many towns, by mid-August, stores are displaying checkered mackinaws, wool shirts, red-flannel underwear, lumberjack peaveys and snowshoes. "Summer up here," said one native mountaineer, "lasts about twenty minutes and *that* seems to come around noon dinner."

Three roads leave Albany, the York State capital, in an east-west course across the rolling hills and river flats that separate the Catskills from the Adirondacks. The northernmost is the Schenectady-Utica-Syracuse turnpike, which runs along the north bank of the historic Mohawk. The southernmost is the Cherry Valley Pike, one of the world's most beautiful highways, which sweeps up and down mile-long hills as if it were the track of a magnificent outsized roller coaster. Between the two, at least part of the way, runs the new Thruway, the comfortable speedway that unhappily bypasses the fine old towns and buildings and the restaurants that serve the distinctive foods and wines of the region.

This is the upstate area. Only the inhabitants, legend claims, can define its boundaries, and they are not given to exactitude in matters of geography. The late Samuel Hopkins Adams, the distinguished author who lived all his years in the area, once said, "Upstate is west of Albany," and considered the subject closed. Upstaters sniff scornfully at New York City's society-page headlines that say, "Upstate Wedding at Peekskill-on-Hudson." They look upon the island of Manhattan as a subject city-state which very properly pays heavy tribute to Albany. As for that other island, called Long, they regard its people as a salt-water breed more closely akin to New England Yankees than to people dwelling beside pure, fresh lake waters.

Some writers claim that the upstater can be distinguished by his physical, mental and social attributes. Not so lean as the New England Yankee (he is too well fed), his manner indicates that he will never stoop to dieting for the sake of vanity. He is hearty and friendly, and his conversation is intelligent and sometimes penetrating except on the subject of fine arts, which he regards as unmanly or at best a lot of foolishness, even if he is a college graduate. ("My wife does the reading for the family.")

Refusal to conform is a cardinal sin to the upstater. He will not let himself be called pretentious by his neighbors. He avoids fancy clothing, nor does he want his wife to be conspicuously dressed. He may go all out in business or in sports without fear of ridicule, but in other areas his self-expression is hampered because he may fail and be laughed at or else succeed and be regarded as one who has tried to set himself above his fellows. Once I heard an upstater admit to a group of friends that he felt that he had done "a pretty good job" on a project. The remark caused a shocked silence.

While the upstater is greatly moved by the subject of food, his tastes run generally to meat, mashed potatoes with gravy, green vegetables and pie. Generous helpings are as likely to win his praise as skilled preparation. Visitors sometimes wail that they cannot find rare beef in the restaurants. ("I'll have rare roast beef," said one. "There isn't any," said the waiter, "and it isn't rare.") Few places serve French or Spanish dishes, and a *spécialité de la maison* is not usually offered. The chief influences on upstate restaurants are Italian, German and tearoom.

Upstate cities follow a pattern too. Through the old part of town runs the chief residential thoroughfare. Here, in lawn-girt rows, stand the sprawling dark Victorian piles built by the old families who made their money early—the tribes referred to, with some awe, as Old Amsterdam, Old Herkimer, Old Rome. Inevitably, some of the elegant mansions have been converted to funeral homes and others have been sold to enterprising immigrant families—and their colorful alterations of conservative façades sometimes startle their neighbors. On the side streets, near this major aisle of aristocracy, stand the expensive new residences of the well-to-do come-latelies whose ranking is less sacrosanct. And on the "other side" of town, in thousands of homes varying little in design, live the employees of the big industries.

Of the smaller upstate cities, many are identified with a single industry. Troy, upriver about ten miles from Albany, is widely recognized as the source of shirts and collars. Schenectady is associated with electric appliances, Gloversville and Johnstown with gloves, Rome with copper, Endicott with business machines, Johnson City with shoes, Little Falls and Herkimer with dairy products, Jamestown with furniture—and so on. All of these vary little from the usual upstate pattern. Three, however, differ very markedly.

The first is Albany. No one who has ever seen wide State Street rise from the Hudson River docks to the Capitol building is likely to forget the sight. It is a sweeping and majestic approach to ornate nothingness—to the three-acre, $25,000,000 gingerbread castle in whose façade the period influences come and go as raggedly as do political influences within. But politics aside—and architecture, too, for most of Albany's other streets are lined with dull look-alike houses of dark red brick or brownstone—Albany has one surpassing distinction. This is Keeler's, the best year-round city restaurant in all upstate, an eating house that feeds sophisticated Manhattanites, rural politicians, foreign diplomats whose palates can be weaned from exotic dishes—and all come away singing the praises of the food. Upstate contains only two other like establishments, and both are in small towns—the Krebs in Skaneateles and Halloway House in East Bloomfield.

The second atypical city is Syracuse, now a center for electronics products and a boom town so overextended that it has hired city-planning experts to ease its growing pains. Syracuse University, city-sized itself and surrounded by the seething town, has retreated skyward—with its 15,000 students—from the slopes where it began to the summit of Mount Olympus, where its newest dormitories look out over the vast reaches, tumbling hills and water-streaked valleys of upstate.

Third is Geneva, the most distinctive of upstate cities. Nowhere else in the Northeast are such gracious city houses standing like Godey's *Lady's Book* matrons in a close row, presenting faces of unquestionable fashion toward the street. Behind them, on sunny days, long narrow Seneca Lake accentuates the white of sails with the blue of water. A genteel provincialism flavors both the houses and their occupants, so that Geneva is something like South Carolina's Charleston, complete with Church of England touches and an "old Geneva" Shintoism of its own.

The two largest upstate cities are Rochester and Buffalo, and the smaller of these, Rochester, is the better organized and the more homogeneous. Although a few miles separate it from Lake Ontario, it has profited from Great Lakes commerce for more than a hundred and fifty years and now seems stabilized on a high level of genial and genteel conformity. Samuel Hopkins Adams, who was brought up there, pronounced Rochester (from his eyrie on Owasco Lake about sixty-five miles away) as nearly perfect as a city may become. Others are not so sure—like the young executive who told me this: "The city hasn't changed. Yesterday I was summoned to an immediate staff meeting. I showed up wearing a yellow shirt under my jacket. I didn't mind that I was the only one in a colored shirt, but I *did* mind that every mother's son there mentioned it."

Downtown Rochester looks more like an enlarged village than a planned city, despite an ill-inspired yellow-brick department store standing like a medieval cathedral at the top of the mall. It is a town of beautiful shade trees and comfortable homes, and in spring its many parks are green and white and purple pleasure-grounds when more than five hundred species of lilacs perfume the whole area and canoes drift in a sun-tinted haze on the river.

Rochester remains the Kodak City, of course, and George Eastman lavished more than $30,000,000 on making it a city of culture. His dream was to provide an art center where his fellow citizens could enjoy fine paintings and great symphonies. Yet little has come of the dream, and Rochester continues on its way, satisfied and comfortable.

At Buffalo, the port may not be denied. Long ships, the ore-bearing "whale-backs," dock in the shadow of towering grain elevators. The lake winds roar into the wide streets. Nights are peppered with the yellow glares of steel furnaces. Delaware Avenue—"Old Buffalo" —is losing face as trade crowds in where society elegants once lived. Impromptu quartettes send *Zwei Herzen im Drei-Viertel Takt* out through the swinging doors of malt-scented German restaurants. And thousands of weathered houses shelter one of the largest Polish populations in the world—a group not to be inhibited by a drab environment. The proof is to see them on a Sunday, walking to their churches with the bulbous spires, or to be a guest at one of their wedding festivals, which run to three full days of gaiety.

Buffalo has a freer "feel" about it than any other York State city. Possibly the wild gusts from the lake, the port atmosphere, the heartiness and *Gemütlichkeit* of the music-loving Germans, the humor and excitability of the Poles are responsible for this. Possibly, too, the English spoken here may be a clue. It abounds in the flat *a* sounds and protracted *r*'s used by the town's Midwestern neighbors, and this would make Buffalo the place where the Midwest begins.

The affection and admiration in which Yorkers hold their state is of a distinctive nature. The breezy enthusiasms of Texans, the lush poesy of Californians and Floridians, the dry assumptions of Down East Yankees are not emulated by natives of my state. Their feeling is articulated by a small voice deep within themselves. The language that a region speaks to its inhabitants is not easily translatable. To a child who discovers all new things in an ecstasy of wonder it is not at first understandable. But to an adult Yorker, who knows that the time of becoming one with the soil inexorably advances, the voice of his own landscape is clear.

Yorkers hear this voice and sometimes, on appropriate occasions illumined by wood fires or by stars, they talk about it. They are, they say modestly, a common-sense people, realistic, thrifty, healthy minded, humorous and easygoing, the very antithesis of mystics. Nevertheless, in those unguarded moments, the honest Yorker will confess that he sometimes feels a "something unnatural" that comes from his natural surroundings. Whether most of his days are spent in the sharp Adirondack clarity of Keene Valley, or among the misty vineyards that line one of the Finger Lakes, or beside the level orchards on blue Ontario's plain, or in the forest shadows where stand the cabins of the Cattauraugus Reservation Indians, this is true.

Your Yorker will point out that, from the time the tribes of the Iroquois Confederacy realized that the Onondagas were more psychic than other Indians, and chose them as the keepers of the eternal fires through whose informing flames the messages of the Creator are translated, men have known that the land which is now upstate holds a peculiar enchantment. He will add that Shakers, Perfectionists, Mormons were only three of more than a dozen religious sects that have burgeoned on the forty-mile-wide east-west strip where beings from another world have spoken to his fellow Yorkers. And to clinch his argument he will assert that drumbeats punctuate the windless air above the Finger Lakes on certain magic days, though no living person has ever beheld the instrument or its player. He will say, truthfully, that he has himself heard the lonesome drum and he will laugh at the science departments of the many colleges roundabout which have considered the phenomenon and propounded several learned explanations, no two alike.

Scoff at him and he will tell you *sotto voce* that, while most of his neighbors have their feet on the ground, like himself, he knows some who appear as sane now as their grandfathers did before they joined the Oneida Community, but who might at any time surprise him—and themselves—by surrendering to mystic influences which never cease to hover in the otherwise salubrious upstate air.

In no other region, I believe, is there a more comprehensive rapport between inhabitant and environment. To its people, rivers and lakes mean boundaries, water traffic, irrigation, pure drinking water, and an intangible something more. Mountains, and valleys between, mean vacation lands and tourism, bottom lands mean fertile soil and rich harvests, cities mean vast industries and wide employment, but all these blessings have an added indefinable and mysterious quality that banishes monotony from York State life.

New Jersey

by CARL L. BIEMILLER

THE NORTH

Few places in the United States are as susceptible to snap judgments as the eleven counties which make up Northern New Jersey. Most people get their first view of North Jersey from the windows of a Pennsylvania Railroad car leaving New York, and a grim view it is. They see a montage of dreary, brackish marsh where tall rushes cover the lower courses of the Hackensack and Passaic Rivers and where the sun glints feebly on the luminescent ooze of mud flats. Pig farms dapple the meadows, vast factories line the polluted rivers, and the skyline is crisscrossed by skeletal radio towers and high-altitude express highways. Fifteen minutes later, the southbound traveler is whisked into a belt of cities—Newark, Elizabeth, Linden, Rahway, New Brunswick—all characterized by a merged blur of factories. At this point, the train rider gives up on North Jersey, and goes back to his newspaper. Yet if he looks up five minutes later he will be astonished to see a pretty, softly rolling countryside beautified by green farms, stands of second-growth oak and pine and patches of brown popple. He may even see a white-tailed deer inquisitively poking its head through the scrub—and this less than half an hour from Manhattan. Northern New Jersey is like that; it is a quick-change artist defying quick analysis.

Now take, for the other side, a motorist driving north toward New

York through the rich and gentle valley farm lands of Hunterdon, Somerset and Morris Counties, or through the aged and forested mountain slopes of Warren and Sussex Counties. Rolling through this countryside, our motorist will decide that this is one part of the East which must be truly loved by its residents, and one which, at the same time, has kept in touch with its historic past.

These neat villages, spacious village greens and tree-shaded walks can have changed but little in two hundred years, and in some sections the place names sound as if they had come right out of medieval England or from the tribal incantations of the Lenni-Lenape, the Delaware Indians who once held the commonwealth. Here, says our motorist, is a sweet bit of country.

Yet no sooner has he made his pronouncement than he finds himself snatched up in a vast complex of concrete-and-steel ramps, high-speed highways, no-speed traffic jams and multilevel bridges. The countryside has vanished, replaced by looming factories, stop lights and vast dumps, where the air is smog-laden with chemical fumes and strange industrial odors. By the time the embittered motorist reaches one of the tunnels or bridges leading into New York he is through with Northern New Jersey. The place, he decides, makes no sense.

He is at least partly right. And if he comes to know more about upper Jersey, he will discover even more startling paradoxes. To wit:

The northernmost counties—Bergen, Essex, Union, Passaic, Hudson and part of Middlesex—contain one of the greatest industrial concentrations in the world; yet here, among the smokestacks, live a good half of the entire population of New Jersey.

Here is a whole section of a state living in the shadow of the world's biggest city. It might be supposed that these north-county residents would have a raging sense of inferiority. Yet North Jerseymen are gusty, independent, inventive, and immensely proud of their own communities. They have built Newark, the biggest and richest city in their state, in plain and defiant view of the colossus across the Hudson.

North Jersey is a commuters' land, a farmers' land, a millworkers' land and a fox-hunters' land. It has produced great prize fighters and great inventors. Its greatest poet is a suburban doctor. It has given birth to engineering impossibilities, medical marvels, agricultural innovations and the movies. It has some entrancing vacation resorts and even a few great country landholdings.

In the hill and valley lands around Somerville, Bedminster, Bernardsville and Morristown are baronial remnants of a lush past that have survived changing times and mounting taxes. They remain as a wistful rear guard fighting for the last real luxury money can buy— simple privacy.

Just how long the classical countryside will remain rural is a matter of much speculation today. A recent census revealed that many of the northern counties have gained new citizens in fantastic numbers. And some of the suburbs which lie within the long shadow of Manhattan have doubled in size.

The growth of the suburbs is understandable. Many New Jersey citizens have good reasons for wanting to move away from the part of their state which is adjacent to New York Harbor, Newark Bay and Raritan Bay. This area holds one of the world's greatest concentrations of industrial capacity. It is a center of electrical machinery-and-equipment production, of chemicals, paints, steel fabrication, food products, textiles, aircraft and automobiles, clocks, instruments, jewelry, drugs and petroleum products. The musk of a motorized nation lies heavy upon it, and the cities within the industrial belt are far from scenic. Railroads bisect them. Trucks pound and crowd their streets. They are immensely productive cities, however, with a neon-lighted vigor, yet most of them are shedding citizens to the suburbs which surround them.

Life within these suburbs is standard suburbia. Montclair, the Oranges, Englewood, Plainfield, Teaneck, Morristown, Summit, Maplewood, Bloomfield, Chatham, Dunellen, Tenafly, and a hundred others belong to the "sundowners." "Sundown citizens" are Jerseymen during evenings and week ends. They decimate whole towns each morning to catch buses or trains to city office or factory. They are earnest breadwinners who travel astronomical miles going nowhere in particular and coming home again to sleep.

The shuttle-minded Jerseyman who commutes to New York daily takes his miracles for granted. Not so the first-time visitor to the North Jersey metropolitan area. The bridges and tunnels across the Hudson are authentic wonders and are appreciated as such. They are operated by the Port of New York Authority, a self-supporting, bi-state agency, without tax burden upon either state. Oldest of the submarine crossings is the Holland Tunnel built at a cost of $50,000,-000, named for its first chief engineer, Clifford M. Holland, and opened to the public in 1927. It links 12th Street, Jersey City, with

Canal Street, New York, and collects approximately 15,000,000 car tolls each year. Newest of the great tunnels is the six-lane, triple-tube Lincoln Tunnel which burrows beneath the river to join Weehawken with midtown Manhattan at 39th Street.

The most glamorous river crossing, however, is the George Washington Bridge. This soaring two-level span links Fort Lee with 178th Street and New York's Riverside Drive and Henry Hudson Parkway. Drivers of the vehicles which pay more than 15,000,000 tolls each year to cross upon this eight-lane highway have a tendency to move a bit slower than usual simply to absorb the view. Here is the sweep of the Hudson River at its finest, with the ruler-straight shadows of the span and the cobweb tracery of the suspension cables blurring the water surface 260 feet below.

Not all North Jerseymen, of course, fall into such simple categories as the gentry, the suburbanites and the city dwellers. The state has produced its full quota of great names. Certainly there is no schoolboy in Northern New Jersey so dull-witted as not to know the name and the saga of Thomas Alva Edison, the "Wizard of Menlo Park," the confidant of presidents, the greatest inventor (*Pravda* notwithstanding) of his time, and the father, incidentally, of a later governor of New Jersey, Charles Edison.

Edison's patents were listed by the hundreds. He was the father of the stock ticker, the mimeograph machine, the grandsire of modern radio. He came close enough to television to warrant an assist. The companies that he founded within the electrical industry became the giant of General Electric and its many subsidiary corporations today. If any man were to try to assay the relative importance of his inventions in their impact upon life in the United States, he would have a herculean job of judgment upon his hands. Perhaps his best known invention was the electric-light bulb, the first practical incandescent lamp which came out of his laboratories in 1879. The Pennsylvania Railroad ran special trains to see its public demonstration at Menlo Park.

However, two years before the electric-light bulb and immediately following his invention of the phonograph, the inventor sought to create "eyes" to go with his mechanical "voice." Assisted by W. K. L. Dickson, a young Englishman, Edison came up with the Kinetoscope, a device that gave pictures the illusion of motion. Almost simultaneously, Hannibal Goodwin, a Newark minister, created a "film" base to take the place of glass plates in cameras. Edison's Kinetoscope, literally a "peep show" device, built a demand for film. By the time his improved Vitascope hit the market, causing the "nickelodeons" to mushroom throughout the East, the North of Jersey was cradling the infant motion-picture industry in no uncertain terms.

Edwin S. Porter, a former Edison employee turned producer, created the industry's pioneer classic. He borrowed a train from the Lackawanna Railroad and took a company on location at Paterson, where a Passaic River bridge was commandeered for a scene in which a man was "thrown from a moving train." Later he moved into the "wilds" of Essex County for some daring horseback sequences. The result was *The Great Train Robbery* with "Broncho Billy" Anderson—the first action-filled movie melodrama.

There are middle-aged Jerseymen who vividly recall the pioneer thrillers made along the scenic Palisades which form the Jersey bank of the Hudson. Fort Lee's Coytesville section was the Hollywood of the East then. The Barrymores lived there: Mr. and Mrs. Maurice, sons Lionel and John, and daughter Ethel. So did the Bennetts: Mr. and Mrs. Richard, and daughter Constance. Early studios erected buildings for such players as Mary Pickford, Theda Bara, Marie Dressler, John Bunny, Charlie Chaplin, "Fatty" Arbuckle, Lon Chaney and Alice Brady, most of whom commuted to New York when the day's grimacing was done. Pearl White's Palisades cliff hanging in the *Perils of Pauline* brought the later term "cliff hangers" into being to describe movie serials.

Edison's invention of the moving picture and the area's pioneer development of the movie-art form is possibly New Jersey's greatest contribution to American culture. But the State has not entirely ignored the individual arts. William Carlos Williams, poet, doctor, and a native of Rutherford, has won a whole cluster of poetry awards while pursuing a very busy and successful practice as a pediatrician. And in Bergen County, in the twenties, Upton Sinclair founded an art colony known as Helicon Hall.

Sinclair and his group of beautiful dreamers took over a huge and dilapidated mansion along the Palisades and opened it to some 300 applicants who came to create. The colonists lacked necessities, but they were long on the intellectual conversations of the times. Some were long on talent too—the late Sinclair Lewis, for instance, who passed briefly through Helicon Hall. The old mansion finally burned to the ground, its only remnant a law suit filed by the colonists for lost manuscripts.

The region's creativeness is mostly professional. The research laboratories scattered throughout North Jersey represent about one tenth of the entire nation's probing into the scientific world of the future. Estimates of the annual research outlay within this region run to several hundred million.

Yet the one research and educational institution closest to the hearts of Jerseymen is no commercial enterprise. It is gray, quiet Rutgers University on the banks of the Raritan River where it winds through New Brunswick. Chartered in 1766 as Queen's College, Rutgers is the eighth-oldest college in the United States. It was selected by the state legislature as a land-grant institution in 1864 and formally designated as the State University of New Jersey in 1945.

It was Rutgers' College of Agriculture which, not long ago, gave Dr. Selman Waksman's now famous antibiotic, streptomycin, to the world and moved mankind another step ahead in the conquest of disease.

Waksman's work is not so well known as other Rutgers contributions, of lesser importance, to American civilization, such as the game of football and its associated declaration which has become a cliché for phony heroism: "I'd die for dear old Rutgers." The first American game of intercollegiate football was played at New Brunswick between Rutgers and its southern neighbor, Princeton, in 1869. Rutgers won that first game, a feat it only sparingly repeats during their now-traditional rivalry.

The character of North Jersey is shaped by factors other than its people and its institutions. Some of the area, for instance, is made lovely by a simple geologic formation known as the Highlands, which is part of the Appalachian foothills. The extreme northwest corner of the state in Warren and Sussex Counties is Appalachian Valley country, with the flat, crested ridge of Kittatinny Mountain overlooking it for more than thirty miles. This reach of ground stretches from the most northerly tip of the state, south to the Delaware Water Gap, where the Delaware River has sliced through rock to form a tourist attraction that annually lures thousands of visitors. More than half of this land is owned by the state and forms the scenic sweep of Stokes State Forest and High Point Park.

High Point, of course, gets its name because its 1823-foot elevation is higher than anything else in Jersey with the possible exception of the state budget. It is a wildlife sanctuary as nearly primitive in character as modern man can comfortably stand, and a camper's delight in the summer. Hikers know it for the section of the Appalachian Trail which enters the park at the New York border and runs south to Stokes Forest. Once a grant from the English king to Lord Rutherford, the land that is now High Point Park was donated to the state in 1923.

The view from High Point is an unbroken one, scanning adjacent Pennsylvania and New York. Enthusiasts claim that from its summit it is possible to see some twenty or more villages, as well as the Alleghenies of Pennsylvania and the Catskills of New York.

It is in the hill country of Northwest Jersey that much of metropolitan and suburban New Jersey plays. Some eighty lakes shimmer in Sussex County. There are forty-one more in Passaic County, including the Pompton Lakes area, ten miles northwest of Paterson, where for years the nation's better prize fighters have conditioned themselves for major bouts. Largest of all the cabin- and resort-lined lakes of the North is Hopatcong, whose forty miles of shoreline ramble from Morris County into Sussex. The coves formed by its indentations make more shoreline than one might expect in a lake that is only nine miles long, but this is a condition that pleases the hundreds of cabin owners. The tiny coves provide green privacy.

Hopatcong in the summer is a recreational mural in tree green and lake blue, a panorama of rafts, floats, canoes and swimmers. It is a giant fresco of small sails, power boats, and grubby boys picking fishing worms out of cans; of moonlight and dance music; of rocking chairs, lighted cigars and cold beer. There are smaller, more exclusive lake colonies in the North, but the recreational pattern, give or take a few tonier facilities, is about the same. Approximately 250,000 vacationists pour into the region annually, many of them "lake families" who have been coming into these playlands since the turn of the century.

It would be wrong to imply that a major proportion of Jersey pleasure seekers spill into the mountain and lake country. As many more go to favored spots along the 120 miles of ocean beaches which stretch the entire length of Jersey.

Many Jerseymen find recreation in other, non-athletic ways. There are probably more amateur historians, antiquarians, folklorists and genealogists in the North of Jersey than in any other American sector, including New England. To them the Jersey hinterlands are one immensely fertile Yesterday. It is not enough to say that preoccupation with the past is a common characteristic. A waspish dowager explained this during a Humus Committee meeting at a local garden club. "My dear," she said. "There are no natives in this community. We are all descendants."

There are, for instance, eighty-five chapters of Daughters of the American Revolution operative within the state, in addition to auxiliary chapters of Sons of, Children of, and other organizations recalling historical data. Only in Jersey would the doughty Daughters be considered a johnny-come-lately group as compared to the Order of Founders and Patriots of America which commemorates "the *founders* of the country as *distinct* from the colonists who reaped the benefit of earlier work and hardships."

The Garden State was properly called "the cockpit of the Revolution." From the time the embattled colonists deposed the last royal governor, William Franklin, to the time George Washington delivered his farewell address to his troops at Rocky Hill outside Princeton, in 1783, Jersey saw the bulk of a rebellious nation's military traffic. More than one hundred battles and skirmishes were fought on the state's soil, most of them in the hinterland of the North, and all of them vital in some manner to control of the all-important Hudson and Delaware River valleys. The campaigning, marked by highway signs, embodied in preserved and restored sites and perpetuated by native fervor for historical gatherings, will never die.

There are places in the North today where so much of the past is physically present that it is possible to believe with a minimum of imagination that Washington and his men never left the state. Morristown, a community of some 17,000 residents and the county seat of Morris County, is such a place. Tourists driving over U. S. Route 202, which runs a diagonal course across Jersey from Lambertville on the Delaware to Suffern in New York State, inevitably dawdle through its tree-lined streets and move cautiously around the Green, which has been the parklike heart of its business center for two centuries. It is not a place for hurry. Even the bustle of its commercial area is a decorous bustle, a mingling of shoppers aware of opportunities to chat.

At one time more millionaires lived within a mile of its environs than in any other similar area in the world, and these were turn-of-the-century millionaires who never knew an income tax. The estates of the Wall Street barons and early industrial leaders have long since moved to the somewhat less-traveled areas around Bedminster and Bernardsville a few miles away, yet Morristown still owns a substantial air of well-being. There is no one to maintain a hundred servants as did the long-gone Otto Kahn, but there is still the foxhunting. Polo, played before World War I at the Whippany River Club, is a middle-aged memory, but genteel dog raising endures in the grand tradition. The one-day show sponsored by Mrs. Marcellus Hartley Dodge at Giralda Farms each May is the best of its type in the country.

Such civic mementos as the $400,000 mansion built by former A. T. & T. president Theodore N. Vail, which now serves as the community's Municipal Building, remind its people of a plush era; but Morristown's affection belongs to a much earlier past, to the days when the Whippany River powered the pre-Revolution iron forges, and the rich ore of West Morris County supplied a hundred mines, forges, furnaces and rolling mills. The county was not only the arsenal of the Continental troops during the Revolution, it was also a major battleground and rest camp, the essence of the Revolution. It saw troop desertions, foraging atrocities and mutiny. It is probably the richest single-source spot of Revolutionary history and lore in the nation. Citizen Tom Paine wrote his crisis papers there. "The times that try men's souls" are impressively recalled by the 1000-acre Morristown National Historical Park established by the Federal Government in 1933, the first of its type created in the United States. Thousands of tourists enter its expanse each year to walk the Colonial camp ground of Jocky Hollow, where, in 1781, the mutiny of the Pennsylvania Line nearly destroyed the Continental war effort, and where Captain Adam Bettin, killed resisting his own men, still lies beneath the "Bettin Oak." The visitors troop across Fort Nonsense, an earthwork boondoggle built, allegedly, to keep Washington's soldiers busy, and see the house that Washington and his wife occupied.

The trim town about the Green is far from being the only gateway to the Jersey past. North of Morristown, where the giant Wanaque Reservoir lies in the folded hills, and the quiet Ramapo River winds through its shaded valley, lies a country seemingly untouched by the metropolitan regions so near in miles, so distant in time.

There is no peace to match a dusk in July along the South Branch of the Raritan River, between Flemington and Washington, when the fireflies are busy in the cornfields and the perfume of new-cut alfalfa hangs on the sloping knolls and the cicadas are drilling holes in the sundown haze, prophesying heat for the morrow. There is no tranquillity to excel a mid-morning in January on the oldest road in America, the Old Mine Road near Montague, with the sun so bright on a fresh fall of snow that the shadows of the hills and trees are black, and the river itself is a vivid green slash on a white blanket. Yet a long tradition of violence, raiding and murder taints the pastoral of the state.

The classic criminal case of modern America was a product of rural Jersey. It happened March 1, 1932, near Hopewell in Mercer County. It was the Lindbergh kidnap case, which reached its climax in the drowsy little town of Flemington in 1935 when Bruno Richard Hauptmann was sentenced to die in the electric chair. The case rocked the political structure of New Jersey, reverberated over the entire country. The story of how 20-month-old Charles Lindbergh, Jr., then the only son of his distinguished parents, was stolen from his crib and found dead on a forest trail is now a national drama.

Jersey folks still remember the roads leading into Flemington blocked, at trial time, by a parade of vehicles which extended across the state. It was a morbid caravan which moved, sometimes as slowly as three miles an hour, and which produced traffic jams that half the State Police was unable to disengage. Applications for trial tickets came from U. S. Senators, Hollywood stars, society luminaries, concert singers and reformers. Reporters covering Flemington sent more than a million words of copy from the scene each day.

The Lindbergh case is matched by only one other in the annals of American crime, and that too was a rural-Jersey murder mystery which to this day remains officially unsolved. It broke in September, 1922, but its impact was so great that it still makes Sunday-supplement copy. No case ever held such bizarre elements or so strange a cast of characters as that which began when the Rev. Edward Wheeler Hall and Mrs. James Mills, one of his choir singers, were found shot and slashed to death on a farm near New Brunswick. Its preliminary investigations turned up dalliant church workers, a Hindu "swami," and a gross proprietor of a nearby farm who was for evermore to be known as "the pig woman."

Not until four years after the original investigations did the Hall-Mills case reach trial. The accused were wealthy Mrs. Hall herself, widow of the slain clergyman, and her brothers. The trial opened in

Somerville, in November, 1926, and a month later Mrs. Hall and her brothers were acquitted.

Such hectic events, of course, do not occur frequently but it would be wrong to assume that any part of North Jersey is entirely calm today. As one Newark bookmaker said when Senator Estes Kefauver's Senate Investigating Committee on organized crime sent agents into the area that lies in the shadow of New York's skyscrapers: "Everything's hassle and risk these days."

But Northern New Jersey has been experiencing hassle and risk for nearly three centuries and thriving on it. The contradictory, quick-changing, vital region remains inured to surprises. They are part of the fascination of its future. At present, North Jersey is trying something new—a re-evaluation of its two, sharply distinctive ways of life. The cities are spreading into the suburbs and the factories are moving into the farmlands. Nervous assembly-line living in the smoky cities and crowded suburbs in the shadow of Manhattan is slowly going out of style, and may some day be as old-fashioned as the baronial way of life on the great estates. There is a new awareness among North Jersey citizens of the beauties and assets of their countryside and perhaps even a longing for the simpler days of the rich New Jersey past.

THE COAST

The most concentrated playtime strand in the United States is a more or less continuous slash of white beach which extends from Sandy Hook, an Army post which rams a fortified finger into New York's Lower Bay, to Cape May. For 125 miles the waters of the Atlantic Ocean are merely a form of liquid money during the months of high summer, and as such are appreciated by the hospitable residents of New Jersey washed by its tides.

Along this coast, dominated by the famous resort towns of Long Branch, Asbury Park, Atlantic City, Wildwood and Cape May, the summer seashore vacation in the United States originated and flowered. Along this coast, each summer, the greatest number of hot-weather holiday rovers in the United States happily congregates.

Cape May is probably the oldest seaside resort in the United States. The Lenni-Lenape Indians were using the cape as a recreation spot before Henry Hudson sailed by the point in 1609 en route to Sandy Hook. Aristocratic Philadelphians, bored with the war years of the

Revolution, sailed Delaware Bay and found recreational pleasure at a fishing village on the same cape before President George Washington took his oath of office. As early as 1788 a boardinghouse at Long Branch on the northern sector of the coast hung out its shingle to attract visitors.

The wild and comparatively isolated coast of Jersey has always been a haven for fishermen, nature lovers, people seeking rest cures, fugitives, and for adventurers who couldn't abide the disciplines of city life. It still is.

Each spring the winter-gray waters of the Atlantic subside into creaming blue swells, which gently lave the Jersey coast as if sorry they spent the winter months eroding chunks out of the beach front. The lead-hued sand dries white and gleaming beneath the high-climbing vernal sun; and from Sandy Hook to Cape May, the shore looks scrubbed. All the days are blue and white and somehow highly tonic.

The sedges of the salt marshes, and the rushes along the fiddler-drilled bay banks wage green war against the brittle browns of winter. On the wilder beaches of the lesser developed resorts the bay-berry bushes sprout leaves and the branches of the beach plums darken with new shoots.

Red-winged blackbirds dart in the meadows. Sandpipers run their skimming gait along the surf, and the black-polled terns fly incredible formations at wave-crest heights. The graceful American egrets fish in the thousands of drainage sloughs in the meadows, the ditches which first began the fight against the Jersey mosquito. Poles of the Jersey Central Power and Light Company and the Atlantic City Electric Company get clumsy adornment as the ospreys rebalance their top-heavy nests.

On 10,000 pilings, pierheads, rickety wharves and fancy docks, the slovenly, lumbering herring gulls bleat, "Put on the blond feathers, kids, the summer folks are coming."

From early June to October, 50,000,000 vacationers move from the cities of the East to the Jersey coast.

Officials of the New Jersey Resort Association—who think nothing of counting each visitor four or five times—estimate that these pleasure seekers spend over a billion dollars each season in the more than fifty-five large, small and eternally hopeful resort communities which line the shore.

The magnitude of this bonanza points up the fact that the genus "guest" is to the resident of the Jersey coast what the reindeer is to the Laplander, his comfort and sustenance. For the big business of the strand is pleasure, and with the possible exception of Ocean Grove (a Methodist resort on the northern reach of the beaches which on Sunday prohibits bathing and stretches chains across its main streets to stop all traffic), few of the coastal towns ever forget it.

Atlantic City, the colossus of the strand, never stops entertaining. This party metropolis, sixty-two miles from Philadelphia and 125 miles from New York by virtually any means of transportation (including one recorded balloon trip in 1906), is not a beautiful resort in the sense that lusher, more verdantly scenic resorts are beautiful. Not all of the luxury hotels along the beach front—including Chalfonte-Haddon Hall, the 1000-room hostel which ranks as the biggest and among the best on the strand—are sleek models of contemporary architecture. No one, however, can deny that they are impressive. And when all of the scenically pampered resorts have run their course up and down the scale of public popularity, this daffy dowager of a town will still be entertaining more guests than any other single resort area in the land. Atlantic City has been harassed by the sea, thumped by national depression, and literally annexed by the military during World War II. Nothing has dampened its monumental vitality or curbed its ebullience.

The 60,000 permanent residents of this gusty town welcome 15,000,000 guests each year, right around the calendar. As Atlantic City goes, so goes the entire Jersey coast. People come to Atlantic City because the town offers a wonderfully infectious brand of foolery, assembly-line entertainment, and a general air of expansiveness not to be found in other places prior to the fourth highball. It is an expansiveness that does not belong to any one segment of society, a democratic euphoria which is just as lifting to the courting couple down for the evening as it is to the retired millionaire registered for the season at the Traymore.

There is no more direct proof that the Jersey coast developed the summer seaside vacation than the mass amusement innovations produced by its biggest resort. The boardwalk, for instance, is an internationally known promenade and an integral part of most seaside resorts. Atlantic City created the original in 1870, at the joint behest of Jacob Keim, a hotel operator who tired of having guests track up his establishment with sandy feet, and Alexander Boardman, a rail-

road conductor with a hypochondriac's dislike of wet shoes. The resort's boardwalk, sixty feet wide and eight miles long, is a bright-light
rialto today where you may buy anything from an ice-cream cone to a
$10,000 piece of Ming pottery.

On a midsummer week end, with the sea breaking within sight of
the strollers and the beaches filled with bathers, it is a timber highway worth going miles to see. But at night, crowded rail to rail with
nearly a half million people and with its incredible bursts of neon
emitting silent screams of color, it is a living lane of light that casts
a radiance far out over the ocean.

The boardwalk is not the only Atlantic City contribution to summertime. The town fostered the invention of the rolling chair (modern versions are mechanized), salt-water taffy, the picture post card,
and what might be termed the first "packaged entertainment" in the
form of the amusement pier.

The best example of the last-mentioned today is George Abou
Hamid's Steel Pier, a sturdy platform structure mounted on pilings
which extends 2000 feet to sea. It has four movie theaters, a dance
floor and assorted features ranging from a zoo to Danny Kaye—all
for one admission price. In the fifty-four years of Steel Pier's existence some 90,000,000 persons have paid to goggle its variety acts—
from the high-diving Hawaiian who one night conked a porpoise on
the way down from his 150-foot perch to "John the Baptist," a diving
horse who made a lesser leap for thirty years without contact with
fish. Steel Pier has offered gorillas, movie horses, flagpole sitters and
crooners by the score.

Performers have been paid as high as $50,000 for a single week's
appearance, and have earned every nickel of it.

Not all of the town's ingenuity has been directed toward the laughing side of resort pleasures. Atlantic City's past shows a shrewd cogni-
zance of such summertime fundamentals as safety for the millions
who use its broad beach. As early as 1855, when the municipality appointed a "constable of the surf" for $117 a year, the lifeguard be-
came a clearly discernible specimen along the strand. Wherever he
may function, today's lifeguard, tanned shoulders and peeled nose, is
an evolutionary product of the Jersey coast.

Atlantic City is the only real year-round resort along the coast, although Asbury Park is a valid pretender. Winter visitors, for the most
part, are convention delegates (by the thousands), sinus sufferers
who find balm in the clean salt air, tired executives who haunt hotel

sun decks and watch the hypnotic sea, and the usual night-out people who drive from nearby cities for a shore dinner at Hackney's Restaurant, a walk on the boards, and a night-club evening.

To remain a twelve-month host, the resort discovered long ago that constant promotion effort is a virtue, and that the best type of resort promotion is feminine either in appeal or content. The annual Palm Sunday and Easter parades are among the biggest fashion shows in the East.

Best known of all the resort's annual events, however, is the Miss America Pageant. In its early days the Pageant was an out-and-out callipygian display, but today it is one of the authentically beautiful, handsomely staged shows of the year. The Pageant, born in the mind of newspaperman Herb Test, in 1921, was the pioneer event which subsequently spread the now-familiar beauty-contest idea from the Jersey shore to every whistle stop in the nation. Pageant officials estimate that there are 25,000 such competitions held annually in the United States, and that since Margaret Gorman, of Washington, D.C., was crowned in 1921, some 500,000 "queens" of everything from cheese to oranges have been selected throughout the country. Further, the "queen" movement in our increasingly matriarchal society shows no signs of abatement. Asbury Park, for instance, has been featuring a *Mrs.* America contest for the past few years.

Gone are the days when the girls competed and were judged by such loose standards as "loveliness, charm and pulchritude." Since 1944, the judges have been coping with the quality known as "talent." Further, it is authentic talent spread over a wide range. By the Saturday night of the official coronation of a new queen in Convention Hall, the judges, and the huge audiences that have paid high for the privilege have usually heard some better-than-good voices. They have seen some intense, if yet unpolished, bits of acting, some creative dancing, and lesser aptitudes ranging from cartooning to water-skiing demonstrations to "chantootsie" versions of hardy perennials like the *Lullaby of Broadway* and *Daddy's Little Girl.*

Despite the nationally known reputations of such resorts as Atlantic City and Asbury Park, and the still warm turn-of-the-century memories of Long Branch and Cape May, many of the fifty-odd shore municipalities are almost one merged entity today.

Municipal distinctions are not as varied as the enthusiasts of individual shore towns might suppose. In fact, there are no really exclusive Jersey resorts, although there are a few minor beach colonies which would like to assume such a cachet.

The huge, landscape-pampered mansions around Rumson in North Jersey and those which line the Ocean Drive through nearby Deal bespeak wealth, as do the scattered, quiet estates which are still sprinkled through the pinelands bordering the strand; but many of the most impressive are valiant remnants of older glories. Bay Head and Mantoloking proclaim reasonably moneyed substantiality mostly in terms of the huge, weather-silvered homes which tower over the dunes. There are luxury hotels and lavish structures from one end of the entire 125-mile surf line to another.

But, by and large, the Jersey coast belongs to the middle-class millions that throng to it from the great metropolitan feeder cities —hard-working, family people.

Naturally, the mink-and-sable set is noticeable among them, but hardly for the tinsel flamboyance which characterizes wintertime along the Florida Gold Coast. The Cadillacs at the Atlantic City Race Track and at Monmouth Park are black, not lavender. The party urge is normally expressed in yacht-club dancing, garden teas and restrained dinner parties at some luxury hotel or surf club. Comfort, rather than excitement, is the keynote of the substantial summer people. Expressed in terms of sloppy game-fishing garb, rumpled golf apparel and denim gardening gear, this comfort disguises if not quite hides the wearers' bank accounts. A genuine air of democracy blows, sweet as the salt breezes, along the Jersey strand, a condition stated succinctly by a retired banker: "There are no wallet pockets in a pair of bathing trunks."

Variations in vacation tastes, and minor geographic distinctions, account for most of the differences between Jersey resorts.

Game fishermen, for instance, flock to Brielle, where the Manasquan Inlet leads offshore to a deep, known as the "mudhole"; here, in season, they troll for school tuna, bluefish, bonita and infrequent marlin.

All the resorts have their individual problems; but from the time the first tourist sat a sundown rocking chair, his head haloed by a nimbus of mosquitos, they all have shared one major concern: that mysterious, capricious element known as "the condition of the beach." Dat Ole Debbil Sea can be a villain as well as a friend. Within a single decade the state has spent almost $7,000,000 on various save-the-sands measures, most of which has been matched, dollar for dollar, by the collective communities involved. And, though there are no exact figures, informed guesses say that private property owners and solvent towns have spent millions more. But, as the horse players at Monmouth Park and Atlantic City race tracks are frequently heard to remark, "Nobody comes here to worry."

There is still virgin beach along the coast, some of it as unspoiled as it was when the shoal reefs of the midcoast were known as "the graveyard of the Atlantic." Perhaps the wildest of all such areas is Island Beach, a nine-mile-long, 2200-acre strip of Barnegat Peninsula, a paradise for marine birds, a haven for dune deer and rabbits, and a wonderful garden where beach heather blooms yellow and the green of cedar and holly seems black against the glaring sands.

The best of the shore's facilities remain the ones nature produced eons ago—beaches and the bays whose "windward-leeward" reaches are dappled with sails each summer. There are still natives shaped by the beaches and bays whose lives remain indigenous to them, but it's pretty hard to tell the year-round residents from the summer people these days. Single-hour access to the big cities over fine highways works both ways.

Once in a while a lucky visitor meets a rawhide-tough old-timer whose life typifies its undefiled saltwater habitat. Not too many years ago the little creeks and the tiny coves held many of them. They lived in snuggish shanty boats at peace with a chunk stove that was winter-red with driftwood. They blessed their walls with cardboard calendars which did double duty as wall caulking, and waited out the time they shared with the sea. Now and again, for tobacco money, they'd remember a minor fish hole for a summer vistor, or confide a favored duck slough to a high-school kid bright with a new shotgun and the memory of a hasty summer promise. They owned an elemental quiet and were jealous of it. They've gone now, but the bays are still building rugged men, and the best of them, in this opinion, are sailors.

There are thousands of power craft operating along the Jersey coast and thousands more sailboats; but the craft best known to the greatest number of people are the rowboats which blanket the back bays with fishermen on a Sunday afternoon or the party boats which chug offshore with rails packed shoulder to shoulder with bottom fishermen.

The railroad which connected Long Branch to New York in 1874, and Monmouth Park race track, opened in 1870, brought social and saloon society from Manhattan.

President Ulysses S. Grant made The Branch a summer home and so did President Garfield, who died here in 1881, after a vain attempt to recover from an assassin's bullet.

Presidents Hayes and Harrison stayed at the old Elberon Hotel and, later, Woodrow Wilson lived at Shadow Lawn, on the west side of the resort. But even presidential patronage could not curb the gusty high jinks which gave The Branch its golden reputation. Lillie Langtry kept a private railroad car on a siding adjoining the home of her current gentleman friend for an entire summer. Diamond Jim Brady bought an electric coupé brightly lighted inside for the benefit of the admiring crowds who watched him and Lillian Russell pass the length of Blue Drive.

While the northern sector of the coast bloomed and blazed with the fulsome antics of the Gay Nineties, the southernmost tip of the strand was entering its second century as a resort, more quietly, more restrained, infinitely more social, as if the Cape itself knew that there were more descendants of the Mayflower colony living in Cape May County than remained in Plymouth, Massachusetts.

The Cape was settled early. Fourteen years after Hudson sailed up the coast in 1609, Captain Cornelius Jacobus Mey arrived in Delaware Bay in the *Good Tidings,* to give the Cape his name and establish settlements. In 1801, Postmaster Ellis Hughes advertised in a Philadelphia newspaper that he had "prepared himself for entertaining company who use sea bathing" and that he was "accommodated with extensive houseroom, with fish, oysters, crabs and good liquors."

Hughes' "extensive houseroom," with coed sleeping quarters divided by a sheet, became the Hotel Atlantic. Stephen Decatur, weary of fighting Barbary pirates, came to it for sixteen years, fought weakfish, croakers and crabs from gentler decks instead. The year after Hughes' advertisement, boats ran regularly from Philadelphia to Cape May. Congress Hall, the same Congress whose painted brick L and impressive, wooden pillars attract visitors today, was erected in 1816. By 1850, Cape May was the leading summer resort in the country, and by 1867, when the West Jersey Railroad linked it with Philadelphia, it had no close rivals, not even New York's Saratoga, which was, in the genteel parlance of the Cape, "a rather fast place."

Cape May lies below the Mason-Dixon line, and much of its custom came from the same place. Antebellum society leaders from Richmond, Washington and Baltimore, as well as Philadelphia, shared its pleasures. To this day there are still soft accents in a few of the hotels where tradition is respected, like the wistfully passé Chalfonte, a gingerbread scrollwork, wooden-frame remnant of the Cape's Southern hospitality.

Hot breads still grace its tables, its cocktails are bourbon and branch water, and on gala occasions it is not uncommon to find the flag of the Confederacy whipping in the sea breeze.

The Cape also knew its presidential sun lovers. Presidents Lincoln, Grant, Pierce, Buchanan and Harrison were among those regally entertained in its hotels. Merchant John Wanamaker summered there as did editor Horace Greeley who, after admonishing young men to head West, climbed a train and went south-by-east.

The grandeur of the Cape as a resort began to fade as early as 1900. Many of its cottagers, however, and many of the guests who have made it part of their lives for succeeding generations prefer its gradual retreat into history.

They love it for its old shade, its historic homes, its narrow, picturesque streets which, even today, seem reminiscent of a New England fishing village. Compared to much of the Jersey shore, Cape May is not bustling beyond ordinary politeness to attract visitors in herd numbers. Its hotels are full enough, the remains of its once broad beaches are adequate; in midsummer it is just properly crowded—no more. After all, there are just so many things nice people can do well, and the Cape does them—fine plays presented by the Cape Theater, one of the oldest and best of the "straw-hat circuit," sailing at the Yacht Club, and the interminable round of parties and teas and dances which distinguish this brine-scented variation of Philadelphia's Main Line.

Cape May's future as a resort lies somewhere between two statements overheard on a porch of the Lafayette Hotel not long ago; one, made by a placid woman wearing a form-fitting rocking chair; the other, rapped out by a young officer from the nearby Coast Guard base. "In two hundred years of history, one should learn perspective," said the first. "Let's go over to Wildwood and see how fast the night goes," remarked the second, "I'm tired of relaxed drinking."

Chances are that the resort towns strung along the 125 miles of Jersey coast will go right on entertaining; the fish will bite, the sails will fill, the breakers will continue to babble along the sand. If it takes new vacation innovations to remain the most popular recreational area in the country, the rollicking, carefree coast will provide.

Pennsylvania

by CONRAD RICHTER

To the very young boy, the word Pennsylvania meant the world.
He saw the red-brick house that he and his brothers were born in,
and the house was Pennsylvania. He looked at the blue-green mountain walls rimming his home town, and the mountains were Pennsylvania. He waded in the Old Lutheran Church run. His mother
told him that the run flowed into Swatara Creek, which flowed into
the Susquehanna River, which flowed more than two hundred winding miles from the northern to the southern border of the Commonwealth, and it was Pennsylvania all the way. Fifteen, fifty and
seventy miles to the east, she said, three other rivers carried Pennsylvania water, the Schuylkill, the Lehigh and the Delaware. A hundred miles or more over the Alleghenies to the west you could find
greater rivers, the Youghiogheny, the Monongahela, the Allegheny
and the Ohio, one pouring into the other, and all this was still
Pennsylvania.

As that boy who was I grew, he had to concede that Pennsylvania didn't constitute the whole known world, but at least it led
the rest. Hadn't the Liberty Bell rung here for all mankind to hear?
Wasn't the Declaration of Independence first read within its boundaries? Weren't the Stars and Stripes supposed to have been first sewn
here? The First Congress of the Republic had taken place on its
sacred soil, not to mention Braddock's Defeat, the Wyoming Mas-

sacre, the winter at Valley Forge and the Battle of Gettysburg. William Penn, the Quaker who treated the Indians according to Scripture, had founded the province much as Moses had the Holy Land, with a sense of divine guidance and brotherly love that made Pennsylvanians a chosen people. As the nation expanded, the sons and daughters of Pennsylvania had gone forth like the disciples in the Gospels and had colonized many of the newer states. One of the Pennsylvania Lincolns had migrated from Berks County, and a descendant in Springfield, Illinois, had become perhaps the most famous of all Americans. Daniel Boone and other Pennsylvanians had taken the Pennsylvania-German rifle south, where it became known as the Kentucky rifle. They took the Conestoga wagon west, where it became known as the prairie schooner, and they carried Pennsylvania pioneer words and phrases both south and west, implanting them in what became Southern, Southwestern and Western speech.

More concessions to the world had to be made as I grew older, but ever while traveling around with horse and buggy and on foot with my preacher father, my understanding of and feeling for my native state grew. Most of my family had been here a long time. From childhood I had heard how my double-great-grandfather—a country blacksmith, squire and member of Congress from Pennsylvania for four terms around the time of Jefferson—would tell stories to the litigants on both sides of a case brought before him until he had them in a good humor and willing to settle their dispute without a hearing; how my great-grandfather, a store and hotel keeper and officer in the War of 1812, later sheltered escaping slaves, and how one of them, Black Hetty, had stayed and lived to nurse me as a baby; and how my grandfather, a passionate gardener, and horseman, whose name is still legend around our home town, preached for nearly fifty years in his one charge, baptized more than six thousand people, and drew such a crowd at his funeral that three sermons had to be preached simultaneously, one in the roped-off street.

But what moved me most deeply about Pennsylvania as a boy, and still does today, is her ancient symbol of freedom, the mountains; not a few isolated ranges, as in some states, but a whole province swarming with them, often one against the other with only narrow valleys between. The sight of their backs raised to the sky, sometimes humped or flared, green and lush in summer, brown, hairy and wild in winter, seldom failed to stir me. I liked to study them and learn the lay of their land, how some ran parallel for twenty or even fifty miles and then turned or joined or threw out spurs to form coves and pinnacles or plateaus; how their aspect changed when seen from different angles; how the benches lay like smaller ridges, often with intervening forest swamps or wild hemlock hollows that the old mountain trails and early roads invariably followed; and how water from one mountain tasted sweeter and purer than that from another.

This wilderness of Pennsylvania, much of it still in woods, which aroused my devotion years ago as it does that of a legion of hunters, fishermen and tourists today, is what excited the imagination of the immigrants from Britain and Germany some two hundred years before. Pennsylvania meant Penn's Woods, and that's what set off the fire in men's breasts, the promise of freedom and free land, virgin woods and more virgin woods, mountains and more mountains. Between the mountains were uncounted valleys, small and large, hidden and open, red and yellow shale valleys, black bottom valleys and white limestone valleys, all rank with timber that attested to the richness of the soil. Meat was for the taking, house and barn timber for the cutting, and land for the clearing, well watered for man and stock.

The Indians had other ideas about the woods, which they had reason to believe belonged to them. My great-aunt Esther had told me about Indians; about her namesake, queen of the Senecas; about the massacres near our home town; and about the Severlings who lived near the covered bridge. Hadn't I noticed the Indian blood in their high cheekbones and coarse black hair? More than a hundred years before, a Severling had taken an Indian girl to wife, and so had a Coover, which was why the Coovers still walked straight as pines, usually with gun and dog, and why they lived as they did, resisting white men's ways.

If you knew the Coovers, you knew why the Indians, after William Penn the Just was gone, had fought his descendants and the other colonists tooth and nail, with arrow and fire, lead and scalping knife. They had tried to contain the white intruders first south of one mountain and then south of another. North and northwestward the conflict ran. The gory border advanced and receded across Pennsylvania's mountains through the long French and Indian wars.

Today you can cross these bloodstained mountains with no danger to your hair. Beyond Philadelphia, traveling northwestward along the path of the early white men, you see at first the low Welsh

Mountains, little more than hills. Then, across the garden spots of Lancaster County, you reach the long broken line of South Mountain, where the fabulous Cornwall iron is mined. Beyond lies the fertile Kittatinny Valley, and north of that, from almost any point on a clear day, you can see a wall of mountain hundreds of miles long. This is the Blue Ridge, called hereabouts the Blue Mountain. From the south it looks like a solitary ridge, but once you cross it you find yourself in a prodigality of mountains, long and slender with narrow valleys between. The crests seem to rise higher as you go on, some of them jumping rivers and changing their names, some stopping short while new ones of great length start farther on.

Finally you reach the still-higher Alleghenies, in the north-central area of the state, and see the orderly northeast-to-southwest pattern break up in violent confusion, the ridges running in any direction they choose. When you are no longer in the mountains, you are probably no longer in Pennsylvania.

Pennsylvania's nickname, the Keystone State, has less meaning in the greatly enlarged Union of today. A more apt name might be the Liberty State, not only because it played a leading part in the achievement of independence but for the tremendously varied mixture of its people and regions, in this resembling the character of the nation. The northwestern section, for example, including Erie, belongs in viewpoint and topography more to the Midwest, while the eastern border, including New Hope, the Poconos and Stroudsburg, is by nature a seasonal suburb of New York City. The state is much too vast and diversified to be portrayed fully here, so this report will set down only that Pennsylvania and its people seen and felt by one observer, boy and man.

You will find the Pennsylvania Dutch in the valleys. Like certain species of plants that grow on a particular kind of rock and nowhere else, they flourish in limestone country. If sometimes a Pennsylvania Dutchman is found tilling other soil, it's because there isn't enough limestone to go around. He and his fellows, for the most part, occupy a broad belt running across the state south of the Blue Mountain. Occasional limestone valleys occur in the mountains farther north, where pockets and sometimes an entire county of these people may be found.

Like the French provincials in Canada and the Spanish Americans in the Southwest, the Pennsylvania Dutch keep alive their own language. It's called a dialect but is really more of a German patois, incomprehensible to visitors. And though they settled here two hundred years ago, their English still carries a peculiar accent and turn of phrase that can stop an outsider in his tracks. The accent varies in different sections; some of the thickest accents may be found in the Hegins Valley in Dauphin County and between Kutztown and Allentown in Berks and Lehigh counties. Nor can the idiom be imitated easily. *Papa Is All* was meant to be a play about the Pennsylvania Dutch, but the title betrays the outlander's heavy hand. Pepper and salt and even vacation may be all, but papa and mamma, never.

Being Pennsylvania Dutch myself, I know how hard it is to get rid of the local (pronounced "logal") speech. Children whose parents have little trace of it, pick it up in school and at play, to be called Dutch the rest of their lives. Native men and women who have lived elsewhere for many years, even college professors of English, find to their dismay that certain inflections cling like birthmarks to betray them, along with telltale phrases such as "come here once," "sprinkle down the clothes," "it will be late till we get home," and referring to one's hair in the plural.

The word "dumb," in the sense of stupid, was in my boyhood purely Pennsylvania Dutch, and our teachers disparaged its use. Similar words used widely in the Pennsylvania Dutch belt by English-speaking people, and which may some day contribute to the American language, are: strubbly, used to describe disheveled, unkempt or rumpled hair; to grex, which means to complain or grunt complainingly; doppick for awkward; spritz for splash and spray; wunnerfitzick for inquisitive; and blutz for jolt and bruise. These words undoubtedly persist because they impart a shade of meaning which the nearest English synonym fails to convey, and also, perhaps chiefly, for their comic expressiveness.

The Pennsylvania Dutch like to laugh. Buildings are erected and automobile engines repaired amid frequent sallies and laughter such as I have heard nowhere else in America. An English traveler of nearly two hundred years ago left a record of the Pennsylvania Dutch custom of standing outside their churches to joke until it was time for the service to start—then coming out and resuming when it was over. Sometimes they laugh over trifles, out of pure animal spirits. Or they may see another meaning unintelligible to outsiders, as in the classic story about the Pennsylvania Dutch woman who came into a store; the clerk asked what he could do for her, and she said, "Oh, I don't want nothing. I just came in to go out."

There is, of course, one class of Pennsylvania Dutch jokes the outsider can understand and laugh at—those at the expense of the natives. These may be such banal and familiar ones as the sign on the door reading, "If the bell don't make, bump," or the remark of a child watching a freight train go by—"Ain't, Mom, when the little red house comes, then it's all?" For every one of these, however, the observing resident of the southern counties knows a dozen that seldom reach print. The woman who cleans our house said triumphantly after killing a snake, "Well, that's one more copperhead less," a statement that shines with succinctness if not with logic.

Tom Lyter, of Ono, tells the story of the widow who was called on by a man who wanted to see her husband.

"You can't see him. He's dead," she said.

"Dead?" the man exclaimed. "Why, when did he die?"

"Well," she said, "if he'd a lived till Thursday he'd be dead two weeks."

Paul Strickler, of Lebanon, relates how he went with a countryman to look for his lost dog, Wasser.

"Now you go up one side of the crick," the man said. "I'll go up the other. You know, he may come back both sides."

If such stories strike you as funny, you have an affinity for Pennsylvania Dutch humor. I have heard these, and many like them, told in my living room until a half score of people, all of them with a dash or more of native blood, shouted with laughter.

On the serious side, the Pennsylvania Dutch have been accused of leaning toward powwowing and hexerei. This is true enough, particularly in the recent past. My grandfather could powwow and was regularly called on to practice his art. He tried to persuade my mother to let me hold a worm in my hand while I was being baptized. This was supposed to give me the power, but my mother, whose maiden name was Henry, declined. As for hex stories, I have heard them all my life, many at firsthand, some told by men and women whose veracity in other matters was unquestioned. I remember as a boy the half-scared sensation of walking past the house of an alleged hex in my home town, and there were others in the surrounding countryside. Some of these reputed hexes, like their counterparts in New England, had a hard time among their fellows, although the

Pennsylvania Dutch, the first to talk against slavery in America, did
not hang their witches.

The traveler may think he sees evidence of hexerei in Pennsylvania
Dutch barn signs, which an enterprising Yankee by name of Wallace
Nutting told the public were witches' feet. Actually, these are harmless symbols of sun and rain and crop fertility. More than that, they
are simply ornaments, of which the Pennsylvania Dutch are very
fond. Their early baptism and marriage certificates, their furniture
and many other articles are decorated with brightly colored designs
of tulips, doves, parrots, roosters, vines and like motifs. They love
color, especially red, as attested by their big bank barns and by their
houses, often of brick and frequently painted over to make the brick
redder.

Pennsylvania Dutch houses are "crazy clean"; porches and cellar
steps are regularly scrubbed; sidewalks, gutters and sometimes the
street are scrupulously swept; even farms and fields look neat as toy
yards under Christmas trees. And the food is something to be remembered in Gath. . . . The tables of the Pennsylvania Dutch groan
with good things to eat, particularly when visitors, no matter how
humble, are being entertained. The legend that seven sweets and
seven sours are served is something of a fantasy, but there are always
plenty of both. If there are many guests at dinner, the fare will probably include chicken accompanied by beef or ham, hard-boiled eggs
in red-beet juice, as well as vegetables, relishes, fruits and several
kinds of pie and cake. Notable Pennsylvania Dutch dishes, for some
of which I still grow hungry in far places, are dandelion greens,
chowchow, chicken corn soup, pannhaas (a kind of richer scrapple
made from country "butchering"), Lebanon bologna, smoked sausage (generally half beef, half pork and cured in an old-fashioned
smokehouse), snitz and knepp, fastnachts, pretzels, and shoofly pie
with deep goo.

Just off the Pennsylvania Dutch belt lies the metropolis of Philadelphia, exiled inland and yet one of the titanic ports of the
world, rich as Croesus and yet quiet and unobtrusive as the Quakers,
the municipality of brotherly love and humility and also of the
haughty tradition, now almost vanished, that no lady or gentleman
would live north of Market Street. A modern center of music and
publishing, medicine, manufacturing and refining, it still has streets
where time has stood still. Crammed with historic spots, tombs,

churches and buildings, as well as with libraries, museums and colleges, Philadelphia's list of firsts tops the nation.

But to me and my fellow townsmen, a hundred miles away, all this was simply "the city." "Are you going to the city today?" we'd say.

North of the Pennsylvania Dutch country, and interlaced by it, lies the rugged hard-coal region. I was born on the southern edge of the anthracite country, and one of my earliest memories is the sound of heavy boots marching up the street to one of the miners' trains that left long before dawn. By afternoon the same trains returned, crowded with homecoming miners like blackface minstrels in overalls, dinner buckets slung over their shoulders, the men dropping off the train before it stopped and breaking into a dogtrot toward home and washtub.

A few years later, we moved to a hard-coal town at the foot of what was known as Fighting Hill, where women during the Great Strike had torn each other's hair in the street. I picked slate in a breaker, swam in a sulphur creek and heard the pioneer union leader, John Mitchell, speak in my home street. My brothers and I found it a kind of storybook country: the man-made mountains of coal dirt down which children of the patch coasted on staves; the "batching" shanties of miners who tramped back and forth to their distant farms on weekends, over forest trails and usually several mountains; the dangerous uncharted air holes in the mountains, where the unwary walker might fall to oblivion; the great sooty collieries; the terrifying mine slopes that dropped into dripping blackness; the endless underground gangways by which miners could come out miles from where they went in; the older, robbed and abandoned workings flooded by water and eternal night; the mules that never saw the light of day; the mine rats born a thousand feet underground that lived on mules' feed; and above all, the brave men who went down into the sunless pits to work and joke while the ghosts of dead men hovered beside them.

Today the hard-coal region has changed. The old-time labor abuses have given way to reform. The price of coal has risen so high that, even in hard-coal mining towns, many oil burners are in use. Other ways of earning a living have been necessarily found. The drab and sordid look of some of the coal towns has changed. Houses that never knew any coating but soot are often painted today, and the white gleam of electric washers and refrigerators may be glimpsed through the rudest cabin doors. But it's still the hard-coal region, the only one of its kind in the country. The picturesque onion steeples of the Greek and Russian Orthodox churches continue to mark the towns. The men and women of the patch, no matter what their ancestry, speak English with an accent that is Welsh in origin. And veteran miners still carry the telltale sign of their calling, a fine sky-blue marking where coal dirt has tattooed them beneath the skin and won't wash off.

The younger generation hasn't wholly rejected the calling. Not long ago, in a supply store near home, I saw a pair of youths come in to buy explosives. It seemed incredible that such smooth-faced lads could be miners. They looked little more than sixteen. They wore miners' caps, and their faces and hands were black. I guessed that they were bootlegging coal on "company" property in some neglected mountain spot, that they had only an old oil drum for a cage and bucket and the engine of some ancient wrecked car for hoist power, that the rope was probably unsafe, the shaft untimbered and the workings uninspected. But they walked into that store like seasoned miners, and their eyes looked out at you with an old-time pride in their calling, something almost vanished from the American scene.

Across the Susquehanna and the Alleghenies, on the western side of the state for the most part, lie the soft-coal fields. My restless father soon moved us here, and I learned to live in a town surrounded by mining patches called camps, where for block after block no blade of grass grew, where the peculiar incense of soft-coal smoke and of burning mine dumps was the familiar home-town atmosphere. The same mixture of nationalities prevailed here as in the hard-coal region, including the Pennsylvania Dutch. Magyar handlebar mustaches moved proudly down the street. Foreign priests muffled in greatcoats with astrakhan collars became friends of my father, and garlic scented the trolley cars and moving-picture houses.

Anecdotes from the two coal fields are nearly interchangeable. In a hard-coal town with a heavy Slav population, Jim Haas tells of a miner named Stosh Chernitsky. At a wedding flowing with cheer in Miners' Hall, Chernitsky fell out of a second-story window and broke some bones. Some of his friends visited him at the hospital.

"How did I get up there, anyway?" the patient asked them.

"You wanted to fly out one window and back through another, like a bird."

"Why did you let me do it?"

"Let you do it?" his friends said. "We even bet ten dollars you'd make it!"

In a play given at the opera house in Shenandoah, a local coal miner was one of the supers. His only part was to be shot and fall dead on the stage. His appreciative miner friends clapped his act, so he got to his feet and dropped dead again as an encore.

Unlike the hard-coal region, the bituminous country has more native products than coal. Flaming coke ovens light up the countryside at night. In my boyhood they flickered on my eyelids when I tried to sleep, as did the flare of blast furnaces in Johnstown later on. More than one evening, from my boardinghouse on the hill, I watched the night-long pageant in the steel yards below, the cars and buckets of melted ore handled like soup, the castings of red-hot metal carried on cars and transmission lines until finally the great hammers pounded and the sparks flew like red-gold fireflies.

A still-better-known Western Pennsylvania product is oil. The derricks run a little farther north than the coal tipples, but in a number of counties both may be seen. The founding of the world oil industry took place here. Oil from this area was peddled as early as the 1700's, but it was not until Colonel Drake drilled his famous well in 1859 that oil-field fever developed, to run like a wild contagion over most of the world. Here, more than a hundred years ago, $1,500,000 was paid for a single farm. The original Coal Oil Johnny was not John D. Rockefeller, Sr., but John W. Steele, a fabulous man who took a company of black-face minstrels along with him for his amusement and bought hotels to lodge them on overnight stops. Wild Ben Hogan had a sign outside his saloon, "The Wickedest Man in the World," and Gib Morgan told his famous stories of the "whickles," a cross between the canary and the bumblebee, and of the "rubber rock" that bounced drills off the richest oil basin in the world.

The giant heart and umbilicus of Western Pennsylvania's soft-coal, iron, oil and gas fields is Pittsburgh, whose mammoth sprawling limbs I knew first as a sixteen-year-old clerk in one of the monster Westinghouse plants; then, later, as a reporter on the now-vanished *Dispatch.* Yet so rapid and immense have the changes been that when I go back I find myself a stranger in a strange land of towers, towering bridges and the cyclopean steel and aluminum hives of commerce and culture.

Of the entire state, the northern-central region was my favorite, an area roughly defined by the railroad that once served it—the old Northern Central. Shaped like a tree, the broad trunk has its roots at Harrisburg, then rises and spreads northeast above the hard-coal region and west above the soft-coal fields. Here, in large, prosperous valleys as well as in smaller ones shut off from the rest of the world, I found people of the old-time pioneer stock, people who had a flavor of individuality and woodsmoke going back hundreds of years. From them I learned the art of leisure and of enjoyment in storytelling, the luxurious extravagance of sitting and talking an afternoon away under a chestnut-shingled roof or a live walnut tree.

In all life, nothing is quite so pleasant to the soul as forgetting the banalities of politics and the artificialities of book learning to lose oneself in an older and realer world concerned with such things as the sagacity of horses and oxen, the natural cunning of wolves, the loyalty of dogs, the value of tanning with hemlock and rock-oak bark, the matchless fur of the mink, marten and fisher, on which no frost would stick and which no cold could penetrate. Many of these people had seen the pine marten, a creature faster than any squirrel on a tree. The extinct passenger pigeons, which they called red breasts, were still a commonplace in their conversation—their long tails and swift flight, how one would make a man a meal, and the way they talked among themselves—"Just like us folks atalkin' together."

The hours here went by for me in pagan deliciousness. These people spoke the meaty old English, Irish and Scotch idiom. They "might as well die with the chills as the fever." Something small was "about as big as a piece of soap after a hard day's washing." Their hounds "blowed like a horn," and they would "sooner see a buck's tail any day than a tavern sign." This was the stock whose great-grandfathers' brothers went south and west taking with them their salty expressions and the time and inclination to figure out new ones. They said things like, "Them folks spend all they have for something to eat and never have a drop of whisky in the house."

In northern-central Pennsylvania, the Pennsylvania Dutch cooking fused with that of the Scotch-Irish and the French to create the best fare I ever tasted. I remember superlative homemade bread and rolls, raw-fried potatoes steamed under a pan lid to a delicacy unknown elsewhere, and home-cured ham so delectable that, after the first taste, a boy I knew would cover his portion with potatoes and pass his plate for a second helping while it was still to be had.

One of the finest cooks I ever knew lived in Lycoming County, a tall, thin, blond woman, half Irish, half Pennsylvania Dutch, who refused to sit with her guests but hovered constantly behind them in a manner that betrayed a nervous pride in her creations.

"Take some of these here potato buns," she would say. "Why, you folks aren't eating! Have some more of them there corn fritters." This, I learned, was ever a sign of special excellence in what she had prepared. But when she said, for example, "My cherry pie didn't get so good today. The store didn't have my regular flour and I had to get along the best I could. But maybe you can eat it"—when she said that, it was the ultimate accolade of humility for something that would melt in your mouth and leave a void that nothing in the future would ever fill.

Her grandmother had had the same hand of genius. She measured nothing, trusting all to her art and the Lord. Her personal salute to a crowning dish, spoken in a ruder and rougher age, was, "It didn't get good today. It's not fit for a hog to eat." Her family, friends, her kin, the hired man and sundry diners were accustomed to such self-immolation and knew what to expect. But a new preacher in his ignorance said bluntly, "If it's not fit for a hog to eat, I don't want any of it," and this practically crucified the woman, who couldn't praise the special dish without praising herself and couldn't endure the thought of her crowning piece of art going untasted and unappreciated by her reverend guest.

There remains one region of the state, the area referred to as the Northern Tier of Counties. The name always cast a spell on my imagination, particularly since we had lived in the shadow of the magic North Mountain, whose formidable battlements stood over the parsonage we occupied in the Muncy Hills.

Every time the buggy crested a hill, my father or I, who often went with him, could see the dark brooding wall, and once, from some poor backwoods parishioner's house where we were spending the night, I had a glimpse of the twinkling lights of Eagles Mere, the rich man's playground on the summit of the unattainable mountain, a never-to-be-forgotten symbol of luxury and ease far above the rude tick of straw and cornhusk on which my father and I were lying.

When I grew older and penetrated beyond North Mountain, I

found the most uniformly high country in the state. As in parts of the region just below it, life in the Northern Tier hadn't greatly changed over the generations. Only the people were different, New England people who had drifted down through New York State, bringing along their taste for gambrel-roof barns, for green tea, sage in sausage, strawberries on biscuits, for New England boiled dinners and New England baked beans. They still read York State rather than Pennsylvania newspapers, and their towns are reminiscent of New England, with wide streets, houses set well back from the sidewalks, with beautiful trees and a common in the center of town.

The legendary lumbering empire of Pennsylvania, once the greatest producer in the Union, sprawled and still sprawls over this and the north-central regions. Here was the famous Black Forest of the New World. As a boy I knew pine and hemlock ravines where the sun never reached the ground, each a natural cathedral which I entered with awe for the work of the Creator and yet with uneasiness lest it be the lair of the devil. But these "dark woods," as they were called locally, paled beside the Black Forest on the west branch of the Susquehanna, which covered hundreds of square miles and some of the most rugged terrain in the Commonwealth.

The Black Forest was the home of the pine marten and silence. The hemlocks were the bearded giants that Longfellow wrote about in *Evangeline*, the white pines such a fabulous stand that they furnished lumber to much of the world of their day, white, strong and yet easily worked; such lumber as no longer exists. An old axman and raftsman of the Black Forest, whose face bore evidence of "loggers' smallpox," the scars left by the spikes of an opponent's boots, told me the white pines stood so close that trees which ran a hundred feet without a knot, and contained up to six thousand board feet of lumber each, often had no more branches than you could pick up in your hands.

Not all the logs were sawed into lumber. The Black Forest furnished masts to the seven seas—spars, they were called in the woods —some a hundred and twenty feet long and nearly two feet in diameter at the small end. The logs were lashed in rafts two and three hundred feet long, and floated down the Susquehanna's spring flood in a wild ride in which the oarsman pilot was king of the river. The masts were shipped to Liverpool, the logs sawed at hundreds of mills scattered down the river to the Chesapeake Bay, and the raftsmen rewarded with four kinds of whisky, Squirrel, Fighting, Sleeping and

Loggers' Delight. The first made you want to climb trees. The last was said to be grain alcohol that had been aged in a barrel with four pounds of fine-cut tobacco to the gallon.

Pennsylvania houses, made more or less from Pennsylvania lumber, vary with their region. One kind that I learned to admire is the old unpainted wooden house, sometimes modest, sometimes of prouder proportions, still to be found in remote valleys of the state.

They were built when white pine was more plentiful than white lead and linseed oil, and now age and weather have stained the clapboards and timbers to a deep shade of brown which, to me at least, furnishes the countryside with an unusual contrast, in summer intensifying the bright colors of the flower garden outside it, in winter enriching the sense of bright life and human warmth within.

Once Pennsylvania had also a wealth of lovely colonial brick houses with fine doorways, windows and chimneys. A few that have escaped the growth of business may still be seen in Carlisle, Bedford, Harrisburg, Philadelphia and other cities and towns. Some noble country houses, erected mostly by Frenchmen in the 1700's, are to be found in the Oley Valley in Berks County. Indeed all through the Southern Pennsylvania countryside, scattered in unexpected and sometimes not easily accessible places, often on minor roads, one comes upon solid old brick and limestone houses built with integrity, their wood carved by loving hands. A modern practice among couples is to beat the countryside for such a find, and then restore it to its original dignity.

The Indian was only one of a long line of Pennsylvania peoples who believed passionately in liberty. Ole Bull, the greatest violinist of his day, founded in Potter County what he called "a new Norway consecrated to liberty, baptized with independence." He brought in eight hundred Norwegian settlers and fiddled all over the world to support the project, which eventually failed. Another refuge, this for victims of the French Revolution, was established by the followers of Marie Antoinette on the North Branch of the Susquehanna. It was being prepared as asylum for the queen herself before tragedy overtook her. Off the beaten path even now, it must then have been an almost inaccessible spot in the American wilderness of the 1700's. Yet it was visited by Louis Philippe, afterward King of France, the Prince de Talleyrand, the Duke de la Rochefoucauld and many others.

Some of the freedom seekers in Pennsylvania came to establish a kind of early communism with its inevitable dictator. One of these was George Rapp of the Harmony Society, founder of Economy, a communal town on the Ohio River. He is most famous for his edict forbidding intercourse between the sexes.

Most of these refuges and utopias have vanished, but one that remains is a showplace today—the Cloisters at Ephrata. Established more than two hundred years ago by a community of Dunkers, it is still a place where the visitor must lower his head in humility to enter the tiny cells, each furnished with a rude bench-cot made purposely short to prevent stretching out in slothful slumber. The passageways are narrow and winding, and the whole effect distills such a medieval atmosphere that it is easy to picture the brothers and sisters moving about in their white friars' robes, woolen in winter and linen in summer, pursuing their daily tasks of baking, printing, hymn-singing and praying; living on vegetables, using goblets, plates, forks, spoons, candlesticks and pillows all of wood. They declined to bear arms, but opened their doors to the wounded at Brandywine during the Revolution. Harder to recapture is the quality of their music—of their thousand and more original compositions which are now lost. The scores were written in many parts, and the choir sounded like an immense organ producing tones that visitors of those days claimed never to have heard before.

On the other hand, the music of the Moravians, a religious society in Bethlehem and Nazareth, was never lost but continues and grows in fame from year to year. Originally a communal colony, it has adapted itself wisely to modern times without losing its religious character. A friend tells me he is constantly impressed by the peace and serenity of Moravian faces. They appear to see beyond the veil. Today, more than two hundred years after the society was founded, their spring festival of Bach music has become famous and draws visitors from all over the world.

Of all the societies which sought religious freedom in Pennsylvania, probably the best known are the Quakers, the "peculiar people," whose Friends Service Committee and Relief Fund, as well as their sympathy for and understanding of other peoples, have won them praise abroad and at home. They stand so high in public confidence that non-Quakers contribute the bulk of the money for their philanthropies, and I know of several Friends today who deny themselves almost to the point of poverty to provide food and clothing for distant destitute people they will never see.

Of all Pennsylvania's tremendous wealth, this spiritual background of refuge and freedom is the greatest of its treasures and goes to the very heart of the nation. Early business deals were sometimes transacted in an unworldly and even poetic spirit. Several religious congregations in Pennsylvania, notably one at Manheim and another near Myerstown, were originally deeded land on which to build their churches for the express sum of one rose to be paid annually to the donor. Similar sentiment sometimes went into commercial transactions. The early owners of the rich Cornwall iron mines made a grant to supply ore free to their small neighboring Robesonia furnace "as long as grass grows green and water flows down hill."

To most native sons, Pennsylvania is the greatest state in the Union. If you come from another, it's your misfortune, not necessarily fatal but too bad. Pennsylvanians are also great travelers, eager to go and eager to get back. They become easily infected with homesickness. A prodigious amount of native food is sent to sons in exile—and not only food. Each spring my father used to mail a shoebox full of arbutus to an old friend who had moved away but pined to see and smell it again. I have heard more than one Pennsylvanian say on his return from a trip, "I've driven six or seven thousand miles and seen a lot of country, but nothing half so pretty as what we've got right here."

Delaware

by JAMES WARNER BELLAH

To understand the Delaware character you will have to know my great-great-uncle, and that will be difficult, for he was born in 1816 and died in 1899—and we have no forwarding address. I never knew the Honorable Edward Tatnall Bellah myself, but he fascinates me. He made his own brandy from his own apples grown for that sole purpose on his own lands outside Brandywine Village, appropriately enough. In his long career as a banker and public servant, he refused ever to take an oath or make a sworn statement. "Such specious approaches to the truth," he wrote, "are the terminal resorts of liars."

His telephone number in Wilmington was 9. He unscrewed the bell at four-thirty in the afternoon and did not let it ring thereafter until half past ten the next morning. "I will not have my home invaded by any means whatever, until a card is first sent in."

By considered choice he left no will. "No heir shall hate my dead hand. Let them hate the courts' live ones instead."

In the mornings, on his way to his seat in the House of Representatives in Dover or to his director's chair in the Union Bank in Wilmington, he would greet his friends on first meeting, but thereafter throughout the day he would cut them cold. "I have made my courtesies. What purpose can be served by hollow repetition?"

But of most lasting memory, this pertinent monument to Uncle Edward: when a deed is searched by the older legal gentry of Wilmington to this day, and Edward Tatnall Bellah's ownership is found of record—no further search is necessary. If he owned the land, *he damned well owned it.*

Uncle Edward was the ultimate native Delawarean. Know the mold—and you will understand the people of the state. Hardheaded with money. Courteous, to minimum requirements, with no urban frills. Completely self-sufficient in private living. Fine judges of good food and drink—in the castles of their own homes, which accounts for the indifferent public eating places throughout the state to this day. Honest at heart—but watch yourself carefully in all business transactions, for Delawareans are, of ancient times, close traders. Comfortably cynical in all basic philosophy. And utterly unchangeable, come hell, high water, the Du Pont overlordship or thermonuclear reaction.

We speak of three small counties, New Castle, Kent and Sussex, on the Delaware River and the Atlantic seaboard, for that is all the state has ever had; or, as was once most uncharitably said, of *two* counties at high tide and three at low, for the loftiest elevation the state attains is a towering 440 feet above sea level at Centerville, north of Wilmington. One hundred and ten miles long, Delaware is only nine miles wide at its narrowest and thirty-five at its widest. But from its earliest beginnings, it has raised a product for which there is no synthesis in chemistry. No substitute. No foreshortened manufacturing process to this day. That basic product is men, and because of their record Delaware has always been called the Diamond State. That is no glib slogan from a latter-day chamber of commerce. It is a treasured heritage from Thomas Jefferson, who coined the glittering term.

Few outsiders have known Delaware (beyond Wilmington) for three centuries past, for like the Eastern Shore of Maryland, it has always lain off the beaten track of north-south travel. But in the last few years the Memorial Bridge from New Jersey and Maryland's Chesapeake Bay Bridge have made it a major link in the motor route from Maine to Florida. This has opened to the world an almost virginal territory of precious colonial architecture, a visible history of our deep past still alive today, under the bounced echo of jet planes —and a world of honest bucolic living, and of fishing and hunting close to home that for years, except to native Delawareans, has remained almost completely unknown.

The land of Delaware is so flat that, from Wilmington for the almost hundred miles south to the Maryland border, the bubble in a spirit level hardly twitches as you go from township to township. But only a geographical snob would object to this flatness, for there are fifty fresh-water lakes spotted through it, with an excellent run of large-mouth bass in season, and there is the long Atlantic coast-line of Sussex County with succulent clams for the raking in un-limited numbers.

The fishing of Delaware, known to the work fleets for generations, is rapidly becoming a newly discovered paradise within everyone's range of fish and pocketbook, from sea trout, ling and porgies, through shad, herring and sturgeon to the offshore drum, marlin and dolphin—with Bowers, Mispillion Light, Lewes, Indian River and Rehoboth the main centers of facility and accommodation.

Quail, reed and railbird—duck if the season is kind—possum and mourning dove can give you excellent gun days in Kent and Sussex counties—as can deer. For over a generation, the deer disappeared almost completely from the state, then a few years ago they multi-plied so prolifically that a brief open season was proclaimed and the freezer chests filled with venison. A Wilmington friend once said to me: "It hardly seems believable but there were a few wild buffalo in Delaware quite a few years after they disappeared for-ever from Texas and the Western plains. I have never seen one, nor do I hope to now—but I have talked to men who have, and if a buffalo is shot in Delaware before I die, I'd like a steak, because my mouth still waters from Bret Harte's description of what they do for a man's inner being."

This primeval approach to Delaware seems the natural one, even though the state is the central ganglion of the world's largest indus-trial chemical empire. In spite of Du Pont, the colonial character of Delaware still exists throughout its length and breadth, with con-tinuous outcroppings of beauty and texture that surprise even native Delawareans—and because of Du Pont roads every corner of the state is accessible.

The Green and the Strand of the ancient town of New Castle re-main much the same today as they were when Delaware's James A. Bayard and the other commissioners took sailing ship there to nego-tiate the Treaty of Ghent.

The pirates Kidd and Teach once skulked the Delaware inlets, and if part of their treasure be not still sequestered somewhere near, then a broached galleon of the Main must lie fathoms deep off the

Sussex shore, for not so many years ago, after a savage Atlantic storm, Spanish coins were picked up on the resort beaches of Bethany and Rehoboth.

On a Saturday evening along Dover's Loockerman Street, you will see bearded Mennonites with their bonneted wives and long-skirted little girls, marketing for the week.

Until a 1915 fire, you could still see bloodstains on an upper stair of gracious Belmont Hall in Smyrna—one of the finest examples of colonial family homes in America. The blood of a Continental sentry, who was shot on the roof walk by a Britisher, and crawled down to give the alarm more than a century and a half ago.

The Green and State Street in Dover are still buttressed by the ancient houses that saw Caesar Rodney tighten cinch to ride to Philadelphia with the crucial deciding vote for colonial independence. Had Delaware *not* voted, the Declaration would have died for want of unanimous support. To this day, only one member of the House of Representatives goes to Washington with Delaware's two senators (the population being less than Rhode Island's) but the state takes precedence over all of the other forty-nine, for it was the first to ratify the Constitution.

One stray enemy plane coming in low from the Pennsylvania border, and jettisoning its stick of bombs before crashing on the outskirts of Wilmington (for somehow a Delawarean would shoot it down), could obliterate one of the most closely knit industrial targets the United States offers. This target is set up almost in a straight line along the Delaware River, from northeast of Wilmington to a few miles southwest, where the bomb run would end logically on the Chrysler Plant near Newark, a few miles from the Maryland line. On the way, in two minutes' close attention, a meticulous bombardier could take out the steel mill of the Colorado Fuel and Iron Company, the plant of Allied Chemical and Dye Corporation, the Du Pont pigments installation at Edge Moor, and the Delaware Power and Light Company. Slight rudder pressure would bring him over the Pusey and Jones shipyards, the Du Pont and Nemours buildings at Wilmington—the Pentagons of the Du Pont empire—Du Pont's experimental station and the experimental station of the Hercules Powder Company. Kicking left again a smidgen, he could add the New Castle Rayon Plant to the destruction, the central research laboratories of Atlas Powder and the American Brake Shoe Company's manganese-steel division. A lucrative bag.

Wilmington has been a mill town since colonial times, because of the water power of the Brandywine. When Washington was President, 400,000 bushels of wheat were ground there every year for years, and Joseph Tatnall of the Tatnall Mills would haul thirty thousand dollars cash from his Quaker small clothes to pay Edward Lloyd of Wye, Maryland, for his standing wheat. (The receipts are still extant at Wye House.) Wilmington has grown steadily in the mill-working tradition, until today thrity-seven out of every 100 working residents are factory laborers. Better than one third of the producing population.

That is not the nation's largest percentage for manufacturing centers, but because Wilmington has a population of only 115,000 concentrated in sixteen square miles, the mark of the belted wheel is inevitable. For years one has come into the city on the Pennsylvania, through slums, junkyards and fish markets. One progresses then through narrow, traffic-jammed streets of tiny wall-to-wall houses toward the few open spaces left in town, where 19th Century middle-class money has added a tower or a cupola to the walls and moated them with "yards." Beyond is the Kennett Pike, where the sprawling du Pont estates stretch full north to the Pennsylvania border and across it in virtually feudal grandeur, with the names of old France on their gateposts. The whole social gamut therefore is Wilmington's —from grinding poverty in the Negro, poor-white and foreign-born sections, through the suffocating country-club midstage—to wealth of astronomical proportions.

One searches in vain in Wilmington history for a past of silk-ruffed and surcoated frimpery, or of gaiety of living such as Annapolis, Baltimore and Philadelphia knew in their time. Although the home of comparative wealth since the earliest days of its shipping history and the mills on the Brandywine, this was fundamentally a Quaker town, subdued by the Quaker approach to the serious and somber business of the journey through this vale of tears.

Wilmington is also a literal town. A woman you have just met will, over a warm Martini, ask you if your father-in-law owns his house in Wawaset—or rents it. But sooner or later a cousin will straighten it all out: "She asked you because she really wanted to know. Her great-grandfather and yours were both caught in the failure of Springer, Morley and Gause. You have much in common."

In Wilmington, let there be a suspicion of the bar sinister in a family, no matter how far back, and the word is passed from mother to daughter so that the shadow still lies across the bloodline to this day —and the next. Let your grandfather have been born on the wrong side of the railroad tracks—fairly easy in three-railroaded Wilmington—and it makes scant difference whether you go to Harvard, join the Wilmington Country Club, live in Wawaset and send your offspring to Friends or Tower Hill School (where they are sure to meet young du Ponts)—there will be those who remember that your ancestors are not buried in Brandywine Cemetery, and there are certain weddings you will never be invited to attend.

But far more important to an essentially Quaker tradition, let there ever have been bankruptcy or financial chicanery of a less heinous nature in a family, and no matter how many generations succeed— the change they make for a dollar is always very carefully counted in Wilmington.

If all of this were a chip-on-the-shoulder attitude, it would be insufferable. But it isn't. Among native Wilmingtonians, it's a family attitude and as they are all members of the same old family, in effect, any objections, appeals, reclaimers will be taken up in family council. Outsiders excluded.

Yet in spite of its deep commercial tradition—rooted in firms like J. E. Rhoads and Sons, founded by John Rhoads in 1702 and the oldest manufactory in America that still does business under the family name, and the Charles Warner Company, founded in 1794, the oldest commercial concern in America still controlled by the founding family—Wilmington was the home of that great American painter, Howard Pyle, who executed his most important canvases with mill smoke in his nostrils. In his tradition, Stanley M. Arthurs, the muralist, spent most of his productive lifetime in Pyle's old studio, still extant. Robert Shaw picked out his fine water-color detail in his house on Penny Hill. Andrew Wyeth, the landscapist, works not far from Wilmington at the present time, as do Gale Hoskins and the amazing Ed Loper, who paints the tortured soul of his transplanted race with terrible, constrained understanding. Scott Fitzgerald once wrote in a rented house on Wilmington's Delaware River, and Victor Thaddeus, whose definitive critique of Voltaire is a modern classic, still lives just outside of town.

So much has been written about Du Pont and the du Ponts, by carpingly critical, coldly objective and servilely subsidized pens, that

almost anything goes, but it shouldn't, for the whole saga is a magnificent American story that echoes now the world around.

For a century they made explosives. For a century "The Company" was a closed family project. The original Eleuthère Irénée
du Pont, who built the first mill on the Brandywine in 1802, was an
apprentice of the great chemist Lavoisier at the French government
powder works at Essone. His son Henry went to West Point for the
finest engineering courses offered in this country. The next generation
went to the University of Pennsylvania for chemistry, and after
Massachusetts Institute of Technology was founded in 1861, subsequent offspring studied there. From the very nature of their business, technical educations were prerequisite, because powder making
is a volatile affair and knowledge is the basic life insurance.

When the company was founded, the original Irénée drew a salary
of $1800 a year. The capitalization was $36,000. By 1809, the profits
had averaged only $7268.94 a year. The War of 1812 increased the
Du Pont gross receipts, of course, but in his lifetime Irénée never
knew real security or complete freedom from debt—only hard and
grueling work and an eternal scramble to meet his obligations.

It is a myth that the du Ponts have always been American rich.
They have not. It is a close but plausible bet that as late as 1900 no
individual du Pont was yet a millionaire. For there are two factors
in making powder. You can build an expensive plant over many
months—and lose it in half a blinding second. Du Pont did, several
times, and started again. And there are two factors in making powder for wars. You can't expand plant fast enough to meet their beginning needs. And you are left fully expanded—with plummeting
demand—when they end.

In a century, Du Pont faced these conditions five times—with the
War of 1812, the Mexican War, the Crimean War, the Civil War and
the Spanish-American War. However, in that same century, the
peacetime market for powder steadily expanded. The vast stumping,
dredging, tunneling, building and mining of a growing country required industrial powder. Du Pont furnished it. Through Henry du
Pont's gunpowder trust, by manufacturers' agreement initially, and
then by slick deals for actual Du Pont ownership of competing companies, they came close to supplying *all* of it—and at their own price.
If a competitor undercut, he was soon working for Du Pont or he
wasn't working. (Such tooth-and-claw methods were so usual at that
time that business itself was like the vast flocks of black sheep in

Connemara: if you see a white one, you wonder what its mother has done.)

In 1907 the Department of Justice took notice and the Government charged the Company had violated the Sherman Anti-Trust Act. The suit showed Du Pont to be either a public benefactor or an industrial monster. Morally, it was never quite decided which, so that you may still take your choice. Du Pont was, however, definitely Big Business by then—although not yet the ultimate giant—the colossus that was to inspire in present times a second anti-trust suit, the hugest in history, and defend itself handsomely, winning against the Government after a five-year battle in the courts.

World War I had to be fought first. By official British admission Du Pont explosives saved the British Empire on the battlefields of France, and Du Pont explosives tilted the balance of victory in favor of the American manpower effort. Capitalization of the Company in 1915 was $60,000,000. After the Armistice of 1918 Du Pont had $90,000,000 of surplus funds in its treasury. The basic Company policy required continuous reinvestment. The fine hand of John Jacob Raskob, who had originally left a $45-a-month job to start with Du Pont as a secretary, found the medium. $49,000,000 was put into Durant's General Motors and Du Pont took financial control.

There is no sanity in going further with figures. Everybody in this world, directly or indirectly, pays Du Pont for something—from the stenographer who buys her nylons for 98 cents a pair to the coolie in Kuala Lumpur who makes his family's sandals from a worn synthetic auto tire he has bought for five Straits cents.

What manner of people are these du Ponts of Delaware, whose collective holdings dominate a larger portion of industry than do those of the Rockefellers, Mellons, Morgans or any other family combine in the United States, including oil-soaked Texas, or any other part of the globe? Forty-five of their individual names appear in the Wilmington telephone book, but without specific census, it can conservatively be said that well over a hundred individuals now comprise the immediate family—those who directly by birth or fortuitously by marriage share the dividends through the medium of Christiana Securities, which is the super holding company for the family's interests. Of this far-flung and prolific clan only a scant half-dozen "of the name" are now active employees of the Company or its subsidiaries. Possibly another half-dozen men of distaff connection are also in active employment, including the president, Crawford Greenewalt.

I have known several du Ponts. One ranks high among the world's most charming hostesses—an incisive mind denying the moated walls of great wealth and living eternally in the reality of the world. One is an insufferable travesty of Chaucer's Eglentyne, eternally prefacing a complete absence of any sound opinion with "As a Dewopawn." One is the victim of sadistic family possessiveness to a point of shuddering almost visibly at the sound of the name. And one, with an excellent war record behind him, works hard at the family trade as his forebears did before him. Some are known intimately and as well in Wilmington as any run-of-the-mill neighbors in any small town. Some are towering swells, only heard of from distant places. Some people in Wilmington whisper the name in awed reverence. One prominent Wilmingtonian who bore it as a middle name never even used the initials.

In the light of Du Pont's complete dominance of present-day Delaware, it is interesting to note how the wheel will turn, given time. How one side of the tracks becomes the other. Who rides the horse who used to walk.

The emigrant du Ponts, if not snubbed by Wilmington, were completely ignored. They were suspect because they borrowed money in Philadelphia, and because they did not live in Wilmington but kept to themselves in a small stone house (successor to their original log cabin) close by their first mill on the Brandywine, and in closely adjacent houses as the family grew.

They were further frowned upon by early Wilmington because not infrequently their mill blew up and destroyed property as well as life and limb. Once, in 1854, three of their powder wagons disintegrated right in town, atomizing the twelve horses, the three drivers and several staid Wilmingtonians passing by.

But be it said for the heroic older breed that the first man into a mill fire that threatened an annihilating blast was always a du Pont, the man who led the rescue party after a blast was always a du Pont, and at least two du Ponts in their time have gone to glory in a holocaust of their mills and several have died indirectly from results, including one du Pont woman. For they were powder-men for almost a century, sweat-stained and charcoal-grimed, living close by their mills, toiling in them personally, giving of their souls to the business.

For this reason, Wilmington's attitude never bothered them much. When they wanted the State of Delaware, they stretched forth a firm hand from the Brandywine and took it. They have never let go.

They took it in 1861, when Major General Henry du Pont, the West Pointer in command of all Delaware militia, changed it from a potential Southern state to a Northern state in a matter of half an hour. Delaware was then a Democratic state and slave owning. In 1860 less than one third of the state's vote supported Lincoln. With war clouds hovering, and with threats of rebellion against the pro-Union minority mounting, General Henry wired the Federal commander in Baltimore, General John A. Dix, for troops. They came at once. Delaware did not secede. She furnished subsequently 13,651 men to the Union—one eighth of her population—and met every Federal tax assessment throughout four years of war.

From that day to this, Delaware has fought and bucked, hated, reviled, admired and fawned upon, ignored and courted the du Ponts, but in the end, it has invariably bowed to Du Pont's benevolent paternalism. Du Pont roads belt Delaware from end to end. Du Pont practical interest in its school system raised the state from thirtieth place in literacy to close to the top. Du Pont endowments to institutions for the sick, handicapped and aged lowered the state's mortality figures drastically. Adding in its lifelong record of fair labor practices, sick and retirement benefits and, in recent years, ownership-participation policies, the Du Pont Company has raised the standard of living directly or indirectly in all three counties.

But the price has been stiff. It is whispered that no candidate of either party running for office in Delaware has a Chinaman's chance of election unless Du Pont approves. (The term is used collectively to indicate a way of life.) That no one is elected to membership in the Wilmington Club, the Vicmead Hunt or the Wilmington Country Club unless, again collectively, Du Pont approves. That nothing is printed in the Du Pont-owned Wilmington papers unless Du Pont approves.

Speaking noncollectively, some Delaware du Ponts live with imposing formality. Some answer their own doorbells. Some dwell in a hundred rooms. Some in three and a kitchenette. At least one has committed suicide. One held the Congressional Medal of Honor. One enclosed his 300 acres of home park with a ten-foot wall topped with jagged inset glass "to keep all the skunks in Delaware out"— as he put it—"most of them named du Pont." Two were United States

senators. One has been married four times (you must be married
five times to be an *officer* of that club). One, for whom du Pont Circle
is named in Washington, broke the Atlantic naval power of the Confederacy from the deck of his flagship. One beat a nasty paternity suit
in the Wilmington courts. One built the Equitable Building in New
York. One tried to sue half the female population of Wilmington for
libel. One is a ranking tennis champion. One married an Irish barmaid between boats at Queenstown—and never came home. One used
to march in uniform in the Wilmington Police Band tooting a French
horn. One even married a Hyde Park Roosevelt, for all the du Ponts'
Republican tradition, and there is the logical place to leave them—if in
Delaware you ever can.

North of Wilmington, there is the Henry Francis du Pont Winterthur Museum, which when it was his home, was admittedly the most
expensively furnished in America.

You may not barge in and ask to be shown through the museum. If
you wish to see it, you must write and receive a card of admission
by mail. You go through in groups of four. The number of groups for
each day is limited and requests are granted in the order of their
receipt. There is an admission charge and ladies must deposit their
handbags before entering.

There are about eighty period rooms on seven floors, and they
cover in the most minute detail the entire spread of American living
from 1640 to the early 19th Century—down to newspapers, magazines and books of the various periods. There is Martha Washington's
cake plate, a book of Cotton Mather's sermons, John Hancock's bedspread, William Penn's bed curtains, several ale tankards made by
Paul Revere. Whole rooms, façades, staircases, hallways and porticoes were moved bodily from their original locales, set up at Winterthur and then furnished to the last detail.

Winterthur was no rich man's hobby, pursued impersonally
through agents. "H.F." was his own ultimate purchaser, his own
agent, his own scout, and still exercises the over-all directorial hand
through his curator. For years he has operated his own line of trucks
to take his treasures to and from seasonal reupholsterings and necessary repairs. He maintains a staff of furniture repairmen and fabric
workers in New York for this purpose. It all started with his rather
meticulous bent for embellishing his own home. From that it has
grown into a $20,000,000 semi-public museum and one of the ulti-
mate shrines of Americana in the entire country.

Delaware in a manner of speaking was a stepchild of the Colonies (but never of the Union) who from her earliest days took care of herself in her own forthright way. The state takes its name from one Thomas West, who, raised to the peerage as Lord de la Warr, was a onetime Royal Governor of Virginia, and under whom the area that is now Delaware became a part of Virginia in 1609. But at seven o'clock on the evening of August 28, 1609, one Henry Hudson, shipmaster in the employ of the Dutch East India Company, let go the *Half Moon's* anchor in lower Delaware Bay, about a mile offshore of the present resort of Bethany Beach. On the strength of that anchoring, two things transpired—a Dutch colony of thirty-three souls was established at Zwaanendael (so called from the wild swans) in 1631, near the latter-day town of Lewes; and New York got a North River on the *west* side of Manhattan—a geographical misplacement which has never seemed to bother New Yorkers one bit.

Eighteen months later the Indians had massacred all but one Dutchman and laid waste the stockade and stores. Nothing remains today except the Zwaanendael House in Lewes, built as a museum and library in 1931 and modeled after a wing of the Town Hall at Hoorn in Holland. It is a must for the traveler, as it is the sole repository of reliquary Dutch culture in America south of New York.

The phrase "south of New York" gives the key to the river enigma. From Henry Hudson's time onward, until the more modern times of great-circle navigation—the direct route from Europe was a departure from the Portuguese coast to the Canaries, passing to the eastward of the Bahamas and to the westward of Bermuda. Your landfall was therefore the bay shores of either the southern river (the Delaware) or the northern river (the Hudson).

Swedes settled in Delaware in 1638 and their colony remained under the Swedish flag for seventeen years until the Dutch took over for nine years again and the British from the Dutch for one hundred and twelve years until the colonists declared their independence from Britain. William Penn, to whom the Duke of York originally indentured the Three Lower Counties for 10,000 years, for a fee of one rose a year, held the upper hand there only about long enough to grant them their demanded autonomy.

History in Delaware, as in Scotland and Ireland, is a close-knit family affair. Touch a man in any of the three counties and you touch my brother. Kinship is ubiquitous and ramified. Cooches still live at Cooch's Bridge where Cornwallis' Hessians tarried five days—where

the Stars and Stripes were first flown in combat. Simplers and Mc-
Cabes still live in Selbyville. Tatnalls teach school or work in banks,
close by their old houses near Wilmington that knew the spur chink
of Washington, Lafayette and "Dandy" Wayne. Ridgelys still sleep
in their ancestral beds at Dover. Judge Richard S. Rodney's law offices overlook Caesar Rodney's equestrian statue in Rodney Square,
Wilmington. A Prettyman still keeps store in Milford—another in Wilmington. The name of Bayard is of some continuing political significance in the land. Bancrofts are abroad in the state to this day,
as are Deputys, Buckalews, Irons, Gilpins, Comegys, Richardsons,
Brinkleys—and Warners.

The pillory as an apparatus for punishment was not officially done
away with in Delaware until 1905. You may still lay yourself open to
strokes of the lash in Delaware for wife beating, burglary, attempted
poisoning and horse stealing—a real enough threat to keep racketeers
well beyond the state's borders. For rape in Delaware, you will be
imprisoned for life, but only if you employ the best trial lawyer in
the state and the jury recommends clemency. Otherwise, you die for
the transgression.

I never cross the Christina River (the "Christeen" still to the native tongue) to head for the southern part of the state but I see the
flying curls of gallant Nancy Hanson once again. (Her hair *must* have
been red.) After Brandywine Battle, Nancy so befuddled a British
officer with blandishment and coquetry that he unwittingly got her a
carriage and two long redingotes to cover the uniforms of two Continental officers in imminent danger of their lives. But the ruse was
discovered and a dozen British dragoons came galloping in pursuit,
with pistols blazing. The Americans had to return the fire—and family
tradition has it that the comely Nancy did some very fancy shooting
herself in close support. One officer was Colonel Tilton. Had the escape not been successful these pages would not have been penned,
for the other was my namesake and progenitor, Captain James Bel-
lach of Caesar Rodney's Regiment. In which there is no simpering
pride but quite an open boast, for, as it is said, ancestry is important
not only in Dover but all over Delaware.

The Christina River which borders the southern reaches of Wilmington divides the two cultures of the state—the starkly industrial
city and the agricultural lower counties.

A detour to the right on the way south brings one into the town of

Newark (accent on the final syllable) wherein Wilmington's industrial overflow encroaches on the academic precincts of the University of Delaware. A state university, Delaware however ranks very high among all state universities in the number of alumni who go on to graduate work—a large percentage in chemistry and engineering—due to practical Du Pont stimulus.

Beyond Newark lie the five tracks of Delaware Park, home of the Delaware Steeplechase and Race Association. A total of fourteen fixture stakes are raced for annually here, ten flat and four between flags, and the track owners do not take a cent of profit. Whatever is made above expenses and taxes is invested in improvement of the installation, so that it is one of the finest tracks in the United States.

A detour to the left on the way south brings one into the ancient town of New Castle, the state's first capital and a town still authentic in its colonial atmosphere. The sprawling modern area encroaches upon the old in a dynamic continuity of history. The spot where William Penn first set foot on the continent, in 1682, is less than a mile from the Bellanca Aircraft Company.

In May of each year, the residents of New Castle open a score or more of the old houses to the public, with guides and hostesses in colonial dress. The George Read house in the Strand is one of the finest examples extant of American Georgian. The Court House dates, in part, to 1682. Packet Alley at dark still whispers with the ghosts of other years—when the boats from Philadelphia connected with the cars of the old Frenchtown railroad to the Chesapeake Bay, one of the first steam railroads in America. The ticket office, about the size of a telephone booth, is still preserved.

Immanuel Episcopal Church in New Castle, with parish records that date to 1689, together with Old Swedes Church in Wilmington, start a chain of significant church buildings that runs southward through the state. Near Odessa, there is old Drawyers Presbyterian Church—one of the earliest in America—built in 1773 on the site of a wooden church built in 1711. At Frederica, there is Barratt's Chapel, known as the "Cradle of Methodism in America." At Broad Creek, there is Christ Episcopal Church, built in 1771, with the original interior woodwork still preserved. And in Dover, the present capital, there is Christ Episcopal Church, dating from 1734, in the cemetery of which are buried Caesar Rodney, the Signer, and those two derring-do officers Miss Nancy Hanson snatched from British nooses so many years ago in Revolutionary Wilmington.

Dover was laid out in 1717, and the old Green at moonrise still gives one the illusion of powdered wigs and crinolines, even though, as in New Castle, the new town grows directly from the old in present leaps and bounds that bid fair to make Dover one of the most important Air Force bases in the United States. The ancient houses are still lived in, in great part by the descendants of the builders, and the old buildings are still used—the State House since 1722. There is no museum flavor, no dead aspect of history as something done with, to be kept apart from life in mothballs. It is all one in both Dover and New Castle, the whole American scene from the beginning, irrevocably intertwined from silver-handled dragoon pistols to Nikes.

They still call in hats and gloves in Dover and drop cards—as they do in Wilmington, but, one thinks, in Wilmington merely to see how you live. When the telephone wires went underground in Dover, the company was required to trench them down the middle of the streets, as side trenching would have damaged the roots of the ancient elms and sycamores—and the complete disruption of traffic was a small price to pay for shade. Possibly ten thousand corporations have their home offices in Dover, for Delaware corporate law is facile and convenient. Lawyers prosper there on this account—in fact almost everyone but the postmen and the police force is a member of the bar. You will note that I have not included the fire department? Purposely. It is volunteer and, at strength, composed of one hundred male citizens. Using the most modern equipment, it is still a gentleman's club. The engine house has billiard tables and card rooms. Its lounge is comfortably appointed in overstuffed chairs and divans, with tapestried walls and curtains of heavy velvet. But Dover has never burned down yet.

Sussex and Kent counties still hold to a certain Southern flavor of living to this day. If you want a tire changed, you may not get it changed, and the reason will be as valid as it would be in the Georgia hinterland. "Cain't, suh. Ain' got no tar arns." In these two southern counties the spoken word is softer than in Wilmington, and life is taken more slowly. There is more time for living—which is to say shooting, fishing, politics and conversation—and ancestry is more an accepted condition than a belligerent major premise, as it is in Wilmington.

Kent and Sussex are largely agricultural, for their climate allows a growing season of about 185 days—a condition that challenges everyone to part-time farming at least. Farms run to between 125 and 150 acres and the most important farm product is broilers, better than 60,000,000 being marketed each year, although 10,000 Southern Delaware acres are planted in fruit trees and 40,000 in truck crops.

A Chicken Festival is held in Harrington each June, with recipe prizes offered to "Chicken Cooks, U. S. A." If you are under the impression that you have eaten chicken in its quintessential succulence, you are sadly mistaken—unless you have been to Harrington, the chicken ganglion of the known world. A "Delawine broiled chicken" done in white wine and apple jelly has brought a first prize—but old-line Delawareans of Sussex and Kent counties are of the considered opinion that no matter how you try to "fancy the bird up" you cannot beat plain old Delaware fricasseed chicken.

At Rehoboth and Bethany beaches there are simple and delightful shore resorts of unpretentious hotels and family cottages. Their flavor is reminiscent of the old Newport, in the days when old New Yorkers went there for the climate—not for the Vanderbilts and the flamboyant horde that followed in their train.

The late Ben Albertson, of Lewes, once refused to sell me a musket that Abraham Lincoln was supposed to have carried as a captain in the Black Hawk War. Said he couldn't in all honesty, because he wasn't sure whether it had been carried by Abe or just by one of the other men in Abe's company. Said he'd still work on it and when he found out for sure, I could have it—because he wasn't particularly a Lincoln man himself. I never got it, for Ben was still working on it when he died.

The British Captain Beresford once tried to dust up Lewes during the War of 1812. He got the dusting himself instead at the hands of the citizenry and left for Bermuda without his fresh water. They had no ammunition, so they picked up the British cannonballs and fired them back. Casualties in Lewes: two chickens and a broken leg.

Delaware has a stubborn, continuing record of producing fighting men that dates well back into the colonial Indian wars. Always with a comparatively small population, she has invariably sent to the colors as large or larger a percentage of troops than any other state in the Union, whenever sovereignty was in jeopardy. The Delaware regiment, which, with the gallant Marylanders, fought the bitter rearguard action at Long Island and saved Washington's army from threatened debacle, carried Delaware fighting cocks with them. A means, one supposes, of eking out their scant and uncertain pay by betting. The best of these game cocks were descended from a traditional blue hen. From her, the Delaware troops were nicknamed the Blue Hen's Chickens. Since that day, the Blue Hen's Chickens have been stubbornly present on every American battlefield. Little men for the most part, but grown tall by circumstances.

Among them, some giants walked as well, nor does the breed die. Delaware's James A. Bayard stands apart in the select company of bygone statesmen—among the Clays, Websters and Calhouns.

So then what have we really? A small but fiercely prideful state with the faint cavalier and bond-servant shadow of Virginia upon its beginnings, a kinship with Maryland's delightful Eastern Shore, the ponderous heritage of Penn's hardheaded Roundheads—a touch of the Dutch, a lacing of Scandinavian, a broad overlay of Scotch, Irish and English, and a self-determined independence of thought and political entity that has given Delaware character and its people individuality for almost three centuries. And still does, in three small counties a hundred and ten miles in over-all length, by nine miles wide at its narrowest and thirty-five at its widest.

So possibly you have come to know my Uncle Edward.

PART III *The East Central States*

Wisconsin

by MARK SCHORER

In Wisconsin, history always seems very near; it is so much a part of daily life that it is never quite remarkable. It has not yet been entombed in monuments, and thus it cannot be resurrected because it has not been buried. It is not something that you come and look at casually; it is something that you live. History is like a green shade in which the little towns of Wisconsin slumber.

Look closely at any town. Look at any lake or river town, for these are the characteristic towns—Sauk City, for example, which lies in a slow bend of the Wisconsin River almost in the center of the southern half of the state. It takes its name from the Indians who abandoned this, their ancient prairie, hardly more than a hundred years ago. Across the river stretch the green rounded hills where they fought their last real battle with the white men, and where village boys still find arrowheads. One hill rises to a sharp and jagged point, where granite rocks are piled like broken statuary. In local myth, this is known as Black Hawk Lookout, after the chief who led his fleeing, stumbling, starving people through this prairie valley.

With the defeat of Black Hawk in 1832, the Wisconsin territory was opened to enterprise, and a bright, wild spirit arrived in Sauk City. He was Agoston Haraszthy, a Hungarian political refugee who came to Wisconsin after reading in Marryat's American travel diary that this was the finest portion of North America. Haraszthy was a tall man, very dark, with a great black mustache and beard, an expert horseman and hunter who charged through the wilderness and across the prairie, wearing a bright green shirt and a red silk sash. A romantic idealist of nearly frantic energies, he established almost singlehanded the enterprises which gave Sauk City its first social pattern.

The main street of the town follows the undulant line of the river where, soon after Haraszthy arrived, lumber rafts drew up in rude processional.

Not far from the edge of the water, between a market and a neon-lighted bar, there is a kind of grass-grown pit. The bar was once a saloon where drunken lumbermen roistered, and the pit was a dugout, branch-and-bough covered, which sheltered first settlers through a long winter. (The term "Badger State" comes down from early miners and others who, like the animal, burrowed in the ground when the icy winter closed in.) The pit is there today, a neglected feature of the street.

In Sauk City you will find a pleasant park of pine and oak, with a large, square, wooden hall in its center, an edifice austerely angular and gray, and behind it a crested, circular bandstand suggestive of communal frivolity. This is the property of the *Freie Gemeinde*, the Freethinkers' Congregation. Organized as The Humanist Society by Agoston Haraszthy in 1842, it was the direct expression of his restless cosmopolitanism and of the liberal views which characterized European revolutionary movements in the 19th century. Largely through this group, Sauk City became known abroad as the atheist's heaven. To the Freethinkers' hall came such famous theorists as Carl Schurz, such notorious atheists as Robert Ingersoll. Liberal professors from the University still come out from Madison to address the members on philosophical and political issues. And even if this group has grown smaller and somewhat staid with the years, even if Reason, which once smiled with such bright promise, has been dusted over by a hundred years of village habit, such occasional intellectual gatherings are as natural to these people as the dances through which they whirl on festival occasions, or the large town picnics in the park, around the bandstand, on the Fourth of July.

In a hundred years Sauk City has grown to only a little more than a thousand people, and in that time its life has become the same as American small-town life everywhere—the neon, the motorcycles roaring through the streets on dead Sundays, the ugly unplanned buildings, the well-kept, dull houses and the neat vegetable gardens behind them, the national highway whose trucks and cars usurp its main street in the summer, and that same street desolate and raw and piled high with snow after stormy winter days.

Yet at night, after the farmers have driven back to their prosperous farms, after the shopkeepers have put out their electric signs, after the townspeople have gone to bed and the small yellow lights flicker out at last, and the town lies asleep on the great breast of the whispering prairie, the presence of the primordial land makes itself felt. The tragic shadow of Black Hawk and the pathos no less than the courage of the pioneers are still in the air as the darkness settles heavily in the empty streets. The little pioneering community of a hundred years ago is not very far back.

This is the character and the quality of a thousand Wisconsin towns.

The name Wisconsin is popularly thought to mean "a gathering of waters." Wisconsin is, indeed, a kind of peninsula: three of its four sides, notched and undulating, are determined by natural waterways —Great Lakes to the east and north, rivers to the north and west. The state is everywhere shot through with rivers, streams and lakes —there are over 8500 counted lakes, 10,000 miles of trout streams— and it is actually bisected from Lake Michigan to the Mississippi by the Fox and Wisconsin rivers.

The peninsular character of the state suggests nearly every economic activity which has developed within it, beginning with Jean Nicolet, the first white man to step upon this ground. He was searching for the mythical northwest waterway to China, and landed near Green Bay in 1634, in the name of the governor of New France. He wore ritual robes to meet expected mandarins, but soon was shooting pistols from both hands when, instead, naked red men appeared. Today Green Bay is a harbor city, snug in the sharp angle of two coast lines dotted with thriving fishing villages.

By way of the Fox-Wisconsin riverway, we cross to the western boundary of the state in the wake of early missionaries like Marquette, and early inland explorers like Jolliet, and of numberless, nameless French and British fur traders. Into Lake Winnebago and out, into the smaller Puckaway and out, past busy mill towns, past somnolent river villages which have grown up on the site of the shacks and cabins of forgotten *coureurs de bois* and company agents, we come to Portage, where the rivers link by a canal, and where the old Indian Agency House reminds us of the bygone importance of this pleasant leafy village.

The Wisconsin River flows through the richest farmland in the state, where wooded valley gives way to rolling hills, and hills to folding prairie. At Spring Green, Taliesin, the Frank Lloyd Wright home, seems to lift itself from the very body of the hills to look down upon the blue river with its yellow sand bars and its green oval islands. Taliesin is a Welsh word meaning "shining brow," and the name suggests the perfect harmony between the house's roofs and the lines of the ridges on which it is built. Here the aging architect, after a life of marked unconventionality and stormy personal tragedies, lived peacefully amid his students, transmitting through the Taliesin Fellowship some of the genius which distinguished his professional career.

Below Spring Green, the Wisconsin River winds through bluffy country, country haunted by the ghost of Whisky Jack. Whisky Jack is a brother of Paul Bunyan and Mike Fink, but of purely local habitation. Born out of the hard life of the river raftsmen, the most reckless, adventurous, dissolute and humorous tribe on the American frontier, Whisky Jack was their mythological ideal. He was a giant in strength and size; he could pick up a grounded raft and set it back in deep water, and he could consume raw liquor—always the test of stature in American folklore—in monstrous quantities without disaster. Yet at least one tale shows this Achilles to have had his heel. Jack believed that when a man had drunk whisky, he was no match for a snake. When he met a huge blue racer in the woods, there was nothing to do but run for it: he ran, swam the river, ran again and swam again, ran and swam, and finally took to leaping from bank to bank, but the snake swam and leaped behind him, until, having covered half the state, Jack was rescued by his fellows, who beat the thirty-two-foot snake to death with cant hooks.

Today this heroic clown is shrunken to the stature of "river rats" who drift through makeshift lives in the lower Wisconsin, in shacks or patchwork boats, living off the fat catfish and other unrespected creatures that thrive in the muddy bottoms. Through this neglected neighborhood, the Wisconsin flows at last into the wooded flood plain to join the Mississippi.

Prairie du Chien, north of the flood plain, is sleepy modern testimony of historical activity. One of the oldest of Wisconsin towns, it was once nearly the most important, the distant sister of Green Bay. Here the agent of the Astor interests, the American Fur Company, gathered in the pelts which Indian trappers shipped from all over the state, and built himself a lordly house, the Villa Louis. The town itself sleeps now in a kind of slow dream of a past that is still too real to escape, too near; and thus most of the Mississippi towns sleep. They are picturesque towns, set in bluffs, many of them terraced to the contours of the bluffs, and all facing out across the wide river to the Minnesota plains. They seem to gaze with dusty melancholy to the westward expanses where the economic forces—the fur trade, lumber, then wheat—which once gave them their life, have vanished.

Northward, the character of the land changes again, as the amplitude and vast placidity of prairie farmland give way to the darker, dramatic landscape of timber. Here in the northwest, the rivers fan out in a great hand—the Chippewa alone has seven important tributaries—and the number of lakes increases, until, in both the northwest and the northeast portions of the state, one has the impression that there is more water than land.

It was inevitable that this entire area should become renowned for sport. Surely it is difficult to think of many other states in the Union where sport is in so large a measure a natural and nearly daily activity of the natives. For every Chicago or Milwaukee amateur who comes here to hunt or fish, for every vacationer who comes to ski or swim, there are a hundred local inhabitants who hunt and fish, ski and swim as naturally as they eat or sleep.

To the ordinary small-town and country people of Wisconsin, who do not take citified vacations, every day provides some out-of-doors pleasure. The bobsled and team which hauls sacks of grain or lumber by day pulls a country singing party through the frosty night, and the hayrick is taken out of the field to consolidate high-school romance on a river lane under the harvest moon. At the end of a summer day, the small-town shopkeeper will row his wife up the river or across the lake, hardly listening to the whippoorwills and frogs. In winter, every spry soul in the village will skate or iceboat on the same river or lake, impervious then to the blue-and-silver splendor of snow and ice which is a daily possession. Infants learn to swim, little girls to fish, and future ski champions begin as small boys on the hill behind the house, using barrel staves that they have smoothed with broken glass.

In the north central and northeast portions, especially, recreation has become a considerable industry. Here every resort inducement is exploited to the full, and in the summer the land is full of strangers. But the winters come early, and they are long, and then—hotels boarded up, cottages half buried in great drifts of snow—the qualities of a more primitive life reassert themselves. Nearly everywhere, at any time, even at the height of the season, there is a curious mingling of the atmosphere of the raw, tough community of the past with that of the modern resort, sometimes the very sophisticated resort.

To the northwest, where commercial exploitation is much less extensive, hardier men pursue their pleasure and their work, in any season, under the most rugged of circumstances. Life is still nearly as primitive as it was when these small communities were lumber towns: a sawmill and a general store, a saloon and a few shacks. This is still the frontier, inhabited by modern frontiersmen. Wolves and bear roam these forests, deer are a commonplace, and the solitary trappers and woodsmen who live deep in the wilderness are almost exact replicas of the earliest *coureurs de bois*, even to their bright wool shirts and fur caps.

Old lumbermen, who can remember when most of the state was covered with virgin timber, live ghost-ridden lives in the haunts of their youthful prowess, and the dream of Paul Bunyan hangs on. Near Wausau, in the north center of the state, the great man is said to be buried under Rib Mountain, while the sons of the wealthier families, who affect the lumberjack's dress and borrow his lingo, ski over him on the best trails in Wisconsin. The sons of the old lumbermen, employed in the woods with a modernly equipped crew or engaged in the production of wood by-products, live easier lives, yet the sight of them absorbed in that most treacherous of physical contests, logrolling, suggests that they delight in maintaining the tradition of their mythical ancestor.

There are whole communities which, even when they will it, cannot shake off their inheritance. It was proverbial among lumbermen in the old days that the four toughest places in the world were Cumberland, Hayward, Hurley and Hell, and that the first three were tougher than the last. Cumberland has managed to reform its lumbercamp morality. In its wild days, a new marshal, to stay in town, had to beat up the strongest saloonkeeper; today, Cumberland boasts more peacefully of its rutabagas, and as a climax to its annual festival, it crowns as Rutabaga King the man who can eat the largest amount of mash. Hayward, too, has mended its manners, and today it is a successful vacation town and enjoys a considerable reputation for its wrought iron, a modern inheritance from logging-camp blacksmiths who preserved a European skill.

Hurley has had a harder time. A phenomenal boom town in the 1880's, it developed a nearly allegorical reputation for viciousness. Edna Ferber's novel *Come and Get It* pictures authentically the rowdy drunkenness and robbery and murder which systematically went on in Hurley's innumerable wooden saloons. When the lumber market collapsed, the population of Hurley shrank, but not its reputation. Prohibition gave it occasion to reassert its historic rowdy role, and throughout the '20's and into the '30's, with over half a hundred speakeasies, it became a haven of gangsters and rumrunners—the one wholly wide-open town in Wisconsin.

Nearby, at a resort called Little Bohemia, John Dillinger and his mob hid out in 1934, and, leaving the molls, shot their way free when the place was surrounded by G-men. The bullet holes in the lodge are shown today in a spirit of local pride. For a time, Dillinger's father operated a small roadside stand where, for twenty-five cents, tourists could inspect the personal possessions of his son and other Chicago notables.

Hurley is exceptional, yet not wholly so. Most of these northern towns have something stark about them, even something rather brutal. They were the products and the victims of the lumber interests, an enterprise too ruthless to allow for geniality or social grace.

The Wisconsin timber industry, controlled by a group of "robber barons" in the old pattern of American avarice, lordly feudal beings who made the law their servant, was like a monster which devoured itself. Alexander, Ross, Spooner, Stephenson, Sawyer, Weyerhaeuser —these are names to conjure with in the development of the state. They are no less the names which repel the Wisconsin citizen today, as his eye sweeps across bleak, cut-over areas and is forced to contemplate the ruthlessness with which these men stripped the forest or, by their neglect, let it burn.

In 1870, five sixths of the state was still covered with virgin forest; forty rapacious years later, there was hardly a stick of it. Fire traveled with the cutters. Almost every northern county has suffered at least one great conflagration. In 1871, a fire which began near the village of Peshtigo spread over six counties, burning a swath forty miles long and ten miles wide within four hours, wiping out entire settlements and killing 1200 people.

The impression of ruin is not, to be sure, persistent. If there are towns today which seem to squat hopelessly in the midst of desolation, there are many more where the surrounding forests seem to crowd down into the very streets. In large measure, this luxuriance is due to state legislation, which belatedly—but then with great progressive brilliance—taught the lesson that timber is a crop. In a spectacular program of conservation, begun under the influence of Charles Van Hise, a social-minded man and one of the greatest of university presidents, the state allowed enormous tax reductions on land that was being reforested. County reforestation projects are tax free, and these, with state and Federal park areas, now comprise almost half the land in Northern Wisconsin.

The spirit of public interest which motivates this program is expressed by the tags which are tied on the thousands of Christmas trees taken each year from the Chequamegon National Forest; these read: "This tree brings a Christmas message from the great outdoors. Its cutting was not destructive but gave needed room for neighboring trees to grow faster and better. It was cut under the supervision of the United States Forest Service from a crowded stand——"

Reforestation is implemented today by an excellent fire-control service, and this, in turn, by intelligent fish-and-game laws.

The lumber industry today is largely concerned with the manufacture of wood products, especially pulp and paper, and this wise economic pursuit is, characteristically, encouraged by the state, and through the magnificent facilities of the Forest Products Laboratory. This is a Federal institution that is appropriately located in the back yard of the University, which aids it and prides itself on its own great commercial and agricultural research. The forest will return to the forest.

The modern dairy farm, in its setting of wooded, rolling land, is the most familiar symbol of Southern Wisconsin. The neat white house, the tidy fences, the enormous red or white barn, the solid, prosperous-looking silo and the cattle standing knee-deep in a stream or pond, or lying in the shade of a cluster of oak in the middle of a meadow—this is the prevailing pastoral image.

The Wisconsin farmer is apt to be a very modern man, as informed about agricultural hygiene or crop rotation as he is about machinery. If he is not himself a University graduate, at least one of his sons is, and the sons return to the farm with expert knowledge. Father and sons are the beneficiaries of the University Extension educational services, and every now and then one or another will go to Madison to attend the famous "short course" for farmers. There he is almost as likely to learn something about regional literature or regional art as he is to pick up the latest information on Bang's disease.

Given even a minimum of co-operation between man and Nature, the chances of agricultural success in Wisconsin are greater than in most states. The very names of the towns suggest the lavish potentialities of earth—Spring Green, Richland Center, Black Earth. Thousands of farms have their own small lake, their own rippling brook, and it is difficult to find one which does not have at least a pond. The prairie that is flat in Iowa and Minnesota rolls richly over domed hills in Wisconsin, and everywhere it is marked by corn or wheat fields flush with a thicket of oak or pine. The landscape begrudges man nothing and almost never plagues him with monotony.

This natural prodigality has found its way from the Wisconsin landscape into the Wisconsin character. The friendly mingling, at a village market or a county fair, is symbolical. There one is likely to see a village banker closing the arrangements for a loan to a shopkeeper, as the two of them pour down a social mug of beer. Or one can hear a farmer, between panting breaths as he rests from mauling a test-your-strength machine, name his fee to a neighbor for putting his stallion at stud. Or two men, pitching balls at rag dolls on a rack, will break off their easy discussion of the indiscretions of a neighbor's girl to take up the lease of pasture rights which one is interested in obtaining from the other.

Fairs in Wisconsin have always been a choice place for political speeches, formal and informal, serving almost as the rural equivalent of the Boston Common, or Union Square in New York, or Hyde Park in London. A common sight at a county fair is some village character haranguing a small crowd on his favorite subject, whether it be Utopian socialism or the sober co-operative movement or a fanatical atheism.

The state fair is not in essence different from the humbler county fair or the tiniest village festival. Behind each of them is the modern farm, and behind the farm is feudal Europe. The midway, with all its gaudy color and noisy rides and sharp-practicing "outsiders," is much like a European village street in carnival mood and infested by mountebanks. The contests of skill and strength, even though their prizes are plaster Kewpie dolls and cheap electric clocks, have their simpler archetypes, and the tug of war for men, the potato or the hobble race for women, the greasy pig or pole for boys are still commonplace. The Central European grandfather who brought his cow or his vegetables to town in the hope of a sale is present still in the scientific grandson who brings his best bull to the county seat in the hope of winning a blue ribbon, or in his wife, whose preserves or pies may get her name into the weekly newspaper. The difference is most eloquently represented in the displays of modern farm equipment.

In many Wisconsin communities, the fair has not yet disassociated itself from European practices. At Sparta, it is held not at a "fairgrounds," but in the streets of the city, and prize cattle are displayed in the courthouse square. The tiny village of Hales Corners, in the southeastern corner of the state, undergoes a metamorphosis on the first Monday of every month, when a fair instituted a hundred years ago by gypsy horse traders usurps the town, and every possible kind of household ware, garden produce and farm animal fill the crowded street. At Watertown, farther inland, a similar event takes place every month, but what was once an ordinary German cattle market now specializes in little pigs and fat, force-fed geese. Abbotsford, in the center of the state, holds a monthly village auction, where anyone can offer anything for sale, and where games and contests share the public interest in bargain prices for a barrel of apples or a bedstead.

Wisconsin's past-in-present character shows clearly in the way its European immigrant groups preserve their national identity. The main groups can be mapped roughly—using climate as a guide—with the Finns and early Poles in the northern timberland, where the winters are sometimes appallingly severe; the Norwegians and Swedes in a loose belt below them, where timber shades to grain; the Swiss and Germans in the milder corn and dairy and orchard regions of the central and southwestern prairie; and the southern Europeans and late-coming Poles in the industrial lake cities to the southeast.

In the 1830's, Cornish miners settled in Mineral Point, and the town was first known as Shake Rag, after its main street. Here the miners built a row of limestone houses precisely as they would have built them in Cornwall, and from their doorsteps their wives called the men home from the hillside mines at mealtime by waving dish-rags. The houses stand occupied today—low cottages of roughly hewn stone, built close together and nearly flush with the street, gleaming pale yellow in the sun—and the town is known as a place where one can buy saffron bread, curdled-cream desserts, and, above all, pasties. The pasty consists of a rather tough pie crust made large and round, then folded over a combination of onions, potatoes, meat and ruta-baga turnips, in a sort of half moon, and baked. The Cornish people of Mineral Point are so stubbornly proud of this national dish that once, when a printer mistakenly set the word "pastries" for "pasties" in a pamphlet advertising a local inn, he was asked to destroy his entire edition.

On Door Peninsula, there is a farming community named Brussels; it was settled by Belgians in the mid-fifties and has lost little of its first flavor. Children learn to weave the complicated maypole dance, the six-week Flemish harvest festival is still celebrated, and on such occasions national costumes are worn with a happy lack of self-con-sciousness. Genoa, on the western boundary of the state, was popu-lated almost entirely by fishermen from the city whose name they brought with them, and the community retains its Italian character. A number of towns in Waukesha County, notably Wales, were settled by groups of Welshmen who were friends and neighbors in the home country, and these people have maintained with a particular fervor not only their domestic and religious ways but the Welsh traditions of poetry and song. Poles settled at Stevens Point, transporting nearly whole their European way of life and preserving much of it into the heart of the 20th century.

In the north, there are the Finns, who likewise brought their man-ners with them. In these lonely areas, Finnish millmen still visit the *sauna,* or wooden bathhouse, on Saturday nights. They sit on benches that line the wall, cooking themselves in steam made by pouring cold water on hot stones. Then they whip one another with branches to stimulate blood flow, and finally they dash outside to roll and tumble and sprawl, naked and shouting, in the great snow drifts.

A more serious Finnish contribution is the co-operative movement, which they imported and developed in nearly every community they entered or established. While the Grange influence, which had native beginnings in the post-Civil War years and has always been strong in

Wisconsin, served as an encouragement, it was no doubt the strong co-operative impulse of the Finns and Scandinavians which created so many active local systems. The city of Superior, where these two groups have always been the most important, has been called "the consumer co-operative center of the United States."

Most tenacious of all are the Swiss-Germans and the Norwegians. In towns like Stoughton and Westby, Norwegian is as commonly spoken as English, Norwegian holidays and feast days are faithfully observed, and food is almost exclusively Norwegian. At Mt. Horeb, which is about evenly divided between Swiss and Norwegians, a game called *Le Hornuss*, which is Swiss for "hornet," has been popular for a half century. It is a kind of elaborate hockey, involving three rubber disks—the buzzing hornets—instead of a puck. One team drives the disks across the field with willow branches, while the other tries to stop them with wooden shields. "Can you take it?" the offense shouts in the dialect of Bern, and, in the same dialect, the defense cries back, "Just try us!"

In the same neighborhood is an establishment called Little Norway, or *Nissedahle*. This is a sentimentalist's dream of a Norwegian valley village, fabricated by the late Isak Dahle, the Chicago businessman who bought the 160 acres on which Little Norway is situated. In 1926 he hired workmen to revise the landscape according to a Norwegian post-card model. His carpenters built a number of small, oak structures with sod roofs and brilliantly painted ginger-bread trimming. Norwegian artisans furnished them with examples of native craftsmanship, and Dahle added his own modest collection of Norwegian furniture, bric-a-brac and silver. Today it is a kind of dollhouse stockade, and the admission fee strengthens the impression that this quaint establishment is some kind of concession at an exposition.

An animated contrast to Little Norway is the community life of a town like near-by Monroe. Monroe, with a large Swiss element, is the center of the Wisconsin cheese industry. It proclaims an annual Cheese Day, has been known to conduct cheese-smelling contests, reeks of limburger on the right breeze, and is not at all averse to publicity. Yet, quite without self-consciousness, its yodeling societies retain the vocal style and skill of their Alpine forebears, and at its Saturday-night dances young men and women mix the traditional folk patterns of Switzerland with jazz. This is no halfhearted attempt to revive a dead past; the past is as vigorous in the life of the community as is the mysterious thing which most of us think of as the present.

Nowhere in Wisconsin is this fact clearer than in New Glarus, a slightly younger Swiss settlement. The site was discovered by *Schweitzers* who were looking for a spot which duplicated as exactly as possible the physical features of the home canton of Glarus. It was settled exclusively by the 100-odd immigrants from this single community, and the present population of about a thousand is largely composed of their descendants. For some years they raised wheat; but the market was fickle, and their soil did not yield an ideal crop. Forced back to what they knew best—dairying—they had such extraordinary success that New Glarus became a kind of ideal dairying community, its settlers wise in the ways of an ancient agricultural tradition and at the same time eager to refresh that tradition with new knowledge.

Nevertheless, while prosperous cheese factories began to spring up around the town, its people preserved an even older homeland industry—lace making. Its farmers pursue the newest methods of dairying and its shops stock the most modern equipment, yet its church continues each year to celebrate the two-day festival of Kilbi, which commemorates the dedication of the Reformed Church in old Glarus centuries ago.

New Glarus represents in quite beautiful miniature the outstanding characteristic of Wisconsin life—a candid love of the past, which preserves the patterns of an ancient European culture; and a lively interest in the present, which expresses itself in some of the most progressive attitudes in America.

In the cities of Wisconsin, old national ties are dispersed and very often dissipated, and the appearance of modern America goes much deeper than the surface. Wisconsin cities are not, in general, distinguishable from small cities anywhere in the United States.

Manitowoc is an example, or Milwaukee, or any of the Lake Michigan ports, which are the chief Wisconsin cities. Manitowoc, first settled because of easy access to water power and transportation, moved through the several stages of farm town, lumber camp, fishing village, ship-construction center and modern industrial city all in just over a hundred years. Today its heavy industry plays a major role in the economic life of Wisconsin; its industrial products have many times the value of its agricultural products.

Yet the accumulated atmosphere of such a city—its persisting mill-town rawness, the farmers in the streets on Saturday night, the old merchant sailors in its water-front saloons—invokes at any moment the whole of its past, even the frontier on which it grew and the European shadow out of which it came.

Milwaukee points up the contrast better, perhaps, than any other city. On almost any busy street the smell of *Apfeltorten* or *Sauerbraten* is mingled with exhaust fumes, and homesick zither strains from the open door of a tavern blend with the imperious blast of a taxi horn outside.

The city combines an insatiable appetite for beer, or for *Gemütlichkeit,* with a passion for art and music, or for political justice. It has a taste for sausages and socialism, for the worst German middle-class vulgarities along with the most enlightened liberal aspirations.

Yet for a sense of the true character of the state as a whole, for the best understanding of what is called the "Wisconsin Idea," one looks to towns like Ephraim, which began as a Moravian settlement with communal ownership of property, or to Sauk City with its Humanist Society, or the hamlet of St. Nazianz, which for twenty years successfully maintained an experiment in Christian communism. Or one looks to Ripon, originally a socialist community, which saw the birth of the Republican Party in 1854, when a coalition of angry Whigs, antislavery Democrats and Free Soilers met to revolt against the extension of slavery under the Kansas-Nebraska Act. Or one looks to the near-by village of Valders, where Thorstein Veblen was born— Veblen, distinguished social economist later dismissed from the University of Chicago for his unconventional private life; or to Watertown, the home of Carl Schurz, a great political theorist who became Lincoln's Minister to Spain. Or one looks to Portage, the birthplace of Frederick Jackson Turner, the famous historian of the American frontier; and of Zona Gale, brilliant liberal spirit in Wisconsin social activity for thirty years, and acid etcher, in her best fiction, of its sometimes petty, sometimes cruel provinciality.

Above all, one looks to the farmland of Primrose Township in Dane County, where, in 1855, Robert La Follette was born and where he lived until he was eighteen. "Old Bob" had the qualities of a lesser Lincoln. Raised in the humblest rural circumstances, he never lost the common touch, as he never lost sight of his one basic principle that democracy rests on a real representation of the popular will. Like Lincoln, he was famous as an orator before he was a political success. His was an old-fashioned kind of oratory, prodigal with rhetoric, full of gesture, nearly fanatic in its intensity, capable of intolerably boring protraction. Unlike Lincoln's speeches, La Follette's do not read well—they depended for their vitality on the style of the man himself, on the physical presence of a personality.

Like Lincoln, again, La Follette held very small office before he held large office, and he had, at times, the same kind of dry humor. When he was asked why he had run for the unprofitable office of district attorney in Dane County, he answered, "For the money," and the humor lay in the fact that this was largely true, for he was penniless. When he at last won the gubernatorial election in 1900, his wife, Belle Case, who was his moral and intellectual prop and an object of positive reverence to the people of Wisconsin, said, "I have been prouder of him when he has suffered defeat." She admired his stanch truculence, even in failure, more than his human grace.

Like Lincoln's personality, La Follette's elicited either loathing or love; there was nothing between these extremes. When, as a young man, he won a Midwest university oratorical contest, his fellow students pulled him home from the railroad station in a triumphal surrey, but not many decades later, when he made his antiwar filibuster in the Senate, students burned him in effigy on the Lower Campus, and in the general hysteria he was denounced for his pacifism in a round-robin statement signed by 399 faculty members. On occasion he was called insane and degenerate, or a chronic drunkard, and sometimes even liberals were convinced that the success of the Progressive movement in Wisconsin meant La Follette was a "crook." Lincoln Steffens thought so until his famous investigation persuaded him that La Follette actually embodied his own ideal of a politician whose aim was truly to represent the will of the people.

What Robert La Follette conspicuously lacked was the broad generosity of Lincoln's character, the enormously relaxed will, that total absence of egotism which puts Lincoln among the very greatest men. Without that, La Follette is left in the second rank of greatness. Yet he had something in place of Lincoln's melancholy resignation and brooding love; he had a kind of dramatic life within himself, a frenzy of faith and self-confidence, an unshakable stubbornness and noisiness of conviction, an inexhaustible reserve of energy which was like fire.

These qualities, taken together, were the perfect expression of the vital unrest and excitement which were fermenting in the intellectual life of Wisconsin at the start of this century. La Follette did not make history so much as he made himself its spearhead.

He came up in politics through the Republican Party, which had dominated the state since the early 1870's and was in turn dominated by the all-powerful lumber and railroad monopolies.

From the beginning, La Follette appealed to the people directly, over the heads of the bosses. When he became a real threat, Philetus Sawyer, the Republican leader, offered him an indiscreet bribe— which brought on the inevitable break with the Party. From then on, until the formation of the Progressive Party itself in 1934, the Republicans were split in two—"stalwarts" and "progressives." It required a six-year battle before La Follette's first election to the governorship in 1900, but antimonopoly legislation followed quickly after that, chiefly in revised railroad taxation and through the newly instituted direct primary.

In his campaign against the railroads, no single event was more important than that of "Scofield's cow." In 1897 it was revealed that Governor Scofield had shipped free of charge, on frank number 2169, from the northern part of the state to Madison in the south, a variety of personal possessions, including a sewing machine, a buggy pole, a barrel of potatoes (small) and a cow (crated). Scofield had not violated the law, but the goods he had shipped dramatized, in a comic way, the privilege he had abused. A storm of public indignation and satire blew up. The cow's picture was printed in the newspapers, and she became, for the people of Wisconsin, the folk symbol of corrupt privilege. Whenever La Follette mentioned "Scofield's cow" he brought down his house in wild laughter.

La Follette embodied the triumph of the "Wisconsin Idea," and in a way, the forces which made it up came to an end with the death of the man, as if his public life had exactly measured the vital extension of an idea in time.

When, on a memorable hot June Sunday in 1925, thousands and thousands of men and women and children from all over the state passed his open bier under the dome of the statehouse in a daylong procession, they were mourning not only the death of a beloved man but a death in their lives as citizens, and the close of an era.

The "Wisconsin Idea" may be defined as the laboratory method in politics. It regards institutions as flexible and government as experimental. It insists that a healthy political life requires that politicians accept the advice of nonpolitical experts. Thus it draws into politics the best available intellectual power and the most experienced minds.

To the older La Follette's administration, the advice of such economics experts as Richard T. Ely and John R. Commons, of such experts in education and public welfare as President Van Hise, and of such specialists in the theory of public administration as Charles McCarthy—all from the University—was nothing less than integral. Commons, for example, was mainly responsible for the writing of Wisconsin's civil-service law, which remains a model in the United States. Together, men such as these were responsible for the long-range planning which went on under La Follette, as the "Wisconsin Idea" developed a systematic program to make the democratic state positively democratic, to keep the public welfare always, and in every detail, in the ascendancy. Much of this program was derived from the most liberal elements in 19th-century German politics, and its appeal to the people of Wisconsin was clearly that it fulfilled here social ambitions which had been frustrated there. It was, in a way, the "best" of Europe, and it came to independent life in Wisconsin.

All this seems less extraordinary today, now that most of the social legislation which Wisconsin first achieved has been written into Federal law and into the law of many states. But in 1912, when Charles McCarthy coined the phrase "Wisconsin Idea" and defined its program in a book of that name, all this was new. When he conceived the idea that a state-university professor has an obligation to counsel a representative in Congress or a governor no less than a farmer, and that the major obligation of the University itself is to serve the state, he was formulating the principles of social idealism which gave Wisconsin in the first quarter of this century its special public quality, and, in effect, created the greatness of its University.

Madison, the capital, dramatizes the "Idea" perfectly. All around it the Wisconsin country rolls in, as it were, to its beautiful center, which is surrounded by three lakes. In the town itself, all streets, by a kind of inverse radiation, lead to the Capitol. This stands on a hill in the heart of the city, facing down a half-mile of straight and open street—State Street—to the University, which, again, is built on a hill. It is as if all the life of the state were being drawn into the statehouse and the University, to flow back out into the state, enlightened and fulfilled.

The "Wisconsin Idea" represents the double strand of practicality and idealism which is woven so deep in the state's character. All through Wisconsin history, its people's feeling toward Europe has been one of nostalgia combined with a deep fear and suspicion. If "grass roots" can throw up great popular leaders like the elder La Follette, they can also foster the most depressed kind of insularity. The antiwar attitude of the elder La Follette and the later attitude of Robert La Follette, Jr., toward President Roosevelt's "twelve obsolete destroyers" were based on the same principle that always guided both father and son: let the people know and let the people choose. Yet many Wisconsin people responded to this position not from allegiance to democratic principle but from a profound provincialism.

No La Follette now occupies public office. The excitement and the vitality of Wisconsin intellectual life of twenty-five years ago are gone. The University still serves the state, but in humbler ways than Charles McCarthy planned—not in ideas so much as in agricultural and economic skills. Something has changed since 1894, when Prof. Richard Ely was, in effect, on trial before the board of regents for economic heresy, and the regents declared, "Whatever may be the limitations which trammel inquiry elsewhere, we believe the great state University of Wisconsin should ever encourage that continual and fearless sifting and winnowing by which alone the truth can be found."

Educational reaction scored a significant triumph over the Experimental College of Alexander Meiklejohn. This was an attempt to set up, within the over-mechanized framework of a vast university, informal methods of study and teaching in place of recitations and the lecture system and, instead of "subjects," the study of entire civilizations. Two hundred students, bright and rather bohemian young men, were selected for the experiment and at once became known as "the guinea pigs." With them came a brilliant faculty—chiefly men who had been sympathetic to Doctor Meiklejohn at Amherst, where he had previously been relieved of the presidency.

The Experimental College, founded in 1928 was one of the first proposals of a new president, Glenn Frank, and it represented the ambitious plans which he had made for his administration. Glenn Frank was not, however, an able administrator, and by 1932, when the experiment was assessed, he had so lost prestige with his faculty, the regents and the people of the state, that the development of Meiklejohn's ideas was doomed to be cut off. The orthodox educational theorists in the University were happy to wield their axes on this monster which had made them so uneasy. Frank did not come to its defense, and in 1933 the experiment was pronounced a failure —and discontinued.

The provincial tendency was revealed more entertainingly in the famous "rocking-chair case." One night the Dean of Women telephoned the Dean of Men to inform him that coeducation was being carried too far by a student couple in a certain private apartment. It was the male dean's duty, she felt, to interfere. The Dean of Men, according to the story which swept the community, went to the indicated apartment and pounded on the door. When the young man would not admit him, the Dean sat down in a rocking chair in the hall and waited until the victims emerged to face expulsion.

The affair reached its peak when the poet William Ellery Leonard, a faculty member, denounced the deans in plain words. The colorful teacher, himself the subject of many scandals, accused the deans of an indecent invasion of sacred human rights. The newspapers loved him for the fuss. Glenn Frank vacillated, and the affair came to a close when he exonerated the Dean of Men and dismissed the Dean of Women. Her comment on Frank's attitude was, "You can't nail a custard pie to the wall."

The problem of academic freedom became acute in the Frank administration. In 1935, the legislature conducted an investigation of subversive political activities in the University, with the implication that President Frank—who, at the time of his death in 1940, was national chairman of the Republican Party program committee—encouraged communism among the faculty and students. This was, of course, nonsense, yet it led to the end of his university career. Whatever his deficiencies, the cause of academic freedom and the reputation of the University were in no way enhanced when Governor Philip La Follette, who was by then Frank's political enemy, forced his resignation.

Something has gone. The State of Wisconsin, like the University, seems today to have slipped into a period of intellectual contraction. Some things, of course, cannot go. The various and brilliant landscape remains, and all that it offers. Old social habits remain. Laws remain. Yet the world moves on, and if social habits and laws merely remain and do not grow, they become old-fashioned.

It is time, perhaps, to look back to certain events in Wisconsin as closed, to certain attitudes as dead. The past, which has always kept itself so alive in the present, may just now be solidifying. If this is true, Wisconsin stands today at the end of its first great period.

Illinois

by CLYDE BRION DAVIS

On a map the state of Illinois is bounded on the west by the Mississippi River and on the east by Indiana and the sycamore-fringed Wabash, but actually, it refuses to be limited by mere geography. It has a faculty for stretching out, and far; so you might say that Illinois is bounded on the west by a ranch house near some such place as Chinook, Montana, and on the east by the Museum of Modern Art on West Fifty-third Street, New York City. You might also say that although the geographical center of the United States is 500 miles to the west, Illinois is the axis of the nation, the hub and vortex of all the wonderful and eccentric hullabaloo that comprises our sweet land of liberty; and it's even possible that this off-center center may account for some of the wabble and vibration in our body politic.

For Illinois is perhaps the most American of all the states. It's the U.S.A. in a capsule. Here our virtues and our faults are most exaggerated and magnified. Here somehow the heroes seem more heroic, the villains more villainous, the buffoons more comic. Here violence is more unrestrained, and the capacity for greatness is as limitless as the sweep of the unending cornfields.

With its great, teeming, beautiful, ugly metropolis on Lake Michigan, Illinois is the economic, agricultural, industrial and cultural heart of America. All roads—steel, concrete and aerial—lead to Chicago. It's the dynamic nucleus of a rich and vital land, the magnet which draws not only millions of cattle from the western plains but talented youth from the valleys of the Mississippi, Missouri, Ohio and Arkansas in search of fame and fortune. The mark of Chicago is on towns and homes that are a thousand miles from the Loop, and on most of the vigorously original American literature written in the 20th Century.

The state of Illinois is a manufacturer, a processor, a distributor and a hog butcher, and one of the great farmers of the world. Central Illinois is the soybean capital of the world, but it is corn that astonishes the summertime traveler. And well it might, for the cornfields of central Illinois are incredible. Mile after mile and county after county of tall, rustling corn, corn, corn, interspersed by big barns, neat farmhouses and rows of cylindrical steel storage bins. The eager black loam of the flat or gently undulating prairie is planted early in May, and in a few weeks of rain and hot weather the corn is taller than a basketball player.

Pull off the highway on a warm, humid night where the road is a mere aisle through a forest of corn, and above the clash and rattle of the shard-like leaves in the constant wind you'll hear a curious brittle popping on every side, a staccato popping like distant firecrackers. That is the corn growing, audibly and enthusiastically. But, unless your sense of direction is exceptionally good, don't wander off between the corn rows or they may not find you until husking time.

As states go, Illinois is not exceptionally large, ranking twenty-fourth in the nation, measuring about four hundred miles from north to south and averaging maybe two hundred miles wide. If Illinois were in Europe it probably would be supporting a population of forty millions or so—when not being invaded by a foreign army. However, nobody is invading Illinois these days except young hopefuls seeking their fortunes and visiting politicians seeking votes.

Yet an invasion should be fairly easy, for the state, and especially its greatest city, is the hub of America—the center of a giant web of railroads, highways and waterways. It was the waterways that first established Illinois and Chicago as the continental axis—for rivers and lakes were the initial highways for the canoes and bateaux of Indian and voyageur. Friendly Indians showed the white man the seven-mile portage from the Chicago to the Des Plaines River, which led to the Illinois River and thence to the Mississippi. The route worked just as well in the opposite direction for those who had come down the Ohio River and up the Mississippi and Illinois to navigate the Great Lakes and the St. Lawrence.

Railroads followed the waterways, turning Chicago into such a bewildering maze of intersecting tracks with seventeen hundred passenger trains entering and leaving seven stations daily—plus heaven only knows how many freight trains—that it's quite understandable how an occasional boxcar gets lost in the shuffle and wanders around the Chicago yards for days. The wonder is that whole passenger trains don't do the same thing.

Easterners naturally regard Illinois as a Western state. And while that seems ridiculous to people in the Pacific and Rocky Mountain regions, the Easterners have a point. Communities like Tombstone, Arizona, and Dodge City, Kansas, bask in their tradition of violence and proudly direct tourists to their "Boot Hills" where rest many early-day characters who died with their boots on. Actually there has been more real Wild West gun-fighting—and gang fighting—over a longer period of time in Illinois than in any state west of the Mississippi.

One incident of many was the Fort Dearborn massacre of 1812, in which sixty-three men, women and children were slaughtered by the Indian allies of the British, for which the late Mayor William Hale (Big Bill) Thompson of Chicago held the late King George V (1865–1936) personally responsible. This indictment was considered too narrow by the late Colonel Robert Rutherford McCormick, proprietor of the Chicago *Tribune* ("the world's greatest newspaper"), to whom all British, including Queen Elizabeth II, Sir Winston Churchill and the Archbishop of Canterbury, were Redcoats. In his newspaper and in addresses before his Chicago Theater of the Air, Colonel McCormick always cherished an active distrust of all Britishers. And Mayor Thompson disliked the English so much that he even pushed a bill through the state legislature making the official tongue of Illinois "the American language."

It would take volumes to recount the spectacular wild western violence of Illinois, but the case of Elijah Lovejoy has a place in any Illinois chronicle because he was a moderate Abolitionist and Illinois was officially an antislave state. Lovejoy, a young clergyman, was publisher of the Alton *Observer*. On Independence Day, 1837, he wrote a Fourth of July editorial which said, "Even the very flag of freedom that waves over our heads is formed from materials cultivated by slaves, on a soil moistened by their blood, drawn from their backs by the whip of the republican task master."

Alton was in free Illinois all right, but there was plenty of Southern thought in that river town. That night a mob broke into the *Observer* office and destroyed the press. Lovejoy's friends bought a new one, but on September 21 a masked mob smashed it to pieces and threw the wreckage into the river. Even then Lovejoy and his backers were not whipped. They raised more money and ordered another press. When it arrived Lovejoy and a dozen friends who were guarding it were attacked by a mob which set the building afire and put an end to Lovejoy's editorials by riddling him with bullets.

Alton is now a city of great manufacturing plants—steel fabrication, oil refining, copper, bronze, dynamite and the Owens-Illinois Glass Company, the biggest bottle plant in the world. It's a hilly country rising from the river bluffs and the principal highways wind this way and that way through the city with hard-working policemen at busy intersections trying desperately to keep the traffic moving. Outside of town, if you get off the main highways you may find yourself on a narrow, horse-and-buggy road of old red brick rambling through the trees, and if it's a hot, muggy night the millions of lightning bugs will make you dizzy.

If you're going South on this muggy night you'll see a strange glow in the sky that does not come from burning barns or oil wells but from big, self-sufficient St. Louis, Missouri, across the river, and from East St. Louis, Illinois, on the eastern flood plain.

East St. Louis is the home of meat packing houses, stockyards, iron foundries, oil refineries and rubber plants. It used to be a quite tough town. But they say now that it has tamed down enough so the old bass-singing canary birds are up to a medium baritone.

About one hundred and fifty miles up the Mississippi from East St. Louis is the strange old town of Nauvoo, once the Zion of Mormonism and the largest city in Illinois—an autonomous state within a state where Joseph Smith's Nauvoo Legion caused some uneasiness because it was bigger and better-trained than the Illinois state militia. Driving up, the most plausible route is U.S. 67, which passes through Jacksonville and Beardstown.

Jacksonville might be called a typical city in America's Midwest heartland. It's neither too large and bustling nor too small and sleepy, but there's a nice balance between industry and agriculture to form a pleasant, well-behaved community. Like many Illinois towns, Jack-

sonville is built around a central square. The city, named for Andrew
Jackson, has three distinctions: The Eli Bridge Company, which
manufactures no bridges but claims to be the only factory on earth
making Ferris wheels; a residential intersection with a church on
each of four corners; and the fact that it was the boyhood home of
"the Great Commoner," William Jennings Bryan, who was graduated
from the State College there.

Forty-three miles on is Beardstown, where a gangling lawyer
named Abraham Lincoln won acquittal on a charge of murder for a
young ruffian named Duff Armstrong by impeaching the prosecu-
tion's star witness with an almanac. That, of course, was the famous
dark-of-the-moon case.

The Keokuk dam stretches across the Mississippi from Hamilton,
Illinois, to Keokuk, Iowa, spreading the river out to a width of perhaps two miles. From the dam it's a beautiful twelve-mile drive
winding up the east shore of this great river to historic Nauvoo. And
the first thing you notice about Mulholland Street in modern Nauvoo
is the number of "clubs"—a situation usually indicative of severe local
restrictions. Modern Nauvoo is known for blue cheese and wine.
Each September a grape festival is held, including a ceremony borrowed from Roquefort, France, called the wedding of the wine and
cheese.

The prophet Joseph Smith said the name Nauvoo was given him
by the Angel Moroni and is Hebrew for "Beautiful Place." Some Hebrew scholars have questioned that, but if it comes to deciding between a scholar's word and an angel's, who wouldn't take the angel's?
"Nauvoo" probably is the lost Hebrew gerund or subjunctive or something for Naturally Beautiful Spot Being Enhanced by Saintly Men.

Led by Joseph Smith and a revelation, a troop of Latter Day Saints
fled persecution in Missouri and bought five thousand acres around
the tiny settlement of Commerce City, Illinois. They changed the
name in accordance with Prophet Smith's revelation and began
building a new Zion in 1840. So many Mormon converts from the
eastern United States and Europe migrated to Nauvoo that the population of the town five years later was 20,000.

All the Mormon property in Nauvoo—the impressive mansion of
Joseph Smith, the part-log, part-frame homestead, just across the
street, he occupied while the big house was abuilding, a large brick
hotel and thousands of residences—now is owned by the Reorganized

Church of Jesus Christ of Latter Day Saints which has headquarters in Independence, Missouri.

There's a sign on the old hotel building saying the Nauvoo House was begun in 1841 and completed in 1869. Then it reads, "It served as the last home of Emma, Joseph Smith's *only* wife. She died in this building in 1879." That "only" is underlined on the sign.

About twenty-five miles away, in Carthage, Illinois, the historic Carthage jail is owned and maintained by the Utah branch of the church. There's a sign on this two-story building of smooth limestone reading, "No smoking. Please remove hats. This is a shrine of the Church of Latter Day Saints." In this old jail Joseph and Hyrum Smith were killed by a mob in 1844.

The two had been arrested after a detachment of the Nauvoo army, under orders from Joseph Smith, had wrecked the office of a newspaper which had attacked his leadership. They were not locked in cells but were given quarters in a second-floor bedroom of the jail. It was there the mob found them.

A volley was fired through the door to their room, and Hyrum fell mortally wounded. Joseph went to the side window with a thought, probably, of leaping to the ground twenty feet below. But the door flew open as the bolt was shot off and Joseph was struck by three bullets.

The caretaker of the jail introduced himself as Elder Matthews of Logan, Utah. Elder Matthews told me, "Joseph cried out, 'Oh, my Lord, my God!' and fell out of the window, landing next to the old well down there." On the floor of the bedroom is a brown stain protected by a glass frame, and this stain, Elder Matthews said reverently, is the sacred blood of brother Hyrum.

No one ever was prosecuted for the murders.

With the slaying of Joseph and Hyrum, Brigham Young, who openly advocated polygamy, took command at Nauvoo and began preparations for the great exodus to a new Zion in the West. Nauvoo became a virtual ghost city, the victim of incendiaries and other vandals.

Up the winding Mississippi a hundred miles or so are the manufacturing cities of Moline, Rock Island and (across the river) Davenport, Iowa.

Moline is especially important historically because a young Vermonter named John Deere established himself there, drawn by the magnet of Illinois, as so very many men of talent, vision and great ideas have been drawn to America's heartland. It was in Moline that Deere perfected his steel plow that made agricultural conquest of the prairie possible. The tough prairie sod had resisted attempts to cultivate it with the old iron and wood plows, but Deere's invention helped to turn the Midwestern prairies into the breadbasket of America and make Moline the farm-machinery capital of the nation.

Eighty-five miles farther up the river, in the junior mountains of Jo Daviess County, is the sleepy town of Galena, known now as the spot where in April of 1860 a stoop-shouldered, middle-aged little man came to clerk for his younger brothers in a leather-goods store after whisky had ruined an Army career. He had failed as a farmer, real-estate agent and tanyard employee, and he was to fail again as clerk. But a year from then he was teaching close-order drill to the Jo Daviess Guards, and five years from then he was to accept the surrender of Robert E. Lee at Appomattox.

There's a sense of age and drowsiness to Galena, with its cobbled streets and houses clinging to the steep hillsides. It is a very old town for the Midwest, and so was spared what has been called the General Grant architecture of the 1870's and 80's, even though it was the general's home town. There are five churches in Galena that are more than a hundred years old, four typically New England in style, the fifth early English Gothic.

Galena is in the northwestern corner of Illinois, close to the Wisconsin border. Swinging south and east, you drive through the famous prairies of Illinois—mile after mile of black loam, gently undulating or as flat as western Kansas or the Texas Panhandle.

A Decatur man told me of riding on the train with a friend from Providence, Rhode Island, who was used to the hill farms and small fields of New England. The friend stared silently from the window as the streamliner whipped past waving corn for the better part of an hour and then he finally turned to the Decatur man and blinked his eyes and said huskily, "What in *hell* can they do with all that corn?"

And that was a good question. What can they do with the five hundred million bushels of corn that are produced annually in Illinois? And what, also, can they do with three hundred million bushels of soybeans, which has become the state's number-two crop?

Of course, human beings consume most of the corn in one way or another. It is fed to stock and poultry and then we eat it as ham and eggs and butter and cheese and ice cream and pork chops and beef-steak. A not inconsiderable amount is also consumed in the form of bourbon whisky. But the only human use I knew for soybeans was the Chinese sauce you douse on chop suey.

Around the corn belt, however, there are a number of processing plants for corn and soybeans, and in Decatur I dropped in on one of the largest, the A. E. Staley Manufacturing Company, to find out the less obvious uses of these crops.

The things made from corn include, of course, cornstarch, laundry starch and corn sirup. And the starches are used by the cotton and synthetic textile industry in sizing fabrics. Paper manufacturers use even more. Cornstarch and dextrin are the binders in aspirin and other pills. Starch is used in smelting minerals, and the reason commercial ice cream doesn't taste like that grandma used to whip up for Sunday dinner is this same good old cornstarch.

Cornstarch and sirup are used in the rubber industry, in cigarettes, in tanning leather, making spark plugs, dynamite and candy. And the "steep water" after corn is soaked for processing is the source of yeast and penicillin.

The once lowly soybean is now America's largest source of vegetable oil, while the meal that's left is used not only in livestock and poultry feed but also in the manufacture of human foods, including pancake flour, spaghetti, sausage, canned soups and peanut butter. And, to round up the subject, soybean oil is also an ingredient of paints, printing ink, linoleum, antiknock gasoline, pharmaceutical products, TNT, candy, mayonnaise and cooking oil.

Decatur is one of the fastest-growing cities in the Midwest. You can scarcely recognize the place after an absence of a couple of years. But Decatur and Macon County were part of the prairie-ringed Sangamon River wilderness when the magnet that is Illinois drew a thin, moody Kentuckian across the Wabash from his boyhood home in Indiana.

The twenty-one-year-old Abe Lincoln drifted into Decatur in 1830 and for a year made a living splitting rails with his cousin John Hanks. Thirty years later this same John Hanks, perhaps prompted by Ward Lamon or Jesse Fell or David Davis, carted a load of fence rails to the famous Wigwam Convention in Chicago and led a parade of Lincoln enthusiasts, each with a rail on his shoulder, to help stampede the convention for the Rail-Splitter. If you wonder where they found timber to split into rails on the treeless prairie, dense forests grew along the Sangamon and other Illinois rivers, and there still is plenty of scrub timber there.

All of Illinois claims Abraham Lincoln for its own and the automobile license plates cry out "Land of Lincoln," but Decatur stands at the southeast corner of the real Lincoln country. Over this whole area—up to Bloomington, over to Peoria, down to Petersburg and the restored log village of New Salem and Springfield—one is never allowed to forget that the Great Emancipator called this home. There are Lincoln theaters, Lincoln hotels, Lincoln parking lots, Lincoln streets and the city of Lincoln. In more than a few restaurants the sad face of Old Abe peers up at you from your dinner plate.

There are so many bronze plaques bearing the Gettysburg Address on public and commercial buildings that one wonders if some enterprising foundry didn't peddle them over the Lincoln country. Once in a while a plaque will contain the Farewell Address or Second Inaugural. And there are other custom jobs which announce that here on such and such a date Lincoln and Stephen A. Douglas engaged in one of their debates.

The town of Bloomington adjoins the town of Normal, the home of Jesse Fell, one of the great characters of Illinois history, who established the normal school that gave Normal its name, and who persuaded Lincoln to write the autobiography which Fell published to acquaint the nation with facts about the tall Rail-Splitter before the 1860 national convention. It was Jesse Fell, with his law partner Judge David Davis, Ward Lamon and Leonard Swett who engineered the nomination of the little-known Lincoln over the distinguished William Henry Seward.

Jesse Fell met Abraham Lincoln early and saw a man of destiny. He conceived the idea of the debates with Douglas, was a leader in forming the Republican Party in Illinois and he put Lincoln's name before the 1858 state convention for United States Senator. Jesse Fell was a self-effacing man of great vision, of great generosity and great creative energy who would never accept public office for himself.

Lincoln first saw New Salem when twenty-two and his flatboat stuck on the mill dam, giving him opportunity to show his mechanical ingenuity in getting it off. It was in this attenuated log village on the hill above the Sangamon River that he clerked in the store, became postmaster, wrestled with Jack Armstrong, borrowed Jack Kelso's books, studied under Mentor Graham and allegedly fell in love with Anne Rutledge. But it was a deserted village and falling to ruin by the time he penned the Emancipation Proclamation.

Now the state of Illinois has done a remarkable job of restoration and the village stands as a sort of national shrine in New Salem State Park. Furniture and utensils stand or lie as if the inhabitants had just walked out from the cabins, mill, store and tavern, but there also is a curious sense of dusty desiccation about New Salem comparable to the ancient cliff dwellings of the Southwest. You feel that New Salem has been a ghost town drying out in the sun for half a millennium.

There is none of that aura of dry antiquity about Lincoln's home in Springfield, though. You really feel as if Abe and Mary and the boys had just stepped out and will be back in an hour or so. You can picture his lanky form on the haircloth sofa or working at his desk. The well-built, two-story frame house is obviously the home of a fairly prosperous professional man. Stick in a couple of bathrooms and modernize the kitchen and it would be that today.

The Lincoln Tomb State Memorial in Springfield's Oak Ridge Cemetery is, of course, a tourist mecca. Mrs. Lincoln and three of their four children also are buried there.

The ancient state capitol, which has been the Sangamon County Court House since 1887 when the "new" Capitol was completed, stands in the old Town Square between Washington and Adams Streets. It was in this building that Lincoln served as a state legislator and pleaded cases before the State Supreme Court.

Springfield itself is one of the most attractive state capitals in America, especially along tree-lined Second Street where the Capitol Building, Centennial Building, Supreme Court and State Armory are grouped behind broad lawns.

There's a 4000-acre artificial lake in beautiful Springfield Park where regattas of national importance to sailboat enthusiasts are held annually.

Fifty miles above New Salem but still in the Lincoln country is Peoria, the second city in Illinois—although Peoria feels the hot breath of Rockford on its neck. Peoria first was an Indian village where the Illinois River widens out to lake proportions, then a French settlement called *Au Pe* for the Peoria Indians, and is now a sizable manufacturing city known for bourbon whisky and caterpillar tractors.

There's a story about a Springfield man whose brother-in-law was an enthusiastic addict of Peoria's principal product. One evening the Springfield man said, "Come on, Joe, let's go for a ride," and they went up to Peoria where they could look down upon the acres and acres of lights of the Hiram Walker and National Distillers and Century Distilling corn-whisky factories, and he said, "Now, look, Joe, you can see you haven't got a chance of drinking all the bourbon they can make." And Joe shook his head sadly. "Gosh," he said, "maybe you're right." Then he brightened. "But, brother, you got to admit I've got 'em working nights."

On the Court House lawn (where Lincoln and Douglas debated) there's one of the most elaborate Civil War monuments I ever saw. It's a high shaft topped by an angry eagle and surrounding the shaft are fourteen bronze figures including a tall, robed gal (one breast bare, of course) in the act of writing, "We write on page of granite what they wrought on field of battle," and the thirteen other people are contorted Peoria soldiers, dead, dying or fighting desperately. One is a young drummer boy with his drumsticks sheathed, firing a large horse pistol right at you.

Roller-coaster addicts never have seen anything until they roll down a steep hill in a barrel or ride the Rock Island Jet Rocket between Peoria and Chicago. It's a beautiful train and how it does travel. A visit to the dining car is a real adventure in eating. Not only is the food good but the service is downright astonishing.

So to Chicago—the second largest city in America. Of course someone has said that Chicago isn't a city at all, but merely a collection of wards. But it looks like a city to me. And—although this may be heresy—I think the "Hog Butcher for the World" is a *beautiful* city, especially around the Loop and Michigan Avenue and Lake Shore Drive. And everywhere it's a city with personality and down-to-earth vigor.

Oh, you can find "arty" things in Chicago, and you pay for them. But mostly Chicago is blunt and real and beautiful. For example, there's a saloon on Addison Street with the most honest sign you ever saw on a saloon. It reads GOOD AND BAD WHISKY.

Of course there's a custom among esthetes to poke sneers at Chicago, even among some esthetes who got their start in Chicago. And, while Rudyard Kipling was not exactly an esthete, he wrote of Chicago, "Having seen it, I urgently desire never to see it again. It is inhabited by savages." Well, I doubt that many Chicago people cried themselves to sleep over that.

It has often been said that the great fire of 1871 was a blessing in disguise to Chicago, that the city had grown too fast and the disaster gave opportunity to rebuild. But Chicago rebuilt pretty fast, too, and a short drive through some of the older North Side residential districts reveals every type of architecture known to man, separately and in weird combination.

The only municipal structure to survive the fire is the well-loved old yellow stone water tower which rises about a hundred and eighty-six feet above North Michigan Avenue. Oscar Wilde, a true esthete, called the water tower "a castellated monstrosity with pepper pots stuck all over it." But they're not pepper pots at all. They're turrets from which the defenders of Chicago can shoot their crossbows and pour boiling oil upon the attackers.

With forty-one railroads homing into Chicago, making it the world's greatest railroad center, it was inevitable that the city should become the livestock and meat-packing capital of America, with the greatest stockyards in the world and headquarters for Armour, Swift, Wilson and other packing houses. G. F. Swift was the Chicago pioneer in meat packing soon after the great fire and, with the new refrigerator car, practically no more Western livestock was shipped east of Chicago. Easterners ate Chicago meat.

For most women of the Midwest who get to Chicago occasionally, the city means Marshall Field's, for Marshall Field & Company is one of the three largest department stores in America, and in some respects the greatest. The first Marshall Field was a Massachusetts farm boy who responded to the pull of the Illinois magnet in 1856 and went to work for a Chicago dry-goods firm. He slept in the store and saved half of his $400 a year salary. Eight years later he was a partner with Potter Palmer in the firm of Field, Palmer and Leiter.

Young Field believed in the "personal touch" and he kept a notebook on the preferences of women customers. He was an originator of the theory that the customer is always right, and the theory paid off. At forty-seven the dignified Marshall Field was one of the richest men in America, and his store was a national institution. In 1893 he established the Field Museum of Natural History, at the southeast extension of Grant Park, and the Field Museum has become one of the nation's greatest scientific assets.

For people of rural America who don't get to Chicago, however, the Midwest metropolis means Sears, Roebuck or Montgomery Ward. In 1872 Montgomery Ward, a young salesman for Marshall

Field, pioneered the mail-order business in Chicago with a capital of $2400 and a one-page catalogue.

Richard W. Sears, a twenty-three-year-old railroad telegrapher, started in business in 1886 when he bought a consignment of cheap watches and sold them up and down the railroad. Then he bought more watchcases and watchworks and hired a tall, thin watch repairer named Alvah Roebuck to assemble them. Presently Sears and Roebuck were in partnership, selling general merchandise by mail and doing quite well despite the antipathy of small-town merchants and newspapers. Ed Howe, the "Sage of Potato Hill," famous editor of the Atchison, Kansas, *Globe,* declared mail-order buying actually was treason to one's community and a greater sin than adultery.

It has been estimated that out of every $100 spent for general merchandise in America today five dollars goes to Sears, Roebuck.

The Chicago World's Fair—meaning the 1893 World's Columbian Fair and Exposition—opened the Midwest to late 19th Century culture and, with railroads offering special excursion rates, brought millions of visitors from every state in the Union and from virtually every country on the globe. Residents of bleak Far-Western communities were dazzled by the beauty of the Great White Plaster City that stood between Jackson and Washington parks; they rode the gigantic Ferris wheel and were properly frightened; they viewed with awe the exhibits and art treasures of all the European nations, the Liberty Bell, the replica of a United States battleship, the wonders of science and agriculture—and they never got over it. Neither have many of their home towns, even after sixty-three years. The late Frank Lloyd Wright said this romantic borrowing from undigested ancient culture, architecturally speaking, was a "national calamity."

The same furious drive and energy which made Chicago the merchandising and railroad capital of America seems somehow to have made it our capital of violence; at least it had that reputation for many years. It was the bootleg era that brought Chicago and Illinois nationwide notoriety. The first of the bootleg-period bosses to be mowed down was Jim Colosimo. His successor, John Torrio, is known now chiefly because he served as agent for the old Illinois magnet in drawing to Chicago a New York gunman called Scarface Al Brown, who later went by his real name, Al Capone. Capone had an early reputation in Chicago for being lazy, not very bright but plenty tough. He retained that last reputation over the years and, like so many others drawn to America's heartland, gained fame and fortune.

On November 10, 1924, a supposedly gentle florist named Dion O'Banion was shot to death amidst his posies. The truth came out at O'Banion's elaborate funeral; he was a former safecracker turned gang leader. At that time it was alleged that fifty dollars would buy a murder in the North Clark Street region. It was in a garage at 2122 North Clark that seven men were lined up on Valentine's Day, 1929, and shot down by a gang wearing police uniforms. That would have been a three-hundred-and-fifty-dollar job.

Chicago may have been the cradle of gang warfare in the United States but the same kind of super-American energy made it the cradle of the most forthright writing in American literature. H. L. Mencken once said that all but two contemporary writers of note sprang "from the Middle Empire that has Chicago for its capital." He mentioned in particular Theodore Dreiser, Sherwood Anderson, Willa Cather and Booth Tarkington.

Hulking, brooding Dreiser was drawn inevitably to Chicago from his native Terre Haute, Indiana, and did newspaper work and wandered the night streets, lonely, lustful and bitter. Dreiser left Chicago for New York, but the influence of Chicago never left him. He was a great bear that wrote like a man—with bearlike clumsiness and bearlike strength. The magnet of Illinois drew the house painter and wanderer, Sherwood Anderson, from Camden, Ohio, and while employed in a Chicago advertising agency he met Dreiser, Carl Sandburg, Floyd Dell, Ben Hecht and others of the Chicago literary colony. Of course Chicago and Illinois ride through Sandburg's greatest works.

Sandburg was born in Galesburg, the son of a poor Scandinavian immigrant, and was tremendously influenced by Abraham Lincoln. He worked as a farm hand, milk-wagon driver and restaurant dishwasher. He served in the Spanish-American War, did newspaper work, and blossomed as a first-rank poet in 1915 with *Chicago Poems* celebrating "the hog butcher for the world." And he's still writing his big, burly, sometimes brawling and often magnificent verse.

Edgar Lee Masters was a lawyer and the son of a lawyer in the Lincoln country. Writing—poetry and prose—was an avocation for him, but his *Spoon River Anthology* broke upon America as a startling innovation in poetry. Both Sandburg and Masters were helped considerably by Harriet Monroe, a dedicated Chicago woman who nurtured talent from 1912 until her death in 1936 in her struggling little magazine *Poetry.* She also gave her poetry prize to a troubled soul in Springfield named Vachel Lindsay whose brain throbbed with jungle rhythms until he pulled the switch in 1931.

Chicago seems forever to be alive with literary talent and even genius. There was young Ernest Hemingway, born in metropolitan Chicago, who became a sort of protégé of Sherwood Anderson before achieving a style that his master never could approach. There was James T. Farrell, who wrote with brutal honesty of adolescence on the South Side; and Ben Hecht, the "Pagliacci of the Fire Escapes," who gained fame in 1923 with his *1001 Afternoons in Chicago* and who in collaboration with the late Charles MacArthur wrote *The Front Page* and probably caused several thousand cub reporters to be fired for trying to act like a Hecht-MacArthur character. And there was Eugene Field, who worked on the *Daily News;* Finley Peter Dunne, who brought *Mr. Dooley* to life in the *Times-Herald;* there was George Ade and his *Fables in Slang;* and the fabulous Ring Lardner, who wrote some of the best short stories in the language.

Talented youngsters not only from the great midland empire but from all over America are drawn by the magnet that is Illinois to its many institutions of higher learning. Chicago has two major ones —Northwestern University at Evanston and the University of Chicago. And, while Northwestern has a student body of about 18,000 as compared with Chicago's some 7000, Chicago has the reputation of shooting the loudest fireworks.

In a way this is strange, for the University of Chicago was founded in 1890 with gifts of thirty-five million dollars from John D. Rockefeller, chiefly to train Baptist missionaries, though this idea became minimized over the years. The fireworks really started popping at the University in 1929 when the old Illinois magnet drew a thirty-year-old Yale bachelor of arts named Robert Maynard Hutchins to Chicago with a "new plan" for education. Young President Hutchins was progressive. And he had a flair for publicity.

First he abolished compulsory class attendance, which met with student approval, and followed that with a program to give students a comprehensive background of the arts and sciences during the first two years of college, specialized work coming later. In 1939 President Hutchins abolished the football team. Then, with young Professor of the Philosophy of Law Mortimer Jerome Adler (later author of *How to Read a Book*) he presented a plan for education which consisted of reading one hundred selected books. Read the hundred and you're educated.

Other educators gave the University of Chicago plans and programs a mixed reception. Some newspapers, notably Colonel McCormick's *Tribune,* were positively hostile, but Hutchins stayed on as president of Chicago until 1945.

Chicago is uniquely Chicago. Almost anything you say about it may be partly true, but nothing the shrewdest analyst or most intuitive poet can say will be more than partly true, for Chicago is too big and too varied and too squalid and too magnificent to fit into a pigeonhole, or a million pigeonholes.

About sixty miles south of Chicago is the old city of Kankakee where the stone walls and buildings of the original French-Canadian settlers still stand, and seventy-five miles farther are the twin cities of Urbana and Champaign with the great University of Illinois and Memorial Stadium where back in the 1920's Red Grange, the "Galloping Ghost," made football history.

South of Decatur you begin to run into the old coal region, and there is the town of Pana which once seemed on the point of death after mining dwindled. Now it is prosperous, and because of roses, of all things. Five major growers ship roses all over the country. Why roses in a coal town? Well, one man liked roses and started a greenhouse; others followed.

Wind in Illinois is not limited to the Chicago region. Driving toward Vandalia, a former state capital, I ran into a curious phenomenon: a rain squall forced the rain to run *up* the sloping windshield. And at a Vandalia filling station a traveler declared the wind had lifted the front wheels of his car off the pavement several times. He seemed perturbed about it.

As a matter of fact a *still* summer day seems ominous in Illinois. The sky is pallid. The trees droop. Then in the afternoon great cumulo-nimbus clouds pile up in the southwest and march forward, and the birds get anxious and fly this way and that. And presently the wind comes back with a rush, an advance guard to the cavalry charge of rain and the mad flash, crash and boom of a Mississippi Valley thunderstorm.

Such a storm is an appropriate accompaniment to entrance into Williamson County in the hills of Little Egypt. For "Bloody Williamson County" over the longest period of time has been the wildest, toughest, gun-fightingest county in the United States, when you count the feud killings after the Civil War, the mine strike riots, the massacres, the Ku Klux Klan operations, the gang wars and plain private murders reaching into the second half of the 20th Century. When you think of violence, you have to think of Williamson County first.

Marion is the county seat. But the old coal mining town of Herrin was the blood-letting center and the scene of the 1922 massacre, which can't be surpassed for cold-blooded brutality. The Herrin massacre took place on the morning of June 22, 1922. Attempting to operate with nonunion labor, the Herrin strip mine of the Southern Illinois Coal Company was besieged by striking union men. There had been considerable gunfire and company guards had killed three strikers before a group of guards and strikebreakers agreed to surrender on the promise of safe conduct out of the county. But as these twenty men were being escorted out of Herrin they picked up a hooting, jeering following that finally got completely out of hand. Men, women and children began throwing stones and beating the marching prisoners. By the time the parade reached the Herrin cemetery east of town, all twenty prisoners had been murdered. A number of trials were held on charges of murder. But no one was convicted.

Prohibition sat lightly on the hills of Williamson County until the advent of the Ku Klux Klan and S. Glenn Young. He was a 140-pound thug from Kansas who wore riding breeches and two pearl-handled forty-fives. He was a brawling braggart who ruled Williamson County as a dictator, mostly without official authority, from 1923 to the time of his death in 1925 in a Herrin cigar-store gun fight.

In the spring of 1923 hooded and robed platoons of the Ku Klux Klan began marching into Protestant churches of Williamson County and making cash contributions to the ministers in the name of "Christian one-hundred-per-cent Americanism." On November 1, 1923, the Klan hired Young to take charge of its "law-enforcement" program and, incredible as it may seem, Young got five hundred members of the Klan deputized as Federal prohibition agents.

Finally, even the state "Grand Dragon" of the Klan, aghast at Williamson County activities, had Young officially expelled from membership. The expulsion meant nothing. Young continued his swaggering two-gun course as leader and hero of the Klan in Williamson County. On January 24, 1925, Deputy Sheriff Ora Thomas, a pale, quiet former bootlegger and gunman, entered a Herrin cigar store to quiet an argument. Inside were several men including Young and two bodyguards. When the gun smoke cleared, Thomas was dead. But so were Young and his bodyguards.

Despite his expulsion from the Klan, Young was buried in the Herrin cemetery in the purple robes of a kleagle. Hundreds of robed Klansmen marched behind the hearse followed by five hundred cars and oceans of flowers. Five Protestant ministers delivered eulogies.

Though the Klan wars virtually ended, rival gang fights and killings continued for the next twenty-five years. The most bitter rivals were the tough Shelton brothers—Carl, Earl, Bernie, and Roy—against the equally tough bank robber, bootlegger and gunman Charlie Birger. At the Herrin police department they say things have been quiet for several years. "All the gangsters are either dead now or have got out of the country."

There is very little coal mining in Williamson County now. But Herrin appears fairly busy with new industry and has a very nice residential district.

South of Herrin and Marion the black Illinois soil often is supplanted by yellow clay hills and swamps with cypress growing from the dark water. And cotton fields make their appearance. It is the deep South except for one thing: a young filling station attendant at Goreville said no Negroes are allowed in the town or immediate vicinity. Six miles south of Goreville is a dreary-looking village with unpainted and sagging wooden awnings over the sidewalk and its extraordinary name is Buncombe. Thirty miles or so beyond, you come to the Ohio River where the Ohio joins the Mississippi and there at Cairo is the end of Illinois.

Cairo (pronounced like the corn sirup) is a busy and noisy city. The region is a haven for Canadian geese, and consequently for goose hunters. Cairo's tourist attraction is Magnolia Manor, the great house built of imported brick in 1869 by the merchant Charles A. Galigher, whose social life was climaxed in 1880 when that little bearded man from upstate Galena was entertained there. They still have the bed in which General and Mrs. Grant slept. Cairo also is known as the town that Huckleberry Finn and Jim passed in the fog, to their sorrow.

Politics is really *politics* in Illinois, and the fainthearted or unwary had better hunt another arena. Even before the days of Abe Lincoln and Steve Douglas it was a tradition that the suave pleasantries of an Illinois politician should be labeled *caveat emptor* to warn against the rugged dose of dynamite under that honeyed cover.

The frontier law of no-holds-barred was in effect with the sinewy boys of old New Salem, and it never has been repealed. In Illinois where they speak the "American language" (with a few casual borrowings from early Saxon) you must be your own bodyguard whether you're in politics, on the Chicago Board of Trade, teaching modern poetry in one of the many colleges or merely driving along one of the excellent highways.

As I said a moment ago, Illinois is the U.S.A. in capsule form—though it's certainly a king-size capsule. It's a distillate of America, the volatile core of Americanism after the lighter substances have been whirled off in the centrifuge of our hurly-burly life.

Thus Illinois is a concentrate of the best of America and the worst of America. Handle with care. Keep away from open flame. Put on the top shelf out of the children's reach.

In other words, the United States of America is a magnificent and astonishing land, spectacularly rich, powerful, generous, God-fearing, lawless, bumbling, emotional, silly and wise. And so, naturally, is Illinois, the heart of America.

Only more so.

Michigan

by BRUCE CATTON

Michigan is perhaps the strangest state in the Union, a place where the past, the present and the future are all tied up together in a hard knot. It is the 20th Century incarnate, and if you look closely you can also see the twenty-first coming in; but it is also the 19th Century, the backward glance and the authentic feel and taste of a day that is gone forever. It killed the past and it is the past; it is the skyscraper, the mass-production line and the frantic rush into what the machine will some day make of all of us, and at the same time it is golden sand, blue water, green pine trees on empty hills, and a wind that comes down from the cold spaces, scented with the forests that were butchered by hard-handed men in checked flannel shirts and floppy pants. It is the North Country wedded to the force that destroyed it.

You enter Michigan, mostly, by way of Detroit, which is something special. It is a profound weight on the land; an enormous city, with great skyscrapers taking the light from Canada, automobile factories and used-car lots scattered across the flat prairies, enough business strewn along the Detroit River to make a Russian's eyes pop; and in the old days, which lasted until World War II, you came into Detroit, usually, by steamboat, which was an experience in itself. The boats came up from the Lake Erie ports, Cleveland and Buffalo and Sandusky, and they gave a theatrical touch to the whole business. Lake Erie is beautiful and shallow and treacherous, with a capacity for whipping up unexpected storms that would bother any mariner who ever lived, although mostly it is pleasant enough; and the old side-wheelers came paddling down its length, usually in the middle of the night—it was nice sleeping, in a snug stateroom on one of those boats, with an air-conditioned wind coming in at the open porthole, and the wash of the paddle wheels beating a quiet rhythm in the darkness—and in the morning the boat came up the Detroit River, and the factories and pumping stations on the bank suddenly made you realize that man had taken over Nature and was trying to make something out of it. Then, a little after breakfast time, the boat docked along the Detroit water front, and no city in America offered a more thrilling or exciting entrance.

The boats are mostly gone, and this is really Detroit's fault. Detroit did not exactly invent the automobile, but it picked the thing up when it was nothing better than a costly and unreliable toy for the rich and made it a necessity for everybody in America, and the automobile—getting slightly out of hand—killed the Great Lakes passenger boats, except for a few cruise ships. You come into Detroit nowadays in your own car, or perhaps by train, and the old impact is gone. The place dawns on you gradually now; it used to hit you between the eyes, with the early light slanting in from beyond Ontario. But even now Detroit clamors at you, arrogantly, with all the confidence that comes to men who know they are really in charge of things and who don't mind enjoying the feeling, and there is something overwhelming about it all.

For here is a foretaste of what the machine is doing to us. Here men picked up the Industrial Revolution and swung it; this place, with its infinite genius for making any sort of contrivance men have ever dreamed of, and making it more cheaply and better than anyone else, is the doorway to the future. Everything goes in a rush, everybody is busy—and the place is big and sprawling and grimy and pulsing with life. Here is where we are going, make no mistake about it, and the big financial centers down East can say what they like and be hanged. Detroit sets the pace because this is where the muscle and the knowledge are; and if you don't think the future belongs to America, you should come here and breathe the air for a while.

Detroit makes its bow to the past, of course. It has such a place as Greenfield Village, in Dearborn, and here the past that Detroit killed forever—the past of wayside inns, one-man machine shops, quiet country villages snuggling by the route of stagecoaches, and rural dancers moving to the wheezy tunes scraped out by self-taught fiddlers—is preserved like a fly in amber, and it is very much worth visiting. But this, after all, is only a gesture. Detroit has been taking us away from that for half a century, and if it shows you Greenfield Village it also shows you the machine-age pace which turned everything Dearborn has on exhibit into museum pieces. Dearborn houses both this fragment of the past and also the Ford Motor Company, which did as much as any one organism could do to put the past in its place.

Detroit's streets come in like the spokes of a wheel, the other half of the wheel having been cut off by the Detroit River. Because the pace has been uneven there are vast skyscrapers standing beside parking lots, with rummy old brick buildings from the Civil War era snuggling up against twenty-story hotels and elongated office buildings; burlesque theaters and sleazy secondhand-book stores rub elbows with the most up-to-date, chromium-and-cutstone buildings that America can build, and the river drifts by, down in front, bearing the iron ore and coal and petroleum on which modern America is built; and whether you like it or not you can feel the hard pulse of America beating up and down these automobile-clogged streets.

Some years ago a civic-minded booster dreamed up the phrase, "dynamic Detroit," to express the essence of this city. He hit it off perfectly. Detroit *is* dynamic. Here is where they call the tune, and it is not a tune the Greenfield Village fiddlers ever quite managed to express.

But Detroit, after all, is not really Michigan. Its industrial empire spraddles over a good part of the state, to be sure—with Flint, and Pontiac, and Jackson and Lansing and Grand Rapids and all the rest—but the tremendous industrial nexus centered here is only half of the story. The other half is something very different—old times, the breath of bygone days and memories that went out of date before the men who remembered them were old—and as a man born out of his proper time I love this other Michigan a good deal more than I love Detroit.

The map of the Lower Peninsula of Michigan is shaped like a fat old-fashioned mitten—a left-hand mitten, placed palm down, with a bulky thumb sticking out into the cold blue of Lake Huron. Detroit is down in the lower right-hand margin, below where the thumb begins, and the great industrial network lies across the lower part of the state: across the upper part of the wrist. But if you will take the map, and draw a line from Bay City—at the bottom of the gap between the bulbous thumb and the rest of the hand—straight west across the state, you will have cut Michigan into its two distinctive parts. Everything below the line is 20th Century; everything above it is North Country—old, half empty, touched by the cold winds that drift down from the Arctic, with trees and sand and crystal-clear water and drowsy small towns as its distinguishing marks. It is a country that will put its seal on you if you are not careful, because it offers a lonely beauty and an escape from almost everything Detroit stands for.

The present falls away, when you go up into this part of the state. Suppose you drive up from Detroit, along U. S. Route 10; it goes through places like Flint and Saginaw and Midland, any one of which would be world-famous if it were in some other country—and then, suddenly, it takes you into the empty cut-over land, where ghost towns cluster by the road, where the rivers flow cold and clear past hills that furnished lumber for half the world a generation or two ago, where cabins nestle down by quiet lakes and where the air drifts straight through you as if nobody had ever soiled it with smoke or grime or gas fumes. From here on north there are not so many farms, the soil is very sandy, excellent for growing pine trees, not often so good for growing anything else, and if it amuses you to count abandoned farms (unpainted shacks going peacefully to ruin amid fields nobody has tilled for a quarter century or more) you can make quite a list in an afternoon's drive. The road leads you out of ambition into peace and contentment; the deceptive light of an eternal summer afternoon lies on the rolling country; the innumerable lakes glitter brightly blue in the fading light, and when you stop your car and listen you hear a blessed quiet.

This part of the state must have been quite a sight, a hundred years ago. Over an area of better than 25,000 square miles there was a magnificent forest—great pines, mostly, with a healthy sprinkling of hardwoods like maples and beeches—like nothing you can find in America today. From lake to lake and for 250 miles from north to south there was an eternal green twilight, with open spaces where the lakes and rivers were; twilight, with the wind forever making an unobtrusive noise in the branches overhead, brown matted needles and leaves underfoot—everything just about as it was shortly after the last ice age.

There is one tiny fragment of it left. If you will go to the little town of Kalkaska, in the northwest part of the state's Lower Peninsula, and drive thirty miles or so to the east, you will reach Hartwick Pines State Park; and here, running down to the bank of the Au Sable River, is an eighty-five-acre tract of virgin timber, the last that remains, preserved for tourists. You leave your car by the park-administration building and suddenly you are in the middle of it, with trees rising 150 feet overhead, and a shaded coolness all about that is proof against the summer's worst heat wave. Walking through it is not unlike walking through a cathedral. It has that effect on people. It is even more moving in the dead of winter, with the big trees coming up out of a white silence that is all but absolute; the trouble is that then you have to use skis or snowshoes to get there.

Anyway, Michigan a century ago was one magnificent forest, and even as recently as the Civil War it had hardly been touched. But then the lumberjacks went to work, and they shaved the countryside the way a razor shaves a man's chin. Where there had been wilderness, boom lumber towns sprang up, with rickety railroad lines threading their way back into the hills. In the springtime, every stream was clogged with logs, with lumberjacks scampering across the treacherous shifting carpet with peavy and cant hook, mounds of sawdust rising beside the busy mills, and a mill town with 1200 inhabitants normally supported from twelve to twenty saloons. Michigan voted for prohibition before the Federal prohibition amendment went into effect in 1920, and anyone who remembers what those saloons did to small-town life can easily understand why. For a time Saginaw was the greatest lumber city in the world, then Muskegon had the title, and then some other place; fresh-cut boards were stacked in endless piles by the railroad sidings or the lake-side wharves . . . and then, all of a sudden, it was all over. The lumber was gone, the mills were dismantled, the booming cities and towns lapsed into drowsiness, store-fronts were boarded up—and the razor which had done all of this shaving had left a stubble of stumps like a frowsy three-day beard across thousands of square miles. Some towns died entirely, some almost died, and the endless whine of the gang saws became quiet forever.

All of which put its mark on a whole generation of people. Here was a region half the size of Ireland which, after only fifty years of history, suddenly found itself at a dead end. A society began to decay before it had matured. Towns dwindled and died before the eyes of the very men who had founded them. Boys who grew to manhood in these dying towns moved off to the city, leaving behind the old folks and the girls—half a century ago it was not so simple for an untrained girl to make a place for herself in a far-off city, and thousands upon thousands of these girls were condemned to lives of unwanted loneliness. They were strong and healthy and they had dreams and high hopes, and these came to very little because life had shoved them off into a side alley, since marriage was just about the only career a girl could hope for in those days. The human cost of a dying boom can be pretty high.

So they killed the infinite forest, once and for all. But there was still the land itself, rolling in vast gentle waves under a clear blue sky; there were the hundreds and hundreds of lakes, blue and cold and sparkling with imitation whitecaps; there was the great stretch of sand, putting a golden border on the water; there were the rivers, so clear you could count bits of gravel ten feet deep, so cold they turned your feet numb if you tried to wade; and there was the air, filtered by its eternal drift down from the ultimate edge of icy nowhere, fresh enough to revive a Peruvian mummy, odorous with the scent of jack pines.

All of this adds up to an earthly paradise for people from the hot cities who want to get away from asphalt and noise and muggy heat when they have a chance and touch base with Mother Nature; and today the tourist trade is the second industry in the entire state, topped only by the exalted automobile industry itself. This place where the wilderness used to be may indeed be the North Country, but it is only a hop-skip-and-jump from enormous centers of population. From Detroit or Chicago, it is a handy one-day drive to any spot in the Lower Peninsula, but at the end of the drive you feel that you have left the city and all of its works in another world.

So the old lumber area has had a rebirth, and the air of defeat and decline has vanished. This change has gone hand in hand with others. For one thing, the trees are coming back; huge state and national forests lie across vast stretches of empty land. In addition, there is a belt of cherry and peach orchards twenty miles wide and 200 miles long down the western side of the state. In spring, when the blossoms are out, the rolling hillsides near Lake Michigan offer a spectacle of breath-taking beauty, and many a town that used to live on its sawmills now lives on its cannery-and-packing plant. Every spring they have a big "cherry festival" at Traverse City—a bright, bustling little city which has made full recovery from the death of the lumber boom—and a pretty girl is named Cherry Queen; her function, usually, in addition to posing for photographs, is to take a cherry pie to Washington and present it to the President. This makes a nice trip for the girl, nets the President a first-rate pie, and presumably makes everybody happy.

But under everything there is this strange, beautiful, lonely land itself, this land of blue sky and clear water, where puff-ball clouds drift lazily overhead, trailing pleasant shadows over water and forest and bright little towns as if nobody ever had to be in a hurry about anything and time had come to a standstill just because what is here and now is too pleasant to leave. This is good country to come from and it is even better to go back to. It is a land of memories and also a land of escape: a place where you can be utterly idle in more pleasant ways than any other place I know.

I was born in Michigan and I grew up there, and not long ago I went back to see what it is like today. I came in through the industrial network in the lower-right hand corner of the state, and after a while I was driving northwest on U. S. Route 10—a fine road which goes for many miles at a stretch without touching a town, and which cannot in any case touch a real, full-dress city because in all of Michigan, north of that east-west line from Bay City, there is not a single place with as many as 20,000 permanent residents.

Beyond Clare, which calls itself the gateway to the northland, I turned right on M 115, which goes on past pleasant little lakes dotted with summer cottages, past a sprinkling of drowsy farms, and past uncounted miles of unused land. Yet a road, after all, takes you where you yourself are going, and not where the road goes, and what you see depends mostly on what's inside of you; and when you go back to re-explore your own country you are likely to find memories and dreams all mixed up with solid reality. I was heading for my own particular corner of the state, where I spent my boyhood, because I wanted to see what the years had done to it; and if in the end I learned more about what the years had done to me—well, that is what usually happens when you go on a pilgrimage.

My own land is mostly Benzie County, which has fewer inhabitants now than it had half a century ago but which has lost its old backwoods isolation and is a homey, friendly sort of country. There is a tiny town with the improbable name of Benzonia, which was

MASSACHUSETTS Stacked rifles on the village green at Lexington, scene of the opening battle of the American Revolution.

CONNECTICUT (*center spread*) *The Charles W. Morgan*, last of the wooden whaling ships, lies peacefully at anchor in the Mystic River.

RHODE ISLAND Some of the many 18th Century houses surviving along Academy Cove, a resort on Narragansett Bay.

NEW JERSEY This beach scene, on the coast between Avalon and Stone Harbor, is one of wind-ruffled dunes and lonely loveliness.

NEW YORK (*center spread*) The Thousand Islands lie like scattered emeralds on the blue St. Lawrence.

DELAWARE   An outdoor tea party enjoyed by costumed ladies at the
Colonial J. Dansforth Bush home in New Castle.

WASHINGTON, D.C. The stately Jefferson Memorial, framed by the Capitol's famed cherry trees.

ILLINOIS (*center spread*) The colossus of Chicago—miracle of the midwest.

VIRGINIA The Blue Ridge Hunt gathers in front of the stunning façade of Carter Hall, near Berryville.

GEORGIA   The Old South lives on—here Mrs. Lester Hardwick graces a lovely tableau of trees and sward and stately mansion at dusk.

FLORIDA   *(center spread)* The water-minded life de luxe in Ft. Lauderdale, with pleasure craft riding in the blue, blue canals.

MISSISSIPPI A crossroad store slumbers under the hot noonday sun near Bentonia.

founded by some eager folk from Oberlin College just before the Civil War when all of this land was new. The air was so clear and good that they wanted a name that would tell about it, so they dipped into their erudition and came up with a Latin-Greek hybrid which means, roughly, fragrant air. They built a little college, and for fifty years it struggled along, graduating eight or ten people a year; then it was turned into a preparatory school, and my father was principal of it when I was a boy, and just after World War I there was no longer any need for this school because the state's high schools had improved, and it quietly died. Nothing is left of it now except a brick building which has been turned into a village community house, but the little town drowses under the long sunlight, with a special flavor that other little towns don't have, touched by the memory of the old-timers who wanted to bring education to the lumber country.

Every man makes his own state—or maybe his state makes him; it is hard to be certain about such things. But you grow up with something on your mind, and it comes out of the place where you were born and reared, and you never can get away from it no matter where you go. And if you go back, long afterward, to the place you knew when you were young, you see it through eyes that were specially conditioned; you cannot be objective about it; you try to write about your background and find that you are really writing about yourself.

I remember, some forty years ago, a January night when the thermometer registered five below and there was a brilliant full moon, and I went to the front door, late at night, to lock up. I stood in the doorway for a moment, looking out at the moonlit landscape, the little grove of trees across the street and the three feet of snow that covered everything. There is not in all America today anything quite as still and quiet as a Michigan small town could be, late on a moonswept night, in January, in the days before World War I. Nobody in all the earth was making a sound, nothing was moving, there was only the white snow, the black trees, the blue shadows lying on the whiteness, and the big moon in a cloudless sky; and to stand there and look out at it was, inexplicably, to be in touch with the Infinite—and, somehow, the Infinite was good, it was lonely but friendly, it meant something you did not have to be afraid of if you understood it. So Michigan means that to me—along with much else—and coldness and loneliness and shattering loveliness go hand in hand, so that while you will always be awed and abashed when you come up against the Infinite you do not really need to be afraid. And maybe that is a fairly good idea to get and take with you.

I can remember another night, in summertime, much earlier, when as a rather small boy my family took me across Lake Michigan on a steamboat from Milwaukee. It was dark and cool and windy, and we came out of the river and out past the breakwater, and the steamer began to rise and fall on the waves of the big lake. For a small child it was quite scary—nothing but water and the dark, with big waves coming in from nowhere and making foaming noises under the bow, and the Michigan shore seemed an unimaginable distance away and the dark sea ahead was what all adventurers have always seen when they pitted themselves against the great emptiness and its wonder and peril, and life itself is an enormous gamble played by people who are eager and frightened at the same time, with nothingness before and above and the chance of a dawn-swept land-fall in the morning lying there, insubstantial and improbable beyond the night, as the possible reward. That is really the truth of it, and that too is good to know.

I am well aware, of course, that, as the world's seas go, Lake Michigan is not really a very large body of water. To cross it by steamer is to spend no more than half a dozen hours afloat, and when the trip is over you have reached only the state of Michigan, which actually is as prosaic a bit of land as you can find. Yet the thoughts of a small boy can be lonely, frightening and touched with unfathomable wonder, and the borders of an unattainable land can glimmer, insubstantial but genuine, over the most matter-of-fact horizon. What you owe the land where you were born and reared is something you can never quite pin down; but if that land can stir dreams and fears and the hints of a completely illogical but convincing promise, you are that much ahead of the game. For what you think and feel when you are very small never quite leaves you, and if it always lures you on to something that the visible landscape does not quite make explicit you are immeasurably the gainer.

All of this means very little, probably, by any rational scheme of things. Yet somehow it is part of the color and the flavor which this strange, light-struck, improbable country gave to me when I was too young to know any better, and it has had its own queer effect on everything I have thought or done ever since. So I bring it in here, along with the pine trees and the cold winds and the everlasting

golden sands, to try to explain why I like to go back to Michigan.
I am probably trying to recapture something unattainable, but that
does not matter; so long as the feel and the gleam of it still lie on the
edge of my subconscious it is real, for me, and the only value in
any dream consists in the fact that you have to keep pursuing it
even though you know that you can never quite reach it. If the real
Michigan keeps getting overlaid with the Michigan I thought I saw
in the old days, I can only say that I am that much better off—for
what I thought I saw then was worth a lifetime's quest.

There is plenty to see up here. Half a mile from this hilltop village
is one of America's loveliest lakes—Crystal Lake, named with an utter
literalness; it is so clear you can see the bottom where it is twenty
feet deep—nine miles long by three miles wide, with wooded hills
all around and a fringe of pleasant summer cottages along its sandy
shores.

Crystal Lake itself will always be something special for me, because it symbolizes an emotion that goes beyond time and space.
When I was very small the minister of the one church in my town of
Benzonia took some months off, and—by dint of what patient frugality
I do not know: the pastor of a country church at that time earned
precious little money—made a trip to the Holy Land. When he returned he made his report, and of it I remember just one thing. The
magical Sea of Galilee, he said, the sea where our Lord walked and
taught and performed miracles, was just about the size and shape of
our Crystal Lake. To be sure, the hills which bordered Galilee were
dun-colored, barren of trees, a bleak and impoverished landscape;
while our hills, green as the heart of a maple leaf, were ringed with
clear water, set about with pleasant little towns, cool and pleasant,
inviting people to linger on their long journey from one mystery to
another. But the resemblance was there, and the lake in which I
caught diminutive perch was very like the lake on which Peter tried
to walk dry-shod; and for some reason my life is richer because a
saintlike little pastor, half a century ago, saw Galilee through innocent eyes which could interpret any lake in terms of Michigan's pine
trees and green open valleys. I have never been to Palestine, but
somehow I have seen the Sea of Galilee, and the Word that was
preached by that Near-Eastern sea has a special sound for me.

Over the range of hills at the western end of my Crystal Lake
there is Lake Michigan itself, and where a little river cuts a channel
through the high bluffs there is Frankfort, a summer-resort town and

a busy little seaport as well. The Ann Arbor Railroad has its terminus here, with a fleet of car ferries that carry whole freight trains across Lake Michigan, and these big black steamers come and go at all hours of the day and night, 365 days a year. In the winter when the big lake is full of ice these boats often have quite a time of it, but they are sturdy icebreakers and they hack their way through regardless, although they sometimes make port with their upper works encased in ice.

From Frankfort you swing up toward Traverse City on route M 22, which cuts up across what is known as the Leelanau Peninsula. Once this was lumber country and now it is cherry country, but mostly it is a region for summer vacationers. Every little town has its lake (Glen Lake, which lies back of Sleeping Bear Point, is a show place) and there are other lakes with no towns at all, locked in by ice and snow for four or five months of the year.

Sleeping Bear Point is an enormous sand dune, five miles long by 500 feet high, jutting out into Lake Michigan. A road of sorts leads to the top, but your car would stall in the deep, fine sand, so you go to the town of Glen Haven and take passage in one of the special low-gear cars with oversized, half-inflated tires, which waddle through the sand as if they were made for it. On the crest there is nothing at all to see but this golden empty ridge and the great blue plain of Lake Michigan far below, with white surf curling on the beach at the foot of the bluff, yet it is one of the finest sights in the Middle West. There is no noise except the lake wind ruffling the spare trees: there is just nothing except a feeling of infinite space and brightness, and utter freedom from the smoke and the rush and the racket of ordinary 20th Century life.

The country north of Traverse City is high and open, with Lake Michigan nearly always in view off to the left, and the little towns and villages along the way reflect the past in a curious manner. First there was the lumber era, in which today's sleepy hamlet was a rip-roaring little city with a solid mile of sawmills along the water front. Then, when the lumber was gone, there was the early summer-resort trade: passenger boats coming up from Chicago or around from Detroit; imposing but flimsy frame hotels, all veranda and white pillars, overlooking every beach; Pullman cars unloading a new consignment of vacationers at the railroad depot every morning . . . and after a while the automobiles came and killed boat lines, passenger trains and most of the hotels, so that these towns which had made one readjustment had to make another. The result is odd. Every town contains echoes of those two vanished eras, and seems to be looking back regretfully to the past; and yet most of them are brighter and more hopeful than they ever were before, the old feeling of backwoods isolation is gone, the people who live here are having a better time of it than ever before and the general level of prosperity is higher and more stable. Yet the feeling of the past does linger, so that in this area which has hardly been settled more than a century there are haunting echoes of antiquity.

Your memory can play queer tricks on you. At Charlevoix I drove east, skirting the south shore of beautiful Lake Charlevoix to reach Boyne City. Boyne City was perhaps the last lumber boom town in the Lower Peninsula. We lived there, for a year or so, when I was about six years old, and it was a lively place then. There were four immense sawmills along the lake front, and a big "chemical plant"— I suppose it was a place where they extracted turpentine and other by-products from the pines—and there was even a blast furnace, although what it may have been doing there I have never been able to understand. Anyway, Boyne City was bustling and exciting, and our back yard ran down to the Boyne River, where the log drives came down in the spring. To my six-year-old eyes that river was immense; it was, I realized, probably smaller than the Mississippi, but it was fascinating, wide, turbulent, somehow menacing—a dangerous river which easily could (and, two or three times, very nearly did) drown a small boy who incautiously tried to play on its treacherous carpet of moving logs. So I returned to the old back yard and took another look at the river—and realized that either the river had shrunk or I had stretched considerably. The river is charming—gentle, crystal-clear, friendly, no more hostile than a brook. Along the lake front there is an uncommonly pleasant park, where the sawmills used to be. A rusted remnant of the old blast furnace still survives, but everything else seems to be gone; and this is not the exciting town where I used to live, it is just a bright, friendly little community where old memories are held in suspension in the sunlight.

Another of my favorite towns in this part of the state is Petoskey, where I was born. No man ever breaks completely away from his birthplace; you carry the mark of your home town with you. I remember it as a sleepy sort of place, built on a spectacular side hill that slants up steeply from the cold blue of Little Traverse Bay, with funny little tourist-bait shops at the bottom where Indian wares

and other trinkets were offered for sale to the "summer people."
These shops always smelled pleasantly of birch bark—there were
baskets, and toy canoes, and other contrivances—and to this day the
odor of birch bark takes me back to tiny stores which must have gone
out of existence a whole generation ago.

Petoskey has grown up to date and prosperous. It is no longer a
lumber center, and the great trains of flatcars piled high with pine
logs no longer go rumbling past what used to be the Grand Rapids
& Indiana depot, and the sprawling summer hotels I remember so
well are not there any more; but because the hill is so high and
because so much of the big lake lies open at the foot of the hill
Petoskey gives you what so much of this part of Michigan always
gives—the strange feeling that you are at an immense altitude, on
some sort of ridge where you can look down on half of the Middle
West and where the wind that never quite dies down has come to
you without touching anything at all along the way from wherever
it is that winds are born.

Even though it always speaks of the past, and seems to look back
toward it in a dreamy sort of way, most of this part of Michigan has
no particular history. But when you go north from Petoskey you
step far back into legend and the distant past. Things were going
on here when the eastern seaboard colonies were still young. La
Salle, Jolliet and Marquette were here nearly three centuries ago.
At Mackinaw City, at the very tip of Michigan's Lower Peninsula,
and an hour's easy drive from Petoskey, there is a lake-front park
with a rebuilt stockade which marks the site of one of early America's
most significant strong points—Fort Michilimackinac. Here, around
1681, missionaries and fur traders and French soldiers and a scattering of just plain adventurers built an outpost of French civilization in a spot which was more remote and isolated than any spot on
earth can be today.

After the French left Canada the British took over, and in 1763
Pontiac's painted warriors broke in, seized stockade and fort, and
massacred the British garrison. Then the fort was abandoned, to be
rebuilt on Mackinac Island, which lies in the center of the straits.
The Americans took it over after the Revolution, and the British re-
captured it in the War of 1812, and then it was returned to American
possession again. Now it stands empty, a tourists' show place, looking out at the unending procession of freighters that cruise slowly
past on their way to and from the lower lakes.

Mackinac Island is a delightful spot, and it is unusual in two ways. In the first place, although it is spelled Mackinac it is, for some incomprehensible reason, pronounced Mackinaw; and in the second place it is the one spot in the whole state of Michigan—one of the very few spots in all the United States—where you never see an automobile. Automobiles are not allowed on the island, and to come to this place, with its hotels and boardinghouses and curio shops lining the quiet streets, and the old-fashioned horse-drawn surreys leisurely wheeling their way in and out, is to step straight back into the Victorian era. To get about the island you walk, or ride behind a horse, or get on a bicycle. More so than any other place in the state, this is a refuge from the present.

Big changes are coming to Upper Michigan and the symbol of their approach is the stupendous five-mile-long bridge across the straits connecting the Lower and Upper Peninsula. The bridge cost around $100,000,000; it at last ties the two halves of the state firmly together. Before, you crossed the straits by one of a fleet of state-owned ferry boats.

Michigan's Upper Peninsula is an immense finger of land running 300 miles from west to east, with cold, steely-blue Lake Superior, the largest lake in the world, lying all along its northern flank. Eighty-five per cent of this area is forested and lumbering is still going on, the Marquette iron range still turns out iron ore, and some copper is still being mined; but comparatively speaking the Upper Peninsula is almost empty, with fewer than 300,000 inhabitants. If the northern half of the Lower Peninsula is North Country the Upper Peninsula is the same thing at treble strength. It is traversed by excellent concrete roads, and you can drive for two hours without seeing a town, or anything that looks like permanent human habitation. For mile after mile there is nothing except clear blue lakes, vast areas of cut-over timber, forests which look as if nobody had ever taken an ax into them, and outcroppings of bleak rock. With Lake Superior so close this country has its own built-in air-conditioning; there is a sharp edge to the air, a feeling of unlimited space and quiet and peace, and that strange quality of half-ominous, half-friendly loneliness is with you all of the time. Now that the bridge is finished, all of this will probably be watered down, but it can never be wholly destroyed. After all, up in this country there is nothing between you and the North Pole except a few thousand miles of totally empty land and water.

One of the interesting things to see up here is the canal at Sault Ste. Marie, whose big locks connect Lake Superior with the lower lakes. The Soo, as everybody calls it, is a lively little city during the eight months of the navigation season; it boasts that its canal handles more traffic than Panama and Suez combined. All day and all night the ships—enormous things, 500 and 600 feet in length—come majestically in from the upper lake, floating high above your head, sinking slowly as the water burbles out of the locks, and then gliding off for the great industrial region hundreds of miles to the south. In an average day, eighty or ninety of them will go through. Day and night, you are forever hearing the deep, haunting bass of their whistles—the inescapable, wholly characteristic and somehow deeply romantic noise of the Soo region. (Progress is taking a hand here, these immense boats are being equipped with air horns, which emit a blatting which carries a great deal farther than the traditional steam whistle but which is pure discord and nothing more.)

Driving west from the Soo, on the broad highway that leads to Marquette and the iron-range country, you pass Seney, a drowsy little country town so unobtrusive that you can go all the way through it before you realize you have reached it. It's quiet and orderly today, but half a century ago Seney was a hell-roaring lumber town, with a reputation for unrestrained misconduct that did not need to take second place to any Western cattle town or mining camp. There is a myth, formerly given wide circulation in the Sunday supplements, about a log stockade that once adorned the town. In it, according to one version, dance-hall girls were kept when not dancing; according to another, captive lumberjacks were immured here between spells in the backwoods. There is one odd thing about these fancy yarns of the high-wide-and-handsome days of the lumber towns; the sins which were committed in these places were never really attractive. It is very hard to glamorize a village rowdy, and the lumberjack tough mugs were at bottom village rowdies and nothing better. Seney's most notorious character, for instance, was a loafer who used to win free drinks in bars by biting the heads off frogs, mice and other vermin. He finally came to a well-merited end, according to the story, when he bit the head off a small owl which was the particular pet of a burly lumberjack, who promptly brought this unattractive character's career to a close by smiting him vigorously over the head with the handle of a peavy.

Marquette is the metropolis of the Upper Peninsula. It is a solid industrial town, with red ore from the great ridges behind it coming down to the docks in red hopper cars, and if it is not the most lovely city in the United States it occupies one of the nation's most beautiful sites. The south shore of Lake Superior curves in and out, along here, with deep bays and jutting, pine-crowned headlands; the old primeval rock breaks through the crust of the land to remind you that this is the backbone of the continent, where rocks so ancient they even lack fossils lie bare under the long summer sunlight, grim and lonely and desolate. Just at sunset, from east of Marquette, you can see the city with the opaque blue panel of Lake Superior silent in front of it and a flaming red sky behind it, lying in the evening stillness like a dream of the city that never was; it is transfigured, a strange light lies on its towers and parapets, and this place that for so long was a Mecca for Cornish miners (the roadside stands still peddle Cornish pasties instead of hot dogs, and very good they are too) becomes an unattainable no-place out of fable, dropping long dark shadows on a silent cold sea.

If you are well-advised, you will head west from Marquette for the copper country. Do it, if possible, early in October when the lonely road will take you through forests aflame with scarlet and gold and bronze, and a wild, doomed beauty that belongs beyond the farthest edge of the world lies on all the landscape; the touch of everlasting winter is in the air and yet for an hour or so the sunlight is still warm, and nothing you will ever see will move you more or linger with you longer. You come out, at last, onto the long spine of the Keweenaw Peninsula—an outcrop of rock and wild trees, reaching far up into Lake Superior, perhaps the oldest land in the new world. The copper mines which caused men to come here in the first place go deep under the lake—some of the shafts go down for more than a mile. You get the feeling of a land that has been passed by, a hard, forbidding and strangely charming bit of country that had a short hectic history and does not especially want any more; and all about is the cold steely blue of the greatest of lakes, and the picturesque little settlements that manage to be both friendly and forsaken at the same moment.

It would be possible, of course, to drive on, noting the points of interest in the Upper Peninsula, mentioning the more unusual towns—like Eagle Harbor, one of the most completely beautiful villages I ever expect to see, with two long headlands enclosing a quiet strip of water and the great angry lake piling destructive surging

waves against the rocks outside—but my state is half reality and half
the dim, enchanted memories of a long-lost boyhood, and anyway
I did not live in the entire state of Michigan. I knew only selected
parts of it, and these parts stay in my memory and call back unforgettable things which were born of the cold emptiness and the
inviting, menacing beauty of this North Country.

They are Upper Michigan, the part that lies north of the automobile belt, the doomed, bewitched country which is surrendering
to the Mackinac bridge and to the superhighway and which, ultimately, will undoubtedly become just another part of the sprawling,
industrialized Middle West. But while today's light lasts it is still
a land apart; there is a pleasantly melancholy flavor of a lost past
to it, and although men murdered the forests with a passionate fe-
rocity the forests somehow still live and put their strange touch on
the countryside. There are cool shadows under the trees and a timeless peace lies on the cutover tracts and the fields where the young
second growth is hiding the stumps.

It is a strange country: lonely enough, even in summer, and cold
as the far side of the moon when winter comes, with the far-off hills
rising pale blue from the frozen white landscape. It offers a chance
to draw a deep breath, to turn around and look back at the traveled
path, to stand on a high hill and be alone with the fresh air and the
sunlight. It is wood and water, golden sand and blue lakes, emptiness and memories and the sort of isolation which it is hard for a
city man to come by, these days. All in all, it is quite a state.

Indiana

by WILLIAM E. WILSON

We were riding—my uncle Clarence A. Cook and I—along a black-topped road from Indianapolis to Turkey Run State Park. It was early morning and there was hardly any traffic. Although the mid-summer day had promised to be fair, the sky was now overcast, a solid, sullen gray, and the air that came through the car window was damp and heavy, almost tropical.

My uncle was driving—"to prove to my sisters-in-law," he said defiantly, "that I am not too old yet to make this trip by myself." He did not have to prove it to me. As I sat beside him, I was thinking that if I could be sure of inheriting his youthfulness of appearance, mind and spirit when I reached my seventies, I'd stop resenting the advance of years.

I knew a great many men and women like him in Indiana. There were the old friends of my father, who himself had lived to be almost seventy-nine, and there were also the chance acquaintances who were continually surprising me by proving to be older than they looked—like the man at the magazine counter in Lafayette who had told me proudly that he was born the day Lee surrendered, and a farmer on a bus out of Fort Wayne who said, "I'll be ninety-two to-morrow, but I can still handle a square meal—or anything else." There must be something in the atmosphere of Indiana as well as the tempo of living that makes for a vigorous longevity.

As we rolled along through Hendricks and Montgomery counties, my uncle kept up a lively comment on the countryside and its people. He was in especially good spirits, for the trip to Turkey Run was one that delighted him. He had been going there for brief holidays ever since it was the Lusk farm, back in 1916.

"All this land round here was once a swamp," my uncle said, as we approached the village of Lizton. "A man that worked for me years ago in Indianapolis came from here. We always kidded him—asked him to take his shoes off and show us his webbed feet."

Farther along, we passed some charred ruins, and my uncle told me a farmer there had lost most of his stock and his corn crop the year before. "But the corn crop will be good again this year," he added. "In fact, there's so much of it that the farmers don't know where they're going to store it."

I gazed out the window. The corn did look good, very tall and green and so thick that the slanting, crosswise pattern of the rows was hardly discernible. Farther north, in the heart of the great, flat corn belt that sweeps across the upper half of Indiana, the corn no doubt looked even better.

My uncle swerved the car expertly round a tractor-drawn hay-rake that was clattering and banging along the side of the road.

"In the Columbia Club the other day," he laughed, "they were telling about a farmer in Putnam County who was finally tracked down by the Federal income-tax people. He owed the United States nineteen hundred dollars. 'You mean I got to send a check to the Guvment?' the farmer said. 'Why, hell, man, the Guvment has always sent checks to me!'"

That was the kind of story members of the Columbia Club in Indianapolis had been telling ever since 1933. In fact, a crack about Cleveland's first administration is probably still good for a laugh in that Republican stronghold.

But at that moment I wasn't interested in the Columbia Club or corn crops or farmers; for in my pleasure in my uncle's companionship on this lonely Indiana road, I had come upon a riddle. Why, I was asking myself, did I always find it so refreshing to be back home again in Indiana?

Previously, on my annual visits to the state, I had supposed I was put at ease primarily by the familiar, rich, warm sound of Hoosier voices. In those days, I was coming "home" from the East, where

I had never learned to speak in the Harvard fashion. But this year, I had come "home" from the West—from Colorado—and had felt the spell of belonging in Indiana just as strong, although the difference in speech was barely noticeable.

True, the Hoosier's "r," like the bosoms of his farm girls, is more robustly developed than the Westerner's, and he has a half-Southern and yet not-Southern way of speaking softly and slowly that is unique. "How are *yew?*" he says; and if you listen closely, you will hear even the best educated of Hoosiers slipping into the pioneer's "whur" for "where" and "git" for "get." Moreover, what Indiana people do to the little word "it" is not duplicated anywhere else in the country. They make it stand up in their sentences like a silo on a low, flat, Hoosier horizon.

I noticed, too, the difference in climate, and that difference was certainly not in Indiana's favor. Indiana's climate, especially in summer, with the heavy, humid stuff that passes for atmosphere, is not designed to put anyone at ease. But after the first gasp or two, I actually relished the Indiana air. Although it clings to you like an impoverished second cousin, it at least has body and character. I even liked the stench of the heaven trees near the Indianapolis airport.

There was no doubt about it; I was a steadfast Hoosier still.

But why, I asked myself, does a Hoosier always remain a Hoosier, even after years of exile?

As we dipped down into Browns Valley, my uncle unwittingly gave me the first clue to an answer.

"A friend of a chap I went to college with lives round here somewhere," he said. "For years I've intended to look him up. Would you mind if we did it now?"

There was the answer—at least, a beginning of it—as plain and understandable as a Hoosier farmer's face.

From Hammond to Rising Sun, from Steuben County to Posey County, there are people whom a returning Hoosier can look up if he wants to take the time. And where there happen to be no such people, he can quickly establish a cordial relationship by announcing to any group of strangers the locality in which he originated. "Then you must know so-and-so," someone will be sure to say. Come to think of it, this is not a bad way to select one's friends in any part of the world. As Abe Martin says, "You kin git a purty fair line on new acquaintances by th' people they ask about."

"Indiana is like a big family," the president of Indiana University once remarked to me. "Being Hoosiers somehow makes us all kin. And that goes for our relatives who have left the family homestead as well as those who have remained in the state."

The family "homestead" of Indiana is actually two houses instead of one. Ask any Hoosier where he is from and the chances are that he will not say simply, "Indiana," but either "Northern Indiana" or "Southern Indiana," depending upon which side of the Old National Road he lives on. The Old National Road, owned by the state since 1839, enters Indiana from the east at Richmond, passes through Indianapolis, and leaves the state for the west at Terre Haute. For years, it was the finest road in the world. Today, as U.S. 40, it is still one of the best east-west thoroughfares. But its importance to Indiana is not the same as its importance to the tourists who traverse it in an endless two-way procession each year. In Indiana, the Old National Road is a kind of boundary.

North of the Old National Road, Indiana has long been populated by descendants of Yankees, New York Staters and immigrants from foreign lands. This is the more vigorous, the more progressive and aggressive, and the more prosperous half of the state. Folks get things done more quickly up here and, by some standards, better. They haven't as much time on their hands as folks in Southern Indiana, and if you stop to ask directions in Gary or South Bend, you may find the busy Hoosier won't walk more than two or three blocks out of his way to direct you.

South of the historic highway, Indiana has been inhabited even longer by descendants of Southerners, with a strong infusion of German and Irish in their blood. Southern Indiana is not so rich as the northern section of the state, but it has a more storied past and more varied scenery. Down here, the Hoosier is more leisurely and more gracious. Also more loquacious. Ask a man in Evansville or New Albany to direct you and he will probably close up his shop for half a day to accompany you to the right road. But he may talk so much while doing it that he will make you late for supper.

But Indiana is not a house divided against itself. Like the double cabins of the pioneers, it has a friendly dogtrot between the two parts. This neutral ground, where the North and the South meet, lies a few miles above and below the Old National Road; and because it blends the elements of the North and the South, it represents most typically what people think of when they hear the word "Hoosier."

(What that word Hoosier originally meant, by the way, has never been authoritatively established. Some say it is a corruption of the pioneer's greeting from his cabin window—"Who's thar?" Others say it was originally "husher," a giant of a man who could hush anybody in a fight. Still others have discovered a contractor named Samuel Hoosier at Louisville in 1825 who hired only Indiana labor and whose men were consequently called "Hoosier men.")

To get back to the two divisions, Northern Indiana is mostly flat land, rich in industry and agriculture. Chicago and the state of Michigan stand atop it, like the legs of a colossus. Ohio borders it on the east—all the way down to the Ohio River, in fact, but with less influence in the southern region. Illinois borders it on the west. In the thick, urban spread of northwest Indiana, it is impossible to tell where one leaves the Hoosier State and enters Illinois. In the South Bend area, eastward, Michigan's significance in trade and commerce is so great that South Benders call the region "Michiana." In Fort Wayne, in the northeast, one sometimes has the feeling that one has already crossed into Ohio. But the people up here are all Hoosiers, just the same, and they don't like being confused with Suckers, Michiganders and Buckeyes.

Traveling the main lines of the New York Central and Pennsylvania railroads through Northern Indiana, I did not feel a sense of homecoming until I got off the trains and talked with the people; for the towns and cities, in the Calumet region particularly, with their miles and miles of steel mills and other industrial plants bordering Lake Michigan, are strung together as tightly as beads in the Indian wampum that used to pass for currency in the neighborhood.

At the turn of the century, Gary, Indiana, was a desolate, uninhabited waste of sand. In the annual report of the United States Steel Corporation for 1905 appeared a statement by Judge Elbert H. Gary: "It has been decided to construct and put in operation a new plant to be located on the south shore of Lake Michigan in Calumet Township, Lake County, Indiana, and a large acreage of land has been purchased for that purpose." Soon afterward great hills of sand were being pulled down and the sloughs between them filled with silt sucked from the bottom of Lake Michigan. A river was picked up bodily and moved one hundred yards out of the way. A tunnel was driven two miles out under the lake for a water supply. By 1907, there was a crude town on the site, and the site itself was fifteen feet higher above sea level than it had been when the work commenced. Today it is one of the largest cities in the state.

Like Gary, every town and city in the north of Indiana makes something—or many things. Hammond is noted for the manufacture of soap. East Chicago, Indiana, is dominated by Cudahy's giant Dutch Girl. Whiting is headquarters of Standard Oil in Indiana. South Bend, which produces Studebaker cars, retains what is left of Indiana's prestige in the automobile industry—a Hoosier enterprise that once produced not only the Studebaker but also the Premier, National, Stutz, Cole, Marmon, Roosevelt, Duesenberg, Haynes, Apperson, Maxwell, Auburn, Cord, Elcar, Davis, McFarlan, Lexington, Reeves, Lambert, Imp, Revere, Zimmerman, Henderson, Marion, Empire, and Waverly Electric, names which are something for oldsters still to conjure with. But South Bend is also famous now for mint distilling and the football teams of Notre Dame University. In Elkhart, Conn musical instruments are manufactured. Fort Wayne, in the northeast, produces radio-phonograph and television equipment—Capehart-Farnsworth and Magnavox—and is the Indiana home of General Electric and International Harvester. South of it is Muncie, maker of bottles, jars and glasses.

It is unfortunate that this northern train view is the only Indiana many East-West travelers get to know; for from the Pullman windows it must seem little different from parts of Ohio and Illinois. It is no wonder that they ask how the Hoosier can be so staunchly lyrical in his local pride. If only these birds of passage would spend the night in South Bend during the football season, or in Gary during the basketball season, if only they would ride a few miles south and meet a few Indiana farmers when the corn is ripe. But they won't. They're in too big a hurry to get to Chicago or New York.

Or these travelers might delay for a week or a month to take a look at the summer resorts of Indiana, most of which are located in the north. Here, just below and to the east of Lake Michigan, are the famous Indiana Dunes, great wastes of singing sands. This northern landscape, beyond the cities' smokestacks, is also studded with lakes having such mellifluous names as Wawasee, Maxinkuckee, Winona, Shipshewanna, Manitou and Koontz.

I shall never forget how we looked forward to our annual two weeks in this magic northern land when I was a boy. Those were the days of the leather-topped car and goggles and the linen duster. The first hazard of the journey from the south was the Reelsville Hill, but if the car surmounted that obstacle and its passengers survived a night in a country hotel, the second day of driving opened up a new world—a world of tamarack and jack pine and blue water.

It was the blue water that impressed me most. Before my first of such journeys, made when I was six, I could hardly believe my father's descriptions of the lakes, for to me at that time all water was brown, like the waters of the muddy Wabash and Ohio rivers. I recall heralding the appearance of the first blue shimmering water with shouts of ecstasy from the back seat of our Reo.

Steel, soap, automobiles, machinery, nationally respected football teams and blue water they boast of up here in the north above the Old National Road. And corn they grow, too, in abundance. But steel is not this country's king, nor are automobiles, nor blue water, nor even the "four horsemen and seven mules" of Knute Rockne's invention. Nor, indeed, is corn. The king of Northern Indiana—of the whole state, in fact, is a phlegmatic individual who troubles himself not at all over the vicissitudes of economics or the applause of multitudes. He never strikes for higher wages or tries to build monopolies. He doesn't come out with a new model each year. He never worries about new maneuvers that the coaches have devised in Texas or California or Minnesota. And as for water, he much prefers it brown. In fact, only the quality and quantity of Indiana corn interest him, for corn is his inseparable companion.

Concerning this stolid monarch, Logan Esarey has written most eloquently: "We may sing the praises of all the heroes of Indiana from La Salle or George Rogers Clark to the present, but the prosperity of our state . . . has depended on Mr. Hog. In fat years and lean years . . . he has come up with his part, even though he does grunt about it considerably. . . ."

A sharp contrast with the north is Southern Indiana. It is mostly hilly land, rich in scenery and tradition. Kentucky bounds it on the south, but the Ohio River is wide enough to prevent the Blue Grass State from dominating the region as Chicago and Michigan dominate the North. There is a constant and not always friendly feud abrewing between Kentuckians and Southern Hoosiers. In the little town of Newburgh on the Ohio, for instance, the fishermen of the two states are often even on shooting terms with each other.

"I says to them fellers," a Newburgh fisherman told me, describing an encounter with Kentucky wardens who were inspecting his lines, "I says, 'I'm asettin' in my boat on Indiana water and I got a gun in my hands,' I says, 'and they ain't a judge nor jury in the whole state of Indiana would convict me if I happened to have a mind to pull the trigger.'"

When I was home on leave in Evansville during the war, my father illustrated to me not only the Southern Hoosiers' suspicion of Kentuckians but also their peculiar pride and sense of justice.

We were enjoying the pleasant Hoosier custom of sitting on the front porch after supper. From the back of the house, where my mother and sister were working, came the clatter of dishes and the low sound of voices. Up the street, a screened door slammed from time to time, and someone thereabouts was playing Hoagy Carmichael's *Stardust* on a piano. It was late summer, and the locusts in the oaks and maples across the way were droning an antiphonal chorus. Occasionally we heard a throaty blast from a towboat whistle down on the river and the shriek and moan of switch engines out in the C. & E. I. yards by the Dixie Bee Highway.

After a long silence, my father stirred in his place beside me in the swing and said, "You know, we're having a crime wave here in Evansville now."

I made no comment.

"It's these Kentuckians," he continued, "come up to work in our war plants, that are causing all the trouble."

"But, father," I said, "there's always been crime in Evansville."

"I know that, son. I've lived in Southern Indiana all my life, and I know Evansville has always had two or three murders a year. But until these Kentuckians came swarming in here across the river, nobody was ever murdered in this town by somebody he didn't know."

Even before the war, Southern Indiana had its industries. Evansville was the nation's biggest producer of refrigerators for a long time, and it once claimed the largest furniture factory in the world. When I was a boy there, the chorus of factory whistles on cold winter mornings was my favorite music, as I lay abed sniffing the fragrance of frying crullers coming up from my mother's kitchen and listening for her final and peremptory call to me to get up and dress for school.

In recent years, New Albany and Jeffersonville, too, have grown into thriving industrial centers. They now boast a shipyard, a U. S. Army quartermaster depot, and a Government ammunition plant so extensive that when a friend drove me past it at ninety-two miles an hour recently, it took us several minutes to go by. At Lawrenceburg, upriver, the whisky industry has practically rebuilt the town since the 1937 flood. Near Bedford and Bloomington, Indiana limestone is quarried, and Terre Haute is prosperous because of beer and bituminous coal.

But the commerce and industry of Southern Indiana, taken all together, don't begin to compare with the concentration of invested capital in the Gary-Hammond region in the north.

To reach Southern Indiana by rail from the east or west, one uses principally the Baltimore & Ohio and the Louisville & Nashville roads, although the New York Central and the Pennsylvania have main lines as far south as Terre Haute. From the windows of these trains, the view of Indiana is different from what one sees in the north. It is a land of thick forest growth in a tangle of rank, subtropical vines, of hills and hollows and, in winter, flooded bottom lands. To anyone who knows the state, there can be no confusion here as to whether the train is in Indiana, Ohio or Illinois.

But these big transcontinental trains cut across only a corner of Indiana. To have a full view of Hoosierland, north as well as south, one must travel on the Monon.

The Monon, which gets its name from an Indian word meaning "swift-running," is a Hoosier institution. Hoosiers used to say that you took the Monon only if you "wanted to go the worst way," but in recent years it has been streamlined and improved. The Monon now ventures into both Chicago and Louisville, but it is still Indiana's own railroad; in fact, no one is really at home in Indiana until he is able to listen without a smile to the brakeman's chant on a Monon local:

"Crawfordsville and Wabash College! Don't forget your valise and parcels!"

In Southern Indiana the farms are smaller and less productive than those in the north, but the farmhouses—some of them, at least—are more interesting in their architecture. I am remembering now the tall, two-story brick houses, set on knolls in groves of oak or hickory trees, their two front doors offering a double welcome and their front porches as ornate with jigsaw work as the deck of an old-time steamboat.

Behind them are the barn lots flanked by big red barns and a half-dozen leaning sheds, and beyond are man-made muddy ponds, where the stock are watered. The hills fling the fields about like colored banners and are dotted with clumps of trees and an occasional single persimmon under whose branches, in the fall, it is sweet to browse. True, the land in some places is almost completely impoverished by soil erosion; but what these rural Southern Hoosiers lack in profits they make up for in scenery.

As one of them in Pike County told me: "Most of the time I ain't very financial, mister, but I got something to look at when I'm tired." Only he said "tard."

Although the southern portion of the state has few summer resorts because of its excessive heat, there is one playground that is nationally famous. It is the French Lick Springs Hotel, once owned by Thomas Taggart and for years the "Tammany Hall of the Middle West," hidden away in the woods of the Orange County hills. It has seven stories, contains a thousand rooms and twenty-five acres of floor space, and looks like something imported from Atlantic City. Its vast dining room will seat several thousand convening Democrats or insurance men at one time. Surrounding the massive yellow-brick building are 4000 acres of well-trimmed lawn and gardens. And in the front yard are the tracks of the ubiquitous Monon.

Though Brown County is also in Southern Indiana, it belongs to the whole state—to the whole nation, in fact. Brown County characterizes Indiana, although it is a caricature too. Certainly it preserves the aspect and atmosphere of Western pioneer life in America better than any other place I know. I doubt whether many Americans can escape a stirring in their hearts as they travel through the county's settlements of Bean Blossom, Bear Wallow, Needmore and Gnaw Bone.

The countryside here is at its best in the fall, when the foliage is aflame with color and the melancholy haze of Indiana autumn blankets the hills. Persimmons lie rotting on the ground then, and walnuts are scattered through the woods for squirrels to gather and small boys to stain their hands with. Wagons loaded with golden pumpkins creak along the steep roads, and in the fields khaki-colored fodder stands in regimented shocks.

Sounds come softly but with a sharp clarity across the hills at this time of year, like words whispered in the night, and the air is perfumed with hickory smoke threading skyward from the chimneys of log cabins tucked in a hundred hollows.

Probably no one has given more fame and reality to Brown County than Kin Hubbard, creator of the legendary Abe Martin. Hubbard kept his Abe Martin feature alive in the Indianapolis *News* for more than twenty-five years, supplementing it with drawings of the characters involved and their Brown County background; and by so doing he populated Brown County. No one who has followed the doings of these rustic folks—or who follows them today in reprint, many years after Kin's death—can forget Lafe Bud, "traveling representative Red Seal Beer Makings," Tell Binkley, salesman of Florida country-club sites and stick-up insurance; Lemmie Peters, "whose graduation essay *We've Left the Bay and the Ocean Lies Before Us* electrified the community in 1913"; Uncle Ez Pash, "lifelong Democrat"; Miss Fawn Lippincutt, "elocutionist," or Honorable Ex-Editor Cale Fluhart.

The owner of an inn at Nashville in Brown County told me that one day a tourist asked him to direct her to the local five-and-ten.

"We don't have a five-and-ten here, ma'am," he explained to her.

"But you must have!" she protested. "That's where Mrs. Lafe Bud works—at the optometrist counter."

Across the street from the country store is the courthouse, a brick building with an outside iron stairway; and behind the courthouse is the log jail, built in 1837. As long as I can remember, it has been in the custody of an overalled ancient who begins his spiel as soon as a sight-seer appears within fifty yards.

Nashville would not be Nashville without the group of loafers who sit on the "Liars' Bench" on the courthouse lawn, ready at all times to assume studied poses for passing photographers. They add to the scenery and the local color and they inevitably remind me of Abe Martin's remark:

"Some fellers have a way of loafin' that makes 'em look indispensable."

About one sixth of Brown County is owned by the state, preserved in one of the most popular of Indiana's fourteen remarkable state parks. The rest is largely inhabited by painters and writers, who live in log cabins, both original and restored. In the dining room of one of the largest of these cabins, on a rise north of Nashville, hangs the only extant copy of the Nashville *Democrat* that announced the victory of Grover Cleveland and Indiana's own Thomas A. Hendricks in 1884.

"GLORY TO GOD!" reads the headline, in letters half a page high. "DEMOCRACY TRIUMPHANT!"

And the Columbia Club in Indianapolis only fifty miles away!

But that is Indiana. While it is not a house divided against itself, politically it is a house divided within itself. In politics, Hoosiers are not notably orginal or idealistic in their thinking, but they are practical, stubborn and always eloquent. Indiana's history is mainly a story of individuals and the loyalty they have inspired; it is not a story of social movements or struggles for causes. When a Hoosier tells you he is a Democrat or a Republican, it usually means that his father was one before him. Or it may mean that he has a friend in the party whom he would like to see in public office—or that he hankers for office himself.

Take the town of Vincennes, on the Wabash halfway between Terre Haute and Evansville. A great deal of Indiana's history is commemorated there, and this history gives you the Hoosier spirit in a microcosm. It is a story of people very much like the people who still inhabit the state—heroes, practical politicians, opportunists, people easily swayed by histrionics or sentiment, but individualists all.

The first inhabitants of Vincennes were French traders and, later, colonists. They came as early as 1700, possibly earlier. In 1763, they shifted their allegiance from France to England without a qualm. And when Father Pierre Gibault, Francis Vigo, and the Piankeshaw chief, Grand Door of the Wabash, helped George Rogers Clark take Vincennes from the British, the citizens and the soldiers who did that heroic job understood little of the principles involved in the American Revolution. They were merely rallying round men in whose good judgment and courage they had confidence.

William Henry Harrison was the next hero of Vincennes. He came more than a century later than the French, as the first governor after Indiana had become a territory. In a somewhat dubious battle at Tippecanoe, Harrison defeated the great Tecumseh's Shawnees while Tecumseh himself was absent in the South; but neither Harrison's men nor Tecumseh's fully realized that the destruction of local Indian unity at Tippecanoe meant the failure of the Indian cause in the whole Northwest.

The French were in Northern Indiana before they established the post of Vincennes. In fact, the first white man to set foot on Indiana soil was probably Robert Cavelier, Sieur de La Salle, who camped in 1679 near the present site of South Bend. But La Salle did not stay. Like so many Hoosiers today, he had the itching foot.

The only northern town that actually rivals Vincennes in antiquity is Fort Wayne. Here, where the St. Joseph and St. Mary's Rivers unite to form the Maumee, the Miami Indians maintained their headquarters in the distant past. Fort Wayne's history has been, first, one of white and Indian skirmishes and, later, one of steady growth as a major Indiana community. Today, like Vincennes, it preserves its past in markers and monuments rather than relics. Fort Wayne has always seemed to me one of the most modern and progressive and perhaps the most livable cities in the state.

After Clark's victory in the Revolution, the age of the flatboat came to Indiana; and after Harrison's triumph over Tecumseh came the steamboat. Most reminiscent of the steamboat's golden age today is the town of Madison on the Ohio. Many Hoosiers will agree with me, I think, that it is also Indiana's prettiest town.

I drove over to Madison one rainy Sunday recently to revisit some of the sites I had seen for the first time eleven years before, when I was collecting material for my Rivers of America book, *The Wabash*. I went through the James F. D. Lanier mansion, which commands a dramatic view of the Ohio through the pillars of its broad portico, and I saw again the Schofield Mansion and the Shrewsbury House. But I was grieved to discover that the Madison Hotel, designed by Francis Costigan, had disappeared and a chain store had taken its place.

Corydon, some fifteen miles north of the Ohio in Harrison County, is another of my favorite Indiana towns. Indiana's first capitol still stands there. Originally the county courthouse, it became the seat of the state's government in 1816 and remained so until 1825, when newly platted Indianapolis on the National Road took over the honor. Corydon today prefers to remember the battle that was fought at its outskirts in 1863—the only Civil War battle on Indiana soil—when John Hunt Morgan, with his 2500 Confederate raiders, crossed the Ohio River at Mauckport and swept northward. At Corydon, he was met by four hundred home guards, who stood him off for an hour.

In sleepy, quiet Corydon today, people still mention the name of

John Morgan somewhat breathlessly. A lad in a dry-goods store recited to me the story of the battle by rote, as he had learned it from his father or his grandfather. An old-timer on the courthouse lawn paused in his whittling long enough to give me a mischievous wink and say: "Know what my pap used to say when I asked him what he did at the Battle of Corydon? Said, 'Why, boy, I ran like a bat out of hell—jist like ever'body else!'"

It is typical of the Hoosiers that, during the Civil War, although Indiana is geographically a Northern state, they were sharply divided in their sympathies; and especially in Southern Indiana there was strong support for the Confederacy in spite of the fact that Abe Lincoln had spent fourteen years of his youth in the state. Knowing the stubborn perversity of the Hoosier spirit, I am almost tempted to say it was true because of that fact. After all, Lincoln did leave Indiana and move over into Illinois.

In Indiana, Lincoln became a giant in body, under the harsh discipline of pioneer life; he became an independent and idealistic thinker, under the influence of his neighbors, who loaned him books, and of his wonderful stepmother, Sarah Bush Lincoln, who saw him through his growing pains. Every time I visit the Nancy Hanks Lincoln Memorial Park in Spencer County, I am deeply moved by thoughts of those formative years of Abe's in my native state. But I am always somewhat disappointed in the park itself. It is beautiful. It is peaceful. It is noble. But it should be equally dedicated to the memory of Sarah Bush Lincoln, and it should have a monument of some kind honoring those two Hoosier qualities—ambition and neighborly helpfulness—that made Lincoln and so many other native and adopted Indianans great.

Indiana people, with their Southern heritage, have a strong sense of family loyalty as well as devotion to friends, and this may explain both the division within themselves and the united front they present to the outside world. My paternal grandfather, who in his youth drove a stagecoach between Princeton and New Harmony, stopped once in the wilderness to dissuade a man from beating his wife. He did not succeed. Instead, he emerged from the man's cabin in a hurry and with two black eyes—one given to him by the husband and the other administered by the wife. Whenever I think about Indiana history, I remember my grandfather's two black eyes.

In regard to family, I think I was for a time the luckiest kid in the whole state. All my uncles and aunts on my father's side lived in the historic little town of New Harmony on the Wabash, and they owned, among them, the only hotel in the village, its only picture show and its best soda fountain. When I went to New Harmony for the summer to visit my relatives, I was in a small boy's seventh heaven.

My aunts conscientiously took me to see the historic Rappite community houses, dating from 1815, and "Gabriel's footprints," which Father George Rapp said were left on the stone by an angel who came down out of the sky to advise him. They exposed me to lectures at the Workingmen's Institute and to the books in the town's remarkable library. But I must confess that what really meant most to me were old Lizzie's good cooking at the Tavern, the delicacies Cousin Clyde concocted at his soda fountain, and *The Perils of Pauline* at Uncle Gene's movie palace, where I was sometimes allowed to sit in the projection booth.

George Rapp's and Robert Owen's communistic experiments failed at New Harmony, and in the years since, that little town has had a curious history. For almost a century it dozed in quiet isolation. The townsfolk, though proud of their history and hospitable to strangers, looked upon the outside world with a kind of aristocratic haughtiness and no small degree of suspicion.

I remember the annual county fair at the edge of town, the watermelon feasts on Mr. Mumford's spacious lawn, the swimming at the Old Dam, cotillions in the Opera House in winter and dances in Arthur Fretageot's store in summer, and the rattle of Fount Hawkins's horse-drawn hack down Church Street, once a day, bringing a drummer or two to The Tavern from the spur-line railroad. But until the 1920's, New Harmony was content to live in proud memories of its past.

Then oil was discovered in the Wabash river bottoms.

Since that time, people in New Harmony have become rich who never dreamed of being rich, and others have taken a new lease on hope. Since that time, too, New Harmony has attempted to restore and preserve the relics of its past. The first of these attempts was by a state historical commission, which New Harmony soon discovered it did not cotton to. What the town likes much better are the individualistic projects of one of its native sons.

Indiana is always proud of its native sons, especially if they never forget, in their successes, to do right by their parents. Even the bandit Dillinger was forgiven a lot on the banks of the Wabash, because it was said that he was always kind to his folks.

Politics has always been in the Hoosier blood. There is a legend in the state that every baby born within its borders announces to the doctor with its first gasp of Indiana air: "While not seeking public office for myself, I will, if elected, serve my country and my party to the best of my ability." I have asked several Hoosier obstetricians if this is true, and I have never got a straight answer, perhaps because the obstetricians themselves had their eyes on public office.

Indiana claims two residents of the White House in the two Harrisons, although neither was a native of the state. And it has been called "the mother of Vice Presidents" because of the election of Schuyler Colfax, Thomas A. Hendricks, Charles W. Fairbanks and Thomas R. Marshall. In Eugene V. Debs of Terre Haute, it has produced one great political visionary and rebel; in Daniel Voorhees of the same city and Albert J. Beveridge of Indianapolis, two great orators; in Thomas Taggart of French Lick, a master of political organization and backstage planning. More recently, the name of Wendell L. Willkie has honored the scroll of Hoosier men in public life.

In the 1920's, Indiana forgot for a while Abe Martin's observation that "actions speak louder'n lodge jewelry" and, under the guise of "100 per cent Americanism" resuscitated the Ku Klux Klan. The Klan flourished cancerously in the state as it did nowhere else, but eventually the Klan was defeated and disgraced in the public eye.

Besides politicking, Hoosiers have two other traditions that distinguish them—providing their children with good educations and writing books. The one, I think, is responsible for the other.

No graduate of an accredited high school in Indiana today is more than twenty-five miles from an institution of higher learning. And it might be added that a very large proportion of Indiana's high-school graduates attend advanced classes of one sort or another after graduation. Besides Indiana University and Purdue, there are, scattered all over the state, many other colleges, large and small. At South Bend, there is the famous Roman Catholic institution of Notre Dame. At Greencastle, there is the Methodists' DePauw, and nearby, at Crawfordsville, is its ancient Presbyterian rival, Wabash. Franklin, founded by the Baptists, shares its name with the town near Indianapolis where it is situated. The Friends have Earlham at Richmond; the Lutherans, Valparaiso at Valparaiso and Concordia at

Fort Wayne. The Presbyterians have another school at Hanover, whose campus, on a high bluff above the Ohio River, is the most beautiful in the state.

Indiana's age of glory in writing came at the end of the nineteenth century and during the first decades of the twentieth. Those were the days of Lew Wallace, author of *Ben-Hur,* whose home in Crawfordsville is now a Hoosier literary shrine; of George Ade, Purdue's benefactor and one of its heroes; of Meredith Nicholson and Charles Major and Maurice Thompson; of Gene Stratton Porter, whose two homes in the "Limberlost" country have made rivals of the towns of Geneva and Rome City; of David Graham Phillips and finally—and most important in Hoosier minds—of Booth Tarkington and James Whitcomb Riley. During those prolific years, the writing fever was at such a height round Indianapolis that on one occasion a visiting lecturer from the East invited all the writers in his audience to join him on the platform, and the entire gathering swarmed up about him.

James Whitcomb Riley's name seems almost synonymous with the word Indiana. He wrote mainly in Hoosier dialect—and with such deceptive ease that thousands of Hoosiers have imitated him ever since. He wrote in the Hoosier tongue and about the Hoosier countryside in all its seasons, when there was "winter without and warmth within," as well as "wortermelon time" and that loveliest of all Indiana months, October, "when the frost is on the punkin and the fodder's in the shock."

But most important of all, Riley wrote about the pleasures of a Hoosier childhood, and that is what makes him The Hoosier Poet. For in Indiana, childhood is a long, long period of delight—a period so long, in fact, that most Hoosiers never completely outgrow it but retain throughout their lives something of its wide-eyed wonder and enjoyment.

Even Theodore Dreiser, in spite of his poverty on the banks of the Wabash and his later gloomy outlook upon life, had a happy Hoosier childhood. If you don't believe that, read his reminiscences in a rare book entitled *A Hoosier Holiday*. And Dreiser also helped his brother, Paul Dresser, compose the sentimental and nostalgic words of that famous Hoosier song, "On the Banks of the Wabash, Far Away."

Since Riley's time, there have been few Indiana writers whose works have been typically Hoosier, although there have continued to be plenty of Indiana writers. It seems hardly possible, for instance, that the sophisticated wit of George Jean Nathan is that of an Indiana man, yet it is. Lloyd Douglas demonstrates a certain preoccupation with the Golden Rule common among Hoosiers, but common also among Americans everywhere. Jessamyn West has artistically portrayed life among the Friends who inhabited the Whitewater Valley a generation ago, but Miss West left Indiana at the age of six, and lives now in California. The late Will Cuppy revealed his Hoosier background in his sense of humor, but it was not typically Hoosier like George Ade's or Kin Hubbard's. Jeanette Covert Nolan of Indianapolis is one of the very few Hoosiers I think of who have used Hoosier themes and at the same time remain in the state. The late Ernie Pyle, of course, was the only Hoosier writer of recent vintage who remained all Hoosier, wherever he went.

In other creative arts, Indiana has excelled chiefly in entertainment—on the radio and the stage and in the writing of popular music. It has produced three renowned composers in Paul Dresser, Cole Porter and Hoagy Carmichael; and in the theater it can boast of such stars as John Olson of Olson and Johnson, Joe Cook, Louise Dresser, Charles Butterworth and Red Skelton. To radio newsbroadcasting it has given several distinguished commentators—among them Elmer Davis, Edwin C. Hill and Claude Mahoney.

It is impossible to talk about Indiana without mentioning names. The state has probably produced more people who get into the news than any other region in the country. Indianans are more interested in people than in anything else. It is a part of their state pride.

Hoosier pride is a peculiar thing; it is not exclusively a pride in the size, the scenery, the antiquity or the climate of the state. It is more like the pride of a man in his home or the house he was born in. He is willing to admit that it may not be the best house in the block. He may even choose not to live in it any longer and he will grant that some members of his family have done wrong and deserve what they got. But he loves that house and that family, and the man who disparages them is in danger of losing his hide.

Indiana combines so many elements and traditions that it can appeal to the taste of Americans of all ages and backgrounds. It blends the Southerner's love of gracious living with the Yankee's industry and devotion to culture, and it assimilates foreign blood and foreign customs quickly, easily and hospitably.

As a result, Indiana strikes a homely American average in most aspects of life. The Lynds chose Muncie as the model for the famous *Middletown,* and even that other exhaustive study of human averages, the Kinsey Report, came out of Indiana. So comfortably American is this state that the most forgotten of all America's forgotten men was a Hoosier—Whistler's father.

Ohio

by BENTZ PLAGEMANN

Ohio is the younger brother who stayed home. When the others had gone off, in search of adventure or fortune in the great world, Ohio is the brother who married the girl next door, raised a family, took care of the old folks, and inherited the family homestead when they died.

No one ever came to Ohio to look for gold. No one even came to Ohio to look for the legendary pot of gold at the end of the rainbow, or stayed there long if he carried the burden of great, impossible dreams. Ohio is the state of middle dreams, the state of normalcy, where it is always eight o'clock on Monday morning, and the factory whistle is blowing, and the school bell is ringing.

Ohio is neither East nor West nor South. It just sits where it is, and never shouts to make itself heard—it just speaks on in its calm, flat, unregional, unaccented, uninflected voice. But what Ohio says in that voice, and what it has said in the past, has affected you, for better or worse, and even whether you like it or not.

Orville and Wilbur Wright built their first airplane, the one they flew at Kitty Hawk, in a bicycle shop in Dayton, Ohio. The Women's Christian Temperance Union began in Hillsboro, Ohio.

Ohio was like that from the very beginning. An engineer and a minister helped organize the Ohio Company in 1786: Gen. Rufus

Putnam, and Dr. Manasseh Cutler. "No colony in America was settled under more favorable auspices," George Washington said gravely, when the sound, practical businessmen of the Ohio Company set out for the wilderness with their titles, deeds, and the patents signed by the Continental Congress. No claim jumping. No land grabbing. No hysteria. "I know many of the settlers personally," Washington added, "and there never were men better calculated to promote the welfare of a community." Welfare and community, strange words for frontier days. And then that word "promote." You hear those three words a lot in Ohio even today. And around Urbana, you can still find descendants of Richard Stanhope, the faithful Negro valet who was with Washington when he died, and who was given his freedom and four hundred acres in the new territory in return for his service.

The first professional baseball team in the country was organized in Ohio. The Red Stockings. They still play. The Cincinnati Reds won every game that first season, 1869.

You might almost say that Ohio wasn't settled; it was developed. It was never really what you might call pioneer country, and in answer to any protests I hasten to point out that the famous *Madonna of the Trail,* the statue of the pioneer woman put up by the Daughters of the American Revolution beside the old National Road near Springfield, Ohio, is walking west, and walking fast—*out* of Ohio. She was undoubtedly the wife of one of those restless, incautious men who weren't satisfied with a piece of land back East, or even out in Ohio. He wanted that pot of gold at the end of the rainbow. He was no Ohio man.

But go back a little way and you'll find the place where the Foos Tavern stood. Griffith Foos was a real Ohio man. He knew what he wanted.

Ohio was a business venture among many other things. It was that tavern, the Foos Tavern, on the old trail West at the end of the National Road; the Last Chance where you unhitched the horses, and the women and children got down from the Conestoga wagons. Ohio was the last warm meal, the last glass of ale at a bar, the last night's sleep in a bed. Ohio was the sensible, ruddy man behind the cash till in the tavern, and the mill where the flour was ground for the bread, and the dry-goods store down the street, and the tinner, and the wheelwright, and the grocery store.

In Dayton, Ohio, James Ritty built his "Incorruptible Cashier," the genesis of the National Cash Register Company. In a woodshed in that same city, Charles Kettering put together his first self-starter, possibly the most typical of all Ohio inventions. You don't have to be told about Thomas Edison of Milan, Ohio, and the light that didn't fail; or Charles Brush of Cleveland, who started the electrical industry with his arc light; or Dietrich Gruen, tinkering with his watches; and Rudolph Wurlitzer with his pianos and organs; and William Proctor and James Gamble building the biggest soap factory in the world, in a state where cleanliness is still next to godliness. Andrew Jergens made a pretty good thing out of his lotion, as Earl Sloan of Zanesville did with his liniment.

They taught me in school that Ohio is the mother of Presidents. (In Virginia, I understand, they teach differently.) There were seven of them. You remember what Grant looked like, but you might say he was an exception. The others were Hayes and Garfield, the last President to be born in a log cabin, and Harrison and McKinley and Taft and Harding; four lawyers and a schoolteacher and a newspaper publisher. A faded memory of beards and business operations. Our own Robert Taft was almost President. Toward the end they called him Mr. Republican. They might well have called him Mr. Ohio. He possessed to an almost classical degree the virtues prized most highly in Ohio: to work hard and mind your own business, never to abandon your convictions no matter who attacks you, or how deluded they try to make you out to be, never to get excited. Robert Taft couldn't understand why the people didn't want him to be President, but he died without making any fuss about it.

William Holmes McGuffey wrote his famous Readers *at Miami University in Oxford, Ohio. What the McGuffey* Readers *taught is still bred in Ohio bones: the virtue of hard work; the sure reward of that virtue.*

The bounty of Lake Erie presses down on the top of Ohio, and the state bends with its weight, and at the bottom the river flows, the Beautiful Ohio, where the moonlight glows, where the barges float by, carrying the hard-earned wealth down to the great Mississippi. Ohio stands straight between its straight borders, plain and full of common sense.

A lot of people came here and stayed awhile, or moved on, or were taken in, but Ohio doesn't change. It's like the old homestead where now the younger brother lives with his family. There isn't much style about the old house—Ohio has always been a little suspicious of style —but it's in excellent condition, and in the spring, when the rains come, the lilac still blooms in the dooryard. Inside in the parlor where the shades are drawn so the sunlight won't fade the Brussels carpet you will find all of the old treasures and curiosities of the house. The magnificent Greek Revival homes with their Adams doorways dream on the commons of the New England villages of the Western Reserve. The Shaker chairs are there, and the old houses where the slaves hid on their way to Canada and freedom in the dark night of the Civil War. The Underground Railway, they called it. The Indian Mounds are there, and the monument to Perry at Put In Bay in Lake Erie. "Don't Give Up the Ship," the banner said. The Mormon Temple at Kirtland is there, the stucco of its surface struck into fire by the setting sun, on the far hill where it stands. The women brought their china and glass to be ground in with the sand and pebbles so it would catch the sunlight.

Platt R. Spencer's tombstone is there, in Geneva, with his name carved on it in the style of handwriting he developed and which everyone in the country once had to learn. The Spencerian Hand: "the tip of the little finger and the ball of the hand touching the surface of the desk as the loops are made." The monument to Betty Zane is there, the girl who carried the gunpowder in her apron.

The curiosities and the treasures are there, but no one pays undue attention to them. Very few people look to the past in Ohio. They'd rather take you outside and show you the improvements, and you will probably have to ride into town to see the post office and the new junior high school and the latest factory.

The Standard Oil Company was begun in Ohio. John D. Rockefeller once gave me a bright new dime when we got off the streetcar together at the same stop on Euclid Avenue in Cleveland. I took it home and put it in my bank. I was a very small boy, but I was an Ohio boy. I hadn't wanted to take the dime, because I hadn't done anything to earn it, but I supposed you had to humor people when

they got old and careless with their money. "Little boys are never
tired," my grandmother said to me one hot summer Ohio day, when
I came in from play and threw myself on the sofa in the back
parlor. I was up and out again, mowing the lawn, before I had time
to bounce. I got a much more respectable dime for that.

You sleep well in Ohio, your brother's house. You know you are
safe there. Everything is under control. The foundation of the old
house is dry and sound, and the roof is good, and the flashing and
the drain spouts and the insulation are checked every year, and the
storm windows are up if it is winter, or the screens in summer, and
it is all so clean, in a favorite Ohio phrase, that you could eat off the
floor.

How proud they would be if they could see it now, the men who
made Ohio what it is! They knew what they wanted when they came
to Ohio, my great-grandfather, and the great-grandfathers of my
neighbors. You can come and look at it, but when you look at it you
must remember clearly that what you see is what they wanted for
their children.

The towns are all beginning to look very much alike now. There
is an airport on the outskirts, and near that there is a development
of new houses, all very much the same. The horizon is smoked with
the factory chimneys, and in town you will find that every Main
Street is the same. There is a J. C. Penney store, and a Woolworth's,
an A&P supermarket, a Sears and Roebuck order office, and a Sohio
station on the corner with its wide apron of cement washed down
and its pumps gleaming, and the young man who works there is leaning on the door of a convertible, talking to a pretty girl. There is a
Bell Telephone office, a Light and Power Company office, a Western
Union office, a Hook and Ladder Company, a Police Station, and a
YMCA with a sign out in front, in winter, telling you when the next
basketball game will be held. There is a movie theater, and if you
want to drive a short distance you can go to the next town, because
the same picture will be showing there.

And afterward, when the picture is finished, and the stores are
closed and their windows are darkened, the light will spill out from
the corner drugstore and you will hear the juke box playing in there,
and the laughter of young people, Ohio's children. They are loved
and cared for, Ohio's children.

The 4-H Club Movement was begun in a basement room in the courthouse in Springfield, Ohio; and the Community Chest was a Cleveland idea. Every year the big thermometer stands on the corner of Ninth and Euclid in Cleveland, in front of the Cleveland Trust Bank, and it stands there like the conscience of its citizens until the red marker climbs to the level they have set for themselves for contributions.

The men who came to Ohio were not the "Pike's Peak or Bust!" men, or the "California, Here I Come!" men. They were farmers and shopkeepers and shoemakers and tavernkeepers and tinkerers, and they didn't count on miracles; they asked only for the land's bounty and equal opportunity for all. They were sound men who respected themselves and who knew what they wanted for their children. Well, they got it. They succeeded. It's all here now. This is what Ohio is. And this is what you must keep in mind when you look at Ohio today.

Let us begin with the pretty girls of Ohio, with their thin, light skin; so fair, often, that the small veins show blue at the temples. (This is to be a very unconventional tour of Ohio, as you can see.) But you imagine, after a while, that you would know an Ohio girl anywhere, with her alternate directness of manner and her shyness —unrelated to coquetry—and the charm of her matter-of-fact way.

Ohio girls don't use the circumstance of their sex in the ordinary exchanges of living, and perhaps that is why they are direct one moment and shy the next, as if they recall unexpectedly now and then that they are women, too, as well as human beings. In Ohio, at a social evening, the men talk together and the women talk together, and if any sustained mixed conversation is required of them they seek each other out afterward with a kind of relief. You will think of that in towns like Youngstown, where the women hurry along the city streets, usually alone, carrying a package or a shopping bag, and probably a list in their pocket, half completed.

The young men of Youngstown, on the other hand (or for Youngstown read Warren, or Canton, or Akron, or Mansfield), the young men wear a very different air as they stroll the streets between shifts at the mill, or during the slack periods when they are laid off. They walk with the unconscious arrogance of admitted lords of the universe in twos or threes or fours, advancing abreast down the sidewalk, so that the hurrying women with the shopping bags must pass close to the shop windows where the mohair living-room sets, and the dinner china with garlands of flowers stamped on a cream-colored background are displayed under the neon signs. They seem unaware of each other, the men and the women, and the young men, walking, or stopping to talk in groups, are loud and uninhibited. But, oh, the sweet, shy, pretty girls, with the clear, white skin, and the fine, light hair. "My land!" you hear one say, as she runs into a friend on the street. "My land, what are you doing here?" And if you are Ohio born you feel a quickening of the blood at that old, familiar phrase. My land, where the men work hard at their jobs, and the women work hard at theirs, and where they meet, the men and the women, and where they are fulfilled, through their children.

Houses are women's things in Ohio, and everything in them is a woman's own, from the paper on the walls, and the furniture, and the rugs, and the pictures, down to the china spoonholder, shaped like a flower, on the stove, where you put the spoon down after you have stirred the broth. You can almost feel that nothing in the history of the world has ever been as clean as these Ohio houses, with their waxed floors, and vacuum-cleaned rugs, and the piece of paper placed on the linoleum inside the kitchen door, to catch any dirt that is on your shoes when you come in the back door; and everything in the whole house picked up and put away, with the newspapers tied in bundles for the Boy Scouts to collect, and the windows washed on the outside, and the curtains laundered and ironed and put back up the very same day.

It is seven-thirty of an evening at the Inn in Oberlin. The members of the Chamber of Commerce, in meeting, have just finished their dinner: fruit cup, breaded veal cutlet, apple pie, and coffee, and now they have settled back for the speaker, after listening to The Barber Shop Quartette sing Back Home in Indiana, *and* Lady of Spain. *The speaker of the evening is a Cleveland department store executive, a typical Ohio citizen, treasurer of his local March of Dimes. The title of his speech is "The Customer Is Always Right." The wife of the president of the Chamber of Commerce is distressed about the audience. "The wives were invited tonight," she explains, "but most of them were too exhausted by their spring housecleaning to come. Of course you couldn't hold your head up in this town if you didn't turn out your house in the spring."*

Oberlin is a college town. Oberlin College was one of the first colleges in America to accept Negro students, but in some ways it is even more significant that Oberlin was the first college in the world —repeat, first college in the world—to accept women students on an equal basis with men students.

Which leads us to the reflection that Columbus, Ohio, produced James Thurber, possibly as a demonstration of the impartiality and balance of nature. Mr. Thurber has devoted his years to curbing the excesses of college-educated women, much as, in nature, the hummingbird keeps us from being overwhelmed by gnats.

It was in Oberlin, too, that Mrs. William Stevenson, wife of the new college president, had to be gently and tactfully told after her arrival that it was considered rather pretentious to allow the maid to answer the telephone if it rang while she was at home herself. "Just let it ring until you get to it yourself," she was told.

The world of the men of Ohio is the world outside. You see them, on Saturdays or Sundays, or in the early evenings, the young husbands and family men, in their old faded Army or Navy clothes, endlessly occupied in all the yards of all the new houses. "They say you're lucky if you've got a good lawn by the time the house is paid for," says young Jim Freeman of Springfield, a Navy veteran, a fireman, working outside on his day off from the Engine House. "We've got good drainage here," he says. "No basement problem. And we changed the floor plans two feet out on the side to give Barbara more closet space," he adds, looking with pride at the garden patch ready for spading, now that spring is here, and at the clothesline poles he put up for Barbara, and at the stacked screens, ready to be put up now that the storm windows can come down.

If the lives of men and women together in Ohio seem sketched out in terms of black and white, without nuance, it is well to remind one's self that Ohio is an industrial state, and that there is always that whistle blowing at dawn. You imagine the young married women at their dressing tables at night, scarcely looking at themselves in the mirror as they take off the make-up, their husbands already in bed and the alarm clocks, set, beside them. Tomorrow night they may all go shopping at the new suburban shopping center, to buy food for the week, or spring clothes, or a new television chair; Jim and Barbara and Cindy and little Joey, happy people, having come to their own terms with life, the parents possessing, in exchange for their hopes and dreams and aspirations, what are surely the healthiest, and the best fed and dressed, and the most indulged children in the world.

But let us look at some of the towns and cities. Let us take as our point of departure Sandusky, that port west of Cleveland on Lake Erie, because it is pleasant there, and if you know New England it will seem familiar to you. The Marblehead Peninsula is rather like Cape Cod, and you cross to it over the water from Bay Bridge to Danbury. There are islands in the bay, and small boats dance on the clear blue waters in the spanking breeze, but in spite of the familiar names there is something alien to New England here, and suddenly you know what it is. This is fresh water, this vast inland sea stretching away to the horizon, and instead of the taste of salt in the air there is a clear, cool, woodland scent.

This is wine country too. In the commercial wine cellars of the city you can see casks which have been in use since the middle of the last century. Not all of the wine cellars are in the city. You can take a boat out to Kelleys Island, or Middle Bass (where the clubroom of the winery is called "The Silenium"), and sit in cool, dark comfort and sample the local product.

Sandusky is a German city, with its brisk air and parks and churches in gray native stone, and the beer is excellent in the restaurants where the good lake fish is served, walleyed pike, and bass, and yellow perch, fresh from the water. The sweet dessert wines are good, the muscatel, and Tokay, and white port. If you want wine, incidentally, you go to the corner drugstore, where you will find the bottles displayed along with the tooth paste and the headache remedies. To buy hard liquor you go to a state store and fill out a form which even asks for your name and address.

East of Sandusky you skirt along the lake shore, seeing the white caps of the waves through the sand dunes and the groves of trees. You cross Old Woman Creek where the rare American lotus grows, its chinalike flower rising on a snaky stem some six or eight inches above the flat green leaves. You cross the Vermilion River, named for the color of the clay in its banks, where the Indians came to paint their faces for war. You are in the country of the Western Reserve now, east as far as the Pennsylvania line, and south to a line just below Akron. The Connecticut people came here, and many a hidden village on a back road, with its dark, blind, old Greek Revival houses facing on elm-shaded commons, is more Connecticut now than Connecticut itself.

The Western Reserve is the architect's and the amateur historian's paradise, a region of America waiting to be discovered by the traveler; where every village has its unrecorded history and its tales and legends passed down from memory to memory. Through towns bearing such names as Norwalk and North Fairfield and New London, you drive in the "Firelands," a tract of land set aside originally for the people of Connecticut whose homes were burned by the British during the Revolution. Good dairy land, where the Classical Revival farmhouses bear the signature of their architects in such unusual details as recessed second-story porches, and fretwork on porticos and pilasters; outlined at night against the setting sun on land flat as the Texas Panhandle, lonely and austere, waiting for a Marquand to record their almost forgotten tales.

The Firelands are only a part of the Western Reserve; all of Northern Ohio bears the stamp of New England, and if you go on, northeast, beyond Cleveland, to Painesville and Willoughby and Mentor, you will find examples of the work of the architect Jonathan Goldsmith, houses whose pillared façades might well serve as a backdrop for O'Neill's *Mourning Becomes Electra*. The blood runs thin in some of these towns, and there is ancestor worship here as pious as any in Massachusetts, where Archibald Willard's *The Spirit of '76* (said to be the most reproduced painting in America) hangs in Abbott Hall, Marblehead, although Mr. Willard himself lived and is buried in Wellington, Ohio, and painted his picture there, in the Western Reserve. (He began it as a cartoon, he said, to be called *Yankee Doodle*, but when he had posed his models an "inspired look" came over their faces, he reported, and he himself was inspired to a solemn and heroic approach.)

Fragments of old stories, and the testimony of lost causes and faded dreams tempt you to turn aside at every corner in the Western Reserve. John Brown's body lies amolderin' in the grave, but his soul goes marching on in Northern Ohio. They will point out the graves of his mother and father to you in Hudson, that jewel of a village in Summit County where the old Academy is, arrested in time, with great elm trees shading the fine old Federal and Greek Revival buildings of soft red brick. John Brown lived in Hudson for twenty-one years; and down in Oberlin they talk of him still, and of their own native son, the Negro killed at Harpers Ferry. Or, in search of stories and the echoes of lost passions, go to Tallmadge, near Akron, where the magnificent Congregational Church stands on the common. The church was built in 1825, but before the church was built, Delia Bacon was born there, in 1811, that wonderful eccentric who died mad after she had succeeded in setting the whole literary world on its ear with her sudden conviction that William Shakespeare hadn't written all those plays after all, but two or three other men, including someone of her own name.

You have to go nearer to Cleveland to see the sustained vigor of the old blood, where a combination of natural resources and water transportation and Yankee enterprise built the fortunes and the manor houses on the heights above the city, and east of that, in the Chagrin River Valley, where blooded horses take the jumps in the paddocks, and where the polo fields glow softly like old, rubbed velvet.

It is Thursday night of the Symphony Season in Cleveland. In the quiet passages of the symphony the audience is so still in its uphol-stered seats in the muted house that you imagine you can almost hear the whistles of the freighters as the ore is brought into the twisted Cuyahoga, or the creaking of the cranes over the coal barges as the night sky is stained by a great sudden flare of light from the mills. After the concert when the audience goes home, it is not to the Goldsmith houses of their ancestors, but possibly to the Norman or Tudor houses of Shaker Heights, with their leaded, mullioned windows, and the half-timbering, and the windows opening out onto gardens, and onto streets named Winchester, or Westchester, or Eaton, or Mannering; or to a "Lane," or a "Place."

The people of wealth, who form the society of Cleveland and the Western Reserve, are a responsible group, bred in the tradition of obligation. They do not wear hair shirts under their discreetly tai-lored clothes, it is true; they do themselves well, and possibly even better than is apparent to the eye, since the key for people of wealth almost everywhere in Ohio is understatement. Ostentation has al-ways been regarded as vulgar. The Livingstons and Hannas, the Eatons and Hoyts and Ingalls, the Wicks and the descendants of Cotton Mather do not produce younger sons given to drinking cham-pagne out of slippers, but over the years they have learned the practice, in their own discreet way, of what Thorstein Veblen called conspicuous consumption. The mansard-roofed Gothic houses of Mil-lionaires Row on Euclid Avenue in Cleveland have long been aban-

doned for Shaker Heights, or for the comfortable life modeled on
the life of the English country squire, in the rambling white frame
houses with their barns and rolling meadows in the villages of Hunting Valley and Gates Mills along the Chagrin.

A young man of society may waste his substance in hunting and
polo, or in the somber, elegant rooms of the soot-darkened Union
Club in town, as long as he turns up on Monday morning, clear-eyed
and shrewd, at his office in the Hanna Building, or the Union Commerce Building or the Terminal Tower; and as long as he takes his
place, and works at it, on the boards of the social agencies and charities, or the civic improvement groups, or the school boards, or the
Symphony Society, or the Art Museum.

Equal responsibility is demanded of the young society matron,
who is trained from the very beginning to take her place in the activities of the Junior League in no superficial way. She is expected
to work, on the hospital committees, or the nursing committees, or on
whatever necessary project is at hand, before she can relax with tennis or golf or garden-club activities.

The character of Cleveland society is, in its way, the character of
the people of the state. Many of the great fortunes were made by
men of background, conditioned to the uses and abuses of money.
They brought their ideals of behavior with them; they set the tone
in their manner of living for the others who followed. They do not,
even today, lust after false gods; they waste no time in idle envy
or emulation of New York or café society. It is a relaxed society, and
not a closed one. The mere making or possession of money is no
entree, but neither are doors closed to newcomers if they learn to
take their place gracefully in the accepted, conservative, responsible
pattern.

The firmly established, largely early German society of Cincinnati
has experienced fewer changes and less influx of outside influence
over the years, and for this reason it may be less flexible than society
elsewhere in Ohio, and possibly even more comfortable in its way,
with its combination of German *Gemütlichkeit*, and Southern graciousness and warmth. Newcomers to the city used to have it explained to them that "the Vanderbilts and the Astors of Cincinnati
are the Schmidlapps and the Hickenloopers." German names still
figure largely in Cincinnati society, although the German families no
longer live in their wonderful "*Sauerbraten* Byzantine" houses in
town.

Wealthy Cincinnatians have moved out to Indian Hill, or to the beautiful prospect above Eden Park, although the social life still revolves around the old, sprawling Country Club, which now sits with its rolling greens almost in the center of town. Here, too, the emphasis for social acceptance is on community responsibility. The Taft family, among others, has set a worthy example for years, and the Family Service Society of Cincinnati recently celebrated seventy-five years of service.

To write of society in Ohio, with a capital S, is a doubtful and rather awkward undertaking. The word is seldom heard in Ohio. The boundaries and the standards of behavior and the code of ethics of Ohio society exist only by tacit agreement, and if it is examined too closely it is likely to vanish, up a dozen avenues of laughter and astonished denial. For responsible as it is, discreet as it is in its activities and its pattern, it risks, knowingly, the disapproval of the defiantly plain, no-nonsense citizens who make up the major part of the state, and who mistrust a broad "a" more than they might mistrust a possibly counterfeit bill. Cleveland is cosmopolitan, and Cincinnati is cosmopolitan, and society there pays a certain penalty for its effort to live in a more fashionable world, or even for the rewards of trying to live in a larger world.

"Sometimes Cleveland acts as if it doesn't belong to Ohio at all," they will tell you in Columbus, or points south of Cleveland. The sons and daughters of wealthy Cleveland families are often sent East to be educated in New England boarding schools, or Ivy League colleges, "but anyone who has gone to an Eastern boarding school, or has a degree from a big Eastern college," they will say, "has a distinct disadvantage here." Towns and cities like Springfield and Columbus and Middletown and Dayton sit stubborn and foursquare on their old foundations, each feeling itself to be unique and self-sufficient, suspicious of the wary visitor, ready with a convenient chip for the shoulder if necessary, every man a king.

There are sections of these cities, and of cities such as Mansfield and Chillicothe and Zanesville and Washington Court House, which have a certain chauvinistic, 19th Century character, with dark, old, eclectic buildings under crenelated false fronts, and with cast-iron pilasters and pediments, and a Gothic-Victorian flavor. Civil War monuments stand in squares, and there are cast-iron fountains in parks, and iron urns filled with geraniums, standing amid plantings of canna lilies or yucca.

Here and there is evidence of some knowledge of a larger world beyond, often brought home to Ohio by the boys who have gone out to war; although it is difficult to account for the occasional "Latin Lounges"—the bars, lighted softly at night, where the boys in the black suède shoes woo the pretty girls with the fair skin, generally in groups of four or six, so that the courtship can be carried on with the comfort and support of one's friends. But you can dine in "Streets of Paris" cafés; and in hotel rooms all over the state you will find framed water-color prints after Dufy, the bright vigor made quaint, with top-hatted gentlemen and women in hoop skirts on the Paris dream streets.

Ohio is not the Middle West, as some deluded Easterners persist in thinking, but it may be that the Middle West begins here. In many respects Ohio is still the Last Chance Town, the place where you are supposed to get down from the stage, and change from your fancy clothes, and begin to talk and act like a natural man. Charles Dickens noted this, in his ill-tempered travels of 1842. Stopping at Colt's Exchange Hotel in Sandusky (it still stands; it is just down the street from the Dorn Winery, facing the lake), he wrote in his journal that the proprietor of the hotel "constantly walked in and out of the room with his hat on . . . and lay down on our sofa, and pulled his newspaper out of his pocket; and read it at his ease; I merely mention these traits as characteristic of the country . . ." An entry which still has the power to amuse the people of Ohio, who thought that Mr. Dickens ought to have known when he was being deliberately baited.

The old republican principles are still deliberately and defiantly practiced in Ohio, and the visitor will regard them as acts of ignorance or boorishness at his own peril. In Chillicothe today, for example, when a man alone hails a taxicab, the driver will open the door to the front seat beside him as he pulls up to the curb. He is not a chauffeur; he is a man doing a job. And you'd better look at him, too, before you decide to tip him. He may not like it; just as any man in Ohio may not like it if you call him by his first name too quickly. It is well to remember here the 18th Century dignity of "Mister," that democratic title which removed the "Esq." from the address on letters, and brought every man up to the same level.

But speaking of democratic and republican virtues, the practice of politics is still highly respected in Ohio. In the fine old State House in Columbus, where the battle flags are furled, with their frayed edges protected by black netting as they stand in the lighted cases, and where a plaque in memory of Andrews' Raiders is fixed to one wall, and where the enormous painting by Powell of Perry's victory at Lake Erie, familiar to all school children, hangs over the east stairway, a kind of mystical quality can almost be felt in the corridors.

Ohio is conservative, conservative, conservative. Ohio is so conservative it sometimes hardly seems to be breathing. You look in vain through almost any Ohio paper for adequate coverage of national or world news. "But it isn't really indifference," perceptive Ohioans will tell you. "Since Robert Taft died," they say, their tone suddenly empty with that genuine sense of loss with which one might speak of a death in one's own family, "we are waiting. We are waiting for our leadership in national and world affairs."

It is night in Columbus, the State Capital, and at the Gayety Burlesque, Miss "Tiny" Burns, "petite, saucy and lovable," the posters say, is doing her grinds and bumps. The dusty, faded old house is almost empty. About forty in the audience, young people, boys and girls together in a group out for a laugh, and a few old creeps. Over at the Deshler-Hilton Hotel a contingent of businessmen has just arrived on a late train for the beginning of a convention in the morning. They have all been given Mexican straw hats with untrimmed edges, and name plates to pin on their lapels. They stand by the elevators, waiting, serious and tired looking, holding the Mexican hats and the name plates absently. As the bellhop picks up the men's bags he looks at the luggage labels carefully and addresses each man by name.

The Pickaway Plains lie south of Columbus, and if you cross them at dusk, where the Scioto flows between its willow-shaded, dreamlike banks, you can almost imagine what this wonderful farm country looked like in the old days when it glowed with the campfires of eight Shawnee villages. You want to forget now that this is bloody land, fought for tenaciously, and that the Logan elm still stands, under which that Mingo chief stood to deliver his famous lament. "Who is there to mourn for Logan?" he said, after his family had been killed by the whites. "Not one."

You cross the Pickaway Plains to get to Chillicothe from Columbus, but if you go to Chillicothe with the memory of its romantic past you are doomed to disappointment. Chillicothe was settled by

Virginia aristocrats, and before the 18th Century had ended there
were bookshops in Chillicothe, with stock from London and the East,
and there were carriages on the streets, and fine houses with win-
dowpanes of glass brought over the mountains.

Some of the old houses still stand, in the city, and on the hills
around, but there are different émigrés in the city now, men who
have come from the South with their families to work on the new
atomic plant going up down on the road to Portsmouth and the river;
enterprising men in an enterprising community, who shame you for
wanting the city to have preserved more of its outlived past. But
you can go to "Adena," if you like, the country house designed by
Latrobe, and completed for Thomas Worthington in 1807, on a hill
northwest of the city. The Duke of Saxe-Weimar visited there, and
the Henry Clays came every summer, and Chief Tecumseh dined in
the State Dining Room, and from this house, the legend goes, after
a night of conversation and cards, Worthington and his friends
stepped out into the cool morning air to see the sun rise over Mount
Logan, and took it at that moment to grace the Seal of the new
state. A good story, but unfortunately the house wasn't finished then.

Now "Adena," like Williamsburg, has been restored within an inch
of its life, to an arbitrary point which probably never existed in its
history, but you leave it with a sense of loss, and go back down toward the city, as the sun strikes its blind, sterile windows. The city
is dominated by the magnificent Court House, built of honey-colored
freestone in 1855, a Greek Revival structure with a superb portico,
and with Mayan touches in the decoration of the stone lintels over
the doors, and other detail so incisive and exquisite that from a distance the whole effect is rather like that of intaglio carving in a gem.
Giants walked this land once, you think; and where are they now,
the men with the vision who made this land?

The director of the Ross County Historical Society gave me the answer to that. "The vision is still here," he said, and from another hill
above the city he pointed out the Mead Paper Plant below, constructed over a prehistoric stream. "For the water they need in their
production of paper they have tapped a river buried long ago under
the glacial moraine," he says. "Ohio is like that, taking its strength
from its buried past."

With these thoughts of the past which, in Ohio, always lead back
to the present, you think of Youngstown again, that apotheosis of
mill towns, a city where almost nothing is beautiful except those

things built by men without any consideration of beauty. The steel mills spread through the valley of the Mahoning like a great shout of masculine defiance, looking, to the uninitiated, with their retorts and caldrons and condensers, like the dream of a mad scientist, and at night the sky of the city is bathed in a clear, cold, flickering light, intense but, at the center of the city, soundless, like a stage effect without thunder for the death of the gods. Even with the blind pulled, the hotel room is bathed in the thin, insistent light of the Bessemer converter, and if you look out you will see in this light torches of flame spurting into the sky, waste gases burning, and other waste gases ascending as smoke.

It is like a symbol of the melting pot itself, you think, and on the streets of the city the faces of the hurrying women and the confident men are new and raw and almost, it seems, without features; difficult to trace or place by racial background. Polish, Czech, Greek, Italian, Serb and Yankee; all are merging into a new visage, a face of light skin and clear flesh, with high color in the cheeks, but with the features still unformed, as if the stamp of the new race had not yet emerged from the soft, mixed clay.

The new race is largely a people without consciousness of background, or even of continuity in history, living on the buried past, living in the sound old house, but having, for the most part, cut themselves off from the abandoned patterns of their fathers. They face only to the future, and they must make up their new ways as they go along, but they possess for this a tremendous wealth of vitality as intense as the heat of the Bessemer converter in which the molten metal is cleansed. Everything they do is new, the clothes they wear, the way they hold their forks when they eat, even their speech, long lost from its Anglo-Saxon source. They do not know themselves yet, and they need isolation in which to develop, an isolation for which they are sometimes criticized. Other than that, in the stubborn old tradition of this Republic, they ask for nothing for themselves. The voice of Ohio is seldom raised outside of its own boundaries, and they are content to have it that way.

PART IV *The Mid South*

Washington, D.C.

by ROGER ANGELL

One spring not too long ago, my wife and I made a trip south to inspect a piece of riverbank real estate of which we are part owners. Along with several hundred thousand of our fellow deed holders, we passed a pleasant April week inspecting our property—asking questions of our tenants and foremen, taking down familiar books from the library shelves, refreshing our memory of old monuments on the estate and admiring the new outbuildings, rereading cherished family letters, and even poking about in the attic. It turned out to be a good idea, this week of rediscovery. We came home in possession of many bright new scenes and rare faces, with the recollection of many moments of seriousness and some of unexpected hilarity, with the feeling that we had learned much about the past and perhaps a little about the present. Best of all, we returned with the happy feeling that our personal fortune was larger than we had known. I recommend the same tour of inspection to everyone who owns a similar share in the city of Washington, D.C.

For an American, Washington is the finest tourist city in the world. There are several reasons for this large claim, but one of the most valid is the fact that Washington is a hedgehog. The fox, you will remember, knows many things, but the hedgehog knows One Big Thing. Applying this old country adage to the realm of cities, one realizes that New York is our finest fox and Washington our one true hedgehog. The complicated, fascinating fox demands a lifetime to study, but if you have only a week or a weekend for your research, the stolid, one-track-mind hedgehog is for you. If you are a tourist, go to Washington.

For all its size, Washington has but a single purpose, a single business—government. It is an artificial creation—a company town, a housing project, a planned city—and for this reason the visitor can see it plain, with few of the confusions which assail him when he enters a city or a village which has grown up on its own and has taken its character from the thousand obscure pressures and subtle nudges of history. But if Washington has unity, it is still not simple; it is not a town to be cracked in an afternoon. It is the city of the One Big Idea.

As you first walk about Washington, you discover countless monuments to this idea, and the figures and words, carved in stone, of men who have believed in it. Seeing the monuments, which are mostly large and mostly marble, you are impressed and reassured by the durability and simplicity of the idea. But then, hours or days later, an important thing happens to you. Watching the capital going about its immense daily labors, watching it at work—in offices and committee rooms and great forums—you come to realize that the One Big Idea is not yet proved. You see that it is still a new concept and one that is besieged daily by countless pressures and problems and the need for difficult decisions. Here, for me, lies the excitement of Washington: in the constant testing of this Big Idea, in the trying out of this brash and dangerous notion that free men are wise enough to govern themselves.

We started with the monuments and the marble. Early on Easter Sunday morning, we taxied to the Washington Monument. It was a fine place to begin, at the exact center of Washington and springtime and tourism—except for one thing: we could not get in. There above us, the immense white paperweight leaned into the spring wind, all 555 feet 5⅛ inches of it, inviting us to elevation and observation, and here on the ground were at least 555 fellow Americans, all standing in a ragged queue that extended from the portal entirely around the foot of the Monument, and all obviously inviting us to get the hell to the end of the line and wait our turn for the elevators. For some reason, we were not annoyed. We abandoned our plans for the summit, and walked slowly around the little hilltop, cricking our necks as we peered upward, shading our eyes as we stared off east and west toward the Capitol and the Lincoln Memorial, both of them quivering slightly in the early morning sunlight, and both more lovely, for all their familiarity, than the heart had remembered. Here, enjoying this carefully contrived, classical and sentimental landscape, I realized (as I was to do again and again on succeeding days) how much of Washington is a cliché—and what a beautiful cliché it is, retaining always its capacity to stir you and to arouse the expected feelings of quiet pride and proprietary excitement. And I was even glad about the crowd of sight-seers, for I suddenly realized that I would be worried about a country whose citizens had become so sophisticated and so bored with the obvious and the patriotic that it could not muster a long line of tourists around the foot of a national shrine on a fine Easter Sunday morning.

We circled the Monument, studying the cars parked around it (bearing license plates from Tennessee and Texas and Montana and Missouri and Vermont and Virginia); admiring the Easter bonnets from Bangor and Boise, the Bon-Ton Shoppe and Saks Fifth Avenue; collecting bits of conversation and accents from East Boston, Puerto Rico and the Great Smokies (the woman who said "White Hoose," we decided, was probably from Virginia). When we walked down the hill to camera range and unshipped our cameras, we found a man beside us on the grass engaged in the same occupation. He was trying to arrange his wife and three restless children and the Monument into A Good Composition, and he was having his troubles. Finally the younger girl began to cry and the photographer lost his patience. "Dammit, Edna," he yelled to his wife, "tell her to shut up. This is for the album!"

But the holiday mood, bright and indestructible, persisted. Down at the Tidal Basin, a strong breeze whipped in off the Potomac, ruffling the waves, which were full of fallen cherry blossoms and, peculiarly, dead fish. A group of soldiers and their girls were stretched out on the grass, eating popsicles, and further on we came upon two Waves sitting under a cherry tree with their shoes off. The President, I had read, was attending divine services and planned a little golf later in the day, and here came another golfer—a secretary who passed us at a brisk pace, wearing tartan shorts and carrying her clubs on her back. Congress was in brief Easter recess and Congressmen were reported to have gone home to see their families and visit constituents, to roll Easter eggs instead of logs. It occurred to me that they might have done better to stay in Washington, for clearly, most of their constituents were here—walking around the Tidal Basin, photographing the cherry trees and the fishermen, lining up for rides on the swan boats, carrying souvenir booklets and hotel-room keys and post cards, and planning to call upon their Congressmen.

We found eleven buses drawn up in front of the Jefferson Memorial, one of them loading up with a troupe of small and cheerful Japanese, another debouching two dozen YMCA men from Mansfield, Ohio, all of whom were attired in Bermuda shorts and Argyle socks. Except for that scene, though, I found the Memorial, which I had never visited before, to be a disappointment. I liked the challenging, dangerous words on the walls (". . . laws and institutions must go hand in hand with the progress of the human mind. As that becomes more developed, more enlightened, as new discoveries are made, new truths discovered and manners and opinions changed, with the change of circumstances, institutions must advance also to keep pace with the times . . ."), and I liked the cool and constant breeze moving through the open colonnades. But I could not help thinking that Jefferson, the architect and patrician, the man of Monticello, would have preferred a statue six feet high instead of nineteen feet, and would have voted for his beloved Virginia brick instead of for glaring white marble.

The Lincoln Memorial was better. Here we found the crowds larger than ever—and somehow less noticeable and obtrusive. Beneath the slim pillars, beneath the soft light falling through the marble ceiling, and, most of all, beneath those great hands and tired, infinitely distant eyes, the hurrying, holidaying, chattering, picture-snapping swarms of our fellow visitors seemed tiny and inconsequential and perhaps only unintentionally boorish. And when at last we began to grow annoyed with the jostling and the heat in the temple, with the whining discussions about ice cream, and with the ugly position of reverence tourists assume when they bend over to focus their cameras, we walked out of the hall and around to the back of the building. Here we were suddenly and totally alone, in cool stone and among the lovely shadows made by fluted columns. We sat down on the new grass, beside rhododendron and pine, and lit cigarettes and wiggled our toes and watched an airplane climbing the bright April air above Arlington. And here, in a moment, I recovered my composure. I thought about Lincoln's face and the words of the Second Inaugural on the wall inside, and I found that I was glad to be a tourist in Washington in the spring.

Government is Washington's first business, its *raison d'être,* but it has a mighty sideline which is now enjoying a permanent and increasing boom—tourism. More than four and a half million tourists come to Washington during the year . . . a figure that has increased by a quarter of a million in the last three years. Over half a million high-school kids descend on the city like eager juncos every spring. Most of them are seniors, traveling in groups, who have raised the money for their expedition through food sales and variety shows back home, and who travel to the capital by bus from as far away as Maine and Oklahoma. With their water pistols, their brush-cuts and pony-tails, their bright sense of history (heightened by Miss Zinsser's course in American Government back home), and their incredible energy, they are Washington's most identifiable and indefatigable visitors.

Then there are conventioneers—members of some 330 conventions that assemble here annually, ranging from the Lions to the WCTU to the Daughters of the American Revolution. The DAR, I discovered, are known as poor tippers but hard workers. "Sometimes I think those old girls must rest up all year for their trip here," one cabdriver said to me. "Because they never get tired. They sure are *strong!*" He shook his head reminiscently. "Big, too," he added.

In spite of the fact that most of Washington's prime attractions are free (or cost a dime or a quarter at the most for admission), these various visitors combine to spend more than 250 million dollars a year in the city. If this figure seems too large to hold in your hand, ponder the following statistics, based on one sidelight of tourism: one photo-finishing agency in Washington processed *14 million* black-and-white snapshot prints one year, plus over 100,000 rolls of color film. *In a single day* one April, at the height of the spring invasion, the same agency processed 112,300 black-and-white prints. Add to this all the color film exposed, all the business done by the other photo agencies in Washington, and all the films that are taken back home to be developed, and you begin to have some idea of the size of Washington's profitable, camera-toting locust swarm.

The fact that so many of these tourists persist in visiting Washington in the spring (almost a million and a half of them in April and May alone) annoys the city's merchants and innkeepers, who would prefer a steadier, year-round business. But I think they are wrong. Washington is perhaps the most beautiful springtime city I have ever seen. It has space, it has air, it has light—a soft and extraordinary April glow that seems to hover just above your head as you stroll the side streets. The city appears to have more trees than Paris, and all the many dozens of parks and circles and squares and malls are alight with geraniums and azaleas, with plum and quince and crab-apple blossom. Coming out of your hotel in the early morning, you turn the corner onto one of the great avenues, and your heart is lifted by Washington's great white distances, by the subtlety and sweep of the genius of L'Enfant, the city's designer.

Forget the crowds and the Kodaks and the conventions; this is Washington's time of year. In the morning, the Government girls pack the long yellow and maroon buses inward bound from Rosslyn and Arlington, filling them with new white straw hats and the hope-ful scent of *Arpège*. In the evening, a visiting high-school senior from Waycross, Georgia, walks hand-in-hand with his steady under the heavy, dark trees on 16th Street, and you are charmed by their slow and graceful accents. In the afternoon, the girls from the Cathedral School turn out for softball practice near 34th Street, wearing bright yellow gym suits, and at the same moment a freshman Congressman from Indiana appears on the floor of the House sporting a new pair of perforated white shoes and carrying in his hand a speech in honor of his State Flower.

Every well-prepared visitor should bring more than his camera and traveler's checks with him to Washington. He should bring along a lively sense of the past. He can acquire this only by reading about the city before he comes here—in any one of a dozen or more books about Washington. His imagination thus prepared, he will be able to see more than simply what comes before his eyes. He cannot then commit the all too common and unfortunate error of believing that Washington's past is what he sees in its monuments—a past that is heroic, impersonal and without human error. I don't think it much matters what particular aspects of Washington's short, furious and often preposterous history he chooses to remember.

It is possible, for example, to look at the "Hobbyhorse" statue of Andrew Jackson in Lafayette Square with a certain lack of rever-ence if you remember that this statue always made Lincoln laugh out loud. . . . Or, walking this same sleepy square, you might choose to recall that this was where the flamboyant Representative Dan Sickles shot and killed his best friend, Philip Barton Key, the son of the author of *The Star-Spangled Banner,* in a fit of rage over Key's illicit relationship with Mrs. Sickles. Dan Sickles pleaded temporary insanity (the first defense of its kind in this country), was acquitted, and went on to become a remarkably second-rate Union general, and to lose a leg at Gettysburg. . . . If you admire the cold, clean beauty of the Washington Monument, then study the original plans for the edifice, which called for a Roman temple and a statue of George Washington riding in a chariot and wearing a toga. And then go on to read how the Know-Nothings managed to postpone the completion of the Monument for decades, because Pope Pius IX had sent a block of marble to be incorporated in the structure. And don't forget that the Monument killed one United States president—old Zachary Taylor. President Taylor attended Fourth of July ceremonies, in 1850, at the foot of the unfinished Monument, where he demolished a bag of cherries while sitting in the hot sun, and washed this down with a pitcher of cold milk. Not surprisingly he was dead within the week. . . . Perhaps you like to believe the unverified story that Andrew Jackson spoiled L'Enfant's magnificent Pennsylvania Avenue by his highhanded settling of the dispute as to where to put the Treasury Building. The legend says that he planted his cane in the middle of the avenue and proclaimed, "Put it here!" . . . But it *is* true that during a slavery debate in 1856 Senator Charles Sumner of Massachusetts was bodily attacked on the floor of the Senate by Representative Preston S. Brooks, who beat him unconscious with a cane and almost killed him.

And always, there are the more vivid pictures from the past, scenes of sadness and sleeplessness and mortal struggle. . . . Robert E. Lee praying all night in his bedroom in the Lee Mansion at Arlington, after he had been offered the field command of the Union Army at the beginning of the Civil War. . . . Julia Ward Howe getting up in the middle of the night in her bedroom in the old Willard Hotel to write *The Battle Hymn of the Republic,* just after visiting the Union encampments outside the same Lee Mansion in Arlington. . . . And Abraham Lincoln sitting up at night, too, to write a long letter urging courage and resolution upon one of his hopeless commanders of the Army of the Potomac—McClellan or Burnside or Hooker—and then tearing up the letter before morning. . . . Woodrow Wilson dying by inches in the White House as his dream died with him. . . . And the silent crowds standing outside the White House where Lincoln lay dead at the end of a great war; and the other, equally silent crowds outside the same house where Franklin Delano Roosevelt lay dead toward the end of another. . . .

Somebody once threw a cat off the top of the Washington Monument. It spun, volplaned, did several half gainers and tucks—and landed, uninjured, on all fours. Several years later, when the cat finally died (probably of boredom), somebody had it stuffed and sent it, of course, to the Smithsonian Institution. The Smithsonian, to the best of anyone's knowledge, has never thrown *anything* away, and for this reason it has been called the Nation's Attic—a description which cannot be improved upon. Like all attics, it is eminently worth a periodic visit. (But let it be clear here that the keeping of trivia and memorabilia is only part of the Smithsonian's job; it runs no less than four museums and art galleries, has a crackerjack department of ethnology, and operates the first-rate National Zoological Park.)

What I like best about the Smithsonian's Arts and Industries Building is its magnificent seediness, its incredible juxtapositions. If you want to see General Sherman's uniforms and Charles A. Lindbergh's *Spirit of St. Louis* at the very same instant, here they are, right next to each other. Here is a tremendous doll's house from 1914 next to Mamie Eisenhower's wedding dress. Here is an exhibit showing how artificial graphite is made, here is a working model of a 1928 Willys engine, and here (buzz!) are some live bees. Here, presumably for purposes of thoughtful comparison, is a Mexican oxcart spang next to the *John Bull* steam engine. Had enough? Or shall we go on and see the scale model of an asphalt-making machine and ponder the influence of the sewing machine upon history?

One good thing about the Smithsonian: you can quit wherever you please, for nobody has ever seen all of the Institution's thirty-million-odd keepsakes. My last and most cherished memory of the place was the sight of a young man and woman wearing identical black jodhpurs, black leather windbreakers and glass-studded kidney belts. They were incredulously examining a pre-1910 motorcycle, and were laughing fit to bust.

The only real way to see the Capitol building is to join one of the guided tours there. Any visitor who fails to do this will become instantly and hopelessly lost among the endless gilded corridors, the double staircases, Senators' barbershops, and the appalling statues of

Phil Kearny, Huey Long, Henry Clay, Elizabeth Cady Stanton and other assorted American deities. All day long in the Capitol, these squads of guided tourists pass each other in the halls—schools of mackerel behind their pilot fish, their eyes on the ceilings and their mouths slightly open.

I went to the Capitol prepared to think about politics and history, and found myself instead thinking about art. For the "official art" in the Capitol is absolutely overpowering, and most of it is overpoweringly bad. Not all of it; I admire the Senate Chamber and the old Supreme Court Chamber; and the President's Room, with its deep colors, its frescoes, its too-big chandelier, and its black leather chairs, is a florid, rococo delight. But the rest—the crawling Brumidi frescoes, the overblown pageants in oil, the Italianate corridors, the stone statesmen in double-breasted suits—must be seen to be disbelieved. Oddly enough, they did not upset me in the least. I had the same feeling about the building itself. The Capitol is all wrong: there are too many banks of stairs, too many wedding-cake tiers of columns; the dome is much too heavy, and the building's best profile, the East Front, faces in the wrong direction. But I could not, for all that, find the Capitol anything but beautiful. I was touched by the rather pathetic bravery of our Government in having set out so confidently to surround itself with nobility and Great Art, and impressed by the dimensions of its effort and the gallantry of its failure.

Later on, I mentioned this feeling of mine to a friend who is an old Washington hand. "I know what you mean," he said. "Come to think of it, I guess I love the Capitol too." And then he pondered for a moment. "I think the Capitol is like the face of somebody you have known and loved for a long time," he said at last. "You *know* that the face isn't beautiful, but you come to think of it as beautiful because of the admiration you feel for the person's fine qualities and for what he has done in his lifetime."

The place in which to recover from the gaucheries of the Smithsonian and the aspirings of Brumidi is the National Gallery of Art. Here is the quietest place in Washington, and one of the richest and most diverse collections of art in the world. Here you find the quality that is so rare in official Washington buildings—attractiveness. The pictures are beautifully hung and lighted, and you walk almost for miles through rich, cool glades of color, and linger gratefully in the galleries containing your favorite works and periods (for me, the Chester Dale Collection of 19th Century French painting). In the

National Gallery one finds oneself, as in so many other buildings in Washington, reflecting upon the individuals behind the institution, the human causes and caprices behind all that marble. The Gallery, the gift of Andrew W. Mellon, is culture bought by capitalism. It is the last, breath-taking (and perhaps atoning) gesture of an old-style American millionaire. It is the American Success Story made respectable, graceful, gentle and possibly immortal. What could be more amusing, more American, more National than this?

The splashiest show in Washington and the favorite with youngsters is the tour of the Federal Bureau of Investigation. I enjoyed it —the death mask of John Dillinger (who was perhaps shot deader than anyone in history), Ma Barker's last stand, the Nazi spies outwitted, the queer money and bad checks traced to their source, and all those busy, anonymous agents behind glass looking into microscopes and examining what?—Human blood? Fingernail scrapings? Prussic acid? Telephone slugs? It is a highly moral show: Crime Never Pays, all the crooks are dead ducks or about to be, and you, the law-abiding American citizen, are always on the winning side. Every tour winds up in a Hollywood finish—with a satisfying burst of Tommy-gun fire and the silhouette of the wrongdoer, at the other end of the range, punctured like a commuter's ticket. For me, in fact, the Warner Brothers overtones of the F.B.I. tour became so strong that I expected at any moment to see Pat O'Brien and J. Edgar Hoover hurry down the hall past us, with their snap-brim hats down and their shoulder holsters bulging, and then to see them return, a few minutes later, carrying the bullet-torn body of James Cagney between them on a shutter.

"Washington is the greatest town for shop talk in the world," said a Government executive to me at a cocktail party. "I know that shop talk is an awful disease, but I think it's better than small talk any day. You have to remember that all of us here, all the hundreds and hundreds of thousands of us, are working in the most fascinating business in the world. And another thing: I think that people work harder here—put in more hours of tough work—than in any other town I've ever seen. That's why all the entertaining is at home, like this. That's why all the parties break up at nine or ten in the evening. That's why Washington has no real night life."

This enthusiasm, this intensity (with the grain of self-doubt), this "awful disease" I encountered among everyone I met in Washington.

Plus the rumors. Washington, as I have said, is the biggest company town in the world, and at every Washington party or gathering I attended, the rumors, the inside dope, the anecdote about what the Senator said to the Admiral, flew about the room with the speed of light. And everybody, both the men and the women, was *doing something* and was identified by his job as much as by his name. ("She's Hell's Canyon," I was told upon being introduced to a pretty, redheaded lawyer.)

And yet for all their contagious and exciting excitement with government, for all their pleasure at being "in on" things and at attending upon and assisting in the making of great decisions, Washingtonians are quick to tell you that they live in what is, in many major respects, a small town. In the same week, three separate people— a Library of Congress curator, an investment banker who has lived in Washington all his life, and a man who had come to work for the Voice of America only two weeks before—all paid the identical tribute to their city: they praised its comfort, its relaxed day-to-day life, its stability, its love of families and gardens, its addiction to slow-going, good talk; all three used the adjective "Middle-Class." And a fourth person, the wife of the Voice of America man, said the same thing in a different way. "I hate it," she said. "It's exactly like Toledo, and I spent years and years of my life just trying to get away from Toledo."

Undoubtedly Washington is closer in many respects to Toledo and Grover's Corners and Main Street than it is to London and the Quai d'Orsay. One explanation for this is that a vast number of Washingtonians have come here from elsewhere and, while they work for the Government, remain no more than semipermanent visitors. There are fifty state societies in Washington, all of them active. For residents of what is today the number-one capital of the world, Washingtonians still show much of the exaggerated chauvinism and accompanying doubt that marks the small-towner. They will boast that the city now has seventeen radio stations and that culture is on the rise ("Have you visited our Contemporary Arts Institute?" . . . "You *must* go to the new Arena Theater!"), while at the same time deploring the lack of a truly great university in the city and squirming over Washington's insatiable fascination with high Society.

But I think many of the doubts are uncalled-for. No city can be really parochial when it has two newspapers of the caliber of the *Star* and the *Post and Times-Herald*. No town can be hick when it includes among its citizens the largest permanent assemblage of newsmen and reporters in the world. The same factors which make for impermanence and lack of continuity in Washington are also responsible, as one lawyer pointed out, for much of its strength. "There is no inherited position here," he said. "The competition and the demand for brains is greater today than ever before. Dilettantism is simply unknown now. A man can rise in the Government just as fast as his ambition and ability will take him. What we have here is an unstable society, under tremendous pressure, and that, to me, is a healthy society."

One thing is certain: nobody who has worked for the Government at a responsible level ever quite recovers from Washington. "They don't go back to Pocatello"—not really, not even after retirement, discouragement or political defeat. A friend of mine who used to work for the Department of Interior told me of once seeing an old, defeated, out of office, Middle Western senator who had returned to attend a committee hearing in Washington. The ex-senator came into the high-ceilinged committee room before the session, wandered vaguely about, and then pointed to the table at the end of the room. "That's where I used to sit," he said to nobody in particular. "That's where my name plate was." There were tears in his eyes. And then my friend, a former New Dealer who is also out of office and out of Washington, smiled and said: "I know how he felt. I feel about Washington these days the way Frenchmen felt about Paris when it was occupied by the Germans."

Settle back in your seat in the Senate Gallery, rest your chin in your hands (but don't lean on the railing—Against the Rules!), and watch your Government at work below. At work? If this is work, you decide at once, you'd like to be paid for the same easy duty. A dozen senators are scattered about the great room; two are standing to be recognized; someone is talking—presumably for pure pleasure, for no one seems to be listening. Two of the club members come in through the swinging doors, stare languidly around, and exchange a joke. A third strolls out, biting the tip off a fresh cigar as he leaves. The faces below leap up at you into recognition, out of newspaper photographs. ("There's the Veep!" . . . "Who's that in the Chair—?" . . . "There's *our* senator.") But what are they *doing*? Surely this is a joke—an expensive, bad joke.

But stick around; listen and learn. And remember that this is only the showcase of the system—the visible tip of the huge legislative ice-berg. And work *is* being done, you begin to realize, amid all the languor, the politeness and the introduction into the Record of a tribute to a retiring judge in Oklahoma. After half an hour, you have heard remarks on a dozen totally diverse and often important subjects—the tax problems of aviators imprisoned in China, the number of life belts to be carried on river steamers, a major Postal Bill, the tension in the Formosa Straits, the possible effects of lingering radiation, a bill for the relief of John Otter, Indian. You find that you cannot keep your eyes off the Majority Leader, for he is on his feet every minute, hard at work, his hands on the controls. He confers at length with his opposite number; he walks back six rows and whispers with a colleague, who then hurries out; he summons a page and loads him down with papers; he nods to the chair; he signals for a roll call. You become aware of a subtle, efficient system of communications. A senator wanders in, seemingly without reason, and takes his seat. A moment later, another senator rises and asks a long and difficult question about a pending appropriations bill, and the man who just came in, a member of the committee that reported out the bill, rises and answers the question in detail. There are mutual thanks; the work goes on.

The Senate does its public work to accompaniment of politeness, protocol, long-windedness and a system of complex and cumbersome rules, but I think there is as much reason for pride as for annoyance in this apparent inefficiency. For democracy and free speech are rarely truly efficient. Quick enactment of legislation is railroading; it is dictatorial. Freedom must go slowly; it must take time for the expression of doubt, for disagreement, even for demagoguery. Pride comes from our realization that the system works nevertheless. The Big Idea is preserved by the rules, and its daily work gets done in the end, even though we are bored to death by its droning voice, its maddening slowness. And all that official politeness down there on the floor ("I yield to no one in my admiration and esteem for the distinguished senior senator from ——") is more than merely charming and old-fashioned. It is a discipline, a highly necessary habit, that allows human and hard-working men to get their work done in a respectable manner, without the intrusion of violent personal and partisan feelings. It is the same rule of excessive politeness that keeps the overcrowded, too proximate Japanese from flying at each other's throats. Watch the Senate at work: it is humankind at work under rules and restraints; it is civilization.

To witness the real labors of Congress, to be instructed (and probably not entertained), one goes to a committee hearing. We went, on a rainy afternoon, to the Senate Committee on Government Operations. We sat beside two elderly ladies carrying reticules, two regulars who had been first in line outside the committee room and who took pages and pages of shorthand notes throughout the long afternoon—self-appointed secretaries keeping tabs on The System. There were no points of order, no disagreements, no drama. We listened to an engineer and heard terribly detailed testimony about the letting of Government contracts for the construction of grain elevators in Pakistan. Like the senators, I tried to pay attention and fought against sleep in the hot room, and then I wished, suddenly and sharply, that this hearing could be seen coast-to-coast, too, in every living room and tavern in the country. For this was the real thing —the painstaking, dreary and vital detail work of a Government whose responsibilities had suddenly spread to the other side of the world, into a corner of a country that most of us could not even place on a map.

There was nothing dreary about the Supreme Court. I was lucky to get in that day, and I shall remember my afternoon there as long as I remember anything about Washington. We stood in line, several hundred of us, to be admitted to the high chamber, for this was a big day—the first day of hearings on the methods whereby desegregation would be carried out in the nation's schools. There was something in the air that morning; you could almost taste it—the flavor of history, the smell of fresh earth as the past was turned under. Almost a year earlier, the Supreme Court had rendered its decision outlawing segregation. But it had posed some questions—How shall it be done? How fast and by whom?—and we were there to see these questions argued.

The doors opened at last and we filed in and sat in silence—lawyers and plaintiffs and attorneys general and citizens, the passionate and the expert and the merely curious—and stared ahead at the high bench and the four columns and the red curtain behind. The press was clustered, four deep and some even standing, along one wall, prepared to relay the tidings to Toledo and to Grover's Corners and to the south side of Chicago and the south side of Mississippi. We waited there upon the power of the law and upon the rights of a few young elementary-school scholars—*Oliver Brown and Twenty Others v. The School Board of Topeka, Kansas.*

Then there was a stir, the black-robed figures appeared, and we rose and heard the ancient, scalp-prickling words of the crier: "Oyez, Oyez, Oyez! . . ." and "God save the United States and this Honorable Court!"

The preliminaries over and the earlier decisions rendered, the attorney general of Kansas arose, and we were at once plunged into details—exactly how the school districts of Topeka had been altered in the last year. The personalities of the nine men facing me made themselves felt with extraordinary power: Warren, looking like a teacher, a polite schoolmaster who hoped there would be no error in recitation . . . Frankfurter, a sharp-eyed terrier, swiveling in his chair, pointing, interrupting, asking questions . . . Douglas, a scratcher and a fidgeter, his pale eyes wandering the room . . . the new boy Harlan, unnaturally quiet and watchful . . . the veteran Black, slumped low and looking pale and exhausted.

The lawyers rose and sat, the quietly phrased recommendations and counter-recommendations succeeded each other, the legalisms swirled about us, and the fervor and anger and hopes of the audience seemed to rise and fall in almost-visible waves.

But no one raised his voice, least of all the lawyers and justices, for no one, I suddenly realized, knew the answers. At that moment, the magnitude, the difficulty and the power of the Big Idea struck me almost like a blow. The personalities meant nothing; the decisions—which would affect the lives of millions of Americans—were yet to be made. Here was simply an assemblage of responsible men, all stricken with very evident self-doubt, all under immense pressure, all trying to bring the order of law to the barbarism of passions and prejudices, all searching for the hard answers to some terribly hard questions. This was the moment that brought Washington alive for me. It made me proud, and it scared me.

At the end of that day, our last day in Washington, my wife and I again went to the Washington Monument. It was windy and cool, and another rainstorm was making up over the river. We got at the end of the line, which was short now, and waited there, with dust and bits of old newspapers whirling about us and the sky getting darker by the minute. But we were still not to get in. The last elevator-load of sight-seers came down, and the guard closed the gate and came out and said, "Closing time, folks. You all come back in the morning."

We stayed on there for another minute, standing in that darkening and artificially dramatic moment before a storm, and watched the lights going on in the White House and in the great office buildings along Constitution Avenue and, away off, in the Capitol. We watched the big buses loading up and the homeward-bound, five-o'clock traffic piling up. But I found that for the first time in that April week, I wasn't thinking about Washington. I thought instead about the rest of the world and how it waited now, at every moment, upon this young and self-conscious and wonderful city. I thought of San Francisco and Moscow and Rome and Jakarta and Bogota and Brazzaville all listening on the other end of the wire, all waiting for the decisions that would have to be made here tonight and tomorrow and the next day. I had a notion that all of them, perhaps even Moscow, were hoping that they would be the right decisions; that someone would choose wisely again, and that the One Big Idea—the idea that men could rule themselves—was still in business.

Maryland

by JAMES WARNER BELLAH

I don't doubt for a moment that almost anyone can move to Baltimore, go into the insurance business, raise a family and lead a reasonably normal life, untroubled by the ghosts of gentlemen in white-sapphire stock buckles, with lace at their cuffs and scabbarded blades under the tails of their velvet coats. But it is far better to allow for their presence, for when the winter fog smokes in from the Chesapeake Bay they are quite likely to fall into step beside you, stand you a rum cobbler at thruppence a merry round, or deftly beguile your lady—if her smile invites. For you cannot hide Maryland under gasoline pumps and Coca-Cola signs—too much of its past is still present to be reckoned with.

Slice the geographer's scalpel across Maryland from southeast to northwest and you come up with a cross section of terrain that is more delightfully varied than in any other state of the Union. Two thirds of Maryland is tidewater. For thirty-two miles of Worcester County the open Atlantic pounds the outer Maryland shore. West from the ocean, the creek-laced Eastern Shore spreads its low and fertile acres to the Chesapeake Bay, a broad land-bound sea that divides the state in twain. West from the Chesapeake the land rises at once, breaks into intermediate rolling valleys and rises again toward the Appalachian Range, which spines the western reaches of Maryland. But before the Appalachians are reached one must traverse the great valley of Washington County. About thirty miles long and twenty wide, this valley is as magnificent in scenery as the storied Shenandoah and as productive as any soil in the world.

Caught as Maryland is between the Republican might of Pennsylvania, the coal baronies of West Virginia, the paternalistic Du Pontism of Delaware and the vast and ancient inertia of the Old Dominion, it is astonishing that her intrinsic character did not long since become hopelessly hybrid. Especially as she embraces, geographically speaking, the District of Columbia. But somehow Maryland has not lost her character. It is a part of her life today as it was her salvation in years gone—a hardy, forthright heritage of self-respecting, well-mannered individualism.

When one speaks of the character of a people, one speaks in intangible generalities that must be brought to earth. There were grand old men in Maryland in my youth. One comes to mind above all others as the epitome of the Maryland way of life: a man in his nineties, as slender and straight as when he surrendered his battery at Appomattox. For thirty years his wife had been bedridden with an arthritis that had stiffened her frame into almost complete immobility. One evening, returning home from the cheer of his club somewhat later than usual, he heard her call, "Is that you?" He stepped to her bedroom door in the dignity of older times, bowed gallantly and said, "And whom were you expecting, my dear?" The twinkle and the tenderness, the subtle compliment and the denial of pain in the memory of gayer years—either the nuance is there for you or it is not.

Charles I, whose towering contempt for the British Parliament eventually cost him his head, gave Maryland—lock, stock and barrel —to his friend George Calvert, first Lord Baltimore, with absolute proprietary powers in matters of government. A scant six years later, in 1638, the sturdy colonists of Maryland moved to take the reins of government in their own hands. They looked upon the right of self-government as so inalienable that, prior to the Declaration of Independence, they defended it vigorously against all comers—the proprietary Calverts, the Royal Governor, the British Parliament, the Crown and the Continental Congress as well. Playing no favorites.

George Calvert himself was a Roman Catholic, but religious tolerance was one of his ideals. The first Maryland law to further it was passed more than three centuries ago. Negroes were enfranchised in slave-owning Maryland sixty years before the Civil War. In 1810 all property qualifications for suffrage were abolished.

Now this is not put down as mere historical record, it is listed as clinical data on a people who progressed swiftly from absolutism to the democratic way of life long before the latter phrase was coined.

I think the reason for it is twofold. The early settlers were of British stock—yeomen sprinkled through with a generous helping of gentlemen. Each knowing the other's tricks and neither impelled too much by a desire to hang witches or to make proselytes. But far more important was this: Maryland is an extremely pleasant part of the world to live in. Marylanders enjoy it immensely and always have. The climate is temperate in the main, the terrain varied, the horses are fast and well blooded, the Chesapeake is a sailing man's paradise and the *spécialités* of food are of such gastronomic legend that to bring Duncan Hines into the discussion would be tantamount to the Gospels rewritten by H. L. Mencken. So with the bounties of God their heritage, Marylanders—from the beginning—lived and let live in self-respecting, well-mannered individualism. They still do.

The climate saves the state from the malarial apathy of the deep South. On an August day, Baltimore heat can addle one's pate beyond the capacity for much else than a frosted julep, but it seldom attains to the cloying steam-room humidity of swamp-built Washington. The vast broad stretch of the Chesapeake's upper reaches is a firming hand on temperature. Nor does a man often freeze to death in the Chesapeake duck blinds, for even late fall kisses Maryland with the courtesy due an old mistress. And winter, especially on the Eastern Shore, is seldom the season that locks Pennsylvania roads tight on occasion, or that drenches the deeper South in tepid rains until all joy leaves one's being. It is a winter of content.

Let us come into Maryland from the south, as General (then Colonel) Washington often did "for the horse races at Annapolis Towne"—where he lost his lace-ruffed shirt more often than he won. The Maryland Jockey Club—1743—the oldest racing organization on the continent and quite possibly the oldest sporting organization of any kind in the United States, held its original meetings in Annapolis, not moving to Pimlico until 1870.

The town of Annapolis today is one of the most amazing architectural olla-podridas in America. Almost literally between Nick the Greek's and a filling station one will come upon a fabulous example

of southern Georgian—still shaded by its ancient elms and not infrequently still occupied by the family that built it seven or eight
generations ago, when Annapolis enjoyed perhaps the most brilliant
and cultivated society in the colonies—certainly one of the wealthiest, due to its sea-borne commerce, until Baltimore became a port of
entry during the Revolution.

By no means has the city's vitality deteriorated with the years.
It is a thriving place that has lived through history and with it, coming
into these times as a prosperous modern town of small businesses,
light manufacture and Bay fishing—with shiny middle-priced cars
and well-dressed stenographers in its ancient narrow streets.

Again the anachronism, because those streets are still called Duke
of Gloucester, Hanover and King George's, and from the thriving
business district rise the spire of St. Anne's Protestant Episcopal
Church—a state church in the time of the Royal Colony—and the
white dome and pillared portico of the State House built four years
before the Revolution and still the seat of government of the State of
Maryland.

St. John's College—one of the nation's oldest educational institutions, occupies twenty-six acres in the heart of the older part of town.
It began as King William's School, founded in 1696. McDowell Hall,
its main building, was erected in the 18th Century as the residence
of the royal governors and is still in use. St. John's College bears
emphasis, for in an age of specialized education, it is devoted solely
to the liberal arts, basing its instruction on the tutorial and seminar
rather than the lecture system and endeavoring to educate broadly.
Limited to three hundred undergraduates, it is coeducational and
non-sectarian and was the first college in Colonial America to pro-
hibit religious discrimination.

Of the United States Naval Academy on the Severn, little can be
said that has not already been said. But for those who go down to
the sea in ships, either in mind or in body, there is a must at the
Academy—the museum of ship models. In days more ancient than
our own the building of a ship began with the building of an exact
model—the scale being usually standard at one quarter inch to one
foot. The model was completed in minute detail to the last copper
spike and the last small block of the running gear and was workable
throughout. Portions of hull planking were left off for access to interior structure, and portions of decking were removable for the same

reason. The model thus became a dynamic three-dimensional blueprint, and the yardmaster worked from it.

The collection of these admiralty models at the Naval Academy is probably the most representative in the world. Most of the little ships whose full-scale counterparts made empire—as well as the ships that challenged it and made the challenge stick—are there. His Majesty's Ship of the Line *Britannia*, 100 guns, and the *U.S.S. Constitution*, *H.M.S. St. George*, 96 guns, and the *Half Moon* and the New Bedford whaler *Niger*, the *U.S.S. Maine*—a whole miniature history of the sea in precise detail.

The worth of the collection in dollars is impossible to estimate. It can be pointed out that such and such fifty-four-inch model would bring $70,000 in the right collector's market, and that $1,000,000 might cover the entire collection. But this is not actually so. So few men are left who can build such ships and time is so short for them.

Leave your car and walk through the Academy grounds to the Museum. Stop at the monuments and read the inscriptions to the men who rose to manhood in the years of other crises, and you will come away more confident of the future, a little lighter of step, a trifle higher of chin. The youthful apprentices you pass will be on the bridges and in the conning towers and cockpits in the years to come, nor will they give up one ringbolt of the ship, either, in their good time.

I never come into Baltimore but once again the fundamental Maryland character comes to mind—self-respecting, well-mannered individualism. Edward Bouchet owned one of the first automobiles in town—a turn-of-the-century Panhard with an open basketwork tonneau and a folding rear step. A thunderous machine of many intrinsic hazards in a day of rutted dirt roads and wooden-planked bridges. Edward and my father and uncle once started for Annapolis in the juggernaut, but a few rollicking miles on the way, my uncle, who had been in the tonneau, turned out to be with them no longer. They retraced their route several miles and found him waiting where a particularly vicious bump had catapulted him. With commendable tribal loyalty to his younger brother, my father suggested to Edward that thereafter he drive more carefully. "Come, come," Edward said. "The car is insured. Everyone who gets into it is insured. Anything or anyone we hit is insured. Why spoil the sport?" Self-respecting, well-mannered individualism.

Baltimore in its older parts is an ugly town unless you love it. If you love it, its personality shines through the scabrous overlay of modern trade and even that attains to beauty by association. Again, even in the old town there are still vignettes of what the city was in the heyday of the Baltimore clipper. Mount Vernon Place still retains a touch of older dignity that would be hard to trump in any other city of the world. So does Washington Place.

There were two Baltimores prior to 1729 but neither one of them took. The exact site of the first is still subject to archaeological debate, and of the second only scant ruins remain. The third and present began life on the north shore of the head of tidewater on the Patapsco River at the point where Jones Falls empties into it and at a time in history when the tobacco and grain planters of the upper Chesapeake country needed a sea terminal nearer than Annapolis. The city grew up around this port function, which still is its modern blood of life. The Patapsco is a deepwater estuary that branches into four arms within the city and offers better than a hundred miles of water front for shipping facilities.

As there were three cities, so there have been three distinct periods in Baltimore history, each leaving its indelible mark upon the modern metropolis. The first was the clipper-ship era, which it knew alike with Boston, New Bedford and Falmouth—when the shipmaster was king of Charles Street, strolling it with a carven gold knob to his ebony stick and a fine powdered wig to his gnarled and weather-beaten head. The fortunes of many old Baltimore families were founded in that period. Boys went aboard Baltimore clippers through the hawsepipe and fought the hard fight aft to the quarterdeck. Shares of cargoes, shares of ships, ships themselves and then whole lines—with the golden profit piling high in vaults blazoned with the old house flags, and no faint shadow of the income tax to lay bony finger upon it.

The second period is stark. The political sentiment of Baltimore was Southern in 1861. Occupied almost from the start by Union troops, the city was harshly disciplined for its political convictions. Its lush trade was disrupted and dissipated by the Union war effort. Private fortunes were broken and pride humbled. Unlike Richmond and Atlanta, Baltimore never had its gallant moment of lost glory. It never took the field for its honor, but lay rather in chains throughout the conflict. The city never fully recovered until after the great fire of 1904.

The final period is today's—Bethlehem Steel's, Alcoa's, United States Industrial Alcohol's and Glenn L. Martin Aircraft's—a teeming metropolis whose telephone book lists branch offices of almost every important industrial operation in the country. It is a prosperous city and a pleasant one. A hard-working city and a playful city. It is a city that graces the fine romantic pen of Van Wyck Mason and the dour vitriol of H. L. Mencken. While the fumes of commerce lace the Bay fog of autumn and tarnish the moon, some of the older men still fence, engaging the sons and grandsons of men they started crossing blades with years ago in the *salles d'armes* of the city. For it is a fencing town still, and beyond New York, Los Angeles, New Orleans, Philadelphia and Chicago, fencing towns are hard to come by, for the sport has no gate to support it, only die-hard devotees, it being an axiom that one must be an accomplished fencer to enjoy watching.

Not so with horses, and Baltimore is a horse town too—with Pimlico the shrine, almost in the heart of the city. The Maryland Jockey Club moved its meetings from Annapolis to Pimlico in 1870, and since then the track has echoed to the hoofbeats of the finest horses of our times—Man o' War, Equipoise, Challedon, Gallant Fox, Citation, Tom Fool, Whirlaway, Count Fleet and Native Dancer. The Preakness gives precedence only to the Kentucky Derby. In fact Man o' War declined the issue in the Derby to wait for the Preakness. And it was at Pimlico that the famous meeting between Seabiscuit and War Admiral took place. "If it's Seabiscuit, take his bit and bridle, Mowbray—and ask him what he'll have."

Laurel has a comfortable sound. Havre de Grace used to tinkle gaily but Pimlico has a joyous whipcrack authenticity—a staccato of turf tradition that has clung to it through the long years and still does. The Futurity, the Pimlico Special, the Dixie, the Baltimore Spring Handicap, the Preakness, the Black-Eyed Susan. *Pimlico*.

In 1650, one Robert Brooke arrived in the Colony from England. He traveled well. With him, in additon to his household and servants, he brought the leading blood of his stable and the cream of his pack. So fox hunting was first introduced to the North American Continent —and the blood of that now-ghostly pack has remained with the Brooke family for three centuries. I would say also that their grand manner of travel had remained unchanged as well, for in an 8000-ton freighter out of Londonderry for Baltimore the winter of 1929, I occupied the next stateroom to a sixteen-hand Irish hunter con-

signed to one of the distaff descendants of the Brookes in the Green
Spring Valley. I wish no misconception made of my use of the word
stateroom. There were eight staterooms off the boat deck. Six were
occupied by ship's officers. I had the seventh. The hunter had the
eighth.

Steeplechasing dates in America from June 7, 1865, at Paterson,
New Jersey; but organized hunt racing in the United States today
is the history of the Maryland Hunt Cup, the most widely known
of the amateur meetings. Long before that unknown Englishman
shouted, "Let's race to yon steeple," meaning in a straight line regardless of intervening obstacles, some mad Irishman had invented the
Wild Goose Chase, which one supposes called for racing cross-
country under the line of flight of an actual wild goose. One likes to
believe so anyway, for there is a demented Irish grandeur to the
concept. Whatever—the steeplechase in Maryland bears closer affinity to the Irish version than to the English. Some fifty years ago,
members of Green Spring Valley Hounds invented a "pounding race"
which was a game of mounted follow-the-leader. By competition,
casualties and cussedness, they eventually developed a club champion and having done so, looked to greener fields. In 1915 the meeting began to take place annually near Glyndon, on the Worthington
Valley estate of J. W. Y. Martin, Esq. From those days to the present,
the Maryland Hunt Cup holds almost the same interest nationally,
in the field of amateur racing between flags, as the Kentucky Derby
and Maryland's own Preakness on the flat. Although the date varies
each year, devotees hold standing reservations at the Belvedere Hotel for the Hunt Cup weekends, whenever they fall.

Baltimore is the sacrosanct portals of the Maryland Club at the
corner of Charles and Eager streets, where the cooling Tom Collins
at one time held military rank. A small one being a Lieutenant Collins, the others progressing in glass size to general-officer rank—and
retirement. It is the Bachelors Cotillon, which ranks with the St.
Cecilia, and horse-drawn vegetable wagons, hawking still, of a Saturday morning. It is the old Shot Tower in the heart of town and the
Baltimore Orioles in the hearts of their fans, and it is the modern
Negro housing projects of the city's slum-clearance program.

Baltimore is also Johns Hopkins University. Although the school is
known the world over for its primacy in medicine, this fame somewhat shadows Hopkins' other departments. In the College, the basic
policy is strong emphasis not on required courses, but on the unity

of knowledge, and on the integration of fields of man's activity with other related fields, so that the undergraduate's horizon of understanding widens steadily as he progresses toward his ultimate specialization. The college itself is in Homewood—a beautiful suburb of the city—and has been planned so well in land purchases and bequests that its quiet academic atmosphere will be preserved for years to come.

Baltimore is also the Dandy Fifth Regiment, now Federally designated the 175th Infantry of the 29th Infantry Division. Its Armory is well worth a long hour, for the regimental history in trophies, battle honors and relics is the history of the United States.

Like New York's Seventh, the First City Troop of Philadelphia, and the Richmond Blues, Baltimore's Fifth is a tradition in the land. A military unit with a record of combat second to none. In some respects a hereditary family responsibility and in others a gentlemen's club. Its military history is unbroken since 1774. With the Blue Hen's Chickens of Delaware it took the brunt of Washington's rear-guard action at Long Island. In 1814 it successfully defended Baltimore against the same British force that burned Washington. Baltimore was *not* burned, and the next day one Francis Scott Key observed that the national colors on the Fort McHenry ramparts were still at full staff. (If "the rockets' red glare" ever confused you, they were Congreve rockets, which were the forerunner of the bazooka and used tactically in much the same way.) In the First World War, the Dandy Fifth fought through the miserable and mist-skeined Argonne, and in World War II it hit the Normandy beaches and continued across Europe to make junction on the Elbe River with the Sixth Cavalry Division of the U.S.S.R.

What are such things as battle honors? An empty parade of past glories? I think not. Rather they are a spiritual bank account passed on from grandsire to sire and son against a time of further threat— which is to say today, in this land of the free and home of the brave.

The University of Maryland sprawls ruggedly in white concrete and red brick across College Park, south of Baltimore on U. S. 1. It is a living, personal monument to almost fifty years of effort on the part of Harry Clifton ("Curly") Byrd, the University's president from 1936 to 1954, when he resigned to enter the Democratic lists for governor. A state university in the broadest sense, Maryland serves well the basic and varied educational needs of the state.

North of Baltimore on U. S. 40, in the northeast corner of the state, lie Havre de Grace and Elkton. Of Havre de Grace one need say nothing to those for whom the sound of it sparks the eye of memory. Of Elkton, a thriving commercial town of late years, one need only say that state law has dimmed its Gretna Green reputation. Time was when every road to Elkton bore signs offering to facilitate marriage, each sign promising to cut more of the necessary time and tape than the preceding sign. Package deals of clerk, minister, witnesses, and flowers were offered on a price-war basis. But times have changed. One can still be married in Elkton, but it is no longer the haven for hasty or exhilarated nuptial decision.

To the west of Baltimore, in fact from well within the city limits, the land begins to rise abruptly into the Piedmont, or the eastern slopes of the Appalachian range. This is the threshold of the old agricultural upland of the state, still rich in grains and dairy products, apples, forests, tobacco and fine cattle. Many of the old upland towns still stand with their main-street façades much the same as they were in the days when the brick was handmade to build them: Taney-town, Thurmont, Hagerstown, Cumberland and Frederick of the Barbara Fritchie interpolation, where the immortality of the old girl is secure today in the sales of Barbara Fritchie candy (story free).

This Western Maryland country, rising as it does into the Allegheny Mountains, offers as magnificent a spread of natural beauty as any other terrain in the East. Adequately road-netted throughout, the western counties still offer a certain primeval majesty to the tourist and a paradise to sportsmen. The farms are prosperous small farms in the main, with the little towns comfortable in the present and breathing still a faint buckskin odor of the past: Indian Springs, Accident, Mount Savage, Funkstown.

There is breathlessness to Western Maryland after one crosses the Appalachian Trailway—a sense of quiet expectance in this meeting of past and present. Skirting the winding road ahead is a young man in a brown coat and the scarlet cap of a hunter, his rifle shouldered for safety over the fences. But it needs only the memory of yesterday to change the scarlet to coonskin and the .30–.06 to a Le-fever long rifle for the fact to come alive again that he is following Indian spoor, not the track of white-tailed deer.

There are twenty-three counties in Maryland—plus Baltimore, which is not part of a county—and with no exception each one offers some private monument of the days of the Cavalier colony—a great house, perhaps, such as Carrollton or Wye or at least a manor house where someone seated his family in days gone, when land was the essence of wealth and servants were to be had by indenture or purchase in any quantity necessary to comfort.

Carrollton, which originally embraced 17,000 acres of extremely choice and varied lands, was the seat of Maryland's senior Catholic layman in his time, Charles Carroll the Signer. On these lands, at Tuscarora, stands the Old Carroll Mansion which, being built of native limestone, is extremely well preserved. The Darnall House is the oldest seat in good condition still standing on the manor. It is at Rocky Fountain and is one of the ancient landmarks. St. Joseph's Church, also on the manor, is well worth a visit and a prayer and a coin dropped in the alms box. The original seat of the Carrolls was, however, in Howard County at Doughoregan Manor, a magnificent two-story great house over 300 feet long from wing to wing. It is there that the original Charles Carroll is buried, in the family chapel.

This is in no sense a guidebook to these old homes, for dozens of such works are readily available, but one or two others should be mentioned in passing, as particularly outstanding monuments of a past way of life, just as legitimate in its time as the subdivision and the FHA loan of today. For prospect, perhaps no house excels Tulip Hall. It commands West River, looking across a broad stretch of Chesapeake Bay to Kent Island and a long run of the distant haze which is the Eastern Shore. Sotterley, in St. Marys County on the Patuxent, is built in the floor-plan shape of the letter z, a design unique in the state. And finally, for present purposes, Homewood in Baltimore—the house Charles Carroll, of Carrollton, built for his son Charles. This house strikes the architectural keynote to the modern Johns Hopkins University which has developed around it. It is distinctly Jeffersonian in concept and is one of the finest houses to be found anywhere in the world.

From the earliest days of the colony there was a necessary geographical separation of the Western Shore and the Eastern Shore of Maryland by virtue of the broad reaches of Chesapeake Bay. The years crystallized this into cultural and economic differences until today there is strong political schism. You are an Eastern Shoreman first and a Marylander second, and if you are a Western Shoreman first and a Marylander second, you probably follow the Mencken doctrine that all Eastern Shoremen are stubborn and slightly, shall one say, reactionary?

Until very recent years, the flat red soil and sandspit of the Eastern Shore was a fishing and agricultural community throughout its width and length, if one excepts the sea-food canneries and the fruit-preserving enterprises that came into being shortly after the turn of the century. The Pennsylvania Railroad has for years operated a main line down the center of the peninsula from Wilmington to Cape Charles in Virginia, but branch lines to the smaller towns were sketchy, hectic and far between. They operated with charming informality. If a farmer's barn was on fire, the train to Oxford has been known, as late as the early 'thirties, to stop while the engineer organized his passengers into a bucket brigade to put the fire out. His reasoning was fundamental. The immediate fact was the fire. There would be no train behind him until the next day and it made no difference when he arrived in Easton or Oxford because none of his passengers were expected until the train got in.

Informality has been characteristic of the Eastern Shore since the earliest days. It is not necessarily laziness or sloth, nor is it for studied effect. Only an Eastern Shoreman fully understands another and beyond that he has small concern for the outside world, although he nods to it in native courtesy as it passes by. His land is good land for small farming, the mourning dove flies in season, as does the duck. He tongs his oysters when the urge is on him, the crab comes up his creek to grow a new shell and the terrapin grows in his own or a neighbor's sequestered bed. His name is Goldsborough or Tilghman or Lloyd somewhere in his ancestry, and that gives him his land by inheritance for over three centuries. Therefore he feels he has the right to live upon it as he sees fit and to raise his glass in the gallant toast—"Here's to Eastern Shoremen, where'er they may be dispersed."

But of recent years his ancient bailiwick has been invaded. When the Chesapeake Bay Bridge was opened, the Eastern Shore became part of the rest of Maryland almost overnight. When the ubiquitous Du Pont interests put in a nylon plant at Seaford, Delaware, the handwriting was firm upon the wall; the economy of all Caroline County, Maryland, was converted literally overnight from agriculture to manufacturing.

It is inevitable that under the lash of commercial necessity much of the ancient charm of the Eastern Shore before long will belong to the memories of very old men—and to history.

How many miles of tidewater wash the Eastern Shore has never been accurately determined, for each one of its rivers is Bay-drowned by the tide, as are their hundreds of branching creeks. Talbot County alone enjoys over 900 miles of tidewater lands. In Talbot three miles by road would at one time bring me from my house to my neighbor's, whereas the same journey was ninety-four miles by boat.

This is why Maryland's oldest yacht club—the Chesapeake Bay Yacht Club—has its clubhouse two miles from the nearest water and has never had a water station. The members kept their boats at their own anchorages, and established their clubhouse at the most central meeting point—Easton, the county seat.

The Miles River Yacht Club is possibly the more active organization at present. Its clubhouse and water station are on the lower Miles, at St. Michaels, which is an ancient town, almost completely of the past. From here one can chug up half a dozen creeks by small boat and see the land still as it was in the days of the Calverts, the rough-cut creek banks broadening to wheat and cattle acres, with an ancient manor house still standing—sometimes in sad disrepair, more often modernized and lived in by more recent owners who carry on a replica of the pleasant living that the original owners knew.

The premier manor house of the Eastern Shore is Wye House in Talbot County. It is not a particularly beautiful structure, but it is imposing. Wye is a "five-part" house of wood, which is to say it has a central block and a corridor leading off from each side to an end wing. In Joan Lloyd's day its interior was much as it had been left by the Lloyds when year-round residence was discontinued. In the office to the right of the main entrance there were cabinet drawers sheafed thick with ancient parchment plantation transactions from days long before the Revolution. Used only as a summer home, Wye was nevertheless alive with living. The priceless knife boxes still stood on the buffet and the portraits of long-dead Lloyds looked down through a faint gray veil of mildew, due to a lack of winter heating.

The house looks across the old bowling green to the brick and lofty arched window bank of the orangery, which is perhaps as fine a piece of architecture as you will find in all America. There are almost three miles of box hedge in the garden, and eight generations of Lloyds lie in the family cemetery.

The Chesapeake retriever is a Shore dog. In point of legend he is probably the first American dog ever bred, for it is generally conceded that he sprang from a *mésalliance* between a Newfoundland bitch who leaped from the rail of an early Colonial ship and swam ashore and a dog from an Indian encampment, breed unknown, who met destiny with her.

If the bar sinister is part of the retriever's heritage, so, too, is heart. He is a lion in his own country. As the pups of Highland sheep dogs start for the Grampian flocks at six weeks, the Chesapeake pup starts for salt water. He is the complete amphibian. He will submerge his head entirely for his first solid food and has been known in maturity to dive to six or eight feet. He sights his game rather than smells it, because water kills scent. His thick, tight-gnarled coat, with self-generated lanolin, keeps him from waterlogging. He can swim for miles in icy waters and would retrieve a DC-6 if it would float behind him. When there is no shooting, he goes for busmen's holidays and you may meet him swimming miles offshore, and there will be mild reproof in his gentle golden eyes if you take him aboard.

He is a gentleman who will lie by your fire and dream with you without talk. He will guard your children when they toddle near the water—less in fear that they cannot swim than in concern that they may drown before they can hold a gun and fulfill their destiny—and his.

The Chesapeake log canoe, the skipjack, the ram and the bugeye are indigenous to the Bay country and you will still see the bugeye on occasion. Her masts rake aft decisively, which is her distant identification. She is extensively broad-beamed to allow for her shallow draft, which was necessary so that she might push well up into shallow creeks to load agricultural freight in the old days of sail. The broad beam kept her seaworthy for outer Bay navigation, for the Bay, like the Great Lakes, is restless water and its sudden squalls and heavy seaways must be met with respect and consummate seamanship. The Bay has myriad minor victories on its long record of ships one will pass no longer.

For a century past, the entire lower peninsula has lived on borrowed time in the march of commercial development. This was a delightful interlude, for it left the Eastern Shore of Maryland as a living museum of what life had once been in these United States. There are a few horses and rigs on the roads, a hazard to the automobile, right up to today. Customs and manners and habits remained much the same as they had been throughout the 19th Century. There was a legitimate landed gentry and a solid, self-respecting yeomanry, and life just was and it was nice to live it—and it was only seven hours by car from New York.

Half a century ago New Yorkers began to discover it. Mr. Sheiffelin Schuyler purchased Bruff's Island in Talbot County and made a delightful home of it, taking the county to his heart and becoming more a part of it than he was of Schuyler, Chadwick and Burnham in later years. Others followed him, finding in the Shore a place of casual delight and a gentle backwater in which to relax. Pittsburgh and Philadelphia families came down and purchased old manor houses, first to summer in, but more often than not, for permanent homes. The Chryslers and the Raskobs came, and in recent years retired regular officers have found it a pleasant place in which to dream of battles they will never fight again.

It is of the very nature of Maryland and of the Shore that there was no rabid attempt to exploit the influx. Land prices rose with the arrival of money, but not outrageously. There was no boom. One could be taken if one were careless—but not too badly. One's manners and address were the passport and if one seemed a good sort, one was taken to the bosom of the Shore.

The Eastern Shore as it was, and as it still is to an extent, was a charming accident of history. It was Pleasant Valley with the marks of horse's hoofs on the grand staircase because one of the last owners was so attached to his hunter that he was known, on occasion, to ride upstairs to bed on him. It was turkey shoots in the fall and fox hunts *to clean out foxes*—with the hunt on foot, on bicycles, in Model T's and on mules, with the only fillip to decorum being one or two red (not faintly pink) sweaters for warmth. It was the Washington Hotel in Princess Anne ("Built 1744, in the Reign of King George II"), with account books running back to the days of £/s/d, and a double staircase to accommodate ladies in hoopskirts. It was old Col. Oswald Tilghman saying, "I have every expectancy of going to Heaven when I die, for I have never cheated at cards, never killed a man who didn't have an even chance of killing me, and never told a lie in my life—except, of course, to a woman." It was sleepy courthouses and World War I names on the American Legion honor roll that were identical with those on the Confederate memorial next to it. It was Cadet Robert E. Lee's initials scratched on a window pane at Wye House with the diamond of betrothal of a girl who did not marry him.

So if it is high time that the oil refineries move in, then they must. And if the fishing grounds must be churned sterile by the screws of tugs and liners, and broad meadows be scored by the steel rails of marshaling yards, and if the manor houses must make way for low-cost real-estate developments, there is still a moment left to raise the glass once more and raise it high *"to all Eastern Shoremen, no matter where dispersed"*—and snap the stem.

Come back with me now across the whole state and pin me down, if you can, to that which I have assiduously avoided except in titillation—food. The ruffed grouse still runs in Garrett County, with the wild turkey and the white-tailed deer in Allegany. There are terrapin beds along the Miles and the Choptank—where the legal size is secondary to the succulence to be enjoyed for a slight infringement of the law, and the soft-shelled crab comes to Hunting Creek like the willing bride in youth. The Bay oyster is still the most delectable this side of anywhere, and a dozen fresh in a pint of pale is still the finest breakfast in the land when the vapors of a rugged night cling to the soul.

I will mention no "best" restaurant; some are better, but those worse cease to exist forthwith. Food anywhere is always what the eater demands, and Maryland food is so dear to the Maryland palate that criteria of quality are pre-established. The crab, the oyster, Bay and offshore fish are a gourmet's delight in almost any hole-in-the-wall in Maryland's Bay towns. For terrapin one had probably better wait to reach Baltimore—and I am fully aware that I take my life in my hands when I say that.

The original and fabulous recipes of Maryland were, in the beginning, the recipes of its homes, kept from generation to generation in the old kitchen books. More often they were never written down, for literacy was not a primary virtue of cooks. They were house dishes. Duck is seldom served in braces, but in dozens rather. Oysters come by the barrel—or the more delicate bushel. Soft-shelled crabs in heaps, and if a dish is to be run down for future duplication, its original source material will probably read "add to taste" or "don't leave in the oven too long." There is esoteric pride in Maryland cooking and justly, because Maryland hospitality, of which Maryland food is a basic ingredient, has almost completely done away with extreme old age as a cause of death.

But then again, in Maryland, extreme old age has its own definition. I call to mind another grand old Marylander who was wont to start his day with a prebreakfast noggin while he shaved himself with straight edge. Then his doctor told him to have done with the breakfast tot, and word of it reached his boy Sam. There was no drink the next morrow. The old man bellowed down the service stairs in no uncertain terms: "I've been having that whisky peg every morning for sixty years and I've lived to be eighty!" And Sam, quaking even in the whites of his eyes, "I know, suh—but doctah say ef you hadn't, you'd be almost ninety now!"

Of oyster races we must have a word, for it is one of the few events I have ever excelled in. The Chincoteagues would come up the Shore by the barrel, consigned to two eaters, in the heyday of the sport. He who consumed the lesser number raw, paid for the whole. I had done moderately well in the preliminaries—well enough to take on the champion. In pregame quarterbacking I made inquiries and got the supreme accolade—"Mistuh Van is an oyster-eatin' man, but yo're the oysterish."

But it is of terrapin that I wish to speak particularly. You may have it in season almost anywhere in Tidewater Maryland and it will be excellently prepared if you choose the most reputable places in the same careful manner you would choose a lady to wife. But few have had it at its supreme best, as I did when the late Murray Lloyd Gainsborough prepared it for me in Candlewood silver, working by spirit lamp under a portrait of his gray-kepied grandfather and using eighty-year-old amontillado. The equation is mathematical. *Terrapin Maryland is as the youth of the terrapin is to the age of the sherry.*

But then again, I don't doubt for a moment that almost anyone can move to Maryland, go into the insurance business, raise a family and lead a reasonably normal life.

Virginia

by CLIFFORD DOWDEY

One afternoon, some years ago, I was slumped on a New York terrace, feeling poorly, trying to soak up some of the thin warmth. It was spring by the calendar, but there was no fragrance in the air, no lilt, and I mentioned to a friend who had stopped by to see me that I felt nostalgic for the sweet, mellow warmth of the Virginia spring.

What was it about Virginia that exerted such a pull on its sons, my friend asked, and I began to explain it.

Three hours later, he said, "It's five o'clock. Let's go have cocktails."

"You forget I'm sick," I protested.

"You forgot it," he said, "when you started to talk about Virginia."

Love of their land is native to all Virginians, whether they live in the flat, river-drained Tidewater of the East, the richest and most populous and oldest part of the state—where the whole country (America as well as Virginia) began—or in the green, rolling middle country of the Piedmont, the "horse country" that's become a sort of Left Bank for equine-minded millionaires; or in the mountain country of the west, the loveliest part of the state, which includes the magnificent and fabled Shenandoah Valley, the Blue Ridge Mountains, the more rugged valley of the southwest, and the Alleghenies climbing into West Virginia and forming a border with the state which broke off from the Old Dominion.

Even to the most urban Virginian, his state is the land. For its first two and a half centuries Virginia was primarily agricultural, and into my time, I knew no one who did not have kinspeople on farms. We visited them in the summer, driving from some small, wooden depot in a surrey, long after cars were commonplace. On the hot, fragrant land, with its strange murmurous sounds, we were laughed at for jumping at the sight of a harmless black snake and forced by pride into unequal tests of strength. Yet when our country cousins visited us in the city they were welcomed with no spirit of vengeance. Even as children we sensed that they represented the enduring nature of our country—Virginia.

Virginians have an almost universal habit of defending anything about their state with: "Why, it's always been that way." Yet, however bitterly it may be lamented in Virginia, the Old Dominion does change, though changes have to be measured by the ages rather than the years. The main point, of course, is that the character of the state does not change, has never changed, and the people resist any change which might affect that character.

The regional culture of Tidewater, the Piedmont and the mountain country varies widely, even to accents; and interests of the three sections not infrequently clash head on. But, though regional natives may regard one another with polite wariness, or even veiled disapproval, the variety of the regions forms for the Virginian a physical self-sufficiency within his own borders which goes a long way toward explaining his character.

It is not that the state boasts of any single physical glory which some other state doesn't have more of or better; it is simply that to the Virginian everything is here. He has the sea and the mountains, the rolling countryside and the flat, relatively plain stretches of Tidewater. Indeed, the native's attachment to his land is not always because it is beautiful, but because of its association; it was settled by people of his blood, and their blood is in the soil.

In my own Tidewater, the beauty is largely in the eye of the beholder. When a family, like my own, has lived almost 350 years in an area covered by four counties, some magic of association accrues to the land. Yet, many people without personal associations also respond to the magic in the hot, miasmic countryside, as if they too can sense the ghosts in the heavily scented mists.

There is almost a lushness in the wildly growing honeysuckle and creeper, in the ivy on red-brick walls, the pink and white dogwood, the redbud, the splashes of azalea, the slumbrous crape myrtle, the roses, and the fragile lavender of wisteria against iron-grill balconies. Some of the world's finest gardens, now in their third century, grow in Tidewater. Spring comes early, in a sudden flowering, and the summers are long, too long, ordeals of damp, steamy heat.

The dampness comes from the water that drains the low-lying land. In the early days of the planters, water was everything, since it carried their tobacco. And water was everywhere, all flowing toward the Atlantic: brooks into streams, creeks into little rivers, and big rivers into the Chesapeake Bay. The big rivers begin with the Potomac, which forms our northern border with Unionist Maryland (except for the two counties on the Eastern Shore of the Bay; and very vain they are of their separateness). The pleasant Rappahannock, across which Washington threw the silver dollar, flows through the middle of the state. Next come the York and the James, and between them lies the Virginia Peninsula, running 100 miles from Richmond to the Bay.

Though the Peninsula was first known nationally in the Civil War, when McClellan tried to take Richmond from there, the narrow, once-fertile strip was the beginning of our country—and I mean both my native state and the whole nation. There on the swampy, malarial island of Jamestown was born the Virginia idea, for Virginia is both a place and an attitude.

The Virginia idea, it must be clearly understood, was not what is today called the American Dream. The Virginian did not dream of a democracy, with its literal meaning of the rule of the people. His dream was to found an aristocratic republic, in which superior individuals would emerge to rule the many.

While his concept of a social order was the first in America, it influenced only Southern states, to which Virginians migrated in frontier days. The rest of America adopted the New England order so completely that it even swallowed the Puritan myth of founding the country at Plymouth Rock in 1620, thirteen years after its actual founding at Jamestown. One of the reasons for the Virginian's indifference to this historical distortion is some doubt in his mind that he wants the United States attributed to him. Having no more promotional zeal than a desiccated member of some old-guard club, the Virginian even permits his children to celebrate Thanksgiving in the style of the Pilgrims, though he knows that the first Thanksgiving in America was celebrated at Berkeley Plantation, up the James River from Jamestown, in 1619—well before the Puritans had even sailed for Virginia and been blown off their course.

To begin at the beginning, the first Britishers to establish a permanent colony of English-speaking people on this continent arrived in Virginia in 1607 in three small ships of twenty, forty, and one hundred tons. Unlike the *Mayflower* descendants, Virginians do not agree even on the names of the ships. One was definitely *Discovery,* the second either *Goodspeed* or *Godspeed,* and the third either *Susan* or *Sarah Constant.* This uncertainty exists because the Virginian, for all the jibes at his "looking backward," has a casual acceptance of his past. To him the past is a continuous stream that flows into and interweaves with the present. Because the same people have been in the same place for three and a half centuries, he can be forgiven if he takes legends about his past for granted rather than trying to prove them. But, as a result, he lives under some awesome misconceptions—though even the misconceptions form part of the attitude.

For instance, the Virginian accepts as dogma that the first settlers to arrive in the naked wilderness were all younger sons of great British families. By record, few great British houses sent sons to Virginia in 1607, and none left any descendants in America. Indeed, not one of Virginia's distinguished families can trace its ancestry to *any* of the 104 tough-bitten adventurers who arrived on those first three ships. A kinsman of my ancestors, Humphrey Blount, came in the first waves, but he was killed by an Indian arrow in 1613. Others died of starvation or malaria, and still others went back to England.

Despite the high mortality of America's first pioneers, others kept coming. More Blounts came, in 1619, and founded one of the half-dozen families who derive from what is called "the early adventurers"—those who came before 1622. These early adventurers were a curious cross section of British life. They were artisans and cutthroats, farmer sons of the minor country gentry, an assortment of minor rogues, London clerks and adventurers such as Captain John Smith, that great swaggerer and agile penman whose life was saved by Pocahontas, and a collection of the useless who could write "Gent." after their names as a symbol that they were above gainful employment. All came as the Forty-Niners went to California two and a half centuries later—to get rich. But they differed from all other American pioneers (except those of South Carolina). They came with the aristocratic dream. As early as 1648, a newly success-ful adventurer was commended because "he lives bravely, keeps a good house, and is a true lover of Virginia." That "true lover" was the ultimate test. It meant identification with the land and accept-ance of the responsibility for the social order.

Even while these "early adventurers" were fighting Indians, starva-tion and malaria, with the dying outnumbering the survivors ten to one, they peered over their crude palisades and dreamed of the grandeur of plantations to be wrought from the rich land. While their London backers were abandoning hope of the Colony's survival, men were staking out plantations in this Indian-infested wilderness, and laying the foundation for an aristocratic society.

The might of their dream is attested by the enduring nature of the society they erected, complete with its myths and legends and dogmas. Nor was the superior individual they expected that society to produce an idle fancy: in its full flowering, the Virginia Dynasty produced more great men in a comparative time and place than ever before or since on this continent. Men who would have been giants in another time and place were overshadowed by such contempo-raries as Jefferson, Washington, Patrick Henry, George Mason, John Marshall, Madison, Monroe and the Lees.

They risked their lives in a Revolution, yet their dream never changed: they wanted freedom from a British king, personal liberty, but no change in their order. Jefferson, because of his grotesquely misinterpreted democratic ideals, was regarded as a dangerous rene-gade by his own family. His cousin, the brilliant eccentric, John Ran-dolph of Roanoke, spoke more typically when he said, "I am an aristocrat; I love liberty; I hate equality."

By 1775, the Colony had spread far beyond the fortified little set-tlement on Jamestown Island, and the capital had shifted to Wil-liamsburg, midway between Jamestown on one river and Yorktown on the other. During the Revolution the capital moved to Richmond, then a trading post at the head of tidewater on the James River, and the splendor of plantation life on the Peninsula began to decline. The rule of the planter class, which instead of giving leadership had clung to its privileges in personal uses of power, was ended, along with so much else, by the Civil War.

"The war," as Virginians still refer to it, was not a matter of two armies fighting to a decision. For an entire decade the state was fought over, lived off, and ruled by occupation forces. Its civilization was destroyed more totally than that of any avowed enemy of the United States.

The planter class, for all its power, had been unable to swing Virginia into the secession column—until Lincoln called on Virginia for troops to invade her sister states. Then, with the soil they loved threatened by invasion, the people themselves rose against the Yankees. In an unsurpassed rush of volunteering, they formed the nucleus of the greatest army man for man in the Western world—Lee's legendary "Army of Northern Virginia." Robert E. Lee, a disbeliever in slavery and a nonsecessionist, became a god of the South not only because he fought off six Union armies and their generals (including Grant), but because he personified the patriarchal leader of the legendary aristocratic society. From that Virginia society came other members of the planter class, like Jeb Stuart and A. P. Hill and the great fox hunter, Turner Ashby; there came members of the then unprivileged class, like Stonewall Jackson and Dick Ewell (a schoolteacher's son whose grandfather had been an intimate of George Washington); there came professional soldiers like Joe Johnston and "Prince John" Magruder and George Pickett.

Virginia lost its ruling class (the good with the evil), its manpower, its wealth, its place in the sun. It did not lose its glory, for the Army of Northern Virginia had no habit of defeat. The state's educated class and its virile young were sacrificed in a cause that was lost, but the only state marker of defeat you'll find in Virginia is on the last retreat that ended at Appomattox Court House.

In coming back from the total wreckage, with cities and even college buildings burned, Virginia started with nothing. Freed Negroes and dispossessed planters followed lean mules on adjoining fields under the merciless sun. Or they trekked in carts and on foot in a melancholy stream into the rebuilding cities, seeking any kind of work.

When my grandfather first came to Richmond, he had only the clothes he had worn at Appomattox. As buttons bearing Confederate insignia were forbidden, and he was too poor to buy buttons or pins, his patched gray jacket was held together by thorns. The Confederate buttons (which I still have) were kept as a secret badge of honor.

Instead of the conquest changing the Virginian, it clarified and accentuated all that he already was. He brought to the city his courtesy, which deepened in this time of trouble; he brought his manners, which grew softer in his gentleness to his fellows; he brought his proudest inner possession, a sense of honor.

There were some with the greed to take advantage of the distress of their countrymen. Even during the brief lifetime of the Confederacy, some cold-headed operators suspected the Rebels' future and hoarded their gold. They broke the creed; they were not true lovers of Virginia. The true lover went down the financial drain and, like virtue, this has its own reward to his descendants.

During the physical and financial rebuilding of Virginia, new powers emerged and took up where the lordly planters left off. Their rise was in the Virginia tradition of the rule of the many by the superior few, for they were superior in about all that counted in those desperate days—money.

It was not until a half century later, in the Great Depression, that the arrogant grip of these neo-Bourbons was cracked by young ambitious Virginians with their way to make and nowhere else to go; yet with all their energy and determination, they could not have done it without help from the North. Under the enchantment of the Virginia way of life, Northerners began buying up old places so that they could live as the planters had. They have come in such numbers that we called the movement "the second invasion." Incredible as it seems to those of us who went North, they come to Virginia for opportunity! They are ambitious for a place for their families rather than for personal fortune.

The center of Virginia's parochial society has always been the family—indeed, the state is something of a family. The basis of this is not, as is commonly thought, "ancestor worship," though certainly there are awesome bores on the subject who reverently muse over familiar genealogical charts in some personal telling of their beads. The family is simply the thing of value, as is wealth (or conspicuous consumption) in a money society. And those qualities regarded most highly by a Virginia family, in addition to honor and gentle manners, are lack of suspiciousness and of pushiness.

It is these standards, as clearly understood and as unarticulated as an unwritten code, that have attracted the new Northerners. In Tidewater, we have been particularly fortunate in those from the North who have bought the great river plantations which grew from the Jamestown dream. By restoring these places to their ancient splen-

dor, they are making the Virginia peninsula even more appealing to
visitors.

This narrow strip of land, between the James and the York rivers,
contains Jamestown, the first settlement, of which little more than
the ruins of the church remain. Across the peninsula, at Yorktown,
are the breastworks where George Washington won our independence. And between the two, Mr. Rockefeller's $61,500,000 dream
shows Williamsburg as it was in Colonial days when it was capital of
Virginia.

In conducting informal tours for friends from the North, I have
found that nothing so stirs the visitor, so evokes the past, as the river
plantations, those individual principalities which formed the dynas-
tic society of Virginia. Today, these show places—Westover, Bran-
don, Berkeley, Shirley and many others—are open to the public
during Garden Week, April 21–28, and the grounds may be seen the
year around.

Probably the purest evocation is captured at Westover, where the
house of most classic beauty in Colonial America was designed by
that learned dandy, William Byrd II. He collected the largest library
in the Colonies, was a good writer himself, and his love of elegance
was matched by an infallible taste.

The neighboring Berkeley Plantation is open the year around to
visitors, and was originally the home of the Harrisons, one of whom
was a signer of the Declaration and another was a President and the
grandfather of a President. The lawn is so vast that McClellan's
army of more than 100,000 camped between the house and the river,
on the retreat from Richmond. Under the influence of its repose, a
Union general and his bugler experimented with a new "Lights Out"
bugle call which, sweeping through the Union army, was adopted as
"Taps."

Taps had long since blown for the grandeur that was Berkeley
when the present owner's father bought it as a summer place around
the turn of the century, and started his son on the career of returning
a plantation to its former glory.

Similar houses are owned by similar converts all over the state,
though some remain in the possession of the original families. Descendants of the famous "King" Carter still live at Sabine Hall, built
in 1730, which continues as a working plantation; and their neighbors the Tayloes still occupy the charming Mount Airy. Both of these
show places are in what Virginians call the Northern Neck, where

George Washington was born at Wakefield and Robert E. Lee grew up in the now state-owned Stratford Hall.

The Neck is bounded on three sides by water—on the east by Chesapeake Bay, on the south by the Rappahannock, on the north by the Potomac—and until bridges and highways were built in recent years it remained, quite deliberately, inaccessible. Perhaps the least known region outside the state, it has the steadiest influx of Northerners who come to settle with neither horses nor old houses on their minds. They are substantial people and they blend without a rift into an order that has never been disturbed even by a railroad.

Though no state of its size includes larger areas of water, and no state was more influenced in its development by the use of waterways, Virginians as a whole were not a seafaring or water-minded people. Of course, fishing, for food and sport, has been a part of Virginia life since Jamestown, and boating has long been a pleasure to many, but it is distinctly within my memory that yacht clubs became fashionable along the countless waters that flow into the Bay.

The slow turn to water sports has a counterpart in Virginia's failure to see the full possibilities of its magnificent Hampton Roads. This immense harbor, with its fifty miles of shoreline, serves Norfolk and Portsmouth on the south bank of the James and Newport News on the north shore. But the shipyards and navy yards have drawn thousands of that "restless proletariat" which the planters feared from the beginning, and which the gentry still fear. As a result there is a stalemate between those who want to change nothing and those who want to change the existing order. And the Hampton Roads area—with nearly one fifth of the state's population and more than one fifth of its purchasing power—has been grievously neglected.

While the Northern Neck is similar to the Peninsula, physically and culturally, both being parts of Tidewater, a marked change comes in the Piedmont, now called "the horse country." The land of the Piedmont is open and rolling, with limestone deposits essential for good grass and for building strong bones. But actually the whole state is horse country. The first Thoroughbred to be imported to America for breeding (Bulle Rock, in 1730) stood near Richmond, and the two greatest Virginia money winners were bred in the Shenandoah Valley and in Hanover County, the land of Patrick Henry.

Racehorses for the commercial tracks, however, are not the abiding interest of Virginians. In typical anachronism, horse to them means "hunter"—a Thoroughbred trained to hunt, to be shown as a hunter, and to race in steeplechases where the prizes are cups and the glory local. As deep in my memory as the legends of the Confederacy are pictures of red-faced women, in severely tailored black hunting clothes, jumping sidesaddle at local horse shows, and of the beauty and excitement of colored silks fluttering in the autumn wind as gentleman riders maneuvered their horses for the start of a race over timber.

In steeplechases, *aficionados* stand beside a jump, and I remember my father holding me up and I wildly shaking as he forgot me to yell to a friend who had fallen right before our eyes: "Go on, Ira, you're still good for second money!"

We rode in childhood, and those who didn't ride knew about horses, as kids today know about automobiles. And, as with kids today, some of us never loved anything else so much. Those who earn their living in other ways make horses (hunters) an avocation. And natives of the so-called "horse country" (more properly hunt country) can support themselves by serving as trainers and riders of hunters for the equine-minded millionaires from the North.

The Piedmont has the best hunter show in America at Warrenton, one of the oldest and probably the best breeding show at Upperville, and long-established horse shows and racing around Leesburg, Middleburg, Culpeper and Berryville. And in those areas are the breeding farms of Mrs. Dodge Sloan, Mike Phipps, Paul Mellon and—at Montpelier, the former home of President Madison, near Orange— of Mrs. Marion du Pont Scott, one of our greatest converts.

The social *éclat* of the horse probably extends from its association with the plantation culture. Since all things in Virginia change by the ages, the native is just facing the fact that horses might, after all, be an anachronism.

From George Washington to Harry Byrd, Defenders of the Faith have been essentially defenders of the status quo. Yet George Washington led a revolution for which he would have been hanged had it failed and Harry Byrd introduced a minor social revolution when he induced industries to come to Virginia. Resistance continues, however, to large-scale industrialization which would change the social structure. "It's better to have more, scattered small industries," Senator Byrd once said. "They are the backbone."

The sharp cleavage between entrenched wealth and the rest of the population does not exist in a state where the drayman (as an actual example) might be the cousin of a former President—and not boast about it either. Families long distinguished produce clerks who prefer scholarship, or hunting, or the bottle to a more solid success. At the Richmond German, a dance assembly at which young ladies are presented to society, the clerk will appear in seedy evening clothes where the tycoon in finest raiment may not enter.

Because of the prevalence of this gentry, there is a body of voters who would so bitterly resent being referred to as "the people" that no demagogue has held power in the history of the state.

The setting of the University of Virginia is in that blandly enchanting countryside of Albemarle County, in the Blue Ridge foothills, where the spirit of the Sage of Monticello mingles with the aura of horse-shows and fox-hunts, old houses and new fashion. The old part of the university—the center unit of Jefferson's design—is probably unequaled by any other American college for its original and classic beauty. There are many colleges in the state—William and Mary, second oldest in the country; Washington and Lee; V.M.I., the only college in the country to possess a battle flag, won at New Market in the Civil War; Hollins and Randolph-Macon, Westhampton and Mary Washington, and the rare loveliness of Sweet Briar. But the university, on its evocative grounds at Charlottesville, exemplifies an undercover struggle between entrenched privilege and the vitality of a people.

This endless struggle is as old as the Old Dominion, though you will never hear a Virginian refer to it on the outside. They all join the myth which goes, "befoh de wah we had plenty of slaves." In the same way the Confederate Army had, as far as I know from listening to stories about my friends' ancestors, only two privates— Margaret Mitchell's grandfather and my own. We had a club called "Sons and Daughters of Men in the Ranks," but we had to take in Yankees to swell the membership.

Once I tried to disentangle history from the legend, in a lecture I gave to a woman's club in Richmond. I praised the courage and the hardihood of our pioneer ancestors who made reality out of a dream. I was nearly run out of town. They were no more eager to be reminded of their rough beginnings than is the lady who has recently escaped from the other side of the tracks.

So provincial-minded is the Virginian that once when I referred to "the Valley," I was astonished at a Mid Westerner who asked, "What Valley?" To the Virginian, there is only one—the Shenandoah. It was the first Great Valley of this country, through which the later-day (18th Century) pioneers passed to the then distant west of Kentucky, and where a unique culture developed among the fugitives from the plantation class in Tidewater and the migrant Dutch, Mennonites and Quakers from Pennsylvania.

The hardy Pennsylvania Dutch placed their impress on the Valley with their self-sufficient farms and self-reliant frontier democracy, but they, too, were swayed by the Jamestown dream. Though it was not plantation country (with slave labor and money crops), the fertile limestone soil yielded a fat competence which gave to the Valley people a continuity of sturdy individualism with manners indistinguishable from those of lordly Tidewater. Like the rest of the state, they have a great love of their region, but unlike most of the state, they live in an area of physical beauty by any standards. Lying between the Blue Ridge and the Alleghenies, it is a magnificently contoured, country where, in the 100-odd miles from Winchester to Lexington, tourists enter pre-Revolutionary towns with time-mellowed red brick houses built flush on the street.

During the Civil War the Valley suffered a devastation so complete that the executioner, a coarse little man named Sheridan, reported that "if a crow flies over the Valley, he'll have to carry his own knapsack." The Valley people had survived Indians before Yankees, and they took in stride the burning of their barns and houses, the running off of their stock—even the loss of their men, who were the nucleus of Stonewall Jackson's army.

If I were going to visit the Valley for the first time I would start on the Skyline Drive, running along the crest of the Blue Ridge, from which you can see the whole incredible panorama. In the Blue Ridge are the only people who speak Elizabethan English in America. Their ancestors were fugitives from the planter control of Tidewater, and they built a rude, aristocratic republic in the hills. They created mountaineer baronies, in a wild version of the James River plantations—for they, too, held the attitude, in their way. They made love and moonshine, played old ballads on the zither, and, illiterate and unknowledgeable of the world, survived with pride and good manners.

These hill clans also held their rude domains southward in the misty Blue Ridge, where Virginia borders Tennessee. This is the land

of John Fox's *Trail of the Lonesome Pine,* of the laurel and rhododendron, galax and hemlock and dogwood, of fine beef cattle, of
deer and bear, wild boar and wild turkey, quail and possum and
rabbit. This handsome country could well become a new garden spot.
The rolling green hills offer the coolest area in those truly epic summers which may be one explanation for the lack of dynamism in the
Old Dominion.

French aristocrats found a haven here from the Revolution, building the lost town of New Paris; Sherwood Anderson found a sanctuary here; and here Bob Porterfield found a unique success. Bob
had gone to New York to take a fling at the theater. When the depression struck, he returned home with a troupe of hungry actors,
and an idea. Abingdon offered him the use of the opera house in the
century-old town hall, with the jail underneath the stage, and the
Barter Theater was born. Nobody made any money that first summer
but they all ate high on the hog. When one of the patrons brought a
young pig, Bob Porterfield raised it and from successive litters produced hams, with which he pays royalties to such playwrights as
Noel Coward and Robert Sherwood. Only G. B. Shaw returned the
ham with the querulous protest, "Don't you know I'm a vegetarian?"
It became the first state-sponsored theater in the country, and one of
its functions today is to take "live theater" to people all over the
state.

Virginia also takes art masterpieces to the people in the nation's
first Artmobile—an air-conditioned trailer provided by that institu-
tional department store, Richmond's Miller & Rhoads, with paintings
belonging to Walter Chrysler, Jr., and operated by the Virginia
Museum of Fine Arts, one of America's finest small museums.

To the West are the Alleghenies, and to the northwest the counties
which seceded from the mother state during the Civil War and
formed West Virginia. When the dividing line was drawn down the
Alleghenies, the story goes, Unionists gave the surveyors such lavish
hospitality that they drew what amounted to a drunken line, veer-
ing east whenever they came to a particularly desirable spot, such as
White Sulphur Springs with its Greenbrier.

The Virginia part of the mountains is the nearest thing, after the
Shenandoah Valley, to the truly spectacular in the state. Certainly
the valley running from Warm Springs to Monterey is one of the
loveliest in our land. This whole section is filled with springs, though
most of the spas, which go back to post-Revolutionary days, today
are ghost towns. You can visit perhaps a dozen abandoned spas

where the grandees and their ladies once waltzed to Strauss after taking the sulphur baths; I never look at these places of vanished grandeur, like Old Sweet and Sweet Chalybeate (Cal-lib-e-at), without a yearning that they might be resurrected. But then there would be neons and gambling-hells, and the ghosts would slink away.

Today there is a new fashion in these hills—fugitives from the cities walk the quiet streams, fishing and lolling, and hoping that no one discovers their favorite spots. There are long-discovered places here, too, that are never out of fashion, like the Homestead at Hot Springs. In these resorts, as in the whole state, there is nothing of what is called "night life," and the Virginian who has tasted the entertainment of New York may groan despairingly at the lack.

In the state that invented the lavish table, where into my grandparents' day dinner lasted from 2:30 to 5:00, its capital was designed for gracious living. Built on a succession of hills rising above the James River and dominated by the white-pillared capitol planned by Jefferson when he was governor, Richmond with its "city villas" (as Dickens called them), was, in the words of a foreign visitor, "a charming, small world capital." Most of the villas are gone now, victims of "progress," and a tourist needs a guide to find the survivors which still evoke the vanished era. With them went the bars, and the hotel restaurants, which survived five Union armies—but not a Methodist bishop named Cannon who brought prohibition to Virginia, and, under stress of World War I, to the United States. Today, even in Virginia's citadel, good food can be found only in homes—and then without taint of French sauces.

Virginia food is both indigenous and a result of the war. In their desperate poverty, the three things they had were corn, hogs and greens. From these came the batterbread, the pork and sausage, and the turnip greens cooked in hog fat. To these were added that curious squash called simlin, a combination of black-eyed peas and stewed tomatoes, fresh- and salt-water fish (with roe herring as a breakfast dish and shad roe as a delicacy), game and fowl, "local beef" and "local liver," fruit and melons, crabs and clams and all varieties of oysters, of which the best are baked with ham, and ham itself—which is a separate subject. The pale meat sold as "Virginia Ham" is a Northern product. The true Virginia ham comes from peanut-fed hogs, and the meat is dark, very strong, and most Virginians can afford it only at Christmas. With a small hot biscuit, it is the favorite of all cocktail hors d'oeuvres.

The thin, crisp biscuit, and all hot bread, takes the place in the

Virginian's diet that sauces occupy in that of the European-minded gourmet. No Virginian, no matter where he lives, ever forgets the hot rolls on his mother's table.

In this, as in all things, the Virginian remains uninfluenced by what other people do or like. In drinks, his bourbon comes from native corn, and if you offer a simple Virginian Scotch, he'll say, "No, I prefer whisky." For my own martinis, I can rarely find a customer (unless a Northern visitor) and this includes the after-church hour of a very light drink. I refer here to the Episcopal Church. The after-church drinking hour of its communicants goes back at least to the early 18th Century when William Byrd at Westover became so overwhelmed with Sunday guests, some of whom stayed on for the following Sunday, that he caused the church to be moved. You can still see it, small and simple and wholly charming, and wonder how so few communicants could have caused one host so much trouble.

The ruralites who voted prohibition to Virginia are no longer in numerical predominance, but they are so solid, so impassioned, and so traditional, that no bloc is strong enough to defy them. They are supported by the bootleggers who flourish in a state where alcohol may not be served in a public place—but only bought by the bottle in a state store. The poor people say: "You can't buy a drink in Virginia: you have to buy a drunk." The rich belong to clubs in which bartenders serve them as long as the members keep bottles in their lockers.

This blight of the rural rule on night life does not apply to the cities' Negro population. Since the Negroes have no intention of abiding by a law they regard as manifestly absurd, the police are said to permit orderly, established fleshpots to remain open. To walk down famed and wide-open Second Street in Richmond after midnight (when the rest of the city is as silent as a graveyard) is to discover one of the complexities of "segregation" in a traditional society composed of two thirds white and one third Negro.

Between the educated, privileged Negro and the ignorant there is a chasm deeper and wider than anything in white society. As everything in Virginia extends from the past, this is an extension of the historic cleavage between the house people and the field hands. But the drivers of Cadillacs are sometimes black people of field-hand heritage who toot imperiously at Negroes of obviously gentle background.

The Negroes have made an art of manners. Except for some of the hostile young and those who stand stiffly on the dignity of new privilege, they equal the whites in courtesy and friendliness, and between the two races there exists a casual intimacy outsiders find difficult to believe. My nurse Edmonia, who had been my father's nurse, had before that been my grandmother's companion, and the two girls had come to Richmond together after the Civil War at the age of sixteen. As Edmonia and my grandmother grew old together, a silent rivalry developed between the old ladies. They occupied adjoining rooms and they vied with each other for the most presents—handkerchiefs, petticoats, stockings, even the bright patches which went into the quilts they made. When they died, the drawers of their bureaus were crowded with objects they had never worn and which seemed to settle the rivalry at a draw. I remember them with enduring love, as my daughters will remember Lucille, their younger version of Edmonia. This is not offered as any pious benediction on "the race problem," but only as a statement of things as they exist in a world changing too fast.

This, then, is the culture which has endured without essential change for nearly three and a half centuries, and which, in the words of Senator Byrd, expects to continue a long time yet. It gave America its greatest revolutionary leaders, it produced more presidents than any other state, it gave to the Confederacy Robert E. Lee, the nation's supreme military leader—yet it makes no great American claims. It is Virginia.

The people of no other state are more passionately identified with their own land place. When traveling abroad and asked their nationality, they will invariably reply, "I am a Virginian." In fact, I know of one internationally famous gentleman who carried this to its ultimate parochialism. When he was presented to the Court and the King asked where he was from, he replied, "Fauquier County, sir—the upper end."

In *The History and Present State of Virginia*, written in 1705, an observer said, "Here is the most Good-nature, and Hospitality practis'd in the World, both towards Friends and Strangers. . . . If there happen to be a Churl, that either out of Covetousness, or Ill-nature, won't comply with this generous Custom, he has a mark of Infamy set upon him. . . ." To our strength and weakness, this could be written today. For even in changing by the ages, Virginia does not change in the attitude.

West Virginia

by JOHN KNOWLES

Many people who have not visited a state think of it as a particular color; for me Florida is bright yellow, Louisiana russet, Alabama clay red. I believe that many who have not seen my home state, West Virginia, think of it as gray. But in fact it is the greenest of states—mountains like tight green clouds, valleys of every shade of green with rivers of plated green moving through them. Lining the banks of the Kanawha River, which flows across the southern part of the state, are gray coal mines and chemical plants in gray towns; but everywhere the natural green encroaches against them, as though to squeeze out the thin line of industry separating the green of the mountains from the green of the river. And right now, in the fall, vivid colors are breaking out from the greenness to bring the whole state alive. Day by day these big hills are brightening, the hues increasing in intensity until you can almost hear the clashing brightnesses—trees of burning scarlet and gentle yellow vying on the hillsides among the rocks and evergreens.

West Virginia is a lovely state to look at and an odd one to think about. Many Americans seem not to be really sure it exists. "West Virginia?" new acquaintances exclaim hazily when I tell them where I'm from. "How far do you live from Richmond?"

This is a very tactless question, and I reply distantly that I have no idea how far I live from Richmond, but that I live seventy-five miles south of Wheeling, and two hundred miles north of Charleston (West Virginia). This rarely helps them to place me geographically, but it clears the air of that specter which haunts the state, the memory of that outraged, abandoned mother, Virginia.

We West Virginians are very tired of being considered inhabitants of just a dominion of the Old Dominion; we would like to make it clear that our state has been independent for ninety years. Some residents take a very strong line about this and always refer to it in conversation as "*West*—By God—Virginia!" We know it is the state people forget when trying to memorize the fifty, that it's the state they aren't sure whether they've driven through or not, that it's one of the hillbilly states. Nevertheless, West Virginia stands right in the middle of American history and development, and has caught and held a great deal of both within its impossibly irregular borders.

The result is a stew, a conglomeration of old-new, radical-conservative, Southern-Northern, rich-poor, ridiculous-dignified American characteristics. That is why West Virginia is "pivotal" politically and gets so much attention during Presidential campaigns. No one can call the turn here; like a completely open-minded man, the state has made a habit of accepting both sides of our national arguments, indiscriminately including Yankees and Rebels, Bourbons and labor agitators, old-stock mountaineers and Sicilian coal miners, beauty and unsightliness. You think you have it when you see the steel mills, the coal mines, the great chemical plants; you think again when you hear the Southern accents, feel the relaxed pace of life, the lazy laissez-faire sociability. Then you see a log-cabin mountain family and you don't know what to think. What you may finally conclude is that this ignored little state somehow incorporates the major elements of life throughout the nation.

On the map my state is probably the funniest-looking state in the Union; it resembles a pork chop with the narrow end splayed. The square southwestern corner of Pennsylvania divides northern West Virginia into two panhandles, one dwindling up between Pennsylvania and Ohio and the other extending eastward like a limp arm between Maryland and Virginia. The northern panhandle, which contains Wheeling with its heavy steel production, points a symbolic finger at the industrial northeast. The quietly rural eastern panhandle curves back toward the Old South. And this is the dual role of the state, bustlingly industrial yet lackadaisically Southern.

But both panhandles spring from the hillbilly heart of the state, the steep little Allegheny Mountains to which old farms and forests cling, and through which dirt roads connect such unassertive villages as Romance and Kentuck, and Losie and Chloe. The names of these quiescent mountain settlements tell something of the state: Alice, Burnt House, Thursday, Shock, Lost Creek (pronounced "crick"), Cucumber, Cyclone, Hurricane, Gip, Heaters, Hominy Falls, Coco, Quick, Lone Cedar. West Virginians are a literal-minded breed, and if Gip seems to be the most appropriate name for their town, that's what they call it, without apology.

I have always wanted to humor those people who insist on finding Li'l Abner in every farm youth, whose ears ring with imagined buckshot on every country road. I've always wanted to bring one of them into my state over a back road with the properly grimy name of Blacksville Road. You approach the Mason-Dixon line from Pittsburgh over a fine Pennsylvania highway, a smooth, wide strip of cement gliding gracefully through pleasant farmland. Suddenly this show-off road ends. There is a kind of dropping sensation; the car springs, which have been relaxing, are thrown into violent action. There is a sharp left turn, a sharper right turn, a stop sign. You are in Blacksville, West Virginia.

Beyond the stop sign you encounter your first real West Virginia turn, a tight hairpin curve starting up the side of a mountain. Reaching the top you plummet straight down into a narrow valley. Now you are really in the hills of West Virginia and the scenery is chaotic. There are few orderly perspectives in this state; the great geological upheavals which buried vast fortunes in minerals underground threw up hills, ridges and mountains every which way on the surface. Valleys start east, turn north, end going west. Hills rise in steep juxtaposition, forested so thickly that it seems you could walk on the treetops. Wide meadows tilt at improbable angles with haystacks perched on them like rakish hats, fences running busily down, around and over, trying to organize the disorder.

As you follow the wanderings of the Blacksville Road, narrowed by now to the interesting West Virginia width of one-and-a-half cars, cows appear grazing almost directly above, while on the other side you look down the chimney of a farmhouse. Surely West Virginia has the only cornfield which is entered by stepladder, the only mule which must be hoisted by block and tackle to the fields. The famous story of the city motorist in the hill-farming country has at least poetic truth. He is driving along the bottom of a steep-walled valley when there is a sudden flurry of dust ahead. He pulls up, and as the cloud settles he sees a rather battered farmer stamping his foot in anger. "What in the world happened?" asks the motorist.

"That's the third time," replies the farmer disgustedly, "I've fell outen that cornfield this mornin'."

The Blacksville Road is stereotyped West Virginia. But presently you wind along a little stream, a "run" as it is called here, pass through a 100-year-old covered bridge, and enter Fairmont, my home town. Here the myth of West Virginia the mountain wilderness must die.

Fairmont is the seventh largest city in the state. The houses are wired for electricity. The streets are paved. This is an important center in the richest bituminous-coal seam in the world, but there are no mines to be seen, they are all in the outlying districts. John L. Lewis commands allegiance underground, and a publication called the *Southern Social Register* attempts to hold sway above. On Saturday nights, good old mountain music twangs out from local hot spots, while in the high-school auditorium the Fairmont Symphony Orchestra plays Mozart. The town has drawn inhabitants from everywhere, Alabama drawls mingling easily with the heightened diction of Massachusetts. Italians, Russians and Poles were brought in to work the mines early in this century, and now their children and grandchildren are being assimilated into Fairmont.

I suppose all these influences make Fairmont a confusing place culturally, but it has a special, typically West Virginia atmosphere which blends them all comfortably. The best term I can think of to describe it is laissez-faire, which would be translated there as "let it be." I saw it most clearly in action one day when I was sixteen. At the time I was taking out a girl who was very attractive but not very mechanically minded, and one afternoon she inadvertently drove her family's new sedan into a grocery store.

"That's terrible," said her mother when she heard of it. "And you children wanted to use the car tonight, didn't you?"

We admitted as much, rather hopelessly now, in view of the accordion folds in the car's front end.

Her father, less easily discouraged, drove the car around the block. "It won't turn left," he reported, "but it turns right well enough."

"That's wonderful," said her mother. She handed me the keys. "*You* do the driving," she said, "and don't try to turn left."

We spent a fine evening going from place to place in large right-hand circles. No one worried about the cost of the repairs. The car would get repaired eventually. And it did.

This balanced ease is one characteristic of West Virginia; another is the ghosts. In Fairmont we consort with the shades of vanished wealth. We grew up with their haunts around us: an empty mansion, modeled after Inverness Castle in Scotland, with crenelated towers and a swimming pool in the basement; pillared homesteads turned into dancing schools; gracious family residences become Red Cross headquarters, or the meeting rooms of the Women's Club, or torn down to make way for gasoline stations. The time was the end of the '30's, and these were the homes built, and during the depression abandoned, by the coal "barons" of Fairmont.

The two most elaborate were within a couple of blocks of our home. Higate, which has become a rest home for nuns, was a majestic place behind its ornate black iron fence, with gravel drives curving through immaculate lawns, its boxwood hedges, tennis court, and the formal vistas of its landscaping. Coal was king in 1910 when J. E. Watson built it, and it was a kingly domicile, a half-timbered Elizabethan country manor house set down in the coal fields.

Next to it is Watson Farms, the original family place. The twenty-room main house ignores its setting just as blandly as the other great Fairmont houses do—it is Spanish Mission design. So are its gatehouse and the carriage house and the other outbuildings. But the grounds, rolling land thick with rhododendron and evergreens, used to be pure West Virginia, and it must have been a fine home at its height, just before the first World War. Clarence Watson was in the Senate then, and William Jennings Bryan came to visit him there.

Today the main house, the carriage house and barn have been broken up into apartments. New ranch-style houses have sprung up like toadstools on the grounds, and the original old log-cabin Watson home, freshly painted, is now a nice suburban residence.

It's all there on Watson Farms—the simple pioneer days, the lush impermanent boom, economic collapse, and then recovery to the pleasant broadened level of middle-class living in the 1950's. It's the social history of Northern West Virginia, and it suggests the social evolution of the United States.

The age of flight presents a real challenge in West Virginia, where nothing is flat except the river surfaces, and not always those. Charleston, the capital, has solved the problem by blasting the tops off three mountains, moving 9,000,000 cubic yards of earth, and setting down on the resultant plateau an $8,500,000 airport. This is Kanawha Airport, the city's current pride. It is served by four air lines and offers what is probably the most comfortable entrance to the state.

With a population of about 90,000 and over 200,000 in the surrounding metropolitan area, Charleston is the center of the state's most thickly settled area. It has more physical dignity than any other West Virginia city, not having been dropped in a hollow or perched on a mountainside. It extends back in an orderly manner from the north bank of the majestic Great Kanawha River, with a splendid, Chicagoesque shore front and a wide boulevard paralleling the river the whole length of the city.

Charleston has a cultural life in keeping with its urbane appearance; a symphony orchestra and even a chamber-music group are maintained, a little theater flourishes, public forums are held, touring Broadway plays come and are welcomed.

The Kanawha Boulevard leads on to the downtown center of Charleston, with the South Hills, a handsome residential district, overlooking it from the opposite bank. Motoring along this drive you pass a symmetrical red-brick house, Georgian colonial in design, graceful and refined in aspect—the governor's residence. And next to it, thoroughly overshadowing it, rises the large, impressive, extensive, ornate, three-winged, U-shaped, Corinthian-pillared, gold-domed, 300-foot-high, $10,000,000 State Capitol.

There are at least two reasons why a small state such as West Virginia should have so elaborate a capitol. One is that, until it was erected in 1932, the official headquarters of the state shuttled four times between Wheeling and Charleston, and the present edifice settles by its sheer size and immovability where the state government will sit for a long time to come. It is also the solidest and weightiest proof that the state is 100 per cent independent of Mother Virginia, a fact which we West Virginians hope to see gain general recognition.

You can also fly into Wheeling, up in the northern panhandle, your plane nosing down on the mountain-surrounded airport like a stalling dive bomber. This is West Virginia's third largest and perhaps best-known city, thanks to its pun-evoking name. (Sample gag: America's most difficult national project is Wheeling West Virginia.) But with its Northern orientation, this original capital of the state doesn't worry over the jokes and wheezes.

Wheeling Downs, the city's race track on an island in the Ohio River, is a beautiful sports center, with its bright grandstand and clubhouse, its landscaped grounds, its shining Thoroughbreds. During the fifty-five days of racing there, which end about October first, the city takes on a dashing air, slightly lawless and western, very big-time for West Virginia.

On the outskirts of town unrolls 808-acre Oglebay Park, a gracious old plantation turned into a municipal playground. For a city of Wheeling's modest size, Oglebay Park is a major accomplishment in recreational diversity. Outdoor operas, folk dancing, flower shows, turkey shoots, swimming carnivals, horse shows, carillon concerts, golf, tennis, riding, hiking and many other sports, symphony programs—it's a very diverse list.

Wheeling has too much to offer to mind being laughed at, and more than enough industries, 400 of them, manufacturing everything from stogies to steel, to be able to afford a few jokes at its expense.

You can come by train from Washington to Grafton, the noted northern West Virginia rail hub, but I cannot recommend this route. The trip could be spectacularly scenic, the train climbing up and plunging down the Alleghenies, curving around horseshoe bends like a dog chasing its own tail. But whenever the scenery has really caught your attention the train is sure to dive into some tunnel, and all becomes gray and black. I think it was Irvin S. Cobb who described this route as the longest tunnel in the world, interrupted by occasional air vents.

Arriving at Grafton will confirm all your worst fears about West Virginia. Here the first battle of the Civil War was fought, or rather not fought: the Confederates evacuated the town before advancing Union troops without firing a shot, pausing only long enough to burn bridges and mess up the town generally. Grafton has been disordered ever since, a gray, sagging place, its narrow streets crawling miserably up a steep hillside. Whatever isn't gray is black, and while it is a busy rail center, it has looked abandoned as long as I can remember.

Grafton is what some outlanders expect of West Virginia, and once they have seen it, especially if it is their first impression of the state, they often develop an irritating habit of gauging everything else by it. "Yes, this is nice," they'll admit when shown one of the state's numberless scenic beauties, "but of course I knew *everything* couldn't

be like Grafton." For them, everything really is; West Virginia remains gray in their imaginations.

But I still haven't pointed out the real way to come to West Virginia. Coming by train to Grafton is not recommended, and the
Blacksville Road should be attempted only by the most expert
drivers. Come instead to Harpers Ferry, at the easternmost tip of the
state, fifty-five miles west of Washington, D.C. Thomas Jefferson
said the view here, where the Shenandoah River flows into the Potomac through a gap in the Blue Ridge Mountains, was worth a trip
across the Atlantic. The main highway by-passes the Ferry now and
you may miss the turn-off, but don't let that worry you for the moment. A few miles farther on is Charles Town and old West Virginia, the farthest outpost of the mint-julep country, the northern
end of that gracious arc of pillars and soft accents and fine horses, the
center of which is somewhere near Atlanta. In its most Rebel moods
this area, the extreme eastern panhandle of the state, considers the
West Virginians beyond the mountains a band of shirt-sleeved Yankee boors and still comes to a boil over the outrage of 1863.

In that pivotal year in our history, just ten days before the Battle
of Gettysburg, West Virginia joined the divided Union. The eastern
panhandle, overwhelmingly sympathetic to the South, had no wish
to be in this oddity of a state, this secession from the Secession. But
they were given no real choice. The Baltimore and Ohio Railroad
passed through these counties, and the Government in Washington,
busily carving West Virginia out of Confederate Virginia, tacked the
eastern panhandle onto the new state so that the B & O would be
officially in northern territory. Charles Town has never forgotten that
it was railroaded into West Virginia.

In West Virginia the conflict was a civil war in the bitterest sense,
a war within a state, with the battles lines of allegiance running down
the center of main streets, through back yards and barnyards, and
cutting cruelly through the middle of family homes. The eastern panhandle, politically in the North, its loyalties and men with the South,
suffered most. Harpers Ferry was battered by successive captures
and recaptures, Romney changed hands fifty-six times, Charles Town
was ruined.

The old wrongs, the dead conflicts, have slowly taken the life from
Harpers Ferry. The state recently bought more than 400 acres in and
around the town and donated them to the country for preservation as

a national monument. Harpers Ferry clusters around the base and climbs up the sides of a steep hump of land between the Shenandoah and Potomac Rivers; the rivers join just beyond the town, Maryland and Virginia are represented across the water by impressive cliffs, and the spirit of John Brown marches on here as nowhere else.

At a time when advocating the abolition of slavery was a most inflammatory attitude, Brown was the most militant of abolitionists. Fresh from the warfare in Kansas over slavery, he attacked Harpers Ferry in 1859 to free the slaves in that area. He also thought he might start a government of his own there, hustling Negroes by this route from Southern slavery to Northern freedom.

John Brown's raid, together with the war it forecast, arrested the development of the town. Harpers Ferry is motionless today; only about 800 inhabitants remain—there is no industry, no business section, no real vitality. Relics of the past are scattered carelessly through it, and nature has moved to take possession again. The handsome early 19th Century houses near the center of town are collapsing, undercut by floods, war and poverty. Old ladies slip along the silent streets, old men hole up with stray dogs in historic, decadent mansions.

Unless the visitor knows something about the raid and about the Civil War in this area, he will find Harpers Ferry only an uninteresting shell. On the bottom land between the town and the river junction, outlined in white flagstones on a sunken lawn, is the site of the Armory which was seized by Brown and his band of twenty-two men, and where they were besieged by United States troops under Brevet Colonel Robert E. Lee. Near the Armory site a small white monument has been erected in memory of John Brown, the great abolitionist and hero of the North. But you can't get away unchallenged with *that* kind of thing in ambiguous West Virginia, so close by it the United Daughters of the Confederacy have placed a boulder to Heywood Shepherd, loyal servant of the South. A Negro, Shepherd was stationmaster at Harpers Ferry, and failed to stop quickly enough when Brown's men cried halt. They shot him. "He exemplifies the character and faithfulness of thousands of Negroes," wrote the United Daughters in their inscription.

A little distance up the street, hewn out of native rock, are the steep natural stone steps which ran with gore during the Civil War. At the top of them is the sagging mansion of the founder of the town, Robert Harper, and beyond it, up a little trail, is the ruin of

St. John's Episcopal Church, which was used as a hospital during the war. The Gothic walls and empty windows remain, the roof is gone, four trees grow up through the nave and vines cling everywhere. Farther along the trail a great rock threatens at any moment to plunge down a cliffside into the Shenandoah River; Jefferson stood on it to make his remark about the view, which is a little obstructed now by the wild fingers of television aerials. It's a fine view, but mortifying as it is to contradict Jefferson, I don't think it was ever worth a trip across the Atlantic.

At the top of the path, on the grounds of Storer College, is John Brown's Fort. Actually a fire-engine house, the fort was down by the river when Brown was besieged and captured in it. After the raid it became famous, and was shipped to the Chicago Exposition of 1893 and moved here and there before winding up on its present site. It's a righteous little structure, one and a half stories high, with arched windows and topped by a cupola. It is a museum today, and also a kind of shrine to the man who achieved such an odd immortality there.

It's interesting that he chose this spot as the place where he could stand to move the whole nation. The raid was a typically West Virginia adventure, very small and irregular, presumptuous, almost silly; yet reverberating outward in all directions, forecasting the future, crystallizing a national dilemma.

John Brown in legend and Tidewater elegance in life dominate this northeastern tip of West Virginia. You will find the Old South in Charles Town today, patched up physically and emotionally, slaveless but still served by Negroes, horsy as ever. The magnificent manor homes built by George Washington's relatives around Charles Town are occupied once more; Claymont Court, erected by his grandnephew Bushrod, has been restored, and a swimming pool and one or two other modern touches added. But it remains antebellum, a spacious yellow-brick mansion with slave quarters attached to the main house by walled courtyards, and a wide veranda, which all plantation homes must have, overlooking a sloping terrace. "Visitors Welcome" reads a sign at the main gate, just as it should at a Southern home.

Apple growing and cattle have restored the prosperity of Charles Town, scenery has drawn the tourists, and horse racing is the main diversion. None of the national front-page horses appear; huge purses are not won. I don't believe the Duke and Duchess of Windsor have ever attended, but people from the panhandle, people from Virginia and Maryland and the District of Columbia enjoy it very much. My sister and a couple of her sheltered friends used to go alone to the races when they were fourteen and no one ever feared for their morals.

Ed Blake, editor of a local newspaper, has a reason for the courtly atmosphere of life around Charles Town. "Good soil," he said recently, "it always draws good people. This is the best farming land in the state, along with the Greenbrier Valley in the south end. They breed wonderful cattle there. Why, down in the Greenbrier Valley there's more bluegrass than in the whole state of Kentucky—and you can quote me on that." I do so with pleasure, and I believe it.

The Greenbrier Valley is another fragment of the Old South in West Virginia, and it has that vivid greenness which bluegrass produces. As in the eastern panhandle, there are the white wooden fences here, but they bring a serene simplicity to this landscape, they seem to be holding it together. It is completely unlike the pitching hills and distracted fences of northern West Virginia; here the hills are in order and at rest, the fences bright and changeless. And here, whitest of all, is the Greenbrier Hotel at White Sulphur Springs, where everything to be painted is painted white, leaving the lawns and shrubbery, the trees and surrounding hills in deep green. It is the vacation pride of West Virginia, and while it has always wished it were a Virginia resort again, as it was before the Civil War, we are glad to have it in our state.

Directly across the state, in the southwestern corner next to Kentucky, life is as different as can be found. Rustic living and revival religion set the tone, people are just folks, and horses are not for racing or riding, they're for work.

Logan, West Virginia, the center of this rugged country, has its own legendary figure—that scourge of the mountains, Devil Anse Hatfield. Captain Anderson Hatfield, as he is referred to on his tombstone, was almost John Brown's equal in righteousness and easily his equal in lawlessness. Both men conceived of themselves as bigger than life, both led bands of killers for reasons their instincts told them were good, and society brought them both to account—well, almost; Brown, who was of course the greater figure and ever uncompromising, was executed. Devil Anse kind of played along with society and died quietly in bed, at the age of eighty-two, from pneumonia. But long before that, he had been stripped of his power as chieftain of the Hatfield clan, the hated McCoys of Kentucky could walk with comparative safety along the streets of Logan, and society had restricted him, like a lesser Napoleon, to a patch of mountains around his home. He used to come into Logan on Saturdays from his farm, his beard spreading down to his chest, "a nice, quiet fellow," one of the elders of Logan told me.

I was glad to hear this because I was just a shade uneasy in Logan. People in Fairmont had filled my ears with warnings. "You'd better carry a gun when you go to Logan," they said. "Don't get drunk on moonshine, don't act like a revenuer, and don't talk Yankee." When I arrived in the narrow, jammed streets of Logan, with mountain bluffs surrounding the town like fortifications, I had a sudden uneasy feeling, as I got out of the car, that I might be lined up in someone's gun sights.

The old-timer briskly dismissed Logan's feuding reputation. Like everyone in that country today, he is anxious to forget the primitive past. Log cabins, he points out, have almost disappeared. The roads have improved to the point where horses are no longer needed to haul cars up the mountains during wet weather. Electricity is everywhere. The children go to school, and the men seldom carry guns.

"My father came here in '71," he said, "and it was quiet, peaceable, neighborly. There were a few fights, what I mean a man might get killed, just like anywhere. But nothing serious."

He spoke in the warm, expressive way of West Virginians, using a wide range of tone, slurring over a few words to descend emphatically on the important one.

"Devil Anse used to call on our family every couple of weeks," he went on, "and I was up to his house once, with my daddy. Very nice old man, Devil Anse was."

He told me that the Hatfield Cemetery, with a monument to Anse, was at Omar, a few miles away. I asked him to describe the monument but he said it was "just another stone to me, I didn't pay it much mind." So I went to see for myself.

On the road I had to stop at an intersection and a tall boy of about thirteen, with red-brown hair and the calm, fine-boned highland face came to the window of the car. "Goin' to Omar?" he asked.

I said I was, and without another word he got in. I asked whether he could show me where the Hatfield Cemetery was, and he said he could. We drove along in silence for a while, and then he said, "Pull in here."

I stopped, and the boy got out and pointed up a steep hillside. "The cemetery's up thar," he said.

I started up the rocky path and the boy followed. "Are you coming along?"

"Yup," he said. We climbed in silence, and at the top of the path saw a No Trespassing sign over the name J. D. Hatfield. Almost secure in the old fellow's peaceful picture of the hills, I went by it with only a momentary jouncing on the nerves, to look at the graves, perhaps thirty of them, ascending the cleared slope. Devil Anse, in white Italian marble, looms over the burial ground. He stands erect, in frock coat and leggings, gazing paternally across the hills. A lone fir tree stands beside him and two of his sons, killed on the same day, are buried at his feet.

"My aunt lies up thar," said the boy suddenly, pointing farther up the hill. I looked at her grave and the others, with withered wreaths on their markers, forgotten bouquets here and there, the grass overgrown all around.

This was the ending then of the bitter vendetta. On Devil Anse's monument his children are listed, among them Jonse, who started it all in 1882 by running off with Rosanna McCoy. Of course fighting had broken out before that between the McCoys on the Kentucky side of the Tug River and the Hatfields on the West Virginia side, but Jonse and Rosanna really ignited it. Then followed the ambushings, the kidnappings and slaughterings, the pitched battles, the burning of the McCoy leader's cabin, the ineffectual indictments (both families controlled law enforcement in their respective counties). Above the din of border warfare the governors of Kentucky and West Virginia argued furiously about who had invaded whose state, and who should surrender which feudist to whom.

The feud simmered down during the '90's, and the coming of the railroad to Logan in 1904 extinguished it. There was too much valuable coal up those narrow hollows to have them a battleground, too much good timber stood on the mountains to leave them forever a no-man's-land. Money dragged law and order willy-nilly into Logan County, and the day came when the Hatfields began laying to rest in their cemetery relatives who had died from natural causes.

The boy and I returned to the car and drove back down the road.

"Bob Hatfield's store," he said, pointing to a little homely country store at the side of the road. We stopped there and met Bob, a jolly fat man in rimless glasses wearing a shirt gaudy as a beach umbrella. He was filling a little girl's order and teasing her affectionately. "Sassiest customer I ever did see," he exclaimed about her to the world in general. I noticed the latest in chlorophylled, ammoniated tooth pastes on his shelves, and thought how far we were from Devil Anse. Then I heard a very un-West Virginia voice coming from the back room, and looking in, saw a television screen occupied by Bishop Fulton J. Sheen, lecturing on Freud.

Right then I abandoned the idea of finding any real mountaineers. Driving away, I mentioned to the boy that, judging from laughing Bob Hatfield, the days of violence were over.

"Yeah, he's always jokin'," agreed the boy. But he added, "One time we's fishing on his land, and he took after us with a shotgun."

That night I drove away from Logan feeling that certainly it was peaceful and all the hillbilly clichés were wrong, but that like a quiet fire far down in a mine, a trace of lonely clannish implacability remained.

So it is in West Virginia—a chopped up, heterogeneous area where each part has only a limited understanding and not much admiration for the other parts. Considering its surface ruggedness, it is something of a tribute to western man that two million people settled there at all.

The Indians didn't try. They reserved it for animals, and judging from the game still there, it must have been a very happy hunting ground. Today armies of deer roam among the mountains and can be seen bounding across busy highways. Grouse, wild turkey, raccoon, black bear and other game fill the state with sport. On autumn days, with the mountainsides celebrating by lighting up the trees, and the lifting wind carrying animal scents and spinning leaves and the blurred crack of shotguns—on such days the notion of West Virginia as a gray industrial hole vanishes.

A state as historically, geographically and culturally ambiguous as West Virginia has a hard time taking a stand on most of our national issues. For example, West Virginia is unshakably on the fence with regard to Negroes. They vote, and they ride where they wish in buses. But they sit in the balconies of theaters, and accept other less obtrusive segregation. They are not second-class citizens and they are not first-class citizens.

The state straddles liquor with equally determined irresoluteness. West Virginia is dry, with liquor legally sold only in state-operated stores. But numberless "clubs" with a couple of dollars membership fee have sprung up where bars operate more or less openly. And then there are just plain bars, without any pretense at being clubs, doing good business. Gambling, rackets, political graft, all have their place in the West Virginia as in the national picture. Being such a compromise of a state, West Virginia is strategically placed to hold a mirror up to our national manners—the gyrations around the green tables of Nevada, the political scandals of New York, the racial inequalities of Mississippi, all are reflected there. Unselective like a mirror, West Virginia catches these images as well as the better ones.

Perhaps then if we could find the typical West Virginian we would have the typical American—what a boon he would be to all the poll takers and opinion samplers and everyone with something to sell. But I cannot find such an essence; it isn't John W. Davis of Clarksburg, who ran for President in 1924; or Louis Johnson of Clarksburg, who was Secretary of Defense for a while; or Jack Dempsey, who loosened up his championship muscles in the Logan coal mines; or Wheeling's gift to the Metropolitan Opera, Eleanor Steber. It's not Ed Blake or Bob Hatfield, or Wib Whited or anyone I know, and it undoubtedly isn't me.

There was a roving pioneer named Adam O'Brien who lived in West Virginia after the Revolution. I don't think he's this archetype, either, but there is something in his last sorrowful judgment of this region which carries across a century and a half. "Those varmints, the sheriffs and constables, are worse than the Indians," he exclaimed, "because you can kill Indians and you dare not kill sheriffs." Times have changed considerably since then—the Indians are gone, for one thing—but this still sounds very much like the natural, not too law-abiding, slightly irreverent voice of West Virginia.

Kentucky

by A. B. GUTHRIE, JR.

The typical Kentuckian is a goateed colonel with a thirst.

He is a barefoot mountain boy with an itchy finger on a flintlock.

He's the owner of a mortgaged plantation and a Thoroughbred foal with the look of eagles in its eyes.

He's a backwoods demagogue who can't spell demagogue.

He's a Southern gentleman.

He's a private enterpriser, a dealer in corn squeezin's, and no revenooer better show his nose.

He's Li'l Abner, Devil Anse Hatfield, the Little Shepherd of Kingdom Come, Private Tussie, Happy Chandler, and Gracious Living by Ancestry out of Bluegrass by Ol' Virginny.

He is all these things, and so, of course, he's none of them.

Kentucky?

It's a heaven of a place (or, to give proper order to an old comparison, heaven is a Kaintuck of a place).

It's a brier patch.

It's Dark and Bloody Ground.

It's bluegrass and juleps and women fair beyond the fortune of any other realm, not excepting the Egyptian.

It is eroded and sequestered hillsides; it is coal mines in the mountains; it is race tracks in the great meadow.

It's all these and none of them, typically, either.

If you must catalogue Kentuckians, go to the writings of the Rev. Mr. Timothy Flint, a New Englander whose summing up defies improvement after more than one hundred and twenty-five years. "The people of this state have a character as strongly marked by nationality as those of any state in the union," he wrote. After respectful passes at their origins, high spirits, courage and tendency to extremes he went on, "When a Kentuckian presents himself in another state, as a candidate for an office, in competition with a candidate from another state, other circumstances being equal, the Kentuckian carries it. Wherever the Kentuckian travels, he earnestly and affectionately remembers his native hills and plains. . . . No country will bear a comparison with his country; no people with his people. The English are said to go into battle with a song about roast beef in their mouths. When the Kentuckian encounters the dangers of battle, or any kind, when he is even on board a foundering ship, his last exclamation is, 'Hurrah for old Kentucky.'"

The resident is likely to divide Kentucky into three regions—Western, Bluegrass, and Eastern. The historian says there are seven natural geographical divisions—the Bluegrass, the Knobs, the Kentucky Mountains, the Pennyroyal, the Western Coal Field, the Jackson Purchase, and the Ohio River Flood Plain. The geologist argues for eight, and, by a stricter re-division, comes out with a total of thirteen.

Either of the two professional lists shows the geographical variety of the state and helps to explain the variety of humanity. The economist could follow with data underscoring the immense differences in per-capita income and natural wealth. The Bluegrass has been called the garden spot of the world. Burley tobacco, the farmer's big cash crop, thrives there as perhaps nowhere else. Beef and lamb grow prime. The Thoroughbred horse develops a stamina unequaled —from the intake of limestone from limestone waters, Bluegrass boosters will tell you. Lexington prospers uncommonly, largely from agriculture. Louisville and Jefferson County are in the big money. They produce or process paint, metals, cigarettes, whisky, beer, machinery, rubber, printing, meat, and chemicals. Paducah, Ashland, and Covington, like smaller towns along the Ohio where industry has tended to concentrate, can boast of factories and payrolls.

When the mines are operating, the coal towns in the eastern and western fields have money, if not always beauty; for coal is Kentucky's biggest export—the biggest, that is, if you exclude the brains the state ships out. Kentucky stands third among the states in coal production, surpassed only by Pennsylvania and West Virginia.

To the list of "have" communities must be added the cities, towns, and counties supported by Kentucky's multi-million-dollar tobacco crop, by the distillation of whisky, by the production of cattle and sheep and hogs, of small grains and corn, by the sale of clay and fluorspar and timber, by the presence of a chance factory or an oil field.

By contrast there are counties desperately poor, so poor that their often dense population can be accounted for only by the absence of known opportunity elsewhere and the countryman's unease outside his old surroundings. There are counties that can't raise enough tax money to operate properly the bare agencies of government. There are towns that can't afford to build sewage systems or to purify water contaminated by people farther up the creek who can't afford sewerage either. There are counties without a bank. There are patches of tobacco and corn on eroding hillsides so steep as to give pause to a goat. There are towns and counties without anything like adequate medical service. There are others without any dentists at all.

A Kentucky newspaperman despondently told me one day that he doubted that Kentucky should have been made a state. It was too various. Bounded for more than half its coast by the crazy meanderings of the Ohio River, it had no unity except touchy loyalty. More than that, its attraction in the west was to St. Louis, in the south to Memphis, Nashville, Knoxville and Chattanooga, in the north to Cincinnati. That last attachment, incidentally, gives to Covington a unique distinction. It's the largest city in the United States without a hotel more ambitious than a rooming house; Cincinnati, just across the river, exerts a corner on the trade. The newsman concluded that only Louisville, pulling on southern Indiana towns, and northern Kentucky, through the tolerated gambling joints that fleece the Ohio lambs, tended to reverse the outbound stream.

He was a little too optimistic. At least four of the clubs in Newport and Covington, including the lush spots, are owned all or in part by a Cleveland syndicate. Thus the stakes lost in Kentucky by Ohioans go back to Ohio along with the losses of Kentuckians.

Beverly Hills, built on a hillside a mile south of Newport, provides investment opportunities in the most elegant of surroundings. It is thickly carpeted. Its long, delicately illuminated oval bar glows with polished glass. Its dining room will seat eight hundred people. Its ceilings are artistically contoured. It puts on a floor show.

Upstairs is the business. Waiting for the man with the dice to roll an eight the hard way, I counted one chuck-a-luck game, two black-jack games, two roulette wheels, and four crap tables. The man sevened. "New shooter," the stick man crooned. "Get your bets down. New shooter coming out." Two dealers sold chips, paid them out and pulled them in. On a raised platform a spotter watched the turn of the dice. Chips sold from a dollar up.

Beverly Hills is just one of perhaps a dozen well-known gambling places and one of scores of spots, ranging down to what are called "Bust-out joints," where a man may risk a buck on a race or a roll of the dice.

Ten days after my researches the games closed down, victims of a combination of politics and righteous wrath. I have spoken of them in the present tense, however, thinking it risky to lay away patients with such demonstrated recuperative powers.

For a variety of good reasons northern Kentucky doesn't give to the state the popular characterization that, say, Butte gives to Montana or Reno to Nevada. One reason is the older and profounder conception of Kentucky as the arch border state, the hapless but difficult neutral of the Civil War, so riven internally that brother fought brother and father fought son, offended, violated, levied on by North and South alike. It was a state without a nation, a tieless territory of ferment, antagonisms, shifting indignations. If the Rebels made Federals of some Rebels, the Federals made Rebels of more Federals. Right after the war northern papers were calling Kentucky the most disloyal state of all. That charge may be argued, but not the statement that Kentuckians nevertheless were a sturdy and independent lot. And not the fact that nowhere was the internal conflict sorer.

Those experiences lie deep, if often unrecognized, in the make-up of Kentucky. The outward signs of the old schism are evident today. Eastern Kentucky, a community of small freeholders without slaves, sided with the Union; today, by and large, it votes Republican. Central and Western Kentucky, with their slave-worked plantations, were sympathetic to the South. Their present political preferences reflect the fact.

The United Daughters of the Confederacy object to "Civil War." They say "War Between the States," thus re-emphasizing the South's answer to a question grown moot. They don't like the Federal Government any too well, either. Lexington members were disturbed just a little while back by the indifferent care given the Confederate plot in the Lexington cemetery. The superintendent advised them that the Government would assume the upkeep if the Daughters would deed the plot to it. Already the Federal burial ground was under such an arrangement.

What! asked the ladies. Give anything to the Union! Never! They didn't either.

Such manifestations, though, are vestigial. Kentucky bears the scars of the 1860's, in places to be suggested later, but they don't hurt much anymore. No longer, except by courtesy to history, is this the arch border state. The rebel yell died with old Colonel Dick Redd, who used to sound off in his cracked voice as he rode his chestnut charger up and down the streets of a Lexington that already in the 1920's regarded him as a curiosity. The term, Yankee, rooted loosely in the old struggle has been extended to designate any rude outlander from beyond the Ohio River, and is employed by Democrat and Republican alike. The descendants of Union men suffer the praises of Stonewall Jackson and Robert E. Lee. I know Democrats who yield to none in their admiration of Lincoln. Negroes vote. They have ever since the War Between the States.

One afternoon I asked a half-dozen all-wool-and-a-yard-wide Kentuckians where I'd find a hotbed of the Confederacy. One said well, maybe Hopkinsville. One guessed, maybe, Danville. One said western Kentucky had a parcel of Rebels—he wouldn't know which town, though. One said he reckoned Lexington had about as much of the old spirit as any place. They agreed that feelings weren't what they used to be; too many things had come between.

The conflict today perhaps can be described best as one of traditionalism versus change. Even the tardiness with which the old political cleavage is yielding to the realities of economics reflects habit more than conviction. It is fashion, not passion. It illustrates not the border quality of Kentucky but the reluctance to change with the changing times.

Examples, big and small, evidence the sentiment that what was good enough for grandpa is good enough for me. Until quite recently Kentuckians built houses like those already built, shying away from experimental and functional architecture, from picture-window modernism. In about 1940, when Dr. Frank L. McVey, then president of the University of Kentucky, put up a flat-topped, functional home, the curious jammed traffic by his door. Business houses were slow to install air conditioning; you almost would have thought they figured to sweat this fancy out. New-fangled apparatus, the gadgets and gimcracks of industry, come late to the state. The citizenry insists on keeping a constitution adopted in 1891. One of its provisions, of course now inoperative under national law, denies suffrage and office to women. Another puts in the oath of office for officials and attorneys a solemn declaration that the oath-taker never has engaged in a duel either as principal or second.

Until the election of 1949 all public officers except the governor were held to a maximum salary of $5000 annually. Variously and reversely construed by the Court of Appeals, this constitutional provision raised hob. The trained men whom the state needed couldn't be suckered into services that paid so little. Public health, road construction, park development, education—nearly every service of state, indeed, was crippled by the limitation. Yet an amendment to liberalize it carried by less than 20,000, despite the efforts of both parties and the vigorous backing of the state administration. Even so, its passage was a great victory. Previous campaigns all had failed. So had a campaign for a constitutional convention. What if the constitution was old? one opponent asked; so were the Ten Commandments.

It is easy but not quite accurate to imagine the citizenry rigidly divided into sides, the traditionalists here, the progressives there, like teams in a tug of war. The split tends to run deeper, into the personality of the individual, who finds himself torn between old loyalties and new attractions and needs. On no issue is the line-up entirely ready-made.

Neither, by any means, are differences in attitudes altogether geographical, though one part of Kentucky is likely to regard another with suspicion, condescension, or even disdain. Tradition has its ancient lovers in industrialized Louisville and the manored Bluegrass as well as in the hinterlands to east and west. The cries for change rise from mountain and municipality.

Into the contest and its recurring results, however, enters the disparity of financial circumstance. By contrast with industrialists, Bluegrass planters, coal-mine operators and professional men in fat surroundings, there are thousands of men scratching for life on leached slopes and worn swales.

Five thousand dollars a year for politicians and professors! That's a fortune! The plight of these people creates a general insufficiency, despite the state's spotted riches.

East and south of the Bluegrass you come quickly to some of the less-favored land. If your route and time are right, you see occasional scrawny livestock, forlorn hillside corn, cabins weathering to pieces in ravines, women, maybe barefoot, in sacklike dresses. And children, of course. Children always. These sights aren't invariable but they're far from rare. Then, if you follow the road I took recently, you come to the coalfields and to Harlan.

Two young miners—Warren Till and Harold Coldiron—were waiting for me there. They were sharp and personable boys, so sharp and personable that it seemed a pity they should have entered an uncertain and static employment from which, the saying is, a man never escapes. They didn't feel that way, though, not altogether. Harlan was home. Other jobs were scarce and, by contrast, dinky. Fourteen seventy-five a day was good money, even if it didn't average out to a great deal, what with strikes and limited work weeks and all. More —and this was my inference—a man who didn't work in the mines might be suspected of cowardice.

Harlan is a small and busy town situated in the valley of the upper Cumberland. Out from it are clusters of uniform frame houses, mostly perched on stilts. These belong to the operators, or sometimes to private investors, and are rented by miners, few of whom own their own homes. Eastward along through the neighboring settlement of Evarts you catch glimpses of mine openings, rubbles of slate, and conveyers angled white on the hillsides. In the summer the valley is green and lovely despite these scars. In the winter, with the flanking mountains whiskered by leafless trees, it is pretty drear.

Here on a May day in 1931 was fought the "Battle of Evarts," a battle which touched off a decade of violence, bloodshed and terrorism. A group of mine guards led by a deputy sheriff encountered a crew of union pickets at an Evarts mine. Someone started shooting. Three mine guards and one miner lay dead when the party was over.

Before comparative peace came to Harlan more men died, the National Guard marched in again and again, the La Follette Civil Liberties Committee held hearings that astonished the nation, Governor Happy Chandler tangled with John L. Lewis, and representatives of the newly formed civil-liberties unit of the Department of Justice appeared on the scene. Meantime, there were wholesale indictments, trials, charges, reports. A state commission said after study, "It is almost unbelievable that anywhere in a free and democratic nation such as ours, conditions can be found as bad as they are in Harlan County."

We drove from downtown Harlan and followed a street like a neglected alley and came to a huddle of dwellings and a front porch where half a dozen Negroes had gathered to pass the Sunday morning. We got out and squatted on the ground and fell into conversation. Most of the Negroes were transplanted Alabamans, and most of them were mine-car loaders and got paid on a tonnage basis. Sometimes they earned more, sometimes less, than shift men.

"This man wants to know about coal mining," Warren said.

A small Negro with a cinnamon skin and yellow eyes and a face without illusion looked me up and down. "It's rough."

"What did you do while the strike was on?" I asked. The strike had ended a few days before.

"Several rabbits in these hills," he said.

The other boys nodded, grinning.

"And some fish in the river. We made out."

"Don' forgit miners' strawberries," someone prompted him.

"What are they?"

"Pinto beans. They go a long way."

I asked about working conditions.

"Ain't nothin' like it used to be," the small man said. "It's safe by what it was. Course, man was killed the day we opened up."

"You ever been trapped in a mine?"

He shook his head. "Got my eye knocked out, though, an' lost fifty-three days."

"How?"

"Slate fell on me. Knocked my eye clean out, but you wouldn't know it now. An' I had to wait while they took the coal out. Coal comes first. There I was, with my eye restin' on my bosom. By and by they come and got me." Unexpectedly he grinned, finding some kind of humor in the case.

"How do you load a car," I asked, "with a shovel or what?"

"Hands, shovel, crowbar, pick, anything." He stepped to the side of the house and picked up a scoop and came back and said, "Me,

I'm a small man. Ceilin' maybe ain't but so high." He held his hand a little above his waist. "Look, I can spraddle my legs out and shovel standin' up."

"What about the others?"

"I'll show you about us," a much bigger man said. He pulled up the leg of his Sunday pants. On his knee was a pad of callus like a pancake.

We had a look at a mine afterwards. It was almost head high at the opening, but quickly pinched down. We stopped before we had gone very far and looked, hunched over, into the tunnel dwindling ahead. There were occasional batteries of dim lights there and, unseen in the darkness, the belch of water. Outside, sawed and split to about fireplace size, were timbers to be used to keep roof and floor apart. Outside, too, was a string of mine cars, squat, wide jobs that looked like little scows.

The outlander is likely to think of the miner as a surly and difficult fellow. Not so. He may believe, and does, that sooner or later his number will come up, but he doesn't live in gloom. Like any fatalist, he lives day by day, enjoying himself while he can.

"A miner spends money when he's got it," Warren told me. "These house-to-house salesmen, they make a killing. A miner'll buy any kind of a gadget."

Out of their border-state experience, perhaps, Kentuckians impose a handicap on the co-operation that their problems demand—they're suspicious of the human animal, including one another. You have only to consult their law books to confirm this point. Neither the governor nor any minor officer of state may succeed himself. Neither may mayors of first- and second-class cities. The constitution lists twenty-eight special prohibitions and, for safety's sake, one catch-all restriction on the powers of the legislature. When, in 1947, a campaign for a constitutional convention was being waged, the antis contended that the state lacked men of sufficient caliber to draft a satisfactory instrument. That was a slander that should have made the pros victorious, but didn't.

The fact is that Kentuckians love politics but have little faith in its principals or performances, including the judicial; as a result, a kind of basic anarchy, the violence of individuality, persists, particularly, one concludes, in the hills and hollows to the east. The conclusion is supportable but still uneasy: in the race for national homicidal honors Kentucky cities outside the mountains have done pretty well through the years. An astonishing number of people carry pistols or blades, just in case. In old families with long years of education and social grace a dark strain of violence occasionally breaks out.

The lawmakers and the courts are duly indulgent. Under the law, crimes of violence are mitigated by the element of "sudden heat and passion." They are in other states, too, but there the offender has to prove provocation. In Kentucky he just has to show that all of a sudden he got mad.

Juries are equally considerate. Comparatively few homicides result in death penalties. At most the defendant is likely to be given a life sentence, which means he can be free in eight years if he's a good boy.

A great deal has been written and said about the mountaineer with his touchy pride and his readiness to act on his own. Outsiders sometimes talk as if every resident would shoot at the drop of a persimmon. Writers, with exceptions, go to extremes. They exaggerate the dark unpredictability of the mountaineer or they make him just too quaint for words, perhaps in the certainty that eastern editors will fall for either version. In neither case do they treat him as a human being, shaped by forces outside his command.

Beneath his usual reserve the mountain man is friendly and obliging. He is hospitable almost to the point of embarrassment to strangers. He has a mind, if an untutored one. In his hills he is frontier America; often he comes out to give leadership to community and state. The risk that a decently disposed and mannerly stranger runs in Kentucky Appalachia is too slight for consideration. It is with himself that the mountaineer has trouble.

He does have it there. No virtues explain it away. It exists—product of ignorance, isolation, poverty, background, social compulsion. Most of all, perhaps, social compulsion, which itself reflects background. At least one historian has ventured the belief that feuds trace directly to the indiscriminate guerrillaism developed by the Civil War. You don't hear of feuds any more, though the clan spirit survives, an injury to a man being considered a personal grievance by kinsmen down to in-laws and second cousins, but associated habits persist. There remain the unruly impulse, the recourse to gun or knife, the carrying of weapons. Warren Till told me—and maybe he was just having fun with a greenhorn—that as a high-school senior he, like his mates, carried a revolver to class.

A Lexington newspaperman and novelist who came out of the fastnesses of Clay County believes the compulsion on the mountain man is the fear of loss of face, the fear of being thought afraid. Scared, he has to prove he isn't. He's not by nature more violent than his outside brothers; he just answers to a different standard. We get back here to Warren Till and Harold Coldiron. They told me that rather than to have anyone think they were afraid to enter a mine they would go in even if they knew beforehand they would never come out.

The Kentuckian's love of politics and such by-products as courthouses and courtrooms and legislation appears to contradict the impulse to anarchy, but it is nonetheless real. No year goes by without an election—school, municipal, county, state, Federal—and nearly every one full-dress. The state abounds in buttonholers, some ambitious for office, some only fascinated. Courthouses ring with promises and denunications. Newspapers tear into the fray. Radios squawk.

It is fitting here to lament the good old days when the late Edwin P. Morrow and Augustus Owsley Stanley were having-at each other. Now there was politics, and there was oratory, and there was fun for everybody, including the antagonists, who got together before and after their debates, it was rumored, for a friendly cup. They were keen and witty adversaries who entered politics joyfully.

Over a Coke or around a fire, older observers of the political scene like to quote a crack of Stanley's. He had beaten Morrow by a nose in the 1915 race for governor. Four years later Morrow again was the Republican nominee. One of his targets was a textbook adopted under the administration of his friend, who could not succeed himself but of course was compelled to defend his record. Morrow said the book contained errors of grammar, which it did. He said the Democrats could not escape responsibility for putting a linguistic monstrosity in the hands of the innocent school children of Kentucky. Stanley, who was more scholarly than Morrow, had his answer. In swelling rhythms he described Morrow's own rhetoric: "Unrelated nouns in open concubinage are crowded into the same sentences, and poor bastard pronouns wander aimlessly through a wilderness of words, vainly seeking their lost antecedents, whom they resemble in neither gender, number nor person."

Morrow was elected, presumably not to Stanley's entire dissatisfaction. Stanley remembers that they "fought mightily" but "ate and drank like friends."

In Kentucky we have no men like them today. They were the last

of the old-fashioned orators, the last, that is, who brought good nature and wit and skill to heightened language.

Kentucky normally is Democratic, but not so Democratic as never
to leave the fold. Union organization, notably that of the Mine
Workers, has increased the Democratic strength in recent years,
though from any gain must be subtracted conservative defections
from the New Deal and Fair Deal. One of these renegades, a prosperous landowner who liked to flash the highly perforated checks
the Government sent him for fencing or conserving or growing or not
growing or whatever, said he glued the checks together one time
and put them through his player piano, and damn if they didn't come
out, *Happy Days Are Here Again.*

What do you do in a state of such extremes? You do the best you
can, or you live in part by myth. In any case, you enjoy yourself.

Satisfaction isn't necessarily bushels to the acre or gain on the hoof
or production on the line. It can be laurel on a mountainside, the
white shower of serviceberry, the wind ripple of bluegrass, the palisades of the Kentucky, the spring festival of redbud and dogwood,
the long haze of autumn, the columned front of old Morrison Chapel
in Lexington. It can be a friend and a julep and a mare in a pasture.
It can be the blaze of old cherry, fashioned after Hepplewhite. It
can be a place where walk the ghosts of better men and worse. It
can be a stage in the great American journey, east to west, where
Dan'l Boone and George Rogers Clark and frontiersmen and soldiers
and seekers tramped history on the land. It can be a day at the
Lexington Trots, at Keeneland, at Churchill Downs, at Dade Park.
It can be old ham and beaten biscuits and fried chicken and corn
pudding.

These things the Kentuckian knows how to appreciate. Problems
exist, troubles arise, but these endure.

The Kentuckian walks down the street of his town and meets
friends along the way, and they stop, wanting to know how things
are, how's the family, why'n't you come and see us, who you pickin'
in the Derby, let's have a cup of coffee.

Or he and his wife call on their neighbors at night and, leaving,
hear the words, "Glad you came. You all hurry back." Answering,
they say, "You all come and see us now. Hear?" The partings are
standard, but the sentiment is honest.

An interest in people, dead and quick, tends to make conversation
personal. Small talk, if you insist on that term, occupies dinner table,

fireplace and corner-drugstore gatherings, if not to the entire exclusion of broader discussion. The tendency perhaps constitutes escapism; in any case it reflects a real curiosity about the individual, a real relish for human vagary. Local historians are as thick as chiggers. But they talk more about personalities than about events and their causes and consequences. And they may turn from the long hunters or Abe Lincoln or Jeff Davis or John G. Carlisle to the more recent and humbler "characters" that Kentucky somehow produces in abundance.

They may tell the story, perhaps apocryphal, of the late Dudley B. Veal, long-time Lexington city detective and later jailer of Fayette County, whose lack of formal education was balanced by imagination and vehemence. Out of his long experience Mr. Veal said he knew the world was round because every damn no-good that ever left Lexington always came back. Or they may trade information about a Louisville *Courier-Journal* reporter who wondered how it was that a black cow can eat green grass and give white milk that churns into yellow butter. For the benefit of his followers—apple-knockers and ridge-runners, he called them, including himself in the classifications —he'd tell whether a hen lays an egg because she wants to or because she has to, or explain why a hound trots with his hind legs out of line. With historians and nonhistorians alike the individual comes before the event. I've never heard one of them contend in defense that the proper study of mankind is man, but the principle seems to have some limited application here.

Man in the form of the local product gives to conversation and culture a provincialism that finds a prior and greater impulse in the feeling of Kentuckians for Kentucky. Any man who had a choice would be a fool to live in any other state. Even heaven can be no more than a Kentucky of a place. By contrast with the facts the Texan's loyalty to Texas becomes a benighted and amusing attachment, to be tolerated on the ground of ignorance. You got to excuse people who haven't had a chance to get around.

This contentment with place to the prejudice of problem, this satisfaction in an imagined isolation from the underprivileged, can be annoying. It's hard, though, to keep a broad social consciousness alive and prickly when candlelight lies soft on old silver, and aged wood whispers under the feeling finger, and women and men honor the ways of ladies and gentlemen and, over coffee or bourbon, the rich, warm anecdotes spill out. Gracious living? It is a name, but more than a name. It is relaxation, ease, escape. At its best it is manners without rigidity. It is hospitality without calculation. If part of it is worshipful of ancestors and the great, gone days, part of it is immediate and fresh, and all of it is beguiling. The jet missile, the hydrogen bomb, the cold war, these join the distant shadows when your host in Louisville or Lexington or Paducah or Ashland or wherever has a mind and the means to entertain traditionally.

There are exceptions to a rule which, though common, isn't general enough to be called a rule anyhow. Obviously not everybody breaks out the rare distillations or gives with the country ham or opens the door on ancestral Chippendale at the honk of a visiting horn. And not all of them by a long shot shy away from the state's debits in enjoyment of its assets. There's Harry W. Schacter, of Louisville, for instance.

Schacter, president of the second-largest department store in the state, thought public knowledge of problems plus democratic co-operation could rescue the commonwealth from half a century of decline. Around him gathered other people, few at first, who thought information more important than the reputation that the patriots would protect. They were professors from the University of Kentucky, farm leaders, newspapermen, representatives of civic, professional and labor groups. They called themselves the Committee for Kentucky. Their aim was to create "a moral climate in which things could happen."

In twelve widely circulated reports they washed the dirty linen. They told the sorry stories of education, agriculture, public health, welfare, housing, legislation, taxation. They discussed the constitution, manufacturing, natural resources. They said: Here's the situation; what do we do about it?

Protests resulted of course. Many citizens were indignant, not so much at the conditions as at the exposure of them. Chambers of commerce growled at the unfavorable publicity. Women's clubs were openly critical.

That response was to be expected. What was astonishing was the strength of the counter-answer. Moved by the reports, people began to concern themselves with the long-neglected troubles of village, city, county and state. Communities began to plan and to act. Officials of state began to give ear, the policies of state to reflect the growing concern. Items of improvement have been substantial if not revolutionary, but more substantial still is the growth in public attitude away from reaction and ostrichism and apathy toward recognition and adjustment.

The myths in which Kentuckians find comfort are the myths of fast horses, good whisky, juleps, old retainers, leisurely graces beneath ancestral porticos. Unlike most myths these have so much basis in fact that a quick condition must be set: These are myths only as the facts are extended and exaggerated.

Not every Kentuckian trots to the race track, his money pulsing in his pocket. Fewer still like a horse because it's a horse rather than a hot thing. Riding isn't a particularly popular pastime. Lexington, "heart of the Bluegrass," never has kept a commercial riding stable in business. It has no public bridle paths. Neither is the citizenry universally attached to the stirrup cup, the evening toddy and the short snort. Ninety of Kentucky's 120 counties legally are dry. More give indications of becoming so. The liberal connotation of horses, whisky and women runs up against the fact of morals-in-action. That is a thing that needs constantly to be remembered—the strength in the state of a Protestant fundamentalism that equates highballs and horse races with sin. Kentucky is the home of good whisky and fast horses, but much of Kentucky is not at home with it and them. Such is the human wish for distinction, though, that even the antis sometimes appear to find pleasure in the reputation the state enjoys among outlanders.

One substantial fact, as distinct from myth, is that Kentucky stands first as a breeder of the Thoroughbred or running horse. And not by accident. Some quality in soil or water must give to horses an extra speed and stamina.

The running horse and to a small extent the harness horse and saddle horse are important to the economy of the Lexington region and not unimportant to that of areas near Louisville, Covington and Hopkinsville. Horses and horse farms probably rank as the No. 1 tourist attraction. Man o' War, in his years at stud outside Lexington, drew more visitors than the tomb of Henry Clay, the first college west of the Alleghenies, the home of John Hunt Morgan, the residence of Mrs. Abraham Lincoln and the college quarters of Jefferson Davis. It used to be said that 50,000 people came to see him yearly. Tourists go now to see the heroic bronze over his grave. They ride to Calumet Farm, home of Whirlaway and Citation, and to Coldstream Stud, and to Mereworth, Elmendorf, Almahurst, Beaumont and Walnut Hall farms, and others that ring Lexington. A tour of them is rewarding in the visual dividend of rich fields, groves and paneled pastures with their mares and foals. And the sight of costly, manicured barns may impress you with man's humanity to beast.

Because Lexington is known as the center of Thoroughbred breeding, many of the uninitiated think the Kentucky Derby is run there. It isn't. It's run at Louisville's Churchill Downs.

Louisville is Kentucky's biggest city and, businesswise at least, its most important. Its residents estimate a metropolitan district that counts more than half a million. It lies on a low plain where the Ohio River broke over falls as lucrative to earlyday pilots, porters and towline hands as they were vexing to vessels and crews. The falls aren't impressive any more. The Government system of locks and dams has reduced them substantially.

Until about 1870 the city's prosperity rose and fell with river traffic, in which the steamboat made its first entrance in 1811. A good many northerners terminated their river journeys at Louisville—which accounts for the fact that the town still casts a lusty if not majority Republican vote.

"Louisville," says the Kentucky WPA guidebook of 1939, "is a border metropolis that blends the commerce and industry of a Northern city with the Southern city's enjoyment of living." It might have said that Louisville is a big, friendly, country town, notable by outward reputation as the home of the *Courier-Journal*, the Louisville Slugger and the Derby.

Even to the man without interest in the turf the Derby is worth seeing at least once, though massed humanity may keep him from catching more than a glimpse of the race. It is horse race, fashion show, spring festival, mob. Notables and nobodies mingle, touts and tycoons, owners and swipes, all beating inwardly to an excitement that old Colonel Matt Winn sedulously cultivated during a long lifetime. A kind of craziness afflicts people, so that even the Kentucky absentee is likely to stay close to his TV or radio until it's over. The crowd is so thick that women caught in its close squirmings lose hats and gain hysterics. More even than it is a horse race, the Derby is a spectacle, a human spectacle the like of which it would be difficult to duplicate.

A second substantial fact, again as distinct from myth, is that Kentucky does make a great deal of whisky, Kentucky in this case being a dozen producing counties among the one hundred and twenty. At times the state manufactured nearly half the whisky distilled in the United States. More, the stereotype of the Kentucky colonel with a cigar in one hand and a glass in the other finds some enforcement in fact. If it's inaccurate to say that Kentuckians are good judges of whisky, it's true that many of them are. Two colonels got to arguing one day about the taste of their drinks. One of them said the whisky had a metallic flavor. The other said no, it smacked of leather. To settle the dispute they drained the barrel, to find at the bottom a leather-washered tack. (The story would have more authority if Cervantes hadn't told it three hundred and fifty years ago.)

It is said of the fractious Thoroughbred that a touch of his blood betters any breed. By something of the same reasoning a similar virtue could be asserted for Kentucky. Through claim of birth or residence the state can boast a list of distinguished men, historical and contemporary, out of all proportion even to its present population of about three million. From this troubled, rich-poor, literate-illiterate, rewarding-distressing, politics-ridden commonwealth have come and still come notables in jurisprudence, national administration, military affairs, science, journalism, literature, education and the arts.

A few years ago three Kentuckians were justices of the United States Supreme Court, a representation that possibly no other state ever could claim. In all, Kentucky has sent nine men to the highest court.

There's no need or room here to call the roll of history. The list of military personages alone would run to dozens. And, anyhow, the distinction doesn't rest exclusively on ancient honors.

This story of the state has run a cycle. We are back to old Brother Timothy Flint, who cited the political squabbling, the clanships, the frequent recourse to violence 130 years ago. But he noted, too, the presence and continuing production of talent and leadership. In words dated only by style, in words that express a hope still current, he said of Kentucky:

"It can not but eventually feel the obligations imposed upon it, to manifest its possession of such men and such talents, by desisting from the petty struggles and broils of party and faction, and acting with a moderation, calmness, and dignity befitting its character."

PART V *The South*

Tennessee

by HODDING CARTER

One summer, a few years ago, an unhappy young Tennessee wife wrote a letter to Mrs. Jean Bruce, the advice-giving columnist of the Nashville *Tennessean*. Her father, complained the young woman, drank heavily—a gallon and a half each week end—constantly abused her mother and had so misbehaved one night that her husband had been compelled to slap him.

"That's a lot of whisky," replied Mrs. Bruce. "Maybe one day he will get too much. Until then you cannot do a thing if your mother does not want to help. . . . I hope your husband hit him hard. It's a pity that someone does not beat him up plenty."

Tennesseans can understand such advice, for theirs has been a tradition of robust living and forceful action throughout a long, honorable and combative history. It is more important to understand this tradition than to memorize statistics, if you want to know the people who came to Tennessee, the country they found and what they have done to it and it to them.

You profit little from learning that Tennessee's population is some 3,500,000, for example, unless you are also aware that fewer than 14,000 Tennesseans are foreign-born and that only a small per cent of the 3,500,000 were born outside of the state; that a majority of its people are the lineal and spiritual descendants of the land-hungry and prideful Scots-Irish and the yeoman English, implacable Presbyterians, Wesleyans and Baptists for the most part, who brought across the contested mountains the demijohn and the fiddle along with the Bible and the rifle, and who shared a bitter mistrust for the King, the Tory, the papist and the dissimilar in blood and tongue.

But the Tennessean's pugnacity is not unrelieved. Hillman, riverman, dirt farmer, he preserves a folkway of courtesy to the stranger.

Once, while lost on a hiking trip one chilly afternoon in the mountains near Sewanee, I came across a mountain home, a split-log, dog-trot house with a rock-and-clay chimney and a long, slanting gallery on which a middle-aged man was playing with a dog. I asked him for directions. He gave them explicitly, his narrow, chiseled face studying my own, and then, probably noting that I was cold, he asked me to have a cup of coffee. I sat on the porch with him, talking about the weather and the autumn hunting, until his sweet-faced wife brought us black coffee in large white mugs. On the wooden tray with the coffee were two pewter receptacles.

"Long sweetenin' or short sweetenin'?" he asked.

"Long sweetening," I replied. A relieved look came into his blue eyes. He handed me one of the two pewter containers. It was filled to the brim with sorghum molasses. "We like it thataway too," he said. I caught a glimpse of the short sweetening in the other container. It was white sugar, and the bowl was all but empty. But there was enough for a guest.

He was a mountain man. There are other Tennesseans. You will not be much the wiser for knowing that the length of Tennessee is a long 430 miles and its breadth about 120, unless you discover that in the rough parallelogram thus formed there is not one Tennessee but three: the East Tennessee of the mountain men, the Middle Tennessee of bluegrass and tobacco and livestock, and the West Tennessee that ends among the cotton plantations and diversified farms along the Mississippi, newer than the others and once shackled to a ruinous one-crop economy.

You need not think of Tennessee's total area of some 42,000 square miles as imposing, for thirty-three states are larger. But in few other places has American soil been so bitterly contested, so darkened by the lifeblood of defenders and conquerors, so vital to the extension and the preservation of a new, continent-spanning nation.

The American Revolution's success in the South was assured at King's Mountain, in South Carolina. John Sevier and his Tennessee

Long Rifles won that battle. The same Long Rifles broke the resistance and the hearts of the courageous Cherokee; Andrew Jackson's Tennesseans destroyed the British at New Orleans in 1815, ending the last European encroachment upon the continental United States; wrested, with some illegality, Spain's Florida from the Dons, destroyed the Seminoles, and assumed a large measure of frontier security from the south Atlantic coast to the Mississippi.

In the Civil War, few states suffered as did Tennessee. Her divided people knew the ultimate horror of civil strife that pitted the slavery-hating Republicans of the East Tennessee highlands against their seceding brothers to the west. Historians agree today that it was at Shiloh—a long, bloody year before Gettysburg and Vicksburg—that the Confederacy was doomed. Tennessee gave the nation its first postwar President, Andrew Johnson, a man whose conciliative spirit was overwhelmed by the vengeful radicals.

In World War I, there was a mountaineer named Alvin York. Though a conscientious objector, he became the nation's best-known hero. In World War II, there rose on Tennessee soil a city named Oak Ridge, a city of mystery whose ultimate contribution to human destiny no man can predict. And it is only 180 years from the Long Rifles to Oak Ridge's Museum of Atomic Energy.

In these and other directions, statistics by themselves grow meaningless. Note that in the Great Smokies there are sixteen peaks of more than 6000 feet. Does such information capture the intransigent beauty of the rhododendron, high in the misty blueness, or the kindred independence of the mountain folk? List the agricultural and industrial products of a state that still relies principally upon the soil. Can this recount the lately joined struggle against ignorant destruction of the land, or the zealous quest for industrial balance? Tennessee had, less than two decades ago, a per capita income that was among the lowest in the nation. But no longer; the figure has quadrupled. Can this reflect the miracle wrought by the Tennessee Valley Authority, the miracle of water working for man in the creation of hydroelectric power for over one million consumers and for nuclear fission, the miracle of flood control and assured water transportation, and land reclaimed and directed to forgotten usefulness?

Here, from just beyond the Appalachians to the Mississippi, was the beckoning pioneer land, the free land of young America. Here, in 1796, was created the sixteenth state; and long before the Decla-

ration of Independence at Philadelphia, angry Tennesseans proclaimed at Watauga an association of free men. Here, Daniel Boone
broke through the Cumberland Gap, the long rifle cradled in his arm,
seeking bear meat and deer and beaver skins and fertile valleys for
those who followed. Here feudal, devout men built the split-log
church and gave brave classical names to their first, one-room academies, and quarreled in the crude courthouses from which strode an
Andrew Jackson, duelist, horse racer, warrior and despotic democrat.
Here roamed forest clearers, Indian scalpers, corn-whisky drinkers
and ballad singers.

Soft people died early on the frontier, their blood wet on the
puncheon floor, the mother grotesquely inert beside the spinning
jenny, the child forever asleep upon the corn-shuck pallet. Only the
hard and the resolute survived. And so the Tennessee frontier
marked its sons with resolution, frequently harsh and unyielding, for
generation after generation. There is a likeness among them all: Tom
Spencer, the seven-foot Long Hunter, and Cordell Hull, the log-
rafter from the Cumberlands; Andy Jackson, the fire-eater, and Andrew Johnson, the Union Democrat; James K. Polk, the second of
Tennessee's presidential triumvirate, who added mightily, through
war and diplomacy, to America's domain, and Sam Houston who
guided an empire of his own; Davy Crockett, the hunter and politician who died at the Alamo, and David Glasgow Farragut, the first
full admiral in the American navy, who damned the torpedoes at
Mobile Bay.

One of Tennessee's best storytelling governors, Bob Taylor, who
knew the toughness of his people and the virtues they most admired,
had a favorite story that had to do with a Tennessee archetype,
Brother Billy Patterson, a new preacher, and Bert Lynch, the bully
of the mountains, who picked fights with all comers.

"In his first sermon in Bert's neck of the woods," Governor Taylor
would recall, "Brother Billy Patterson hurled his anathemas against
Satan and sin and every kind of wickedness. He denounced whisky;
he branded the bully as a brute and a moral coward, and personated
Bert. This was too much for the champion. He resolved to thrash
Brother Patterson, and in a few days they met. Bert squared himself and said:

" 'Parson, you had your turn last Sunday; it's mine today. Pull off that broadcloth an' take your medicine! I'm agwine to suck the marrow out'n them old bones o' yourn.'

"The pious preacher pleaded for peace, but without avail. At last he said: 'Then if nothing but a fight will satisfy you, will you allow me to kneel down and say my prayer before we fight?'

"'All right, parson,' said Bert. 'But cut yer prayer short.'

"The preacher knelt and thus began to pray:

"'O Lord, Thou knowest that when I killed Bill Cummings and John Brown and Jerry Smith and Levi Bottles that I did it in self-defense. Thou knowest, O Lord, that when I cut the heart out of young Slinger and strewed the ground with the brains of Paddy Miles, that it was forced upon me and that I did it in great agony of soul. And now, O Lord, I am about to be forced to put in his coffin this poor, miserable wretch, who has attacked me here today. O Lord, have mercy upon his soul and take care of his helpless widow and orphans when he is gone.'

"And he arose, whetting his knife on his shoe sole, singing:

> "'Hark! from the tombs a doleful sound;
> Mine ears attend the cry.'

"But when he looked around, Bert was gone. There was nothing in sight but a little cloud of dust far up the road, following in the wake of the vanishing champion."

Upon them all, the stamp of the frontier, the outdoor stamp. Tennessee is the land of the hunters of the coon and the possum and the fox. It is a land where a mountain man may compete in a turkey shoot today with a rifle fashioned by John Bull of Bull's Gap some 135 years ago; where the West Tennessee tenant may grabble naked in a slough for a mess of fish and where the vacationing fisherman and huntsman swap lies at Reelfoot Lake over a bottle of Jack Daniel's whisky, that potent sour-mash distillation whose long-ago creator remains a patron saint. And in the Cumberland Mountains, the revenuers again stalk the resurgent whisky makers, who reason that when the tax on corn liquor gets so high, it's time again for a man to make and drink and sell his own.

There are other less innocent manifestations of the frontier's stamp: The shameful, though limited, outrages of the Klan; the sound and fury of Tennessee's politics, where factionalism and personal venom and the lethargy of the nonvoting majority are more apparent than are issues; racial conflict in Columbia; the GIs' armed uprising in Athens; the long-ago evolution-law trial at Dayton. Distant people envision the mountaineer caricature and do not see the rising cities, the hopeful towns, the sure forging ahead.

In perspective, even the aberrations can be understood. Go back a short time, as time is reckoned in the history books and the recollections of men. Remember again the frontier, and remember also that this frontier was bloody and raw and that it began to recede only about 135 years ago. On this frontier, vices and virtues were alike primitive. Leadership, political or military, was violent, personal and immediate, and there was scant time for meditation upon good and bad. Culture, in its softer definitions, was a thing that came later. But not before the frontier had marked her sons.

What the Long Hunters saw first of Tennessee were the mountains, shrouded in blue haze, guarding the eastward approaches, north and south.

Some of the hunters surrendered to the beauty or the primal independence of the mountains, and settled among the giant tulip poplars and beside the cold, quick streams of the Great Smokies and the Cumberlands. Their more restless fellows roamed the Land of Peaceful Hunting, slaying the bear and deer and bison, or possessing and clearing the fertile valleys and plateaus and lowlands beyond the eastern peaks. But all who came by way of the eastern passes remembered the mountains: remembered the flame azalea, the purple rhododendron and the dark leaves of the laurel that grew along their slopes. Here was East Tennessee, a land of great heights and twisting, narrow valleys and solitude.

The settlers and travelers and adventurers who came northward along the Natchez Trace to Middle Tennessee remembered best the rich plateaus and rolling bluegrass country, lying between the eastern and western loops of the Tennessee River; a gentler, more fertile land than the mountain valleys, a land where a man might prosper and build a great house among the oaks and the cedars, with the iris and yellow jasmine and honeysuckle thick in the woods that border meadow and field. Here was the pulsing heart of a state.

Once during the war I swapped some homesick bragging overseas with a young Tennessean, a fighter pilot in the Ninth Air Force.

"There's only one place worth living in, and that's Middle Tennessee," he said. "When I get out I'm going back there. I'm going to marry a Nashville gal. I'm going to buy some Middle Tennessee land and raise Tennessee Walking Horses and Tennessee babies. I'm going to cure Tennessee hams with Tennessee hickory, and I'm not going to drink anything but old Jack Daniel sour-mash Tennessee whisky. And if my wife ever talks about leaving Middle Tennessee, I'll drag her clean over to the Tennessee River and drown her. Hell, I'm so homesick I could root for the University and I'm a Vanderbilt man."

The later settlers found a third Tennessee; a country to be reached either by long, overland journey, or roundabout by water or land or both. Here was West Tennessee, a land of black bottom lands and river swamps and long, undulant valleys between unimposing hills. Here was a lusher, wilder growth; lilies and Indian rye, orchids and wild rice and cypress. Here was proper earth for cotton's planting, a land to which the slave could be brought, where the river outranked the overland road or the mountain pass, and the price of cotton determined the price of man.

Give me the rivers, says the West Tennessean, the borderline Cumberland, the Tennessee, and the yellow Mississippi, the lush bottom lands and the wonder of Reelfoot Lake. In the narrow, eighteen-mile-long lake live the alligator gar, the huge spoonbill catfish, the savage water moccasin, the terrapin and a profusion of game fish. To dark Reelfoot wing the mallard and teal and the Canadian goose, the bittern, the rail and the purple gallinule. Here soar the bald eagle, the blue heron and the fish hawk; and in the forest tangle the coon and opossum hide from man. Reelfoot is a sportsman's heaven today.

Middle Tennessee is more tranquil than its rivals; it is a land where man's own mark seems permanent and nature more normally lavish. But on the eastern borders of this more placid countryside rise mountains, too, the rugged, outer plateau of the Cumberlands, and there is no softness to beauty here. This middle land is girt by the Tennessee River, tamed now and reshaped and bent to man's full use; but the river once spelled travail and blood. And here men seem to remember the past most lovingly, though they are not bemused by it; and it comes to life readily, in a score of towns, a hundred landmarks, a thousand folk tales remembered.

Here, in Middle Tennessee, a man can speak unashamedly of culture. To the colleges and universities of Nashville come annually about 9600 nonresident students, white and Negro. In Nashville, a symphony orchestra flourishes, and a children's museum, one of the most beguiling in the country. Middle Tennessee is the cosmopolitan region of the state. It seems also to rest upon the firmest foundations. The Middle Tennessee farmhouse is solider and more extensive than its counterparts to the east and the west. Its landowners appear to be more secure, its folkways and even its sports more deeply rooted.

East Tennessee, Middle Tennessee, West Tennessee. So much in each of which a man might boast. The refashioned river itself; Fall Creek Falls, with a water drop of 256 feet, the highest east of the Rockies. And Lookout Mountain dominating Chattanooga and Moccasin Bend, a lofty rock-faced promontory carved through thousands of years by the downrushing Tennessee. From Lookout Mountain, a man can see seven states on a clear day. If he is a good Tennessean, he will prefer the nearest.

And within the state, he will prefer his section and the city which dominates it. Time was when the four principal cities of Tennessee could be defined by characteristics as well as by location. This is less true now, for a common industrialization tends to level their differences. They share a determination to grow, to industrialize.

Nevertheless, certain differences persist. Nashville, the second largest city and capital of the state and of Middle Tennessee, has a serene, Athenian quality, as if it were more attuned to its eight universities and colleges than to its industrial plants. A Nashvillian speaks more readily of his city's book houses and writers, its symphony and its statelier past, than of its more material promise. Memphis lacks this quiet assurance, for it grew from a brawling boom town on the river to the state's largest city so hurriedly that it has hardly had time to assess itself. Energetic, clean and preoccupied with its almost incredible industrial expansion, Memphis seems—despite its Beale Street, its heavy Negro population, its Cotton Carnival and a commanding position as the deep South's cotton-trade center—more like a bustling Midwestern city than the mecca of Mississippi planters.

Chattanooga and Knoxville have more in common than do the others. They are only 100 miles apart, the one lying on the border of Middle and East Tennessee and the other in the shadow of the Great Smoky Mountains. Chattanooga derives spiritually and economically from both sections; it profited after the Civil War because perceptive Northerners, sensing the industrial advantages of her location, joined hands in a real reconstruction, so that cosmopolitan

Chattanooga became one of the first of the South's industrial cities. Today it shares with diversified Knoxville the benefits of being in the heart of the TVA country; both prosper in no small part because of TVA's reclamation and recreational enterprises.

Gentleness and compassion were not among the virtues of the early Tennesseans. Courage and hardihood were. And the tough breed which survived produced a hero's roll: Nolichucky Jack Sevier, who was the first governor of the unique, independent state of Franklin and six times governor of Tennessee; Evans and Isaac Shelby, scourges of the Southern Tories; James Robertson, revered even in his lifetime as the father of Tennessee; Colonel John Donelson and the surviving companions of the unbelievable winter voyage by flatboat and pirogue down the Tennessee to the Ohio and up the Cumberland to the site of Nashville; Daniel Boone, blazing the Wilderness Road; Davy Crockett, roaring, fighting drunk on the Memphis bluffs.

But none of them left such a mark as did a spare Carolinian, a redheaded lawyer who came riding into Tennessee near the end of the century. In Andy Jackson were reflected all the vices and virtues of the Tennessee frontier. He dominated his adopted state for thirty years, and all the United States for half as long. Duelist Andy Jackson, who feuded with Calhoun, and dipped unwholesomely in land speculation with his friend John Overton, encouraged the rape of the Cherokees, and bossed Tennessee's politics down to county and town, and spoke for the common man; childless, pain-wracked Andy Jackson, playing the flute in The Hermitage at Nashville, for his neighbor's children to dance by, and dreaming of his dead love.

It is not implausible to conjecture that had Jackson been in power a generation later he might have avoided the Civil War; for he had a spirit that could cow the South Carolina cockerels and the venomous abolitionists of New England alike. But he was dead in 1861, and across his state raged the desperate fury of civil strife.

Most of Tennessee had been lukewarm to secession. Its mountain Republicans had actively opposed withdrawal from the Union. And Tennessee had been the last state to secede.

But this sane reluctance did not spare it from some of the most terrible destruction of the war. From the capture of Fort Donelson in February, 1862, to the battle for Nashville in December, 1864,

Tennessee was a battleground. Bloody, decisive Shiloh . . . Murfreesboro, Chattanooga, Lookout Mountain and Missionary Ridge . . . Chickamauga . . . and Franklin.

In Tennessee, Grant experimented in the strategy of the bludgeon, and Sherman condoned sack and pillage. And Nathan Bedford Forrest, slave dealer and cavalryman, with his "critter company" baffled and enraged the overwhelming forces of conquest and occupation.

"Two hundred recruits wanted," Forrest advertised in the Memphis *Appeal* soon after disastrous Shiloh. "I will receive 200 ablebodied men if they will present themselves at my headquarters by the first of June with good horse and gun. . . . Come on, boys, if you want a heap of fun and kill some Yankees. (signed) N. B. Forrest, colonel commanding Forrest's regiment."

Tennessee, the last state to leave the Union, one of the longest occupied and worst ravaged, became the first to re-enter. Her debasement under the Reconstruction governor, Parson Brownlow, a fanatical loyalist, was not so long-lasting as was that of many of her sister states; but it was complete for its duration. And out of the humiliation and desperation of the disenfranchised white, rose the ghostly Ku Klux Klan, born as a prankish fellowship of young Confederate veterans, and expanded and diverted to an awesome, extralegal striking force against misled Negro and predatory carpetbagger and scalawag.

The story of Tennessee has another chapter. The Bible rested also on the log mantel beside the powder horn, and when the town sites were cleared, the preacher-teacher came to instruct in reading and writing and figuring and piety. The frontiersman hungered for more than land. He coveted for his sons what he had lacked on the seaboard and beyond the ocean.

The culture of Tennessee is oriented in part toward the wilderness past, in part toward what the wilderness denied. Its folklore relates to storied fighters and hunters, patriots and orators; though the mountaineer's individuality is being lost as the highway and the radio, the craft shop and the newspapers intrude, the Tennessean takes pride in the olden virtues of the mountain people, in the ballad preserved and the riflemen's turkey shoot and the fiddler calling the reel. In these and less subtle ways is evidenced the frontier temper, the agricultural base, the rural savor of the state's lifeway.

In a state that was once prostrate and has been long exploited there are now forty-nine institutions of higher learning. Twenty-eight of them are colleges and universities, seven are professional schools, five are teachers' colleges and nine, junior colleges. Eight are for Negroes and these include the noted Fisk University, Meharry Medical School and Tennessee Agricultural and Mechanical College, one of the largest Negro institutions in the world. All three are in Nashville.

The record of educational expansion is impressive, and all the more because of the small and harassed beginnings. The first regular school west of the Alleghenies was not opened until 1780, when a fighting preacher named Samuel Doak began conducting graded classes at his farm near Jonesboro. It was not until Reconstruction that a public-school system began to compete with the little academies, in great part sectarian, that for almost a hundred years afforded the young Tennesseans their only schooling. The public-school system is weak still, for almost everywhere there are too few schools and too great a difference between the best and the worst. But that, too, is changing.

The origins of some of the institutions of note are of more than passing interest. The splendid University of Tennessee began as Blount College in 1794, one of the earliest nonsectarian and co-educational schools in the United States. Vanderbilt University, founded as a Methodist Episcopal church school, was later endowed by old Cornelius Vanderbilt, renamed in his honor and made nonsectarian. The proud little University of the South at Sewanee in the Cumberlands, was founded by the Protestant Episcopal Church just before the Civil War. Bishop Leonidas Polk, one of its founders, went to the war as a general, and Union troops burned the new college down to its cornerstone. It was rebuilt principally with British contributions. At Bell Buckle is Webb School, unique among Southern preparatory schools, whose classical-minded founder, "Sawney" Webb, was the father of preparatory-school education in the South. Near Monteagle in the Cumberlands is the Highlander Folk School, a training school for industrial leaders, founded by Myles Horton, which works closely with the mountain people in preserving the old crafts. At Nashville is the principal teaching-training school in the South, George Peabody College for Teachers, which, as the University of Nashville, received a large bequest from the estate of George Peabody of Massachusetts, and like Vanderbilt, took the name of its benefactor. And at Nashville also is Fisk University for Negroes, which was founded after the Civil War by the American Missionary Association, and has prospered from its own indomitable purpose and a lasting good will. There is a happy symbolism in the announcement that Fisk, whose first students were former slaves who studied the simplest of curriculums, has recently received one of the best modern-art collections in the United States, including works of Picasso, Rivera, Cézanne and Georgia O'Keeffe. It is a long way from *Swing Low, Sweet Chariot* to the Fisk art gallery.

A cosmopolitan diversity reflects the origins and objectives of these Tennessee institutions. Contrarily, the creative spirit in the state has been largely regional in outlook. Writing fares best among the arts. Out of Tennessee in the recent past have come T. S. Stribling, the hill realist, Harry Harrison Kroll, John Porter Fort, Leland Crabb and Jennings Perry; and from West Tennessee, Roark Bradford, and sensitive Anne Goodwin Winslow, of Raleigh. It was from West Tennessee that Joseph Wood Krutch went to New York. And young Peter Taylor is a Tennessean.

Of all these Tennessee contributors to the arts and letters, I would single out the late Roark Bradford, the gentle, honest interpreter of the Negroes of the lower Mississippi Valley. The ignorant intelligentsia suspected him on the grounds that he mocked the Negro. The evaluation was shallow and unjust. He never caricatured or ridiculed the primitive, amiable folk whom he knew so well. He laughed with them and not at them, and the laughter which he set down was as real as the Mississippi.

I suppose that I am prejudiced, because he was my good friend, and because he gave me some newspaper advice long ago which I have tried to follow.

"Don't go after the ordinary folks," he said. "Most people get hurt often enough without having writers go out of their way to hurt them. Go after the people who do the hurting."

In a nation so extensive as ours, the American of one region often finds it difficult to understand the people of another. What little he thinks he knows is frequently true only in part or is a cruel caricature. So with the notion of Tennessee as a tragicomical area populated by shaggy-eared mountaineers, book-burning fundamentalists and political monstrosities, a backward land of social absurdities and racial discrimination, where the Klansman, the political boss, the landowner and the fundamentalist conspire against economic and moral evolution.

Begin with the position of the Negro in Tennessee. Among the Southern states Tennessee is unusual in that its Negro population does not constitute an omnipresent problem, nor do its politicians emphasize the racial issue to any appreciable extent.

A clue to this relative tranquillity lies in the composition of early Tennessee agriculture and the accompanying role of the Negro slave. A majority of Tennessee's farms—and even its western plantations—have always been relatively small. The farmer and planter owned but few slaves, and were in direct contact with them; and this closer, individual association had a humanizing effect upon master and slave alike, so that compassion was developed in the one and a more diverse capability in the other.

An obvious result of the small-farm composition of Tennessee was a lower ratio of Negro to white than elsewhere in the cotton South. The Negro was never in a majority in Tennessee, and today the state's 550,000 Negroes are only one sixth of its population, the lowest proportion in the Deep South. The social taboos are rigidly observed, but, particularly in Middle Tennessee, the Negro enjoys a happier status as landowner, voter and independent citizen than do his brothers in most of the rest of the South. More hopefully significant than anything else, perhaps, is the number and the quality of Tennessee's educational institutions for Negroes and the general acceptance of Negro suffrage.

But statistics on educational development cannot indicate the personal, human element of white-Negro relationships in Tennessee— nor the friendship and respect that are accorded the outstanding Negro. It is unlikely that any Tennessee citizen is more esteemed than Dr. Charles S. Johnson, the president of Fisk University, a patient, scholarly scientist and educator whose faculty is bi-racial and whose school is the meeting ground for a yearly interracial conference of men of good will and hopeful purpose. I doubt that any Tennessean is more liked by his patrons than is aged Aaron Taylor, custodian of the state law library, the only Negro in the United States to hold such a post.

Nor was any musician, in or out of Tennessee, more loved than the late William C. Handy, the timeless genius of the mournful blues— young Bill Handy, Alabama-born, who refused to follow the steps of his minister father and grandfather, preferring the "sinful music" of the rivermen and the improvisations of his first battered cornet; gaunt Bill Handy, hungry roustabout and day laborer, heading north on a freight train at twenty-one with the blues moaning in his head, to sing and play for dimes in saloons of Chicago.

As for the ballot, Tennessee has offered less resistance to the Negro

vote than has any other Southern state with the possible exception of
Virginia.

The rioting in Columbia in 1946 is still an open wound. In the back
country, hoodlums in masks and sheets prowl on occasion again,
and men dare to boast that they are Klansmen. But their numbers
are few and their vicious beatings and intimidation have claimed as
many white as Negro victims.

Such matters make headlines. Others do not. In Nashville I talked
with a young Fisk student, a war veteran who planned to be a
teacher. We discussed a city election in which he had voted. He
waved his hand expressively at the campus.

"That's all we're asking," he said. "A decent, equal education, and
the ballot. We can win everything we deserve to win with schools
and the vote. And we won't scare anybody when we do it."

The headline curse extends to Tennessee's politics. To the casual,
distant critic, Tennessee politics means the shrewd, vitriolic Edward
H. Crump of Memphis who rode herd over his city for forty years
and for fifteen years bossed his state. It means eastern Tennessee's
election-day gunfights, and the pitched battle in Athens between
young veterans and the thugs of the county machine which sought
to steal the election. It means the poll tax, and the oldest unamended
constitution in the United States—not a comma changed since 1870
—a hopelessly outdated document which denies duelists the right to
hold office, forbids the election of a minister to the legislature and
relieves the citizen of the duty to bear arms "provided he will pay
an equivalent to be determined by law."

Certainly self-government in Tennessee suffers greatly from indifference, petty venality, and factionalism. More than one governor,
senator and congressman have been the creatures of the autocratic
Red Snapper of Memphis. How strong has been his hold, up to the
recent past, is humorously illustrated by the story of a gubernatorial
candidate who had expected Ed Crump's backing and after happily
announcing his candidacy, learned that the Memphis machine would
support his opponent. "Man," commiserated a friend, "that sure puts
you out on a limb."

"Limb, hell," observed the wretched candidate. "I'm out on a twig."

But it is also fair to point out that Mister Crump's town is not boss-
ridden in the corrupt sense that characterized Hague's Jersey City

and the Kansas City of Pendergast. Memphis is a well-run, orderly, and relatively uncorrupt city—though that itself is dangerous, since it made Mr. Crump's totalitarian regime so attractive. And the boss man got his comeuppance some years ago in 1948, when the progressive Estes Kefauver won the United States senatorship, and Gordon Browning, once a Crump-backed governor, whom Crump hated most of all, became governor again.

The angry campaign was vividly Tennessean. Crump compared Browning to Judas Iscariot and called Kefauver the darling of the communists. But when the smoke cleared away, Kefauver and Browning were elected.

Most Tennesseans resemble their fellow mortals elsewhere in effecting a workable compromise between religion and human frailty. This adjustment with reality is in the heroic tradition. A group of Memphis ladies of more than a century ago whose little Presbyterian church was heavily in debt decided to organize themselves into a sewing society and hold a fair at which their handiwork would be sold. Near the church was a saloon owned by a generous citizen named Hart. The saloon was better equipped for holding a fair than was the church. So the ladies went to Mr. Hart, who readily consented to let them use the saloon. While the devil looked the other way, the Presbyterian ladies sold $700 worth of their work; and it may be hoped that the gentlemen of the church thenceforth gave Mr. Hart their patronage.

Even the most unearthly character in Tennessee folklore made much the same kind of compromise. She was the Bell Witch, the spirit of old Kate Batts who after her death harried John Bell, his family and even his good friend Andy Jackson because she fancied that she had been cheated in a land deal. The Bell Witch didn't restrict herself to hounding them alone, but spent her spare time attending every revival in Robertson County, moaning and shouting with the best; and raiding the county stills and getting unbelievably drunk. Since there were about as many stills as there were revivals, she must have been the busiest spirit in occult history.

The Bell Witch's divided devotion to the spiritual and the spirituous was not without more earthy emulation. The religious fervor, particularly of rural Tennesseans, is nevertheless real, and the majority of churchgoers worship simply and unaffectedly. Yet some do not. Tennessee has no monopoly on the masochists whose interpretation of Biblical passages leads them to extraordinary and sometimes fatal lengths; but these extremists do seem to thrive mightily in the Tennessee back country, and their performances are enough to chill the believer and the skeptic alike.

Once I witnessed a Holy Roller revival held in a field at nighttime, and the preachers and performing laymen—eight or ten of them— stood behind a long table on a crude, roofless platform. On the table burned yellowly a half-dozen kerosene lamps, the only illumination except for the stars. The five hundred or so worshipers and curious spectators sat on soap boxes, logs and the ground itself. It didn't take the preachers long to work themselves and many of their audience into a gibbering frenzy. Leaders and participants alike broke into the weird unintelligible supplication that they call speaking in the Unknown Tongue; and as the frenzy increased, men and women began grunting and moaning and laughing insanely. Here and there transfigured believers jerked uncontrollably, a chant of "Oh, sweet Jesus, sweet Jesus" keeping time with the gyrations. The lamps were white hot. At the climax, the preachers lifted the searing lamp globes from their bases and fondled them with their bare hands.

It is difficult sometimes to laugh without also marveling. And sometimes one wonders at the laughter. A quarter of a century has passed since the trial of young John T. Scopes in Dayton, a pleasant, hill-girdled little Tennessee city, tree-lined, thriving, remote from the outside world. No other event in Tennessee's history brought it so much notoriety.

Among the citizens of Dayton was George Rappleyea, a distinguished engineer, who in the spring of 1925 found himself vexed by a new state law which forbade the teaching of any theory of man's beginnings that ran counter to the Biblical story of creation. It occurred to Mr. Rappleyea that it would be good publicity for Dayton if a test case were to be made there. In a Dayton drugstore, he suggested to young John Scopes, a Northerner and biology teacher in the high school, that he put his head on the chopping block. Rappleyea would bring charges against Scopes. Scopes agreed.

Dayton got all the publicity that the little group had bargained for, and more. Overnight, John Scopes became a martyred hero to the Eastern press, and Tennessee a target for derisive onslaught. The American Civil Liberties Union rushed to Scopes' aid; Arthur Garfield Hays and Dudley Field Malone joined the defense forces. They were to be overshadowed by Clarence Darrow, who had also immediately volunteered his services. The state prosecutors found a no less notable ally in William Jennings Bryan, who in his later years had increasingly concerned himself with the defense of fundamentalist beliefs.

With the trial, Dayton became a carnival town and a crank's paradise as fundamentalism mobilized against the invaders, twice damned as atheists and Yankees. Across the main street hung a banner: "The Sweetheart Love of Jesus Christ and Paradise Street is At Hand. Do You Want to be a Sweet Angel? Itemize Your Sins and Iniquities for Eternal Life. If You Come Clean God Will Talk Back to You in Voice." The little city's pretty streets were lined with peanut, hot-dog and lemonade stands. Quasi-religious barkers peddled pamphlets bearing such provocative titles as "Hell and the High Schools," and "God or Gorilla?" In the hot July night, revivalists shouted from beneath swinging lanterns, and white and Negro minstrels sang the praises of the Lord.

Darrow and Bryan, once political allies and friends, shouted their contempt for each other in the sweltering courtroom and on the lawn to which court was moved. "Bigots and ignoramuses," cried Darrow. "The only purpose Mr. Darrow has," spoke the tormented Bryan, "is to slur at the Bible." Once they came near exchanging blows.

The audience movingly and unexpectedly gave Dudley Field Malone the greatest ovation of the trial when he pleaded for the defense:

"There is never a duel with truth. The truth always wins and we are not afraid of it; the truth is no coward. The truth does not need the law. The truth does not need the forces of government. The truth does not need Mr. Bryan. The truth is imperishable, eternal and immortal, and needs no human agency to support it. . . ."

The jury found John Scopes guilty, as he and his associates expected. He was fined $100. Five days later William Jennings Bryan died in his sleep on a Sunday afternoon, exhausted in mind and body and shocked to the breaking point by the savage disbelief of his adversary.

The case was appealed to the State Supreme Court which upheld the constitutionality of the statute. But the court made further appeal impossible. It found that the trial judge had erred in assessing the $100 fine, as that should have been the jury's prerogative, and recommended a nollepros to the Attorney General.

"The Court is informed," the Chief Justice said, "that the plaintiff in error is no longer in the service of the state. We see nothing to be gained by prolonging the life of this bizarre case."

The Attorney General accepted the recommendation, precluding appeal to the United States Supreme Court. And the law remains on the books.

The ballad's tune is Old English, but the words are as new as a miracle that came into being only twenty-seven years ago; and above them throbs another and wordless song, the ballad of water at work for man. Here is man's ballad, as genuine as any that was handed down from mountain father to remembering son:

> *My name is William Edwards.*
> *I live down Cove Creek way,*
> *I'm working on a project*
> *They call the TVA.*
>
> *The government begun it*
> *When I was just a child,*
> *But now they are in earnest*
> *And Tennessee's gone wild.*
>
> *Oh, see them boys a-comin'*
> *Their government they trust.*
> *Just hear their hammers ringing,*
> *They'll build that dam or bust.*

The clean, purposeful dams tower high in the land of a continuing miracle, the land of the Tennessee Valley Authority. "You can't tear those dams down," said Wendell Willkie, who tried, as president of Commonwealth and Southern, to keep them from rising; tried understandably and with conviction, in a gigantic battle of economic concepts and of survival. He lost his fight, but not his stature. Tennessee won the fight and gained also in stature; and in the long run no American has been in reality a loser.

Consider first the valley of the Tennessee. Its area is four fifths as large as all England. Upon the mountains which shadow the sources of the Tennessee there fall annually 6000 tons of water to the acre. From the mountains, the water seeks its own level, rushing down the green slopes in a thousand creeks, into a host of small rivers, and thence into the Tennessee. In the wake of the eroding water, two and a half million acres have been lost. Another four and a half million have been reduced to submarginal usefulness. The Tennessee, roaring downhill—it descends nearly 600 feet from Knoxville to Paducah—was no friend to the harassed valley.

For almost a hundred years the shoal-infested river into which the mountain rainfall emptied has fascinated and challenged the engineer, the dreamer and the land planner with its potential power, its defiance of the navigator, its unpredictable rampages. No agency, public or private, seemingly possessed the resources, the vision and the capability to conquer the perverse, unorthodox river.

And then, early in his first term, President Roosevelt asked for the creation of a Tennessee Valley Authority. The long fight of Sen. George Norris of Nebraska neared an end. The TVA's objectives were to be "maximum flood control, maximum development of the river for navigation, maximum generation of electric power consistent with flood control and navigation, proper use of marginal lands, proper methods of reforestation of all lands in the drainage basin suitable for reforestation, and the economic and social well-being of the people living in the basin."

Before the end of 1949 TVA had its millionth consumer. Not customer, but consumer, for TVA sells only to municipalities and cooperatives and these sell to the million customers.

"Maximum generation of electric power. . . ."

This is what the President of the United States said on August 6, 1945: "It is an atomic bomb. It is a harnessing of the basic power of the universe. The force from which the sun draws its powers has been loosed against those who brought war to the Far East."

Two days later, Colonel K. D. Nichols, district engineer at a place of which most Americans had never heard—a place in Tennessee named Oak Ridge—added a little more to the awesome story that the world was piecing together.

"The nearby sources of electricity in large amounts from the TVA has been the chief factor in locating the plant at Oak Ridge," he said.

A model for military brevity. Behind it lay the saga of new, urgent dams, completed far ahead of schedule out of men's sweat and guts and lives—massive Fontana and Kentucky and Douglas and Cherokee—so that more power might be generated in the Tennessee Valley. Behind it the unwritten history of a secret city that sprang up in a place called Happy Valley, a remote, unsettled and peaceful region eighteen miles from Knoxville. Behind it, the key to victory in an awesome race among nations. At the peak of what was known as the Manhattan Project, 75,000 people lived in the guarded, austere settlement, themselves ignorant of the task at which they labored and conscious only that its purpose was dreadful, vital, linked to the winning of a war that seemed so far away.

Oak Ridge is, in great part, still a place of mystery, but it is now an open city too. Its population, shrunk to a stable core has begun an orderly growth. Permanent homes and business buildings rise; it has its own newspaper; and almost in the shadow of the guarded plants women work their rose gardens, and men sit in their shirt sleeves on cool porches.

And there is one especial place in Oak Ridge where the visitor can say, "This is understandable, this is American, this is part of my past, part of my children's future—I pray." Surprisingly, it is the Museum of Atomic Energy, the first permanent center devoted to telling only the story of the atom.

I do not say there is reassurance in the scale models, the maps and the diagrams which depict and superficially explain the plants in which U-235 is separated, the uranium chain-reacting pile, the preparation of radioisotopes and the creation of power from nuclear energy. But there are two moments in the museum which all can understand. The first comes when a guide asks the visitor for a dime. The dime is made radioactive before the donor's eyes and returned to him in a souvenir mounting. The second comes in the exhibit for the youngsters. There the atom-splitting process is explained in cartoons and dialogue by Dagwood and other beloved cartoon-strip characters.

Step right up, folks, see the atom demonstration, only twenty-five cents for adults, five cents for children—and dear God, let it go on like this. . . .

Visionary Senator Norris could not have foreseen the outcome of his struggle "waged on behalf of the common people against the combined forces of monopoly and human greed." The distant enemy which TVA helped destroy had carried monopoly and greed to a far ghastlier extreme than the Nebraskan who loved humanity could have even imagined. Nor could he have envisioned or understood more hopeful ends, the promise of the radioactive isotopes from the laboratories of Oak Ridge, for the healing of man and the enrichment of society.

Maximum generation of electric power. . . . A great cloud over Hiroshima, a secret weapon that is secret no longer, a crossroads that branches from Happy Valley in Tennessee to the outer reaches of the earth.

Surely David Lilienthal was thinking of such matters long ago, in his first speech on the social implications of TVA.

"Those who believe that things as they are cannot be improved will wonder why we are concerned with a better planning of economic and social life," he mused. "But those with a sense of humanity, who see all about them want in the midst of plenty—factories idle while men need the products which manufacturers want to produce, millions of farmers desperate because they have produced too much while other millions of men go hungry for lack of these very crops— those who see these distressing facts and are perplexed and troubled by them will join in any intelligent effort to bring a bit more order into a world which so desperately cries for it."

A bit more order. Fields rustling with green, thick pastures where once the red gullies tore away earth's life. . . . White-faced Herefords and heavy-uddered Jerseys where a cotton farmer once told the tax collector to take the land and be damned. . . . The sheen of a fat bass in the sunlight on Norris Lake. . . . The tinted-glass windows of small factories, and large, in a valley that once begged for industry at any cost . . . the yellow glow of electric lights, high on a mountainside at night, the hum of the washing machine and the refrigerator in a tenant's cabin, the swelling deposits, the proud towns . . . the stately parade of the steel transmission towers of TVA . . . the red and yellow and green lights on the switchboard of the control room at Chickamauga. . . .

"We wanted those dams to have the honest beauty of a fine tool, for TVA was a tool to do a job for men in a democracy," said David Lilienthal.

People have to play even while they work out their destiny—and that means, among other things, that you don't need to approve TVA in whole or in part to enjoy it. Ask anyone who has gone on the annual TV-Ho! cruise upriver from Paducah to Knoxville, 630 miles of fun and adventure and surprise.

On the waterfront of river-wise Paducah, a Negro baptism ceremony among the willows; beyond the shrieking penitents, the oil barges, the present that is background for the past. . . . Lake Ken-

tucky, a long, blue 184 miles from Kentucky Dam to Pickwick; and on it a trim small ketch, heeling to a sudden squall, its sails rare yet on the transformed river. . . . Storm-whipped whitecaps scudding across Lake Pickwick, toward the overtaken foothills, while the smaller craft, shepherded by the TVA and Coast Guard patrol boats, make for the snug, well-marked safety harbors. . . .

We came ashore the first night, in a warm, drenching rain, at Johnsonville. The rain couldn't halt the first of the catfish and hushpuppy receptions for the most pampered voyagers in the history of navigation. The rain just made the fish and the barbecue, the crisp hot cornmeal slabs and coffee taste better.

Always in Tennessee the past intruding upon the present.

On this site, General Forrest and his cavalry ambushed a Federal flotilla, sinking some gunboats and supply boats and capturing others. The sunken craft lie deep now beneath the higher waters of the lake, and far from the newer shoreline, too deep for boys to dive, as they once did, for mementos of the dead; and on the shore here will rise a generative force a thousand thousand times as powerful as ever were the broken boats that strew the river bottom.

The first night, Johnsonville. The second, Pickwick Landing, where the dead fish bobbed crazily as we rose in the swirling waters of the lock; where in the sheltered cove, the voyagers sang and fished and swam in the dying rain; where only a few miles from Shiloh battlefield—so green and tended now above its buried thousands—a mammoth automobile carrier churned upstream with its glistening load.

And then the thriving little cities of Alabama, where the river curves southward, loops eastward and rises again toward Tennessee. Chickamauga Dam at Chattanooga, in the shadow of Lookout Mountain after the mountain-girt passage that they rightly call the Grand Canyon of the Tennessee. Watts Bar. And great Norris Dam.

Everywhere the pride and the confidence, the friendly hosts talking of plants and pay rolls and a burgeoning agriculture. Everywhere the fish fries, the barbecues, the whole-souled entertainment of friendly people who want you to know how far they've come and how much further they intend to go. And everywhere the pleasant shock of contrast. Boys swim yet in the subdued waters, bobbing distantly in the waves of the Diesel-powered tows. Men in skiffs fish within earshot of the droning turbines at Wilson Dam, the nucleus of the noble dream; the hillman's cabin looks down upon the nitrate plant; the workmen on the new country club can see below them the long-ragged farm that now responds to guidance, and Knoxville, journey's end.

North Carolina

by OVID WILLIAMS PIERCE

North Carolina begins with the brightness of sea sands and ends with the loneliness of the Smokies reaching in chill and cloud to the sky. It stretches from the break of the Atlantic to the still of mountain coves, from sunlit capes to shadowed valleys five hundred miles away—from the low river-fed acres of the Coastal Plain to the rocky Piedmont and on to the hanging slopes of the Blue Ridge.

The state's outer banks are long golden strips of sand pointing into the Atlantic to form treacherous capes—Hatteras, Lookout and Fear. Nothing can dramatize their remoteness from the rest of the world so much as storm. This was true especially at Nags Head in the days before bridges and highways, when the sense of isolation there was almost complete. But the Coast Guardsmen gave you ample warning: in hoods and raincoats they rode the beaches on horseback, stopping at the old cottages (then there were long stretches of sand and sea oats in between) and telling the silent little groups on the porches the news that had just come in.

For two days the beach had been deserted, even in front of the old Arlington Hotel. People gathered on the porches and wore sweaters and jackets against the dampness and chill. Wind-whipped waves filled the air with spray. And there, just a little way over the sand, was the dark, tortured, twisting sea.

The terror of this day was the height the water reached. If you stood midway between house and beach, you had to look up at the waves. They rose unbelievably above you, held their towering height for a second, then in crash and thunder and torrents of spray rolled higher and higher over the beach. And all the while you knew the real winds were still at sea, that during the night they would lash across the sands, already a diminishing strip beneath you, and carry the Atlantic over into Albemarle Sound.

So, during the long night you watch through the blackness. Kerosene lamps in the windows, hardly more than match flames, intermittently identify the cottages which lonely watchers have not yet abandoned to night and wind. The circle of yellow light within the thin walls of your cottage is like an island now riding in blackness, spray and roar. Once or twice you look out at the black, beaten shapes of the houses near you and can only wonder what the storm has done.

But first light brings calm and view of another world. Waters of the Albemarle and Atlantic have met. To the east, out to sea, to the west, across the Sound, the surface of the water is unbroken, a great glittering mirror now to hold the sky. The long stretch of sand which bore a strip of road, a path to the outside world, has been washed from the earth. Hotels, cottages, garages, chicken coops, which rose out of the sand on stilts, are now sliced from the bottom, low and flat. Even the great dune along the highway, Jockey's Ridge, a little mountain of sand, is an island with the water lapping round it, diminishing its command of the earth.

You know that in a short time people will begin to appear on this unpeopled scene, to break into the unworldly emptiness with tentative exploratory surveys, two or three in a boat, to assess what the night has done. Just for a moment longer will this silence hold. Already there in the distance is a boat. Two men are rowing, one is standing, pointing across the mirror of water that stretches as far as he can see.

You are a visitor. As you look out over the little hills of sand spotting the horizon, it comes to you again with a shock of surprise that this rib of the continent, reaching down from Nags Head, past Oregon Inlet, down and down to Hatteras, Lookout and Cape Fear, has been closed to the world for almost two hundred years.

On the stretch from Whalebone Junction to Hatteras there are seven tiny villages like beads on a string, hardly more than clusters of houses around a store or two. They've had no governments, no taxes, no jails. A hard-surfaced road has recently made them accessible. But earlier the only chance of approaching them through the sand was to follow the daily mail truck, with its tires nearly flat, and not allow it to get too far ahead. With it out of sight, you were faced with a bewildering maze of disappearing tracks across a desert of sand. Far in the distance, the village itself was hardly more than a mirage, simmering in glare and heat.

Inhabitants of this region still speak with a Devon accent, a full-vowel dialect to carry against wind and "toide." Their songs, for the outsider, need almost as much translation as Chaucer:

> *The noight was doark and hoizy,*
> *When the* Pickodully Doizy
> *Went daown with the cap-tun and the cre-uw.*
> *Oi'm sure the water drow-uned 'em*
> *For we never, never found 'em,*
> *And Oi know they didn't come ashore with Oi.*

Folk tales in the region are endless. In the stories the old pirates, Stede Bonnet and Blackbeard, who would frequently retreat through the inlets to safe waters, live again. So, too, are the land pirates remembered: those who hung the lantern on the old nag's neck and made her walk the beaches at night, hoping that her light would be mistaken for a beacon which would lure lonely ships upon the sands. A headless horseman gallops the dunes. Virginia Dare, the first child of white parents on this continent, appears at midnight reincarnated as a white doe, for those who know where to look. Offshore, there is a phantom ship, a modern Flying Dutchman that has never been named. In the little village of Rodanthe, Christmas even now is celebrated on Twelfth Night.

An old man, ninety-one, ninety-five, he couldn't remember—nobody left to tell him—was sitting in a cottage on the mainland. Far out across the Sound lay the little spot of sand which had for eighty years been his home. Yes, grandchildren made him come to the mainland. Lost his wife seven years ago. Now he was just waiting, just looking out over the water, as though the place where he'd done all his living had been swallowed up in the earth. Falling mustaches framed his chin; his eyes blinked.

You call it a ghost town—Portsmouth? Hunh, once it was all the world. His father? He shook his head. Had tried to find out too late where he came from. Trouble was, hadn't nothing been written on paper. Memory was all.

Sure, out there, every man had to do everything. Hunt, fish, carpenter, plant, save lives at sea in storm. Doctor, preach and bury. Found three dead men in my time, one of them caught in a net. Just like they come from another world, so far as anybody could say. No questions asked. No law to ask it, not in them days.

Ghosts? Didn't believe in 'em himself. Plenty did. Couldn't tell another man what was or wasn't, not on the outer banks. Every man made his own world. Bring a man dying in a sailboat across the water at midnight, wind and no stars, is ghost enough.

Did he ever expect to cross the Sound again to see what was left?

The old man blinked again, a little confused by the question. Go back? He shook his head slowly.

But now North Carolina has embraced its ragged fringes. Long bridges reach across the glare of the Sounds, ferries ride the choppy inlets; and hard-surfaced roads, like spines down wind-blown strands, bear the traffic of the world outside into this lost corner of earth. Kitty Hawk, Nags Head, Hatteras, Ocracoke Island, have all become a summer world of beaches, of swimming and fishing. In the last few years the stretches of summer cottages, filling stations, motor courts, cafés, hotels with concrete aprons for parking, dance halls opening to the sea, have reached deeper and deeper into the old desolation of sand.

At night during the summer months on Roanoke Island (reached now by bridge from Nags Head to the east), hundreds of people assemble at the Waterside Theater for a performance of *The Lost Colony*, a pageant by Paul Green, which celebrates with dignity and insight North Carolina's first story, the story of the 117 men and women who settled the "Citie of Ralegh" on this spot in 1587, only to vanish without a trace, leaving nothing but the cryptic word CROATOAN carved on a tree, not as a key nor as a guide but as a token, perhaps, that the dark soil of American forests had already received English blood.

For this last scene the forlorn little group of colonists assembles mid-stage. They shoulder their bundles and packs. Already the site which they have cleared—this "Citie of Ralegh"—looks abandoned, its fires cold. One by one, they turn away. But, suddenly, with the banners of England flying, their voices raised to God—"We walk this way of death alone"—they march into the forest, which is waiting to receive them, to hide them forever from later years.

Now the stage is darkened, and the audience feels the silence reclaiming the land.

Then, as if by a miracle of timing, over the Sound, far down the beach, lights from a great granite shaft play across the sky. It is the Wright Brothers National Memorial Monument rising from Kill Devil Hill, marking the site of the dunes from which Orville and Wilbur Wright sent man's first power-driven plane into the air. On December 17, 1903, their fragile machine flew for twelve seconds, one hundred and twenty feet. On a fourth try, it flew eight hundred and fifty-two feet into windy space.

The audience still sitting in the darkness of Elizabeth's century looks for a brief moment with fresh wonder upon its own.

The Coastal Plain of North Carolina lies between the Sounds and the fall line, a distance of a hundred and fifty miles inland up the broad muddy rivers. This area of lowland, crossed by the Chowan, the Roanoke, the Tar, the Neuse, the Cape Fear, like so many highways to the sea, is the Old South of North Carolina, the agricultural South of river plantations, of small towns, of counties predominantly Negro, of long stretches of nothing but swamp, heat and pine.

The Great Dismal Swamp, lying at the upper edge of the Coastal Plain (and across the Virginia line), is thirty miles long and averages ten miles in width—a quagmire, a vast spongy surface that is neither water nor land. For two hundred years lumber companies have tried to subdue it but the swamp remains as inaccessible, at its secret heart, as it ever was. Sunlight can barely filter through the density of its inner growth: cypress, black gum and juniper. Stained for centuries by the leachings of trees, the water has become a deep wine. The region is in fact an unearthly darkness lying across sunlit land.

Perhaps this secret swamp is a symbol in an area where the past still presides visibly upon the landscape, where the past still looks out from abandoned oak groves, from the skeletons of old resort hotels, from chimneys rising starkly in the middle of plowed fields.

Perhaps this untracked path across the east is a symbol, too, of the Negro world, which for so long has coexisted with that of the white but which has remained forever closed, a river, its banks ever widening, mysterious, uncharted, across the Southern states.

Just off the highway near Halifax, an old Negro was sitting under a shed in his back yard. He was weaving a cane bottom on a kitchen chair. Obviously this was something he could do now without having to move around. He had all his paraphernalia conveniently within reach. Even his chair had been placed to miss the sun, which lay neatly at his feet.

"Uncle Jim."

His hand jerked, but his face showed no surprise. Many stood here to watch, many from the passing world.

"You don't know me?"

"Naw-suh." He was intent again on his chair. "Sit down. Company welcome here. Folks stops all time. From way off. Can't remember countries. Kentucky and Baltimore. Which country you?"

When I told him, knowing that it was the place of his birth, he took both hands from his work, holding the palms out toward me, as though to reject what he'd heard. "Hish yo' mouth. Sweet Jesus, I know." Then he looked at me hard, finally nodding. "To be sure, to be sure."

And, so, we were a part of that most lasting fraternity, sons of a remembered place and time. Recent faces, recent years had hardly the substance of reality for him. These days now were merely the shells of empty moments around a remembered living core—a core made of people larger than life.

"That was Miss Julia said that. Miss Julia, to be sure. Her pa was the one married the second time. Yas-suh. Married him a rich lady from way off. Kin see 'em right now in that surrey, coming into town. Folks didn't think he done right, marrying so soon. Wouldn't even pay no calls out there. Just like they'd be turning against Miss Cora, lying in her grave under the cedar tree for not more'n a year, Miss Cora that had been the prettiest lady of anybody's remembering around here. Couldn't understand how come he done it, was what it was. Lawd! Lawd!"

Finally he looked up, shook his head sadly. "Don't nobody know what we talking 'bout."

Was it only the magic of remembering which made the lives of people of this post-Civil War generation seem more dramatic, their manners more distinctive, that made them "characters" capable of dominating a place and time?

In any case, people in eastern Carolina have lived under long shadows of old figures, belonging now to time and myth.

The surest sign of the past in the eastern counties is an oak grove, an old company of trees, rising like a great tent swollen with wind. Mounds of brick and clay show where chimneys stood. But nobody will be there to give the grove a name.

Yet in the heart of the back country, completely hidden from view, at the end of a strangled road, stands the shell of a once great house—windowless, porchless, long since gray and warped, open to wind and rain—but containing still (if it has not been sacked) rare pine flooring, fine cornices, medallions clinging to water-soaked walls.

You will be surprised, as you stand there on this spot from which life so long ago fled, when a little Negro boy pulling a sardine can at the end of a string appears from behind the house. He is as startled as you. For a second he is incapable of retreat. Then he is gone, his boat of a sardine can abandoned.

In a moment the others come, no nearer than they must, just out from the corner. They make a little group, as though they moved as a body around this silent place. The mother is surrounded by a half dozen children holding to her skirt and to one another. She is neither young nor old. She will speak your language, but she knows another of her own. She is out of time, belonging neither to the crumble of the world in which she survives nor to that which your presence has brought to this isolated place.

A little off to the side, beyond the limits of the yard, three or four dark cedars are drawn together in a group, as if forever bound in retreat. A tangle of vine has almost completely claimed them. Underneath that choking green the graves lie—nameless even to them who watch the hanging cemetery gate.

"Lady ain't gonna sell this place. Ain't never gonna sell. Gonna stay here until lady dies. Ma say her pa 'longed to lady's pa. Us gonna stay here until lady dies." The Negro woman speaks with a deadened monotony, delivering a part rehearsed, revealing in her words the seekers who had stopped here before.

As though disbelief on your part provoked her, she adds, "Ma tell you. She tell how come can't nobody buy."

She turns then, indicating for you to follow.

Three or four rooms, opening upon a porch which makes an L at the back, have been kept nearly habitable by makeshifts of patchings: tin in lightless windows, loose planking for walkways across gaps in the flooring, a discarded automobile seat for a porch chair.

Here, enthroned, sits Ma. Even the approach to her is somehow deferential. "Ma, here man. Tells him lady ain't gonna sell."

She begins shaking her head. "Won't 'low no selling, lady don't. Says old Jane die here. Says keep dis place for old Jane. Bring lady, too, some day, that graveyard. Then time for old Jane to go. Old Jane sets here watch. Waiting for lady to come back home. Den old Jane go too. Don't live after lady. Dey sell. Sons, daughters. Watches now, waiting for time. Keep ghost off nighttime. Puts knife graveyard gate."

Old Jane sits presiding over a little realm as dark as time. It is hard for you to believe that not too far away runs a great highway bearing the traffic of the world.

Of course, Old Jane's diminished kingdom of lady and spirits is an exception. But it is true that, since the War Between the States, the second and third generations of owners have moved to town. Many old sites have been cut into small farms. In Halifax, Northampton, Warren and Bertie fine old houses have been dismantled and shipped north. In some cases Northern money has come in and saved old houses for the South. Many a mansion would be lost except in fiction but for outside help.

So, if this part of North Carolina is no longer a land of country sites, it has become a land of little towns. Some are raw and ugly under the Southern sun. But there are, too, the old towns: the county seats of softness and charm, of wide shaded streets, empty in the noonday sun except for some old Negro passing by, of pleasant white houses with green blinds drawn, of old heavy trees without motion in August heat, of Confederate monuments on lonely watch now in unused parks, and of molding yellow courthouses with square clock towers and cupolas enveloped in the fluttering shadows of pigeons and sparrows.

But the most striking feature of the little eastern town—something common to them all—is the straggling fringe of houses known as "colored section," spilling over into a ravine or clustering around a dead-end road, each bearing a name: Scott's Bottom, Harper's Field, Smith's Stretch.

In winter these sections look cold and deserted. All doors on the sagging porches are shut. A broken pane is stuffed with newspaper. Thin smoke rises from a chimney here and there to remind you that some of the older residents don't go out to work. But in spring when doors and windows are open, the road out front is everybody's yard. The air is alive with swinging clotheslines, colors flapping in the sun, the misty smoke of a pot boiling, thick smoke of trash fire, and white and pink of fruit trees flowering (all winter they've been no more than black wet sticks).

But the ragged edges of the towns are buttressed with new brick schoolhouses, shiny and sharp-angled and surrounded by gleaming yellow buses, too bright in the Southern sun, buses that started early in the morning to gather the little groups of Negro children waiting far out in the country at mailbox, crossroad and store.

It would be a mistake to assume that this eastern half of North Carolina has only the past to give the state, only the remnant of a plantation culture. This east has for long been growing and marketing one of the greatest shares of the world's tobacco, so here, too, is the area of the markets: Kinston and Greenville, Wilson, Henderson and Rocky Mount, and dozens of lesser size.

All have round their outer edges flat sprawling warehouses with acres of cement flooring and cavernous doors—doors to which in the fall the farmers will deliver load after load—wagons, trucks and trailers piled high—of "golden leaf"—the labor of months, actually, from the last of the winter to the fall of the year. No farming requires harder work, longer hours or greater skill.

A farmer who looked to be about sixty-five was standing in the doorway to one of the big tobacco warehouses in Rocky Mount on the day the market opened.

"Been coming all my life," he said to me. "Started coming in a wagon. Them days coming to tobacco market was a business and a holiday too.

"See that street here. Now ain't nothing but automobiles as far as you can see. Folks can get in 'em and go home or go to a café. Don't have to bother about nothing to eat. Used to be folks would bring something to eat to you. Sell it, I mean. Had stands all up and down this street. Great big tubs of barbecue, corn bread. Great big tubs of lemonade, hunks of ice floating around in it as big as your head. Sell you anything else too. They was folks that didn't do nothing but study ways to get your money. Money you done work the whole year for. Got it sometimes too. Would roll dice. Would even sell you oil land.

"Them days, got here, we had to stay a while. Us boys come sitting up on a top of a load of tobacco with the mules pulling us durn near all night long. Get here little 'fore sunrise, time to put tobacco on the floor. Warehouse had stables for the team. A little liquor passed around. See folks you hadn't seen in a year. Man, it was better'n August meeting any day.

"Now, got to wait till they tell you to come. What day. Just like you got a 'pointment with the doctor or something. Tell you when they got floor space for you. Man, I reckon it is better. I seen wagons lined up on this street here for a mile back—all waiting to get in and unload. But, seems like, waiting warn't so much of a burden them days as folks make out it is now."

Inside there was a sudden pulling of the crowd toward a corner of the warehouse. A group had formed at the head of the first row: the warehousemen, the auctioneer, the buyers. They were assembling as a machine now, every man having a part. Suddenly, as a group, impatience gripped them. "All right! Let's go! Let's go!" And the machinery was in motion, the chanting, sinuous rhythm of buying and selling had begun.

If this eastern half of North Carolina is self-contained, agricultural, and living within reach of its past, it is a proper complement to the Piedmont, a higher, rockier land, cut by sharper, swifter streams— the Yadkin, Saluda, Catawba and Broad. This is the region of cities, not farms; of factories and mills, of youth and growth, not of decaying houses standing miles and miles from any town. And all the roads lead here, to Raleigh and Durham, to Charlotte, Greensboro, Winston-Salem—and to Chapel Hill.

If North Carolina has a center, it is the town of Chapel Hill. But when the site for the university was selected in 1792, it was less of a center than a frontier. The rolling Piedmont and the unknown mountains rose to the west. The old towns of the east were behind it, lost in the distance and the green of the land.

What has Chapel Hill become in the South today?

My guide, a member of the faculty recently retired and a man whose affection for the university is balanced with understanding, sat across from me in a quiet pleasant corner of the Carolina Inn. Outside, Chapel Hill's great old trees properly shaded the veranda across the front, diminishing the urgency of the students' cars that filled the village streets.

Was there any other place which could claim Chapel Hill's title as "The Capital of the Southern Mind"?

"Suppose you name the place." And he pointed out the work that had been done by The Institute for Research in Social Science, under the late Howard Odum. Nowhere had more searching studies been made of Southern life; nowhere could a survey of a culture have been made more objectively, especially of a region for so long misrepresented and misunderstood.

How about the Carolina Playmakers?

Here was a subject close to his heart. Certainly. A significant part of the intellectual ferment for which the university is known. Frederick Koch, it was, who began it. What he had to say was that a man should write about himself. On this proposition the whole creative movement started. The mountains of the west and the cotton and tobacco farms of the east—areas which had rarely had any spokesmen except in the rhetoric of their orators pursuing the ghosts of Northern armies long after the Civil War, now had ably trained, devoted writers to interpret them realistically for the rest of the world. The Playmakers, reaching the farthest limits of the state, helped to make folk drama a graceful, natural voice in everyday life.

Even a partial listing of Koch's students is impressive: Thomas Wolfe, Jonathan Daniels, Frances Gray Patton, Bernice Kelly Harris. Oh, yes, my informant went on, it was here that Wolfe wrote his first play, *The Return of Buck Gavin*. Not a good play, but a start. As a matter of fact, he was the only boy in Koch's first class. But there was something about Tom Wolfe that should be corrected, a false notion arising, perhaps, from the vast loneliness which so concerned him as a novelist. He was not a recluse. Not a tormented spirit shunning others and in turn being shunned. Tom Wolfe, on the contrary, was one of the most conspicuous men on the campus. He acted in his own plays. He debated throughout his college years, certainly without any show of shyness. He joined practically everything there was to join on the campus, social and honorary. And he was with his other accomplishments something of a clown. It is safe to say that none at the time could foresee that this lad, down from the mountains, six-feet-three with boyish face, would later command the angels of Milton to look homeward and melt with rue.

For over fifty years the university has held the intense affection of its people, a fact suggesting that there no longer exists a single school but, perhaps, the myth of many, made out of the needs and imaginings of different men. Old students not only want to return to Chapel Hill to live but many of them do. Elderly couples, retired and well to do, have found the village charm. Writers have made there a considerable colony.

But the really important thing—the conversation continued—was that the university had survived as a great liberal institution, in an area where one wouldn't expect to find it. No one man could do it, could make a university. The university was the sum of all its people living in pursuit of ends unseen and knowing the purity of freedom of search.

Taking the winding road downward, away from the town, was like returning to an everyday world which had—quite surprisingly—known how to protect its citadel on the hill.

Barely twelve miles away another university lies hidden in the trees—Duke. Beginning at a circular drive, there is a long beautiful approach to the tower. The road rides high above the slopes and gardens below, which, in spring, drop down and down in terraces of color. The tower ahead reaches up, overlooks the forest around. Then, suddenly, to the right and left, the quadrangle, perhaps the largest university court in the world, has received you—a vast greensward enclosed by buildings of greenish-gray stone.

It is strange to pass a tobacco barn, a crossroads store, a little white church in a grove as fresh as a primer drawing, and to come suddenly to the center of this Gothic world. Here in the middle of the North Carolina woods is a re-creation of the Middle Ages, as complete as a town.

The story is that in 1925 James B. Duke looked over the forests around Durham and, coming upon this spot, exclaimed, "Here's where it ought to be." Here, accordingly, a complete university sprang from the woods.

The chapel tower reaches above the lesser towers. Arches and cloisters are worked into a unifying design. Flagstone walks cross the green. Chimneys and spires rising from the deep slope of moss-gray slate reach into the sky with the tops of the pines. And there inside the chapel are the bodies of the founders of the Duke dynasty, each marble sarcophagus as cold, as permanent as that of any European saint.

Comparison with the University of North Carolina is of course inevitable. By its very nearness to Chapel Hill, Duke has had a difficult role to play. To many, it has seemed to be a foreign thing on native soil. But Duke, too, is North Carolina—an old school, in fact, founded in 1838 as Union Institute, with a history of more than a hundred years of service to the South.

Now as you follow the serpentine road around the campus, you see the cars of all the states. Here is a school for the Eastern seaboard: New York, New Jersey, Pennsylvania, as well as the South. A little farther around the circle is the hospital area, one of the great medical centers of the South, a complete world within itself.

You can't help remembering again what a short time ago it was that Mr. Duke walked into this forest and said, "Here's where it ought to be." The making of a myth out of marble tombs inside the Duke Chapel seems not so strange as the story of this school translated from tobacco farms, from North Carolina land.

Quite abruptly, to the west, above this Piedmont plateau, above the mill towns, above the new highways endlessly bearing the traffic of a growing land, rises the ragged escarpment of the Blue Ridge. It rises suddenly. There it is before you, a great wall, the boundary of still another world: North Carolina's western fringe.

For a hundred years the isolation of this mountain region was as complete as that of the eastern sea-reaching strands. But now this heavily forested, cloud-wrapped land, too, has been embraced. The young have come out of the valleys to the mills and colleges of the Piedmont. Picture shows, beauty parlors, radios have reached to the farthest village to compromise old purities of manner and speech. And highways are bearing more and more of the world outside to regions which only a short time ago were known only in name.

One of the most beautiful drives in America is that along the Blue Ridge Parkway, coming out of Virginia, past Asheville to the Smokies below. Frequently high above clouds, the highway winds down and around the folds of the mountains, showing its own path far below, cuts gracefully through rock, and turns time and again above canyon and valley that unexpectedly open the world as far as you can see. The distance is a pale blue range above a range, hardly more than a deeper breath upon the sky.

Round the glittering lakes in sunlit valleys are dozens of summer camps bearing the names of Indians, mountains, waterfalls—names on swinging signs over rustic cedar gateways, on sweaters, on writing paper for weekly letters home. Little clusters of white shacks, tennis courts, bridle trails circle the shining lakes. The young are discovering themselves away from home, expanding with new-made friends as swimmers, riders, and sleepers under the night stars along old Indian trails.

Halfway up the mountains, on the verandas of the hotels, 19th Century white-frame buildings, all windows, row above row, rising out of rhododendron and laurel, the elderly are sitting in the circles of rockers—gray-haired ladies and a few gentlemen, wearing light coats against the chill. They have come up to spend the hot months, as they have been doing for years, to this same porch, wrapped in afternoon mist, to remember those once here, to whom the circle of chairs earlier belonged. Sisters and widows of the state's illustrious, theirs is a close-knit little clan, one of the last aristocracies to be found. Their tales, their recollections, reaching back and forth from plantation to town, touching here an old judge, there an old bishop, a governor or two, tell the story of a North Carolina that is just disappearing, that is, perhaps, nowhere more real than here.

A short turn off the Blue Ridge Parkway will bring you to such a retreat. The small hotel looks out through mist-hung trees across the valley to Linville. The clouds are not always beyond the reach of the trees, so the little terraced area of paths and mountain laurel is quite often shut off from the world, from the valley which lies just below, from the mountains rising beyond. The balsam and cedars are black with dripping chill.

But inside, in a great stone fireplace, a fire is burning. Two elderly ladies, removing their cloaks, are just returning to its warmth. Thickening mist has kept them from their walk. Beyond a point the path is completely lost as though it had disappeared into space.

For thirty years the older of the two ladies has been coming here, first as companion to an aging, distinguished husband, then with a companion of her own, a distant cousin. For years and years the hotel sheltered a closed society made up of those who remembered the lady's distinguished husband, and circled round her, perpetuating a former day. There was a time when all remembered him, when the lady received the deference of all. But with the years the circle diminished; and finally only the lady came, each year searching the new faces, but turning away always with increased bewilderment. How could such a time have passed so completely away, not even remembered today?

Below the hotel, on a hairpin turn down the mountain, in a little recess against the rock, there is a wayside stand. From overhead there is a fern-and-moss-lined trickle of water. Myrtle capping an overhang is dark and thick; it reaches up as far as you can see. The mountaineer is sitting beside his display of wares, in this misty heart of the mountains, already blue-shadowed in the afternoon. You wonder how he got there; there hasn't been a cabin for miles. Pottery and baskets, cane-bottom chairs, blankets and rugs. The blankets and rugs with bright flowery patterns are strung and waving as though on a country clothesline.

These mountains have been called the greatest reservoir of folk manufacturing in America. The long isolation of this region, inaccessible by water or roads, accounts for the fact that crafts have survived here as in no other part of the land.

The same isolation also perpetuated Old English folk songs, kept alive in memory here for over two hundred years, to be rediscovered in our day by the outside world. Also, in some of these areas, off from any beaten track, fragments of early English speech linger even now: the pronoun *hit* is still extant; *Ey God,* from which "egad" presumably derives, is current; and so are *mazard,* meaning head; *poke,* meaning bag; and *peart*—lively or well. Certainly these words are disappearing. But it is interesting to note that the word "mazard," which appeared in the gravediggers' scene in *Hamlet,* should reappear in the mountains of North Carolina after three hundred years.

An estimate has been made that within one hundred miles of Asheville, the capital of these mountains, ten thousand highlanders are making their living from pioneer handcrafts once pursued in isolation in places known only on maps. And crafts, it should be added, practiced in need, to supply mountain cabins with what there were no roads to bring. Hand loom and ax, needle and hoe, afforded a self-sufficiency rarely more complete in this nation than in this mountain land.

Now summer visitors come from half the states, from the whole Eastern seaboard, to well-organized handicraft schools, to study with native craftsmen in metalwork, weaving, pottery, wood carving, marquetry and dyeing, to learn from the natives the source of colors from hulls, berries, sage and goldenrod.

"Oh, yes." An elderly man from Ohio was speaking. "I come every year. See what I've learned at my age." He was weaving an intricate pattern, one that required great patience and care. He looked up for a moment, taking off his eye shade. "My wife and I started coming. Better do this now than bother your children. Sleep up here? Never slept better in all my life."

In Asheville, it isn't necessary any longer to search for the path of Thomas Wolfe. The same public libraries which wouldn't have *Look Homeward, Angel* upon their shelves now have his picture upon their walls. A historical marker rises near the busy traffic of Pack Square to point toward his old residence a block or two away. "Dixieland," once a boardinghouse run by his mother, is now a shrine.

For a group of visitors the author's surviving kin were standing on the steps of the house, answering questions, restating the story of the child and the youth. Inside, some of the little group which had come to pay its respects were looking at the bare, almost stark interior, at the plain, worn furniture. Glimpses of long-lost days were restored. Fragments of conversation were recorded. A schoolmate, a neighbor, a friend who received him when he returned—they all remembered. And you know you are present at the making of a legend, the legend of a poet who loved his mountain land.

On beyond, farther than Thomas Wolfe could see from the center of his town, rises the state's last wall—the Great Smokies, ancient, mysterious, forever remote, lying under purple haze. The Qualla Reservation, a tract of sixty-three thousand acres, lies in the heart of this forbidding land. This is the home of 3700 Cherokee Indians, the finally diminished corner of their earth. They are descended from rebellious Cherokees who refused to be uprooted by the white man and escaped from the bitter march to Oklahoma known as the "Trail of Tears."

Now the icy streams, the dark forests, the patches of corn are theirs. They are self-governing: a tribal council administers their affairs. But as you ride through the little town of Cherokee, on the reservation, it is a final humiliation that you see. All along the street, with beads and trinkets and drums and feathers, the Indians are waiting for tourists.

A mountain man was standing near me, seeing the moth-eaten finery of a Cherokee chieftain selling his baskets and pots—seeing him with the eyes of an outsider, as though for the first time.

"Played with him as a boy many a time." He nodded toward the now strange figure in the chieftain's role. "What made 'em different from us when we were kids? Nothing! Only him right there was the slickest trout fisherman you ever saw. *Walked* different from us, one thing—with toes pointing in a little. Go through the grass along them mountain streams, smoother'n a snake. Not make a sound. Could spot the trout he wanted, pick him out in clear water like looking through a glass bowl. Never showed himself against open sky. Always kept dark behind so the fish wouldn't see. What else was different? Nothing till he grew up and saw what he had to be."

And you know that these heirs of an old race, bedecked in gaudy headdress, with the dust and noise of the road enveloping them, are lost forever, belonging neither to the world of their forefathers nor to that of their neighbors outside.

Between these old mountains of the Cherokees and far Hatteras on the eastern shore, there lies a long stretch of land, three regions independent geographically which were for so long only in name a state. The Tidewater was closed to the Piedmont; the Piedmont to the Blue Ridge and Smokies beyond. Mountaineer, small farmer, planter; log cabin, growing town, river house; ax, mill, land. So the regions ran.

But these early diversities have in their longest reach helped to weld, to unite. North Carolina today has attained a degree of wholeness, a unity in its differences that is rare for any state. The past of the east is there to question the direction of the Piedmont, the Piedmont to define the withdrawing west. There is an aristocratic condescension of family toward a new aristocracy of wealth. In the colleges there is an enlightened intellectual liberalism pulling against an old conservatism of the Bible Belt. There is challenge of change against a counseling past.

In the village of Burnsville, high in the mountains, you find one of the earliest visions of a state that would someday be. In the middle of the town there is a pleasant little square. You approach the statue in its center, a little surprised to see that it is a naval figure. For the sands of Hatteras lie far away.

But there before you stands a forgotten hero of 1812—Otway Burns, captain of a privateer, a man of the coast surrounded now with hills.

The inscription reads: "He guarded well our seas. Let our mountains honor him."

South Carolina

by WILLIAM FRANCIS GUESS

Years ago, when school let out in June and at Christmas, my brother and I traveled from a cotton-mill town in Piedmont, South Carolina, to a cotton plantation in the coastal pinelands, from the red Catawba River in the north to the black Edisto in the south. It was a fine and fearful journey: we braved two clangorous trains and taxied alone through Columbia, our state capital, a city risen, we knew even then, from the ashes of Sherman's march northward from Georgia.

But it was a symbolic journey, too, as I think we also knew. It took us, at Columbia, over the "fall line," a visible drop in the land across our triangular state, dividing the stern Presbyteric upcountry from the easygoing Cavalier coast. It took us from the stoic presence of one grandmother, whose affection did not save us from labors with the compost heap, to the capacious lap of another, who sent Negroes with waffles and milk to sustain us while we watched the cotton gin.

Blood and affection, however, reconciled the differences for us. And training. We were taught to be South Carolinians, Ca-ro-li-ni-ans, mind you, and not, please God, the Tarheel slur, Calinians. (An impious people who even boiled their rice to a glutinous soup.)

An old Charlestonian may think of his city first and last, his heart bound to the palm-lined Battery, where echoes linger from the blasts

of the guns his forebears trained on two meddling foreign powers—
Great Britain and the United States. (The half-foreign power of
South Carolina seldom meddles.) But by and large the people of
this state are tribal in their loyalties, whether their ancestors shucked
corn in Pickens County or ruled slaves along the Waccamaw. There
are, to be sure, tribes within tribes, and Negroes might disclaim with
some justice any membership at all. Though once at a New England
school a young Harlem Negro remarked, "You know us two"—meaning himself and me—"will get along fine. We both come from good
South Carolina families." A romanticism, perhaps, but not a fiction,
and we did get along. Admittedly, however, we would not have
shared quarters in South Carolina, and in most encounters here he
would have done the getting along.

South Carolinians don't speak of themselves as a tribe, but their
sense of identity and kinship, their contented possession of a fair and
historic land, distinguishes their character as a people. To judge them
content with themselves, however, is not to challenge their fame
as a fighting race, mythically descended from General Sumter, the
Gamecock of the Revolution. Only an angry people, after all, could
claim such a record. They fired the first—if not the last—shot of the
Civil War, they died on the dueling field till 1880; and in wrath at
the Democrats in 1948 they helped dig a third-party grave for their
Governor Strom Thurmond, only to resurrect him in 1954 for the
U. S. Senate in a protest write-in jubilee remarkable in American
elections.

The people of this state are still strongly homogeneous, Protestant
and Anglo-Saxon, though the terms are obviously more cultural than
racial. Most have similar origins and traditions, and most are caught
up happily in vast intertwining kinships.

An alien soon trips on the tribal lines. Replying with accustomed
brevity "Ohio" to the ladylike inquiry of his hostess, "And where do
you come from, sir?" a visiting gentleman from the Western Reserve
got in return a blank "Ohio, uh-hunh," along with a Lord-help-me
rolling of the eyes. He said he felt like a casteless Hindu.

But that was surely not her intention. As a lady, she wished him
to feel at home, but people you know just don't come from Ohio,
and South Carolina conversations begin and end with the people you
know. If only he could have said Georgetown or Chester or Florence:
what sweet extended vistas then of piazza talk. Her sister Blanche
and his Aunt Cecile might have slid down the spiral fire escapes together at Winthrop College, gripping their skirts to thwart the male

dean below. Their Kingstree cousins might have summered with
Mrs. McGregor at Pawleys Island. True South Carolinians, in other
words, can talk endlessly about themselves and their state.

They cherish the theory of social cleavage, but in practice they
mix a great deal, because they've all been poor together, at least since
the Civil—or rather, the War Between the States. Most have hop-
scotched together in the public schools, and most collegians have
shared rooms in state institutions: the University, Clemson, Winthrop
or the Citadel. They don't even begrudge the claims of lineage, even
though a family tree may prove nothing beyond the indisputable fact
of generation. "Nice" South Carolinians would rather die than admit
belonging to the middle class. They're aristocrats or nothing, and
many of them feel about outsiders the way Stark Young's planter
(in *So Red the Rose*) felt about his Yankee visitors: "It's not so much
that these people are not wellborn, they don't want to be wellborn."

But South Carolinians aren't stuffy about it. In fact, they can make
fun of themselves, their shibboleths and proprieties in an often racy
and perceptive talk. South Carolina talk can be admittedly special.
If you never sat at a country table around hog-killing time, you won't
admire, I suppose, a great lady talker's sketch of a county bachelor:
"Look at old Archie, poor old thing—looks like a hemstitched chitlin."

Her kind is special, of course, even in South Carolina. I've sat en-
tranced for whole August afternoons while she aired off the gnats
with a palm-leaf fan and entertained a stream of callers. She and
her husband kept open house, in the face even of calamity. Returning home one summer noon with the mail, he said, "Honey, guess
who's coming." "I don't have to guess," she said, "I can tell by the look
on your face it's Cassie." (Cassie was a pious female of the blood.)
"Well," he said, "if you'll sit up and talk to her all day, I'll sit up and
talk to her all night. But I can't talk to her day and night."

I've thought their sort was dying out, but just the other day a young
woman said to me of a tiresomely stylish and talkative old lady,
"Child, I ran into her last week on the street wearing one of those
low-cut dresses that showed the little blue veins in her bosom. She
gabbled at me so I couldn't stick in so much as a whistle, and I
thought to myself, 'My Lord, she's gotten so old and shriveled there's
nothing left but tongue, eyes and tongue.'"

In addition to genealogy, South Carolinians are addicted to romance, in politics as well as in love and religion. And the object and
source of much of their romancing is the low country. Vestiges remain

here of the great indigo, rice and cotton plantations of Colonial and ante-bellum days, and also the legend of a culture inspired by the Fundamental Constitution of 1669, in which English planners for Carolina ordained an elaborate aristocracy "that we may avoid erecting a numerous democracy."

If you enter South Carolina from the north by the coastal route, the former King's Highway, you will begin to feel the low-country atmosphere not far below Myrtle Beach, perhaps when you see two live oaks mingling their branches high over the road and trailing Spanish moss like veils of mourning.

More than any other feature, perhaps, they enchant, though it sticks in the craw of a local lady that a visitor from Altoona, Pa., inquired of those incomparable oaks at Brookgreen Gardens, "Why don't they clean that stuff out of the trees?" For those who live there the danger has been that the veils and soft airs from the sea cast too opiate a spell: one might recline like a lotus-eater while the Doric columns behind rotted away.

And some did after the spoilage of the Civil War, at least till Yankee wealth came seeking quail and ostentatious quiet; an invasion, incidentally, that prompted a new criterion of caste: Yankee plantation owners could not be gentlemen because "gentlemen sell plantations, they don't buy them." And when an upcountry South Carolinian, occupying a plantation in the early '30's, reached for his checkbook to pay his food bill, the country storekeeper said, "Mister, when you first come down here, we thought you was a rich Yankee. But now we know you're just as po' as the rest of us. The check you gave me last month bounced."

To many South Carolinians, however, plantation country is merely beach country. Summer colonies dot the entire coast, and many of the larger ones display increasingly swank establishments. (Many white South Carolinians share the hedonism that was ascribed by a Negro philosopher to his own race, "You white folks buy what you need, but we colored people buy what we want and beg the rest.")

Myrtle Beach, the largest of these resorts, now offers such enticements as a motel trying to look like the Governor's Palace at Williamsburg and a restaurant using the effete come-on "No fried foods ever." So Myrtle Beach obviously gets a sizable out-of-state trade. I can't imagine South Carolinians upholding a prissy aversion to fried oysters and shrimp and red-horse bread (known as hush-puppies elsewhere) or, for that matter, fried chicken.

As a South Carolinian traveling the King's Highway I would have to stop off at Murrells Inlet, a curving resort shore on which a single line of cottages spreads in a quiet grove of oaks and longleaf pines. There's not a joint on the shoreline—no jukeboxes tear up the night. (Dancing collegians ride down the highway, take off their shoes and join in the barefoot frenzies at the Pawleys Island pavilion.) Nothing stirs after dark, in fact, but the occasional boat of a fisherman gigging for flounder by flashlight.

Most who frequent the Inlet own their cottages and go year after year to fish, to eat their daily catch of crab and shrimp and to sit on their screened porches and talk to the neighbors. The crab are especially plentiful, and you can laze in a boat and bring them up on a drop line or rake them out of the "pluff" mud in the marshes at low tide, a sport for the doe-footed, since a pause to puff on your cigarette can sink you in slime at least as deep as the grave.

At the Inlet I like to visit with "Miss Julia" Peterkin (Mrs. William Peterkin, but the polite usage is "Miss" for older ladies, married or single), the Pulitzer-prize author of *Scarlet Sister Mary*, who has moved down every summer from Lang Syne plantation at Fort Motte for half a century: I'm a little grieved now to find her in a louvered-glass breezeway: she looked more natural rocking on the porch of the old faded red house, with its wooden shutters and weathered roof sloping down like the brim of her wide straw hat. She regrets the change, too, I think, but as she said it would not have been proper to let a visitor cave in with the rotting floor. In other words Miss Julia is a South Carolina lady, in spite of her novelistic career and the excursions she used to make North into the ulcerated circles of the literati, but she's not a rose without thorns. Her wit pricks at fakery and sham, though she always remains within the limits of the aristocractic code she espouses.

And that code, with its "realistic" stratifications, may induce its own unreality. Thus, her novels of Negro life, for all the realism for which they were acclaimed in the '20's, were written out of sympathetic condescension, presenting the Negro as a human being, but leaving out the all-obtrusive background of white society.

But her stories are beguiling and poignant. Better in the telling, perhaps, than in the writing, for her voice is sweet and low, and her blue eyes are magnetic.

One she tells concerns a plantation laborer, a magnificent black figure who lost his legs to gangrene and afterward pined away in idleness, having to bear the pain of his wife's lovemaking to another man in the next room. And finally, sinking toward death, he said to Miss Julia on one of her visits to his sickroom, "Missy, please, please bury me in a man-size casket. You know I was six foot tall."

And there's the story of her Inlet cook, Wallace, an ageless little Gullah, who succumbed during the last war to the sumptuous wages at the Myrtle Beach airfield. Every weekend, though, he brought his pay home to Miss Julia to keep for him. Accepting the envelope one Saturday, she said, "Wallace, how do you know I'm not going to spend this money?" And Wallace replied, "Miss Julia, any little thing you want you jes' buy it for yo'self. You'se the only mamma I'se got."

From the Inlet on down the coast it's old-plantation country, a thirty-mile strip including the barrier Sea Islands and centering on Charleston. It is also a Yankee domain, a sort of vast private hunting preserve. Bernard Baruch, for instance—actually he's South Carolina born—bought up all but three of the plantations carved out of Hobcaw Barony, one of the feudal domains apportioned to the Lords Proprietors. Though Lord Carteret never occupied his Carolina lands, Mr. Baruch does from time to time; and his daughter, Miss Belle, occupies her private seat, Bellefield, in a state of seclusion which she guards with her commission as reportedly the only woman constable in the state; in fact, not too long ago she arrested a Georgetown citizen who tied up at her boat landing.

But I don't mean to paint her as an ogress. She probably takes at face value the classic American right to be left alone. And if she totes a pistol, she's in the vein of plantation women of older days—like my grandmother, who kept a loaded six-shooter by her bedside till the day she died at the age of eighty-one.

And this may be a good place to remark on the nature of plantation life, which I knew in a fairly modest form.

In the first place the plantation was big, by general American, if not by Texan, standards—500 up to 5000 acres. Its crops, mainly cotton, were grown by Negro tenants, forty acres to the family, living in weathered shanties. People I knew and liked and who I thought liked me went in and out of those shanties: the waddling cook, for instance, whose "toting" pan yielded up every afternoon a succulent slab of cornbread and who sometimes indulged my forbidden heart's desire to bang at the little pump organ in her front room, gorgeously papered with magazine pictures.

At the center of plantation life stood the "big house," sometimes manorial, comely in proportion and richly appointed but more often just big and comfortable, if drafty in the winter. But there were fire-places in all the rooms and Negro boys to haul in "light'ud knots" and hickory logs. Plantation life was opulent and cultivated—at certain times and in certain places. There were hunt balls and races and libraries and trips to Paris, but these graces were fewer and less continuous than legend would have it. Both planters and their wives had to labor, in the first place, to make a wasteful system pay, since neither slaves nor share-cropping tenants toiled with philanthropic zeal. As an ante-bellum hostess remarked to a British visitor, "When people talk of my having so many slaves, I always tell them it is the slaves who own me . . . I'm obliged to look after them, to doctor them, to attend them in every way."

But if plantation life as most knew it wasn't so grand, it was rich and pleasant. At Christmas the family gathered, twenty-five or thirty strong, for a week, and ate and talked and laughed and shot fire-works and hunted partridges. We drank persimmon beer and ate ginger-flavored sausage and fresh squab and tipsy squire and all the cakes that are too much trouble to make any more: Lane and Lady Baltimore and Japanese fruitcake. On summer nights we ate, among other delectables, boiled pinders, green peanuts boiled for hours in salty water.

But plantation hospitality has declined with the flight of Negro hands, and you aren't likely to find twenty-five at Sunday dinner around the most baronial of boards. In fact, you probably won't be asked to dinner.

Old-plantation country is still quiet and thickly wooded, opening up best to the mannerly explorer. Some of the homes are on spring-tour display and some that aren't yield through the good offices of somebody who knows somebody. One plantation which welcomes the traveler is Mepkin, the old Henry Laurens (Revolutionary states-man) place near Moncks Corner, now a Trappist monastery. (To replace the vanished house Mr. and Mrs. Henry Luce, Mepkin's former owners, built a flat picture-windowed lodge which makes an arresting sight in the context of towering moss-hung oaks.)

Many planters formed summer colonies in the scattered islands of pineland in the low country. These were the nuclei of such atmospheric towns as Summerville and Pinopolis. Pinopolis seems quaintly retired from the world, its cottages turning their whitewashed shoulders to a single road meandering through a continuous grove of pines. A favorite local event the past few years has been a tilting tournament presented by the Pinopolis Lancing Association on the splendidly capacious lawn of the Doric-columned Gippy plantation house. These tourneys had been a fairly common low-country sport—with crownings of the queen of love and beauty, and bootleg corn flowing from the hip—but the Pinopolis affairs are conscious salutes to the past, making much of colonial finery and genealogical luster: blooded horsemen tilt at the rings in knee breeches and Cavalier hats.

A few miles from Gippy stands Mulberry Castle, the only "mansion" surviving of those built with the first crop of low-country fortunes in the early 18th Century, and, with its pseudomedieval towers, a fine example of Jacobean baroque architecture. And the road past Mulberry Castle plantation leads, as do all low-country roads, to Charleston, the region's Holy City, South Carolina's first capital and always in the minds of its own a kind of Greek city-state.

So much has been written of Charleston, and Charlestonians are so touchy, that you sometimes wonder what to say. Still, there is one very evident thing about Charleston: it is the most glamorous city in America, a city with an antique grace so discreetly guarded it makes one think of heirlooms in daily use, a city that has blessedly escaped both the bulldozers and the ministrations of antiquarian wealth.

Its colonial aspect seems less glamorous, however, than its fame for Castilian pride of birth. Old Charlestonians are admittedly complacent, but less remote often than the families of softdrink barons with villas at Myrtle Beach. Content with their own company, they can and do receive cordially; and sometimes they even mix their blue blood in marriage with outlander red. But the myth seduces. Most Americans are homesick for lords and ladies; they like to think that somewhere lofty beings fit their ideal of nobility. So what is Charleston more famous for than the St. Cecilia Society, the ball-giving social fortress which legend erects to Trojan heights of impregnability?

The myth is implicit in these doggerel lines:

> *In Boston the Lodges speak to the Cabots*
> *And the Cabots speak only to God;*
> *In Charleston the Pinckneys speak to the Rhetts*
> *And the Rhetts don't bother about God.*

When the fury of the 1938 tornado damaged the roof of a tony Episcopal church, a wit explained: "God has been trying to get in for 200 years, and he finally had to come in through the roof." But to counter the notion that it's all myth, take the notation that one of the Middletons who was president of the College of Charleston made in his diary nearly a hundred years ago: "When Edward, Prince of Wales, visited in New York, he had the honor of dancing with my cousin Hattie Aspinwall."

Old Charleston retains the aspect of an 18th Century town, the area between Broad Street and the Battery has as many fine buildings of the period as any similar plot of ground in America. Georgian porticoes open from the street onto columned piazzas repeated for one or two stories above, facing south to catch the breeze and over-looking walled gardens. Gardens where azalea hues are not nearly so prized as the fragrances of tea olive and banana shrub or the ambrosial bounty of a Turkey fig.

To offer a dissenting word on Charleston's culture is to risk turning up the dampers of hell, but the truth is that neither in the past nor in modern times has Charleston, or the state of South Carolina for that matter, produced a major American novelist or poet or musician or painter. And it is picayune to mourn the failure or to blow up the minor literary figures into major ones. Because Charleston is a part of the South and the United States, and her great novelist might well be not William Gilmore Simms, good as he was for his time, but William Faulkner or even Herman Melville.

I will try to atone by remarking that only Charleston, of all the towns in the state, violates the restrictive liquor laws to offer the visitor a civilized drink over the bar; and by quoting the late Ludwig Lewisohn: "A race lived here that loved dignity without ostentation, books and wine and human distinction. Its sins, which were many, fade into the past. They were always less vulgar and ugly than the sins of those who have come after."

Less than fifty miles below Charleston—longer if you drive by the famous Magnolia and Middleton Place gardens—the town of Beaufort (pronounced Bewfort) clings to another curving bay with something of Charleston's grace. Many of its houses have an architectural kinship, though their tiered piazzas generally face the street.

Most of them were built by planters to escape their often isolated and dull establishments on the Sea Islands. They were saved from General Sherman by their usefulness as quarters for Union forces which occupied the town throughout the Civil War. Their owners scattered, and their descendants might still claim Beaufort to be an occupied town, since few of the planters had the cash left to redeem their homes from the vindictive Federal taxes.

But few clouds linger from the storm: the chief relics of the past in Beaufort are the piazzas looking out across the bay and the live oaks and such serenely neutral monuments as St. Helena's Episcopal Church (founded 1712), which lifts its Yankee-donated spire over dead Confederate soldiers. Men and women of three centuries lie there, but one thinks first of the soldiers; here, for example, is an inscription which almost unbearably epitomizes the old regime, its virtues, its graces, and its limitations:

CAPT. PAUL HAMILTON—20 years
(30 battles)

Special Order

On his last battlefield, he displayed as he has done on every occasion every quality which adorns the perfect soldier. In his death our cause has lost an ardent defender, his state a devoted son, and this brigade is called to mourn the untimely fall of a brave, a loved and honored comrade.

By order Wade Hampton
Brig. Gen. Commdg.

From Beaufort to Columbia you follow a route which many plantation refugees took in 1861 and units of Sherman's Army traveled in 1865. But Columbia these days dwells little on the past; it's too busy trying to merit its status as the largest city in the state. It sports not one but two "skyscraper" apartment houses and a real, live supper club with talent imported weekly from up North (no drinks sold by the house—you tote your own bottle).

A visitor in the previous decade called Columbia the "city of philosophy and flowers," a description still pleasing to old Columbians, who look upon their city as a sociable grove of academe, boasting such urbane institutions as the Kosmos Club, whose town-and-gown membership meets twice a month for dinner and a scholarly paper; and cultural attractions as a growing museum of art and a Town Theater that since 1918 has boldly mixed a little Ibsen with the usual Broadway froth.

These graces, though scarcely Athenian, are all connected in one way or another with the presence in Columbia of the University of South Carolina, now showing signs of ancestral vigor. As South Carolina College it had a first-rate reputation for liberal learning until the Civil War, when carpetbag rule and subsequent attacks on its aristocratic leanings pushed it toward futility. Today it is encouraging the growth of graduate departments, and it was one of the first state schools in the Southeast bold enough to give entrance examinations. The University's alumni, however, are more devoted to the facts of football and are generally satisfied if their team can beat Clemson on the State Fair's Big Thursday.

The intense rivalries of that match are sometimes reflected in legislative voting, especially in the wrangling over college appropriations. But wrangling is a prime note in all South Carolina politics, a note intensified by the county-to-county canvass, a Democratic-party requirement for joint debates since 1890. The canvass was conceived by Governor Pitchfork Ben Tillman partially as an honest move to inform the politically ignorant masses, but it quickly degenerated into a kind of medicine show with overtones of a gospel-camp meeting. Crowds would gather for all-day rhetoric, and when the steam was up, the wool-hat boys would urge on the favorites—"Go to it, boy! Burn 'im up!"—while their wives fanned the flies off the waiting fried chicken and jelly cake.

I knew the canvass in its already declining days, the '30's, but it still offered at least one of the old warhorses, Ellison D. (Cotton Ed) Smith, who rode to the U. S. Senate for more than thirty years on a wagonload of cotton, brandishing the buggy whip of White Supremacy. When he parted his lips and bellowed those long rhythmic periods of hypnotic sound and fury, "I—am—an—un—reconstructed Southerner—from the top of my head—to the heels of my shoes," his opponents might as well have climbed down from the stump.

Many of the intracounty canvasses had the obscene flavor of a two-bit carnival. The biggest clowns got the vote. I remember one who shouted in a humble precinct, "I'm one of you boys and you know it. I was born down here and raised down here and you know it. And, by God, I'm still one of you boys, even though I *have* moved up with a better class of people." It was so good they voted for him to the man.

But I don't intend to malign all South Carolina politicians. Many are able, educated men, and those who got by on clowning alone are surrendering to the competition of television.

Modern South Carolina politics may have given the state Pitchfork Ben Tillman and his successors, but the people of the Pee Dee section, several eastern counties lying along the Pee Dee River, gave the state David R. Coker, who in turn gave the world the "priceless boon of pedigreed seed." In his efforts to improve strains of cotton and tobacco and in his support of manufacturing interests, Mr. Coker (1870–1938) carried on in the tradition of Governor David R. Williams, the scientific farmer said to have introduced the mule to the South in the early 19th Century, and of his father, Major James Lide Coker, experimental planter whose benefactions made possible, among other things, the founding of Coker College for Women at Hartsville.

The upcountry proper spreads out northwest from the Pee Dee. Traveling from Columbia, you recognize it as you strike the long green hills of Fairfield County. Though the character of upcountry life still betrays a more rigorous and a plainer heritage, scattered towns and houses show traces of low-country ease; Camden, for instance, thinks of itself as a piny refuge of Charleston manners. The town's present distinction lies in its grove-shaded ante-bellum houses, and in at least one public building, the gracefully plain Presbyterian Church designed by South Carolina's only architect of genius, Robert Mills. Many of the country's fine race horses are trained in Camden, and fashionable South Carolina turns the spring Carolina Cup running into a "twenty-five-acre cocktail party."

But in Camden I always get an upcountry chip on my shoulder. I'm done with white columns and trailing moss and homesick for red waters and rain-gray houses and hickory-nut trees. I suffer the dual loyalties that author John Rice said moved his father, who would remark after some social humiliation, "I have often wished I had been a gentleman," but who when telling a favorite story of Tillman's jibe at a lordly opponent would become the proud, poor boy of his origins.

When I say rain-gray houses, I'm aware that most of the houses in the upcountry are painted. What I mean to imply is that the upcountry heritage returns to plain houses, plain living and a plain religion, much as the silver-service set of Rock Hill or Spartanburg or Greenville might wish to deny it. And I do mean plain, not debased and surely not humble, though pretension can't tell the difference. A Georgia lady, joined up with a preposterous band of bluebloods tracing their lines to the Magna Carta, visibly shrank when I told her the church of her ancestor was a plain, unpainted affair, suitable to a God-fearing people. I suspect she promptly dropped him and took up an ancestor of more acceptable denomination.

Cotton grows on upcountry hills as well as in the lowlands, though decreasingly now since competition from the deeper South has drained the profit away. The farms have always been small, generally under 300 acres, and worked not only by Negro field hands but by the owners themselves. But when the upcountry farmer as I used to know him came in from the fields at night he washed himself and sat down to a polite and plenteous supper, laid out, probably, on a walnut drop-leaf table handed down from his great-grandfather. His wife might have toiled as hard as he, but over a wood stove in the kitchen, not at his side in the fields. For she was a South Carolina lady, and ladies don't chop weeds in the cotton patch.

Those two went to church every Sunday, the Presbyterian or the Baptist, and sent their sons and daughters to college if they could squeeze enough money from the cotton. They believed in education but preferred the utilitarian variety. (Their folks had always been too righteous and poor to care much for the classical South Carolina College at Columbia, and Pitchfork Ben Tillman built Clemson and Winthrop to suit their needs.)

As a child I often visited such people; I recall especially one couple. Their home was a spacious cottage built about 1825, with dormers in the roof, a long front piazza and interior paneling of mellowed pine. They lived a simpler life than I knew in the low country, they had harder soil to dig their living from and less time and substance for pleasure; but they loved their lands, they enjoyed their neighbors and they ate well. They talked out of long, humorous and affectionate memories; and they ate hominy and fried smoked ham and corn bread and turnip greens and an ambrosial pie they made up for hot summer Sundays, preserved damsons or scuppernong peels and whipped cream on squares of cold piecrust. They admired plain speech and honest intentions and hated sham. But it was a peril to mistake them for humble people. Their ancestors had fought for their country and held it: they were as proud in their way as were the coastal gentry.

And they had their caste distinctions even as Charleston. My grandfather, for instance, loved to quote an old upcountry farmer's slyly discriminating record of his children's marriages. "My son Alex," he would say, "married Louisa Bolton, sister of Thad and Thomas Bolton —mighty fine men they are—and they live up thar. Now my daughter Lavinia, she married Evans Curtis—good man to make a crop, he is—and they live over thar. But my son Hap, by the Lord God Almighty, married Sadie Suggs, old Coot Suggs' daughter, and they live down thar."

Many of these upcountry people were Dissenters of such dissidence that they backed into whatever causes they joined. During the Revolution they could scarcely decide which tyranny they hated most, that of George III or of their highhanded brothers in Charleston. (At least George, they often thought, was farther removed.) And during the Secession period some wavered between the evils of greedy industrialism and the myth of injured chivalry, fighting ultimately in a cause they never made. My mother has a stack of old Aunt Hannah Wylie's letters which belabor the secession movement and often in language surprisingly Anglo-Saxon for a lady. She reports attending a secession debate that was "more like a cornhusking than anything I can compare it to" and ridicules the argument of Barnwell Rhett (South Carolina Senator, often called the "father of secession") that departure from the Union would make them rich. He was cheered, she says, for "every puke anecdote he told." She was a typical upcountry Scotch-Irish Presbyterian Dissenter.

But today the cotton-mill towns—Spartanburg, Greenville, Anderson, Rock Hill and Lancaster—characterize the upcountry perhaps even more than the small farms of Scotch-Irish Dissenters. Mills thrived on the hill country's two principal resources—water power, and poor whites in flight from their grudging corn patches to the northwest. They rattled down on their mountain wagons, the purest Anglo-Saxon stock in the world, in a pioneering migration from the servitude of poverty to the servitude of the looms. There were quarters for the family in villages around the factory and jobs for all, too, for children of eight and ten and pregnant wives and the lean, overalled men with ancestral blue eyes and the grave mouths of defeated pride.

These millworkers gave South Carolina its first proletarian element, that is a distinct and almost alien body within the body politic. And they became a proletarian political force as Negroes never could, if for no other reason than that they had the vote and Negroes didn't.

But, of course, for the more potent reason that they were free men reduced to a kind of slavery and knew it.

One of their bosses, the late Colonel Elliott White Springs, described their heroic record in his miscellany *Clothes Make the Man:* "They fought with Braddock on the Monongahela; they killed Ferguson at Kings Mountain; they went with their Cousin Andrew Jackson to New Orleans; they went to Mexico for Cousin James K. Polk; they flung the gauntlet at Cousin Abe Lincoln, and they refused to be reconstructed by Cousin Andrew Johnson; they joined their North Carolina and Tennessee cousins in the Thirtieth Division to break the Hindenburg Line; they saddled Halsey's white horse at Tokyo; and they are ready to take on Joe Stalin or anyone else who attempts to exploit them. Every spinner could be a Colonial Dame, a D.A.R., or a U.D.C., if she wished."

The point is they could not take on the mill owners, who in the old days did exploit them. And through isolation in the company villages they were made a race of social pariahs. In my boyhood they were "lint-heads" and "mill-tacks," set off by the mountain twang of their speech, their faded ginghams and overalls and their snuff-dipping suspicion of the world in general. But as I found out when my mother taught some of their daddies and mammas and grandmas to read and write, they were often kind, loyal and quietly self-respecting. Their increasing assimilation is one of the most striking notes of change in upcountry towns. You can't tell them on the street now from anybody else.

They get good wages today, of course, from their remote corporation employers as they did from such intensely personal bosses as Colonel Springs, one of the last of the old race of cotton-mill kings, who ran his tri-county empire from Fort Mill in the eastern corner of Piedmont, South Carolina. With a great many millions to his name and absolute control of the business in his restless hands, the colonel could afford the tribal South Carolina right to tell any man to go to hell.

When the unions moved up their big guns, the Flying Ace of World War I is said to have warned the help that if they chose the enemy's ranks, they could eat the enemy's chow. And they stood fast. In return for their loyalty they get most of the benefits unions have won and some they haven't, such as the use of resort facilities at Myrtle Beach and college scholarships for their sons and daughters.

In addition they got what is rare for industrial workers these days, the sense of laboring for a man rather than a machine, a man many have known all their lives and one who called more than a few by name. And they got a lot of free entertainment. The colonel was at heart a Princeton Triangle man who grew up to be a *College Humor* man in an age that had lost its taste for John Held, Jr., and Clara Bow. He was also, probably, just a writer gone wrong; the only personal boast in his *Clothes Make the Man* is that he once earned the highest price ever paid for a short story up to that time, sixty-two hundred and fifty dollars. He was modest enough not to remind readers of the several films made from his stories, including one called *Body and Soul*. He did, however, offer gratis to office visitors copies of his *War Birds*.

The ads he composed for his bed sheets sometimes looked as though they had strayed from old-time *Ballyhoo*, but they had the virtue at least of spoofing the slick pieties of Madison Avenue and apparently they sold the goods. I daresay they also pleased the help, as did, no doubt, his legendary local stunts. When his daughter was married, for instance, he had her descend to the Fort Mill plant in her wedding regalia and parade among the looms.

About twenty-five miles from the colonel's desk lies the site of the important Revolutionary battle, Kings Mountain, in which some of his forebears undoubtedly fought, and I'm sure he would agree with other South Carolinians that the battle was the turning point of the Revolution.

From Kings Mountain southwest you follow a stretch of what Jonathan Daniels called the Gold Avenue, the South's rich industrial artery from Danville to Atlanta. Of the cities in this area the almost twin towns of Spartanburg and Greenville are the fourth and third largest in the state, but Greenville, with more than a 20,000 lead over her rival, is so busy that, to hear the natives talk, their only worry is where the next million dollars is coming from.

Almost every approach to Greenville displays the brand-new plants of brand-new enterprises. On one of these approaches you pass a sign not only of Greenville's prosperity but of a kind of luxury South Carolina has never before been able to afford: a 1000-acre tract on which is rising a $22,800,000 plant for Furman University. That South Carolina Baptists, who support Furman, are raising such a pile of money testifies to their strength in the state and symbolizes their strength in the Greenville section, often referred to as the Bible Belt of the Bible Belt. It's so Biblically inclined, a bookstore proprietor told me, that the only important theft she ever suffered was a seventeen-dollar copy of the Good Book.

Twenty-five miles southwest of Greenville a comfortable inn, supermodern in aspect, stands unexpectedly on a steep rise of the Clemson College campus. Built and operated by the college, the Clemson House is only one sign of a general face-lifting of the agricultural and mechanical college which Tillman pressured into being. The college is located on the grounds of Fort Hill, the John C. Calhoun estate left to South Carolina by Thomas G. Clemson, the Philadelphia scientist who married Calhoun's daughter. Though the college has a huge new agricultural center, it is probably giving more attention these days to supplying engineers for the state's new industries. Some time ago, for instance, it completed a new center for training in ceramics. But the most impressive change is the replacement of the old barracks with a dormitory of a thousand rooms, resembling the Gropius-planned Graduate Center at Harvard.

In its role as the state's chief engineering college Clemson was shaped by upcountry industrial needs. But it has always drawn students from every section, as Tillman might have ranted, "between the palm-lined shores of Hilton Head and the rock-ribbed brow of Caesars Head." It has furthered, in other words, that reconciliation between upcountry and low which the college aimed at in its early days by drawing together sons of the Cavalier coast and sons of the Calvinist hills.

It is fitting, therefore, that two symbolic houses should stand on the Clemson campus: Fort Hill, the home of John C. Calhoun, first and last an upcountry Scotch-Irish Dissenter, though he came to address the nation as spokesman of the slave-rich coastal sires; and Hanover, the transplanted home of Paul de Julien, a low-country planter who pioneered in the early 1700's on lands now lying beneath the Santee-Cooper power development's Lake Moultrie. The Calhouns epitomized the stern Scotch-Irish breed which settled the backcountry Carolina; and the de Juliens epitomized one strain of the French-English breed which wrought *Peu à Peu* ("Little by Little," the words Paul de Julien inscribed on a Hanover chimney) a graceful culture in the low-country swamps. (It is fitting, too, that Calhoun's wife, a low-country aristocrat of Huguenot descent, should lie among the hills her husband plowed as a boy and that the fierce old statesman himself should rest in her home city, Charleston, which came to love him as well as any native son.)

But if their energies flowered in different patterns of life, the two breeds shared courage and the love of freedom. And however science may belittle the claims of blood, South Carolinians have bravely defended the worth of theirs. And they will keep on believing—I know as one of them—that to be a South Carolinian born and bred, with Cavalier and Huguenot and Scotch-Irish blood in one's veins, is to stand not appreciably lower than the angels in the Great Chain of Being.

Georgia

by CALDER WILLINGHAM

"Aha," said Cousin Virginia. "Come all this way to write us up, h'm? What's it going to be—the truth, or are you going to struggle real hard to find something good to say about old Georgia?"

"Aw, naow, hon," said Cousin Gary, with a broad and beamy grin. "Ain't nothing bad could be said about old Georgia. What you mean, the truth?"

"I mean," said Cousin Virginia, "that it's hot, dull, hellish and horrible, and couldn't possibly interest anybody who isn't so unfortunate as to have to live here."

"Aw, shucks!" said Gary. "Go on, hon. Shucks!"

The heat of Georgia's flatlands has given its mountains a special meaning to Georgians. There in those hills is a cool green paradise of forest, lake and hidden, cloud-hung cove; of air like champagne, of waterfalls and rhododendron, and fieldstone fireplaces with logs burning on a summer night. It is fitting that any tour of Georgia, any "march to the sea" by an ex-Southerner such as myself, should originate in the mountains. That's how Sherman did it, and while I have neither his motives nor his destructive powers, his path is still a good one to follow.

Georgia is physically the most complex Eastern state. It is the largest east of the Mississippi; the city of Rome, in its northwest corner, is almost midway between Miami and Chicago. Its surface is a long, wide table sloping gradually down from the mountains to the sea. Tilt the table erect, North above and South below. High to the left and right are heavily forested mountains, separated by a region of hills and valleys that blend into a wide, gently undulating band. The line of demarcation is clearly visible: above the band are hills and mountains; below it, is an almost perfectly level area reaching to the swamps of Florida and the coastal tidelands of the Atlantic.

The mountains, the hills and valleys, the Piedmont belt, the coastal plain, and the tidelands and sea isles—these are the five geographic divisions of Georgia. Each is an area unto itself. Enormous differences in physical appearance, climate, occupation and way of life distinguish them. Such distinctions indicate the inexactness of the term "Georgian," and atop these distinctions must be added the crucial though diminishing contrast between city and country. The surprising thing is that, vast and varied as Georgia is, its people have a continuous identity as Georgians.

Let us go on a fishing trip, a Georgia fishing trip, to Jack's River in the mountains. There is no better place to settle life's deepest problems, and simultaneously drink hearty and discuss the fair sex far from the delicate ears of Southern ladies. Here is as wild a spot as you will find anywhere in the East. We will go from the heart of the valley-and-hill region deep into the mountains, over good highways to black-tops, and from black-tops to a forest-ranger road, and on to a mere wagon-trail excuse for a road, on till Cousin Billy's new car trembles and heaves as we head upward to the smoky blue hills.

The hills and mountains of Georgia occupy roughly a tenth of its area—a considerable piece of real estate. And note that they are *not* the "foothills" of the Smokies; they are too high and wild for that. They are a continuation of the Appalachian chain.

Wildflowers of incredible variety thrive on their slopes, with almost tropical masses of rhododendron and other flowering shrubs. The original hardwood continental forest, untouched by the glaciers that scoured New England, still grows here, a forest that once may have been world-wide: close relatives of trees found here grow today in China. Humus accumulated through the ages, Southern sunshine, and the torrential rainfall that gave both the Blue Ridge and the nearby Smokies their names, have produced a forest here that is taller, larger and more lush than the northern hardwood forest of New England.

At dawn, we drive from the deserted, gray streets of Rome to Calhoun. On either side of the highway we see rich farmland, rolling pastures dewy-silver in the dawn, and fat, high-bred dairy cattle. The earth is a shocking Technicolor red—not shocking to me, because I was brought up in this country and regard bright red as the natural color of earth; but shocking to those who think the "red hills of Georgia" are a fable. No fable. Red. Very red.

On we go, past the Indian ruins of the Cherokee capital, New Echota, where a type of the Cherokee language has recently been discovered—or so I was told at Cousin Virginia's party. We are still in pine country, the yellow or loblolly or field pine is everywhere, but we see enormous willow oaks along the streets of Dalton, the "chenille-bedspread capital of the world." This is a nice place to stop and get a bedspread with tufts forming a multicolored outline of a peacock, in case you happen to want such a bedspread. Millions do. But we continue north on a black-top, on through the bright-gold early-morning sunshine. Since this is a fishing trip, lazy Southern profanity comes into play, emanating a secret, delicious hilarity.

The scene is changing, the valley has become narrower and we see blue mountains in the distance. We by-pass Blue Ridge in midmorning as the fishing language becomes all the headier. There is a certain pure art to this talk, at times a kind of poetry; it is not really vulgar, though all of us would collapse with horror if some madness should drive us to speak this way back home.

The valley narrows again as we turn upon a smaller hard-top. We are out of red-clay country now; the earth is brown. The mountains are much closer, the farms wilder. It is already cooler. Then the hard-top vanishes and we are on a good dirt road. We turn again, now upon a road maintained by the Forest Service; it is narrow but passable, and we are rising and winding through unbelievably dense woods. Tulip trees a hundred and twenty feet tall rise like high thin columns on every side, with hickories, oaks, ash, maples, ironwood—it would be hard for the car to fall very far down the steep mountainside, and that is a reassuring thought since Cousin Billy, our driver, has tossed caution to the winds and gotten fully into the fishing spirit. Later he will jump into the campfire, but fortunately this reckless gay mood has not seized him yet.

The Forest Service road comes to an abrupt ending. A wagon trail, a bear path—no, an indistinct foot trail that a bear once passed over—winds ahead, jagged with boulders and writhing crazily this way and that, a dark tunnel through the trees. On we go, lurching and jouncing through country that looks undiscovered even by the Indians. A mile, two miles, a hairpin turn and another car; back up, stop; pistol practice, down the old hatch, pile in, boys; a dip, a turn, and finally and amazingly we are at the Jack's River camp: there is the musty-smelling old cabin with its rock fireplace, and the river itself in the glade below. A quarter of a mile away is George Schuler's farm, and that is all; mountains like smoky giants stand all around and loom overhead. Gone are telephones, electricity, television, movies. We are among the bear and the deer, the mountain laurel and dark hemlock groves.

The Jack's River is a typical stream of the Southern mountains, as George Schuler is a typical Southern mountain man. The Jack's is fast-flowing dark water, filled with boulders and stones polished smooth. Trout pools are not so deep that they cannot be walked for the mile or so of the river that is fished. In midsummer, one sleeps under blankets here.

A flash flood once swept down the Jack's, isolating George Schuler and a group of city fishermen. The party half forded and half swam the stream and got back to camp, all but George, a little bright-eyed man in his late sixties, who stayed and slept on the ground, rose in the morning with the birds and crossed the stream at its normal depth.

"I'm too old a man," said George, "to drown right yet."

Mountain men for the most part swim as well as old British tars; water is regarded as a dangerous element in contact with the skin. Spending the night on damp ground, however, soaked to the bones, is nothing to worry about—so long as you don't make the fatal error of changing later into dry clothes: that's asking for pneumonia. The thing to do is "let 'em dry on ye."

What George lives on is a mystery. Fish, game, a few vegetables from the small mountain-ringed farm. Of course, some people in George's position might stir a little "smoke" once in a while, but if George has ever done that sort of thing, he has turned his back on it today. Whisky, says George, leads to disputes between man and wife. "We don't drink it," he declares, "nor make it ary one." A small, soft-spoken man with a hand the size of a doll's, clad in antediluvian overalls, George peers like a wise old woods creature from below a "wool" hat, a faint smile on his face. Perhaps he is thinking that fishing expeditions are an amusing joke.

Rome, in north Georgia, is the capital of the valley-and-hill region, a town built among hills at the junction of the Oostanaula and Etowah rivers, which form the Coosa. The town is known, among other things, for the nearby Berry Schools and College, a fabulous educational empire created out of nothing, except an iron will and vision, by Miss Martha Berry. The students are chosen almost entirely from the rural South and do not pay to attend; but they all contribute by working (in the field of agriculture, mostly), and thus gain experience along with book learning—an educational system widely admired for many reasons. The campus of Berry Schools has been called, with justice, the most beautiful in America. It is certainly one of the largest. Miss Martha, by the time of her death, had accumulated more than thirty thousand acres for the "grounds" of her schools.

I was born in Atlanta but grew up in Rome from the age of three, all through the depression years. I remember the vacant stores on Broad Street, empty and dusty in the oppressive heat of summer. Model A's coughing up and down the street by the war monuments. Red-necked farmers in faded and patched overalls leaning against the red brick buildings on the Cotton Block, hopelessness in their eyes, tobacco juice dribbling down the stubble on their chins, the shade an angled dark line across their wool hats, as their wives, gaunt and pathetic with two or three or four dirty little tow-haired children, walk down the hot sidewalk to the ten-cent store for stick candy. They go past the old Rivoli Theater, whose patrons' summer-bare feet may or may not get bitten, as my own were, by gigantic rats the size of fox terriers. Cowboy pictures, with Buck Jones and Hoot Gibson, are showing, along with Boris Karloff as *The Mummy*.

Outside, the sun bakes down with blinding power, a power that would put half of New York City in the hospital. The ultraviolet whams down like a physical force, and atmospheric "lazy lulus" shimmer on the horizon. The blue asphalt on Broad Street softens, becomes mushy, and black bubbles rise in the tar patches. It won't rain, though the air is drenched with moisture, because "it's too *hot* to rain." Hot is the word: it's a hundred and five, a hundred and six, a hundred and seven in the shade, and who knows what in the sun. There is not a breath of air, not the hint of a breeze. The heavy moisture will drift on to become rain in the mountains, replaced by more moisture from the Gulf.

Life is at a standstill. The burning days and wet nights pass in a kind of delirium. Businessmen huddle in little clumps at the dining room of the Hotel General Forrest. Here and there are the Blue Eagle signs of the NRA. An occasional truck of CCC boys rides by. The sun bakes down and nothing happens. The stores stay empty and dusty, the Coosa Country Club limps along, as the grass burns brown and the members resign or fail to send in their dues. Old trees die in the heat, the corn in the red fields outside town is withered and yellow and runted two feet high, the cotton sickly, the peach orchards a dismal yellow-green . . . and dust rises in choking clouds from every country road around.

Dust is in the tall willow oaks and hackberries on Second, Third and Fourth avenues, and there is no money anywhere. Store clerks struggle against suicide if they're fired from an eight-dollar-a-week job, the Elks Club almost collapses, while nice ladies sip ice-cold Coca-Cola at bridge parties and deplore home relief, which after all is so spiritually demoralizing—a man can always find something to do if he has a little git-up, even if it's only cutting grass.

Call it an area of basic economic weakness hit doubly hard by a national calamity, but there stand those dusty, empty stores, the plate glass all dirty and dead flies on the display counters, their feet stuck up in the air. We have one, an empty one, and there is no one to rent it. But there was someone, finally: a traveling magician, for a week. He makes sparks come out of an apple in your hand; it's *electrical*, that's what it is.

"A million volts, little girl, are passing even now through your body cells and fluids. Do you feel them emerge through the fibers of your hand?"

"Eek!" said the little girl.

"Folks, that there electricity has just leapt out of that apple through this little girl's hand, right through space and you have seen it your own selves, or call me a liar and a tadpole!"

That summer never ended; it went on forever. But somehow fall was there, and the rain came, and flooded West Rome, and there were nine thousand tons of mud distributed evenly over Fourth Ward.

The Rome of the depression years is gone as though it never existed. Now the stores on Broad Street are not only rented but are remodeled with new plate glass, curved brick and stainless steel. The old Rivoli Theater has vanished. A trim new dress shop stands in its place. The businessmen don't huddle now, they get together and smoke cigars and slam each other on the back, and smile faintly at the memory of the grim past. There are several new millionaires, and quite a few new multi-hundred-thousandaires, not all of them from "nice old families," but it doesn't seem to matter so much any more.

Everything is different. Cousin Donald's employees at Lindale make more Lady Pepperell sheets than ever before at salaries many times depression pay; the huge General Electric plant has arrived; and a kraft-paper mill. Subdivisions spread in all directions. The war monuments are gone off Broad Street: there are too many cars, and not old Model A's but shining chrome-covered new cars by the thousands. There is no mud in Fourth Ward any more, because a levee has tamed the Etowah, the Oostanaula and the Coosa. On those acres of dismal mud have been built a housing project, a new state hospital and an entire new business district. The deserted, run-down country club is a paradise of emerald green, flourishing with new members. The country roads around town have all been hard-topped and dust doesn't blow into the town any more—only it isn't a town now, but a booming bona fide city. What's more, it isn't *hot*, either —why, the climate is downright balmy and delightful. It was the depression that was hot. And besides, with so much air conditioning, who cares if it gets mildly and healthfully warm now and then?

The Georgia Piedmont, an undulating plain that stretches like a huge band across the center of the state, was not only the scene of *Gone With the Wind* and *Tobacco Road*, it is also the most vital area of Georgia in an economic way. With the exception of Savannah, the largest Georgia cities are located in the Piedmont: Atlanta, Augusta, Macon, Columbus, Athens, La Grange, Milledgeville.

As a child, I remember riding on dirt roads through the Piedmont, past old homes of the "Tara" type, as well as past dilapidated, awful, unpainted shacks of poor tenant farmers. This was before the days of good road maps. You had to ask constantly where you were, how to get to your destination, if the road was passable, and if the bridge ahead would hold a car. This meant stopping at a farm house, having a glass of buttermilk with the farmer, praising his coon dogs, commenting on the weather, telling an anecdote about Uncle So-and-So who used to live in this area—all of this in the deep shade of the front porch, as cicadas droned and sang and hummed in the Georgia summertime. Finally the farmer would give his "calc'lations" about how to "git thar," and then a prolonged good-by-that-sho-was-good-buttermilk, and back into the Model A, whereupon the coon dogs that were friendly on the porch would go mad with indignation and come racing, and follow along howling and barking and snapping at the tires for three or four hundred yards.

I also can recall visits to old mansions in the Piedmont countryside, old columned brick homes spared for one reason or another by Sherman. Many of these had fallen almost into ruins. But there they stood, magnificent gnarled oaks and hackberries around them, needing paint and with leaks in the roof, musty-smelling, stamped with poverty. Why, I wondered as a child, was it always considered such a treat to take visitors out and show them "the old slave quarters"? Invariably, these were in even worse disrepair than the main houses, with tattered tar-paper roofs, bare dirt floors, broken windows and doors of rough-cut pine hanging askew on crude hand-forged hinges long gone to rust. What was so fascinating, I wondered, about this? Why that glow of quiet pride? "Naow, suh, Ah will take you and yoah li'l boy out to see *the old slave quarters.*" And the solemn procession, as if on the way to behold the Holy Grail, would begin. I can see now the expression on my father's face as he looked solemnly at *the old slave quarters,* nodded with a grave air, and said, "H'm-m-m-m-m-m." Very noncommittal, but this was always considered an adequate response; the host, usually some old gentleman with rheumy eyes and white hair and perhaps a little yellowish goatee, would inevitably give my father a grateful look, and back then we would go, mission accomplished.

Yankees and new-rich Southerners (and a few old-time "family type" Southerners) have taken over these old homes now. They are remodeled and furnished in the best of taste. It's big medicine socially, heap big strong medicine, to have one of these places, especially if it was "in the family." This claim is not too hard to make. Southerners in general and Georgians in particular can establish a blood relationship with nearly anyone: "The cousin of some distant great-great-aunt, I will have you know, brought up a whole crew of wild niggers from New Orleans, and built Red Roof Hall himself. It's been in the family for years. . . ."

The city of Atlanta is the capital of the Piedmont, and thus logically also the capital of Georgia. Atlanta is perhaps not quite, to the Southeast, what Boston is to New England, but it is not far from it. Along with New Orleans and Houston, it is one of the great cities in the South. Georgia Tech, Rich's department store, Emory University, Agnes Scott, many other schools and many good hospitals help make Atlanta today the hub of Georgia, financially and culturally. This was not always true. Just yesterday, Atlanta was an ugly railroad center. The growth of the city, along with the industrialization of the Piedmont since the end of the depression, is probably the most spectacular development in Georgia in recent years.

Ralph McGill, the celebrated editor of the Atlanta *Constitution*, takes an interest in many things, including Georgia novelists. He takes them to lunch at the Capital City Club, and usually gets them buzzed.

This of course puts them in a mood to love Georgia, and to love Atlanta and the Capital City Club, and the Bobby Jones Golf Course, and the South—above all else, the South!

"We understand the South," says McGill, "you and I. It isn't a backward, benighted hell hole, now is it? Problems? Sure, tragic problems, but don't tell me the South isn't changing and growing. What's more, my friend, where else in this country are you going to find people who are kinder, more honest or more human than the people of this damned and condemned and glamorized and glorified state? Is it true, or not? Do we understand the South, and Georgia, or don't we? Be frank with me. Do we or don't we?"

"Ralph, we understand Georgia. I might not know much in this world, Ralph, but I know one thing. When it comes to understanding Georgia, Ralph, we are in there."

The brilliant comprehension of Georgia that Ralph McGill inspired at the Capital City Club is a bit dimmed now. Too bad. But I think, in all seriousness, that if other sections of the country listened more to Ralph McGill and others like him, many misconceptions about Georgia would vanish, or at least a more balanced picture of the state would prevail.

In any event, there is no doubt today that the buttermilk-on-the-porch Piedmont has disappeared. Today's sophisticated farm dogs wouldn't dream of barking at the cars that zoom down the new highways, and perhaps even the old slave quarters have collapsed into dust.

Savannah is one of the most attractive cities in the South for a number of reasons, one being the large number of separate, small parks scattered through the downtown area. Besides, one of the greatest trees in America grows well there, and Savannah has taken inspired advantage of it: *Quercus virginiana,* the great live oak. The city is graced with several major park boulevards of four lanes separated by double rows of spreading oaks. The majesty and charm and beauty of these trees defies description. They make Savannah one of the most pleasant places to live in the entire United States.

The city is "picturesque," too, and like other seacoast cities, has almost an Old World atmosphere. Much that can be said about New Orleans or Charleston can also be said about Savannah: quiet, "gracious" living, a highly refined society of old families, excellent restaurants, a dash of night life. Today, however, Savannah is in commercial turmoil. An old friend, whose insurance offices are located in truly Old World surroundings, expressed the thought that perhaps he should modernize; and when a man of his traditionalism, talks of modernizing, Savannah *is* in turmoil.

There are two especially remarkable sights in or near Savannah. One is the Bonaventure Cemetery, which surely must be the most eerily beautiful cemetery in the world. Its enormous, gnarled live oaks, with their almost horizontal limbs hung and draped and shrouded in Spanish moss, form a landscape like a fantastic dream. Outside Savannah, at the Isle of Hope, lies another dream realm: Wormsloe Plantation, regarded by many as the most fabulous home in the South. Wormsloe is the sort of place that, if used as the background of a movie, would provoke the ironic comment: "Hollywood exaggerates so." It is hard to believe that such a place exists, even if you are actually there, enjoying a Scotch and soda with its owner and discussing (of all things) modern American writing.

The central residence is built on eight hundred acres adjacent to the Inland Waterway. The entrance to the grounds is approximately a mile from the house, which is reached by a drive lined with live oaks that create an effect of unbelievable grandeur and magnificence. And on the grounds immediately around the house are even larger live oaks—huge, spreading, gnarled, moss-draped giants that overshadow gardens of azalea and other flowering shrubs. The house itself has a raised front porch with tall white columns and curved steps on either side. Inside, the marble mantels, the furnishings and family portraits are ante-bellum.

The setting for all this is a twenty-acre park lovely with huge oaks, camellia-japonica trees, climbing purple wisteria and a dense carpet of Algerian ivy. The estate also has many acres of junglelike wild forestland—tropical bamboo growth among palms and oaks—as well as a private yacht basin on the Inland Waterway and the ruins of pre-Revolutionary Fort Wimberley. Wormsloe, incidentally, is one instance of an old Southern home owned by the same family that built it originally.

The sea isles of Georgia, the "Golden Isles," are one step from Savannah. Exactly what Sherman did to them I do not know. Perhaps he went over and had a swim and thought about the hell of war. In any case, the sea isles are there, and they are utterly different from northern Georgia. There is no denying their beauty or their tremendous assets as vacation areas, but Sea Island, the best-known of the Golden Isles, seems hardly Southern or Georgian in atmosphere, since most of its "cottage" owners come from such places as Philadelphia. (Eugene O'Neill's old "cottage" at Sea Island is indistinguishable from others built in the same period.) The place reminded me of Beverly Hills plus a beach. It is frankly at the service of the well-to-do—of "correct religious background," as one of its publicity officials told me. The famous hotel there, the Cloister, is a splendid establishment with luxurious grounds, a superb beach and swimming pool, and wonderful food. It also offers riding, tennis, a beautiful golf course, and in general much solid comfort to those who can get in.

I asked a woman at the Cloister for information about nearby Jekyll Island, the one-time haunt of millionaires that is now a Georgia state park.

"Jekyll Island," she replied, "is of no interest, and I would not go there, indeed not. I haven't been there myself since the days when Jekyll was Jekyll. It's not Jekyll any more. It's now going to be run over by hordes of Georgia crackers, and I assure you, sir, that nice Northern people, if they read your publication, couldn't have the least interest in it."

I went to Jekyll, the island paradise of the day of J. P. Morgan, Sr. The story is that J.P. and a few of his friends assembled a squad of doctors from Johns Hopkins and told them, "Find the healthiest and most beautiful spot on earth. We want to buy it."

The doctors looked long and far. They found one promising area somewhere in the South of France, but then discovered that it was not for sale. They found another in Egypt, but Egypt was too far away. Finally the doctors settled on Jekyll Island, off the south Georgia coast not far from Brunswick, and thus was born the most exclusive social nonesuch of modern times, the Jekyll Island Club.

Millions of dollars were spent there to build "cottages" and a big gingerbread clubhouse. No one except a select group of the incredibly rich was allowed to set a foot on the island. To be invited there in the old days was It. But new days came and wore away the substance of the Club. Perhaps, as Cleveland Amory has remarked, the Club was so exclusive it bored itself to death.

Now anyone can cross the new causeway to Jekyll and its huge old "cottages" from an era that has passed. Even the ghosts of the Morgans, Vanderbilts, Bakers, Hills, Pulitzers, McCormicks, Goulds and Goodyears seem to have fled this beautiful island and its once sacrosanct beaches, and all the visitor feels is that the luxury of yesteryear looks a little silly now. Georgia's crackers, however, should enjoy the island's eleven miles of spectacular beach, down which J. P. Morgan, Sr., used to putt-putt grandly on his little electric scooter bug, if they only keep an eye peeled for the descendants of the 300 wild boars sent to him by King Umberto of Italy.

Those born and bred on the south Georgia coastal plain (which Sherman had the good sense to avoid) are more likely to admire it than outsiders. The landscape, as any motorist driving through to Florida knows, is rather depressing. There seems to be nothing in it except millions and millions of slash pines, used in the production of turpentine, and the vast Okefenokee Swamp, used as the background for Hollywood movies.

There is more than that, however, to the region, and one place to see its true appeal is in the virgin pine stands of the great estates around Thomasville. Many Presidents have come to the area to hunt quail. Incomparably the most delicious of all game birds of the South, quail are hunted here on horseback through slash and longleaf pine, even by north Georgians who can afford to make the trip. In fact, it is a kind of index of your financial standing in north Georgia; if you are anybody at all, you pile your bird dogs in the back of the station wagon and head for these southern happy hunting grounds.

Also in south Georgia is one of the most interesting places I saw in the entire state—the private project for public happiness known as the Ida Cason Callaway Gardens. Located not far from Columbus and southwest of Atlanta, the Gardens are beyond all question the most remarkable thing of this kind in Georgia. One finds here thousands of acres of magnificent forestland, a five-mile drive of excellent paved road, and wildflower, holly, magnolia and azalea trails; also superb fishing, a beautiful golf course as good as any in the South, a large and attractive clubhouse with excellent food, boats to rent, a sight-seeing barge, a miniature train for children, a country store with country-cured hams and water-ground meal and delicacies from everywhere, and much, much more, including a snow-white man-made beach. And what price admits you to all of this? Fifty cents.

The puzzle, to me, was why Cason J. Callaway, an extremely able and successful businessman, spent five years and millions of dollars creating beauty in the wilderness. I talked for many hours with Mr. Callaway.

"We have set out here," he said gently, "to build the most beautiful gardens till Gabriel blows his horn." He took me all over the premises. And he told me why he had done it all.

First, the Gardens are a memorial to Mr. Callaway's mother. Second, Mr. Callaway feels, "If our children have something pretty to look at, if they have some inspiration when they're young, maybe they will see what life can be. Our country needs great men, and maybe a Ben Franklin will come as a child and play here."

Finally, however, I came upon the real reason, the real truth. We were walking on the huge beach, as Mr. Callaway told me how many train-loads of sand it took to make it. The Gardens were crowded that day, and many, many children were running and playing near the water. In the midst of our conversation, Mr. Callaway turned and looked at them in silence. I stood there with him, reflecting that many of these south Georgia boys and girls had probably never seen a lake before, or beautiful white sand, or so many slides and toys and miniature trains. They could not imagine the painstaking care, the hours and days and weeks of planning, the labor of love that went into building this natural wonderland, but they were having the very time of their lives.

And then Mr. Callaway's deepest motive came out. "It just gives me a thrill," he said, "to see these children having so much fun." That thrill was in his voice, and in his eyes.

"Well!" said Cousin Virginia. "Talk! Say something! What did y'all see, runnin' all around Georgia?"

"Saw the bes' ole state in the Union!" grinned Cousin Gary. He leaned forward with a grave air, polite and Southern; grave, and very solemn and soft. "Take yo' glass?" he said. "And get you another?"

Florida

by BUDD SCHULBERG

Did you know that the northernmost part of Florida is south of the southernmost part of California? I didn't know it myself until I drove from Jacksonville to Key West and back along the Tamiami Trail to St. Petersburg and on up the West Coast last winter. Then I heard it all the time and not from the Chamber of Commerce either. I heard it from gas-station attendants, from a waitress in Kissimmee, in Punta Gorda, and motel owners from Wisconsin or Ohio who were tourists themselves just a few years back. The Florida Chamber of Commerce is not known for modesty or lack of civic enthusiasm, but every town I stopped in had a flourishing chamber of unofficial hosts eager to sing the praises of their adopted state. Here and there, of course, one encounters a native Floridian—a cracker in the pine country rolling west of Tallahassee; a third-generation descendant of a founding family of Sarasota—but since the state population has trebled from a million and a half twenty-five years ago to about four and a half million today, and is growing at the rate of fourteen thousand new settlers each month, your Florida booster usually turns out to be a fellow who finally got tired of Great Lakes winters, or just moved his family down from the Bronx.

Florida has the oldest history and the newest population of any state in the Union. The Spanish conquistadors came here a full century before the English exiles found haven in Massachusetts. In the

1820's the energetic (and often ruthless) American frontiersmen displaced the demoralized Spanish. But the real colonization of Florida is a 20th Century phenomenon. There were only half a million people in Florida at the dawn of the century. Miami was a sleepy subtropical outpost on the banks of the Miami River flowing out of the unknown Everglades. Today Miami is America's fastest growing city, and Greater Miami now has a population greater than that of all of Florida in 1920, on the eve of the first boom.

First boom, we say, because almost unobtrusively a second has spread across Florida. You feel it on the Keys, where the little fishing village of Marathon seems to change its architectural face at least once a week. You feel it on the road north from Miami, where recently open country has been transformed into a connected series of modern-house, middle-class communities, all the way to Palm Beach; there are new motels and modest houses even in that aristocrat of winter resorts, and not far from superexclusive Hobe Sound there's a new low-cost housing development. The East Coast has long monopolized the tourists and the building programs, and the West Coast—Clearwater, St. Petersburg, Sarasota, Fort Myers, Naples—has prided itself on its quieter rhythm, its more conservative recreations. But the West Coast is no longer a chain of relaxed and complacent water-front towns staring drowsy-eyed into the Gulf. The spectacular fifteen-mile Sunshine Skyway out of St. Petersburg across Tampa Bay is a symbol of West Coast initiative. Now motorists, no longer bottlenecked in St. Petersburg and Pinellas Peninsula, can stream south into Bradenton and on down the easy-riding Tamiami Trail. Dozens of Gulf Coast towns that slept through the first boom are feeling the effects of the second.

In the Everglades country in February 1955 buildings lots between Sarasota and Ft. Myers were offered for $250. Three months later those bargains had been painted out. The choice, newly cleared palmetto waste extending from the highway to the Gulf was selling by the foot now, and the little towns were doubling, tripling and quadrupling their populations. "We don't call it a boom," said a lady real-estate operator (from Massachusetts). *Boom* is still a dirty word in Florida, and 1926 was a black year. "In the twenties people were buying and selling land they never even bothered to see. A lot might change hands ten times in a week. *You* remember. But here on the West Coast we have what you might call a solid boom. Nothing frantic or hysterical. But more northern visitors come here every season, and tourists on this coast soon get the retirement bug and shop for land. Or they sell their businesses up north and look around for something to do down here. Anyway, we're growing so fast that some of the old-timers are afraid we're going to end up as hectic and over-developed as the East Coast."

The Florida growth is so spectacular (25 per cent population jump in five years) and the tourist business is so well publicized (more than eight million vacationists a year make Florida the world's all-time pleasure dome) that many Northerners think of Florida as an overballyhooed vacation resort with crowded beaches and the sound of midnight trumpets blending with the race-track bugles. Actually the almost four and a half million permanent residents and the eight-million-plus vacationists are pretty well scattered in a state with 3750 miles of coast line, from the broad beaches of Fernandina, just below the Georgia line, down the 400-mile peninsula and up the Gulf side 600 miles to the rolling white sands of Pensacola, near the Alabama line. Seen from the air, Florida looks like a long jagged finger reaching into the tropics and the Caribbean. It fails by a few miles and a couple of degrees to qualify as on-the-level tropical, but Floridians import the tropics in the form of vivid flowers, lush fruit, varieties of palms and even a siesta-fiesta culture that blends nicely with Northern energy to form a new kind of American. He brings with him his Middle Western production skills and his New England education, and he puts them to work, but not at the frantic clip he knew back home.

"I saw my partner hurry up and die," a fifty-year-old motel owner told me outside Tampa. "Right then and there I decided to sell out my plumbing-fixture business and move down here. We had been coming to St. Petersburg for our winter vacations, so last winter we just stayed. Wouldn't go back now for a million dollars. I bought this place, but I got some new ideas for building a better one. Next winter I'll sell out when the market is high and build me the snazziest-looking motel on the Gulf."

There's a world of difference between the upper and lower East Coasts, between the Gold Coast and what they are beginning to call the *Platinum* Coast, between the citrus country and the Everglades, the big-city bustle of Jacksonville and the Old South mansion-house mood of Tallahassee—but this Northern-flavor-with-a-Southern-accent mood was one I encountered from border to border. The

billion-dollar-a-year tourist trade, the fusion of the Old South and
the restless North is rapidly producing a new kind of state which is
neither Southern nor Northern, Middle Western nor Western, yet
with discernible elements of all four. In fact, Florida is to the United
States today what the United States was to Europe a hundred years
ago—a melting pot, a frontier, a place to improve your health or
your luck.

Florida is the world's greatest amusement park, of course, and a
hundred pleasure-seeking images crowd around my head as I write
—from the guests in the Fontainebleau's La Ronde Room enjoying
high-class opera, to gut-bucket-strip tease, to thousands of local
Negroes and Northern tourists spending only time to pull the shiny
black bass out of the Tamiami Canal between Miami and Ft. Myers.
But what impressed me most was the dreaming of big dreams. People may lie on the beach and bask and doze but they don't go to
sleep in Florida. There's something un-Southern in the atmosphere
that calls men to jump over the moon. King-size frustrations, or
youthful dreams of glory, no matter how grandiose or touched with
madness, have a way of taking root and enjoying fantastic growth
in Florida. In fact, you might say Florida has been built by obsessive
Northerners as balmy as the climate they came south to enjoy. Or to
put it more kindly, people of rare daring have found in Florida a
last frontier to challenge their will and resourcefulness.

Take Julia Tuttle who, as a wealthy young widow about seventy
years ago, landed her family from a barge at Fort Dallas, a Seminole
trading post on the wild shores of the Miami. To this post she brought
all her worldly goods, her extensive library and art collection, her
imported china, piano, housekeeper and two Jersey cows. Julia Tuttle
cleared the jungle undergrowth, planted a lawn, and began dreaming one of those Brobdingnagian dreams that seem generic to this
part of the country. She looked at her virgin beach and uninhibited
tropical growth and wrote a Northern friend:

*It may seem strange to you but it is the dream of my life to see
this wilderness turned into a prosperous country and where this
tangled mass of vine, brush, trees and rocks now are to see homes with
modern improvements surrounded by beautiful grassy lawns, flowers, shrubs and shade trees.*

Like the pioneers who were to follow, Julia plunged ahead. She
went to work on Henry Flagler, the restless Standard Oil tycoon who

had brought his railroad and the first of his great resort hotels to St. Augustine. Flagler had thought of St. Augustine as his American Riviera, until he pushed his railroad down the coast to Palm Beach. The irrepressible Julia had made up her mind that the railroad must reach her beloved Miami. Flagler held out until the famous frost of '95, when Julia sent sprigs of orange blossoms to prove that her home-site lay south of the frost line. Miami was a frontier village with a few sand trails and a shabby row of pine shacks and tents when Flagler's railroad arrived there sixty years ago. Overnight the town began to grow as Julia Tuttle envisioned it, and the handful of fron-tiersmen who had tapped their temples when "Jack-ass Julia" passed found themselves in on the ground floor of what was to become the vacation capital of the world in less than twenty-five years.

Julia Tuttle died in 1898; twenty years later Miami was a flourish-ing town of 29,000, and her dream of a garden metropolis on the banks of Biscayne Bay was realized, though not even her prophetic soul could have foreseen a day when four hundred of the most luxuri-ous hotels in the world would create a gleaming seven-mile sky line along Miami and Miami Beach. Built literally in Julia's back yard is a beanstalk city of pastel skyscrapers with a Greater Miami popu-lation of one million and four million transients flocking in each year.

Flagler went on to indulge an even more precarious dream, the extension of his railroad to Key West, a hundred and fifty miles to the south, across a limestone necklace of odd-shaped islands divided by deep-water channels, many of them a mile wide and one demanding a seven-mile span. This venture was rightfully called Flagler's Folly— there were mosquitoes and heat and tropical storms and seemingly impossible engineering obstacles—but Flagler pushed his 4000 men to do the job in seven years, and Key West, that fine old island city, was connected to the mainland for the first time in its picaresque history. More than 700 men were washed away by storms, and ships and precious materials were lost, but in 1912 the "eighth wonder of the world" was completed, and Flagler, a dying man of eighty-two, proudly rode into Key West on his single-track dream line, an enter-prise that was doomed to operate at a loss until it was swept away in the terrible hurricane of '35. But old Henry's single-track obsession had doomed Key West's splendid isolation. The Flagler roadbed was used for the extension of U.S. 1 across the subtropical keys, and today Flagler's dream is vibrantly alive as the Overseas Highway, a breath-takingly beautiful drive of 130 miles between the Atlantic and the

Bay of Florida, comes tantalizingly close to turning your motor car into a boat as the islands fall away behind and you are surrounded by the sparkling sea, dotted with mangrove islands to the horizon.

There is something about Florida's lush and fertile climate that grows limes as big as oranges, that magnifies the size of the flame-red flowers of the royal poinciana, that multiplies the variety of wild orchids and blows up to near-bursting the expansiveness of human dreams. People had laughed at Julia Tuttle and Henry Flagler, and they laughed at John Collins when he built his rattly wooden bridge between Miami and Miami Beach some forty years ago. The Beach was a forsaken swamp, a playground only for mosquitoes. Collins ran out of money, and another irrepressible Floridian (from Indianapolis), Carl Fisher, bolstered his sagging dream. Fisher had been racing most of his life, on bicycles, motorcycles, automobiles, and making money (Prest-O-Lite, and the Indianapolis race track which he founded), and when he got to Florida at the age of forty, he was badly bitten by the Florida dream-bug. They laughed when Carl Fisher had the idea that the despised sand bar could be turned into the world's favorite vacationland. Bridges had to be built, marsh had to be filled, canals and islands had to be made, and doubters had to be convinced. There were people who said Carl Fisher was pouring $50,000 a day down a sinkhole. He offered a city block free to anyone who would build a first-class resort hotel. Today the land he was offering free—with no takers—is worth thousands of dollars a foot.

The Julia Tuttle to Flagler to Collins to Fisher parlay started paying off in the Steve Hannagan era when Miami Beach and the bathing beauty in the scandalous one-piece bathing suit became interrelated symbols of escape from winter temperatures and Northern pressures. Now this incredible island, which harbors one fourth of all the hotels in Florida, has settled down to a sane, durable and expanding economy. There is a substantial middle class living in semiluxury on the man-made islands of Biscayne Bay, and insurance companies are moving their national headquarters into the area. "It's just as easy to handle the business by mail or phone in a modern sun-lit building. In five years," I was told, "this will be the insurance capital of the world."

But the old-time tradition (the 1920's are medieval history to the hopped-up 60-year-old Miami) of hoopla press agentry has not flagged. When Miami Beach celebrated its fortieth birthday by opening the fifteen-million-dollar, fourteen-floor, fabulous-is-putting-it-mild Hotel Fontainebleau, Leo Morrison, vice-president in charge of fanfare, flew a hundred New York notables down. This hardy group of later-day pioneers, rendezvoused at "21" for lunch and liquids, were catered to on the flight down by the "21" staff, were welcomed at a cocktail party in the new hotel's Salle de Josephine, enjoyed an informal dinner—if such a thing is possible—in the grandiloquent Fleur-de-Lis Room, went to sea next afternoon in "a fleet of private yachts," watched from private boxes the Fontainebleau Race at Tropical Park and staggered down that evening to the Grand Bal de Fontainebleau. That's the way it went from Saturday to Monday.

The Fontainebleau, a daring, massive elliptical structure was designed by Morris Lapidus, a sober architectural experimenter who confessed that the Fontainebleau was fun to build but he wasn't sure he'd choose it for his own vacation. "Personally I like smaller places," he said. "And of course I realize it's a little overdone inside. But"—he paused and smiled knowingly—"this seems to be what the people want." Guess Mr. Lapidus is right. The Fontainebleau's plush-ultra 565 rooms have been filled since it opened. Of course there is an established system of hotel social climbing, which permits tourists less flush to bed down on the west side of Collins Avenue (away from the ocean) where rooms are $12 instead of $40 but spend their days roaming the Fontainebleau lobby, using the stationery, ogling the guests, dropping in at the Caribbean-type Boom-Boom Room or even paying $3 to sit in the Fontainebleau sun by the Olympic-size pool. "Why should I pay forty dollars just to sleep here? I pay twelve down the street and get the benefit of all *this*," a rotund New Yorker told me in the Fontainebleau gardens (modeled on the gardens of Fontainebleau, with tropical embellishments).

"That's my biggest headache, sight-seers," Morrison complained. "We have to station bellboys just to keep people from coming in and feeling the drapes." The lobby of the Fontainebleau must be seen to be believed. It's French Empire, of course, with certain modern improvements that were not available to Louis XIV. The furniture is elegant French period reproduction with a smattering of *moderne*, and there are pillars that are Greek and pillars that are Romanesque, and some square ones covered with crackled gold- and silver-leaf paper that are pure Lapidus. There are stone statuettes of Grecian ladies wearing a wisp more clothes than the girlies (that's what they call them) on Dade Boulevard. There's an 18th Century music room, and in the Fleur-de-Lis dining room the décor, according to the menu, is "designed to capture the spirit of the court elegance of the time of Louis XIV." The Sun King is there along with "various ladies and courtiers, symbolizing Sea Power, Land Power, Music and Court Pomp."

Every year in Miami Beach there is a new hotel and a new hotel joke about "this year's hotel." When it was the Fontainebleau, the story was: "In the lobby of the Fontainebleau, if you drop a quarter, you have to give the bellboy a dollar to pick it up for you." Pretty true too. One bellboy, who may be buying into the place any day now, told me he wanted to be a writer and was saving $50 a week during the season so he could take a year off and write a novel. "And boy, could I write a novel about this place," he said menacingly. The Fontainebleau also boasts the most luxurious ice-cream parlor in the world, the Bon-Bon Room. It's all delicate roseate pink and white, and gives you some idea what it might be like to get inside of a strawberry-ice-cream soda served in a milk-white glass.

"On this room and three straight strawberry milkshakes you can get drunk," I heard a guest cry out from a nearby booth.

Personally, I preferred rum at the ocean-front bar. I was perched there one afternoon when a freak storm blew up out of an ominous yellow-gray sky. In a few minutes there was a sixty-mile wind blowing, and hail as large as golf balls. Charley the bartender went on mixing fancy drinks, using the outlandish hail in his cocktail shaker.

"This storm must be doing an awful lot of damage," said a young lady schoolteacher from Chicago, who had saved an entire year for these few days.

"It's only going on at the hotel," the bartender insisted. "There's nothing the Fontainebleau won't do to amuse its guests."

As we prepared to leave the Fontainebleau for Happy Jack's Cabins on the fringe of the Everglades, we identified our car as a convertible Cadillac. "Are you kiddin'?" said the indignant bellboy. "Whaddya think we got down there except convertible Cadillacs?"

Followers of the Beach's hotel rat-race tell you the third year is the test for every new hotel. "The first year everyone wants to get in the act. The second year the momentum carries you. By the third year there is usually a newer, bigger or flossier hotel and the race is on." Never in world history has there been a building program like the boom on the Beach. On the West Coast, where there is more stability, a hotel remains as it was built, and even in modern Florida's brief history begins to take on a look of age and solidity. The John Ringling Hotel in Sarasota, the Vinoy Park in St. Petersburg, or the San Carlos over in Pensacola are first-boom hotels which have come to look lived-in and respectable. But a Miami Beach hotel is outdated in six or seven years, and must be remodeled inside and out to keep up with the new-look neuroses of the Beach's restless tourists.

North Miami Beach, which is neither a beach nor north of Miami Beach, is another of the many dream towns from the first boom that only now are springing to life. Boca Raton, Hollywood-by-the-Sea, Coral Gables, were all laid out in a spurt of Roaring Twenties optimism, with broad avenues, elaborate parks and stucco-elegant towers and archways. The collapse of the boom left them as perhaps the most unusual ghost towns in the world. Hollywood, for instance, had the widest boulevard in the country, and almost no population. The manic history of Florida's last thirty-five years is reflected in this community's rise, fall and phoenixlike rebirth.

Joe Young, who planned a full-blown metropolis north of Miami, poured million after million into his dream. Before there were houses he brought a symphony orchestra to his circular park in the center of the city; prospective settlers were brought down by the busload and lived in tents while they picked out homesites. The hotel was palatial and the paved streets and the sidewalks were wide enough and numerous enough for a city of 60,000. Joe Young was going to have his own Miami, but not even a fortune of forty million could contain this Bunyanesque dream, and when the boom suddenly blew up, Joe Young couldn't pay his cement bills. His largest creditor, Samuel A. Horvitz, from Cleveland, found himself in the real-estate business, and to this day Horvitz's company—Hollywood, Inc.—dominates the town. Hollywood was condemned as an impractical dream three decades ago, but now there are lines of new cars and busy shops along business streets that were thought ridiculously wide during the late 20's.

Because palm trees and tropical flowers were planted during the boom, Hollywood doesn't have the bare, sprung-up-overnight look of so many of the new boom towns spreading north from Miami. Its fine six-mile beach and adjacent deep-water harbor of Port Everglades, its location on the edge of the Gulf Stream between Miami and Fort Lauderdale make it an ideal resort-retirement city. So many New York policemen and firemen have settled in Hollywood that the sound of a siren is said to stir eighty per cent of the population to grab their old uniforms.

In the last few years American know-how has revolutionized the life of Florida. Two innovations—air conditioning and frozen orange juice—have brought stability to a land that previously lived it up from Christmas until the end of March, and then marked time until the next influx of Northern sun worshipers. Air conditioning makes Florida bearable through the summer (which loyal, transplanted Floridians insist is no hotter than New York or Philadelphia), and retirement developments are mushrooming along both coasts as Northern pensioners discover they can live longer, more comfortably and certainly more cheaply by investing in one of the $7500 (or $6990) houses multiplying in identical rows from Hollywood to St. Petersburg.

But man is the most industrious of all mammals, and the dream of dozing his life away in the sun soon tires. "I came down to die. Now I'm back in the building business and making as much money as I ever made up North." I heard those words at least a dozen times while wandering from Jacksonville to Key West and up the Mangrove Coast through the prospering beach-water towns from Naples to Clearwater.

At the Earl Gresh Wood Parade and Museum, in St. Petersburg, a dignified elderly gentleman showed us the remarkable wood mosaics of Biblical scenes, all worked in natural-wood colors from shiny black ebony to delicately tinted rosewood. I asked our guide how he got into this work. "I came down seven years ago as a retired minister," he said, "and after a year or so I got a little fidgety to be useful again."

A Midwestern industrialist by the name of Curt Joa has instituted the *Curt Joa Plan,* by which retired mechanics who no longer can stand the grind of a full working day spend a few hours a day teaching their skills to apprentices. Now men of sixty-five who had felt banished from productive society work twenty hours a week, and supplement their retirement checks. "I enjoy Florida twice as much now that I don't feel I'm on the rubbish heap," a seventy-year-old machine-tool craftsman at Lakeland told me.

Between Miami and Homestead we encountered a retired businessman who did not mind being outside the pale of productive society. He was as lean and brown as the Seminoles who once traveled this edge of the Everglades. He was on foot, and he pulled a covered wagon about six feet long and four feet high, just big enough to sleep in. On its side was painted, "Dick Cook, the Walking Man." Cook had been a contractor in Michigan, where he had suffered a nervous breakdown after a construction bid turned out disastrously. That decided him to chuck the whole thing and just walk. This was his fourth year and he had done nearly 20,000 miles. This year he's walking up one side of the Mississippi Valley and down the other. I pulled the wagon a few feet to get the feel of it; it was heavy. The life he had staked out for himself sounded like an endless highway of drudgery, but Dick Cook seemed happier than some of the crowd we had fallen in with at the Fontainebleau.

"You can't really enjoy the scenery when you're in one of them things," Cook said, pointing contemptuously at our resplendent rented Cadillac. Was he ever going to settle down again? "Yes," said this peripatetic marvel, "one of these years I'm going to build me a little shack in Marathon down on Key Vaca."

The first time I saw Marathon, it was a crudely built fishing village of a few hundred people, with a motel for the deep-sea fishermen. Today it's a glamour-tag area, Marathon Shores, headed by Key Colony Beach, a whole community constructed "from the ocean's depth" by a Detroiter named Phil Sadowsky and his associates: fine hotels and motels, marinas, restaurants, charter fleets, and an 18-hole golf course.

Side roads still wind through the mangroves to isolated lagoons known only to herons and bonefish, and some of the Keys retain the tropical-island-away-from-it-all feeling that captured my imagination just after the last war when I drove down the lonely highway into the heart of the Keys. But today the Carl Fisher fever has seized the Keys. The wild cry of the gull and tern is drowned out by the roar of giant dredges coaxing the waters of the Gulf into man-made channels so that advertisements can offer "waterfront lots with your own boat dock." The Keys were a hideaway, getaway land before the new boom, and beach property was being sold for taxes. Now they have been discovered. The rich-rich come ashore from their sleek eighty-foot ocean-going yachts to window shop at Marathon. Islets lying off the Overseas Highway are now a string of tropical suburbs and a fisherman's paradise.

Lying west of the Keys, across the island-strewn Florida Bay, the glades rolling west of Homestead, the unofficial Everglades capital, are being cleared, drained and reclaimed into black muck-rich farming lands. And west of this new tomato and celery belt is a tropical wilderness that has fascinated me ever since I cruised around virgin Cape Sable and followed brackish Shark River into the heart of the Everglades, through the Seminole State Indian Reservation.

This is one of the most remote and primitive areas in the United States. Here the resourceful Seminoles finally found sanctuary in the trackless sawgrass prairies (which they aptly called "grass water") out of which rise fertile hammocks, or islands, heavily grown with royal palms, mahogany, tamarind, the red-barked gumbo-limbo, and the cruelly beautiful strangler fig. Here the Indians who refused the indignity of being removed en masse to Oklahoma built their villages and planted their squash and bananas, confident that this insidious marsh country of the redbug and the moccasin would be theirs by default because it was the one section of Florida the white man could not endure. The only other inhabitants of these impenetrable mangrove swamps were squatters, outcasts, moonshiners who lived in shacks raised on stilts over the shallow Florida Bay flats at a now vanished community well-named Snake Bite, or in lawless little bands on the islands of Whitewater Bay.

The Everglades squatter may represent one of the last Americans uncontaminated by modern civilization. One day on the Keys I met a West Coast fisherman who told me of a fishing village at the edge of the Big Cypress Swamp where criminals were welcomed and Federal men dared not enter. "We got our own ways and our own laws," he said. "If you want to go in there I'll write you out a passport." The broken coastline from Naples to Cape Sable is last-stand country for ragged individualists, where the roots of the mangrove trees look like a thousand gnarled fingers reaching into the dark still waters of the silent glade rivers.

To preserve this timeless stretch of grasslands, sloughs and tropical vegetation, where the rarest of the long-legged birds still breed and perch in the giant cypress, and wild orchids in hundreds of brilliant varieties burst from old stumps and tree hollows, is the dream of still another transplanted Northerner. Dan Beard, worthy descendant of the founder of the Boy Scouts, is a scholarly outdoorsman who first dreamed of an Everglades National Park when he was sent here on a survey twenty years ago. He was convinced that if this strange wonderland of the pink ibis and the snowy egret, of the sleepy 'gators and the vicious crocodiles, of the wildcat and the almost extinct roseate spoonbill was not protected by Government purchase and National Park Rangers, it would eventually become just another piece of Florida real estate. "We got it just in time," Dan Beard told us when we stopped by his office in Homestead. "We have acquired over a million acres in the Everglades; we have the squatter problem just about licked; we have new roads and our new National Park is in business. We're working to make it the most interesting wildlife sanctuary in the country." In a single year half a million tourists, including many attracted by the Audubon wildlife tours, have entered this primeval world to fish for tarpon, study the tropical growth and bird-watch the droll, impressive, stilt-legged wading birds found here in greater numbers than any other place on the globe. As the Park extends its roads and services, the once-dreaded Everglades may draw as many visitors as now flock to Cypress Gardens or Silver Springs.

Dan Beard, a naturalist with no thought of personal gain, may seem a very different type from city planners like George Merrick of Coral Gables and Joe Young of Hollywood, but when he talks of Florida he has something in common with these other pioneers. "You'll find all over the state," he says, "a creative spirit, a youthful daring, a frontier enthusiasm for new ideas. The Everglades, of course, are a real frontier, but the whole state is a frontier. The bulldozers are pushing back the tropical forest, and people go plunging into schemes that would scare them half to death back home.

"I'm from Flushing, New York, but this Everglades National Park is my home now. We're working hard to make it the most interesting wildlife sanctuary in America."

Yes, in Florida the imagination has a way of busting out all over, in shapes and colors as strange and vigorous as the blossoms of the Bird of Paradise and the passion flower.

Millions who come to Florida to find the sun and idle winter pleasures hardly have time to appreciate the drive and the vision that lie behind some of the state's favorite attractions. Cypress Gardens, for instance, is a miracle in what has come to be the Florida tradition. Thirty years ago Dick Pope was a real estate and advertising man who had gone bust after the blow of '28. To stimulate interest in the Winter Haven section Pope got the idea of developing the cypress swampland around Lake Eloise into an incomparable tropical garden. There were folks in Winter Haven who laughed at him as "The Swami of the Swamp." Today this "swamp" is Cypress

Gardens, one of the wonders of Florida, annually attracting more than a million visitors who come to watch the water-ski ballets, and the spectacular ski-jumping from the lakeside grandstand, and to enjoy the beauty of the ancient cypress trees rising out of the water, with their fantastically shaped "knees" spreading around them like a family of elves, and the winding paths and waterways bordered by rare and brilliantly colored plants gathered from all over the world.

Lake Eloise is one of a hundred lakes in a five-mile radius, and the city limits of Winter Haven embrace dozens of fresh-water lakes connected by channels that make possible an unusual water journey of seventy-five miles. The coastal beaches have become so famous that one has to sail, ski, swim and fish these inland waters to realize that Florida has three times as many lakes as Minnesota. From the Georgia line down the middle of the state to 700-square-mile Lake Okeechobee, there are 30,000 lakes and an entirely different tourist world from that of either coast.

To these lovely inland lakes come the quiet-type tourists who like small-boat fishing for large-mouthed bass. Here tourists are sedately called "winter visitors," and the residents are proud that their quiet towns are as different from the elegance of Palm Beach as they are from the carnival life of Miami Beach. "This is the real Florida," you will hear them say.

Mile on mile of orange trees perfume the air, and you aren't surprised to learn that one third of the world's orange crop comes out of Florida, and three out of every four oranges grown in the United States come from Florida's citrus belt. My old home state of California has almost been pushed off the citrus map by the dynamic growth of Florida's breakfast-fruit business. Along with eighty-nine million boxes of oranges, it contributes nine tenths of the grapefruit (forty-two million boxes), all the limes and tangerines. "All the fruit juice you can drink for ten cents" is still a come-on for motorists.

In Florida ultramodern architecture is taken for granted. Because South Florida, especially, is a 20th Century phenomenon, it's naturally receptive to the idea of drive-in banks, bird-cage houses and even open-air churches.

Some years ago the Florida Power and Light Company brought down a trainload of bankers from New York to observe the industrial possibilities of a state with hundreds of miles of wide-open spaces. The bankers boarded the train in style, complete with Homburgs. A Florida press agent, with an eye for direct action, went through the train flinging the stylish chapeaux out the windows to demonstrate that Florida is still a fishing-cap, open-shirt country, even for Wall Street bankers.

"There's something about the place that relaxes your prejudices and opens your mind," a public-relations man told me at their state convention at St. Petersburg Beach.

"The chairmen of the boards of northern insurance companies and banks come down here and insist on modern designs for buildings that they wouldn't be caught dead with in Chicago or Detroit. It's like a businessman putting on a Hawaiian sports shirt and yellow slacks. The modern architects are having a ball."

They're building modern on the West Coast, too, but like everything else on that gentler, less commercialized strand, the architecture is less radical, less flamboyant. There are people of great wealth along this coast, hidden away at St. Armand's Key off Sarasota, at Captiva Island and Naples, but you will not find the conscious style of Palm Beach, or the upper-middle snobbishness of Venetian Fort Lauderdale. Simplicity and informality are the keynotes of the West Coast. The motels make no attempt to ape the grandeur that is Miami Beach, and the winter guests on the beaches of Clearwater, St. Petersburg and Sarasota-by-the-Sea, paying less than their East Coast cousins, seem to enjoy the contemplative recreations—sun-bathing, shuffleboard, shell collecting, bridge fishing, and watching the sun take its evening plunge in the Gulf of Mexico, leaving behind it a trail of purple and rose and gold.

St. Petersburg is a growing city, and Sarasota, with a younger, more cosmopolitan population, with its writers, painters, little theater, and the spangled atmosphere of the Ringling Circus, is expanding at such a pace as to alarm the "old settlers," like MacKinlay Kantor, who came down to Siesta Key when it was a slumbering island in the 30's. Kantor, not a man to express his opinions *sotto voce*, is convinced that "progress" may yet destroy the original, Southern, unhurried atmosphere of Sarasota. Sarasota is growing rapidly but soundly. "We can't help growing," says a prominent Sarasotan. "With Sarasota's natural beauty, with the circus in our back yard, with a great variety of interesting people, and the easygoing tempo everybody feels as soon as he arrives, with wonderful beaches and good schools, we're much more than just a nice place to spend a few weeks in the winter. The West Coast is the future of Florida and Sarasota is the future of the West Coast."

It's tempting but perhaps misleading to generalize about this beguiling border of the Gulf. It's the avenue of royal palms through venerable Fort Myers on the banks of the broad Caloosahatchee. It's the new medical center at Sarasota. It's the thousands of old men and women drowsing and chatting on the green benches of St. Petersburg. It's the sprawling trailer camp of Bradenton, a caravan city with its dances, sports events and community sings. It's Steak Capuchina at Tampa's superb Spanish restaurant, Las Novedades. It's Webb City in St. Petersburg, a "drug-store" with a public-relations director, a radio director, fashion models, a roof-garden floor show, Arthur Murray instructors, a beauty parlor and barber shop, a bakery, ice-cream and coffee-roasting plants.

The West Coast is also unspoiled Mullet Key, off St. Petersburg, which has only one old-fashioned white-frame hotel for the few guests who want to enjoy isolated beaches, superb fishing and the absence of automobiles. It's a sign on a motel between Bradenton and Sarasota, "We're from Indiana and Illinois—where are you from?" It's tall Florida cowboys rounding up the humpbacked, exotic looking Brahman cattle around Punta Gorda. It's the St. Louis Cardinals and the New York Yankees battling for the spring-training championship of St. Petersburg. It's the snub-nosed, orange-painted Greek sponge boats putting to sea from their "little Greek" harbor at Tarpon Springs. It's 300 species of fish from combative but inedible tarpon to delicious pompano and bluefish.

The West Coast is also the fresh-water rivers that flow from subterranean caverns in a continuous outpouring of hundreds of millions of gallons a day. It is Homosassa Springs, nature's giant fish bowl, where you look through a glass wall into a fresh-water pool alive with what seems to be an infinity of fish, including salt-water varieties like snook and jacks and sea trout that mysteriously leave their native Gulf for this fresh-water basin. It's Weekiwachee, with its daily flow of 144 million gallons of fresh, crystal-clear water, where "mermaids" perform a remarkable underwater ballet, working from a novel underwater stage. The West Coast is the teeming harbor of Tampa; the sleepy fishing village of Cedar Keys; and the fisherman's dream, Crystal River, halfway between Weekiwachee and Cedar Keys, in lovely, unspoiled Gulf country where St. Petersburgers go for a weekend's fishing and camping when they want to take a vacation from the tourists.

Farther up the coast, and halfway between Tallahassee and Tampa, is the mouth of the Suwannee River, the lazy, lovely, picture-book river that Stephen Foster never saw, the river that weaves its languorous way from Georgia's dank Okefenokee Swamp through the Old Florida of White Springs, a quiet, 19th Century health resort, past Ellaville, a once-prosperous river town now slumbering on the banks of the widely sung but little-known river, and other century-old cracker towns that had their little booms in the 70's and 80's and are now curled up in sleep.

The hundred-odd miles on the East Coast from St. Augustine to Daytona are urbanized, commercialized and suburbanized. The West Coast is still adventure country. The East Coast has had its adventure and is settling down to its orderly, civic comforts.

The Northern stereotype of Florida too often fixes on Miami Beach or some other highly developed beach-colony life. Actually there are a thousand Floridas, and as one of the five million who take the state over in the winter and spring (and even in summer now that Northern piggybank vacationists and Southerners by the hundreds of thousands flock to the Gulf and Atlantic to escape the inland heat) you have a choice of crowded beaches and a full calendar of organized activities or the peace of a deserted stretch of sand where you can cast a line into the sea and reel in—maybe a bonefish or a pompano, maybe only an hour or two of contentment as you daydream by some of the world's most pure blue, pure green waters. Or you may find your Florida in the crystal-clear depths of Rainbow Springs, as you stare in wonder through the submarine porthole at the other-worldly underwater scenery, while a local Negro guide describes what you are seeing in language that strikes the ear as deliciously original native poetry.

Throwing bread into the water to attract the smaller fish, he says, "Now look at the little sunnies come up to eat the bread. Now look at the big-mouth bass comin' up behind to eat the sunnies. Now if we're lucky we'll see the giant leopard-gar comin' out to eat the big-mouth bass. On the Rainbow River we say only the man can catch the giant leopard-gar and only the Good Lord can catch the man."

If New England lives on its past and the West enjoys a vibrant present, Florida basks in its future. It is the only state which claims tourism as its major industry and sunshine as its principal commodity. It is a state with a sunny disposition; people are constantly telling you how much better they feel. The population of other states is made up of people who were born there. Florida is peopled mostly by those who pulled up roots and moved there.

Except in the hibernating communities in the northwest corner, optimism infuses the atmosphere. One night my wife and I were trying to reach Collier City, still a primitive fishing port on the lower West Coast. The dirt road grew bumpier, rockier and narrower and finally, along the water front, became impassable. A sign said "Road under construction" but the legend under it wasn't "Proceed at your own risk." Instead it was, "A sign of progress."

"That is what I love about Florida," said my wife, Vicki. "'Travel at your own risk' always sounds so dismal. This road looks dismal but you have to admire their attitude."

In increasing numbers people who come to Florida to play are coming back to stay, including the Schulbergs, who had been wintering in Florida for years but finally took the plunge and moved to Sarasota.

labama

by CARL CARMER

I had not seen the red hills of northern Alabama for more than thirty years when I returned to them on a Sunday in early June. I drove in from Chattanooga and took the little ferry that lurches across the Tennessee River into Bridgeport, just south of the Alabama state line. The freshets of spring had not entirely subsided and the water was still picking up a pinkish brown from the clay banks. On the road down from Bridgeport to Scottsboro familiar signs advised travelers to drink Dr. Pepper when thirsty and use Clabber Girl baking powder when baking.

Northern Alabama when I first knew it was a mountain country with a river running through it. Hill cabins perched dangerously on steep acres high above the Tennessee ("Fire your shotgun up the chimley and your punkin crop'll drop into the fireplace"). It was a land of fiddlers' conventions and all-day sings and square dances and court weeks. Few Negroes lived here—their homes were in the Black Belt towns where their slave ancestors had worked for rich white folks. The mountain people plowed their acres six days a week and on the seventh attended little unpainted churches where the wrath of a jealous God was expounded with emphasis. Now this area, because of the damming of the Tennessee River, is a lake country. The rutted roads that once ran near the river are gone, and blacktops run smooth along the ridges from which motorists look down on families picnicking beside clear water.

Scottsboro is larger and obviously more prosperous than in 1931, when nine Negro boys from counties to the south were tried in the Scottsboro Courthouse and found guilty of rape. To the west, in a valley, lies Huntsville—a city of old, pillared mansions and new, clean business buildings, and the road to Decatur, farther on, offers long foothills and dramatic views of rippling surfaces over which small boats skitter and water skiers swing in long arcs. Blue lake, blue sky, red earth, white blossoms, green grass—make sunny days garish. Neat motels have sprung up along the way. Planes drone into a modern airport at Decatur. The towns in this area are crowded with new dwellings, small and grim, a picture window staring from each cottage forehead. There are fewer cabins on the slopes. Many of the hill people now live in "housing development" suburbs and listen to artificial folk music on the radio. Their aerials, lifted by tall rods above their roofs, twist and curve like nests of mountain snakes.

Industry has brought its not always welcome blessings to this hilly region. Teeming cities make its farms sure of markets for their produce. Corn whispers over wide acres that used to grow cotton. Cows graze where once were stump-dotted marshes. Businessmen who have made fortunes in the town factories grow Black Angus cattle in the meadows above their country homes, and sell the beef to expensive city restaurants. The shining silo towers of dairy farms hold feed for herds of Guernseys, and milk trucks roll silver-colored tubes of white cargo along the highways. Fertile pastures and new crops—corn, peanuts, beans—have emancipated the white serfs of the old Alabama economy. And the land has added its concealed treasures. Portland cement, coal, iron ore have pointed the way to wealth in Birmingham, the state's largest city.

Not as old as Mobile or Montgomery, Birmingham labors under a sense of inferiority which the two other cities delight in fostering. "We don't scrabble so hard for a dollar as Birmingham does," they say. "We have age and cultural background. Birmingham is *nouveau riche* and acts that way." As a consequence this "Pittsburgh of the South" self-consciously, but eagerly, goes about improving its cultural standing. Its riches help, and it has rolled colonies of expensive and often beautiful homes up and down the suburban ridges of Red Mountain and Shades Mountain, each of which, according to the city's detractors, bears an example of Birmingham's culture.

On Red Mountain stands an enormous statue of Vulcan—sixty tons of iron coated with eye-dazzling aluminum paint. Though it is called the "second largest statue in the world," it hardly improves the general opinion of the city's taste. The huge figure, an early work of the Italian sculptor Giuseppi Moretti ("He is bored with whirling in his grave," says a former disciple), was a marvel at the St. Louis World's Fair, in 1904, before it arrived eventually at its 120-foot-high platform on the summit of the mountain. To Birmingham it is a symbol of the bigness of its major industry.

Shades Mountain has another memorial of Roman classic culture—Vestavia, a replica of the pillared temple of Vesta beside the Tiber River. The structure lures visitors to see the sculptured figures of Roman gods and goddesses in its interior. Built by an eccentric citizen who chose to live among his togaed servants as a Roman prince, it remains one of the city's major curiosities.

A newer attraction on the same mountain is The Club, a glass-walled building of neo-Miami character. Here patrons may dine listening to the music of violins and a mother-of-pearl piano and looking down into the valley where the steel furnaces flare in the night ("You get the same thrill that Nero got—the fiddles play while the city burns").

The grime of a steel city persists in downtown Birmingham. Only here and there does it give promise of the city its riches will erect. A new art gallery, happily situated among the buildings of the city government, a Little Theater that has existed long enough to establish a tradition, a few clean-cut towers of business—these are the beginnings.

I had planned, when I set out for Alabama, to write a nostalgic, atmospheric, sentimental piece about it. It was in Birmingham, my first stop of considerable length, that I discovered this would be impossible. Almost no one would talk of the past, not even the past of a quarter century ago.

"There's a new spirit here," a Birmingham businessman told me. "The reason? Money for one thing. And in the wake of that—air conditioning. I know you used to think that heat gave Alabamians some of their characteristics—quick tempers but slow movements and slow minds. Well, now our offices, our stores, our homes, our automobiles are cooled through all the hot months. Nobody is exposed to the heat any longer than it takes to walk from an office building to his car. And in some companies the ten-thirty Coke break has become a coffee break—just like in New York City. An air conditioner costs no more than a television set. And I've seen one-room shacks that have both."

"Negro shacks?"

"I guess so—though Negroes can stand heat better than anybody else."

The approach to Montgomery from the west was a long "strip," sure omen of entrance to an American city—motels (TV in every room), drive-in movies, curb-service stands offering frozen custard, palm-reading "parlors"—forming a one-story jungle of soiled concrete and neon tubing.

Montgomery, however, I found much as I had left it. There are few apartment houses. Most families live in homes of their own, be they elegant or simple. The wooden awnings that sheltered shoppers for a century on the main business streets of the town have disappeared, but the tradition of providing shade continues; many of the new and modern shops use variegated awnings or jutting wooden shelving to fend off the sunlight.

On a Monday morning I visited the State Capitol and found that the old building, domed and white, had become the center of a wide circle of other Government houses, also white. No one was moving about (the state legislature was not in session) and no wind stirred the misty sunlight that struck between the tall white pillars. I was reminded of the Civil War and of my limping grandfather who had tried to destroy this temple and its creed of slavery; and I recalled a passage from a poem by Marianne Moore—"white is the colour of worship and of mourning." There was something, I thought, which had departed—and the empty shrine seemed to be waiting for it to return.

That night, at a dinner in a Montgomery country club, I told a new acquaintance of the impression the white buildings had made.

"You're right," he said, "and what the capitol is waiting for is the homecoming of distinction and dignity and honor. A hundred years ago the Deep South was governed by gentlemen of family and of classical education, champions of the humanities. Now we live, with accidental exceptions, under the tyranny of guitar twangers, gallus snappers, baby kissers and sockless barbecue orators. Beneath that Yankee mask of yours you know as well as I do that white knights should inhabit those white buildings. We've got them, but they haven't a chance against politicians who call them sissies, dudes and eggheads in order to get the gutless clowns elected."

"Isn't that kind of talk subversive?" I asked.

"It's the juleps talking," he said, "but *in juleps veritas*. Let's get down to what we've been avoiding—all we think or talk about—segregation. When the National Association for the Advancement of Colored People sent that girl to the University of Alabama in a limousine all dyked out in orchids they were stupid. But the thoughtful people of Alabama were stupider. On the night before the disorders on the campus I called on one of the grand old jurists of our state.

" 'What's going to happen?' I said.

" 'Violence,' he said. 'The roughnecks will try to stop her.'

" 'You and I are good citizens,' I said. 'We detest illegal violence. So what are we doing here?'

" 'Sitting home and hoping the roughnecks will win,' he said. 'Instead of listening to the opinions of our best minds—arguments that even the Supreme Court would respect—we're letting a mob take over.' "

My companion paused for a moment, then said pathetically, "What do we do now? What do all the intelligent earnest Alabamians do now?"

"Don't let this hotspur upset you," said a nearby friend. "He's one of our local radicals. I know where there's another drink and a pretty lady waiting."

The next morning I saw the gardens of the city. Montgomerians take gardening seriously and their rich soil rewards them mightily. No artist would dare to combine so many clashing hues—the red of japonicas, the pink of oleanders, the coral of Roses of Montanta, the purple and scarlet of begonias—yet somehow, relieved by the yellow of Cape jasmine, the blue of larkspur, the white of magnolias, sweet olives and Cherokee roses, and the garish alternating tones of the azalea, Montgomery gardens are choirs of singing color.

Later I stopped at a cemetery—a green carpet of grass, dotted with headstones, stretching toward the summit of a gentle hill. I asked to be brought here, to revisit the graves of seven Royal Air Force fliers who had come to Montgomery's Maxwell Field for training during World War II. A storm of wind and rain had brought darkness early on the afternoon of May 21, 1942, and the young men, lost in a trackless sky, had crashed to their deaths. Now I read on the simple gravestones the moving epitaphs their families had chosen—"For love of Freedom," "That is forever England," "He left the Vivid Air signed with his honor."

Beside these markers stands a tall and startling monument. Hank Williams is the name on the stone, and carved below are a guitar, a few notes of music, a ten-gallon hat. Hank was an idol of the millions of young Americans whose emotions are stirred by hillbilly music. The titles of his songs are worked into the stone here, too, among them *Luke the Drifter* (he used to call himself that), *Your Cheatin' Heart, Kaw Liga, I'll Never Get Out of This World Alive.*

"He had Montgomery's biggest funeral," said one of my guides. "No church was big enough—so it was held at Cramton Bowl, our stadium. Boys and girls from here and Georgia and Mississippi and Tennessee crowded it to the brim."

"He was a natural," said the other, "an untutored Mozart. But money gave him a way of life that killed him."

In the six years I had spent in Alabama during the Twenties, no one could buy a good dinner there. Southern hospitality was no myth and home cooking was superlative—but restaurant food was heavy, greasy, tasteless. There has been a considerable change, at least in Montgomery, where nowadays a traveler can find the exquisite food that the great cooks of Alabama (white and black) provide daily and as a matter of course in family homes. At Leila Dowe's Blue Moon Inn, for instance, an old-style residence on Goode Street, the gourmet (if he orders in advance) may feast on crabmeat soup, chicken Country Captain, asparagus ring with mushrooms, and other delicacies that convince him he has dined in the distinguished plantation-house tradition.

I took a wandering journey through many byways on my way to Mobile. I passed Snow Hill and Rose Bud, where the road offered grotesque vistas of landscapes shrouded by a broad-leaved vine called kudzu. Like flames of green fire, its swift tendrils had licked over stumps and dead trees, hooding them with green, blunting their pointed tops, creating ominous sculptural patterns. Near Uriah and Blacksher the muddy overflow of Little River lay in shallow pools defended by battalions of jacks-in-the-pulpit. At State Prison Farm, just outside Atmore, the corn stood high and the wide level fields looked neat and fertile. The tiny Styx River laves the town of Bay Minette and a few miles beyond it lie seemingly measureless stretches of tall yellow-green grasses. Ocean odors permeate the air above them. A few houses stand very much alone and the landscape looks as if it had been painted by an artist who meant to emphasize their aloneness. Even in sunlight the impression is ominous—a sense of moving through the setting of a bad dream.

Suddenly the traveler is in a long gleaming tunnel that dips under Mobile Bay and emerges into Government Street. He feels the miracle—in a few seconds he has left a nightmare of the present for Mobile's dream of the past. The long and gnarled limbs of the live oaks shade the street, admitting occasional spatters of sunshine. The mottled pavement leads through an aisle of public buildings and houses that display their gardens and wrought-iron galleries where they may be seen. Smaller and more intimate than New Orleans, Mobile holds the enchantment of its Latin past but has not yet felt the compulsion to exploit it. The old thoroughfare is longer than it used to be, but building in its northern stretches has been in keeping with the city's tradition.

Mobile Bay tells the story of the new Mobile. One morning I sought out my old friend Earl McGowin, the Commissioner of State Docks, and we set out, water-borne, on a tour of the port. As the fog burned off we made out nearly thirty vessels, among them the Dutch *Gran Río,* bound for Haiti with a cargo of bedsprings and aluminum sashes; the *Hadrian,* Norway's largest vessel, her vast tanks cleaned out to receive wheat, milo, corn and beans; the Japanese *Kyowei Maru* discharging a mixed cargo that included two exquisite Chinese junks; the American *Sue Lykes,* bearing British automobiles and Scotch whisky; the Costa Rican *Spidola,* exchanging Colombian mahogany for Alabama coal; the Liberian *Yucatán,* ready to transport milk bottles, cotton cloth and chicken feed to Cuba. These were only symbols of the port's swift growth. The hundreds of ships that crowd its wharves during the year carry natives of almost every country in the world. This bay, most remembered by Americans for a romantic barbershop ballad, *On Mobile Bay,* is now as exotic and cosmopolitan as Marseille or Port Saïd.

The seas have brought riches to Mobile, and business booms. Progress is a watchword, but it brings a danger with it. Near Earl McGowin's office, later that day, I heard a woman say to her male companion, "They're trying to save the oaks on Government Street. They ought to realize no trees can stand in the way of progress."

That night I boarded a larger and more elegant craft which went speeding on the glittering ripples among the dark hulks of the freighters into boundless moonlight. The dinner served on board was memorable. The Negro chef and his assistant prepared crab-meat with a chopped-vegetable sauce of puzzling flavor, and then broiled large snapper throats, which I had never before regarded as the astonishing fish-course delicacy they are.

After coffee I went on deck to chat with a fellow guest. Suddenly he asked me point-blank, "Are you a spy for a Yankee magazine?"

"No," I said.

"I need to tell you something," he said. "Stop trying to strangle us. All those men and women inside are against segregation—but not for the reasons the Northern press howls about. If our group could only win a primary we could put up an argument Yankees might consider. Our best candidate won't run because he'd be beaten. I think we ought to put him up anyway and go down fighting. Then some of you ruthless and irrational fanatics might know we tried. Let's join the ladies."

I spent the night in Earl McGowin's cottage at Point Clear, on the east side of the Bay. Next morning, not far away, I saw a huge star-shaped structure—the Grand Hotel.

"They kept the name out of sentiment," said Earl. "The old inn on the same site was rambling and Victorian. What do you think of this one?"

We went over for a closer look. The place seemed to belie its name. There is no grandeur about it—only a concealed elegance. The colors—rust for the roof and green-blue for the walls—are muted. Blue water bounds it on three sides. There is an outdoor auditorium far out on Julep Point, and the golf club (near the main building) is paneled in natural woods. The boat basin is roomy. Whoever planned the Grand Hotel evidently meant it to lure people of dignity and taste. I found it restful.

The home of the McGowin family is at Chapman, a tiny cross-roads community south of Montgomery about sixty miles.

They live in a tree-shaded park stretching back from a white fence bordering the highway. Here a big brick house with white pillars still shelters Miss Essie, widow of the Greeley McGowin who built a prosperous sawmill business at Chapman. Behind the main house, in a long arc on the shores of a little lake, are the comfortable homes of his sons and their families.

When the late Greeley McGowin set his saws to screaming through Alabama logs at Chapman, he had at least three definite purposes in mind. One was to make money in the lumber business. A second was to keep a steady and lasting supply of logs moving into his mill by replanting the areas he had cut. A third was to provide his four sons with education of a superior sort. He sent them all to the University of Alabama and thence overseas to Oxford.

Dusk was settling as Earl and I approached the door of Floyd McGowin, eldest of the brothers. Inside were all the McGowin clan, a welcoming swarm. The McGowin wives are not only pretty but well read, so the conversation was gay and intelligent. After dinner my host took me into his library and we talked books. His interests ranged from Chaucer to Joyce—and his collection alone of the works and critical appraisals of Joyce struck me as extensive and important.

Hours later I sat with Earl on the terrace of his home while fireflies doodled on the blackboard of the darkness.

"Despite all you Yankees hear about us," he said, "Alabama is a booming state. The towns you used to love for their sleepy charm are awake and thrashing about. We have water—not only on the coast but on inland lakes and rivers now made navigable. We have electric power, lumber, oil, chemical plants. Being an ardent states' rights man I sort of hate to admit that our Federal air centers—such as Brooks and Maxwell Fields—stimulate our economy with big payrolls. Yankees may disapprove of us—but there's a lot of Yankee money invested here. When you were teaching at the University our percentage of illiteracy was high. Now we have almost wiped it out. If it weren't for——"

"For what?" I said.

"What's your solution of this integration business?"

"I have none. To me it's insoluble."

"That's the word," he said. "Let's go to bed."

Chapman is not the only small community in Alabama where intellectual interests and industrial vigor reach a high level. As I was leaving I remembered the pronunciamento of the late "Uncle Louis" Davidson, world traveler, bon vivant, sage of the Black Belt counties: "There are only two towns in the world where a civilized man may live happily—Paris and Uniontown, Alabama." Alabamians of education take pride in the cultural tradition of the pre-Civil War South, though too many of them believe that they have inherited it and so do nothing about it. The new culture—represented by museums, the interest in contemporary arts, the appreciation of William Faulkner (twenty years ago his novels were generally denounced here)—has almost no relationship to the old-time planter's preoccupation with the Greek and Latin classics or Shakespeare.

Back through the gargoyles of kudzu I went, through Pine Apple and Snow Hill and the wide Main Street of Selma ("Never a homely girl from Selma"). Westward then—through Demopolis, whose past claims a romantic Vine and Olive Colony of aristocratic refugees from the French Revolution (they tried their unaccustomed hands at growing wine grapes and olives, with little success) and whose present boasts "the liveliest Junior Chamber of Commerce in the state," and thence northwest into the old Black Belt town of Livingston. There was the courthouse on the old square, the drugstore that has borne the same family name for many generations, the "bored well" ("Drink from it for what ails you")—and finally the home of Pratt and Ruby Tartt, with Miss Ruby standing in the doorway.

It was years since she and I had had a good long talk, but we took up almost where we had left off. Miss Ruby was in her eightieth year when I visited her but she had defied her aging. We sat under a tree in her garden while Lizzie, her Negro cook, turned the smell of frying chicken into a promise of joy. Had I heard about Jesse, a local boy who went into the Army and took to boasting that he was a leading citizen back home? When two of his buddies happened to pass through on the "doodle," the one train that stops at Livingston, they got off and asked at the depot about their pal. No one knew him, and this they reported back in camp.

"I didn't say I come from smack dab up to the courthouse," said Jesse.

As we sat down to eat, Miss Ruby said, "By the way, I don't know how our train got its name but everybody calls it the doodle. Our only other train doesn't stop here, so it's called the through-doodle. One day a boy stepped up to the station master and said: 'Do the doodle come before the through-doodle do or do the through-doodle come before the doodle do?' The whole county has been chanting that one ever since."

On the next morning Miss Ruby and I returned to our old routine of seeking folk materials. We visited Gainesville, once the prosperous center of a cotton empire, now almost a ghost town. In a general store there, while the odors of tobacco, coffee, candy, snuff enchanted us,

Miss Beth (Mrs. O. K. Murray) sang for us an ancient English ballad each stanza of which begins with a question from a wife and ends with an unmusical answer in monosyllables from her husband. The woman draws from him the information that he intends to go downtown to get drunk and that on his return he expects her to have cooked a bushel of peas for dinner. When she remonstrates they— the peas, that is—will kill him the husband replies, "Let them kill me," and when she asks where to bury him he replies, "Throw me away." This is the last stanza:

> *The buzzards will eat you, my kind old husband,*
> *The buzzards will eat you, she called him aloud.*
> *The buzzards will eat you, my kind old husband,*
> *The best old fellow in the land.*

It ends with the husband's shout: *"Let them eat me."*

In Gainesville, too, we pieced together the materials of an early melodramatic story—one of the dark, plantation-house tragedies that Alabama porch-sitters have always delighted in.

In the early spring of 1847 a plantation owner took the river steamer *Lamplighter* to Mobile, where business and politics would detain him for several months. His lovely but frail wife he left in the care of his best friend, a distinguished physician. The smoke of the side-wheeler's stacks had hardly blown from the sky before the two left behind were lovers. Though he was himself married, the physician wooed the lonely girl "in prose and verse," and soon the couple could not conceal their wild infatuation. All Gainesville was set gossiping when the doctor began wearing a ring marked with his sweetheart's initials, having had it enlarged to fit his finger.

By late May a friend of the betrayed husband arrived in Mobile. The next upstream packet, the *Ophelia*, bore an armed passenger. Striding up River Street from the Gainesville dock, the planter shot his rival dead, then ordered his wife out of his home. The Alabama courts exonerated him for the killing and soon thereafter granted him a divorce.

The story, like an ancient ballad, has had continuing life for more than a century. Most Black Belt Alabamians have forgotten about Dancing Rabbit Creek Treaty, by which the Choctaws gave Sumter County to the nation in 1831. Few could describe the surrender of General Nathan Bedford Forrest and his dashing command at Gainesville in 1865. But the tale of the planter, the doctor and the beautiful but faithless wife is a folk legend that will be told as long as people live in Alabama.

I saved my visit to Tuscaloosa, home of the University of Alabama, where for six years I had been a professor, for the last few days before I set out for home. Long-time friends awaited me there, and I knew it would be difficult to look upon the old town objectively. When a man comes back after years to a place he has loved, nostalgia compels mourning over things that are no longer the same.

I arrived on a gray hour when the pavements were still shining from a recent shower and the clouds were breaking to show patches of blue. Immediately I felt grieved because many of the oaks—the Druid Oaks, the town once called them—had disappeared. Now a tall hotel—promise of comfort and elegance—stood in a cement desert streaked by white parking lines.

My room was pleasant, my dinner good, and I set out as once I had in 1921 to see the town. Tuscaloosa has grown more at its center than on its edges. The lawns that once separated its big houses are now occupied by small houses that shoulder their way into the narrow "frontage." The magic atmosphere I had felt long ago was gone. I had to remind myself that time dispels enchantment.

The University, which had held two thousand students, each known by name to President George Denny, now boasts an enrollment of eight thousand. Its new president—handsome Frank A. Rose —came recommended to the board of trustees as a former football player and former minister ("They needed both," say Tuscaloosans).

Gradually I became reconciled to the changes that disturbed me. As I sat on the back gallery of the Moody House, first of the pillared homes I came to love, I was reminded by its owner that the president's home—most beautiful of all Alabama houses—and the Gorgas house with its graceful iron railings, enchanted more students than ever. The old Governor's Mansion, built in 1829, is now beautifully restored and has become the University Faculty Club. I lunched with friends there the next day, and afterward we stood for a while on the steps beneath the second-story iron balcony that is shaded by graceful pillars.

"Back when Tuscaloosa was the capital of Alabama," said one of our party, "the old capitol building used to stand at the other end of the street. Do you remember when it burned in 1923?"

"Yes," I said.

"We all gathered here to watch the fire and old white-haired Judge Foster stood in front of us. Tears were streaming down his cheeks."

"I remember," I said.

"We used to live in the glory of our past," said my friend. "Now we live on the promise of our future."

Mississippi

by WILLIAM FAULKNER

Mississippi begins in the lobby of a Memphis, Tennessee, hotel and extends south to the Gulf of Mexico. It is dotted with little towns concentric about the ghosts of the horses and mules once tethered to the hitch-rail enclosing the county courthouse and it might almost be said to have only two directions, north and south, since until a few years ago it was impossible to travel east or west in it unless you walked or rode one of the horses or mules. Even in the boy's early manhood, to reach by rail either of the adjacent county towns thirty miles away to the east or west, you had to travel ninety miles in three different directions on three different railroads.

In the beginning it was virgin—to the west, along the Big River, the alluvial swamps threaded by black, almost motionless bayous and impenetrable with cane and buckvine and cypress and ash and oak and gum; to the east, the hardwood ridges and the prairies where the Appalachian Mountains died and buffalo grazed; to the south, the pine barrens and the moss-hung live oaks and the greater swamps, less of earth than water and lurking with alligators and water moccasins, where Louisiana in its time would begin.

And where in the beginning the predecessors crept with their simple artifacts, and built the mounds and vanished, bequeathing only the mounds in which the succeeding recordable Muskhogean stock would leave the skulls of their warriors and chiefs and babies and

slain bears, and the shards of pots, and hammer- and arrow-heads
and now and then a heavy silver Spanish spur.

There were deer to drift in herds alarmless as smoke then, and
bear and panther and wolves in the brakes and bottoms, and all the
lesser beasts—coon and possum and beaver and mink and mushrat
(not muskrat: mushrat); they were still there and some of the land
was still virgin in the early nineteen hundreds when the boy himself
began to hunt. But except for looking occasionally out from behind
the face of a white man or a Negro, the Chickasaws and Choctaws
and Natchez and Yazoos were as gone as the predecessors; and the
people the boy crept with were the descendants of the Sartorises and
de Spains and Compsons who had commanded the Manassas and
Sharpsburg and Shiloh and Chickamauga regiments, and the Mc-
Caslins and Ewells and Holstons and Hogganbecks whose fathers
and grandfathers had manned them, and now and then a Snopes too
because by the beginning of the twentieth century Snopeses were
everywhere: not only behind the counters of grubby little side-street
stores patronized mostly by Negroes, but behind the presidents'
desks of banks and the directors' tables of wholesale grocery corporations and in the deaconries of Baptist churches, buying up the
decayed Georgian houses and chopping them into apartments and
on their deathbeds decreeing annexes and baptismal fonts to the
churches as mementoes to themselves or maybe out of simple terror.

The Snopeses hunted too. They too were in the camps where the
de Spains and Compsons and McCaslins and Ewells were masters
in their hierarchal turn, shooting the does not only when law but
the Master too said not, shooting them not even because the meat
was needed but leaving the meat itself to be eaten by scavengers
in the woods, shooting it simply because it was big and moving and
alien, of an older time than the little grubby stores and the accumulating and compounding money; the boy a man now and in his hierarchal turn Master of the camp and coping, having to cope, not with
the diminishing wilderness where there was less and less game, but
with the Snopeses who were destroying that little which did remain.

These elected the Bilboes and voted indefatigably for the Varda-
mans, naming their sons after both. Their origin was in bitter hatred
and fear and economic rivalry of the Negroes who farmed little farms
no larger than and adjacent to their own, because the Negro, remembering when he had not been free at all, was therefore capable of
valuing what he had of freedom enough to struggle to retain even

that little and had taught himself how to do more with less: to raise more cotton with less money to spend and food to eat and fewer or inferior tools to work with; this, until he, the Snopes, could escape from the land into the little grubby side-street store where he could live not beside the Negro but on him by marking up on the inferior meat and meal and molasses the price which he, the Negro, could not even always read.

In the beginning, the obsolescent, dispossessed tomorrow by the already obsolete: the wild Muskhogean—Chickasaw and Choctaw and Natchez and Pascagoula—looked down from the tall Mississippi bluffs at a Chippeway canoe containing three Frenchmen—and had barely time to whirl and look behind him at a thousand Spaniards come overland from the Atlantic Ocean, and for a little while longer had the privilege of watching an ebb-flux-ebb-flux of alien nationalities as rapid as the magician's spill and evanishment of inconstant cards: the Frenchman for a second, then the Spaniard for perhaps two, then the Frenchman for another two and then the Spaniard again and then the Frenchman again for that last half-breath before the Anglo-Saxon, who would come to stay, to endure: the tall man roaring with Protestant Scripture and boiled whisky, Bible and jug in one hand and like as not an Indian tomahawk in the other, brawling, turbulent, uxorious and polygamous: a married invincible bachelor without destination but only motion, advancement, dragging his gravid wife and most of his mother-in-law's kin behind him into the trackless wilderness, to spawn that child behind a log-crotched rifle and then get her with another one before they moved again, and at the same time scattering his inexhaustible other seed in three hundred miles of dusky bellies: without avarice or compassion or forethought either: felling a tree which took two hundred years to grow, to extract from it a bear or a capful of wild honey.

He endured, even after he too was obsolete, the younger sons of Virginia and Carolina planters coming to replace him in wagons laden with slaves and indigo seedlings over the very roads he had hacked out with little else but the tomahawk. Then someone gave a Natchez doctor a Mexican cotton seed (maybe with the boll weevil already in it since, like the Snopeses, it too has taken over the Southern earth) and changed the whole face of Mississippi. Slaves were clearing rapidly now the virgin land, lurking still—in 1850—with the ghosts of Murrell and Mason and Hare and the two Harpes, into

plantation fields for profit where he, the displaced and obsolete, had
wanted only the bear and the deer and the sweetening for his tooth.
But he remained, hung on still; he is still there even in the boy's
middle-age, living in a log or plank or tin hut on the edge of what
remains of the fading wilderness, by and on the tolerance and sometimes even the bounty of the plantation owner to whom, in his in-
tractable way and even with a certain dignity and independence,
he is a sycophant, trapping coons and muskrats, now that the bear
and the panther are almost gone too, improvident still, felling still
the two-hundred-year-old tree even though it has only a coon or a
squirrel in it now.

Manning, when that time came, not the Manassas and Shiloh regiments but confederating into irregular bands and gangs owning not
much allegiance to anyone or anything, unified instead into the one
rite and aim of stealing horses from Federal picket lines; this in the
intervals of raiding (or trying to) the plantation house of the very
man to whom he had been the independent sycophant and intended
to be again, once the war was over and presuming that the man came
back from his Sharpsburg or Chickamauga majority or colonelcy or
whatever it had been. Trying to raid, that is, until the major's or
colonel's wife or aunt or mother-in-law, who had buried the silver
in the orchard and still held together a few of the older slaves,
fended him off and dispersed him, and when necessary even shot
him, with the absent husband's or nephew's or son-in-law's hunting
gun or dueling pistols. The women: the indomitable, the undefeated,
who never surrendered, refusing to allow the Yankee *minie* balls to
be dug out of portico column or mantelpiece or lintel, who seventy
years later would get up and walk out of *Gone With the Wind* as
soon as Sherman's name was mentioned; irreconcilable and enraged
and still talking about it long after the weary exhausted men who
had fought and lost it gave up trying to make them hush: even in
the boy's time the boy himself knowing about Vicksburg and Corinth
and exactly where his grandfather's regiment had been at First Manassas before he remembered hearing very much about Santa Claus.

In those days—1901 and '02 and '03 and '04—Santa Claus occurred
only at Christmas, not like now, and for the rest of the year children
played with what they could find or contrive or make, though just
as now, they still played, aped in miniature, what they had been
exposed to, heard or seen or been moved by most. Which was true
in the child's time and case too: the indomitable unsurrendered old

women holding together still, thirty-five and forty years later, a few of the old house slaves: women too who, like the white ones, refused to give up the old ways and forget the old anguishes. The child himself remembered one of them: Caroline: free these many years but who had declined to leave. Nor would she ever accept in full her weekly Saturday wages; the family never knew why unless the true reason was the one which appeared: for the simple pleasure of keeping the entire family reminded constantly that they were in arrears to her, compelling the boy's grandfather then his father and finally himself in his turn to be not only her banker but her bookkeeper too, having got the figure of eighty-nine dollars into her head somehow or for some reason, and though the sum itself altered, sometimes more and sometimes less, and sometimes it would be she herself who would be several weeks in arrears, it never changed: one of the children, white or Negro, liable to appear at any time, usually when most of the family would be gathered at a meal, with the message: "Mammy says to tell you not to forget you owe her eighty-nine dollars."

To the child, even at that time, she seemed already older than God, calling his grandsire "colonel" but never the child's father nor the father's brother and sister by anything but their Christian names even when they themselves had become grandparents: a matriarch with a score of descendants (and probably half that many more whom she had forgotten or outlived), one of them a boy too, whether a great grandson or merely a grandson even she did not remember, born in the same week with the white child and both bearing the same (the white child's grandsire's) name, suckled at the same black breast and sleeping and eating together and playing together the game which was the most important thing the white child knew at that time since at four and five and six his world was still a female world and he had heard nothing else that he could remember: with empty spools and chips and sticks and a scraped trench filled with well water for the River, playing over again in miniature the War, the old irremediable battles—Shiloh and Vicksburg, and Brice's Crossroads which was not far from where the child (both of them) had been born, the boy because he was white arrogating to himself the right to be the Confederate General—Pemberton or Johnston or Forrest—twice to the black child's once, else, lacking that once in three, the black one would not play at all.

Not the tall man, he was still the hunter, the man of the woods; and not the slave because he was free now; but that Mexican cotton seed which someone had given the Natchez doctor was clearing the land fast now, plowing under the buffalo grass of the eastern prairies and the brier and switch cane of the creek and river bottoms of the central hills and deswamping the whole vast flat alluvial delta-shaped sweep of land along the Big River, the Old Man: building the levees to hold him off the land long enough to plant and harvest the crop: he taking another foot of slope in his new dimension for every foot man constricted him in the old, so that the steamboats carrying the baled cotton to Memphis or New Orleans seemed to crawl along the sky itself.

And little steamboats on the smaller rivers, too, penetrating the Tallahatchie as far up as Wylie's Crossing above Jefferson. Though most of the cotton from that section—and on to the east to that point of no economic return where it was more expedient to continue on east to the Tombigbee and then south to Mobile—went the sixty miles overland to Memphis by mule and wagon; there was a settlement—a tavern of sorts and a smithy and a few gaunt cabins—on the bluff above Wylie's, at the exact distance where a wagon or a train of them loaded with cotton either starting or resuming the journey in the vicinity of Jefferson, would have to halt for the night. Or not even a settlement but rather a den, whose denizens lurked unseen by day in the brakes and thickets of the river bottom, appearing only at night and even then only long enough to enter the tavern kitchen where the driver of the day's cotton wagon sat unsuspecting before the fire, whereupon driver, wagon, mules and cotton and all would vanish: the body into the river probably and the wagon burned and the mules sold days or weeks later in a Memphis stockyard and the unidentifiable cotton already on its way to the Liverpool mill.

At the same time, sixteen miles away in Jefferson, there was a pre-Snopes, one of the tall men actually, a giant of a man in fact: a dedicated lay Baptist preacher but furious not with a furious un-sleeping dream of paradise nor even for universal Order with an upper-case O, but for simple civic security. He was warned by every-one not to go in there because not only could he accomplish nothing, he would very likely lose his own life trying it. But he did go, alone, and talked not of gospel nor God nor even virtue, but simply selected the biggest and boldest and by appearance, anyway, the most vil-lainous there and said to him: "I'll fight you. If you lick me, you take

what money I have. If I lick you, I baptize you into my church":
and battered and mauled and gouged that one into sanctity and
civic virtue then challenged the next biggest and most villainous and
then the next; and the following Sunday baptized the entire settlement in the river, the cotton wagons now crossing on Wylie's hand-
powered ferry and passing peacefully and unchallenged on to
Memphis until the railroad came and took the bales away from them.

That was in the seventies. The Negro was a free farmer and a
political entity now; one, he could not sign his name, was Federal
marshal at Jefferson. Afterward he became the town's official bootlegger (Mississippi was one of the first to essay the noble experiment,
along with Maine), resuming—he had never really quitted it—his old
allegiance to his old master and gaining his professional name, Mulberry, from the huge old tree behind Doctor Habersham's drugstore,
in the gallerylike tunnels among the roots of which he cached the
bottled units of his commerce.

Soon he (the Negro) would even forge ahead in that economic
rivalry with Snopes which was to send Snopes in droves into the
Ku Klux Klan—not the old original one of the war's chaotic and desperate end which, measured against the desperate times, was at least
honest and serious in its desperate aim, but into the later base one
of the twenties whose only kinship to the old one was the old name.
And a little money to build railroads was in the land now, brought
there by the man who in '66 had been a carpetbagger but who now
was a citizen; his children would speak the soft consonantless Negro
tongue as the children of parents who had lived below the Potomac
and Ohio Rivers since Captain John Smith, and their children would
boast of their Southern heritage.

In Jefferson his name was Redmond. He had found the money
with which Colonel Sartoris had opened the local cotton fields to
Europe by building his connecting line up to the main railroad from
Memphis to the Atlantic Ocean—narrow gauge, like a toy, with three
tiny locomotives like toys, too, named after Colonel Sartoris' three
daughters, each with its silver-plated oilcan engraved with the
daughter's Christian name: like toys, the standard-sized cars jacked
up at the junction, then lowered onto the narrow trucks, the tiny
locomotive now invisible ahead of its charges so that they appeared
in process of being snatched headlong among the fields they served
by an arrogant plume of smoke and the arrogant shrieking of a
whistle. It was Redmond who, after the inevitable quarrel, finally

shot Colonel Sartoris dead on a Jefferson street, driven, everyone believed, to the desperate act by the same arrogance and intolerance which had driven Colonel Sartoris' regiment to demote him from its colonelcy in the fall elections after Second Manassas and Sharpsburg.

So there were railroads in the land now; now couples who used to go overland by carriage to the River landings and the steamboats for the traditional New Orleans honeymoon could take the train from almost anywhere. And presently Pullmans, too, all the way from Chicago and the Northern cities where the cash, the money was, so that the rich Northerners could come down in comfort and open the land indeed: setting up with their Yankee dollars the vast lumbering plants and mills in the Southern-pine section, the little towns which had been hamlets without change or alteration for fifty years, booming and soaring into cities overnight above the stump-pocked barrens which would remain until in simple economic desperation people taught themselves to farm pine trees as in other sections they had already learned to farm corn and cotton.

And Northern lumber mills in the Delta too: the mid-twenties now and the Delta booming with cotton and timber both. But mostly booming with simple money: increment a troglodyte which had fathered twin troglodytes: solvency and bankruptcy, the three of them booming money into the land so fast that the problem was how to get rid of it before it whelmed you into suffocation. Until in something almost resembling self-defense, seven or eight of the bigger Delta towns formed a baseball league, presently raiding as far away—and successfully too—for pitchers and shortstops and slugging outfielders as the two major leagues; the boy, a young man now, making acquaintance with this league and one of the big Northern lumber companies not only coincidentally with one another but because of one another.

At this time the young man's attitude was that of most other young men who had been around twenty-one years of age in April, 1917, even though at times he did admit to himself that he was possibly using the fact that he had been nineteen on that day as an excuse to follow the avocation he was coming more and more to know would be forever his true one: to be a tramp, a harmless possessionless vagabond. In any case, he was quite ripe to make the acquaintance of the league; it began with that of the lumber company, which at the moment was taking a leisurely bankruptcy. A lawyer had been appointed referee in the bankruptcy: a friend of the young man's family and older than he, yet who had taken a liking to the young man and so invited him to come along for the ride too. His official capacity was that of interpreter, since he had a little French and the defuncting company had European connections. But no interpreting was ever done, since the entourage did not go to Europe but moved instead into a single floor of a Memphis hotel, where all—including the interpreter—had the privilege of signing chits for food and theater tickets and even the bootleg whisky (Tennessee was in its dry mutation then) which the bellboys would produce, though not of course at the discreet and innocent-looking places clustered a few miles away just below the Mississippi state line, where roulette and dice and blackjack were available.

Then suddenly Mr. Sells Wales was in it, too, bringing the baseball league with him. The young man never did know what connection (if any) Mr. Wales had with the bankruptcy, nor really bothered to wonder, let alone care and ask, not only because he had developed already that sense of *noblesse oblige* toward the avocation which he knew was his true one, which would have been reason enough, but because Mr. Wales himself was already a legend in the Delta. Owner of a plantation measured not in acres but in miles and reputedly sole owner of one of the league baseball teams or anyway most of its players, certainly of the catcher and the base-stealing shortstop and the .340-hitting outfielder ravished or pirated, it was said, from the Chicago Cubs, his ordinary costume seven days a week was a two or three days' beard and muddy high boots and a corduroy hunting coat, the tale, the legend telling of how he entered a swank St. Louis hotel in that costume late one night and demanded a room of a dinner-jacketed clerk, who looked once at the beard and the muddy boots but probably mostly at Mr. Wales' face and said they were filled up: whereupon Mr. Wales asked how much they wanted for the hotel and was told, superciliously, in tens of thousands, and—so told the legend—drew from his corduroy hip a wad of thousand-dollar bills sufficient to have bought the hotel half again at the price stated and told the clerk he wanted every room in the building vacated in ten minutes.

That one of course was apocryphal, but the young man himself saw this one: Mr. Wales and himself having a leisurely breakfast one noon in the Memphis hotel when Mr. Wales remembered suddenly that his private ball club was playing one of its most important games at a town about sixty miles away at three o'clock that after-

noon and telephoned to the railroad station to have a special train
ready for them in thirty minutes, which it was: an engine and a
caboose: reaching Coahoma about three o'clock with a mile still to
the ball park: a man (there were no taxis at the station at that hour
and few in Mississippi anywhere at that time) sitting behind the
wheel of a dingy though still sound Cadillac car, and Mr. Wales
said:

"What do you want for it?"

"What?" the man in the car said.

"Your automobile," Mr. Wales said.

"Twelve fifty," the man said.

"All right," Mr. Wales said, opening the door.

"I mean twelve hundred and fifty dollars," the man said.

"All right," Mr. Wales said, then to the young man: "Jump in."

"Hold up here, mister," the man said.

"I've bought it," Mr. Wales said, getting in too. "The ball park," he
said. "Hurry."

The young man never saw the Cadillac again, though he became
quite familiar with the engine and caboose during the next succeeding weeks while the league pennant race waxed hotter and hotter,
Mr. Wales keeping the special train on call in the Memphis yards
as twenty-five years earlier a city-dwelling millionaire might have
hacked a carriage and pair to his instant nod, so that it seemed to the
young man that he would barely get back to Memphis to rest before
they would be rushing once more down the Delta to another baseball game.

"I ought to be interpreting, sometime," he said once.

"Interpret, then," Mr. Wales said. "Interpret what this goddamn
cotton market is going to do tomorrow, and we can both quit chasing
this blank blank sand-lot ball team."

The cotton seed and the lumber mills were clearing the rest of
the delta, too, pushing what remained of the wilderness farther and
farther southward into the V of Big River and the hills. When the
young man, a youth of sixteen and seventeen then, was first accepted
into that hunting club of which he in his hierarchal time would be
Master, the hunting grounds, haunt of deer and bear and wild turkey,
could be reached in a single day or night in a mule-drawn wagon.
Now they were using automobiles: a hundred miles then two hundred southward and still southward as the wilderness dwindled into
the confluence of the Yazoo River and the big one, the Old Man.

The Old Man: all his little contributing streams levee'd too, along with him, and paying none of the dykes any heed at all when it suited his mood and fancy, gathering water all the way from Montana to Pennsylvania every generation or so and rolling it down the artificial gut of his victims' puny and baseless hoping, piling the water up, not fast, just inexorably, giving plenty of time to measure his crest and telegraph ahead, even warning of the exact day almost when he would enter the house and float the piano out of it and the pictures off the walls, and even remove the house itself if it were not securely fastened down.

Inexorable and unhurried, overpassing one by one his little confluent feeders and shoving the water into them until for days their current would flow backward, upstream: as far upstream as Wylie's Crossing above Jefferson. The little rivers were dyked, too, but back here was the land of individualists: remnants and descendants of the tall men now taken to farming, and of Snopeses who were more than individualists: they were Snopeses, so that where the owners of the thousand-acre plantations along the Big River confederated as one man with sandbags and machines and their Negro tenants and wage-hands to hold the sandboils and the cracks, back here the owner of the hundred- or two-hundred-acre farm patrolled his section of levee with a sandbag in one hand and his shotgun in the other, lest his upstream neighbor dynamite it to save his (the upstream neighbor's) own.

Piling up the water while white man and Negro worked side by side in shifts in the mud and the rain, with automobile headlights and gasoline flares and kegs of whisky and coffee boiling in fifty-gallon batches in scoured and scalded oil drums; lapping, tentative, almost innocently, merely inexorable (no hurry, his) among and beneath and between and finally over the frantic sandbags, as if his whole purpose had been merely to give man another chance to prove, not to him but to man, just how much the human body could bear, stand, endure; then, having let man prove it, doing what he could have done at any time these past weeks if so minded: removing with no haste, nor any particular malice or fury either, a mile or two miles of levee and coffee drums and whisky kegs and gas flares in one sloughing collapse, gleaming dully for a little while yet among the parallel cotton middles until the fields vanished along with the roads and lanes and at last the towns themselves.

Vanished, gone beneath one vast yellow motionless expanse, out of which projected only the tops of trees and telephone poles and the decapitations of human dwelling-places like enigmatic objects placed by inscrutable and impenetrable design on a dirty mirror; and the mounds of the predecessors on which, among a tangle of moccasins, bear and horses and deer and mules and wild turkeys and cows and domestic chickens waited patient in mutual armistice; and the levees themselves, where among a jumble of uxorious flotsam the young continued to be born and the old to die, not from exposure but from simple and normal time and decay, as if man and his destiny were in the end stronger even than the river which had dispossessed him, inviolable by and invincible to alteration.

Then, having proved that too, he—the Old Man—would withdraw, not retreat: subside, back from the land slowly and inexorably too, emptying the confluent rivers and bayous back into the old vain hopeful gut, but so slowly and gradually that not the waters seemed to fall but the flat earth itself to rise, creep in one plane back into light and air again: one constant stain of yellow-brown at one constant altitude on telephone poles and the walls of gins and houses and stores as though the line had been laid off with a transit and painted in one gigantic unbroken brush stroke, the earth itself one alluvial inch higher, the rich dirt one inch deeper, drying into long cracks beneath the hot fierce glare of May: but not for long, because almost at once came the plow, the plowing and planting already two months late but that did not matter: the cotton man-tall once more by August and whiter and denser still by picking time, as if the Old Man said, "I do what I want to, when I want to. But I pay my way."

And the boats, of course, they projected above that yellow and liquid plane and even moved upon it: the skiffs and scows of fishermen and trappers, the launches of the United States Engineers who operated the Levee Commission, and one small shallow-draught steamboat steaming in paradox among and across the cotton fields themselves, its pilot not a riverman but a farmer who knew where the submerged fences were, its masthead lookout a mechanic with a pair of pliers to cut the telephone wires to pass the smokestack through: no paradox really, since on the River it had resembled a house to begin with, so that here it looked no different from the baseless houses it steamed among and on occasion even strained at top boiler pressure to overtake, like a mallard drake after a fleeing mallard hen.

But these boats were not enough, very quickly not near enough, the Old Man meant business indeed this time. So now there began to arrive from the Gulf ports the shrimp trawlers and pleasure cruisers and Coast Guard cutters whose bottoms had known only salt water and the mouths of tidal rivers, to be run still by their salt-water crews but conned by the men who knew where the submerged roads and fences were for the good reason that they had been running mule-plow furrows along them or up to them all their lives; sailing among the swollen carcasses of horses and mules and deer and cows and sheep to pluck the Old Man's patient flotsam, black and white, out of trees and the roofs of gins and cotton sheds and floating cabins and the second-story windows of houses and office buildings; then—the salt-water men, to whom land was either a featureless treeless salt marsh or a snake- and alligator-infested swamp impenetrable with trumpet vine and Spanish moss, some of whom had never even seen the earth into which were driven the spiles supporting the houses they lived in—staying on even after they were no longer needed, as though waiting to see emerge from the water what sort of country it was which bore the economy on which the people—men and women, black and white, more of black than white even, ten to one more—lived whom they had saved; seeing the land for that moment before mule and plow altered it right up to the water's receding edge, then back into the River again before the trawlers and cruisers and cutters became marooned into canted and useless rubble too along with the ruined hencoops and cowsheds and privies; back onto the Old Man, shrunken once more into his normal banks, drowsing and even innocent looking, as if it were something else besides him that had changed, for a little time anyway, the whole face of the adjacent earth.

They were homeward bound now, passing the river towns, some of which were respectable in age when South Mississippi was a Spanish wilderness: Greenville and Vicksburg, Natchez and Grand Gulf and Petit Gulf (vanished now and even the old site known by a different name) which had known Mason and one at least of the Harpes and from or on which Murrell had based his abortive slave insurrection intended to efface the white people from the land and leave him emperor of it—the land sinking away beyond the levee until presently you could no longer say where water began and earth stopped: only that these lush and verdant sunny savannas would no longer bear your weight. The rivers flowed no longer west, but south now, no longer yellow or brown, but black, threading the miles of yellow salt marsh from which, on an off-shore breeze, mosquitoes came in such clouds that in your itching and burning anguish it would seem that you could actually see them in faint adumbration crossing the earth; and met tide and then the uncorrupted salt: not the Gulf quite yet but at least the Sound behind the long barrier of the islands—Ship and Horn and Petit Bois, the trawler and cruiser bottoms home again now among the lighthouses and channel markers and shipyards and drying nets and processing plants for fish.

The man remembered that from his youth too: one summer spent being blown innocently over in catboats since, born and bred for generations in the north Mississippi hinterland, he did not recognize the edge of a squall until he already had one. The next summer he returned because he found that he liked that much water, this time as a hand in one of the trawlers; remembering: a four-gallon iron pot over a red bed of charcoal on the foredeck, in which decapitated shrimp boiled among handfuls of salt and black pepper, never emptied, never washed and constantly renewed, so that you ate them all day long in passing like peanuts; remembering: the predawn, to be broken presently by the violent near-subtropical yellow-and-crimson day almost like an audible explosion, but still dark for a little while yet, the dark ship creeping onto the shrimp grounds in a soundless sternward swirl of phosphorus like a drowning tumble of fireflies, the youth lying face down on the peak staring into the dark water watching the disturbed shrimp burst outward-shooting in fiery and fading fans like the trails of tiny rockets.

He learned the barrier islands too; one of a crew of five amateurs sailing a big sloop in offshore races, he learned not only how to keep a hull on its keel and moving but how to get it from one place to another and bring it back: so that, a professional now, living in New Orleans, he commanded for pay a power launch belonging to a bootlegger (this was the twenties), whose crew consisted of a Negro cook-deckhand-stevedore and the bootlegger's younger brother Pete: a slim twenty-one-or-two-year-old Italian with yellow eyes like a cat and a silk shirt bulged faintly by an armpit-holstered pistol too small in calibre to have done anything but got them all killed, even if the captain or the cook had dreamed of resisting or resenting trouble if and when it came; the captain or the cook would extract the pistol from the holster and hide it at the first opportunity (not concealed really: just dropped into the oily bilge under the engine, where, even though Pete soon discovered where it would be, it was safe because he refused to thrust his hand and arm into the oil-fouled water but instead merely lay about the cockpit, sulking); taking the launch across Pontchartrain and down the Rigolets cut to the Gulf, the Sound, then lying-to with no lights showing until the Coast Guard cutter (it ran almost on schedule; theirs was a job, too, even if it was, comparatively speaking, a hopeless one) made its fast haughty eastward rush, going, they always liked to believe, to Mobile, to a dance; then by compass on to the island (it was little more than a sandspit bearing a line of ragged and shabby pines thrashing always in the windy crash and roar of the true Gulf on the other side of it) where the Caribbean schooner would bury the casks of green alcohol which the bootlegger's mother back in New Orleans would convert and bottle and label into Scotch or Bourbon or gin. There were a few wild cattle on the island which they would have to watch for, the Negro digging and Pete still sulking and refusing to help at all because of the pistol, and the captain watching for the charge (they couldn't risk showing a light) which every three or four trips would come—the gaunt wild half-seen shapes charging suddenly and with no warning down at them as they turned and ran through the nightmare sand and hurled themselves into the dinghy, to pull along parallel to the shore, the animals following, until they had tolled them far enough away for the Negro to go back ashore for the remaining casks. Then they would heave-to again and lie until the cutter passed back westward, the dance obviously over now, in the same haughty and imperious rush.

That was Mississippi too, though a different one from where the child had been bred; the people were Catholics, the Spanish and French blood still showed in the names and faces. But it was not a deep one, if you did not count the sea and the boats on it: a curve of beach, a thin unbroken line of estates and apartment hotels owned and inhabited by Chicago millionaires, standing back to back with another thin line, this time of tenements inhabited by Negroes and whites who ran the boats and worked in the fish-processing plants.

Then the Mississippi which the young man knew began: the fading purlieus inhabited by a people whom the young man recognized because their like was in his country too: descendants, heirs at least in spirit, of the tall men, who worked in no factories and farmed no land nor even truck patches, living not out of the earth but on its denizens: fishing guides and individual professional fishermen, trappers of muskrats and alligator hunters and poachers of deer, the land rising now, once more earth instead of half water, vista-ed and arras-ed with the long-leaf pines which Northern capital would convert into dollars in Ohio and Indiana and Illinois banks. Though not all of it. Some of it would alter hamlets and villages into cities and even build whole new ones almost overnight, cities with Mississippi names but patterned on Ohio and Indiana and Illinois because they were bigger than Mississippi towns, rising, standing today among the tall pines which created them, then tomorrow (that quick, that fast, that rapid) among the stumpy pock-age to which they were monuments. Because the land had made its one crop: the soil too fine and light to compete seriously in cotton: until people discovered that it would grow what other soils would not: the tomatoes and strawberries and the fine cane for sugar: not the sorghum of the northern and western counties which people of the true cane country called hog feed, but the true sweet cane which made the sugarhouse molasses.

Big towns, for Mississippi: cities, we called them: Hattiesburg, and Laurel, and Meridian, and Canton; and towns deriving by name from farther away than Ohio: Kosciusko named after a Polish general who thought that people should be free who wanted to be; and Egypt because there was corn there when it was nowhere else in the bad lean times of the old war which the old women had still never surrendered; and Philadelphia where the Neshoba Indians whose name the county bears still remain for the simple reason that they did not mind living in peace with other people, no matter what their color or politics. This was the hills now: Jones County which old Newt Knight, its principal proprietor and first citizen or denizen, whichever you liked, seceded from the Confederacy in 1862, establishing still a third republic within the boundaries of the United States until a Confederate military force subdued him in his embattled log-castle capital; and Sullivan's Hollow: a long narrow glen where a few clans or families with North Ireland and Highland names feuded and slew one another in the old pre-Culloden fashion, yet banding together immediately and always to resist any outsider in the pre-Culloden fashion too: *vide* the legend of the revenue officer hunting illicit whisky stills, captured and held prisoner in a stable and worked in traces as the mate to a plow mule. No Negro ever let darkness catch him in Sullivan's Hollow. In fact, there were few Negroes in this country at all: a narrow strip of which extended up into the young man's own section: a remote district there through which Negroes passed infrequently and rapidly and only by daylight.

It is not very wide, because almost at once there begins to the east of it the prairie country which sheds its water into Alabama and Mobile Bay, with its old tight intermarried towns and plantation houses columned and porticoed in the traditional Georgian manner of Virginia and Carolina in place of the Spanish and French influence of Natchez. These towns are Columbus and Aberdeen and West Point, and Shuqualak, where the good quail shooting is and the good bird dogs are bred and trained—horses too: hunters; Dancing Rabbit is here, too, where the treaty dispossessing them of Mississippi was made between the Choctaws and the United States; and in one of the towns lived a kinsman of the young man, dead now, rest him: an invincible and incorrigible bachelor, a leader of cotillions and an inveterate diner-out since any time an extra single man was needed, any hostess thought of him first.

But he was a man's man, too, and even more: a young man's man, who played poker and matched glasses with the town's young bachelors and the apostates still young enough in time to still resist the wedlock; who walked not only in spats and a stick and yellow gloves and a Homburg hat, but an air of sardonic and inviolable atheism, too, until at last he was forced to the final desperate resort of prayer: sitting after supper one night among the drummers in the row of chairs on the sidewalk before the Gilmer Hotel, waiting to see what (if anything) the evening would bring, when two of the young bachelors passing in a Model T Ford stopped and invited him to drive across the line into the Alabama hills for a gallon of moonshine whisky. Which they did. But the still they sought was not in hills because these were not hills: it was the dying tail of the Appalachian mountain range. But since the Model T's engine had to be running fast anyway for it to have any headlights, going up the mountain was an actual improvement, especially after they had to drop to low gear. And coming from the generation before the motor car, it never occurred to him that coming back down would be any different until they got the gallon and had a drink from it and turned around and started back down. Or maybe it was the whisky, he said, telling it: the little car rushing faster and faster behind a thin wash of light of about the same volume that two lightning bugs would have made, around the plunging curves which, the faster the car ran, became only the more frequent and sharp and plunging, whipping around the nearly right-angle bends with a rock wall on one hand and several hundred feet of vertical and empty night on the other, until at last he prayed; he said: "Lord, You know I haven't worried You in over forty years, and if You'll just get me back to Columbus I promise never to bother You again."

And now the young man, middle-aged now or anyway middle-aging, is back home, too, where they who altered the swamps and forests of his youth have now altered the face of the earth itself; what he remembered as dense river-bottom jungle and rich farmland is now an artificial lake twenty-five miles long: a flood-control project for the cotton fields below the huge earth dam, with a few more outboard-powered fishing skiffs on it each year, and at last a sailboat. On his way in to town from his home the middle-aging man (now a professional fiction writer: who had wanted to remain the tramp and the possessionless vagabond of his young manhood but time and success and the hardening of his arteries had beaten him) would pass the back yard of a doctor friend whose son was an undergraduate at Harvard. One day the undergraduate stopped him and invited him in and showed him the unfinished hull of a twenty-foot sloop, saying, "When I get her finished, Mr. Bill, I want you to help me sail her." And each time he passed after that, the undergraduate would repeat: "Remember, Mr. Bill, I want you to help me sail her as soon as I get her in the water": to which the middle-aging would answer as always: "Fine, Arthur. Just let me know."

Then one day he came out of the post office: a voice called him from a taxicab, which in small Mississippi towns was any motor car owned by any foot-loose young man who liked to drive, who decreed himself a cabbie as Napoleon decreed himself emperor; in the car with the driver was the undergraduate and a young man whose father had vanished recently somewhere in the West out of the ruins of the bank of which he had been president, and a fourth young man whose type is universal: the town clown, comedian, whose humor is without viciousness and quite often witty and always funny. "She's in the water, Mr. Bill," the undergraduate said. "Are you ready to go now?" And he was, and the sloop was, too; the undergraduate had sewn his own sails on his mother's machine; they worked her out into the lake and got her on course all tight and drawing, when suddenly it seemed to the middle-aging that part of him was no longer in the sloop but about ten feet away, looking at what he saw: a Harvard undergraduate, a taxi driver, the son of an absconded banker and a village clown and a middle-aged novelist sailing a homemade boat on an artificial lake in the depths of the north Mississippi hills: and he thought that that was something which did not happen to you more than once in your life.

Home again, his native land; he was born of it and his bones will sleep in it; loving it even while hating some of it: the river jungle and the bordering hills where, still a child, he had ridden behind his father on the horse after the bobcat or fox or coon or whatever was ahead of the belling hounds, and where he had hunted alone when he got big enough to be trusted with a gun—all this now the bottom of a muddy lake being raised gradually and steadily every year by another layer of beer cans and bottle caps and lost bass plugs. And the wilderness, the two weeks in the woods, in camp, the rough food and the rough sleeping, the life of men and horses and hounds among men and horses and hounds, not to slay the game but to pursue it, touch and let go, never satiety—moved now even farther away than that down the flat Delta so that the mile-long freight trains, visible for miles across the fields where the cotton is mortgaged in February, planted in May, harvested in September and put into the Farm Loan in October in order to pay off February's mortgage in order to mortgage next year's crop, seem to be passing two or even three of the little Indian-named hamlets at once over the very ground where, a youth now capable of being trusted even with a rifle, he had shared in the yearly ritual of Old Ben: the big old bear with one trap-ruined foot who had earned for himself a name, a designation like a living man through the legend of the deadfalls and traps he had wrecked and the hounds he had slain and the shots he had survived, until Boon Hogganbeck, the youth's father's stable foreman, ran in and killed it with a hunting knife to save a hound which he, Boon Hogganbeck, loved.

But most of all he hated the intolerance and injustice: the lynching of Negroes not for the crimes they committed but because their skins were black (the lynchings were becoming fewer and fewer and soon there would be no more of them but the evil would have been done and irrevocable because there should never have been any); the inequality: the poor schools they had then when they had any, the hovels they had to live in unless they wanted to live outdoors: who could worship the white man's God but not in the white man's church; pay taxes in the white man's courthouse but couldn't vote in it or for it; working by the white man's clock but having to take his pay by the white man's counting (Captain Joe Thoms, a Delta planter though not one of the big ones, who after a bad crop year drew a thousand silver dollars from the bank and called his five tenants one by one into the dining room where two hundred of the dollars were spread carelessly out on the table beneath the lamp, saying: "Well, Jim, that's what we made this year." Then the Negro: "Gret God, Cap'n Joe, is all that mine?" And Captain Thoms: "No, no, just half of it is yours. The other half belongs to me, remember."); the bigotry which could send to Washington some of the Senators and Congressmen we sent there and which could erect in a town no bigger than Jefferson five separate denominations of churches but set aside not one square foot of ground where children could play and old people could sit and watch them.

But he loves it, it is his, remembering: the trying to, having to, stay in bed until the crack of dawn would bring Christmas; and of the other times almost as good as Christmas: of being waked at three o'clock to have breakfast by lamplight in order to drive by surrey into town and the depot to take the morning train for the three or four days in Memphis where he would see automobiles, and the day in 1910 when, twelve years old, he watched John Moissant land a bicycle-wheeled aileronless (you warped the whole wing tip to bank it or hold it level) Bleriot monoplane on the infield of the Memphis race track and knew forever after that someday he too would have to fly alone; remembering: his first sweetheart, aged eight, plump and honey-haired and demure and named Mary, the two of them sitting side by side on the kitchen steps eating ice cream; and another one, Minnie this time, granddaughter of the old hillman from whom, a man himself now, he bought moonshine whisky, come to town at seventeen to take a job behind the soda counter of the drugstore, watching her virginal and innocent and without self-consciousness pour Coca-Cola sirup into the lifted glass by hooking her thumb through the ring of the jug and swinging it back and up in one unbroken motion onto her horizontal upper arm exactly as he had seen her grandfather pour whisky from a jug a thousand times.

Even while hating it, because for every Joe Thoms with two hundred silver dollars and every Snopes in a hooded nightshirt, somewhere in Mississippi there was this too: remembering: Ned, born in a cabin in the back yard in 1865, in the time of the middle-aged's great-grandfather, and who had outlived three generations of them, who had not only walked and talked so constantly for so many years with the three generations that he walked and talked like them, he had two tremendous trunks filled with the clothes which they had worn—not only the blue brass-buttoned frock coat and the plug hat in which he had been the great-grandfather's and the grandfather's coachman, but the broadcloth frock coats which the great-grand-father himself had worn, and the pigeon-tailed ones of the grand-father's time and the short coat of his father's which the middle-aged could remember on the backs for which they had been tailored, along with the hats in their eighty years of mutation too: so that, glancing idly up and out the library window, the middle-aged would see that back, that stride, that coat and hat going down the drive toward the road, and his heart would stop and even turn over. He (Ned) was eighty-four now and in these last few years he had begun to get a little mixed up, calling the middle-aged not only Master but some-times Master Murry, who was the middle-aged's father, and Colonel too, coming once a week through the kitchen and into the parlor, saying: "Here's where I wants to lay, right here where I can be facing out that window. And I wants it to be a sunny day, so the sun can come in on me. And I wants you to preach the sermon. I wants you to take a dram of whisky for me, and lay yourself back and preach the best sermon you ever preached."

And Caroline too, whom the middle-aged had inherited too in his hierarchal turn, nobody knowing any more exactly how many more years than a hundred she was. But not mixed up, she: who had for-gotten nothing, calling the middle-aged "Memmy" still, from fifty-odd years ago when that was as close as his brothers could come to "William"; his youngest daughter, aged four and five and six, coming in to the house and saying, "Pappy, Mammy said to tell you not to forget you owe her eighty-nine dollars."

"I won't," the middle-aged would say. "What are you all doing now?"

"Piecing a quilt," the daughter answered. Which they were. There was electricity in her cabin now, but she would not use it, insisting still on the kerosene lamps which she had always known. Nor would she use the spectacles either, wearing them merely as an ornament across the brow of the immaculate white cloth—head-rag—which bound her now hairless head. She did not need them: a smolder of

wood ashes on the hearth winter and summer in which sweet potatoes roasted, the five-year-old white child in a miniature rocking
chair at one side of it and the aged Negress, not a great deal larger,
in her chair at the other, the basket bright with scraps and fragments
of cloth between them and in that dim light in which the middle-
aged himself could not have read his own name without his glasses,
the two of them with infinitesimal and tedious and patient stitches
annealing the bright stars and squares and diamonds into another
pattern to be folded away among the cedar shavings in the trunk.

Then it was the Fourth of July, the kitchen was closed after breakfast so the cook and houseman had rallied, and that morning the
generations of her loins began to arrive, from her own seventy- and
eighty-year-old children, down through their great- and twice-great-
grandchildren, faces which the middle-aged had never seen before,
until the cabin would no longer hold them: the women and girls
sleeping on the floor inside and the men and boys sleeping on the
ground in front of it, Caroline herself conscious now and presently
sitting up in bed: who had forgotten nothing: matriarchal and imperial, and more: imperious: ten and even eleven o'clock at night
and the middle-aged himself undressed and in bed, reading, when
sure enough he would hear the slow quiet stockinged or naked feet
mounting the back stairs; presently the strange dark face—never the
same one of two nights ago or the two or three nights before that—
would look in the door at him, and the quiet, courteous, never servile
voice would say: "She want the ice cream." And he would rise and
dress and drive in to the village; he would even drive through the
village although he knew that everything there would have long
been closed and he would do what he had done two nights ago;
drive thirty miles on to the arterial highway and then up or down
it until he found an open drive-in or hot-dog stand to sell him the
quart of ice cream.

But that stroke was not the one; she was walking again presently,
even, despite the houseman's standing order to forestall her with the
automobile, all the way in to town to sit with his, the middle-aging's,
mother, talking, he liked to think, of the old days of his father and
himself and the three younger brothers, the two of them, two women
who together had never weighed two hundred pounds, in a house
roaring with five men: though they probably didn't, since women,
unlike men, have learned how to live uncomplicated by that sort of
sentimentality. But it was as if she knew herself that the summer's

stroke was like the throat-clearing sound inside the grandfather clock preceding the stroke of midnight or of noon, because she never touched the last unfinished quilt again. Presently it had vanished, no one knew where, and as the cold came and the shortening days she began to spend more and more time in the house, not her cabin but the big house, sitting in a corner of the kitchen while the cook and houseman were about, then in the middle-aging's wife's sewing room until the family gathered for the evening meal, the houseman carrying her rocking chair into the dining room to sit there while they ate: until suddenly (it was almost Christmas now) she insisted on sitting in the parlor until the meal was ready, none knew why, until at last she told them, through the wife: "Miss Hestelle, when them niggers lays me out, I want you to make me a fresh clean cap and apron to lay in." That was her valedictory; two days after Christmas the stroke came which was the one; two days after that she lay in the parlor in the fresh cap and apron she would not see, and the middle-aging did indeed lay back and preach the sermon, the oration, hoping that when his turn came there would be someone in the world to owe him the sermon owed to her by all who had been, as he had been from infancy, within the scope and range of that fidelity and that devotion and that rectitude.

Loving all of it even while he had to hate some of it because he knows now that you don't love because: you love despite; not for the virtues, but despite the faults.

American Panorama

West of the Mississippi

AMERICAN PANORAMA

WEST OF THE MISSISSIPPI

A HOLIDAY MAGAZINE BOOK

DOUBLEDAY & COMPANY, INC.
Garden City, New York

Contents

Introduction

The United States is divided naturally into broad geographical regions—mountains, plains, deserts; the broad coastal areas and the great river basins. The pattern of states that has been overlaid seems puny and artificial in comparison. More often than not the borders are odd and arbitrary, reflecting political connivance or geometrical convenience rather than the plain geographical realities.

But these fifty states are more than mere patches of color on the map. In the crucial moments of American history it has been the states that have assumed the leadership. It was, after all, thirteen of them who brought the nation into existence. Less than a century later those same states and many more engaged in a long and bitter war to defend their individual rights, beliefs and habits.

Now as in the beginning there are differences between the states. For a hundred years the differences have been expressed in pride and achievement rather than in hostility, but they have by no means disappeared.

Over the years Holiday has published portraits of all of the states of the Union including the two newest—portraits which reflected their history, their people and their personalities. This series, written by some of America's most gifted writers, has formed the outline of the magazine's continuing mosaic of America.

This volume is part of that total picture—the twenty-four states west of the Mississippi. It is representative of the whole for at least two reasons. It dramatizes our continual differences—the difference between Wyoming and Louisiana, for example, or Minnesota and New Mexico. It also sounds another and greater theme, the theme of unity which in combination has formed and defined this country.

The Editors

American Panorama

West of the Mississippi

PART I *The New States*

by JAMES WARNER BELLAH

Alaska should be entered slowly, by boat or by road; its vast spread makes it impossible to assimilate in the four easy flying hours from Seattle to Anchorage. Its magnitude is untrammeled; its grandeur grows upon the consciousness, like hunger. It cannot be explained by comparison. It offers no common denominator to past experience. There is no instant Alaska.

By ship from Vancouver to Juneau, the capital, you steam three days between the islanded shores of the Inside Passage, through thick-growing timber, and along that entire eight hundred miles there is no scar of forest-fire damage, no smoke wisp of a campfire. You hear no honk of a car horn, no whistle of a train. No one is there to drop a cigarette, to be careless with firesmolder. No one is there at all. In places, no one has *ever* been there.

The Tongass National Forest, in the southeastern part of the state, says the Forestry Service, alone could provide much of the newsprint for the newspapers of the world. United States Army Engineers estimate that a Yukon River dam at Rampart would form a lake as large as Ontario, that would take nine years to fill; and the resulting water power would produce half as many kilowatt-hours as are produced at present in all the other forty-nine states.

Yet in Nome, on the Bering Sea, a guide, after spotting a polar bear from the air, can telephone a Wall Street broker that if he will hop a plane he can enjoy some fine shooting and be back at his desk a few days later.

Arrived at Juneau, you have barely entered Alaska. You must continue westerly about *thirty-four degrees* of longitude before you reach Little Diomede Island in Bering Strait—a scant two and a half miles from the U.S.S.R. You must travel north more than a thousand miles across the entire northwest shoulder of North America before you reach Point Barrow on the Arctic Ocean. You must go almost to Asia before you reach Adak in the Aleutians. Alaska is a *damn* big land.

Despite Edna Ferber's implication to the contrary, there are many respectably-come-by mink coats in Fairbanks and considerably more in larger Anchorage (although the parka is more suitable winter garb). Lilly Daché hats and Irene gowns are sold in both towns— and to prove that this fringe of luxurious insanity is no latter-day innovation, Klondike Kate wore a Worth gown brought from Paris at Dawson's St. Andrew's Day Ball back in 1900—and every gentleman with her in the extant photograph wore tails, except one who came black tie deliberately or was a waiter. And Dawson, fifty miles or so across the line in Canada's Yukon Territory, is a bare 128 miles south of the Arctic Circle.

Alaska is a solidly, stubbornly, prideful American land. You can live and work there in reasonable comfort the year around—despite the mere two hours of summer darkness and the scant two hours of winter daylight.

There is no Skid Row in any Alaskan town. With seasonal employment a condition of life, some Alaskans plan their living better than others, thus live more comfortably in the slack winter season. Some have more, some less—but there are few bums; it is not an environment in which a bum can survive.

Newcomers have difficulty adjusting to the high costs of food, clothing and rent; but wages are high, too, and it isn't long before a balance is struck. Then life settles into a routine much like that in any small town Stateside. There are Scout troops, Cub packs, the Y.M.C.A., bridge clubs, cocktail parties, lodges, luncheon clubs and country clubs of sorts.

The first winter can be a morale hazard if you make it one. Children go to school in darkness and return in darkness. But again, in compensation, the sun is still shining in summer when you come out of the night picture show.

Alaskans work hard, on a seasonal schedule; they are imbued consciously or unconsciously with the challenge of their vast land. They marry young, raise large families and their children for the most part remain in Alaska.

There is a cheerful get-rich-quick flavor to life that seldom pays off; it probably persists from the gold-rush days which never paid off either. This may be due to the absence of huge corporations to dominate commerce and mold organization men. A young Alaskan will get a local job—but he usually keeps one hand free for himself. He fishes and hunts as a routine of life and, as a further routine, he eternally casts about for an opportunity to go into business for himself —however modestly. He has an extremely self-confident and independent character. You cannot be otherwise in the eternal grandeur of this vast land.

There have long been two schools of thought in Alaska about statehood—for and against. The "Fors" wanted their destiny in their own hands, regardless of the taxes needed to support a state. They wanted to be rid of territorial status, to pass their own laws to govern their living—for there is a Great Dream in Alaska, and it can come true only if the individual is untrammeled by Federal paternalism.

The "Againsts" were acutely conscious that the permanent population of Alaska is small and they believed that the economic health was due in great part to the vast military and naval installations. They wanted no curtailment in the largess of Uncle Sam. They saw financial ruin in statehood.

The "Fors" wanted statehood now. The "Againsts" wanted it too— but after a while. Now that the die has been cast, however, most Alaskans seem gratified. They have attained voting representation at last—as a balance to their taxation. Statehood is American—no matter what it costs.

Now that Alaska is a state, it is experiencing a great influx of visitors. There is no Hilton Hotel yet in Alaska and no Forum of the Twelve Caesars to dine in, but if you write for summer-travel information, you'll get enough material on off-trail sights—natural wonders, totem poles, fish, moose, bear and Mount McKinley—to top seven pounds on the bathroom scales. For to Alaska tourism is an essential industry highly organized by the Alaska Visitors Association.

From June to September you can travel Alaska's tenuous net of paint-shy, neon-lighted towns by your own car, hitchhiker's thumb, bus, boat, train or any of a dozen airlines in a reasonable expectancy of comfort. In winter, hitchhiking will freeze your thumb stiff, and the waterways are iced in, but with foresight and respect for weather, travel is not entirely restricted.

There will be a virile echo of the raw frontier in this Alaskan junket, a sense perhaps of the latent sacrifice that has always attended the March of Empire, a feeling that the Donner Passes and the Death Valleys that have been long forgotten Stateside are still nebulously just around the corner in Alaska, in a grandsire's living memory.

Before you reach Ketchikan on the Inside Passage, there is the rusted wreck of the steamer *North Sea* on the easterly shore a few miles north of the Indian Village of Bella Bella. She went down in 1947—with no loss of life. In Juneau, at the Museum, there are two water-stained life rings of the *Princess Sophia*. She sank above Juneau in 1918—and there were no survivors. The North Country can be a hard country.

Ketchikan is the first port of call on the Inside Passage, and there the frontier forthrightness strikes you abruptly in a hand-lettered sign: "No dogs. No drunks allowed." This is not tourist stuff. The proprietor means it. It bears the indelible mark of anger—of long-suffering patience exhausted at last. You *feel* for the man who lettered that sign.

The average age of the Alaskan today is twenty-seven, which in all sports—including the challenging one of making a new country—is about the peak championship age. Bred in Alaska, in many instances for three generations, his grandfather knew the '98 Gold Rush. His father knew the lean years after 1918—and his children find the houses too big when they visit the older States, and the waters too warm for good swimming. "Outside" for a few weeks, they want to go home—to the snow-capped mountains, the salmon, the fast, trout-thick creeks, the bear and moose in the broad and empty reaches of the Big Land—a land that has already grown its own vital people.

There is the natural friendliness of youth in the Alaskan. It is innate to his character that he offers himself and accepts you without guile. He passes you from town to town to his friends and neighbors. Alaska is the biggest small town in the world. Trump your partner's ace on Monday in Petersburg and it's known—by mukluk telegraph—in Kotzebue on Tuesday.

Its Main Street is only four blocks long—Southeast Alaska, the Interior, the Arctic and "Westward"—which ends at the tip of the Aleutian Islands, close against Asia. This Main Street, though, has a cultural texture that could give a scholar a lifetime of research.

Aboriginally, there are the ancient Indian tribes of Southeast Alaska and the offshore islands that shelter the Inside Passage. There are the Eskimos of the northern Arctic rim. There are the Aleuts (give that three syllables, please), an Eskimo stock differing from the Arctic Eskimo in head shape and in development of basic language, with their culture adapted to a raw, wet climate rather than to subzero cold. The islands of the Aleuts curve under Siberia—almost to Kamchatka.

In hill-sprawled, jumbled Juneau—named for Joe Juneau who discovered gold there in 1880—it is easy to go back the first ninety-two years of American Alaska's culture. You can do it in conversation with the curator of the Museum—or academically with the records and exhibits kept under his helpful and scholarly hand. Or you can climb up to Ruth Allman's house and cover the subject informally over sourdough waffles and Russian tea. Ruth's house hangs on the hillside with most of Juneau below, framed by the bow windows in which Judge James Wickersham's old desk and chair still sit. Her stepfather, James Wickersham, was a United States District judge in Alaska from 1900 to 1908—often as not riding circuit by dog team— and thereafter delegate to Congress from Alaska for fourteen years. He introduced the first statehood bill in 1916—forty-two years before final passage. He was the moving spirit in the founding of the University of Alaska. His old house is a pleasant home still and a repository crammed with mementos of his service to Alaska—including a five-foot shelf of his personal diaries.

In the judge's files, there is a photostat of a document that had long been mislaid in Washington, and which the judge finally located when he was a delegate: "To the Treasurer of the United States, greeting. Pay to Edward de Stoekle, Envoy Extraordinary and Minister Plenipotentiary of His Majesty the Emperor of Russia, or order, out of the appropriation named in the margin—Seven million, two hundred thousand dollars, being in consideration of certain territory ceded by the Emperor of Russia to the United States as described in treaty of 30th March 1867." That Warrant, Number 9759, made Alaska a part of the United States at a price of about two cents an acre. A right smart real-estate deal.

Item—from Ruth Allman's conversation: "To make a 'starter' for sourdough cakes," says Ruth, "you boil a few potatoes pretty much away and put the residue in a jar until it ferments. This you carry with you on the trail for the rest of your life.

"You next stir a pinch of soda in a shot glass of water and you stir it with your left little finger as a matter of tradition because that finger is usually cleaner than the others and there were few spoons in the Yukon in Ninety-eight. Add this to a flour-and-water mix laced from your 'starter' and whop it up fast. As you whop it you can hear the batter thicken, for what you are actually going to eat when sour-dough cakes are baked is fifty per cent hot air."

In Juneau the people jump to the fire siren faster than in any other town in the world, for the heterogeneous, closely packed, well-weathered buildings are mostly of wood, and the hill funnel in which the town is built can become a roaring chimney if the wind is right. The engine sirens begin with the first sick-cow bellow of the fire alarm, which faintly echoes the urgency of London air-raid warnings during the blitz.

Behind Juneau are the upper workings of the now-idle Alaska Juneau Mine—at one time the biggest gold-mining operation in the world. You can walk through the entire mountain to the water-hung outer workings you first saw from the steamer. It's possible to take sharp photographs in Juneau at half past nine of a summer's night and play baseball by daylight until almost eleven—and if you want a frontier echo after dark, there is the galloping Red Dog Saloon. You will probably eat your first grilled king-salmon steak in Alaska at Mike's, across the bridge in Douglas, and you will never forget its succulence.

You can drive up to Alaska over the Alaska Highway, once called the Alcan, as you can drive through much of interior Alaska. From Canada the Haines Cut-Off connects over the mountains to Haines, where a car ferry with Florida, New Jersey, Alabama, Colorado and other remote license plates carries your car into Juneau.

The Alaska Highway is not a hard-surface road, and in the dry season it is dusty. It is a long road and, if you are easily bored, monotonous. There are, however, gas stations, repair shops and mo-tels every fifty miles or so—and your face will be exceedingly red if, before you started, you were talked into buying do-it-yourself repair kits, extra fan belts and a spare battery, four spare tires and two five-gallon cans of extra gasoline.

Every hundred miles or so in the Yukon Territory there are camping points with water, cooking facilities, trailer courts and a cottage for emergency shelter. Ambulance, nursing and medical service are supplied by the Canadian Army. The Royal Canadian Mounted Police patrols the highway in Canada. The Alaskan Police patrols it in Alaska. There may be a detour or two, and in the dry season forest fires, but you will see retired couples traveling the highway in expensive sedans, women driving it alone, families with children touring in station wagons, and tourists bussing it by scheduled bus.

From Vancouver to Fairbanks, Alaska, it is about 2300 miles of almost breathlessly beautiful country. It is not U.S. 66, and you won't find heated swimming pools at the motels, but there always will be hot water for a bath, and on occasion excellent food and service—and you will have had a safe adventure the like of which is not offered to you anywhere else in the world at this late date.

In Juneau we have pecked lightly at Alaska's nearly one hundred years of American culture. Let us go farther back. Fifty minutes of bush-pilot flying time, westerly beyond the Inside Passage to the open North Pacific Ocean, will land you in Sitka—the old Imperial Russian capital of Alaska. The first Russian governor was Alexandr Baranov. His castle is gone and so is the Russian fort—all but some miscellaneous smooth-bore artillery—but the line of the palisades can still be traced with the help of the National Park Service. The inscriptions on some of the Russian graves are still legible, and more tangibly, there is no telephone book in the towns of Alaska that does not carry some Russian names to this day, many of them American descendants of the Tsar's traders and military. M. L. "Duke" Mitrovich was the mayor of Sitka when I was there and Mrs. Margaret Federoff his very competent city clerk. If you fancy carved wood and inlay work, you know her husband's bowls, table tops and candle holders—even if you have never been farther west than Madison Avenue, New York.

Sitka was founded in 1799 as New Archangelsk, but it was not until 1816 that Father Alexis Sokoloff arrived with an icon of the Archangel Michael and converted the Russian-Orthodox chapel into a church. St. Michael's Cathedral is the direct descendant of that original chapel. Regular services are still held there. It is a log structure, clapboarded outside and lined inside with painted canvas, and if you make a modest altar donation, you will be permitted to inspect the interior.

Inside, you will see the Chapel of Our Lady of Kazan, the Chapel of St. Michael and the Chapel of St. John the Baptist—each with its painted icons embellished magnificently with silver-gilt *repoussé* work, appliquéd to the iconostas, which is the wall that closes off the sanctuary into which no woman may pass. The book of the four Gospels which is used at St. Michael's only at Easter and Christmas is so heavy with silver decoration that it weighs more than twenty-five pounds.

In the National Military Cemetery, at Sitka, the runner, Captain Charles William Paddock, USMC, is buried, the onetime "fastest human," who died in a plane crash during World War II. Not far from his grave lies Lieutenant B. W. Livermore, 2nd U. S. Artillery, said to have been killed in a duel on June 30, 1868—with a whisper to this day that the cause was a woman—to be more precise, a Russian princess, or in the vernacular of the times, a squaw.

The transfer of Alaska from Russian to United States sovereignty took place in Sitka; the Army withdrew in 1877 and then the United States Navy took over.

A Presbyterian missionary named Fannie Kellogg started a school for Indian children, and a United States Naval officer became the first truant officer. Some time during each school day the officer turned up in Miss Fannie's classroom. If the full quota of children was not present from each house, he imposed a five-blanket fine for each absent child.

How much that was in dollars in 1880 is hard to say, but a Thlinget (pronounced Klinket) blanket today is worth as much as a thousand dollars and more. Truancy, therefore, decelerated to zero. (No one remembers what the Navy did with the blankets.)

Close by the flagpole across from the Federal Building are two stone slabs that bear petroglyphs from the deep mists of antiquity—stones marked by a people of whom the Sitka Thlinget Indians have no knowledge in song or legend. All they know is that the marks were made by people who lived in the Big Land long before they themselves came—and the Thlingets have forgotten how many centuries *they* have been there.

They have not forgotten, however, that on the beach outside Sitka, more than a hundred and fifty years ago, they once beat the caviar out of the Russians (the Sitka National Monument marks the spot)—and if the Russians should come back they will do it again at the drop of a Thlinget ceremonial dance hat.

I cannot leave Sitka without mentioning the eating place that was run by Bill Shields when I was there. We had a mess of shrimp and a fillet of grilled sockeye salmon that were so delicious we almost ate ourselves into a delightful decline. A night's sleep, however, and the palate was ready for cold, cracked Dungeness crab at the Bills Club in Haines, which you reach by a fifty-minute bush-pilot flight north.

This country between Juneau and Haines—a mountain-girt land free from the distractions of the outside world—is as beautiful as any on earth.

The air is invigorating; you need no tranquilizers. Snow never leaves these bald mountaintops, nor do the mountain sheep and goats. There are brown, black and grizzly bear in the timber and a profusion of moose in the flatlands, and fish swim thick in the waters.

Alaska is in the glacier business. The Mendenhall outside of Juneau is a must for visitors, and near Haines is the equally dramatic Davidson, and the high-hung Rainbow. Little more than thirty years ago the Rainbow reached down to the waters of the Chilkat; now it nestles along the upper slopes, a kaleidoscope of color when the sun strikes it—and a roar of ice-spewing thunder when it stirs. When there is an earthquake in this country, the mountains dance to the glory of God. They smoke from base to summit with the saffron dust of tumbling rocks and there is an awesome grandeur to the spectacle.

The first permanent Army post in Alaska—Fort William H. Seward, sometimes called Chilkoot Barracks—was established near Haines, in 1898. At one time it was garrisoned by the Second Battalion of my old Regiment, the 16th Infantry, and it was commanded around 1912 by an old Army character who appears in special orders merely as Colonel Gardener. To eke out a much lower pay scale than the Army enjoys today, Colonel Gardener would make a weekly round of the Haines bars, ostensibly on duty checks, but actually to empty into his tobacco pouch the clipped ends from the permanently installed cigar clippers of the day; they supplied his pipe tobacco for the following week. I rather like that homely touch.

"Fiji" Carl Heinmiller—who left an eye and part of a hand in the South Pacific when he fought the Japanese War for a shirtful of medals—and four other World War II veterans purchased Fort Seward from the War Assets Administration in 1946. It is now the town of Port Chilkoot, and Carl is the mayor and the activating spirit of Alaska Youth, Inc. This organization supplies summer jobs for teen-agers, offers craft and trade instruction and has developed

Chilkat Thlinget Indian dancing—done by Explorer Scouts and Explorettes—into a decidedly worth-while cultural attraction.

Since the older Indians no longer dance and the tribal teen-agers regard ceremonial as distinctly old headdress, Port Chilkoot is now the only place in Alaska where you may regularly see these ancient dances. They are as authentic as the midnight sun, for tribal elders have painstakingly coached the youngsters, in many of whom the tribal blood still flows.

If big-game hunting lures you to Alaska you need base no farther north than Haines or Port Chilkoot; the Chilkat River's upper reaches offer bear, moose and mountain sheep and goat in abundance. It was near here, a few years ago, that Forrest Young was mauled by a giant grizzly—chewed from head to foot, with his lungs exposed, one of his ribs torn completely out and two ripped loose. He survived, and enjoys life today, thoroughly.

If you hunt with a camera, this same Forrest Young will take you to Mosquito Lake in his air boat; you can flush moose in the flats and chase them at twenty-five miles an hour while your camera purrs from thirty yards away—until their not-too-nimble brains prompt them to crash to cover. You need no license for this sport.

Or you can photograph mountain goat from a chartered sport plane. You spot a flock and then bank over and flap down, and, if the wind is right, hover. They start then, with the kids scampering after their rapidly curdling suppers. Then you dive after them, leaving the goats with the conviction that the Chilkat eagles suddenly have grown very large and noisy.

Alaska is such a youthfully challenging country that it seems somehow incongruous that the average age of its tourists is around sixty. It would appear that young America should accept this challenge, as it has met the challenge of other frontiers, for this is a young man's land.

At Port Chilkoot, if you are tired of high-priced real estate, you can still buy an Army-built two-family house on a 60-by-170-foot lot for $6000, rent half and hunt and fish for the rest of your life. Or you can buy a barracks building that once housed two infantry companies, if you have a large family, as most Alaskans do. If you like strawberries, the Haines variety (the Festival is in early July) often grows so large that one will fill a coffee cup—and still maintain its delicate sweetness.

At the Thlinget village of Klukwan, a few miles north of Haines, you can watch old Dan Katzeek, chief of the Killer Whale Fin tribe, work on his dugout canoe. This is no tourist act; Dan needs a new canoe. Two of his adzes are Russian trade goods that date back to the time the Killer Whales helped beat the Russians on the Chilkat—but his axes are strictly Sears Roebuck. It takes him two to three months from the felling of the cottonwood log. Pared to an inch in thickness, baked in the sun in the oldest manner, thinned and soaked, the cottonwood shell stretches almost like hide.

The old legends still prevail around Port Chilkoot and Haines. Martin Madsen was in the gold stampede of '98, and Steve Sheldon —who smokes his after-breakfast pipe on the Hotel Hälsingland's veranda—knew Rex Beach. ("Nice fellow who wrote some pretty far-fetched stuff.") He once met Jack London, and understood he was a pretty nice fellow too. ("Drank a bit, however.")

We have walked the length of the first block of Alaska's Main Street, for even though Skagway—about eighteen miles above Haines —is still a part of Southeast Alaska, it belongs immortally to the Yukon and the Klondike. Skagway and nearby Dyea were the ports of entry for the '98 Gold Rush.

They will tell you that Skagway is a ghost town—but if it is, its ghosts are wonderful. At the Pack Train Inn you can drink a mug of ale with the shades of Alex Pantages, Philadelphia Jack O'Brien, Tex Rickard and (according to the sign) Robert E. Service (although I always thought he was Robert W. because his middle name was William when he was a bank clerk in Dawson), and you can hear the echo of the shot that killed Soapy Smith, the gambler who fleeced the gold stampeders.

Judge Wickersham in his book, *Old Yukon,* says that Frank Reid, the vigilante, fired four shots and Soapy fired four shots; but Mary Pullen Kopanskí—who will show you the old Pullen Hotel where President Harding stopped in Skagway, and her grandmother's museum—tells an eyewitness version of the yarn, because her grandmother, Harriet Pullen, was so close she almost got hit. Frank misfired first, and Soapy shot him. Then Frank, still on his feet, smoked one into Soapy and Soapy was dead before he hit the ground. Frank lived eight days after he fell. One of Soapy's hand guns, with two notches, is in the Pullen Museum, as are his roulette, faro and crap tables. Las Vegas would do well to send up to Mary for the design of that crap table. Kidney-shaped and bowled, it swings the dice around almost 180 degrees for a sweet run.

When a shipload of tourists arrives at the Skagway terminal of the Inside Passage almost the whole town puts on the "Days of Ninety-Eight" show. For a dollar admission you get a hundred dollars in stage money to gamble with. Top winner gets a prize.

Townsfolk play all the old '98 characters; they have acted the parts so long they are almost professionals—especially the cancan girls, theatrically speaking, that is. Dance with the "wrong 'uns" and you are mock-tried by kangaroo court. The show's finale is the "Shooting of Dan McGrew"—acted out in detail—then the whole cast goes down and sees the ship off, with community singing.

In Skagway, at Kirmse's Curio Shop, you can hold Pat Renwick's watch chain in your hand. It is made of huge, linked gold nuggets—the largest nugget watch chain of record—and it weighs more than three pounds. Pat was a gambler and he hocked that chain so many times during the gold rush that H. D. Kirmse, who made the chain, used to keep two thousand in cash in his safe in case Pat came in. In a single day, Pat hocked and redeemed it three times.

A hundred thousand men, along with many women and children, hit the gold trail of '98 (there had been only 200 white men in all of Alaska thirteen years before) and the bulk of them landed at Skagway or nearby Dyea. From Dyea they packed on foot over the murderous Chilkoot Pass into the Yukon. From Skagway they packed over the White Pass.

J. C. (Jack) Hoyt, the superintendent of the narrow-gauge White Pass and Yukon Railroad, had read a book I wrote years ago and because he still remembered it vividly, he gave me the courtesy of his line and a seat in the engineer's cab to go over White Pass.

This, my masters, is a trip; if you haven't made it, you haven't lived. Diesel electrics pull the long train with a "helper" engine midway in the string of cars. Hairpinning up through the high pass, it takes two hours to go the first twenty miles. A grouse sat the tracks until the engine's snow scoop was five feet away, then it walked off in contempt. The day before, they told me, it was a brown bear cub. In places, you can look straight down from the cab window—several hundred feet. In the first twenty-one miles, on grades as steep as 4 per cent, the train climbs 2885 feet up mountains of almost solid rock—paralleling the Trail of '98. Joe Sheleby, an old 7th Cavalryman, was the engineer, which was comforting, for that throttle is no place for a fancy-pants soldier. The train runs almost every day winter and summer, taking supplies in and ore out, and has been derailed a number of times by weather as the marks on the ties attest, but no passenger has been lost in a wreck, though two cars were once actually blown off the track by high winds.

Six hours and a hundred and ten miles later, after passing out of Alaska into British Columbia and out of British Columbia into Canada's Yukon Territory, you are in Whitehorse, on the Alaska Highway—the land of the ptarmigan and the devilish wolverine, of the giant rainbow trout, the Great Northern pike, the lake trout and the twenty-pound arctic char, of the elk, the caribou, the bear and the convolute-horned mountain sheep. (If you want any of these, call Mike Nolan at Marsh Lake Lodge—an ex-R.C.M.P. sergeant turned guide.)

Sam McGee's cabin is in Whitehorse. You are twenty-five miles from "the marge of Lake Labarge" and just a step from tailors, dry cleaners, good inns, taxi stands and a branch of Toronto's Eaton's department store. Whitehorse is Canadian, with the deep monarchic tradition which republican America never seems quite to understand; but it is still linked closely with Alaska, for the Yukon races by the White Pass and Yukon Railroad station to its confluence with the Klondike and both territories were opened by gold. Bill McBride's museum holds the mementos of the gold-rush days and Bill is still around to tell you the story.

From Whitehorse's International Airport you can fly the second block of Main Street—to Fairbanks, in interior Alaska. You do this in a little more than two hours, passing slightly north of the village of Snag, where the lowest temperature ever recorded in North America—minus 81°—was clocked in 1947.

Fairbanks is an authentic deep-Alaska town, for it, too, started with gold—from 1902 until about 1917 every store in town had a scale to weigh gold dust against purchases. Miners' log cabins, still lived in, dot the business streets. The United States Smelting, Refining and Mining Company still mines gold in the Fairbanks area; but it is dug by multimillion-dollar dredges from the frozen ground, sold by law only to the Government, which immediately puts it back underground at Fort Knox.

There is a Mode-O-Day dress shop in Fairbanks and apartments and modern business buildings. There are flower shops and the

Travelers Inn—as comfortable a motel as you would want. Or you can sleep aboard the old stern-wheeler *Nenana*, which used to make the run to Fort Yukon, but is now a boatel.

It is risky to give the population of any Alaskan town, for people come and go continually, but we might guess Fairbanks at between 15,000 and 20,000. There's no guesswork, however, about Fairbanks' having the highest cost of living of any community under the American flag; that's supported by Government figures. When I was there beer cost seventy-five cents a can and a haircut $2.50. Cigarettes were thirty-five cents and Coca-Cola twenty cents. A taxi ride that would be eighty cents outside cost two dollars. There is no greedy attempt at the deep gouge, in any of this. They charge steeply because they must pay steeply. Freight rates to Fairbanks are high because of distance. Labor costs are heavy because there are only 120 outdoor working days a year. They have to make a living but they'll give you their shirts if they like you—and they like everyone who likes them—*and they are extremely likable people*.

Only an hour and six minutes by Russian jet bomber from the nearest Siberian Base, the ladies of Fairbanks do not sleep in terror of invasion, with guns under their pillows, as one opportunist correspondent reported. The attitude of interior Alaskans is expressed by a red card you see in stores: "In the event of atomic attack, be calm, complete your purchase, pay your bill—then run like hell!"

All the short-run, scheduled-airline, small-aircraft pilots in Alaska call themselves bush pilots—and proudly, for their safety record is exemplary. Originally there were three leading bush pilots in the Fairbanks area—Noel Wien, Joe Crosson and Ben Eielson—and to them go the laurels for opening interior Alaska to air travel. They blazed the trails. Eielson Air Force Base and the aeronautical engineering building at the University in which the Alaskan Museum is located are named for Ben. Joe Crosson brought back the bodies of Will Rogers and Wiley Post from their crash at Point Barrow; his memorial stands in Fairbanks. Noel Wien's Airline—with Noel occasionally at the C-46 controls—makes it possible for your Aunt Emma to get to Nome and Kotzebue and Point Barrow on the Arctic almost as easily as she gets downtown to shop.

Arctic Alaska is the comparatively small strip along the Bering Sea and the Arctic Ocean that gave the forty-ninth state its "outside" trade-mark of the igloo. The word means house but the Eskimo's permanent home is not of ice. It is a fairly large skin-and-driftwood shelter tunneled into from beneath. Or it can be a cottage, or a Nissen hut, or an apartment in Fairbanks, depending on his job. He builds small igloos of ice blocks only when hunting far from home. He is a pleasant, round-faced person with the ready, incandescent smile of the Himalayan Gurkha—and a capacity for technical education that, in the opinion of Air Force officers, could eventually qualify him to handle any specialized job on the installations of the D.E.W. Line. He has inherited a flair for tools and engines from his Oriental ancestors who, thousands of years ago, probably helped invent the wheel.

He has been reviled in the past for his "barbarity" in leaving his old folks in provisional ice igloos when hunting was bad. But to him it was not barbarism. It was for the good of the greater number; the handicapped being left so the others could go on and survive. He has been reviled, too, for polygamy; but this again was self-preservation. In mid-June and July he goes after whale. Last year some Point Barrow hunters were caught on rotten shore ice with an offshore wind; they were saved, but in years gone all the men of a village have been lost. So polygamy was a matter of survival too.

Of all the original people of Alaska, the Eskimos cling most tenaciously to their tribal customs and their language—probably because their race memory is deeper. They have held precariously to life along the Arctic and Bering Sea littorals for centuries, sustaining themselves on game, fish, berries and roots, and the transition to modern dietary habits at first caused a high incidence of previously unknown diseases—especially tuberculosis. But medical science came with the change of diet and soon brought things into balance.

There is an unfathomable plasticity to the Eskimo mind that is probably the fundamental ingredient of his survival. He adapts. A product of primitive tribal government since the beginning of known history, he was amenable to the overlay of democratic concepts. Early in territorial history he began to sit in the Legislature, so that his place was firmly established when Alaska became the forty-ninth state. He *is* the Alaska National Guard—organized in Scout Battalions with modern light weapons—and he knows how to handle modern heavy equipment. Eskimo teen-age girls look more at home in sweaters, nylons and high heels than Indian girls do.

At Point Barrow, a two-day or a three-day packaged air tour from Fairbanks in July will give you a chance to witness the Nulikatuk, that celebration of a successful whale hunt which is supposed to appease the whale spirits so that there may be a successful hunt next year. It's a time of laughter and roughhousing. Take a sweater.

The Eskimo from time immemorial has made tools and weapons of walrus-tusk ivory and the whale-bone of long-gone corset days—his only durable materials. Then the traders got after him to turn out tourist catchalls, and today the shops are full of all sorts of ivory gewgaws that the Eskimo himself never uses.

Nome, which is only about 130 miles from the nearest point in the U.S.S.R., and is not connected by road or railroad to the rest of Alaska, boasts the oldest newspaper in Alaska—the Nome *Nugget*. The latest movie hit was showing at the Nomerama, from whose door you can pitch a stone into the Bering Sea. The current crop of TV sagas were on KNOM-TV—canned. At the Polaris Dining Room you can try a charcoal-broiled reindeer steak. To get a cab, call Main 170—a soda, go to the Glue Pot fountain—a Martini, the Bering Sea Club.

Come back from the Arctic to Fairbanks and look in on the University of Alaska. Judge James Wickersham, after years of selling the project to Congress, laid the cornerstone in 1915. It was originally an Agricultural School and a School of Mines, but has expanded its courses into Arts and Letters, Biological Science, Business Administration, Chemical, Civil and Electrical Engineering, Education and Geophysics—with graduate work in most of them. The summer-school students may make an air trip over the North Pole which is almost as painless as going out to Montauk, Long Island, from Columbia University in New York.

In interior Alaska, around Fairbanks and Anchorage—eight hours south of Fairbanks by train—you pick up the huge installations of the Armed Services. Eielson and Ladd Air Force Bases near Fairbanks, Fort Richardson and Elmendorf Air Force Bases near Anchorage. These are huge, self-contained military cities, the nuclei of the outer line of defense for the entire continent. Here the line is held along the entire westerly and northerly front of the Cold War. Daylight or dark, winter and summer, defensive air patrols are maintained. Our pilots see the red-starred planes patrolling their side. A thin line of dynamic alertness lies between the two—vast sinews of retaliation tense and readied.

Anchorage is much larger than Fairbanks—but it started as a camp for the construction of the Alaska Railroad, so the aristocratic gold-grubbing tradition does not cling to it. The frontier feeling does, however. There are forty-four bars on Fourth Street, the main drag.

Anchorage has log cabins that are still lived in and two of them stand in the shadow of the fourteen-story Mount McKinley Building. If you want Jack London texture surge into the Cheechako Bar on Fourth Street, just a short step from the svelte Chart Room of the Westward Hotel.

There are smart dress shops and it is a growing town of new apartment houses and housing developments. Drive through Turn-again-by-the-Sea and you might well be in a new California subdivision, except that the ranch houses are smaller for the $30,000 or $50,000 they bring. Smaller, therefore easier to heat against the deep-freeze of winter.

You can drive from anywhere in the United States to Anchorage, by way of Fairbanks. The road roughly parallels the railroad, through the beautiful Mount McKinley country. The Department of the Interior runs the railroad.

In Anchorage you are two hours by air from Kodiak Island, the United States Navy and those Big Bear. They weigh considerably over half a ton and the pelt cures to more than eleven by ten feet. A hundred and twenty-seven pounds of rug, without the head. Call Alf Madsen—and if he's not home he's at Karluk Lake after bear. Alf is in his thirty-eighth year of guiding with no client hurt beyond a mosquito bite—and fourteen-year-old boys have killed their bears under his competent hand.

Donnelley and Acheson in the town of Kodiak is the oldest store in Alaska. Only the Spanish missions outdate it in point of outlander establishment along the American Pacific littoral. It has been at its present location since 1796. You can buy anything there from a Cadillac to a package of chewing gum.

Up the street is the B and B Bar, the seventeenth-oldest licensed bar in Alaska, which is like holding a low-numbered *Fédération Aeronautique Internationale* flying license, for there are as many bars in Alaska as there are lakes on the Kenai Peninsula—or mosquitoes in summer.

Off Kodiak Island the halibut weigh hundreds of pounds, delectable king crab measure six feet across, salmon are thick in season and the Dolly Varden trout follows them upstream to feed on their eggs. The green of Kodiak is as brightly iridescent as in Ireland and Scotland. It shines wet green even at night.

The Navy's Alaskan Sea Frontier—the utterly last frontier in America—stretches down the Aleutians to hang under Asia. This is the last block on Alaska's Main Street. Here are the tiny fishing towns of the beckoning names—Dutch Harbor and Scotch Cap, Ouzinkie, Halibut Bay, Kanatak, False Pass, Squaw Harbor and Unga—down to Adak, which again is Navy and the only installation west of Kodiak that approaches the dimension of civilization, with good docking, good housing, good food, four-engined strips and the finest harbor in the Aleutians. There is no bear or moose or reindeer at Adak, but the Marines have put a caribou herd out to breed. Lonely and isolated under a not unusual seventy-knot wind, and the williwaw that blows 125 knots on occasion, Adak is the farthest western reach of the tangible sovereign dignity of the United States, but children are born here, men work here and this *is* the United States—under the new 49th star.

A Big Land, my masters, which is what Alaska has been called in the language of its older people since long before Christ. The *Main Land* as opposed to the islands that fringe its coast, hence the *Big Land* as opposed to the smaller land of the islands—for that is what the word Alaska means.

awaii

by FRANK J. TAYLOR

It's another Hawaii today—this new state—no longer the drowsing and glamorous tropical haven remembered so nostalgically by travelers of past years; different also from the booming, money-mad military outpost on which a million soldiers, sailors, airmen, Wacs and Waves waste no love. In the years since the end of the war the Islanders have performed a near miracle in removing the shambles —barbed wire on beaches, mountains of military junk, miles of drab barracks. But they have not been able to work the miracle of recapturing the prewar Arcadia of the travel folders, and probably never will be.

"I'm selling out and moving to Samoa or some place where civilization hasn't regimented life," one of Hawaii's unhappy *kamaainas* declared, as we gazed out the plate-glass window of her living room at Honolulu, Pearl Harbor, and the blue Pacific with the pastel peaks of Oahu in the distance, a truly breath-taking scene. "The *malihinis* have ruined the old Hawaii forever."

Kamaainas are the old-timers, "children of the soil," in the mellifluous tongue of the native Hawaiians. *Malihinis* are newcomers, the "strangers."

Throughout the Islands, the *kamaainas* mourn the passing of the white-man's paradise, the Hawaii that faded into memory with the war. But the new conquerors of the Islands—*malihinis* and native workers—want no going back—believe they are going forward to a better, common-people's Hawaii with the fiftieth star in the American flag.

Despite the *kamaainas'* complaint, Hawaii is still much the same physically—a beautiful semitropic archipelago of eight main islands 2400 miles southwest of San Francisco. All together, they're about the size of Connecticut and Rhode Island combined, and they're populated by over a half a million people. Hawaii, called by natives the Big Island, is at the southeastern end of the chain and is larger than all of the other islands together. Maui, second largest of the group and having some of the most important plantations, is northwest of the Big Island and is flanked by three smaller islands: Kahoolawe, on the southwest; Lanai, on the west; and Molokai, on the northwest. Oahu, third largest island, is roughly thirty miles northwest of Molokai, and is the richest and most densely populated, with the city of Honolulu. Kauai, called the Garden Island, is still farther to the northwest, and across a channel from Kauai is the mystery island of Niihau, farthest west of the main Hawaiian Islands. Beyond, for about a thousand miles to the northwest, stretches a chain of uninhabited lava and coral islets which were set apart by President Theodore Roosevelt in 1909 as the Hawaiian Islands Bird Reservation.

To the tourist's eye, the Hawaiian archipelago still looks like an unparalleled spot to spend a vacation or a lifetime. To appreciate the *kamaainas'* lament, you have to consider the violent social upheaval wrought by the war in the Islands. The day before Pearl Harbor, Hawaii was a paternalistic, almost feudal, pastoral realm; the day after, it was a human beehive in state of siege, with all civil rights ignored by the military autocracy. Emerging after V-J Day, the Islanders heaved paternalism out the window, adopted collective bargaining, hiked wages to near-mainland standards regardless of the shade of the worker's color, and saw the pendulum of power swing from the big employers to flushed union leaders. Nurses, clerks, cooks, laundresses and employees of 150 industries pinned on buttons of the International Longshoremen and Warehousemen's Union. Because Hawaii depends upon shipping for food, fuel, clothing and supplies, the CIO-ILWU became the big voice in the Islands. Now the pendulum is swinging back part way.

Hawaiians have been trying to digest in one gulp reforms that normally would take a lifetime. They have economic, social and political stomach-aches, but things may not be so bad as the *kamaainas* fear. There is still a lot of *aloha* awaiting the visitor to these perpetually summertime shores. The eight Hawaiian isles still loll in the same sparkling sunshine, are still cooled by the same soft northeasterly trade winds as before. The white clouds still hitchhike across the Pacific on these same gentle winds and drop their life-giving moisture upon contact with Hawaii's steep peaks. You can still push up through the clouds on the road to Haleakala Crater on the island of Maui and see this rain in the making, or you can watch the fascinating meteorological show on a still grander scale from an inter-island plane.

From these vantage points, a glance will reveal why the larger islands are lush and jungle-clothed on the windward slopes; parched and semidesert on the lee side, which gets only the moisture leavings. On the windward side of the Nuuanu Pali, a startlingly steep pass in Oahu's mountains, where on occasions you may toss a penny to the winds and have it blown back to your hands, these same winds may whip up a cloudburst in ten minutes, while back of you in protected Honolulu seven miles away the sun is burning brightly. Frequently in Honolulu you can cross the street and step from rain to sunbeams, so localized is Hawaii's "liquid sunshine."

The big news for you, if you are holiday-bent, is that, though the man-made geography of the islands has been somewhat transformed with the dredging of airfields, naval bases, terminals and building sites from the ocean, Honolulu's weather is unchanged. The average temperature is still 74.6° F. and there is only 6.5° difference between summer and winter, which adds up to the fact that here is the most equable and enjoyable climate on the globe for avoiding work. It's not too humid, not too dry. The trees and vines still bloom the year around, the lei makers still string flowers by their gas-lighted carts. Every little girl has a hibiscus in her hair, and the little boys still dive for quarters as your ship docks or sails, but let dimes sink to the bottom. The coconut palms still shimmer in the moonlight, you can still dance under the stars, and the sun tan you pick up in January is just as brown as July's.

The isles of the archipelago are just as different from one another as they were before the war, and some of them still offer you chunks of old Hawaii. Somewhere on the Islands the traveler with gumption and sense enough to evade the Honolulu-Waikiki merry-go-round may find almost anything he seeks, from a 13,000-foot ski slide to a fishing village whose easygoing Polynesian inhabitants live almost as primitively as did their ancestors in 1778 when Captain Cook first stumbled upon the Hawaiian group and named it the Sandwich Islands after his patron, the Earl of Sandwich.

You have to go out and find the real Hawaii; it won't come to you at the Royal Hawaiian Hotel. Too many visitors discover this too late. By the time they arrive on Oahu, the *aloha* or welcoming isle, where everyone first sets foot either from plane or steamer, they are tied by the American Plan or other commitments to Waikiki, a Coney Island-like mile-long assembly of littered beach, hotels, restaurants and shops, pathetically less glamorous in reality than in song and story.

Four out of five visitors to Hawaii are sun seekers. If you are an average *malihini*, you have bought your *aloha* shirt and bright beach towel and are out on the sand within an hour after being shown to your room. But after the first day on too-narrow, too-crowded Waikiki you begin to look around and wonder how a group of islands with 956 miles of coastline could have so few top-flight beaches. There is an answer to that: the Islands are merely the projecting peaks of a vast submerged mountain range. They fall off abruptly into the depths, except where sea life has built up protecting coral reefs. Elsewhere, the waves crash against sheer cliffs or pound with fury against lava rocks, sometimes blowing spray out of holes above underwater caves in jets that look like Yellowstone's geysers.

In windward Oahu, for instance, there stretch many miles of white coral beaches on which crash breakers like those of the mainland. These breakers look inviting, but are dangerous for any but the strongest swimmers, because of the undertow. The island of Kauai has bathing beaches protected by coral reefs, but few visitors stop to swim there as they whip past them on sight-seeing excursions. Hawaii, the Big Island, offers the weird phenomenon of coconut-fringed beaches of jet-black sand, churned up out of old lava flows by the waves. Here, as on the other islands, sea swimming is usually *kapu*, as the "Keep Out" signs warn you in the native lingo. Even in the protected coves, it is wise to take along a native surfer who knows the reefs and rocks and holes.

This explains why three fourths of Hawaii's sun seekers are inevitably packed around Waikiki, in the sheltering lee of Diamond Head, right in the city of Honolulu. Waikiki is pretty disappointing because it is so small. But it has always been popular and will probably stay that way. Waikiki is made by the coral reef, a mile out, that protects it from the sea. Inside the reef, the water is so safe and shallow that you can put a foot down after swimming a quarter of a mile and make the astonishing discovery that it is only shoulder deep, after all. The waves that break over the reef are smooth and even, perfect for surfboards and outrigger canoes. Catch a wave as it breaks over the reef and you are off on an exhilarating thirty-mile-an-hour ride ending at the water's edge—if you are skilled enough to stay aboard that long.

Mainlanders are not the only sun seekers who congregate like gony birds on Waikiki. Islanders are there, too, especially on week ends—Caucasians, Hawaiians, Japanese, Filipinos. On Saturday and Sunday the water is alive with surfboards and outriggers. Those pictures you see of boys carrying girls on their shoulders, on surfboards riding dizzily on the crest of the wave, aren't just stunts for the camera. The Hawaiians do it for fun and for free, and you can watch them for hours, riding, spilling and splashing.

You must see Hawaii—all of it—to comprehend the extent of its beauty and the extent of its problems. Nature has scattered Hawaii with extraordinary sights, from snow-covered mountains to black beaches, but what seems lovely to the tourist is often just more trouble to the local folk. Instead of flattening out, once they pushed through the surf, the suboceanic mountains that rose up to make the Hawaiian Islands lifted themselves still higher in precipitous peaks. Hawaii, the Big Island, comprising almost two thirds of the area of all the islands and still growing, is a good example. Its sky-scraping, often snow-covered craters, Mauna Kea (13,784 feet) and Mauna Loa (13,680 feet), burst into eruption every few years, piling cinders still higher and pouring lava down the slopes to the sea in seething caldrons, to make the Big Island still bigger. At Kilauea Crater, if you are lucky in your timing, you can drive up to the rim and see some of this red-hot earth cooking.

Islanders never call Hawaii by its name; it is always "the Big Island." Until recently, geologists considered Hawaii the youngest of the islands to emerge from the sea. Now they are not so sure. Parts of the Big Island, such as the Kohala Peninsula and the moist, verdant Hamakua Coast, may have been pinprick landmarks in the Pacific before the "older" islands—Kauai, Oahu and Maui—emerged.

The Big Island is easily the most fascinating of the group, because it has everything. You drive through tropical jungles, stroll through fern-tree forests, detour to primitive native villages in coconut groves by black-sand beaches. You can fish (swordfish, tuna, dolphin) or hunt (wild pigs, goats, or sheep) or climb snow-capped volcanic peaks. You can lose yourself on roads winding through waving, tasseled cane fields. Orchids and a dozen other flowers, mostly trees and vines, bloom year-round and in wild profusion. Nobody has to plant them. The Big Island offers deserts, cactus, wilderness, and history, but it takes time to track them down. Hawaii is so big it takes two days to drive around the island in a car, and a flight from Honolulu to Hilo, moist and verdant second city of the Islands, isn't a fair sample of the Big Island.

The always sparkling Kona Coast, across the island from Hilo, is just as different from the wet Hamakua Coast as it is possible for two sides of the same island to be. Protected by Hawaii's two monster volcanic peaks, Mauna Loa and Mauna Kea, Kona gets only the leavings of the rainstorms that drench the north coast of the island almost daily. Water is so precious that every house has a galvanized roof feeding the captured raindrops into gutters which in turn empty into tanks. When the Kona ranchers speak of watersheds, they mean just that; acres of galvanized-iron sheds high on the slopes, where the showers are more frequent, catch water, delivering it into tanks, sometimes enough to store a million gallons on one ranch. Kona's volcanic soils are so porous that rain sinks into them as through a sieve.

Yet there are enough passing showers to keep trees, vines, bushes and flowers in bloom year-round and the dry-land taro, the waxy-leafed coffee bushes, the papaya, mango, avocado and *lauhala* (pandanus) trees thriving. Kona has probably the nearest-perfect climate in the Hawaiian group; it is where every Islander is going to retire someday to the little grass shack under a breadfruit tree by a taro patch above a fishing cove at Kealakekua. Life is still simple and easy at Kona, and the *pilikia* (the catchall word for trouble) that complicates existence elsewhere hasn't gained a foothold yet. It may never gain one, because at Kona, Nature provides a living—taro root for *poi*, breadfruit, fish, coffee and fruits—and time to enjoy it.

It has been the same since Kamehameha I, the Conqueror of the Islands, returned to his birthplace at sleepy Kailua, on the Big Island about a century and a half ago, after his strenuous years of battle, to live out his days. At near-by Honaunau, you can picnic on what is left of Kamehameha's City of Refuge, where great mounds of volcanic rock rear on a jutting point. Here the kings held court and subjects found protection from *kapus* and vindictive chieftains. The City and another at Kawaihae are the nearest thing to an engineered town the primitive Hawaiians achieved.

Near by is Kealakekua Bay where a monument marks the spot on which Captain James Cook, after being greeted as a white god, lost his life and the white man's prestige in a sudden and foolish battle with native warriors in 1779. In a later expedition, two English sailors, Isaac Davis and John Young, were seized and spared to shoot captured cannon in local wars. They proved the edge in weapons that enabled the Great Kamehameha to purge Hawaii, Maui and Oahu of rival kings.

Prowling the peaceful coast of the Big Island and Kona's slopes, dotted with tiny farms, you have to flex your imagination to conjure this peaceful scene as the militant hub of Hawaii in Polynesian days, the center from which Kamehameha ran a fleet of 600 outrigger canoes, carved from solid trunks of koa trees grown high on the mountainside, to carry commerce to and from the other islands.

Kauai, at the northwestern extreme of the Hawaiian group, is the antithesis of the Big Island. Small, only 555 square miles in area (fourth in size of the Hawaiian Islands), it is rank jungle or plantations from the Nawiliwili tip to the Barking Sands Airport on the other side. Hence its sobriquet, "the Garden Island." Even Lihue, the county seat, over which wafts a pungent molasses odor from the near-by sugar mill, is only a crossroads in the cane fields, with a traffic cop at the intersection and a huge Kress store rising out of the jungle. The near-by town of Nawiliwili, with the name that intrigues every passer-by, is a sugar port on a sheltered bay, from which put out fishing boats whose Hawaiian skippers guarantee that their passengers will always catch something.

The volcanoes that reared Kauai have long since gone to rest, their lavas have eroded into rich red and black soil, which the constant rains have carved into spectacular canyons and rich valleys. Red-hued, precipitous Waimea Canyon is one of the earth's spectacular exhibits of rain erosion. Rainwater, which falls at over 460 inches a year at the peak of Mt. Waialeale, slowly chiseled this 3000-foot "Little Grand Canyon" and the near-by Napali Cliffs which plunge dramatically into the blue Pacific. Time has given them a vast silence, so quiet you can hear it. At Barking Sands Airport, fifteen miles away as the mynah bird flies, the rainfall often is only some twenty inches a year. This contrast between the rain-soaked windward slopes and the sun-parched leeward side is marked on all the larger Hawaiian Islands. The windward side is invariably rank tropics; the leeward side is parched desert. Only on Kauai is the moisture evenly enough distributed by showers and rivers to keep the entire island verdant. After heavy rains, dozens of streams crash over cliffs in foamy waterfalls.

On the Garden Island you roll through waving cane fields, past pineapple plantations, rice paddies, and miles of flowering trees and vines. At Waimea, a monument marks the spot where Captain Cook first set foot on Hawaiian soil. Here Cook was greeted with characteristic Polynesian hospitality, and sailed away to return and meet his end on the Big Island the following year. On Kauai you ponder over the origin of the rock-hewn irrigation ditches, which according to Hawaiian lore were built by a race of dwarfs, the Menehunes, who preceded the Polynesians. Scientists scoff at the idea, but there are the ditches, lined with rocks square-hewn and neatly fitted with a stone craftsmanship the Hawaiians never mastered. Kauai's Barking Sands are another gee-whiz; the sand makes strange noises when you walk across it, or if you put some of it in a bottle and shake it. Part of the explanation is that the grains of sand, as they dry out after each soaking by sea or rain, pick up a thin film of condensed gases which can vibrate with considerable resonance. The shape and outside surface of each individual grain give the sand its peculiar pitch and volume, which suggest a poodle's bark.

Maui, second largest of the Hawaiian group, is nicknamed the Valley Island, a misnomer that ranks with the best Hawaiian paradoxes. Maui has no valleys to compare with those of Oahu or Kauai. The island's big show is the 9318-foot Haleakala Crater, where, according to native lore, a fire-resistant mythological Polynesian hero trapped the sun and harnessed it to shine overtime for Hawaii. Hence, Haleakala's name, "House of the Sun." Maui was probably two island peaks in prehistoric times, each with its belching volcano. Haleakala, with a crater large enough to gulp Manhattan Island, must have been terrifying when on a rampage. After it stilled, the sea between the two isles filled in and Maui acquired what is called "the Valley," but which is in reality a low plain with coast at each end, an area intensely planted to sugar cane and pineapples.

Maui's sugar-cane belt has fingers that fringe the mountains, which are eroded into jungle-covered peaks and spectacular clefts, such as Iao Canyon, and its inexplicable 1200-foot rock needle resembling Rio's Sugar Loaf. Wailuku, nestling at the Iao's mouth, is a good place to see a sugar plantation at its best—cane fields, mills, company towns, the manager's magnificent residence. Around the mountain is Lahaina, a picturesque town basking around a plaza almost covered by an enormous banyan tree. Rugged windward Maui, a narrow, cliff-bound plateau, is cut by deep gorges, each the boundary of a plantation that is a little world to itself. So, likewise, is Hana, at the easternmost tip of the island.

Maui has three satellite islands, Molokai, Lanai and Kahoolawe. All three were short-changed when Madame Pele's volcanic fires were forging new terra firma. None has high enough cliffs to precipitate adequate rains. On the eastern half of Molokai, rising above the Kalaupapa Valley, is a mountain range that some consider the most beautiful spot in all the Islands. Not many people see it, because here is located the famed leper colony, accessible only from the sea. The other end of Molokai is a sloping semiarid plain, with barely enough moisture for pineapples and cattle ranching.

In the lee of Molokai and Maui hovers Lanai, the Pineapple Island, which offers one of the world's best demonstrations of soil conservation. About a quarter of a century ago, Lanai was slowly blowing into the sea. Mormon pioneers had tried growing sugar there and had failed for want of water. Subsequent owners grazed cattle. The cattle and wild goats wiped out the grass, turning the island into a seagirt dust bowl. In 1922, James D. Dole, founder of the Hawaiian Pineapple Company, bought what was left of the island. Company engineers laid out the rolling central plateau in contours, planted pineapples with mulch paper to keep out the weeds and hold down the soil when the wind blew. They planted thousands of Norfolk pines on the slopes to hold the hills in place, sowed grass seed, developed wells. Today, "Hawaiian Pine" has 14,000 acres in pineapple, rated the largest cultivated farm in one piece in the territory. The rest of Lanai is a cattle ranch on which the company raises beef for the island's population. The Hawaiian Pineapple Company, including its plantations on Oahu and its cannery, is Hawaii's biggest single enterprise, employing at the peak of the season thousands of workers, most of whom wouldn't have been on the pay roll

if Jim Dole hadn't tackled the job of saving the island that was blowing away.

Kahoolawe, only fifteen miles from Lanai, is an island that nobody
saved. It is still blowing out to sea, often in red banners that hang
over the ocean for many miles. Only goats now inhabit the island,
which has too little grass for cattle. Yet Kahoolawe served its purpose. Thousands of Army and Navy bombardiers and pilots sharpened their sights on the island, which became a bombing range for
fliers finishing their training on Oahu, Maui and Hawaii.

In spite of the attractions of the other seven islands, Oahu is still
the hub of Hawaii. It is the "Populous Isle" because at Honolulu
and contiguous Pearl Harbor are the two safest deep-water harbors
in all eight islands. They nestle on the lee side, and escape the
oceanic rollers that sweep down from Alaska to pound the windward
coasts with an occasional tidal fury such as that which made a
shambles of the Big Island's Hilo harbor and Maui's Kahului harbor
some years ago.

Oahu is the Hawaii most visitors know, because they never get
any farther. Oahu is where you see what the restless whites can do
to remake the Polynesians' tropics. When the white men arrived,
the ground on which Honolulu stands was a dry, dusty plain. The
whites drove tunnels into Oahu's mountains to capture underground
waters, which made Honolulu a city of flowering trees, hibiscus,
poinsettias.

They filled the swamps, dredged new land from the sea, built the
harbor and the impressive office buildings which make Honolulu's
Little Wall Street, clustered at Fort and Merchant Streets.

Driving past Pearl Harbor to Wahiawa, through swaying cane
fields and stubby, monotonous pineapple plantations, past experimental gardens of Macadamia nuts, litchi and papaya trees, with
the rugged green peaks on either side, you see how white men's
ideas and natives' industry have turned this gently sloping saddle
from jungle into one of the most productive stretches of earth anywhere. Drive a score of miles on the good highway that skirts the
island, and you slip from unreclaimed jungle and precipitous cliffs
to more plantations, flower-bedecked villages on low stilts, gay beach
homes, rocky foam-swept coast, coconut palms, banana and papaya
farms, open-air homes hidden in planned jungles, Diamond Head
(a long-dead crater)—all this, and more, you see in one morning's
brief drive out of Honolulu.

The varied landscape, so pleasing to the traveler, accounts for much of Hawaii's troubles. The mountains that kept growing and never flattened out left altogether too little land for cultivation. Of Hawaii's 6435 square miles, less than a tenth is suitable for crop agriculture. Another tenth is forage land for cattle and sheep. Eighty per cent is precipitous mountains, uninviting lava flows, semibarren desert. The Islands have no mineral deposits, no other resources than the fish that are found in such abundance in the surrounding sea.

When the Hawaiian Islands were discovered, the white men guessed that they were inhabited by 350,000 natives, a figure that historians later whittled down to 250,000. However many Hawaiians there were in Captain Cook's day, they lived a simple existence, pulling most of their food from the taro patches and from the sea.

Today the productive two tenths of Hawaii is hard-pressed to support the half million population, which is roughly one fifth white, one third Japanese, one sixth Hawaiian and part Hawaiian, the balance being Chinese, Filipino, Korean, Portuguese and Puerto Rican.

The Hawaiian land-tenure system, under which enormous landholdings have been built up, has its roots in a momentous event a century back in the reign of Kamehameha III. This liberal-minded monarch was Hawaii's Franklin D. Roosevelt. His particular New Deal is still known as the Great *Mahele,* which means "the redistribution." Under previous Hawaiian sovereigns, title to all the land was vested in the king, who assigned it to his chiefs, and they in turn were charged with seeing that every Hawaiian family had its taro patch and its fishing hole. Disapproving of this paternalism, Kamehameha divided all Hawaii in three parts, one third for the crown, one third for the chiefs, and one third for the people. The king then cut his slice in two, ceding half to the state and keeping half, an example followed by some of the chiefs.

In the years that followed, this well-meant New Deal went askew. The state clung to its lands until the end of the kingdom, through the limited days of the Hawaiian Republic under a flag that is a curious combination of the Union Jack and the Stars and Stripes, and finally delivered them to the United States Department of the Interior when Hawaii was annexed in 1898.

The natives, never having felt the need of private ownership of land anywhere in Polynesia, soon sold their land for pittances to opportunistic whites. The latter were mostly traders and fortune seekers, and not missionaries, as is popularly believed. The whites experimented with crops and eventually built up, after many failures, the cane and pineapple plantations that now support many Islanders. The few natives who held their lands did well, particularly those daughters of the *alii*, or nobles, who married white husbands wise enough to manage and increase estates.

The Hawaiian Islanders' most persistent *pilikia*, is the land famine. There just isn't enough good earth for enough farms or enough home sites. The tightly held holdings have resulted in land values that would be fantastic for comparable ground on the mainland. The demand for home sites, sold on the square-foot basis, has been so urgent in the Honolulu area that the enterprising Dillinghams, who struck it rich building railroads, dredging harbors and constructing breakwaters, have been using their equipment to dredge new subdivisions out of what was ocean shallows or swamp land a short time ago. Spread with a thin frosting of top soil, these coral beach fronts become fabulously priced building sites overnight.

The restless whites have been wresting land from the sea, the jungle or the desert ever since they arrived on the Islands. To the easygoing Polynesians, this seemed like an unnecessary struggle with Nature. The natives would have none of it. There were fish in the sea and taro root in the swamp. The Hawaiians, at the time the whites arrived, were sprung from a seagoing race, who, when their homelands became too crowded, took off in fleets of outrigger canoes on long sea voyages that still baffle the anthropologists. They brought their children, dogs, plants and foodstuffs, and after multiplying prodigiously in the hospitable Hawaiian Islands, lost their ancient navigating skill.

Before the whites arrived to settle in the Islands, the local kings and chiefs had been purged in a series of bloody invasions by Kamehameha I, the Conqueror, who died in 1819. The Hawaiian Islands were a kingdom, and the king owned everything in feudal totalitarianism. He owned his subjects, men and women alike, if he wanted them. He held his people in constant fear of taboos punishable by death.

When the first New England missionaries reached the Islands in 1820, the old taboos had broken down. The Hawaiians were hungry for a new religion. It was a rugged paradise, in which the missionaries soon found themselves combating not only the Devil but the raucous sailormen of whaling and trading ships. Gradually the missionaries, by their steadfastness and industry, gained the upper hand, only to be cut off by the Mission Board in New England and forced to earn their own living. Some tried the agriculture in which they had attempted unsuccessfully to interest the Hawaiians. They were joined by traders and other white settlers, and from this struggling start grew the sugar industry that is Hawaii's largest source of support.

Before they could grow cane, the pioneers had to clear away the jungle, or turn deserts into gardens by building spectacular canal systems that tapped mountain streams. They had to build mills to crush the cane and refine the juice into sugar. This called for capital, which few of them had. They found it in Honolulu, where other pioneers had established agencies, first to service trading and whaling ships and later the isolated plantations. The agencies, or factoring companies, bought and stocked supplies for the plantations and marketed their crops. They also invested in the plantations and mills.

Statehood for Hawaii was not a matter of economics, for the territory was not only self-supporting but paid more Federal income tax than did any one of a dozen states. The big problem was to convince prejudiced groups that statehood for such a geographically distant area was feasible, and that the national ballot should be given to the Japanese, Chinese, Filipinos and Koreans, as well as the Hawaiians. Statehood supporters point out that there is virtually no race problem in the territory itself, that there is no area under United States jurisdiction where a greater complexity of races lives so harmoniously.

The cosmopolitan complexion of the Islands today stems not so much from this international background as from the fact that the native Hawaiians dislike heavy field labor and repetitious chores. No Hawaiian can see why he should sweat out a living in a cane field or a sugar mill when he can earn his livelihood fishing, sailing a boat, riding a cow pony, holding public office, or blowing a police whistle. After the first futile efforts to make farmers of the Hawaiians, the early plantation operators gave up and imported Chinese.

For a few cents a day, the coolies built the ditches, planted the cane, hoed the weeds, harvested the crops. Their sons and grandsons moved to the towns and cities, became merchants, lawyers, doctors—some of Hawaii's outstanding business and professional men. The planters brought in Portuguese from the Madeira Islands, good workers whose sons likewise preferred the town. Japanese were the next and largest wave. They, too, were industrious, dependable plantation labor; but their sons and daughters, the second largest pure racial block in the Islands, went to town. As a last resort, the plantations brought in Koreans, Puerto Ricans and Filipinos. They too, are migrating off the land, and machines are taking their place.

The younger generation finds no lure in agriculture, and this is one of Hawaii's top problems today. The University of Hawaii, which offers excellent courses in agronomy, can't interest students in the training for the Islands' basic industry. As a substitute for manpower, managements have built ingenious and expensive machines, many of which are operated by whites, among them ex-servicemen who became intrigued with plantation life while on duty in Hawaii. Nearly every plantation is operating with one third fewer employees. The rest have gone to town. These fugitives from agriculture became the work force for the hundreds of postwar enterprises that sprang up almost overnight. They found higher-paying jobs in the 55 new manufacturing establishments turning out garments, jewelry, jam and jelly—these being but a few of the products that were not being made on the island at all when the war ended.

For years a serious lack of good hotel space had hampered Hawaii's tourist trade. More mainlanders wanted to go to Honolulu than Honolulu could accommodate; that is until 1954, when the dynamic Henry J. Kaiser turned a run-down motel into his fabulous Hawaiian Village. Later Mr. Hilton and the Sheraton chain descended on Waikiki. Between them they have bought and reconditioned or are building anew thousands of hotel rooms to handle the jet-boosted tourist trade.

Meantime, the Islanders are organizing their traditional *aloha,* which can mean welcome, hospitality, love and good-by, all rolled into one neat word, to meet the changed conditions. They have revived the Hawaii Visitors Bureau, supported by the community not only to lure travelers but to help them find rooms, food, transportation, souvenirs or toothbrushes.

The Bureau's manager, promises that no visitor will set foot on the Islands or leave them without a lei around his or her neck. The lei makers, mostly Hawaiian women, are lined up again on Fort Street outside the pier on steamer day.

Before the whites came, Hawaiian music consisted of chants to the accompaniment of beating drums and calabashes. The songs and the dances were to propitiate the gods or to extol the prowess of the chiefs. The missionaries turned this love of pagan music to love for hymns. Queen Liliuokalani gave it another turn; inspired by a touching parting of lovers at the palace gate, she retired to her room one night and wrote what is perhaps Hawaii's most haunting melody, *Aloha Oe*. Half Hawaiian and half English, with a refrain from an old hymn, it was the pacesetter for the outpouring of *hapa-haole* songs so popular in the Islands today.

Hapa-haole is a word that means literally "half white," but by usage, "part Hawaiian." Anyone with a few drops of Hawaiian blood is a *hapa-haole*. So is a song with a few Hawaiian words. Many of them sprang spontaneously out of an evening strumming of guitars and ukuleles, the latter being the Portuguese contribution to Hawaii's music lore. Every new song, serious or comic, inspires its own interpretive hula dance, in which gracefully flowing hands speak a language to the rhythm of swaying bodies, a language part pagan, part missionary, part night club.

The Islanders, regardless of ancestry, love the rhythmic symbolism of the hula. They use the slightest pretext—parties, welcomes, farewells, politics—to activate a hula.

✿ ✿ ✿

Not surprisingly, the two faces Hawaii presents to the world—bustling boomland and leisurely tourist paradise—do not always smile at each other. It is one of the problems—more of the *pilikia*—of coming of age. Yet there is a truism that every traveler, Hawaii bound, could well remember:

"If you love Hawaii, Hawaii will surely love you and greet you always with *aloha*."

PART II *The Pacific Coast*

California

by IRVING STONE

So much has been written about California there is little left to be told: except the truth. In a state where the hyperboles are picked green and allowed to ripen en route to the Eastern market, an ounce of astringency is worth a pound of praise.

Northern California is a lean, hard-bitten mountain man, a Jedediah Smith or Joseph Walker fighting his way across the snow-clad Sierras with a hunter's gun slung on his back; male, rugged, disciplined, carrying the indestructible seed of a new civilization. Southern California is a lush, red-lipped, sensual female who came up from Acapulco in the cabin of a well-rigged Spanish ship, and now suns herself in a patio surrounded by bougainvillaea, her gown cut sufficiently low to intimate how abundantly the coming generations may be nourished.

This love affair and marriage have been passionate and prolific, but not always peaceful; there have been quarrels, bills of divorcement; yet the partners have remained in wedlock because of the magic and wealth of the family name.

Intemperate Californians have been heard to say (it's not enough to be on your guard against the natives, the converts are the worst exaggerators) that their state is another Valley of the Nile or Euphrates, cradle of a civilization richer than any the world has ever known; a land of milk and honey and ripe orange groves, green fields, shining streams, sun-drenched ocean beaches: the Promised Land.

Can there be even a smidgen of truth in such outlandish claims?

Everyone knows about our North and South Poles, those two charming geographical concepts. If Moscow is the East Pole, and certainly the Kremlin is calling the tunes for the Orient, then California is the West Pole, the heartland of the new and fresh democracy we feel is being fashioned in the Far West.

What are its components?

It is the life of the individual homeowner, who is not buffeted or mastered by the changes of the economic or political cycle, to whom democracy means neighborliness, getting along with the people next door. It means living with lack of tension, suspicion, hostility, in a largely informal and classless society: for there is food and space, mountains and sea, fertile valleys, cities and villages, sunshine for everyone. We are not a cramped people, in spite of the staggering onslaught of newcomers into the state; neither are we pushed, harried or harassed.

It is living with nature, yet without the constant conflict with the elements, of drought and flood, of ice and sleet. It is the joy of going to work in the daylight and returning in the daylight, with the chance to recoup one's energies in the sun, the surf, the pines, the streams, or just cultivating one's garden.

California fashions have contributed to the nation a picture of the casual life, the gay and informal: the easily cared-for costume, colorful slacks and sports jacket for men, the cotton skirt and thonged shoe for women, the servantless home with the kitchen a part of the living room so that the housewife, in her brightly hued, tapered pants and peasant shirt, can chat with her guests as she tosses a Caesar salad while her husband broils the steaks on the barbecue.

The big houses are being torn down, the grounds subdivided to make room for twenty modern homes. So too with antiquated social distinctions: few Californians try to keep up with the nabob Joneses; now they try to uncomplicate their lives and keep their pretensions down with the democratic Smiths. When each man owns his own garden, his sacred little piece of the good earth, he is anybody's equal.

Be forewarned: when all the facts about California are piled on top of each other, they will constitute a volume thicker and more amazing than Baron Munchausen's book of travels. Along with the Texan, the Californian identifies himself so strongly with his state that he constitutes himself an individual chamber of commerce, sometimes permitting a soupçon of braggadocio to enter his otherwise cool and objective appraisal of his birthright.

The state is almost eight hundred miles long (longer than Italy), embracing within its boundaries staggering contrasts: the stark, barren, primordial rock mountains towering above the sand and creosote-bush wastes of the Mojave Desert to the south; in the north, the dense green forests of redwood and *Sequoia gigantea*, the largest trees in the world, the epitome of long life, of the power of growth and survival.

The Californian offers equally astonishing contrasts: he came during the gold rush in a flash flood of humanity representing almost every race on earth: the Italians in the Sonoma and Napa valleys, the Armenians around Fresno, the Chinese of San Francisco and the Sacramento Valley, the Mexicans of Los Angeles and the Imperial Valley, the Germans around Sunland, the Scandinavians in the lumber towns and around Twin Peaks, the Japanese wherever flowers and vegetables will grow, the Portuguese and Finns of the northern fishing villages, so like the rugged coast of Wales; as well as the thousands of New Englanders, New Yorkers, Pennsylvanians, Southerners. Each group brought its mores, its heritage, the flavor and tone of its state or national character, creating in the Far West a cosmopolitan culture; for the state has the same assimilative powers as the ocean that rolls in from the Sea of Okhotsk and the Tasman Sea.

It was not the billions in gold taken out of the state that enriched California, it was the wealth of humanity that poured in.

Californians see themselves in the large; in their own minds they are all Paul Bunyans who can swing allegorical axes and level forests. Aside from those born here, which requires only modest courage, most of the people who made the long journey to the state were hardy, adventuresome souls. Courage is at the base of California character: the lone coward I've met in all my journeying up and down the state is myself, during the years I had to cross the cemetery on my way home from a night job.

One measure of people is how much they dare, and Californians have dared greatly: Isadora Duncan revolutionized the dance; Frank Norris (we consider any man who has lived here for five years

as a true Californian, though of course not with all of the privileges
pertaining to the native) liberated the American novel from sentimentality to realism; Jack London blueprinted the coming world of
authoritarianism; Gertrude Stein released the American language
from its outmoded word-forms; Luther Burbank created edible cactus, plumcots, stoneless prunes; John Muir, the naturalist, saved
Yosemite and some hundred million acres of forest reserves for the
nation; Upton Sinclair, at sixty, began an eleven-volume historical
novel.

We have Chief Justice of the U. S. Supreme Court Earl Warren,
who helped bring in a unanimous antisegregation law; writers
Saroyan and Steinbeck of Fresno and Salinas origin; Nobel Prize
winner Ralph Bunche of the U.N.; Nobel Prize winners Ernest
Lawrence, developer of the cyclotron, Glenn T. Seaborg and Edwin
M. McMillan, discoverers of plutonium; Jackie Robinson, who pioneered the way for Negro athletes into big-league baseball; Beni-
amino Bufano, whose vast sculptures have kept San Francisco in an
uproar; Richard Neutra, who has carried forward magnificently creative Frank Lloyd Wright's revolution in modern architecture, and
says that nowhere else in the entire world could he have had as great
an opportunity to experiment in living forms and materials. Many
of these men were born elsewhere, but came to California to mature
and do their work; did they come because they knew they could find
the freedom and strength to accomplish or does being plunged into
the inspirited atmosphere of the state increase a man's courage and
scope?

On the pediment of the State Office Building in Sacramento is the
line: *"Bring Me Men To Match My Mountains."* A tall order: for the
Sierras go up to the greatest heights in North America.

How would you like to enter California? From what direction, in
what area of time, by what means? By Spanish ship with Cabrillo in
1542, around the Horn in an English ship with Drake in 1579, on
foot from Lower California in 1769 with Padre Junípero Serra, by
foot and horseback with Captain Juan Bautista de Anza from Mexico
in the spring of 1774; down from the Bering Strait in a Russian ship
to found Fort Ross in 1812, to remain until 1841 and then sell out just
before the discovery of gold; into the harbor of San Diego with Richard Henry Dana (*Two Years Before the Mast*) in 1834, or in the
hundreds of ships that sailed through the Golden Gate Strait into
San Francisco Bay, true womb of California, with the thousands of

gold miners in 1850? Would you prefer to come down from the north, after crossing the Oregon Trail with Parkman, or from the south, across the blazing heat of Death Valley with the Jayhawkers, or over the Sierras with John Bidwell, in covered wagons down the Humboldt with the Chiles-Walker Party in 1843, or with what remained uneaten of the Donner Party in 1847? Would you prefer an automobile on Highway 66, crossing bleak California deserts until you're sure you've been had by the chamber of commerce, and then suddenly come to the top of a bluff and see spread below you a land of ripe orange groves, green meadows and sparkling streams? Or perhaps you want the last word, the jet that leaves New York in midafternoon and reaches California that evening when, replete with Martinis and pheasant under glass, you will circle the phantasmagoria of lights that is San Francisco or Los Angeles, and be taken in a limousine to a swank hotel.

The name California, like so much else in the state, is the invention of a fiction writer, one Ordoñez de Montalvo, who wrote around 1510, "At the right hand of the Indies there is an island called California, very near to the Terrestrial Paradise. This island is inhabited by robust dark women of great strength and great warm hearts; when children are born the females are preserved but the males are killed at once, saving only those required to guard against depopulation . . ." Sounds a little like present-day Hollywood.

The first inhabitants of California found it anything but a terrestrial paradise; the thirty-odd tribes of Indians were the sorriest to stumble onto the North American continent: poverty-stricken, living largely on nuts and berries, without the skill to grow food or make tools or weapons. The only characteristic they shared with their smarter cousins to the east was that they managed to get their squaws to do the work. When the Spanish arrived, the Indians would gladly have closed out the whole state for the same twenty-four dollars that bought Manhattan. Instead, the Spanish put the braves to work building missions, whereupon most of them folded their wretched huts and vanished. The best-known Indians remaining in California today are those who get themselves shot by studio cowboys protecting covered-wagon trains.

Cabrillo, sailing around the Horn in 1542, claimed California for the Spanish and set a four-hundred-year tourist precedent by exclaiming when he saw the coast at Carmel:

"The mountains seem to reach the heavens!"

By 1769, Junípero Serra began to build the missions that became California's first permanent settlements: San Diego, San Juan Capistrano, San Fernando, Santa Barbara, San Luis Obispo near Monterey, Mission Dolores in San Francisco, Sonoma, most of them now rebuilt. Aside from the missions, and the sparsely manned military presidios at San Diego, Santa Barbara, Monterey and San Francisco, the Spanish thought little of California: it was too remote, too undeveloped, without any of the golden wealth they had drained out of Mexico and Peru.

The Mexicans were barely settled when *americanos* began filtering in from the northern mountains or the southern desert: Jedediah Smith, a trapper, in 1826; James Pattie, a fur trapper, in 1828; Ewing Young in 1829, Joseph Walker in 1833, John Frémont and Kit Carson and John Bidwell in 1841, then American sailors who jumped ship when their barks anchored in California ports, and those put ashore sick and left to die. They did not die; of all the multitudes sent to California by their family doctors back home, not one has been known (publicly) to succumb. Many of the Americans became *Californios:* and why not, with thousands of acres of fertile land for the taking, and beautiful black-eyed *señoritas* languishing for husbands?

The first revolt of Americans for independence from Mexico was started by the wrong social set; that's probably why we hear so little about it. Isaac Graham, their leader, was the owner of a distillery, described by Hubert Howe Bancroft, our fabulous source historian, as "a wild and unprincipled man, with no good qualities except personal bravery." Graham and his followers wound up in a flea-infested jail in San Blas, Mexico.

But six years later there were some seven hundred Americans in California, owning a great deal of land, restive under Mexican rule. In 1846, Colonel John C. Frémont, son-in-law of Thomas Hart Benton of Missouri, the most rabid western expansionist in the Congress, having appeared from over the mountains with a band of well-armed explorers and cartographers, had a brush with General Castro, the military commander of California, and raised the American flag on Gabilan Peak for three days of defiance. Then, moving northward, he was overtaken by Marine Lieutenant Gillespie, who had confidential dispatches from Secretary of State Buchanan. Frémont turned south, united the *americanos*, and so began the story of modern California.

Very soon thereafter an excitable young wheelwright by the name of James Marshall, while building a sawmill at Coloma for his Swiss boss, John Sutter, glanced over at the tailrace he had built across a bend in the American River, and noticed a number of flecks of yellow where the water was sluicing through a sandbar. If the Flower of the Pacific was wrested from Mexico through rape, and its birth as an American state must be branded as illegitimate, there was no questioning the legitimacy of that gold; it started a rush that has never slackened, and will not abate until some fifty million people call themselves Californians.

Superlatives are indigestible; let's sample a few, and have done with them.

We have the largest number of owner-occupied dwelling units of any state, the widest diversification of agricultural crops and livestock, bringing the highest cash farm income; the widest diversification of minerals, of recreational facilities; the largest number of automobiles, driven by the wackiest drivers; the largest bank, the lowest land point, Death Valley; the tallest trees, the tallest storytellers, starting with Mark Twain and his *Jumping Frog of Calaveras County*. We spend more money than any other state for public services: education, public welfare, highways. California is the third largest state geographically (alas, we can never become first), embraces 158,693 square miles, bigger than New England with New York and Ohio thrown in for friendly measure; has the second highest per capita income of the major states. . . .

What do these facts and figures mean? What is their true significance? The Himalayas are big, but they have produced no Athens or Florence, while I have yet to meet an elephant who has written *The Brothers Karamazov* or a dinosaur who has painted Van Gogh's *Vegetable Gardens*. Size and wealth are meaningless unless translated into terms of the good life for a whole people.

The best way to know California is from within, by working its veins and arteries, as the original gold miners did, and as this writer did; drive a San Francisco grocery wagon and have the horse fall down in its harness when you attempt to take him down the perpendicular Haight Street hill; dig holes for electric poles across the hot Central Valley; oil dynamos at a Kern River power plant in the mountains above Bakersfield; whitewash the trunks of apricot trees in Hollister, pick peaches in Marysville in the farm belt, wrap meat in a Los Angeles packing plant and watch the hams and bacons dance on the rack when an earthquake rocks the building; or check

vacationers in and out of a swank Lake Tahoe mountain resort as a
desk clerk. Deliver suits for Pauson's and fling a package up a long
dark flight of stairs on Grant Avenue in San Francisco's Chinatown,
fleeing in terror because you've been brought up to believe the stories of Chinese opium dens and white-slave trade; some years later
play *Smiles* and *Margie* for an Italian wedding in a Grant Avenue
hall with your back against a lattice-work partition, on the other side
of which a Chinese orchestra is playing Old Country music for one
of their weddings; blow a saxophone at the Orange Show in the lush
southern citrus land of the San Bernardino Valley for ten days and
nights, or on the back of a truck helping to gather Central California
crowds in Benicia, Vallejo, Napa and Sacramento, so that political
haranguers can tell the people why they should vote for John W.
Davis for president; entertain with a traveling vaudeville troupe
through the mining regions of Angels Camp and Chinese Camp, the
mountain and lumber towns of Jamestown, Sonora, Tuolumne; work
as a stock boy in one of San Francisco's oldest bookstores where you
unpack hundreds of copies of Ibañez' *Four Horsemen of the Apoca-
lypse,* the best seller of the day, and at every opportunity read a
few pages in the storage stacks until the manager tells you to take
a copy home and read it on your own time; be signaled out of an
8 A.M. senior discussion group in economics at the University of
California at Berkeley, unshaven, and be asked by the professor to
take the rostrum and replace the Teaching Fellow whose appendix
had been removed an hour before, thus stumbling into the noble
profession of teaching.

California is actually five different states, with a variety of cultures: the sun worship of the vast southern desert; the semitropical
life of Los Angeles with its hundred-mile aura of influence; the valley
culture of the five-hundred-mile-long, rich agricultural land between
the Coast Range and the Sierras; the fog culture; the mountain and
big-timber culture of the north.

San Francisco is the capital of the fog culture, though its natives
will tell you that it has no fog, or if they are confronted with the
sight of it rolling in from the beach at fourteen miles an hour, that
they find it exhilarating. You will be driving north from Los Angeles,
with the top of your convertible down, baking in the hot sun; you
reach the south end of the suction cup, perhaps five miles down the
peninsula from San Francisco, and find yourself engulfed in raw
penetrating cold. The fog will blanket the whole city as you drive

over the Mission hills, past the ball park, across Market Street, by the Civic Center with the beautiful Opera House, and out automobile row. The waters of the strait will be milk gray, with only the tips of the vast steel girders of the Golden Gate Bridge visible, as though they were hung downward from the sky. Yet once across the bridge, and through the cut in the hills, a matter of a mile or two, and you are again in the hot clear sunshine.

Every man writes a biographical novel with the blood of his spent hours; but if you have freedom of choice, San Francisco is a good town in which to be born.

My first memory of the city is at the age of three, when I stood on top of Twin Peaks with my mother on an April night in 1906, watching San Francisco burn to the ground. My mother said: "We will never live like civilized people again; we'll roam these hills like wild animals, foraging for our food."

On the ashes arose the city in which I grew up, the ugliest city in the world, built of hard wood and harder gray stone, a grim-visaged masculine town with its houses glued together in long, tall, dark, narrow rows, the steps emerging out of the very sidewalks, mounting the hills like the rungs of ladders, with no blade of grass, no tree, no flower, no touch of soft feminine earth. The architecture was haphazard; district after district was plain, austere, heavy, unbeautiful.

But you turned a corner and unexpectedly you found yourself on the crest of a hill. Below lay the bay, with its islands bold and clear in the brilliant sunshine; in the docks along the Embarcadero nestled the dozens of ships being loaded for Oriental ports, and the quaint ferry boats plying the waters; beyond were the green hills of Oakland and Berkeley. And suddenly the irresilience dropped away, the street and the people grew soft and friendly, and you knew that you lived in a city with mood, with tone, with style, with beauty: the most beautiful city in the world.

San Franciscans, like the amazing hills they have climbed these several generations, are a hard, stony people, astonishingly like New Englanders: stubborn, proud, willful, self-contained, tenacious, fiercely independent, rooted in rocky tradition; not the kind of hardness that is mean or uncharitable, but rather the kind that demands so terribly much of itself. Easterners say, "We can always tell a San Franciscan: there is a touch of accent, of Boston thrown into a crude pioneer settlement; a touch of the arrogance of people who can flourish under difficult circumstances; a submerged grimness of purpose, a shortness of humor, cultivated"—we natives like to boast that we had an opera house and a first-rate literary magazine, the *Golden Era,* before we paved our streets—"and yet at the same time curiously insular, almost like an island folk."

Do not gather the impression that San Francisco is a cold city; actually it is one of the warmest communities in the world, with the old Spanish tradition of the latchstring always being on the outside still predominant. San Francisco is warm and hospitable to strangers, trusts newcomers and takes them at face value. When you have done raving about the tiny tart shrimp at Fisherman's Wharf, the cable cars clanging up Powell and California streets, the view of the Golden Gate Strait from Pacific Heights with tramp steamers coming through the narrows, the Bay Bridge seen from Coit Tower or the Top of the Mark, the soignée San Francisco women, among the best groomed in the world, the breath-taking panorama of Market Street extending from the foot of Twin Peaks all the way down to the now obsolete Ferry Building; when all of this has been recounted, it still does not disclose the secret of why San Francisco is one of the world's most beloved cities: the incredible fact that after an hour you feel that you belong, that this city which embodies and projects a quality of delight, could be your home forever.

A lot of folks did. They came originally to find gold, but when they grew bored with digging, or the gold did not pan out, they resumed the trades they had practiced at home: carpentering, farming, doctoring, trading, bookkeeping, schoolteaching, the law.

Few came with any great wealth, and whatever social position they may have enjoyed at home they necessarily left behind them. San Francisco created its own wealth, its own society, its own erudition. Class lines never had much chance to solidify, for the great lady in the mansion up on Washington Street was probably as newly arrived as the mining, sugar, railroad-shipping or real-estate money with which her husband built the ornate forty-room house.

When I told my mother, who had read from cover to cover but one book in her life, Mary Antin's *Promised Land,* that I was determined to become a writer, she wept with fear for her only son: for in one of my Aunt Julia's flats lived a writer with his wife and three daughters. They had no furniture except two beds, a kitchen table and chairs, no carpets on the floor. When the writer ran out of food money he would pick up a tray of toilet waters and peddle them to the wives of chicken farmers around Petaluma. To my mother's objection I replied:

"San Francisco is a good place for writers to be born." What more can any city give its children than the unshatterable faith that they can accomplish whatever they may set their minds and hearts to?

In 1923, when I was an economics instructor at the University of Southern California in Los Angeles, sharing an office with three other instructors, two handsomely dressed young men from the Janss Investment Corporation made us an offer: they would give each of us a large lot free, in something that was to be called Westwood Village, where a southern branch of the University of California was purportedly to be built, if we would contract to erect a $10,000 business building within three years. Though the four of us could not have collected ten thousand jelly beans, we piled into my Model T, drove through the miles of open plains on either side of Wilshire Boulevard, then trudged over the sand dunes wondering why these slick operators did not confine their confidence games to wildcat oil wells.

Today Westwood Village is one of the most sparklingly beautiful and prosperous communities in the state; you can't buy a lot there with money, let alone jelly beans, and the faculty complains that it is the only university town in America where the rentals are too high for the professors to live.

I, for one, should have known better: as a child I stood on a high sand dune in San Francisco overlooking the Pacific with my grandfather telling me how, in 1870, he had stood on this very dune waiting for sight of the ship, reported lost, coming from around the Horn with his wife and children. To my question of whether there ever would be houses on these miles and miles of lonely dunes, my grandfather replied:

"Never. There aren't enough people in the world to fill them up."

The only sand you can find today is on the beach south of the Cliff House.

Not long ago I drove through Los Angeles to the International airport, out Sepulveda Boulevard past open fields and dunes where I had been horseback riding the day before. I flew to New York and remained long enough to send a book to press, three months at the most; when I returned I found the same countryside occupied by several thousand bungalows, with the streets in, trees planted, lawns and flowers already up, kids playing under the sprinklers.

Why do they come? Why are they willing to give up home, family, friends, jobs, clientele, roots? Why do so few become disappointed and return to the place of their birth?

The climate is one of the two commanding factors: in Southern California, the weather is a friend with whom you can have a delightful time the year around. People say, "If I'm going to have to work for a living I might as well do it where it is warm and pleasant all year." There are other reasons: most of our cities are new, clean and sun-drenched; our buildings rarely go over two to four stories and those coming from skyscraper cities can see their world horizontally instead of vertically, surrounded by a huge bowl of sky instead of cement walls. There is no snow to be shoveled, coal and oil to be burned, soot to be fought; men don't have to wear heavy overcoats and rubbers, women don't have to bundle up the children in wools and ear muffs. Folks live in their own homes, with flowers in front and a back yard where the kids can play in safety all year round. Many middle-cost builders are replacing the rumpus room or extra bedroom with a small swimming pool.

The second motivation is exemplified by my own family: my mother and stepfather moved down to Los Angeles from San Francisco in 1919 because Los Angeles, then a sleepy village, was just beginning to offer fresh business opportunities. With expanding aviation, automobile, steel, oil, motion-picture, real-estate and a hundred other industries there is work for all, and opportunity aplenty.

Some years ago, when some friends moved to Los Angeles from New York and I asked their sons what they were majoring in at school, they replied disdainfully, "Recess. Every time we turn around we have to go outside and play," to which their mother added, "Apparently you Southern Californians are trying to develop a race of seven-foot dopes." This is no longer true: in a leisurely two-hour drive from the beautiful U.C.L.A. campus in Westwood one can circle past Los Angeles City College, U.S.C., and go east through the San Bernardino Valley past Occidental, California Institute of Technology, Whittier, Scripps, Pomona, Redlands and now the new liberal-arts branch of the University of California at Riverside, all fine educational institutions.

Los Angeles was once the capital of bad taste in America, with all manner of vulgar architecture, restaurants in the shape of hot dogs and tamales, with bastard Spanish or Moorish monstrosities for residences. In towns like Beverly Hills the original builders built thick-walled, narrow-windowed Spanish houses, black dungeons which are being ripped out and converted to moderns to make way for the sun and light. The intellectual tone of the community, totally insular and isolationist, was dictated by senior citizens retired from the rigors of the Midwest farm states, who came because living was cheap.

Though Los Angeles still has to borrow San Francisco's opera company for two weeks out of the year, it now has its own symphony orchestra, growing art museums, many little theaters, vigorous bookstores, superb private collections of paintings and sculpture available for local showings. The motion-picture industry has helped to make the change, bringing in creative artists from all over the world.

Even in California, the democratic West Pole of the world, we have our dissenters and defeatists and crackpots. In spite of the maturing of our arts and education, Los Angeles still remains one of the most powerful anti-intellectual centers in the country.

Yet there is a vitality abroad that is building new schools, libraries, whole outlying communities: a vitality that says make way for life, the California life.

The country for 120 miles south of Los Angeles to the Mexican border, the first half dominated by the oil derricks of Culver City, Signal Hill and Huntington Beach and the wells out in the ocean, is a narrow strip with houses hugging the mountains overlooking the sea. Behind this wall of mountain there are tremendous valleys where only a few cattle graze. In South Laguna you can have your own private beach and catch fish from the rocks; in La Jolla you can skin-dive for abalone and put out your lobster traps. San Diego has beautiful views of the ocean and bay wherever you turn and the most exciting zoo in the world.

The most beautiful and cultivated trio of towns in the Los Angeles area are Santa Barbara, Pasadena and La Jolla, generically alike and formerly known as the "Three R's": rich, Republican and reactionary. This canard can no longer be charged; the cities are extremely prosperous, but many of the great Eastern and Midwest fortunes that founded them have gone to their rewards: the Treasury Department. Pasadena's big estates are being broken up for handsome two-story modern apartment houses, while whole suburbs of precision-instrument workers are moving in to man the new plants. La Jolla is being settled by the overflow of middle-class families from San Diego, while Santa Barbara is becoming an important college center with its new University of California campus.

A hundred miles of magnificent beaches are a half hour's drive from anywhere in the Los Angeles area; so are the mountains with good fishing in summer and skiing in winter. Except for Old Los Angeles, Southern California is sparkling new, with the gleaming whiteness of house and market and street, a constant joy to the newcomer.

The word "slum" has dropped out of the language in California; even the rundown sections have a bit of lawn, shrubs, a few flowers in front of the houses.

Southern California families live as much outdoors as they do in; modern architecture includes the out-of-doors as part of the interior decoration. This willingness to experiment, to try the new and different has helped to lessen the tightness and the tensions of a more rigid world. *California's greatest difference is that we are on the way to creating an anxiety-free people.*

And in Southern California there is Hollywood.

California has always been a romantic area and concept, from the beginning romance of its name, through the discovery of romantically free gold, the romance of its semitropical flowers and brilliant sunshine, its golden oranges and golden poppies, its Mediterranean-date crop around Indio in the Coachella Valley, and finally that great romance breeder which has made the name of Hollywood famous in the remotest villages of Afghanistan.

The proper way to describe Hollywood is in terms of the motion-picture industry: the various companies are only ostensibly in competition. Actors, producers, directors, writers shift from M-G-M to Fox to Warners to Paramount to Columbia to Universal-International and back to M-G-M without changing a picture on their desks or knowing that they have actually moved. The steady and secure core of the industry are the technicians, the engineers, sound men, electricians, property men, all well but not exorbitantly paid, and enjoying almost full security. These are the gentle folk, the soft-spoken, the totally decent and reliable.

Do the movie big shots have a more amoral set of values than the leaders of other industries? If you were playing poker with twenty dollars in the pot and saw an opportunity to cut a corner in order to win, you probably would not be tempted to take advantage; but if there were two hundred thousand dollars in the pot, and you saw a chance to cheat. . . . Only in Hollywood can a man who is earning five thousand dollars a week be unemployed the following Monday, the man who is broke and cannot meet the payment on his home suddenly get a contract or sell a property to the movies and have a hundred and fifty thousand dollars in the bank.

Only in the motion-picture industry are millions spent each year on promoting individual personalities, until actors and actresses believe their own press notices and come to regard themselves as kings and queens with the divine right of royalty. Imagine what this does to the integrity of human beings; imagine what these men and women will not do to remain at the heart of the greatest romance creator of our age, and to reap its fabulous harvest—even though in their hearts they know they really earn but the smallest portion.

What is the effect of living in Southern California, through whose communities are spread the thousands of people engaged in the motion-picture industry? It is a pleasant one; at the sneak preview at your nearby movie house you will see the entire cast of big pictures as well as the director, producer and cameraman of the film which will be splashed across the newspapers three months hence. Not even the gala international world *premières,* with the lights and the stars and the special stands, can make any shattering change in your life; but all these things are fun, they are gay, they lend color and character to Southern California.

Picture to yourself two high walls of mountains, the Coast Range and the Sierra Nevada, going up over 14,000 feet at Mount Whitney; and between the two a mammoth valley some five hundred miles long and forty wide—roughly half the size of England.

Two thirds of the state's agricultural lands are here, irrigated by the Central Valley Water Project, which stores water high on the Sacramento and San Joaquin rivers and carries it five hundred miles south to the once desert lands around Bakersfield. Every species of temperate-zone and subtropical fruit, vegetable or field crop is produced: pears, asparagus, celery, beans, onions, rice, lettuce, grapes, prunes, peaches, apricots, plums, olives, cotton (we produce more cotton than any state in the South, except Texas), oranges, lemons, pomegranates, figs, avocados, loquats, guavas, almonds, walnuts, dates, artichokes, cherries, honeydew melons, cantaloupes, tomatoes, cauliflower, spinach, dry beans, garlic, alfalfa, apples, sugar beets, grapefruit, barley.

In this earthly paradise have grown prosperous, modern communities whose millions of people live free of insecurity and want. The three most important towns of the Central Valley are Sacramento, about a hundred miles northeast of San Francisco, which grew up around Sutter's Fort, with orange and magnolia trees shading the streets, architecturally half old, half new, with hundreds of suburban ranch-style houses; Stockton, an inland port, important as a trading post long before the gold rush; and Fresno, center of the billion-dollars-a-year trade of the San Joaquin Valley, halfway between San Francisco and Los Angeles, a young, vigorous, almost completely new city.

In towns like San Jose, forty miles south of San Francisco, a center of canning, dried fruits and wineries, three quarters of the families own their own homes, as they do in Sacramento and such prosperous southern towns as Pomona, with its colleges, Redlands, Riverside and San Bernardino. Millions of Californians want no part of the life in the world-known cities of San Francisco and Los Angeles; they like the intimacy and camaraderie of the coastal towns or the hot, small communities of the Central Valley: Marysville, Lodi, Stockton, Modesto, Merced, Fresno, Visalia, Salinas, San Louis Obispo and a hundred others, many of them with a single shopping center and conventional neon signs which are slowly draining their individuality. In towns like these you can know nearly everyone of your own generation; you need never live among strangers. You can, and do, marry young, frequently out of high school. Friendship is strong because it underlies almost every social activity. There is a homogeneity, not merely of ideas and values, but of income levels as well. No one need get lost. The weekly poker game you start during the last year of high school will still be going twenty years later with the same fellows, and probably the same gags. You won't enjoy much privacy; the other women will know exactly how much your wife spends on clothes and when you and she last quarreled. And you will also know everything about them.

Without this Central Valley, this modern-day Valley of the Nile, California would be a magnificent front, able to support less than half its population, hollow at its economic core.

The newest culture in the state, and perhaps the most exciting, is the life of the desert. The desert can be cruel; to many newcomers it appears hostile, fruitless. But the desert is also intensely alive, mysterious, masterful. Palm Springs is the center of the vacation area; no hospitals or sanitariums or industrial plants or farms are permitted in this particular mountain-enclosed valley. Palm Springs is attracting more devotees each year by what they like to call its optimum climate: the greatest amount of beneficent clear sunlight and the least humidity in the United States; but what is not generally known is that thousands of families are exchanging the business-suit-and-necktie life of formal cities for the open-sport-shirt-and-sandal life of the Coachella Valley, which includes Indio, heart of the date palm.

You drive through the eye-burning smog of Los Angeles, then climb up the San Gorgonio Pass, through Beaumont and Banning into the desert itself, with its towering wall of sheer brown rock; and suddenly you can breathe deeper, suddenly you are in a world of brilliant sunlight and color, the openness of vast areas where no person or object can fence in your body or your thinking. No matter how tired or ill you may be, or possessed by *Weltschmerz*, your troubles and complaints fall away: for there is little tension on the desert, pressures dissolve in the hot sun, as do the nervous confusions of a competitive world.

The recuperative power of the desert, its ability to bring one closer to the eternalities of nature, the ever-shifting forms of the sand, and the shadows on the mountains, with the sun on your back during the day, the warm silk-soft air of the night on your face, have caused thousands of people to move into the area around Palm Springs and make it their permanent home. There will be hundreds of thousands more in the balance of the Coachella and Imperial valleys, now that they are watered from the Colorado River through the new All-American Canal.

The desert is one vast *Kaffeeklatsch;* everyone is friendly and helpful because everyone is himself a new arrival, remembering how it felt to be lonely. When you live with the vastness of sky and sun and mountain, with the magnificent panorama of changing pastel colors, vivid purple sunsets, skies so thick with stars you can reach up and pick them like bunches of grapes, you stop worrying about Russians, hydrogen bombs, income taxes; you become, instead, in your own simple way, a philosopher. The products of philosophy, alas, cannot be boxed and shipped like the superb Coachella grapefruit and dates or the Imperial Valley melons; but by breeding an anxiety-free man, the desert is adding a new dimension and a new health-drenched culture to the complex geographical and mystical entity of California.

Northern California, the third of the state that lies north of San Francisco, is as different from Southern California as New Hampshire is from Florida. The mountains and stands of pine, redwood, Douglas fir, incense cedar, western yew, mountain birch and white oak are majestic, the towns and people few. There is privacy and solitude, great hunting, fishing, camping for a hardy stock that can take thirty-five below zero in winter, ninety-eight above in summer, and will not hesitate to brave the worst of these extremes to bag a fine mule buck or catch a large brown trout, or be averse to taking a wee drop now and then. The people living in the far north conceive of themselves as still living in an almost-frontier country; they enjoy the romantic conception of the hardy, robust, difficult life.

Northern Californians, too, live close to nature; it is an outdoor interest that explains the presence of most of the residents, particularly among the professional classes, yet the rugged four-season life is the exact opposite of that led by the new desert dwellers. They are never more than a few minutes away from upland meadows, mountain torrents, rock gorges through which the Kings and Kern rivers have cut their beds, high Sierra peaks and passes often snow-laden, nearly impenetrable forests carpeted with swordfern, huckle-berries, buckthorn, elderberry, teeming with bear, antelope, mountain sheep and mountain lions, fox, beaver and muskrat.

The towns of Northern California are old and so inbred that if you have an argument with a merchant or city clerk in Alturas you find that you have offended half the families of Modoc County. The people here are harder, sterner, more ruggedly set than the soft, easy-going, fast-changing but slower-moving and slower-talking Southern Californians.

The social life is exhausting: bridge parties, community concerts, baseball, bowling and rifleshoot competitions, an endless round of luncheons, cocktail parties, dinners, dances and picnic suppers. In a town like Ukiah, a hundred miles north of San Francisco, the community life of the churches, P.T.A., fraternal, scouting, political organizations and volunteer government committees is so highly organized that there is almost never a free hour; while the most often repeated line in Alturas is, "I got a meeting tonight." There are few book or music shops in these northern towns; however, the book clubs do a flourishing business and many middle-class families maintain credit accounts at San Francisco and Oakland bookstores.

The people of Northern California are a little like their redwoods: lean in temperament, resentful of intruders though exhaustingly hospitable to friends; opposed to change, to the new or different, disdaining the Southern California backyard-barbecue and swimming-pool set. To the Southern Californian, anything that is not built tomorrow is old-fashioned; to North Californians that which smells of paint, the most cherished of all perfumes in the south, is parvenu.

Around Lake Tahoe, where California and Nevada make an elbow bend, the rings on the *Sequoia gigantea* add up to four thousand years, probably the oldest inhabitants of the state; the northern people have somewhat the same solidity of tradition, priding themselves on being an "old" culture. This is true all the way down to Fresno, about midway in the state, after which the pride comes in being spanking-new.

California is not Utopia, yet it is a land to dream on; seventeen co-operative colonies, from the religious Fountain Grove near Santa Rosa in Northern California to Madame Modjeska's agricultural colony near Anaheim in Southern California, have been essayed in the past hundred years. When you drive through the gold-rush regions, pass abandoned mines and the high piles of rock displaced by hydraulic mining, and the river beds where millions in golden dust were taken out, it's all you can do to restrain yourself from jumping out of the car, grabbing a shovel and commencing to dig.

The state is changing: subdividers are ripping out walnut orchards and orange groves in the south for residential tracts, prune orchards and vineyards in the north for drive-in theaters or hardboard factories. The old-timers in Mendocino County don't want to be industrialized any more than the original settlers of San Diego want their two-lane roads expanded to superhighways.

Sentiment in the East used to be, "You can live cheaply in California, but you can't earn a living there." Today there is work for all, but the cost of living is high.

When I grew up in San Francisco a human being was a precious commodity, there were so few of them on Market Street or Powell. When I moved to New York in 1926 I was stunned by the hordes of humanity jammed on Fifth Avenue or 42nd Street during the day and on Broadway at night. If there are so many people in the world, I thought, can any one of them be truly valuable?

A Californian moving to New York today would not be so stunned by the difference: for we are fast acquiring people. By the year 2000 we should have a population of 50,000,000, outnumbering most of the countries of Europe.

To this writer, who has spent his summers in the north since he was six, the Sonoma and Napa valleys, and Jack London's Valley of the Moon, are the most beautiful parts of California, surpassed only by the view of the Lombardy plain from the top of Assisi. The immigrating Italians, back in the seventies and eighties, searching all over America for their native Italy, found it in these valleys, cleared the mountainsides of first stand redwood and pine, manzanita and madroña, planted their vineyards and made some of the world's finest wines, enriching the country with the best of their native character, particularly gastronomically. But the third generation no longer wants to plow the fields or cultivate the grapes; they've become Americanized and prefer to work in factories. The superb little wineries, with some exceptions, have been sold to the larger distilleries.

What is the character of the state today?

Californians are by nature a tender and gentle people somehow given to violence, doubtless a vestige of the pioneer days when folks had to take care of their own hangings. If you feel the urge to blow up your parents on their yacht, or poison the milk of your best friend because you're in love with his wife, California is far and away your best bet: true-blooded Californians are too close to the pioneer days to convict anyone for a crime of passion.

Politically, it is clean; it would be after fifteen years of Earl Warren as attorney general and governor; yet we are not too aseptic to elect an occasional hack politician to high office, and have him celebrate his victory on election night by getting falling-down drunk in one of the swankier night clubs.

In the early part of the century, California was so predominantly Republican that we hardly knew there was a two-party system. I was first introduced at the age of nine to the Democrats by a gang of Mission district boys who grabbed me and shouted, "Who are you for?" I was for Teddy Roosevelt, but since it appeared obvious that they would not have grabbed me had I been for the right candidate I answered, "Taft!" Their leader bulked his fist in front of my face and cried, "You be for Woodrow Wilson, or I'll punch your nose in."

I had never heard of Mr. Wilson, but I quickly changed my registration.

Like my entry into active politics, I was first rudely introduced to the California labor problems by being showered with broken glass from a rock thrown through a Masonic Avenue streetcar by striking motormen. San Francisco has always been known as a tough labor town; over the years there has been violence on the water front, swinging fists and swinging clubs, and the biggest general strike ever conducted in the United States. After persuading my wife, who was born in decorous Minnesota, that we should live in California because it was a peace-loving state, we spent our first day driving over a roadbed of crushed lettuce leaves, having bumped spang into an agricultural workers' strike in the Salinas Valley lettuce bowl.

Today management nor union is going to the wars quite as frequently as it used to: they are rather like the married couple that sits in the living room all night and holds hands, each afraid to let go for fear the other will haul off.

Los Angeles, by direct contrast, was kept an open-shop town for decades; to attract industry, the city advertised nationally that there were no unions there. As late as 1936 Los Angeles had one of the most docile and underpaid labor forces in America; grocery clerks, for example, earned eighteen dollars for a seventy-two hour week. Today, Southern California is organized, wages are high; the unions have achieved solidity without bloodshed or too agonized cries from management. Doubtless the influence of the benign climate.

Probably the most recognizable connecting links between the towns of string-bean-long California are the 540 or so Bank of America buildings, which stretch from Yreka, just south of the Oregon border, to National City, just north of the Mexican border. Though it has spread-eagled the state, it has managed to escape the charge of "octopus" both by keeping out of politics and by fulfilling A. P. Giannini's dictum that his bank must be for the little fellow: in truth, it is the common man's bank.

Started in 1904 by A. P. Giannini as the Bank of Italy in a modest building in the North Beach Italian section, it has since become the largest bank in the world, having revolutionized the whole concept of banking by creating branch banking, thus giving it statewide billions to finance vineyards, irrigation districts and a thousand businesses. In 1944 when I had used up all my available cash in completing *Immortal Wife*, my own happily mortal wife informed me that we were overdrawn a hundred or so dollars. We drove from our home in San Fernando Valley to Hollywood to see the manager, a Mr. Grillo who presided over the tiny branch in what had formerly been a corner grocery store. We told Mr. Grillo that we were overdrawn. He replied: "Why don't you go home and finish your book, and let me worry about the banking business?"

A few weeks later he loaned us fifteen hundred dollars to take our completed manuscript to New York, the money enabling us to live and work there until publication: probably the first time in history that a bank midwived a successful biographical novel.

This illustrated another difference in California life: the neighborhood bank, branch department store and supermarket as against the impersonal, coldly formal, monolithic downtown bank or shop.

Nor, in our economic prosperity, are we trying to live by bread alone. Bookstores were opened in the Sacramento Valley during the very height of the gold rush by men who thought it more important to sell and disseminate literature than to dig a fortune out of the ground. Probably no state, with the possible exception of Indiana, has bred more creative writers. The great University of California, which literally teems with creativity in the humanities and sciences, and has eight campuses stretching throughout the state, accessible free of charge to all of California's youngsters, was started a full century ago, also while gold was available for the digging.

We have our art colonies at Carmel in the north, Laguna Beach in the south, Idyllwild high in the mountains, the music academy of the West in a beautiful Santa Barbara garden. Open-air art exhibits in the neighborhood parks of Los Angeles have attracted thousands of paintings and sculptures; granted little of it has anything more than therapeutic value for its creators, but even the most modest practice of an art is the first step toward its understanding.

The Californian today is assuredly not what he was during the gold-rush days, nor during the sleepy sun-baked 1880's when Los Angeles was an adobe village, nor yet what he was during the rambunctious days of San Francisco after the turn of the century with its Barbary Coast. The Californian today has been widely crossbred; in many parts of the state, prior to the second World War, it was almost impossible to find anyone except a native son; today in Southern California, for example, almost 90 per cent of the adult population is from out of the state.

Our faith in the absorptive powers of the state is strong. With our magnificent dams and irrigation systems, with our new chemical marvels and improved farm machinery, we can raise enough food to sustain an empire. The Pacific Ocean is so vast that it is able to dissipate whatever poisons may be dumped onto its broad bosom; our mountains, deserts, valleys, hundred bustling little towns have the same powers of assimilation.

If Frank Lloyd Wright was correct in saying that only the Far West is vital because it is still growing, then perhaps out here in California we can evolve a breed of human being who is healthy in his mind as well as in his body; who can live a vigorous outdoor life, close to the beauties and mysteries of the desert, the mountains, the redwoods, the fertile valleys and the sea, and at the same time work prodigiously in the creative arts and intellects. Perhaps we can sire a breed of *homo sapiens* who does not want to fight and destroy but to construct and live at peace with his neighbor, be he next door in Santa Ana or Eureka, in Athens, Bangkok or Tokyo.

This is why we have the temerity to suggest that California is the West Pole. With half the world shutting down on freedom, California is offering ever increasing freedoms to all its people, those here and those on the way.

The line forms on the right. Build yourself a modern home of steel and glass so that you can cook your dinner in a kitchen overlooking the Golden Gate Strait and the hills of Marin County, or go to sleep in a bedroom in the hills of Altadena overlooking the light-studded plains of Southern California.

So much has been written about California there is little left to be told: except the truth. But would you look for truth in the eyes of a man in love?

Oregon

by H. L. DAVIS

It used to be a saying in Oregon that people who lived there could change their whole order of life—climate, scenery, diet, complexions, emotions, even reproductive faculties—by merely moving a couple of hundred miles in any direction inside the state. Maybe they still can, but there is not that feeling about coming back to it after a long time away. I have tried returning from three different directions now, and touching it at any point unfailingly brings all of it back on me, not a collection of separate localities but always as one single and indivisible experience. Everything belongs in it, and it all comes together: the gray high-country sagebrush ridges of the Great Basin where I once herded cattle, the rolling wheatlands fronting on the Columbia River to the north where I lived as a youngster, the green-timbered valley country between the high Cascade Mountains and the Coast Range where I was born and grew up—where people sometimes lived all their lives without having any idea what the naked earth looked like. Except for the cultivated tracts, there were not a dozen acres in the country without a stand of Douglas fir trees.

Beyond the Coast Range is the open coast, and it belongs in the experience too. I used to hunt deer there every fall. My grandfather homesteaded down one of the little coastal rivers in the 1870's, and my mother lived there as a girl. The country was not logged off then, and there were no roads. The family marketing had to be done by taking a homemade canoe down the river, and the children explored the neighborhood by walking on fallen logs where hundreds of gaily colored garter snakes collected to sun themselves during the afternoon. It must have been an intrusive kind of place to grow up in, with white-topped combers jarring the granite cliffs like dynamite blasts and the long wall of black spruce and cedar tossing and roaring in the spring gales, and swarms of huge gulls screaming and fighting over the salmon that got washed out on the sand bars in the spring spawning runs. It would be the same now, probably. Cliffs and combers and gulls are still there, and so is the timber, black spruce or fir or cedar, not bent or twisted by the sea wind but standing straight and rigid against it as the gray cliffs in which they are rooted. They do let down a little along the creeks and old clearings; there are intervals where they leave room for masses of grayish-green alder and dogwood and maple. There is not much variety of color in the country. Except when the flowers are out, it is mostly variations of green, and even autumn alters it very little: a few blots of yellow in the maples, sometimes verging on white, a few streaks of pink in the dogwoods, though hardly enough of either to break the monotony. The extremes of temperature are too small to color leaves very brilliantly. In some places the alder leaves merely die and fall off without coloring at all.

The wild flowers do make a difference. They are all through the woods and grasslands when spring opens: dogwood, wild cherry, sweetbrier, flowering currant, mock orange; ground flowers like lamb's-tongues, cat ears, blue camas lilies, red bird bills, patches of buttercups and St.-John's-wort, wild violets that are not purplish like garden violets, but the intense sky blue of jaybird feathers, and yellow violets, trilliums, blue lilies of the valley and pink swamp mallow, besides skunk cabbage and water lily, which are mostly ugly. Wild asters, foxgloves, azaleas and rhododendrons come later in the summer when the berries are beginning to ripen—wild blackberries, black raspberries, black haws, wild strawberries, red and black huckleberries.

Wild berries were a staple article of diet for farm families in Western Oregon a generation ago. Some species, like the native wild blackberry, were scarce in many sections then, because hurried and careless picking destroyed the vines. They should be taking a fresh hold now. Picking them always took hard work and time, and it is easier nowadays to buy such things at the market, so the berries

are left for the blue grouse and bears, which don't object to hard
work and have more time than they know what to do with anyway.
People in some areas used to depend on the mountain Indians to
come through the country with their pack trains every fall, peddling
huckleberries and wild blackberries, as they always wandered
through peddling muddy water cress out of dripping gunny sacks
every spring, but those signs of the changing seasons ended a good
many years ago. Indians nowadays do their wandering mostly in
automobiles, the same as everybody else, and seldom with anything
to sell.

The berries go on growing, nevertheless. There are places in the
scrub oak and bracken of the red-earth foothills where, in late April
or early May, the wild strawberries are crowded so close together
under the broom grass and bracken that you will crush a handful at
every step; there are huckleberry swales in the higher mountains
where the bushes are bent flat to the ground with the weight of
their berries, and trails show where the bears have had to fill up on
bitter ashberries as a corrective against overindulgence in them;
there are wild blackberry patches in the old timber burns of the back
country where, in the late spring, the drumming of ruffed grouse
sounds like a battery of rivet guns running full blast.

Some of the country's most common and useless-looking types of
vegetation have stories back of them. The evergreen blackberry vine,
which tangles itself over all the old fences and abandoned homestead clearings, was brought across the plains by the women of the
first emigrant train in 1843, and watered and tended carefully during
the entire journey as something to plant in their new gardens. Once
it was started, they discovered that the native wild blackberry was
far superior to it in size, flavor and accessibility, so it was left to run
wild, and in many parts of the country it has become a serious pest.
The Spanish moss, which grows in long skeins and festoons on the
oak trees of the lower valleys, belongs on the opposite side of the
ledger. None of the early settlers had imagined there could be any
possible use for it until one winter in the early 1850's, when a deep
snow buried all their pastures and they discovered that their cattle
were keeping alive by eating Spanish moss from the low-hanging
tree branches. Since most of the moss grew higher, the settlers took
to cutting the trees down to keep a supply of it within reach. After
the first few days, the cattle would come charging through the snow
whenever they heard the crack of a tree about to fall, and the chil-

dren of the settlement had to be stationed around it with clubs to keep the cattle from stampeding in and being crushed under the tree when it came down.

The moss has never been used for anything since, but the memory of help given in need takes a long time to wear off. A great-uncle of mine, who came to Western Oregon as a youngster in 1852 and lived there till he was past ninety, told me once about standing guard in the snow with the other children during that winter, and added that he had never since been able to look at Spanish moss without a vague stir of gratitude, or at cattle without a deep feeling of dislike. He had five or six children, all born and brought up in the valley country where he spent nearly all of a long and useful life. None of them stayed there after they were grown. They all moved away, and scattered according to the usual pattern for such families: one to New York, one to Washington, D.C., a couple to Los Angeles, one to some city in the Middle West. They used to come back on visits sometimes. They are all elderly now; some may be dead.

The constant drifting away of second generations from this country, and the influx of new people from other states, may have something to do with its persistent sense of newness, of everything being done for the first time. The growth of the towns probably helps too. Many Western Oregon towns have trebled in size since the war; most have doubled. There are old buildings still left in them, but they are usually overshadowed by an environing swarm of new stucco supermarkets, car and tractor showrooms, chain-saw and logging-truck repair shops, real-estate offices, Assembly of God tabernacles, drive-in movie-theaters (generally referred to as passion pits), country-club residence subdivisions, antique and curio shops, and places offering such out-of-the-way amenities as fortunetelling, agate testing, and streamlined bull service.

Even if it were possible to account for all these new and varied enterprises in detail (what, for instance, is there about bull service that anybody could streamline?), trying to trace out the original lines of these towns runs into all kinds of confusions and bewilderments. The local residents are usually not much help. Traveling through the lower valley country last spring, I stopped at one of the newer towns to have a surgical dressing put on an infected finger. The doctor's office was upstairs over the drugstore. From the window, there was a view of two motels, a service station, the highway bridge over a small creek, and a gaunt old three-story frame hotel, tall and shabby and narrow-windowed, shedding loose boards and patches of ugly yellow paint behind a clump of huge half-dead pear trees. The doctor saw me looking at it as he worked, and remarked that it was a real relic. It had been a kind of roadhouse for gold miners back in the early days, he had heard: saloon, dance hall, gambling house, that kind of business.

"Some rip-roaring old times there when it was new, I guess," he said. "Shootings, big-money gambling, one thing and another. Dance-hall girls, and all that. It could tell some wild old stories, I guess, if it could talk. It is a kind of an eyesore, the shape it's in; a firetrap too. It ought to be fixed up or got rid of, or something. We could have a real town here if these State people weren't so fussy with their restrictions."

He was young, sociable, and interested in a lot of things. He was originally from Wisconsin, had come out during the war as medical officer in an armored division that carried on field training in the desert around Fort Rock, and had decided to stay on afterward and grow up with the country. I asked which State people seemed the most bothersome, and whether there weren't other places where they were less stringent. He said it was the highway department, mostly, though none of them were easy to get along with if you wanted to do anything.

"All their regulations about what you can build and where, and what you can do and what you can't do, till you'd think we were some bunch of mental cases that had to be told to come in out of the rain," he said. "There are other places, I suppose. Still, I don't know. I like this one. All this new country, and seeing things to do with it. You don't get that in the older places. It's worth something. There's a kind of a feeling about it."

New country, I thought. Down the little creek that was visible from his office window was part of the old trail over which Ewing Young and ten herders drove 600 head of cattle in from California in 1837. It was something of an achievement, by all accounts. His herders quarreled among themselves so fiercely that he had to sit up nights with a loaded gun to keep them from killing each other, and he dared not attempt to reconcile them for fear they might get together and decide to kill him. He got cattle and herders in safely, despite difficulties, and other herds followed. By 1842, the trail was a main route of travel. And not over an hour away was a town on the Umpqua River where the Hudson's Bay Company had a fort and

trading post in 1834, and French Prairie near Salem was all wheatfields and orchards by then. . . . What was Wisconsin in 1834? Indian country, like most of Maine, and Minnesota, and Louisiana, and
Northern New York, and all of the Tennessee Valley. Oregon is not
new; it is older than most of them. Its population turnover gives it an
illusion of newness, that is all. However, the doctor was right about
one thing: there is the illusion, the same as in the beginning, and an
illusion is enough, if it can be made to last.

His ideas about the old hotel having had a rip-roaring past were
all wrong, though: colored by too many moving pictures, probably,
or by some older resident trying to make the country sound interesting. Merely a hotel was all it had ever been: an overnight stop on the
old stage line across the mountains from the coast, with the usual
accommodations for man and beast. There had never been anything
rip-roaring about it: no wild times, no dance-hall girls, no big-money
gambling, probably no great amount of money to gamble with, if
gold mining had been its main source. There was gold mining back
in the hills in the early days, and some even up to a few years ago,
when high operating expenses forced most of it to close down, but
none of it ever produced much. A sheep herder prodding around
in a dry creek bed on the Upper Rogue River in the early 1930's took
out more actual gold in a single afternoon than most of the early-day
miners ever saw, or the old hotel either. My grandfather, who was a
Hard-Shell Baptist clergyman, used to hold religious services in its
main lobby every month or so when he was circuit rider for the
district. He was not in the least rip-roaring, though he was responsible for the only shooting the place ever had recorded against it; not
exactly a conventional one, though it was disastrous enough in its
results.

It happened, according to family tradition, one night after a wedding in the hotel at which he had been invited to officiate. After the
ceremony, he withdrew to an upstairs room and went to bed, leaving
the guests to their dancing and celebrating, which usually lasted till
daylight. Along past midnight, he was roused by some disturbance
in the horse corral that sounded as if prowlers might be sneaking up
to spring the gate and stampede the horses. Raising an alarm seemed
a waste of time in such an emergency, so he rummaged an old
muzzle-loading shotgun out of a closet, rammed down a double load
of powder and shot, leaned out of the window and let go both barrels
at the shadows outside the corral gate. Nobody ever found out

whether he hit anything or not because, loading the gun hurriedly in the dark, he had rammed the tail of his nightshirt down one barrel along with the powder, so the shot yanked him out of the window headfirst. He fell three floors into the middle of the wedding celebration with his shirttail in flames around his neck and scared everybody almost to death. Several guests collapsed, and some ran eight or ten miles without stopping. My grandfather sustained a broken arm and second-degree burns, and miscarriages were claimed by two ladies, and denied heatedly by three others, including the bride.

The difference between that uncolored incident and the riproaring type of conventionalized fantasy is the difference between tradition and illusion. Tradition is what a country produces out of itself; illusion is what people bring into it from somewhere else. On the record, the illusions have considerably the better of it. People keep bringing them in. Those who kept the traditions going keep drifting away and scattering, to New York and Washington and California and places in the Middle West. Still, it will go on producing new ones, probably. It always has.

There used to be an old sawmill and logging settlement back in the deep timber on the eastern fringe of the valley country, where my father taught school when I was not much over two years old. It was a small-scale sort of operation, with no prospects of expansion, because its local market was limited to a scattering of homesteaders and cattlemen around the neighborhood, and distance and bad roads made hauling its lumber out to the railroad impossible. Still, between the homesteaders and some half-breed fragments of an old Indian tribe back in the hills, there was enough to run a school on while it lasted. Afterward, the mill closed down, the homesteaders moved away, the Indians were rounded up and shipped north to the collective reservation at Siletz, and the school and settlement were abandoned for a good many years. Recently, after back-country logging had been put back on its feet by such new wrinkles as tractors, hard-surfaced roads, power chain saws, truck transportation and a rising market for building material, a big lumber company bought up the old camp and the timber back of it, built a fence between it and the main road, and hired a watchman with experience in handling firearms to keep campers and hobos and log pirates out.

There was nothing about the old logging camp that I wanted particularly to see. I had lived in it when too young to remember it; the stories people used to tell about it afterward were associated with them, not with the place. It was the lumber company's watchman I went up there to call on. I had known him from years back, when I was on a Government survey in one of the national forests up in northern Oregon, and he was guide and camp wrangler for a symphony-orchestra conductor from New York who liked trout fishing, or thought he did: a strutty, playful old gentleman who sang resonantly while fishing, and naturally never caught anything.

The watchman didn't have to work as a guide, being very well off from speculating in orchard lands around the Cascade foothills, but he liked the woods and would rather be working at something than sitting around doing nothing. He used to come over to our camp of an evening and tell stories about being sent out to track down people who had got themselves lost back in the deep timber. He held that anybody could get lost in the woods, there was nothing disgraceful about it, he had been lost in that very country half a dozen times himself, though he was accounted an authority on its geography and landmarks. Whether it turned out seriously or not depended on the kind of intelligence a man used after he got lost. A fool would never admit that he was lost; no matter how completely bushed he was, he always knew his location and directions exactly, and got himself worse lost trying to make them work out. The watchman said he had brought out lost hunting parties in almost a dying condition who were so positive he was taking them in the wrong direction that some of them had to be dragged to get them started. His stories were not only diverting but helpful. I have been lost in the woods a couple of times since then myself, and without them I would undoubtedly have done pretty much what he said the fools always did.

The hard-surfaced road back to the old logging camp had strung the twenty-mile stretch of adjoining country so full of small cottages and shacks and chicken-farm lean-tos that there was hardly any country left until I got within sight of the old logging-camp buildings and the lumber company's fence and padlocked gate. Beyond that, everything changed. There was a dirt road, sprinkled with dead fir needles, with a dusty spot showing where quail had wallowed. The big Douglas firs stood straight and tall and motionless up the sidehill, not crowded together as they are in the rainier mountains near the coast, but scattered out between clumps of hazel and vine maple and open patches of white-top grass and pink fireweed. There were no rusty car bodies or can dumps or barnyard manure piles in the creek. It rattled past clear and bright and untroubled, reaching back through thickets of red willow and gray alder and sweet bush to some old stump land overgrown with evergreen blackberry vines. There was a grouse clucking somewhere up the hill, in a sort of anxiously persistent tone that for some reason was restful to listen to. It was impossible to tell where it was coming from: sounds in timber country have a curious way of seeming to come from the air itself rather than from any tangible thing in it.

The old logging camp buildings were all nailed up and deserted, except the one nearest the road. It had its windows unboarded, with a school election notice tacked to the door above a wooden-seated chair, and a tin tobacco box alongside containing a few rusty nails, a fire warden's badge, a carpenter's pencil, some loose cigarette papers, and a half-box of .22 cartridges. The watchman was nowhere around. I left my car at the gate and climbed over it and walked up the road a few hundred yards to look around.

There were deer tracks in the road, a doe and two fawns, and big-foot rabbit tracks, and a blue grouse hooting in the firs somewhere, but it was not altogether as the Lord had left it. People had lived here once, up the dirt road for miles back into the hills. My mother used to tell about some of them: an old cattleman, enormously wealthy, who kept eight squaws, one at each of his line camps, and had children by all of them regularly, though he was then past seventy, and a town named after him which is still flourishing. And one of the young half-breeds who drew a knife on my father in school, and then tried to make up for it by bringing him presents—potted plants, ornamented mustache cups, dressed turkeys —all of which turned out to be stolen; and another half-breed, a youngster of about fifteen, who used to write poems, each stanza in a different-colored ink, and peddle them around the settlement at two bits a copy. People used to buy them and never read them. And another cattleman, middle-aged and quarrelsome, was supposed to have set himself up in business by murdering and robbing an old Chinese peddler, and had a mania for giving expensive wedding presents to every young married couple in the community, even those whose fathers he was sworn to shoot on sight. . . . There were more of them. It had been a big community once. There had probably been as many people in it as there were in the chicken-farm cottages down the creek, and they had stayed there at least as long. But they had marked it less, or maybe the marks they made were the kind that healed over more easily. A few were still visible: some old stumps grown over with vines, some half-burned fence posts showing through the fir needles, part of an old corduroy wood road running uphill into the salal with rabbit fur scattered in it where a hawk had struck. The creek had taken out some of the old marks, seemingly. A tangle of whitened driftwood piled high above a cut-bank showed that it had sometimes flooded. There were scuff marks across a strip of sand below the cutbank where some beavers had dragged sticks to use in building a dam.

They had their dam finished, and the cutbank was partly under-mined where they had started a tunnel to their nest. It was nothing to be proud of, as far as workmanship went. I had always heard that beavers had a sort of obsession for work, and spent all their time at it because they enjoyed doing it, but the dam didn't show it. They hadn't cut down any trees for it at all, though there were dozens of alder and willow saplings within easy reach. They had merely made it a tangle of dry sticks from the driftwood, most of them no bigger than a lead pencil. The whole thing was so childish and flimsy that they had to weight it down with rocks to keep the creek from wash-ing it away. It was some sort of commentary on modern times, prob-ably, but a man gets tired of having the same thing proved over and over again. It was time for me to go back, anyway.

The company watchman was sitting in his chair by the door when I got back to the gate. There is always a certain trepidation about meeting somebody you haven't seen for twenty years, but he hadn't changed much. He had always been grayish and scrawny, and he was merely a little grayer and scrawnier. He apologized for being out when I came, and said he had been down arguing with some of the chicken-farm people who kept trying to sneak through the company fence and dump garbage upstream in the creek. He didn't know why it meant so much to them to dump it upstream, and they hadn't been able to explain it very convincingly themselves. Their main argument seemed to be that it was a free country and the creek belonged to everybody, and the lumber company had no right to go around telling people what they could do and what they couldn't. It looked sometimes as if they couldn't stand to see anything in the country left as it had been before they got there. It preyed on their minds, or something.

"There's not much left for them to worry about," I said. "Not around here, anyway."

"It's no better up north," he said. "There's highways crisscrossed all through the mountains up there. A highway into the mountains lets people see what wild country looks like, if they can find room to drive between the log trucks. Nobody ever figures that the wild country might not want to see what people look like. It's like that old saloonkeeper up on the Columbia River that had himself buried in an Indian graveyard when he died, because he'd decided that Indians were better to associate with than white people."

I remembered the story. Everybody had been deeply impressed by his wish to associate with Indians after he died. Nobody had thought to find out how the Indians felt about associating with him. It turned out that they were not impressed by the prospect at all. After he had been buried in their tribal graveyard, they moved all their graves somewhere else and let him have it all to himself. Building a main highway into a wild country is like driving a red-hot poker into a tree and expecting the sap to start circulating in it. The living tissue of the tree draws back from it, and the sap goes on circulating around it; or else the tree dies.

"There's wild country left," the watchman said. "More than you'd think, from the way they've fixed things down the creek below here. It's not much different than it used to be, if you figure it right. You've got to figure it in time instead of mileage, that's all. It used to take a day for a man to drive up here from the railroad with a team and wagon. You probably drove it in less than an hour, and you're surprised that it's all built up. If you'll take a team and wagon and take out on some of these old corduroy wood roads into the hills for a day, the way you'd have done twenty years ago, you'll run into all the wild country you want. You may have to chop some logs out of the road and fight yellow jackets off the horses, but it'll be wild. The animals and everything else."

"Not all the animals," I said, and told him about the beaver and their scamped job of dam building up the creek.

"They're Oklahoma beavers, I expect," he said. "Moved out from the Dust Bowl back in the hard times, more than likely. You've got to remember that they've been through a lot, and that it don't do any good to stand around and criticize. What they need is help. You ought to have chewed down a few trees for 'em, to get 'em started off on the right foot."

It was not the first tribute to the Oklahoma temperament I had heard, though most were less indirect. "Are they as bad as that?" I said.

"We're none of us perfect," he said mildly. "They're not exactly the kind of company I'd pick to be shipwrecked on a desert island with, but there's points about 'em. I had a crew of sixty of 'em fighting a little brush fire in some second-growth timber on Thief Creek last fall, and they were as conscientious as anybody could ask in a lot of ways. Paydays and mealtimes they never missed. They even fought fire off and on, till it got within about three-quarters of a mile of 'em. Then they dropped everything and legged it out of there at a gallop. Well, they have to learn. It takes time."

"It sounds as if it might take a lot of it," I said. "More than either of us will ever see, probably."

"I've seen 'em come in like this before," he said. "Some as bad, and some worse. They spread back into places like this and dumped garbage and slashed trees and strung fences and tore up grasslands and fixed everything around to suit themselves. Then they got old, and their kids grew up and moved away somewhere else and sent for 'em and a lot of 'em died out, and now they're all gone. They never last. They think they will, but they never do. They swarm in here with their car wrecks and bellyaches and litters of children, and they pile in to fix the whole country over, and it civilizes 'em in spite of themselves. Then they pick up and go somewhere else to show it off. I may live long enough to see it here yet. Hell, lots of people live to be over ninety nowadays. It'll happen, anyway."

It was looking past externals to an underlying purpose in the country, whether it was the right one or not. And it may have been the right one. Years before, when I was timekeeper for a Greek extra gang on the old Deschutes Railroad, the foreman of the outfit used almost the same terms in trying to explain about some squabble that had got stirred up among the men. The details were a little involved, and he finally brushed them aside and attacked the root of the problem.

"The trouble with these fellows is that they ain't been over here in this country long enough to know anything," he said.

He was Greek himself, from some small coastal village in the province of Corinth. He had left home when he was young, because of some parental difficulty: he had sneaked his father's muzzle-loading pistol out to see how it shot, and the load of slugs and scrap iron tore all the bark off two of the old man's best olive trees, so he ran away to keep from being skinned alive. "All these fellows know is how things are back in the old country. They think that's all they need to know, and it ain't anything. They ain't civilized back in the old country."

The idea that an expanse of Eastern Oregon sagebrush where horse-Indians still wandered around living in tepees and digging camas could represent a higher stage of civilization than the land that had cradled Sophocles and Plato was so startling that I laughed.

"Well, it's the truth," he said, "them people in the old country ain't civilized. They don't know what it is to be civilized till they've been over here awhile. It takes a long time for some of 'em."

"You ought to be civilized by now, anyway," I said. "You've been over here a long time."

"If I was, I wouldn't be out in a place like this," he said. "I didn't say this country got people civilized. I said they found out what it was like to be civilized, that's all. That's as far as I've got."

It did work out to some kind of system. The older generation found out what civilization was; the younger absorbed it, and moved away somewhere else to show it off: Joaquin Miller from his parents' farm in the Willamette Valley to Canyon City, and to England, and to his final exhibitionistic years in California: Edwin Markham from Oregon City to California and to his end in New York; John Reed from Portland to New York and Mexico and to his tomb in Red Square in Moscow. . . . Civilization? At any rate, it was something.

I got a camera from the car to take some pictures of the old logging camp buildings. It was not difficult to pick out the one we had lived in from the stories my mother had told about it. It was the one with the high front porch; she had told about two drunk half-breed Indians rolling and fighting under it one night on their way home from town, and how she lay in bed listening while one of them beat the other to death with a rock. She was alone in the house; my father was away at a teachers' conference in Roseburg, the county seat.

The watchman looked the camera over, and said he had been intending to get one himself. He wanted to take some pictures of the country to send his son, who lived in Hollywood.

"San Fernando, I guess it is, but it's the same thing," he said. "He works in Hollywood. He's got one of these television shows, Know Your Neighbors, or something like that; interviews with people, and things like that. He's doing well at it, but it don't leave him much time for anything else. He can't get away much. It'll be a big thing some of these days, but you have to stay with it. If you don't you lose out."

The country north through the Willamette Valley is lovely in the spring, with long expanses of green meadowland and flocks of sheep and dairy herds and clumps of wild apple and plum and cherry flowering against the dark fir thickets along the streams. The towns have a certain New Englandish look about them, emphasizing a difference between their culture and that of the country around them that has existed from the earliest days. The townspeople came originally from New England, and were traders and small merchants and artisans. The settlers in the rural areas were mostly open-country cattle raisers from the Mississippi Valley—Missouri, Arkansas, Tennessee, Kentucky. The two cultures have never mixed, and there has been little sympathy or understanding developed between them. Each is admittedly indispensable to the other: country people need towns, and towns have to live on the country, but there is not much enthusiasm in accepting the necessity.

A highway turns east from Salem across the Cascade Mountains by the Santiam Pass, following an old toll road built by cattlemen in the 1850's as a driveway by which to move their herds from the Willamette Valley to the open-country sagebrush and bunch-grass ranges of Eastern Oregon. It couldn't have looked like much of a move, as far as appearances went. The Willamette Valley grasslands are green, luxuriant, well-watered, and usually open for grazing throughout the entire year. East of the mountains the country is arid, colorless, baked dry in summer and whipped by blizzards in winter, its sparse clumps of whitish-green bunch grass not sodded, but spaced out two or three feet apart from each other with naked red earth showing between each clump, or sometimes hidden so close among the sagebrush roots that an outsider will wonder how cattle turned out on it are managing to keep alive, when they may have been put there to fatten for market. There is not much nutriment in grass that has had too easy a time of it; it will keep cattle alive, but not put weight on them. The bunch grass, which has had to fight for every inch of its growth, is far superior in nutritive value to any of the deep sod grasses west of the mountains. There might be some suspicion of a moral back of this, except that cattlemen are not interested in the moralistic aspects of the subject. Nor are their cattle.

One spring I drove east by the highway over the mountains through Santiam Pass. Deep snow all through the pass and in scattered drifts far down into the timber. Blue Lake down in a deep basin to the south, still and deserted; the snow roofs of the summer cabins looked peaceful and attractive. Not a living soul in any of them. Mount Washington towering back of the lake, its huge snowy peak striking into the blue sky like a spear. Snow in patches even below the level where the fir timber changes to yellow pine; salal bushes in bloom among the pines, hanging full of little pink bells like heather, the shallow drifts of old snow under them splotched with pale yellow where their pollen had shed. No wild life in the fir timber, not even birds. A few magpies among the pines, and a tiny lilac-throated hummingbird working on the salal blossoms. Near where the pine thins out into scattering juniper, a little town called Sisters, where sheepmen used to load their pack trains for the camps in the mountains; remote, quiet and dusty, a movie theater showing some tired B-Western picture. A youngster of about sixteen at the gas station gave me some directions about roads, and then said, "What does television look like?" . . .

North through the Warm Springs Indian Reservation. Open juniper and grassland, the timbered Cascade Mountains off to the west, a few cattle and some scattering wheatfields. The agency was about the same as it was twenty years ago: the store and gas station probably new. Some young Indians in a car, apparently from Klamath or somewhere south, were on their way to a spring salmon festival at Celilo on the Columbia River. I noticed that a couple of them had their hair marcelled, apparently to get rid of the Indian straightness. It didn't seem much of an improvement. Until recent years there were only dirt roads through the reservation, and it was even lonelier than it is now.

. . . North to the Columbia River at Celilo. It was late afternoon, and twenty years had not changed it much: the gigantic blue shadows reaching down from the gray-black cliffs over the white sand and dark water were still enough to make a man catch his breath and forget to let go of it. No picture can do what the place itself does; the pen-and-ink drawing that Theodore Winthrop made of it for his *The Canoe and the Saddle* in 1860 comes no farther from it than any of the modern photographs. They all miss the intensity of tones, and the scale—the cliffs a thousand feet high, the shadows half a mile deep and twenty miles long, the rapids thundering spray into the air higher than a man can see. The houses scattered in the rifts of cold sunlight have a helpless look, as if the whole thing stunned them. . . .

The salmon festival appeared to be all over with. Several dozen out-of-state cars were pulled up alongside the old Indian village (a huddle of unpainted board shacks along the river, dirt-floored and completely unsanitary, which seem now to have become merely a show piece; the Indians live in some large white corrugated-iron barracks on higher ground, which look very clean and thoroughly dull) and tourists were poking around asking questions of a few middle-aged Indians, with some squaws watching from an old Cadillac sedan. They had on their best clothes, and seemed prim and a little self-conscious. It couldn't have been much of a salmon festival. In the old days, the centerpiece of a salmon festival was always a wagonload of canned heat, and the ceremonies usually wound up in a big free-for-all fight. It was a little dangerous sometimes, but the guests did have something to talk about for the rest of the year.

. . . South through the Sherman County wheatfields to Antelope. The wheat towns remain unchanged, at least: no new buildings, the old ones all still standing, though some seemed vacant. The great divisions of color in the wheatfields were beautiful: bright green winter wheat, black summer fallow, white stubble, running long curves and undulations across the ridges to the sky line and into the gray sagebrush to the south. A flock of sheep grazing along a little creek bed at the edge of the sagebrush, with the herder's camp wagon drawn up behind a clump of junipers; not much of a camp wagon, merely a small high-wheeled trailer with a stovepipe stuck through the roof. The herder came out and stopped to talk for a minute: an elderly man, gray and stocky and taciturn. He complained of the long winter, which had been hard on the sheep, and offered to trade his high-powered rifle for my .22 pistol, because there was no longer anything around that a man could use a high-powered rifle on. He had herded sheep most of his life, he said, and didn't mind it. A man could get used to anything. It was easier nowadays, with cars and radios, than it had been. He had a radio in his camp wagon, and liked to listen to it, except the commercials, which made him want to buy things when he was miles from the nearest town and couldn't. His son was in college, he said, studying law; in Los Angeles.

Antelope had not changed in appearance since I lived there as a youngster. It was still a quiet, grayish little town with tall poplars lining the streets and a creek valley spread out below it. The only thing different was the people. They had been mostly Indians and

Highland Scots: big lumbering men, some with the reddest hair I
have ever seen, who talked English in a curious half-falsetto tone,
when they could talk it at all. The only languages one commonly
heard on the street were Gaelic and Chinook jargon. It had been a
homesick experience, trying to get used to them at first. Now it was
a homesick feeling not to find any of them left.

The newspapers had a follow-up story about the salmon festival
at Celilo. There were a few touches of the old tradition in it, after
all; according to the reports, some of the guests got drunk and got
to fighting, and the venerable Celilo chief got poked in the jaw
and was confined to his bed, feeling terrible. The stories gave his
age as somewhere around eighty-two. It must have been all of
twenty-five years before that he appeared as a witness in a Federal-
court hearing involving some old fishing-rights treaty, and gave his
age as eighty-eight. Still, anybody is entitled to feel younger at a
party than at a Federal-court hearing.

. . . South to Bend. The road follows the high country along the
rim of the Deschutes River canyon, with a view of all the big snow
peaks to the west: Mount Adams, Mount Jefferson, Mount Hood,
Mount Washington, the Three Sisters, Broken Top. Sometimes, when
the air is clear and the wind from the north, you can see Mount
Shasta to the south. A man working in this country during the summer falls into the habit of counting these peaks from the north to
south regularly every day, and watching to see how their snow lines
are holding out against the heat.

In the irrigated lands north of Bend, there were ring-necked
pheasants all along the road. They stay close to it, knowing that it
is against the law to shoot from a public highway, but not knowing
enough to keep out of the way of traffic. I counted eight that had
been killed by cars, in ten miles.

The general notion about company towns is that they are ugly,
spirit-destroying, and deliberately sordid and monotonous. Bend
and Klamath Falls are both sawmill towns, dominated by big lumber
companies. They are the two loveliest towns in Eastern Oregon, and
perhaps in the entire West. Certainly there is nothing in California
that can come anywhere near either of them.

. . . Southeast to Lakeview. The road from the Deschutes River
into the Great Basin is through two great national forests, the
Deschutes and the Fremont, with pine timber for miles on both sides

of it. There are ice caves off to the north a few miles, probably originally blown into some body of molten lava by imprisoned steam, and not much to see. A cave is a hole in the ground, and ice is ice. The short dark-colored underbrush among the pines is used as summer grazing by the cattle herds east in the Great Basin, its foliage being highly esteemed for its meat-building properties. The stockmen call it chamisa; erroneously, since it bears no resemblance to the chamisa of Arizona and California, which is worthless as forage, is pale gray instead of dark, and grows only on ground open to the sun, never in woods.

This country has never been notably accurate in picking names for things. The little blue-flowered ground plant known here as "filaree" is not in the least like the afilerilla of the Southwest, and is not even the same botanical species. Nobody could possibly confuse the two, one being a flowering plant and the other a flowerless grass, so the misnaming must have been accomplished in the dark, or maybe it was mere cussedness. There are dozens of similar cases. The Douglas fir is not a fir, but a spruce; the Port Orford cedar is not cedar, but a sub-species of redwood; the sagebrush is not sage, but wormwood. Some local breeds of trout are really grilse, what the restaurants serve as filet of sole is either sea perch or flounder, and their lobster (which has no claws, merely antennae) is probably some kind of overgrown prawn.

. . . There are a few little towns scattered along this corner of the Great Basin: Silver Lake, Paisley, Valley Falls. They are old and a long way apart, with a subdued sort of charm about them—gray poplars lining the streets, old houses set back against the willows along the creek, lilacs and bleeding-heart and white iris coming into bloom behind the gray picket fences. The little creeks hurry past bright and swift and eager, though there is nothing much for them to hurry to. Since the waters of the Great Basin have no outlet to the ocean, the only end its creeks can look forward to is stagnation in some of the alkali lakes down in the desert.

One of the towns had a small roadside lunch stand run by an elderly couple who had owned a cattle ranch in one of the valleys back in the old wagon-freighting days. The old gentleman came out and visited while I had lunch. He was bright, alert, and quiet-spoken. Nobody would have guessed him to be much over fifty, though he must have been considerably past that to have been running a cattle ranch so far back. He spoke of some of the old wagon-freighters, and said he had lost his ranch in the depression, and had been in the country so long he couldn't bring himself to strike out for a new one. There was no chance of starting over again where he was; all the small ranches had been wiped out in the bad times, and the country had fallen into the hands of four or five big cattle syndicates, which ran it to suit themselves. They had everything bought up—homesteads, small ranches, Government land leases—and they hung onto it. A small outfit would not stand a dog's chance trying to buck them. They were the main reason that the town was dead. With the syndicates sitting on everything, there was nothing for new people to come in for.

"They must bring in some business themselves," I said. "You can't run cattle outfits that size without a payroll."

"It don't amount to much," he said. "Not the way they run things, with cross fences and branding chutes and trucks and tractors and everything done by machinery. When they hire a cowboy, they don't ask him if he can stay on a horse or handle a rope. What they want to know is whether he can repair a truck and dig postholes. In the old days, any of those outfits would have kept seventy or eighty men on regular. Now they get by with a dozen apiece; fifteen, maybe. They pay 'em well, I hear. More than they're worth, to my notion. Most of 'em couldn't work for me for nothing. Assembly-line mechanics, that's all there is to 'em."

We talked about men we had both known. One had started a bootlegging business in a small sheep town up north, and when things began to slow up and the businessmen began to close down and move out, he decided to take over all their businesses and run them himself, to keep the place going. Now, in addition to his bar, he ran the drugstore, the grocery, a hay and feed business and the barbershop, besides handling a small line of dry goods, notions, plumbing supplies and fuel. He also repaired shoes, sold hunting and fishing licenses, ran a branch of the county library, and was agent for a laundry and dry cleaner in one of the bigger towns.

"I hope he stands it, handling all that," I said. "He must be old by now."

"A man will stand a lot to hang on in a place he's got used to," the restaurant man said. "Anyway, he's not old. He can't be much over sixty."

. . . All the Great Basin is high country. The altitude of the flatlands around Picture Rock Pass is over 4000 feet, and the mountains
are twice that. In the short timber northeast of Picture Rock Pass
are mule deer: to the southeast, around Hart Mountain, there are antelope. In between, lying under the huge hundred-mile length of
mountain scarp known as the Abert Rim, is a chain of big alkali
lakes—Silver Lake, Summer Lake, Abert Lake, Goose Lake. Some
are over thirty miles long. During cycles of scant rainfall, they are
dry beds of white alkali, as they were during the 1930's, and in 1858
when Lieutenant Philip H. Sheridan camped in the area on some
obscure Indian campaign. When the cycle turns, they run full of
water again, as they are beginning to do now. The water is too alka-
line for any use except as scenery, and Abert Lake has a pronounced
odor, but it is pleasanter to live with than the dust clouds, and the
uselessness seems a small thing when the great flocks of wild ducks
and geese and black-headed trumpeter swans begin to come down
on it in their northward migration every spring.

There is something wild and freakish and exaggerated about this
entire lake region in the spring. The colors are unimaginably vivid:
deep blues, ferocious greens, blinding whites. Mallard ducks bob
serenely on mud puddles a few feet from the road, indifferent to
everybody. Sheep and wild geese are scattered out in a grass
meadow together, cropping the grass side by side in a spirit of complete tolerance. Horses and cattle stand knee-deep in a roadside
marsh, their heads submerged to the eyes, pasturing the growth of
grass underneath the water. A tractor plowing a field moves through
a cloud of white Mormon sea gulls, little sharp-winged creatures, no
bigger than pigeons and as tame, following the fresh-turned furrow
in search of worms. A flock of white snow geese turning in the high
sunlight after the earth has gone into shadow looks like an explosion
of silver.

The black-headed swans trumpeting sound like a thousand French
taxi horns all going at once. If you happen to be close when they
come down, the gigantic wings sinking past into the shadows will
scare the life out of you. It is no wonder that the Indians of this
country spent so much of their time starting new religions.

. . . Frenchglen, Steens Mountains. Nobody hears much about the
Steens Mountains. They are near the southeastern corner of the
state, a 10,000-foot wall separating the Great Basin on the west from
the tributaries of the Snake River on the east. There is a wild-game

refuge in a creek valley along the western rim, with antelope and pheasants and flocks of wild ducks and geese scattered all through it.

. . . The little lake high up in the mountains looked about as it did when we used to ride up over an old wagon road in the late summer to fish for speckled trout. It was small, not over a quarter of a mile long, and not shown on most maps at all. The thickets of dwarf cottonwood around it had not grown or dwindled, the water was rough and dark and piercingly cold, and the remains of old snowdrifts in the gullies back of it still had the curiously regular shapes that looked, at a little distance, like spires and towers and gables in a white town. There was no town anywhere near; the closest was over a hundred miles away. It looked as quiet as it always had at sundown—the dark water, the ghostly cottonwoods, the scrub willows along the bank, a few scrawny flowers spotting the coarse grass. About dark, a wind came up, and it began to rain and kept it up all night. By morning it had eased up a little, but the wind was stronger and it was spitting sleet. Being snowed in in such a place was not a tempting prospect. I loaded the soggy camp rig into the car, turned it around gingerly in the mud, and headed out.

There was a sheep camp in the cottonwoods at the head of the lake where the road turned down the mountain. The camp tender was striking camp to pull out, the tent hanging limp on the ridgepole and flapping cumbrously when the wind struck it, the pack mules standing humped against the grains of sleet and gouts of foam from the lake that kept pelting them. The sheep were already on the way out; they were jammed so close together down the road that it was impossible to get the car into it. I stopped, and the herder called his dog and went ahead to clear a lane through them.

It was slow work trying to crowd them off into the cottonwood thicket and there was open ground beyond, so I waved to him to drive them on through to where they would have room to spread out. He nodded, and came back to stir up the tail-enders. It was not a big herd; three hundred, maybe, mostly old ewes, hardly enough for two full-grown men to be spending their time on. He got the tail-enders started, and stood back and dropped the cottonwood branch he had been urging them along with. I expected him to say something, but he looked away, watching the dog round up a few stragglers. He was about forty, heavy-boned and slow-looking and bashful, as if he was trying to avoid being spoken to. It struck me what the reason might be, and I took a chance on it.

"*¿De Vascondaga, verdad?*" I said.

That was it. He had been trying to dodge around admitting that he didn't know English. A good many Basque sheepherders in that country didn't.

"*Sí, Vizcaya,*" he said. "*Aldeano de Zarauz.*"

Vizcaya was one of the Basque provinces. Vascondaga was the collective name for all of them. He was from the country adjoining some town named Zarauz.

"*¿Hace mucho?*" I said.

"*Dos años,*" he said. "*Más o menos.*"

He was not being exactly co-operative. I would have given a good deal to be able to sling a sentence or two of Euskera at him, just to see him jump, but wishing did no good. Spanish was the best I could manage. I tried a change of subject.

"It is slow moving a camp with pack mules," I said.

"We work with what we have," he said.

There didn't seem much left to say on that. I tried the weather.

"*Que tiempo malo,*" I said.

"*Hay cosas peores,*" he said. "There are worse things." He was loosening up a little.

He had something specific in mind, I thought. If he had been over here only two years—— "You saw the Civil War in Spain?"

He nodded, and took a deep breath. "Nobody sees all of a war. I saw people shot. I saw our house burned. My father was shot. I didn't see that, but I saw enough."

"You are *desterrado?*" I said. It was a polite expression the Spaniards used for a political refugee. It meant something like exile.

"A little," he said. Then he took it back. "No. I am not *desterrado*. This is my country, here. It is the only one I need."

His handful of lumbering old ewes plodded down the open slope in the wind. The mules flinched and humped uneasily as a blast rattled sleet against them. Some torn leaves from the cottonwoods skimmed past.

"Some people would call it bleak," I said. "Weather as cold as this."

"Nobody can know what is good until he has seen what is bad," he said. "Some people don't know. I do."

He went to help the camp tender with the packs. I drove out of the cottonwoods and through the sheep and on down the mountain.

It was Oregon, all right: the place where stories end that began somewhere else, the place where stories begin that end somewhere else. It has no history of its own, only endings of histories from other places; it has no complete lives, only beginnings. There are worse things.

Washington

by NARD JONES

Washington is called "the Evergreen State"—and on the water side of the Cascade Range, which divides the state almost equally north and south, the land is truly evergreen. In Eastern Washington are deciduous trees whose boughs become bleak and barren in winter, and there are plenty of areas in the state where the rhododendron, the official flower, is never seen.

However, the western half of the state is verdant with cedar and Douglas fir, with marsh grasses and tall ferns. Even the beaches are green rather than sand-colored, for the kelp is plentiful, and pebbles and driftwood take on a salt-emerald sheen. Of course, the sea and the inlets are often green.

The contrast begins at the horizon. The sky may be blue, but it is more likely to be gray. A gray sky does not mean rain necessarily, but strangers may find this "dry gray" too ominous for complete relaxation. If they prefer actual dampness, they will get it, sooner or later, on the coast. From October until May it rains intermittently for days at a time. Thus arises the canard which affronts Washingtonians when they travel: "Rains all the time out where you come from, doesn't it?" When the Washingtonian looks startled, the query may be defended: "Well, I was there for several days a couple of years ago and it rained the whole time." This could be the truth. But if it does rain long, the natives say, it rains light.

It is a mild climate, well suited to work and play. This is borne out by the fact that several hundred thousand war workers, together with earlier immigrants who came from dust-bowl areas in the 30's, have decided to stay for good.

Older Washingtonians are not thrilled by the rise in population since the beginning of the war. Despite the spaciousness offered by 66,836 square miles, the average Washington man is decidedly nervous about crowds. He was the same after the first World War, when Washington did not even dream of a population of more than two million.

In his hesitance to accept new population in sizable chunks, the average native forgets the original cosmopolitan character of the state.

When Washington became a state it was much nearer Foochow and Hong Kong than to our own Midwest. Chinese heard of opportunity in the new country and drifted down through Victoria, in British Columbia. The woods were full of Swedes and Norwegians, naturally attracted to the logging. But there were Scots and Irish, too, who arrived on foot or muleback across the Isthmus and up the west coast. The mills, the mines and the fisheries attracted Finns and Poles, Dalmatians and Yugoslavs. The Japanese came later, and were to take over truck gardening and the business of being servants or houseboys in the clubs. Filipinos, too, were later arrivals. Such trade as there was in the pioneer days was international. Washington was sending lumber to South America, China and Australia, as well as to San Francisco. It was furnishing Douglas-fir spars for the British Navy.

All these have been absorbed to a much greater degree than have their racial kin on the Atlantic seaboard. Older generations speak the native tongue in their homes, but in public they use English, even among themselves. The newness of the cities, with their shifting residential areas, makes colonies rather impractical. However, in most of the larger cities there is a well-defined Chinatown. Before the war the Japanese were clannish, although relatively few have returned.

About two fifths of the present population were born in the state. The rest come mainly from Iowa, Minnesota, Wisconsin, Illinois and Missouri, in about that order. In pioneer days many came from Maine and New Hampshire and Vermont, and this New England heritage explains a great deal about Washington people that might otherwise appear paradoxical.

Contrary to the outsider's conception, many Washingtonians prefer the status quo, a definite heritage from the New England pioneers. There is another strong group, more typically Western, which hankers to see new things happening and rather enjoys the arguments and bitter schisms which occasionally startle a stranger. Originally most of these came from the Midwest and the mountain states. Their clashes with the New England heritage create the social paradox that is Washington. Yet in both groups you can find the well-publicized Washington liberals and progressives who leaven the regional political scene.

More recent arrivals are content to look on; they came chiefly for a milder climate and more elbow room. Almost all Washingtonians, however, have one trait in common. They are boosters. They like the state and they want visitors to like it. If you do not want to live there they find it difficult to understand why, and they may even cross-examine you on this point.

They are a friendly people, generally. They are quick with confidences and inclined to be miffed if the stranger does not respond in kind. They own a robust suspicion of the intellectual and the pompous. They are usually healthy, for the climate is conducive to health yet does not attract the ailing. And—to shatter a myth—they are no bigger or stronger or more silent than inhabitants of other regions, though the female younger generation is taller than average and athletic. The women pay more attention to sports clothes than to street wear and formal gowns. Like the English women in a similar climate, they have remarkable complexions.

The main thing to keep remembering about Washington is its youth. Only eighty some years ago there was only one dwelling on the shores of Lake Washington, and the owner of that house reached the village of Seattle over an Indian trail that is now Madison Street. There are men and women still living who remember this house. About sixty years ago Seattle had its very first tea party. The occasion was to honor Miss Kate Field, a correspondent for the New York *Tribune* and a lecturer who knew George Eliot and the Brownings and Trollope, and in her lectures she discussed Mormon polygamy, temperance and the Hawaiian annexation.

A hundred years ago the State of Washington was largely unexplored. Hudson's Bay men had been there, and so had Astor's fur traders. Factors of the Northwest Company had been there, too, and one of them brought the first white woman to set foot in the Pacific Northwest. She was Jane Barnes, a Portsmouth barmaid, and wilder than any Indian squaw on the Columbia. Jane hated the Evergreen land and soon sailed away to China with a British lieutenant. Washington prefers to remember another as its first white woman, one who established a hallowed household—Narcissa Whitman, wife of Marcus Whitman, the missionary. Narcissa liked her new surroundings, and stayed on to be murdered by Indians.

Lewis and Clark had followed the River of the West, but it could not be said that they explored the state. Captain Robert Gray of Boston had discovered the Columbia in a sloop called the *Washington,* but had not ventured far inland. Even today there are large areas virtually unexplored. A hundred years ago the eastern half of the state was nothing but sage and bunchgrass populated by prairie dogs, rattlesnakes, coyotes and a few thousand Indians into whose midst a dozen or so missionaries had come. There were savages on the coast, too, but far different from the plains Indians, who were stalwart and fiery horsemen. The coast tribes were "canoe Indians," squat of figure and sometimes with foreheads flattened in infancy according to tribal custom.

Washington is really two states in one. Eastern and Western Washington are as different as night and day. There are Washingtonians who insist that the eastern boundary of the state should meander along the peaks of the Cascades, and that Eastern Washington should join up with the narrow northern strip of Idaho. It is an old idea, and even today you can find supporters for it on either side of the Cascades.

The people of Eastern Washington are interested primarily in grain and cattle and fruit. They live on the plains and the hills, in open country, and while they are aware of the coastal area they feel no close kinship to it. Their climate is different, too, with long warm summers and rugged winters. Their feeling of entity and independence is expressed unconsciously in the name they chose years ago for their section of the state. They call it the "Inland Empire."

To tens of thousands of Washingtonians on the coast, the whole eastern half of the state is a kind of no man's land which contains the Grand Coulee Dam. These coastal Washingtonians are knit together by interests of their own: commercial fishing, logging and lumbering, pulp and paper manufacturing, shipbuilding and shipping. The area is affected by the metropolitan character of Seattle and Tacoma, as well as of Portland, Oregon.

There are marked subdivisions, too, in Washington—seven of them, in fact. Three are in the western half of the state, three are in the eastern half, and the seventh—the Cascade Range area—does the splitting. On the west, the Puget Sound basin is the best known of the areas, and is the most heavily populated area in the state. The sound itself is eighty miles long, about five wide, and up to 100 fathoms in depth. It is dotted with more than 300 islands, 172 of them in the picturesque San Juan group. Whidbey is the fourth largest island in the United States. On Puget Sound are the two largest cities of this section, Seattle and Tacoma, as well as the capital city, Olympia. Up the Sound are Everett and Bellingham; and on the Strait of Juan de Fuca, which leads from the Sound into the Pacific Ocean, are Port Townsend and Port Angeles. Many visitors to Seattle believe they are on the western beach of the continent and that Puget Sound is the Pacific Ocean. Actually, the Pacific is a hundred miles due west.

Between it and the Puget Sound basin spreads the Olympic Peninsula. This is *Egg and I* country, and Betty MacDonald has given it the best description yet devised: "the most rugged, most westerly, greatest, deepest, largest, wildest, gamiest, richest, most fertile, loneliest, and most desolate" in all the known world.

At the center of the peninsula the sun seldom reaches the floor of the dense forest. It is a region where man and his works seem anachronisms. In its glacial valleys the dark-green ferns grow as high as young trees. It is so isolated that few names have been given to places that lie within its deeper recesses. The names that you do find are derived from the Indian tongues—names like Elwha, Duckabush, Dosewallips, Hoh and Queets. News comes late out of the depths of this peninsula bounded on the west by the Pacific, on the north by Juan de Fuca's Strait, and on the east by deep-reaching Puget Sound.

If Puget Sound residents are "city folks and dude campers" and Eastern Washingtonians "sagebrushers and apple knockers"—the terms are their own—then the inhabitants of the peninsula are the vestiges of the iron men and women of the Washington Territory of the old days.

There is, in fact, an Olympian septuagenarian known as the "Iron

Man." He comes to civilization only when he needs a new iron stove, trudging out of the woods to the nearest settlement. Into the stove he packs a sack of flour, a side of bacon and a bag of salt. Then he lifts the stove onto his shoulders and heads back into the woods.

Once Harold Ickes, then Secretary of the Interior, took a cabin on the peninsula with his wife. He did not stay long, for the settlers, who are the pioneer type, began looking for him. They had heard that his national-park plans would force them to move. One strapping woman followed him as far as Seattle, bringing the ax with which she had cleared her land. "I want to discuss this business with the Secretary," she told reporters.

"Why the ax?" they wanted to know.

"Well," she said, "I dunno. But it may be my rebuttal."

Just south of the peninsula are the Willapa Hills, the third distinct geographical division of the state. Bounded on the south by the Columbia River, it boasts two sizable ship havens—Grays Harbor, with its lumber ports of Aberdeen and Hoquiam, and Willapa Bay, with Raymond, another timber port. The mouth of the Columbia, six miles wide at one point, is a harbor of importance, but it is shared with Oregon and most of the fishing-vessel work is around Astoria, in the neighboring state.

Up the river, however, is Vancouver, Washington, a shipbuilding and manufacturing center. Sixty miles from the Columbia's mouth is the deepwater port of Longview, newest of the lumber towns, built in 1922. Four years later it had 10,000 population.

In the Puget Sound basin, the peninsula and the Willapa Hills are the well-worn tourist paths and the greatest concentration of population. In these areas lumber is king, with commercial fishing running a close second. Here, with few exceptions, are the manufactories, and here natives and visitors play.

The Cascade Mountains are more than a dividing line between the eastern and western halves of the state, for they, too, are important for lumbering and recreation. They have been thrust up in the shape of an hourglass, sixty to more than 100 miles wide at the Canadian and Oregon boundaries and half that width in the center of the state. Rainier is, of course, the highest volcanic peak, but there are others almost as imposing. Mount Adams, Mount St. Helens, Mount Baker and Glacier Peak are, as the poets say, eternally capped with snow; and there are several others ranging from 6000 to 8000 feet.

It took the Columbia River several million years to get through the Cascades, and the project has not been too easy for man; yet there are three transcontinental-train tunnels, and three motor-highway passes—known as the Snoqualmie, the Chinook and the Stevens —at least one of which is kept open in the dead of winter.

East of the Cascades are the three other distinct sections of the state: the Okanogan Highlands, the Columbia Basin and the Blue Mountains. The Okanogan Highlands roll from the Cascades to the Rocky Mountains on the east and lie north of the Big Bend of the Columbia. These gently rising hills attain heights of 6000 feet. Their forests are open and parklike, with very little undergrowth. The Highlands, too, are an apple country and a vast cattle range. Here you find some of the last truly old-time cowboys. The Methow Valley was the setting for *The Virginian*.

South of the Okanogan Highlands is the Columbia Basin, site of the biggest thing ever built by man, the Grand Coulee Dam. But even the dam faded in the minds of Washingtonians when it was discovered that the Hanford Engineer Works, now operated by General Electric, was manufacturing plutonium for the atomic bomb in another part of the state.

For years beyond count the Columbia Basin had been 1,500,000 acres of scabland suitable only for cattle grazing and dry-land farming, and, where irrigated, for apples and other fruit. The Grand Coulee Dam changed all that, and its irrigation system, interrupted by the war, is now bringing into cultivation an area of "new land" the size of Connecticut. This has altered not only the face of Eastern Washington but its whole thinking. Spokane no longer sees itself merely as a transportation center and one of the largest cities in the state. It is now what it has been calling itself bravely for twenty-five years—the heart of an "Inland Empire." In the Columbia Basin country there is a real-estate boom bigger than took place on Puget Sound when the railroads were coming in. Towns like Ephrata, Coulee City, Almira and Wilbur are transformed from sleepy dry-land farming towns into jumping Western-frontier communities. The boom will bust and they all know it, but meanwhile it is fun—and they are very clear about the shape of the future when the dust settles and the land is green. Vast areas of scabland are being broken into small irrigated farms on which families, many of them refugees from the dry years in the north and central tiers of states, may live in abundance.

The final distinct region in the state is a relatively small area down in the southeast corner known as the Blue Mountains. To a Westerner they are not mountains at all, but hills. The "capital" of the region is the town they liked so well they named it twice, Walla Walla. It means "many waters" and that is valid, for the rounded hills get enough rainfall to support a timber crop and there are many streams in the valleys. It is a rich grain and vegetable country.

There is little to hold these seven areas together except the boundary lines of the state and the feeling of belonging to the far Northwest. In a sense, however, the Columbia River ties some of them together. The Columbia rises in a mountain lake in Canada. It flows into Washington, then west, and then south again to the Oregon border. There, at the Wallula Gateway, it veers sharply west for the second time and heads for the Pacific, plunging into the sea after 1400 tortuous, adventurous miles. Unlike other streams, it reaches its peak flow in the warm growing season, and that is very significant to the Evergreen State.

This characteristic was one of the big reasons for the Grand Coulee Dam; there would be water when water was needed. For the Grand Coulee (*coolie* in Washington) was never primarily a power project. Unlike the Bonneville Dam, which lies far below it on the Columbia and belongs as much to Oregon as to Washington, Coulee was planned as the key to a giant irrigation project. Bonneville, on the other hand, was a power dam from the beginning. A law enacted by initiative in 1930 made possible the establishment of public water-power districts and began a long struggle between private and public power interests. The building of municipal power plants at Tacoma and Seattle heightened the battle, but it was the completion of Bonneville in 1937 which tipped the scales in favor of public power in Washington. Coulee Dam went into power service in 1941, just in time to serve war industries. Now, in peacetime, engineers have resumed the reclamation phases of the project.

The Columbia's watershed covers an area equal to New York, Pennsylvania, Ohio, Virginia, West Virginia, Delaware, Kentucky and Maryland. It falls 1300 feet in a stallion rush to marry the Pacific, and 1000 feet of that fall are between the Canadian border and the Snake River which joins it near the Oregon border. It has been a mighty river in history. Now, after years of being little more than a scenic wonder, the Columbia has again taken a hand in the state's affairs. This is not alone because of the power and irrigation from two dams. Before the coming of the railroads the Columbia boasted steamboats almost as grand as those on the Mississippi. Lumber freighters had plied for years between Vancouver and Longview and world ports around the Pacific. Now there is something new: Diesel-powered tugs and barges carry petroleum products as far inland as Wallula, and haul wheat and wool and canned fruits to Portland, Oregon.

Each of the seven distinct regions of Washington has its principal city or cities, and they differ just as the regions in which they are located differ. The Puget Sound basin has several, of which Seattle and Tacoma are the chief. The focal point of the Columbia basin is Spokane, and there is little real relationship between it and the two big Puget Sound cities. Walla Walla, leading city of the Blue Mountain area, feels more akin to Portland, Oregon, than to Spokane, Seattle or Tacoma. It is a cultural affinity quite as much as a kinship of commerce and agriculture, because Walla Walla and Portland, despite their difference in size, more closely resemble New England towns than any other community of the Far West.

Okanogan is the leading town of the Highlands, although Spokane lays claim to the area as part of its "Inland Empire." Wenatchee and Yakima, of apple-blossom fame, are the key towns of the eastern slope of the Cascades. The twin cities, Aberdeen and Hoquiam, share honors in the Willapa Hills. Only the wild Olympic Peninsula remains uncitified. Bremerton, site of the Puget Sound Navy Yard, sits on the eastern edge, and Port Angeles and Port Townsend cling to its northern shore, but in culture and commerce they are allied with the Puget basin rather than the interior of the peninsula. Residents of the peninsula find small trading centers sufficient to their needs—places like Forks, Ozette, Sappho, Quinault and Pysht. This last delights the stranger. But it really has a meaning—river of fish.

Rural settlements are important to the state even though they suffered some decline with the building of paved highways. The war, with gas rationing and decentralization of activities, gave them a new lease on life. Some, particularly in the eastern half of Washington, are bigger than ever. All are "cities" or "towns"—the self-consciousness of the Pacific Northwest and municipal rivalry won't allow any community to call itself a village.

Most Washington towns were planned for definite purposes. Thus Everett was designed as a center for lumbering and iron working. Kelso was planned for agriculture and lumber. Longview was laid out for lumbering and the shipment of lumber. The founding fathers foresaw that Wenatchee would be the center of great apple orchards, and that Walla Walla would be the center of wheat.

The plans of men, however, are subject to change. Everett did not become an iron-working center, but it became, in addition to a sawmill town, the site of a pulp mill which contributes considerably to Washington's place as the first wood-pulp-producing state, a record once held by Maine. Walla Walla never dreamed that it would be the center of vegetable-canning factories that pack one sixth of the tinned peas of the United States.

Sometimes the plans did not come off at all. Once Washington had towns called Branham, Buckeye, Cedarville, Day City and Clipper. They are no longer on the map. On the other hand there are towns that refused to die. Shelton, in the western part of the state, is a case in point. It is one of the "revived" lumber towns, and for that reason of particular interest. It was once a temporary, ramshackle mill town. False-front buildings meandered along a muddy street from which the larger stumps had not been removed. Normally it should have been a ghost town sixty years after the first big logging around 1880. As late as 1941 the Washington *State Guide* gave it more of an obituary than a description. "For a number of years it grew and prospered," the *Guide* said, "as a . . . center of logging operations, which ate their way steadily inland, consuming in less than a generation forests that had taken hundreds of years to grow."

Sixty years finished off many a lumber town in Maine or Pennsylvania or Wisconsin. But Mark Reed, a lumberman from the East, thought it shouldn't be that way at Shelton, and he refused to sell cut-over lands. Instead he kept them and protected them from fire. Seedlings grew. In that lush black soil they were soon saplings. Now there is a new forest more than eighty feet tall. Today private owners of timber have joined with the Government in a co-operative plan whereby both private and Federal lands will be logged selectively. It is the first contract of its kind in the United States and insures full production for wood-using industries in Mason County for at least a hundred years.

Shelton had a fire in 1910, and after the town was razed Mark Reed began it again by building his own home there. Many lumber tycoons no longer lived in their mill towns but had put up mansions in Tacoma or Seattle. Shelton began to grow; it squeezed through the depression, a tough job for a lumber town. Today, a modern little city with fireproof buildings, it sits proudly on the shore of a bay. Highways radiate to the outside world. In addition to logging and lumbering, it boasts a pulp mill and a wallboard plant.

What has happened around Shelton is one reason why Washington is confident that it can go right on being a leading lumber producer and the first pulp producer in the nation. The state has only recently begun to realize that trees do not have to be gigantic for profitable lumber operations. For years the Northeast and the South have been logging and lumbering and making pulp from trees which are pygmies beside those of the Puget Sound country. It may well be that, except in state and national park areas, the days of heroic trees are passing in the Evergreen land—but not the days of the forest industries. Already there are 2,000,000 acres of "tree farms" in Washington, and there will be more. One pioneer logger of seventy has a tell-tale new slogan. It is, "Here today, and here tomorrow."

The old-time, bearded, irresponsible logger may have been a colorful figure, but the ones who stayed on to insist, "There must be timber here for our sons to work on," are more significant. Because of them, the man in the Washington woods today can stay put and raise a family if he has a mind to.

This is not to say that there has been no "hell and high water" logging in the state in years gone by. There was plenty of it, but recently the lumbermen themselves began to get religion. They had cut in the Northeast and moved on. They had cut in the Lake States and moved on. Now they were up against the Pacific and there was no place else to move.

Today in Washington there is tree planting, and reforestation, and careful re-logging by the large companies. The timber barons, the conservationists and the United States Forest Service now seem to see pretty much eye to eye on forestry practice. Arguments still rage, however, on timber taxation, and some of the timber-worker unions make the lumbermen red-eyed by advocating complete Government ownership of all timber.

Trees are still the leading business of the state, whether you speak of the fir, spruce, hemlock and cedar of the western slopes, or the short log trees east of the Cascades—the white pine and the ponderosa, the cottonwood and larch. There have been many changes in methods. In the 60's loggers were still hacking away with axes at the foot of the tree. Then they began to rig platforms high on the tree so they could use a two-man saw. Visitors see these old fifteen-foot stumps, assume they were cut in a fifteen-foot snow, and go home to tell untrue tales about Washington winters. Nowadays the fallers and buckers work close to the ground again, with power saws. Washington logging equipment is gigantic and modern.

In the Washington mills, too, there are great electric and hydraulic machines which handle the forest giants like toothpicks by means of push buttons and levers. In the pulp mills trees are stripped of bark by hydraulic machinery, and ground to bits in huge chippers.

Lumber, pulp, sash and doors and chairs are only the beginning, Washingtonians will tell you; scores of cellulose products and by-products, unknown now in the Evergreen State, will be in production tomorrow. The leaders of the industry see no end to the trees, nor to the things that can be done with them.

The next biggest job of work, as they say in Washington, is commercial fishing. Your Washington fisherman is more than a hardy and simple man who fishes because it is in his blood or because he knows nothing else. He invests from $15,000 to $500,000 in his vessel, which certainly qualifies him as a businessman. Sometimes a fisherman's boat will be worth more than the packing plant to which he sells his fish.

Yet even the Puget Sound fish buyer is no ordinary fishmonger. The plants where the catch is canned or frozen are food factories. The fish business is second in Washington, as in the pioneer days, and salmon is king. Canned salmon in the Northwest and Alaska is a $60,000,000 annual industry. Pilchards, or sardines, are first in volume of fish—about a billion pounds yearly. Somehow, however, it is the halibut fleet which captures the fancy of visitors and natives alike. Almost all of America's halibut comes from the North Pacific, out of waters that extend south from the Aleutians to the Northern California line.

Up-to-date equipment has made the life of the logger a little easier, but a modern vessel has not lessened the hard lot of the fisherman. He can still lose the whole pilothouse, and his life, by hitting a wave a little off center around Scotch Cap. The compensation is money. One man's share on 100,000 pounds of halibut may be over $1500.

The Washington fisherman admits that Gloucester schooners under full canvas are a grand sight, but he was never one to follow tradition blindly, even in such a traditional calling as the sea. He has developed his own type of ship for what he needs to do—the squat-sterned purse seiner, the trim tuna clipper, the stocky halibut schooner and the little gill-netter. He was using an internal-combustion engine while the older Eastern fisheries were still in sail, and he was first to try the Diesel engine instead of gasoline power.

Apples and wheat were once the only sizable agricultural activities in Washington, although the state is certainly a cow and chicken commonwealth and famous for berries, nuts, hops and potatoes. Farming, overshadowed by the early fur trade and the later mining booms, got off to a slow start during the Civil War.

Now a vegetable-canning industry and prepackaging of fresh foods vie with dry-land grains, and the Columbia Basin irrigation canals will further change the character of the state's agriculture.

As for apples, many a middle-aged citizen of Washington is the son or daughter of parents who rushed West to raise apples so they could be independent and maybe rich. Jim Hill, the railroad builder, had promoted a big Apple Show in Spokane and, himself, bought all the apples on exhibit for ten dollars a box. Naturally word got around the whole United States: "Buy an orchard in Washington!" The anticlimax came in the early 30's when apples brought ninety cents a box, and the man on the street corner selling them became the symbol of the Great Depression.

That was the beginning, not the end, of the apple industry. Much has been learned about soil conservation, irrigation, the care of trees. Today Wenatchee deserves the title of apple capital of the world.

Washington is not satisfied with its lumbering, its fisheries, its agricultural activities alone. It talks now of light metals, of chemical and metallurgical plants, and "chemurgy." These carry the same excitement today that "salt fish" and "Douglas-fir spars" held for the first settlers. For years the small manufactories—the ironworks, the foundries, the engine shops—were content with local business. Then the war brought national prominence to many a factory that had been known only locally. Washington factory owners (not just the big lumbermen and canners) began flying to the United States capital and to New York to meet Government and industrial bigwigs. Now they plan on a nation-wide scale. They know that East and West are coming closer. The best defense against Eastern competition, they are saying in the tall timber and around the Big Bend, is a strong offense.

There are those who warn that Washington cannot always expect to be saved by wars, by dams and other Federal projects, by gold rushes and by immigration. That is why Washington wants a backstop to its wood and fish and farm economy. It dreams of industrialization more nearly comparable with the East.

Washington was not always favored by big appropriations. Its early history is one of faith shown by a few men and women, of neglect by the Government and of ignorance on the part of the rest of the country. There were plenty of valid reasons, of course, for the neglect and the ignorance. Until very recently it was a very, very long way from the East and South to the Pacific Northwest. It is a long trip even by rail. By foot and canoe it was a distance to stagger the imagination, and wagons encumbered the journey rather than accelerated it.

Now it is a matter of a few hours between New York and Seattle. But more important to Washington than the development of air transport is the fact that now everybody has bridged the continent with his mind. When people have tried to understand the immensity of World War II, and have struggled with problems of uniting nations all over the globe, they begin to feel that it is only a little way across our continent.

Washingtonians have been in almost constant rebellion against neglect. Washington Territory was once a part of the Oregon Territory which was established in 1848. Only three years later a band of discontented pioneers met on the Cowlitz Prairie, up north of the Columbia, and petitioned Congress to form a separate territory with a government of its own on Puget Sound. "Columbia" was suggested as a name for the new territory, and Stephen A. Douglas, a fancy man with words, suggested "Washingtonia." But it was called Washington Territory in the measure that President Fillmore signed on March 2, 1853, and its boundaries then included parts of what are now Idaho and Montana.

When Oregon became a state its sister territory to the north waited patiently for two years. Then it presented another memorial to Congress. For years nothing happened. Then came the news in 1888 of Federal appropriations for rivers and harbors. California, a state, got $1,500,000. Oregon, a state, got more than $500,000. Washington Territory received a little over $5000! Immediately a clamor of protest was heard from Puget Sound. On February 22, 1889, Congress passed an act enabling Washington to organize itself as a state.

Washingtonians have never stopped protesting, for it is natural that a state in the upper left-hand corner of the map should feel neglected by the far-off seat of government. In 1933, however, work began on the Grand Coulee Dam, and Washington could no longer complain that it was merely a colony. The appropriation was huge— $174,000,000 to start—and it would erect the biggest thing ever built by man. Washington's exhilaration was expressed by the Big Bend farmer who said, "Well, by God, we got her! The biggest thing man ever built. *That* ought to be big enough for us!"

When Congress threatened to cut drastically the budget of the Department of the Interior, endangering Western reclamation projects, it was the then Governor Mon Wallgren of Washington who blew the bugle that brought Pacific Coast governors and lawmakers to a protest meeting in Seattle's Olympic Hotel. The shades of those Cowlitz Prairie pioneers must have nodded in approval.

The big dam across the Grand Coulee is not the only thing which makes modern Washingtonians feel they are important in the national picture. The Boeing bombers built at Seattle, the sleek destroyers from Tacoma, the gigantic growth and strategic importance of the Bremerton Navy Yard, the mysterious plutonium pile at Hanford, and a war in which the enemy had to be ousted from the world's attic in the Aleutians—these have made Washington more certain that it is genuinely a part of the nation, and perhaps even important to the whole world.

Nowadays Washingtonians listen intently when the phrasemakers speak of "the Arctic influence on national security." They gaze at the maps of air-age geography in which the Arctic is revealed as a center rather than a frontier. They have always had a proprietary air toward Alaska, toward British Columbia and the Yukon. The north country is a part of Washington's history, a part of its people. It is in the bloodstream of all its commerce. The idiom of Alaska and the Yukon is in Washington speech.

From the day in 1897 when the steamer *Portland* put in at Seattle with news of a gold strike in the north, Seattle was "The Gateway to Alaska." The character and tempo of the western half of the state changed overnight. Puget Sound became the mecca for thousands of gold-seekers and bloodsuckers, the jumping-off place for the north, a cross-roads of the world. Years before, Spokane had known the throb of a gold rush when yellow veins were found in the Coeur d'Alene country. Now it was Seattle's turn, and this gold strike was higher, wider and handsomer. A region that has experienced a gold rush never quite loses its air of expectancy. Washington has been through it twice.

Today Washington's bond with the north is enhanced by the continual passage of people back and forth across the border. Klondikers make regular trips to Seattle in the spring. Citizens of Tacoma and Everett golf at Vancouver, British Columbia and spend Christmas at the Empress Hotel in Victoria. Washington border towns are sprinkled with Canadians shopping for styles a little sharper than Mother England supplies. A Washington pleasure-boat owner thinks of the famous "Inside Passage" to Alaska as his private canal.

So naturally, whatever is going to happen in the north country, for good or bad, Washington feels it is in dead center. It is a sobering thought, and it fills Washingtonians with an ambition to be ready to fulfill their destiny. This would be easier, as a Tacoma businessman said, "if only we knew what the hell it was going to be!"

Meanwhile life goes on as usual, simpler and less harassing in Washington than in many other sections. The visitor is astonished at the great number of outdoor celebrations. Hickory Hat Days, Daffodil Jamborees and similar "potlaches" extend from January through December. Most of them extoll and perpetuate the virtues of the pioneer life or the region's natural beauty.

Visitors to the state find liquor customs irritating, and often say so. Hard liquor sales are state controlled. Sunday (which begins at midnight Saturday) is utterly dry everywhere. Washingtonians are untroubled. They keep right on with their simple relaxations. These are—and in about this order—motoring, fishing and hunting, skiing, boating, swimming, hiking and beach activities.

With such mountains, Washington is naturally a skiing paradise. National championships have been decided here, but the general public gets in on the sport to the extent of possibly 80,000 men, women and children—and some claim more. There are enthusiastic and daring mountain climbers too.

Many a Washington citizen is a tourist who went there to fish and never got away. There is stream fishing, lake fishing and a rugged type of river fishing which includes outwitting the sturgeon. But it is salmon fishing that attracts the majority—a light rod and drag reel for spinning; and a heavy-test line of several hundred feet for trolling from the stern of a boat usually outboard powered. Both men and women enter the annual Salmon Derbies which attain the prominence of major athletic events.

The hunter can find as much variety as the fisherman. In the mountains are bear, deer and cougar. There is a short deer season (twenty-one days) and a limit of one buck. There is a ten-day open season on elk. In the eastern half of the state there are quail, pheasant and grouse. The lowlands of the Cascades attract duck hunters, and geese shooting is a popular sport on some of the ranches.

Washingtonians don't call it "yachting," but thousands engage in boating—with sailing dinghies, outboard-powered skiffs, shiny runabouts and small cabin cruisers. Boating is not confined to Puget Sound and the coastal towns. At Coulee Dam there was a boat club even before the formation of Roosevelt Lake, the new 151-mile-long body of water backed up behind the dam. Spokanites sail on Lake Coeur d'Alene, just over the line in Idaho, or Lake Pend Oreille. Chelan Lake is the mecca for boating fans from Wenatchee and Yakima. Almost every Washington town on water has a boat club, and there are literally thousands of miles of sheltered waterways in the state.

Olympic National Park and Mount Rainier National Park are both in Washington. Besides, there are more than fifty state parks, and over a score of recreational areas in national forests. Washingtonians also consider themselves close to other great parks and resorts. Seattlites run over to Sun Valley in Idaho when they tire of skiing on home slopes, for distance means little in the Far West. Banff in Canada is only 300 miles north of Spokane, and Jasper a little more. Yellowstone is just a two day's drive to a Washingtonian.

It is the outdoor pleasures which attract and hold people to Washington. Their play, not their work, is the best index to their character. Some of them have given up things to live in Washington—the excitement and stimulation and color of the giant cities, and some of the cultural advantages of the greater population centers—but the true Washingtonian considers none of them as important as what he has gained. A man with $5000 a year in Washington was a wealthy man before the last war. He could own a home in the country (really in the country, yet not far from town), a car and a modest sailboat or cruiser.

Washington approaches culture with frontier impatience. From the earliest days it has listened attentively to imported wits and sages, but it keeps its sense of humor. Your Washingtonian, realizing his weakness, is fond of the saying, "An expert is a fellow from out of town."

There was a time, not so long ago, when a fake duke or a spurious European tycoon could easily get his feet under some of the best tables in the Pacific Northwest. This was not because Washingtonians were more gullible than citizens elsewhere, but simply because they were out of the main stream of travel. Nowadays the fakers have hard going. But the genuine article still gets a glorious welcome in the Evergreen land. This is possibly because Washington professions are not glamorous. Washingtonians are merely lumbermen, lawyers, insurance brokers, salesmen.

Washington showed its interest in the theater early. In Territorial days it offered enthusiastic audiences to the traveling "professors" and lecturers. At one point in its history, Seattle boasted several stock companies in one of which the late Laurette Taylor learned her profession. Seattle's enthusiasm for the theater is revealed in a favorite anecdote of Alexander Woollcott's. Ticketholders waited in the lobby of the Olympic Hotel until two in the morning when a blizzard delayed the arrival of Katharine Cornell and her *Barretts* company. But Washington's fascination with the theater dates back at least to the 90's, when a monkey escaped from an animal act and expired beneath the floor of the old Casino in Spokane. The floor was not taken up for a year, and the presence of the monkey's remains grew sharply apparent. Yet, it is reported, attendance did not decline.

The increasing costs of putting a show on the road have naturally shaded Washington's current theatrical history, for it is a long way from New York when transporting actors and scenery. So Washington carries on with civic-theater enterprises and little-theater movements which may be found in cities of such varying sizes as Seattle, Spokane, and Walla Walla. The University of Washington's Penthouse Theatre and the Showboat are recognized nationally; they have graduated players both to Broadway and Hollywood.

The state boasts several symphony orchestras and Seattle and Tacoma, at least, have been able to attract internationally famous conductors for them.

Washington painters and art lovers were made happier in 1933 when the Seattle Art Museum was erected in Volunteer Park. It was donated to the city by Dr. Richard E. Fuller and his mother, Mrs.

Eugene Fuller. More than 200,000 are said to visit the museum annually. It has been a springboard for many Washington artists through its regional exhibits.

Although there are a number of scattered local historical museums there has been no single building which would reflect the state's historical, cultural and industrial growth. However, a Seattle site has been selected and money is now being raised for the building.

Washington is like all new lands, a mixture of many other lands. It is still plastic and imitative, and sometimes it appears uncertain. It is still young. In 1929, on the eve of the Great Depression, Washington as a state was only forty years old. Whether beneath the depression and two wars it has been weaving a pattern peculiar to itself remains to be seen. Perhaps now it is too close to its sister states, to Canada, to Alaska and the Far East, ever to develop a pattern of its own. The whole world has fallen in on Washington before it knew what it was, much less what it wants to become.

Yet the very lack of pattern can be Washington's pattern. And Washingtonians can say truthfully that no other people in the nation have done so much and come so far in so short a time.

PART III *The Mountain States*

ℐ*daho*

by A. B. GUTHRIE, JR.

Idaho, they will tell you, means sunrise; and the sun, they will agree, must be astonished each time he lifts his bright face on the place. No state can surpass, if any can equal, its contrasts, its extremes, its huge natural fancies that exist as if to stun wonder.

Here is a land wrought by fire and ice, by the slow force of glacier and the eruptive energy of volcano, a land of rivers and of deserts, of forests and of barrens, of mountains and flats, of sterility and fruitfulness, of cold zone and temperate, of growing settlement and eternal wilderness.

There are lovely subalpine lakes in the north—Pend Oreille, Coeur d'Alene, Priest; southward are reaches of stone and dust that frazzled the fiber of man and beast in the days when men strained overland to Oregon. The Palouse, out of the university city of Moscow, is wheat-farmed to the last good inch, but the plow hasn't been made nor the man crazy enough to turn the dark rock in and around the Craters of the Moon near Arco. The Boise Valley is fat and peaceful, but just south is the torn waste of Owyhee County, where antelope and wild horses range and for miles the Bruneau flows between walls that would stay a mountain climber. Mt. Borah rises to 12,655 feet; Lewiston, on the Snake, nestles within 738 feet of sea level.

The Snake, the Mad River of the French, helped along by its little sister, the Salmon, subscribes to the policy of contrast. Once the outlet for prehistoric Lake Bonneville—shrunk now to the comparative puddle of Great Salt Lake—it goes its prehistoric, uncivilized way, now complacent, now raging, now gentle with its shores, now scouring deeper the chasms scoured long, long ago.

Hell's Canyon, upriver from Lewiston, is the deepest gorge on the North American continent. Here, between walls of basalt, greenstone, rhyolite and andesite, the Snake digs at a bed already more than a mile below its rims.

More striking than all, Idaho is a state broken in two, broken by a grand wilderness of crag and canyon that railroads barely nudge and that pavement hardly more than edges. The division isn't merely geographic or climatic, though geography and climate are basic. Northern Idaho is the land of the miner and logger; Southern Idaho is the land of the orchardist, the farmer, the stockman, the occasional industrialist and, lately, the digger of phosphates and other industrial chemicals. It follows almost as a matter of course that the north is less conservative than the south, even without considering the south's large Mormon population, known for its thrift and reserve.

But to revert. Rugged is the term that promoters use for Idaho. It fits but doesn't suffice. Add majestic to it. Add magnificent. Add incredible. You might almost add undiscovered, too, for reasons later to be stated.

Lewis and Clark came here, not without chagrin. Lemhi Pass over the Continental Divide was easy enough, but west and north of it—not so far from what today's traveler on State Road 28 sees advertised as the birthplace of Sacajawea, the Indian girl guide—real trouble arose. Salmon River trouble. West lay the Pacific, but before it such a madness of chasm and climb that even the dedicated explorers turned away. They pushed north along Montana's Bitterroot River and struck west over Lolo Pass and, entering Idaho again, came to the Clearwater.

Not far, or not long, behind Lewis and Clark came the pelt hunters, the seekers of the furred wealth that was beaver. They built their posts and set their traps north and south, but early learned to avoid the drainage of the Salmon. Cutrock country, they called it, because the shards sliced through their moccasins.

To the south came the Astorians, financed by John Jacob Astor, who would build, so they planned, a great trading house where the Columbia flowed into the sea. They reckoned insufficiently with geography and with climate. They weren't prepared for what's now Southern Idaho, or for the Snake. They hungered and chilled and sickened, and some of them drowned; and the fort finally built at Astoria passed to the British in the War of 1812.

For three decades and more thereafter the British dominated all that great Oregon country of which Idaho was a part, dominated it though the tides ran more and more against them. Americans were too venturesome, too independent, too ambitious and too ready at hand to be deterred long or much by the minions of a foreign power.

Oregon was joint territory anyhow, no matter what the Hudson's Bay Company pretended. Old H.B.C., the Americans said. H.B.C., meaning Here Before Christ. So American trappers poached on Hudson's Bay preserves. They dickered with Hudson's Bay Indians. By practices called sharp they made away with Empire peltries.

That was the beginning. Next the eyes of American farmers and businessmen and promoters and missionaries, of Midwesterners and Midsoutherners and New Englanders, turned to Oregon. Fruitful soil was there, resources untapped, possibilities unthought-of, adventure, pitiful savages hungry for grace, freedom from the fevers of the Mississippi and Ohio, freedom, too, from debts if one would dodge them. There, in a word, was Opportunity.

In 1846 came compromise and resolution. The north-and-south dividing line between American and British holdings would be the 49th parallel.

Fourteen years later the first permanent agricultural settlement was established in present Idaho. A party of Mormon homeseekers traveled up from Utah and camped just north of the Utah boundary, at Franklin. Gold was discovered at the same time, on Orofino Creek. The country boomed. Lewiston, the port, came into being. Idaho won territorial status.

As Indians went those days, the Indians had been peaceful. For a few years they remained so, and then the pressures were too great. Three outbreaks occurred between 1870 and 1880. Out of them, heroic and heart-wrenching, emerges now the figure of Chief Joseph, leader of the Nez Percés. He was a man of peace, and he was a born tactician, and he had dignity and understanding and the capacity and courage to act in the face of grievance. After a two-day battle with the whites near Kamiah, he led his people over the Lolo Pass and far through Montana in one of the most masterly retreats (it covered 1300 miles) on record. And at the last, defeated in the Bear

Paw Mountains, sick of butchery, bereaved, he spoke words of surrender so simple and so eloquent as to haunt the white reader yet. At the end he said, "From where the sun now stands I will fight no more forever."

But even earlier the cattlemen had taken over the ranges of Idaho. By 1875, grazing lands were well stocked. In the following year the first drove went east, the Durhams descendant from the tame family animals that the first settlers of Oregon took with them. Shorthorns, they call these Durhams now. In the early '80's the railroads came— the Northern Pacific, through north Idaho in 1880–82; the Oregon Short Line, across south Idaho two years later.

So, if not the present day, the early dawn of it. From Lewis and Clark to the iron horse in one not-uncommon lifetime.

You can see a part of Idaho—the cities and the settled countryside and something of the woods and mountains and waste places—by sticking to the pavement. You can see more and learn more and gain a truer sense if, on occasion, you take side trips on dirt and gravel roads. A fuller knowledge would demand pack horses, and lots of time besides. But side trips help. And they're fun if you have a taste for the byways.

I like a sashay that I took with friends to Pierce, an old and not-quite-ghost gold camp kept alive by lumber. In our party were C. K. Lyman of Missoula, Montana, supervisor of the Lolo National Forest; George V. Jackson of Choteau, Montana, a friend since boyhood, and myself. Ours was a journey of discovery, at least for me who had lived next door to Idaho for years but, like others, knew too little of the state. The discovery was rewarding and Pierce not the least nugget picked up on the trip.

We arrived there after dark and made arrangements for the night and afterwards visited a little bar and over beers brought up the theme of gold. Gold is not a major metal in Idaho any more, not from the standpoint of production. It definitely is in point of interest, however, there in the once-flush Orofino country where men hark back to placer strikes and dazzling color in the pan and themselves go out and try the gravel and find hope in a yellow flake worth a cent or so.

One by one the innkeeper and his three or four patrons warmed up, and Charles Johnson, a mustached Scandinavian whose eyes showed weather and the search for wealth, told us with smiling ruefulness that first came the white man, who got the cream, and next came the Chinaman, who collected the skimmed milk, and finally came the Swede. L. R. Davis, the proprietor of the place, said that back in 1942 and 1943 he used to buy gold in small amounts, paying $26 an ounce and receiving $27.50 and sometimes $28. We asked if he had any remainders to show us.

And all of a sudden little glass vials of it began appearing and going the rounds, each containing a fraction of an ounce. They weren't Davis' alone; everyone, it appeared, had his sample and, somewhere, his claim.

We mined a heap of gold that night in the bar. Dust, nuggets, mother lodes, we found them all. And still it seemed to me it wasn't gold that held us there, any more than it was truly gold that sent men out with pans and shovels in the placer years. Gold was a symbol; it was the wildwood hope, the ultimate ecstasy, the sum of dreams. Find it, and it is no more than greasy metal, and far off lies the strike that answers all, over the next mountain, in the next valley, on the shore of some secret stream.

There are many gold camps in Idaho, some hanging to the thread of life, some gone to dust, and one of the more interesting is the town of Silver City where, at the time of my tour, two people lived of the thousands that once jammed the place.

If gold has petered out, silver hasn't, or lead, or zinc. The Coeur d'Alene mining district in the north though almost the only hard-metal district in the state, is one of but eight in the world that have produced more than a billion dollars in gross value, and it is still a-goin'. It lies along the south fork of the Coeur d'Alene River and is about twenty-five miles long and four or five wide and supports the towns of Mullan, Kellogg and Wallace. Once a brawling community where labor and capital toughed it out, the district appears ordered and steady these days, and men vote bonds whose predecessors voted with bullets.

But for a runaway, three-dollar jackass the Coeur d'Alene strike wouldn't have been made when it was. One night the animal took leave of N. S. Kellogg, a destitute carpenter turned prospector. Exhausted after he had tracked it down next morning, Kellogg sat down to rest and listlessly picked up a loose rock. Beneath it he found galena, the outcrop of a silver-lead vein, and still more galena. He was in.

The jackass, once because of its hellish bray regarded as a nuisance in the town of Murray, became a privileged character after the strike. But only for a time. After its hour of glory someone tied a few sticks of dynamite to it, lighted a long fuse and sent it on its way.

Years later some joker or jokers erected a sign:

> You are now near KELLOGG
> The town that was discovered
> by a JACKASS
> and which is inhabited
> by its Descendants.

The humor was too strong. The sign came down.

A new type of mining, identified as industrial mineral mining, promises in time an importance greater than all the others, for well over half the nation's known reserves of phosphate lies in the southeast section of the state, in the vicinities of Soda Springs and Pocatello. Millions of dollars have been put into development—by Monsanto, Anaconda Copper, the San Francisco Chemical Company, the J. R. Simplot Company and others. More millions will be spent, not to bring out phosphate alone but barite and fluorspar and the rare earth, monazite, which the Government is stockpiling for atomic purposes.

Here, in a large sense, is Idaho's first really big industrialization. It is a thing to celebrate, no doubt. But Soda Springs is the old Beer Springs of the Oregon trailers, and Pocatello stands near the site of famous old Fort Hall, and Arco, close neighbor to the Atomic Energy Commission Reactor Testing Station, once served Injun whisky to dusty drovers bound for Montana and Wyoming. History going down before history, vestige before venture, sentiment before necessity. All right and good. But in a certain mood and for a moment the passerby may be allowed to wonder which will blow up first, the new atomic testing station or the old volcano near it.

What you notice first in northern Idaho are the noble stands of timber, of white and yellow pine, of larch and fir, of cedar and hemlock and spruce. They rise majestically, even awesomely, and you find yourself speaking quietly in the felt presence of the forest gods. Here and there are mills, and now and again big trucks come rolling by, laden high with fine, clean logs, and the air tastes of pitch and needle and sawn wood, and you feel humble and exhilarated and altogether good.

In national forests alone are more than twenty million acres, or over thirty-three per cent of the state's land area, all to be protected, managed, marked for logging and let for grazing under the experienced direction of the Forest Service. Merchantable timber on Idaho national-forest lands is worth one billion dollars to the American public in stumpage value alone. Some interests, not all, regard this standing wealth with the wistful hunger of a gold miner situated next door to Fort Knox. Isn't public ownership socialism? Don't we believe in private enterprise? But questions like these, together with their persuasiveness, appear to have diminished with years and evidence. Though companies of real standing—and they are more than a few—have learned and are learning the wisdom of logging their own lands on a basis of sustained yield, ghosts haunt them, ghosts like the dead timber towns of Spirit Lake and Laclede, which ate their cake at a sitting and thereupon expired. It is hard to argue in the face of such examples, and I got the idea that commercial loggers weren't too much inclined to argue anyhow. For whatever reasons—experience, wider awareness, social sentiment, the integrity and quiet competence of the Forest Service—they seemed to hold a taciturn respect for the Service and to acknowledge, if with reservations, the necessity of its being.

Overgrazing presents no such open and easy examples of folly as greedy logging. It takes knowledge to know that weeds grow now where native and nutritious grasses grew before, to see that erosion is recent and wanton, to note the deterioration of the soil. Like neighboring states, Idaho has its bald and rootless and weedy and worthless ranges, cowed down and sheeped off and all but hopeless. Here again, within its domain, the Forest Service through controlled grazing attempts to preserve and rebuild. And it is to the credit of Idaho that its chamber of commerce and most of its stockmen have kept apart from any efforts to grab the land and to escape the discipline.

The Forest Service in explaining its multiple program doesn't lead with timber these days, or with forage or public recreation. It leads with healthy water. Healthy water. Little water, restrained along its origins by root and blade and matted leaf and flowing clear and cold and without haste and so in time becoming big water. Healthy big water, miles and miles and maybe states away from where it started. We can't have such water, we people anywhere, without trees and grass in the watersheds. Minus them we have the mad, feverish, flood-and-mud corruption that stupid and grasping exploitation, abetted by forest fires, has made of many streams. A quicker and more immediately exciting interest is fire. Take a parched and breezy August day with the conifers like tinder and dry thunderheads sailing up! There's not much thought of timber cruising then, or of range management or healthy water. Everything is fire, and maybe, anxious in regional office or ranger station or makeshift camp, the men will talk of famous fires in Idaho.

Careless campers, known now as guberifs (omit the *s* and spell it backward), set the woods afire on a summer day in 1931. In one blazing white-and-red-hot afternoon 22,000 acres of fine timber, mostly white pine, went up in smoke. By extraordinary work the Forest Service got the blaze in hand and later came along with plantings that have thrived. You can still see dead, black trunks, though, and moldering stumps, and you can mark the course of the fire which foresters refer to as the Freeman Lake burn. It occurred about six miles north of the little town of Priest River.

Worse was the fire of 1910, which laid waste not only part of north Idaho but parts of Eastern Washington and Western Montana as well. It is an individual, though, a ranger, a man, that emerges first from the mist of history. His name was E. C. Pulaski, and he was in charge of forty fire fighters whose fire lines southwest of Wallace were broken by a sudden gale. He ordered a retreat toward the town, to find there was no avenue of retreat. On all sides the fire raged. The one hope of survival was a small mine tunnel that Pulaski knew about. Go there, he said.

Now of terrifying experiences perhaps none is more unmanning than a forest fire. People of real courage quail. They act strangely and insanely, with no more wit than horses in a barn blaze. Now, and later in the smoldering tunnel, men screamed for help from someone, any someone, the someone who was no one and nowhere except in the person and presence of Pulaski. They wept. They begged. They shouted they were dying. One refused to enter the tunnel. Inside, others tried to break out when the portal timbers started smoking. But this Pulaski was a man. By example and by word—and persuasion with his revolver—he saved the lives of all but six, though himself blinded in one eye.

Recent retellings of the Pulaski story provide a quaint footnote. F. B. Foltz of Coeur d'Alene, cook with the crew and to his knowledge the last survivor of it, wrote in the *Spokesman-Review* of Spokane, Washington: "When I checked in for my pay Superintendent Weigle told me that the rate was only twenty-five cents an hour, but that he would allow me twenty-four hours a day, so that I could receive a larger sum."

Hell's Canyon is Idaho's greatest spectacle. We didn't want to miss it, and so, at Lewiston, the starting point, I inquired of a travel service about the ninety-nine-mile boat trip up the Snake. Two outfits operated, I was told, but neither on daily schedule and neither on the day we wished to go. Special arrangements could be made though.

As I left the desk an earnest gentleman collared me. Had he heard me asking about Hell's Canyon? I answered yes.

"Don't go!" he said. A rugged trip. Poor accommodations. Miserable sanitation. His sister from the East had just suffered the experience.

We went anyway, under the captaincy of John Olney and in company with his wife and daughter, who were as pert and at home with water as water ouzels.

Scenery is a little word. It applies to things comprehensible to eye and brain, to familiar, embraceable things like pastures and peaceful sky lines, to things subject to measure and to placement. It won't do for Hell's Canyon or even for the miles of introduction to it. The Snake runs too crazy. Its walls push too close and too high, and their blacks and their yellows, their grays and their greens speak too much of time and the coldness of time. This isn't scenery. It is desperate grandeur. It is remorseless manifestation. It is wild water and wild stone, wild beyond the reach of belief, and it is beautiful.

The walls are not always sheer. Above and between the perpendiculars frequent benches slant where wild grasses climb and mountain mahogany catches root-hold; and on one of them, high above, a deer appeared from somewhere and gazed down at us, a figurine imperious with altitude, a sentinel of Pan's.

The river tore at our little cruiser. From bend to bend it came tearing, now lean and green with strength, now white with fury, as if to wash us to the mother sea. The engines growled and the craft trembled at test on harder test; and, imperturbable at the helm, Olney skittered us along the lips of rapids, along eddying shores and, if need be, straight up the white-maned current. To faculties numbed by enormity he stood as Man against Nature, the close, real, resourceful mite against the world's blind might. By some miracle of power and cunning we arrived at the rustic, unpretentious lodge which was terminus.

We started back, back between the crowding lifts, giving ourselves now up to the river, planing over rapids we had had to churn up, wind in our faces, great banks running by, the roller-coaster pitch and drop of wave and trough. The worst of the rapids, and the boat spanking hard, and one of the girls calling to Olney, "Let 'er go, Pappy!" Yeah, let 'er go, boy! Away to the Columbia! Away to the sea!

We came home at evening, tired and needing time to appraise and place what we had seen. Now we had no words but shotgun words like great and grand, majestic and magnificent. And, lifting our stiff bones to the bank, we agreed this was no journey for the delicate or crotchety, even though the ordinary schedule covered two days, not our one. So the complainer at the hotel was partly right. But wrong too. Mighty wrong. Fatigue had bought a bargain.

We had visited the Diamond Match Company's lumber mills in Idaho and so it seemed time to go back along the line of production, to have a look at one of the camps where men by old reputation fell trees by day and one another by night and sin is the rule without exception and the classes struggle and you'll get pie in the sky when you die.

It was latish when we showed up at the Gold Creek camp of the Diamond Match Company sixty miles from Moscow and most of the men had had supper. The cook was in the cookhouse, though, along with a couple of helpers and three or four tardy diners, and we were made welcome. The room, big enough to accommodate both kitchen and dining hall, was plain and plainly furnished, as you would expect, but clean and tidy. On stoves and tables was an assortment of food fit for both finicky and famished. I made a list: Beef, potatoes, beans, cauliflower, tomatoes, celery, apple sauce, prunes, cake, doughnuts, pie, homemade bread, crackers, butter, fresh milk, coffee. The vegetables were fresh, the dishes well cooked.

The men we ate with weren't too ready with a word, being serious about the serious business of food and restrained before strangers, but by and by, with appetite and unease allayed, they opened up somewhat. The outdoor season, they said, ran roughly from May to October, when winter shut down operations. I asked one young fellow how he made out then.

"I go on armchair money and see the football and basketball games," he answered cheerfully.

By "armchair money" he meant unemployment insurance.

The men looked at me strangely when I inquired about the professional female visitors of whom I'd read and heard.

"A lot of us commute to our homes," one of them said, "and most of us are married men." He shook his head and added, not righteously but as a matter of judgment, "One wouldn't get far here."

What about working conditions? What about labor-management relations? What about the old I.W.W.?

All agreed that camp improvement began with the I.W.W., though none of them as modern union men seemed to want any part of the old organization now. They appeared satisfied with their work and working conditions. Wages? A matter of bargaining, of course.

My questions troubled an older man, however. "Ah-h," he said, speaking of those older, ruder times. "Dirt! Black bean soup! Ah-h!"

He didn't go further. He got up, unhappy with his memories, and strode out.

It was 8:30 or thereabouts when we left. The camp was just about asleep. No fights. No assignations. No ranting against capitalists. From somewhere in the dark came the whisper of a radio.

Agriculture, lumber and mining—these, barring the come-lately tourist business, are the Big Three of Idaho's economics. Of them agriculture is first. Just get water on that thirsty lava dust, and, as old overlanders used to say about Oregon, a nail planted today will come up a spike tomorrow.

They've got water on quite an acreage of dust, and the figurative spike appears in row on row of sacked russets, in bag after bag of onions, in crates of fruit, in crops of seed peas, beans and even corn which supply the demands of localities better known than Idaho for the mass-market production of these very items.

Wheat in the Palouse, without benefit of irrigation. Potatoes from Ashton to Pocatello. Potatoes around Burley and Twin Falls and Rupert and Jerome and Gooding. Onions too. Seed crops and dairies in the gentle valley of the Boise. Fruit north to Lewiston and farther. This rugged state of Idaho can smile and, smiling, is all the more engaging for its usual severity.

The character and irrelation of the major economic interests make for towns and little cities. Boise, capital and biggest place in Idaho, numbers less than 40,000. Pocatello, its closest rival, a little better than half that many. Idaho Falls, perhaps commercially the liveliest of the lot, runs a close third.

Residents don't fret. Size doesn't count for much. These are good towns, these and others like Sandpoint and Caldwell, Blackfoot and Moscow, Twin Falls and Coeur d'Alene. All are distinguished by setting as their residents are influenced by it. Men live pretty close to nature, even city men. When not working they are likely to be out with rod or gun, to be on boat or saddle horse, to be hiking or prospecting or just letting the lonesome wind blow them. The cause of ulcers, indeed, may be the fear of growth, the fear that unspoiled places will fill with picnickers and empty beer cans.

Such a sentiment, for all the warm friendliness of the state, does exist—though its holders will concede their cause is lost. Glenn Balch of Boise, writer and student of a variety of folklore, told me he hoped this story never would appear in print. Just bring a lot of people in, he said, and maybe some of them would stay. All right to let them visit, maybe, but then shoo them out.

Throughout Idaho are men who have settled in the state and natives who refuse to leave simply because the side rewards of living there are greater than the greater money they might make outside. They like small-town and small-city associations, and they like free space, and they fill their eyes with grandeur and their ears with the great silence of the mountains.

The rivers of Idaho provide extraordinary fishing for salmon and steelhead and other varieties of trout, but it is the lakes of the north that are really sensational both in size and number of fish and fishing records. Lake Pend Oreille has yielded the world's record rainbow —37 pounds—and the world's record Dolly Varden or bull trout— 32 pounds. Priest Lake set the American record for Mackinaw or lake trout with a specimen weighing fifty-one pounds. More, an innumerable concentration of Kokanee or bluebacks inhabit the waters of Lake Pend Oreille. They are a tasty, smallish, up-to-14-inch salmon and once there was no limit on the catch. Nowadays you're risking trouble if you yank out more than fifty in one day.

The story of the Kamloops is a story of private enterprise and public astonishment. The fish, a rainbow in everything but size, is a native of British Columbia. In 1941, a group of Sandpoint citizens brought in some eggs. For four years thereafter nothing untoward happened, and then one day in 1945 a man came into town lugging a thirty-two-pounder. It was a sensation, and no wonder. For twenty-nine years the world's record for rainbow had stood at twenty-six pounds. Since then, of course, the record has risen, and each year at the opening of the season there's a big to-do at which the taker of the biggest trout is duly honored.

One of these honorees won additional distinction in the spring of 1947. Here he was ashore with the record fish, and photographers were popping bulbs around him, and for a final shot it was suggested that he stand holding his prize in the stern of his boat. He was an obliging man. He did so. And somehow the trout slipped from his grasp. Somehow, though dead, it sank like a stone, and in deep water. There was a moment of paralyzed incredulity. Then the man, Lord love him, shrugged and turned away and said, "I always heard they threw 'em back unless they weighed forty pounds." P.S. They dredged the fish out later.

A tour of discovery uncovers items unrelated one to another except by the common quality of orphanhood. A few we came across: Thayne Robertson, of Boise, a manufacturer of fancy pipes, now and then turns out a cigar-store Indian. . . . Unlike some produced elsewhere, Idaho potatoes never lacked a market. . . . Thousand Springs, which gush from the bank of the Snake west of Twin Falls, probably are unique in the world. . . . Yell "Timber" in an Idaho barroom and you buy a round for all. . . . "Savage" is a common word. Hewers of poles are cedar savages. River recluses are river savages. . . . A timber contractor is a gyppo logger. . . . Sun Valley is in but not of Idaho. Nice resort, where men in summer wear pedal pushers and cameras. . . . In dust-bowl days refugees traveling by way of Missoula, Montana, and Wallace, Idaho, came to Lake Coeur d'Alene. Boy, it was good enough! They've got along just fine too. . . .

. . . In the unlikely agricultural town of Caldwell, was and is the Caxton Printers—J. H. Gipson, president—which for more than 20 years has been putting out trade books as a sort of indulgent and extravagant side line to a general-printing and textbook business. Good books, too, a very considerable number of them. Needed books. Books, however, more likely to show loss than profit because publishing in any circumstances is risky nowadays and stingy with dividends. Mr. Gipson, a lively and hospitable gentleman who rolls his own cigarettes, said he kind of drifted into trade books just out of a love for books. From a start as a dinky newspaper his business had thrived to the point at which he was willing and able to risk a loss of maybe thirty thousand dollars a year in the publication of trade books. The loss, it developed, was real enough. To date it amounts to around two hundred thousand dollars. "But," Mr. Gipson explained without regret, "we've had two million dollars' worth of fun." He showed no intention of quitting, either.

. . . The last saw-log drive of any size left in the state and maybe the nation starts on the north fork of the Clearwater and terminates at Lewiston. . . . Only vestiges remain of the old Farragut Naval Base on the shores of Lake Pend Oreille where thousands of boys trained in the war years. . . . Lewiston promotes the Appaloosa horse, that spotted pride of the old Nez Percés. . . . Food's good in Idaho. Try Hurschell's Lighthouse on Lake Pend Oreille. . . . The biggest concentration of Basques outside Spain is to be found in and around Boise. A non-Basque observation: "Everybody loves the Basques." . . .

. . . At least two roads in Idaho will take your breath away. One loops like an immense snake, its coils now and then hidden by knolls, up and down the hill high above Lewiston. The other winds the divide between the Clearwater and Salmon. Ten miles and more long, both these hill roads. They are exhilarating but likely to scare flatlanders. We encountered one driver who just couldn't nerve herself for the Lewiston Hill. . . . Down the divide from the Clearwater to the Salmon you come to the Whitebird battleground where Nez Percé and paleface fought in one of the last of the Indian wars. A sign there tells you this is the spot "where 35 white men lost their lives June 17, 1877." No mention of Indian losses. They didn't matter, I guess.

. . . On the north edge of Latah County south of St. Maries is a small but lofty stand of timber, kept inviolate by the Forest Service for the eyes of the American public. This virgin growth includes white pine, cedar and hemlock. All are magnificent, but one tops the rest. It is a white pine 168 feet high and 72 inches through at breast height. A marker says it was a seedling when Columbus discovered America.

Earlier I said Idaho was almost undiscovered. It isn't that its 83,557 square miles are tenanted by roughly 600,000 people, for there are states with sparser populations. And it isn't altogether that

Easterners, hearing you're from Idaho, are likely to ask if you know Uncle Ben in Oklahoma. It is, rather, that population seems disproportionate to opportunity and attraction. More, it is that the state appears to belong to a younger and elsewhere long-gone time, to a time when energies were fresh and hopeful and the raw stuff of fortunes lay about and the limit of achievement was the limit of ambition.

These impressions find a doleful disagreement in an old Idaho guidebook which tells us that the state's greatest development "must rest upon its potential wealth as a national playground."

National playground, to be sure. But there is land still to be watered and timber still to be reached and minerals still to be mined, and who knows what elements will be found in mountain and desert and what new uses will be discovered? And there is power to be generated, and, though it may not figure in the bloodless arithmetic of economic analysts, there is the spirit of the people, the confident and forward spirit.

I don't mean the booster spirit. There's astonishingly little of that in Idaho, even among chamber-of-commerce secretaries. Their attitude sums up to this: we like it here and hope that you do.

Names and places, and out of them good memories. Rich and reminiscent names like Lochsa, like Selway and Clearwater, like Lemhi and Lost. Names cradled by mountains, flanked by long plains. Names echoing yet the first wonder of men at the wonder of regions still wonderful. Lonely names, some of them, for places of good loneliness.

We were south of Troy, in expansive, rolling country patched with yellow wheat and full-leafed autumn groves, and away and away, purple in the purple distance, swam the hills of the Clearwater. And for an instant this was eternity. This was time and place suspended so that a man could have a look and give himself to both.

We tooled toward Riggins along the Salmon River, the River of No Return, and the stream flowed fine and green and spray-white among the shouldering heights, and no men were around and no sign of men except the road we rolled on. By that wild stream, deep in those impersonal hills, we were lucky sparks of consciousness, lucky atoms somehow made aware of the bulk and force of senseless atoms.

We pushed north for the Lemhi and, pushing, saw Portland Mountain and Flatiron to the west and the great break of the main range to the east. We stopped at a roadside restaurant and beer hall, and an old sprite waited on us, saying you just dam betcha he had what we wanted. A Sharps buffalo gun hung on the wall, and it led to talk of old times. Long ago, our ancient waiter told us, he had trailed horse herds over the divide into Montana and driven others back. "It was branded stock," he said, grinning. "All legal, of course." He gave us a big wink then. "Oh, they'll find my marks on this country all right," he went on. "You dam betcha they'll find my marks."

Would they? The marks we found were the marks the country had left on him. It had weathered his skin and bowed his legs, and, far more important, had given him that certain cast of mind and spirit that space and nature face to face give men.

The quality perhaps can best be called resilience. It is an ability to accept what comes in a kind of life in which anything may come and many things do. The isolated Westerner, the self-dependent Idahoan—and his city brother through exposure to him—more often than not learns to take it and, what's more, to make the best of it. He can dismiss misfortune with a crack. He dares nature to wipe the grin off his face.

So the quality isn't submissiveness. It is closer to defiance, and it is a triumph of the man, not over nature, but over himself. He has risen superior to self-pity; he can see the humor in adversity.

Best of all, he isn't posing. His reactions are unstudied and almost automatic, their origins so lost to him that, marked by country as he is, he still can think he marked the country.

If you have followed me this far, you have gathered that I like Idaho. The crystal streams. The rushing rivers. The forests. The mountains. The lakes as blue as paint. The splash of mountain ash or maple. The foam of the syringa, the state's official flower. The awesome wastes. The fruitful fields. The warm friendliness of crossroads and town. The high sky over all.

Montana

by A. B. GUTHRIE, JR.

Buy the boys a round in the extra-sovereign state of Montana, and you leave the change—in silver dollars—on the bar, presumably to show you're ready to put out for another. Even though petty chiselers —Easterners, of course—sometimes make the practice costly, it's not the best of form to pocket your money till your thirst is quenched. The rule goes for the official of the Anaconda Copper Mining Company and the blue-jeaned hay hand, who, incidentally, would insist he has as much right and obligation to set 'em up as any nabob.

The amenity is revealing. Free spending is a habit among Montanans, an attitude toward money perhaps stemming from the mountain man, who was contemptuous of possessions, or from the gold miner, who thought he always could make another strike, or from the stockman, who might be broke but never was broken.

One night in the small wheat-cattle town of Choteau a character we will call Pete asked the bartender to set out a round. Pete was a first-generation American. Money came hard to him. All his life he had done the world's drudge work.

"What's the matter, Pete?" the bartender asked. "Don't you love money?"

"Luff money!" Pete answered, drawing himself up. "Luff money! I hate da dom stuff."

His fellows may not hate it, but neither do they hoard it. And yet, or hence, few Montanans are even moderately rich. The state is prosperous. Farmers—pardon, ranchers—the biggest single element of population, do better individually than those in any of the other Northwestern states except Wyoming.

To discourage an influx of outside plowmen and mail-order wranglers, it might be well to remark here that though income is high, so are costs. The Montana rancher, whether wheat grower or stockman, buys a lot of things that other farmers produce for themselves. He does so partly because he dislikes petty jobs, partly because land and climate in many cases discourage side lines to cereals. So he buys canned vegetables. Maybe he even buys evaporated milk. Yep, milk—and even if he is a stockman. The Montanan, even the Montanan whose place will support a cow, hates the chore of milking just as the old-time puncher did before him. He buys canned cow.

If few men are rich, though, the total income's well divided, among stock growers, wheat ranchers, small businessmen. The only economic giants in the state are the Anaconda Copper Mining Company and its close relative, the Montana Power Company. More than four fifths of Montana farms are owner-operated.

Along with openhandedness goes the bent elbow. The bar, by custom and preference, is both social and business headquarters. Some men, only half jokingly, call it the office. Drinks come fast. If you dawdle, you may find them stacked two and three deep in front of you. If you're known, and often if you're not, the solitary drink with which you'd thought to calm yourself becomes a half-dozen. It's hardly necessary to add that you get very calm indeed.

Don't ask for fancy drinks, though, not in the little cow-and-wheat towns. A Martini? Nope. Manhattan? Nope. Stinger? What's that? You can order a John Collins or a Tom Collins or a gin stirrup, but the almost universal drink is the ditchwater highball, often shortened to ditch.

The name came into being about twenty years ago when two judges who were sober as judges and a stockman long absent from the office met at their car after a hunting trip. They dug out a bottle.

The stockman didn't like his whisky neat. He walked over to a nearby irrigation ditch to dilute it. So did the judges. Hence the ditchwater highball. Hence ditch. By extension the term means tap water plus bourbon.

One of the reasons the Montanan can drink as he does without having to repent or to engage a specialist to search his psyche is that he spends much of his time out of doors. Another may be that the country's high and dry. The boiling point is low. Alcohol won't stay in the system very long. You have to apply yourself to insure an authentic hangover.

The open hand and the bent elbow, or some related and undefined habit of feeling, encourage another indulgence—the feeding of slot machines. In bars, restaurants, clubs, beer joints you'll see the machines ranked against the walls—the five-center, the ten-center, the two-bitter, the four-bitter, the one-bucker—with cherries, plums, bars and lemons wheeling as players work the cranks. You get so you can almost tell the addicts; they suffer from what might be called the slot-machine twitch.

Admittedly the things are bandits. Players cuss them, but keep on playing. So many a club in Montana exists in very fine style, and many an entrepreneur earns his overhead and more. Illegal? No one seems to know about that. The original legislation, loosely drawn, had restricted the machines to clubs. But it was no problem to set up a club, or to join one. Just enter a bar and stare at the slot machines, and someone would make out a ticket and you'd find yourself a member of the Cheerio or How-De-Do Club.

The bar is not only social and business headquarters; in the little wheat-elevatored towns sitting lonely in the roll of plains, in the small settlements walled in by mountains, it is often the single downtown place that stays alive at night. The drugstores, where youngsters used to gather, close early. Pool halls, those imagined hell holes of yesterday, exist as vestiges, if at all. The young man or woman abroad at night sees just the garish neon of what, by a great feat of the imagination, may be named the cocktail lounge.

Montanans have a certain tough gaiety, an almost automatic refusal to be downed by circumstances. The Montanan's bloody head, unbowed, sees something funny in the blood. He makes a joke out of it. He buys a drink, not for escape but as defiance. One of them, who knew what it was to be lost in the mountains, said he'd always take a deck of cards with him thereafter. If he got lost, he'd start a game of solitaire, in the certainty that some damn fool would look over his shoulder to ask why he didn't play the red ten on the black jack.

For all the sometimes rowdy conviviality, a curious distinction still tends to exist between the proper and the improper. Montanans are free if not especially imaginative cussers. Yet I heard an old-timer object to the word "pregnant" in a speech. Wasn't talk for mixed company, he said. Maybe that distinction, now disappearing, arose in earlier days, out of the troubled, lonely minds of men who seldom saw a woman except for an occasional untidy squaw. The early comer, living alone, keeping his own cabin, doing his own cooking, washing his clothes by stringing a wire and suspending his underwear and pants in an irrigation ditch, developed strongly marked attitudes. He still has some of them.

Another, and different, contradiction exists. Nowhere more than in Montana is sentiment so vociferous for private enterprise, for rugged individualism; yet crimes of violence are rare. Here where the memory of the Henry Rifle—and the Colt—is recent, no one but a game hunter carries a weapon. A man would think as quickly of carrying a grenade as a six-shooter. He would think it crazy to arm himself with a blade. It is the boast of boisterous Butte that women on the streets at night are safer there than almost anywhere else in the nation. In this direction, in the surrender of the private impulse for justice or vengeance or plain orneriness, in the recognition of the police power, Montanans are not nearly so rugged individually as the longer-settled hillbillies of the Appalachians.

In Montana the reliance on group action goes back a long way— to the 1860's and the gold fields and the road agents, and the Vigilantes who strung the bandits up, including one Henry Plummer, who held the combined posts of sheriff and chief of the outlaws.

Yet the sentiment for individuality is real. Montanans may come closest still to believing that any boy can grow up to be President. The reason seems pretty obvious. So many residents of the Treasure State, coming from the East, coming from Norway, Sweden, Denmark, Germany, Scotland, Ireland, found opportunity waiting. They incline to forget that those were the days of the open range, of free land, undiscovered ore, unclaimed water. They forget that every available acre worth a nickel has been taken up. They made out for themselves, didn't they? Anyone ought to be able to do the same.

The memory of natural riches waiting for the claiming is recent. It accounts not only for this faith in self-determinism but also for the fact that Montanans don't take too much stock in plundered-planet talk. The stockman finds it hard to believe that ranges can be overgrazed. All we need is rain, he says, searching the dry, blue sky. He doesn't always realize that once the streams ran clear that now run rusty. He'll agree with an ag-college man I talked to who ventured the opinion that, although trees and cows and people might all die, the native grasses, as natural-selection survivors of the hordes of buffalo, would go on forever. What bothers the stockman is Government interference. Lord, how he hates it; except, of course, for the tariff, which doesn't strike him as interference, anyhow.

Elsewhere you find this confidence in the adequacy of resources. Or perhaps you find myopia. The mining man thinks—and maybe rightly—that there's ore in plenty yet, considering the new and more efficient processes of extraction. The sawmill operator wants new roads to standing timber; there's no money to be made in stumps.

Today Montana grass-fed beef is as good as any, no matter how the "any" may be stuffed with Iowa corn. Try it if you're in Montana. Dempsey's at Great Falls will serve a steak the like of which you've seldom eaten.

The problem of conservation is made more difficult by the character of a great deal of the land. It's difficult, not to say impossible, to establish a livable home on a wheat ranch where a tree won't grow, where a well-driller often can't drive down to drinking water. The consequence is that, in a good many sections, the dry-land farmer, encouraged by his recent prosperity, has moved to town. Why live on the sun-baked, snow-banked ranch? he asks himself. Wheat ranching takes but three or four months of the year. Let the old house go, or roll it into town. A tool shed and a granary are enough.

Someone will ask, how come these rugged individualists elected liberal senators like James E. Murray and the early Burton K. Wheeler?

For lots of reasons. Because depression hit Montana. Because prosperity did. Because no state is single-minded, no matter how reporters may generalize. Montana has its mixture of convictions. It has Democrats, new style and old. It has its union men, its wage earners of Butte and Great Falls and Anaconda, its New Dealers in education, its independent free lances, its rebel-stock Southerners from Missouri and Kentucky and Texas. Yet, on the spot, you feel somehow this liberal sentiment isn't potent, isn't representative, re-

gardless of the ballot boxes. It isn't old-time; it didn't come across
the plains in a covered wagon. It seems upstart and a little alien,
especially to a resident of the eastern slope, to whom Butte and its
doings appear outlandish and alien. Around the bars, gibes at the
welfare state are as common as the clank of silver dollars. Maybe
there's the reason for the impression the visitor gets—the conservatives are just noisier.

There's another reason for the Murrays and the one-time
Wheelers. Until the Federal Government began brooding over the
provinces, the Anaconda Copper Mining Company and the Montana
Power preferred Washington to the state capital as the abiding place
of a dangerous man. On the local front they've managed pretty well,
thanks to a remarkably shrewd public-relations staff, thanks to the
support of stockmen and wheat growers who can't see a great deal
of difference between their situations and the companies'. Live and
let live, these latter will argue. A company, like an individual, has
a right to the fruits of labor and of luck. It is out of long experience that Montana's two giants of industry call on the cow counties
across the mountains when trouble threatens.

Despite the affinity, it needs to be emphasized that Butte isn't
Montana, though you'd almost think so as a consequence of the
disproportionate reams that have been written about it. Butte exists
of itself, a place of sporty extravagances, a settlement on a scarred
and ugly hill in a hairpin of the Continental Divide where nature
deposited such a load of metals as no man can imagine and chance
brought together a cast of brash and colorful characters.

Out of the scarred hill has come between three and one half and
four billion dollars in copper and zinc and silver and gold and
manganese. How much remains nobody knows, but the company
says it has no cause to worry. Conflicts have raged in Butte and
vice has flourished and men have gambled for fortunes, and the
political influence of copper kings and companies has been felt from
border to border—and all have been reported and extended and
speculated on. But Butte isn't Montana. It isn't even one of the up-
and-coming cities of Montana. The flourishing cities are Great Falls
and Billings and, more quietly, the state-university site, Missoula.
Butte is Butte.

There, in these more peaceful if still not-too-inhibited times, you
have the feeling that the old mine kings—Marcus Daly or William
Andrews Clark or Frederick Augustus Heinze—may be looking over

your shoulder at the bar or footing the night's drink bill for the town, though all three long since have passed to a place no doubt paved with copper. Your mind hears a song, composed before mechanisms drove mules from the mines:

> *My sweetheart's a mule in the mine.*
> *I drive her with only one line.*
> *On the dashboard I sit*
> *And tobacco I spit,*
> *All over my sweetheart's behind.*

Daly and Clark and Heinze, with a late but lusty assist from Henry H. Rogers and the Standard Oil Company, did a lot for Butte and the state, not all of it to their greater glory. Clark and Daly fought over the site of the state capital. Clark was for Helena, Daly for Anaconda. Clark won. They warred over public office, not as rival candidates, for Daly didn't seek the limelight that Clark did, but as candidate and constitutional enemy. In 1899, Clark finally bought his way to Washington, only to submit a strategic resignation of the senatorship when he learned that a Senate investigating committee was ready to report his election null and void. He ran again, in 1900, and again was chosen by the legislature, the electoral agency of those days. This time he held his seat; but Daly had died meantime, and Clark's satisfaction must have been much diminished.

During their long feud a personality and a company that were to be mortal enemies appeared on the scene. The first was Heinze, the second the Standard Oil Company, represented by Rogers. Their aims were make or break. The methods were money, litigation, propaganda, public pressure, trickery, legislation, all of which were used by one side or the other or both. It stands on the record of Montana that the governor was coerced into calling a session of the legislature to enact a change-of-venue bill, the alternative being an indefinite idleness on the part of Standard Oil properties employing 20,000 men, a number estimated at four fifths of the wage earners of the state. Heinze, the last of the copper kings to come to terms with Standard, finally nicked the company for $10,500,000 and went to New York and Wall Street, there to lose his roll.

No state, perhaps, ever found itself more generally or generously corrupted than did Montana during these financial and political battles. Legislatures were bought, newspapers, editors, individuals, minions of government. Clark once was quoted as saying he never bought a man who wasn't for sale. He found plenty who were—but at fancy prices. According to one reporter, he spent $431,000 in eighteen days for the forty-seven legislative votes that sent him to Washington. Another report, also probably reasonably accurate, says Clark and Daly spent almost $3,000,000 in the fight over the capital site. The figure becomes all the more impressive in the light of Montana's total vote, which barely exceeded 50,000.

But there's a difference—or there was a difference—between selling out and stealing, in the code of the Montanans of the time. In this very period, in the little Montana settlement in which I grew up, Joseph Hirshberg and Company, general merchandisers, kept a box in the front of the store. Into it customers tossed the keys to the door latches they bought. No one ever locked a house or cabin. To do so would have been to manifest an unworthy suspicion of Western mankind.

While the copper magnates fought, and afterwards, unionism had its ups and downs and bumps and bloodlettings in Butte. At first, organization was encouraged and leaders were courted by employers who needed the support of labor in their fights with one another. Witness that Clark and Heinze inaugurated the eight-hour day before the legislature made it mandatory in 1901.

Long before then, though, in 1878, a group of fewer than 100 miners organized. By the years 1900 to 1906 the number had grown to more than 8000, composing the largest and strongest association of metal workers in the West. Butte held Charter No. 1 in the old Western Federation of Miners and is still Local No. 1 in its successor, the International Union of Mine, Mill and Smelter Workers, CIO.

In 1914, as a consequence of union rivalry that brought violence, bloodshed and the blasting of two buildings, martial law was proclaimed. Under its protection Butte, "the strongest union town on earth," reverted to the open shop.

In the summer of 1917, a fire deep in the Speculator Mine smothered 164 men. The workers struck, at not the happiest of times, for World War I had broken out and the public took with less than a grain of salt the consequent charges of anarchism and pro-Germanism. That suspicion was increased by the involvement of the Industrial Workers of the World, the Wobblies, who were the open enemies of the capitalistic system. Martial law again was proclaimed. Vigilante organizations attacked miners and their allies. Newspapers whipped up hysterical sentiment.

While the strike was in progress, a gang broke into the room of Frank W. Little, an IWW organizer suffering from a broken leg, and hanged him to a trestle, pinning on him the old Vigilante number, 3-7-77, meaning three feet by seven feet by seventy-seven inches, the dimensions of a grave. The strike ended in about six months, but martial law remained in effect for more than a year.

More blood was shed three years later, when gunmen fired into a picket line near the Butte city limits, killing two men and wounding nineteen. The most recent disturbance occurred in the spring of 1946. During the course of a ten-day strike, houses were stoned, windows broken, furniture moved from homes, families threatened. The mob outbreak lasted sixty hours, amid outraged cries of communism and unanswered demands for martial law. The union disavowed responsibility, denounced the destroyers of property and offered its help. One hundred of its men were sworn in as special deputies. Property damage was considerable, but personal injuries few and slight unless counted among them was the fatal injury of a boy by a stray bullet.

Twelve years before that time, after the inauguration of the National Recovery Administration, Butte returned to the closed shop and again became a union stronghold. Earlier than that, following reports of the Bureau of Mines and the Public Health Service, the operators agreed to spend millions of dollars in equipment and practices to reduce the incidence of pneumonia, tuberculosis and silicosis.

Violence in Butte seems pretty far away today. So does the old wholesale corruption, if you except the sportiness that still prevails, if less extravagantly. You could conclude that more amicable relationships were likely to prevail. The Anaconda Copper Mining Company, divorced from Standard Oil through Teddy Roosevelt's trust-busting, has announced an interest, aside from copper, in the community of Butte. It has projected long-range plans that contrast with the philosophy and practice of the mere exploiter. It has established for employees a clubhouse, complete with theater, bowling lanes, library and game rooms, that comparatively few men could afford to belong to anywhere.

But Butte, in spite of change, remains Butte, more cosmopolitan, more outlandish, different in make-up and temperament from other cities in the state. It is an immensely interesting, hearty, friendly place; but it isn't Montana.

Neither is the western slope quite the genuine article. It belongs more to Idaho and Oregon. Men are known to raise cherries there, and apples, which may be the finest in the land but still aren't wheat or beef or mutton. It is hard to think of a Montanan as a cherry picker or an apple knocker. He needs to have wheat straw in his hair and cottonseed cake in his whiskers. He needs to have the print of wind in his face and the mark of the saddle on his pants or the smell of sheep in his Mackinaw.

Most of Montana, more than four fifths of it, I'd estimate, lies east of the Continental Divide. And it is here that you get the feel and color and smell of Montana. It is here that the west wind blows and the sky is high, where you know that space is something no one can understand, not even Albert Einstein. It's here, too, that you keep your directions straight, provided you live within sight of the front range of the Rockies, for west always are the mountains, stony and blue and beautiful against the arch of sky.

Great Falls is both more flourishing and more Montanaish than Butte. So is Billings. Geography and people have the more nearly typical stamp. Here you see and remember the men who wear outdoors indoors.

Great Falls lies in a bend of the Missouri, close to the mouth of Sun River. The main range of the Rockies rears to the west. East and southeast are other ranges, the Highwoods and the Little Belts.

On a flat above the town lies East Base, selected and installed by the military for the special training of flyers because so many days are clear.

Great Falls didn't start as a mushroom town, generated by gold or copper. It started slowly, planned by a man who saw its industrial possibilities. The man was Paris Gibson. In 1883, three years after he had looked at the site, he came back from Minneapolis with a surveyor and an attorney and plotted the townsite. It wasn't long until a hydroelectric plant—the first of the present-day four—was installed at one of the numerous falls that break the nearby Missouri. Before then a flour mill, planing mill, lumberyard, school, bank and newspaper had started operations. Here, in what a few years before had been the heartland of the savage Blackfeet, white institutions took root.

The greatest institution, though, is not dams or refineries or industries of any sort. It is the memory of a man—of Charlie Russell, cowboy artist, sculptor, author, wit and hearty liver, who combined in one personality the characteristics Montanans most admire. His paintings command big figures now. So does his sculpture. His books have entertained thousands and thousands. But it isn't his work that the Montanan particularly likes to talk about. It is Charlie, dead since 1926—Charlie with his easy conviviality, his store of stories, his love for the old Montana, his Will Rogerish ability to point up a situation with a crack.

A rancher who was a friend of Charlie's leased his place to a character reputed to be an honest prohibition farmer. In the course of a couple of years the farmer made off with nearly all the equipment on the ranch.

Charlie commented: "It looks like the only thing that honest prohibition farmer won't take is a drink."

High on the rimrock above Billings, bronze Bill Hart sits his bronze cayuse while airplanes drone in and out of the airport nearby. Let them ride the sky. He is the Range Rider of the Yellowstone, overlooking the great reaches that cowpunchers used to work. Four hundred feet down, on the bank of the Yellowstone, rests the town, prosperous in a valley that a reporter of 1874 termed "valuable for neither agriculture, grazing, nor minerals. . . ." The reporter was wrong about grazing, and he didn't reckon with irrigation. Billings is cow country and sugar-beet country and alfalfa country and wool country. And it is Montana country. Here again you see the marks of horse and hayrack.

In a state like Montana, where population is small and space great, human affairs are immediate and personal. Welfare legislation is not an imponderable, written in answer to statistics. The man who draws unemployment money, the oldster who receives assistance—these are known to their communities, not always favorably. The Montanan, especially the old-timer, is apt to sniff and ask what things are coming to. Physically his world is large; population-wise it is small. He gets a look at things. Both the largeness and the smallness affect him. He finds it hard to imagine a crowded world, difficult to think of humanity en masse. And so, I might add, would you. This is a different world from the Midwest and East. Different circumstances bear on judgment. You feel isolated, happily isolated, free of the frets of our time. Let the world go hang. It is at this point that you need to remind yourself that we tried to let it go hang before.

Part of the citizenry is glad that the ratio of space to population is high. They don't want a lot of outlanders to people the unpeopled places, to fish out the trout streams and spoil the hunting. Another part wants to promote the state, but even the promoters, like the Montana Chamber of Commerce, speak rather cautiously of small, home-owned industry that would help to solve the seasonal unemployment problem. With syndicate operations and mechanization growing both on farms and in lumber areas, they foresee even fewer seasonal jobs.

In part, it is perhaps space and climate that give the Montana resident his humor, his readiness to accept, his disinclination to exaggerate the importance of self. Montana, the fourth-largest state in the Union, is a various and mighty country—146,997 square miles of badlands, high plains, foothills, mountain spurs, glaciered mountains, valleys. The tourist finds the drive from border to border, north and south, a fair day's wheeling. The Great Northern's crack Empire Builder, toiling east across the mountains by way of Marias Pass and dropping to the endless plain, takes just ten minutes short of twelve hours getting from Troy, on the western edge, to Glasgow, which is still one hundred and twenty crow-flight miles from the North Dakota border. The state is rugged. It possesses a grim beauty. Any way the eye looks, it is filled—with nothing, said an Easterner who couldn't see. The grandeur of the place makes self-concern incongruous.

Weather does too. You never can tell what will happen to your prospects in a country in which the temperature ranges from 50° below zero to 110° above. What you do come to realize is that nature isn't overly concerned with you. Montanans take the climate without even due complaint. Cold? Hell, the eastern sloper will tell you, there isn't a month in Montana without at least one day in which a man will be comfortable in his shirt sleeves. Ever feel a chinook? he asks. Chinook? It's a warm wind from the west. Last time it started up, a rancher who'd come to town by sled just managed, going home, to keep his front bobs on the snow. Like to killed his horses doing it.

The exaggeration isn't so extreme. Balmy days do come in midwinter. Snow doesn't often stay on the ground very long except at high altitudes.

Another element helps to mould the Montanan. It is the element of peril—peril from climate, animals, geography, seclusion. In nearly any graveyard can be found markers to sheepherders who died in blizzards with their bands. One July night a Dupuyer sheepman named Broadhurst Smith left his summer-range camp to relieve the night herder. He took a .30-.30 carbine with him. He had settled down for the night when he heard a disturbance in the band. Two grizzly bears were there. He ran at them, shouting, and scared one away. The other began to circle him. As it reared, he shot it down, worked the lever of his rifle and advanced to administer the *coup de grâce*. The hammer clicked on an empty chamber. The sound brought the bear up. It charged Smith and mauled him badly. When it had left him, Smith started, too soon, to crawl away, fearful that if he waited he'd die from loss of blood. The bear came back, fiercer than before. It tore his scalp away. It bit him, bone-deep, on arms and legs and shoulders. It clawed his face. Afterward Smith somehow got to camp and climbed a horse and rode for help. He survived the horseback ride, survived an eighty-mile automobile trip to a Great Falls hospital, survived wounds and shock and loss of blood. The last I heard, he was back on his ranch.

The frontier is so close that social stratification hardly exists in Montana. The man of money and command plays poker with his barber. There's no worship of ancestors, of landholders, little kowtowing to money, not much regard for the dubious bases that snobbery rests on.

There are exceptions. The Indian, for instance, the mixed-blood. No absolute cleavage exists here; the aborigine may win to brotherhood; but some Montanans are likely to feel, without assessing causes, that Indians and "breeds" are thieves and no-goods, for whom nothing can or need be done. Too bad, they'll say, the way the South treats Negroes.

The Montanan has escaped the evangelical religions. He allows his neighbor the right to believe and the right to live in his belief—unless the neighbor happens to be a Hutterite.

The Hutterites are a sect, agrarian and socialistic. They won't bear arms. They live apart, in barracks, refusing to participate in the lives of the communities in which they've settled. And more and more of them have been entering Montana as a consequence of restrictive legislation in Canada.

Montanans don't like them, don't like their whiskers, their dowdy, uniform dress, their seclusion, their socialism. They say they spoil a country. They say there ought to be a law.

If religious convictions, with this exception, are respected, if snobbery scarcely exists, there remains a rigidity in political and economic opinions, a tendency to damn a man if he dares differ from the bunch, a kind of intellectual Vigilanteism. The defender of the Hutterites, for whom something certainly can be said, is likely to be regarded as a crackpot or a rascal. Up to a point you can be free and have friends. Beyond that point you have to pay a price. People haven't time or temper for fool ideas.

Not until recent years did Montana begin to pay real attention to its past, perhaps for the reason that history just walked out the door. People still living can remember when Paris Gibson founded Great Falls. Within the lifetimes of others occurred the massacre on the Marias River, where a band of friendly Piegans were savagely and senselessly slaughtered. It isn't so far back to General Custer and the Battle of the Little Big Horn, nor so far from there to gold strikes on Grasshopper Creek and in Alder and Last Chance gulches. History? It had hardly happened yet.

Along came a man named Bob Fletcher, though, with both interest in and knowledge of the state's past. Then on the staff of the highway department, he had an idea. He wanted to put signs—big ones—along the roads to tell tourists about the country they were passing through. Now, on road signs widely copied elsewhere, motorists, pulling up at convenient driveouts, get pieces of information written humorously and accurately by Fletcher himself.

Along came another man, out of St. Paul, to raise wheat in Cascade County. Charlie Bovey got interested in history, too, so interested that at Great Falls he established Old Town, a re-creation of the Montana settlement of the 1880's or 1890's, complete with barbershop, saloon, smithy, general merchandising establishment and the outmoded goods and fittings that went with them. Not content with that, he revived Virginia City, a moldering mining camp where road agents and Vigilantes once raised Ned. The old spots there have been restored, the furniture and trappings rounded up and put in place. The town swarms now with tourists. Plays are put on; family nights are held at the old brewery. One bartender wears a mustache like a longhorn's points. Hurdy-gurdies and music boxes play. Peepshow machines hold pictures that, from this point in time, are more comic than risqué. Quite a place.

A passionate expatriate Montanan like me asks himself what binds him to the state. Is it just my interest in a time and activity, in the mind-heard echoes of old trappers on the beavered streams, in the imagined grind of prairie schooners? Is it the rise of a trout to a royal coachman? Is it a buck's antlers showing through the quaking asp? Is it scenery, space, the opportunity for solitude? Is it friends? Is it old and rich associations with places and with people?

It is these: It is mountain water over shining rock. It is stars like campfires in the sky. It is the riffle of the west wind in the redtop. It is clouds among the peaks of Glacier Park. It is a cottontail at the edge of a thicket. It is a pack trail to the Chinese Wall and the Continental Divide. It is a horseman and a bronc. It is the Blackfoot Big Lake's grave on the benchland. It is limpid fishing streams like the Madison and the Flathead and Sun River and the Teton. It is a round of ditchwaters with old-timers who by and by will get to reminiscing. It is the aching roll of badlands. It is Lewis and Clark and the things they saw that I see now. It is the girls, the lithe young girls, goldened by the blood of Scandinavia, coppered by the touch of *voyageur* and Indian. It is a bar of song remembered from some long-ago country-schoolhouse dance. It is the wild geese V-ing before a storm. It is the cool summer nights with the coyotes crying.

It is the informal cordiality that a man encounters from border to border. It is the grease monkey and the hasher saying "You betcha" to a request. It is the unknown rancher in a pickup who stops to ask if he can help you with a flat.

It is all these, and it is more than these. It is something else, something that makes others love the state though they recognize its shortcomings, that gives to visitors the sense of living in a different, a less fretful, and a better world. It is, as I think I've already indicated, that here one feels an individual superiority to event, a be-damned attitude toward mischance, a freedom from or ascendancy over the anxieties that press so hard elsewhere. Montanans somehow stay on top of life.

A rancher I know lived in town. He had a great wheat-crop prospect one year—six hundred acres standing thick, almost ready for the combine and the elevator. Wheat was high, almost three dollars a bushel. The ranch foreman came to the house early one morning. He roused the rancher, to tell him hail had felled every straw during the night.

"Oscar," the rancher said, "why'd you want to wake me up to tell me this? There's plenty of time to worry when I'm ready to get up." With that he turned over and went back to sleep.

I know the man. I know he'd do it. He's pure Montana, out of Norway.

Wyoming

by HAMILTON BASSO

James Runningwater is a Crow Indian. He is somewhat heavier than the average run, stands close to six feet, and looks considerably older than his twenty-nine years. An infantryman in the last war, he lives on the Crow Agency in Montana. He has a mother, a wife, two children, four horses, and a battered, rheumatic, 1937 sedan. Every year, in the third week in July, he piles his family into his car, along with as many extra passengers as he can squeeze into it, and heads south for the three-day rodeo in Sheridan, Wyoming. The rodeo is known as the Bots Sots Stampede; Bots Sots is Crow for "very best."

My impression is that the Sheridan rodeo is the year's most exciting occasion for many of the Crows. Several hundreds of them come down from Montana and pitch a tepee village just outside the rodeo grounds. They do a moderately brisk trade in beaded moccasins, leatherwork and other Indian crafts, cheer those of their number who participate in the various events, and, strictly for tourists, perform some of their tribal dances at night.

I first met Runningwater at the rodeo while hunting for a bathroom for a ten-year-old boy. He gave me the directions I needed. Later, while admiring a particularly handsome buckskin pony that was part of the string the Crows had brought down to run in the bareback relay race—one of the high spots of the program—I saw him again. Thanks to Runningwater, I became a Crow man. We exchanged congratulations when their jockey came in first. The following afternoon I set out for a late ride from the ranch where I was staying. After an hour or so of cross-country ambling, I made my way back along a dirt road that forms one boundary of the ranch. It was just before sunset. The huge outcroppings of rock that rib the slopes of the Big Horn Mountains shone in the slanting light, that immense solitude so characteristic of the West hung over everything, and except for the clopping of my horse's hoofs and the distant chatter of a magpie there wasn't a sound. I was startled to find a battered, dusty automobile parked ahead of me as I rounded a curve in the road where it mounted the crest of a hill.

A man was standing beside the car, absolutely motionless. He was dressed in the ordinary, workaday costume of the American West— the blue jeans, blue shirt, plow boots, and moderately big hat that used to be common from the Mexican border to both Dakotas before the corrupting influence of Hopalong Cassidy.

As I approached and he turned in my direction, I saw that it was James Runningwater. I also saw that the car was stuffed with Indians. I noticed three youngish men dressed as Runningwater was, an old brave with braided hair, and a woman and two children.

Staring across the hills, they gave me hardly a glance. Runningwater recognized me and we greeted each other. He apparently guessed what was on my mind. "We are looking," he said, "at the grass."

I suppose there are those—especially those who put signs in their shop windows saying "No Indian Or Mexican Trade Solicited"—who will find this incident another example, even a "perfect example," of loco Indian behavior. I don't think so. As I see it, Runningwater and his friends were looking at the most important thing in the whole state of Wyoming. So far as its character and personality are concerned, there isn't anything in its 97,548 square miles nearly as significant as grass.

In relation to Wyoming, the usual batch of statistics are only of moderate value. It is helpful to know that it lies midway between the Mississippi River and the Pacific Ocean, and that it ranks ninth among the fifty states in size. Nor does it do any harm to remember that three great river systems—the Columbia, the Colorado, and the Missouri—have their sources in its mountains, or that it is one of the most sparsely populated areas in the country. The most vital fact about it, however, is that in some sections it is overspread by more than 150 kinds of grass. Because of their scarcity, small size, and inaccessibility, most of these are unimportant. But the blue grasses, the wheat grasses, the fescues and the redtops—these are enough to make an Indian's heart stand still. Or a white man's heart, too, for that matter, provided grass has ever meant more to him than the cheerful greenery that brightens front lawns.

The whole of Wyoming's history, until very recent times, can be told in terms of grass. First the original nomads, then the Indians, and finally the latter-day white men—grass is what brought them to Wyoming and grass is what kept them there. The story of the trek into Wyoming is too large and complicated to be told here, but its outlines are simple enough: the buffalo followed the grass, the Indians followed the buffalo, and the cattlemen followed the Indians. That tattered, worn-out term, "grass roots," has consequently a very special meaning in Wyoming. It is from these roots that the state has sprung.

Compared with certain other states that have been completely transformed during the past fifty years—Texas and California, for instance—Wyoming cannot be said to have sprung very far. In the entire state, which is seventy-eight times the size of Rhode Island, there are only slightly over 200 settlements. Less than 100 of these are lived in by more than one hundred people, and only three towns in the state, Cheyenne, Laramie and Casper, have a population of more than 15,000. Nearly all of its settlements, moreover, are from thirty to fifty miles apart. I have driven more than one hundred miles in Wyoming without seeing a single habitation—or, indeed, a single living thing—and I know of no place where man's passage has left so little imprint on the earth. Everywhere his footprints are lost in the grass. And where there is no grass—in the badlands of the northeastern part of the state; in certain sections near the even yet not completely explored Wind River Mountains; in those big, semiarid reaches where the cover is so sparse that it requires forty to fifty acres to support a horse or cow—there is no sign or indication that man has ever been. It is hard to escape the feeling that were Wyoming's first aboriginal inhabitants to return today, along with the Indians who came after them—the Crow, the Blackfeet, the Sioux, the Cheyennes and others—they would find the country much as they left it.

Yet, in common with the rest of the West, Wyoming has had a

vivid history. Furthermore, many chapters of its history are a part of living memory. There are wrinkled braves still living who rode on the buffalo hunts. There are others, younger, who remember the gathering of the tribes for the Battle of the Little Big Horn. There are men and women who saw the first Union Pacific train arrive in Cheyenne in 1867, and there are still a handful of grizzled veterans who drove the longhorns up the Texas Trail in the days of the open range.

So the feeling of emptiness one gets in Wyoming—the ache of vastness and of solitude—is not because it has no past. It is rather because the signs and monuments of the past are so meager and so few. The characters in its cavalcade—the Indians, the trappers, the miners, the scouts, the bullwhackers, the mule skinners, and the cowboys—left hardly a trace in their passing. They came, they did, and they went. The decaying logs of an old fur press, rotting sluice boxes, the stone abutments of an old railroad trestle, a rusty beaver trap lying in the weeds along a river, a broken arrowhead kicked up in a field—these are the relics of Wyoming's history. Nearly everything else is scenery, emptiness, and the ever-enduring grass.

The history of Wyoming divides itself, schoolbook fashion, into four convenient parts—exploration and fur trading; emigration along the Oregon-California and Overland trails; Indian campaigns; territorial days and statehood.

Nobody knows the name or identity of the first white man who got to what is now Wyoming; the chances are that nobody ever will know. Two French-Canadian fur traders, François Vérendrye and Louis Joseph Vérendrye, may have made their way to the central part of the state in the winter of 1742–43. It seems more likely, however, that their wanderings did not take them any farther west than the Black Hills of South Dakota—which, it might be added, was pretty far west. After them, in the early part of the 19th Century, came other trappers and traders—great doers and great talkers like John Colter, Jacques La Ramie, Jim Bridger, and various others. They made the first maps and opened up the first trails; they went where no others had been before.

Back in St. Louis—the center of the fur trade, the warehouse and arsenal and jumping-off place—the news of an untapped, virgin, beaver-rich country began to get around. Bald-headed Benjamin Bonneville—Benjamin Louis Eulalie de Bonneville: the son of a French refugee who went to West Point, graduated in 1815, and worked his way up to Captain of the Seventh Infantry, U.S.A.—knew a good thing when he heard of it. The years he had spent on frontier duty hadn't gone for nothing. Taking two years' leave from the Army in 1832, Bonneville, backed by one of John Jacob Astor's partners, led a fur-trading expedition of 110 men into the Wyoming region. He also made a radical, farsighted, notable experiment—he took twenty wagons along. He had trouble along the way, the same kind of trouble that was later to dog the fortunes of thousands of emigrants, but he got his vehicles to and over the Continental Divide. The tracks they made ran straight across history; once again the impossible had been done; a new era was in the making.

By 1840, with Martin Van Buren in the White House and the war with Mexico six years off, the Federal Government began to think of looking into the region. Officially, that is. Then, as today, the machinery of government moved with something less than startling speed. It was not until 1842 that an exploration party was sent into Wyoming. At its head was a young, good-looking Southern-reared lieutenant named John Frémont. It marked the beginning of the career and reputation that was to cause Frémont eventually to aspire to the presidency and signaled Wyoming's entry into the second phase of its history—emigration along the Oregon-California and Overland trails.

Those who went westward along these trails, however, were restless, far-seeking people. Wyoming was merely a stretch of country they had to pass through. The land of heart's desire, along with the gold fields of California, lay farther to the west. The first permanent settlers in Wyoming were a party of Mormons who established themselves at Fort Bridger in 1853. Even they did not stay long. Pursued by the bitterness that met them at every turn, and also by a small U. S. Army, they burned their homes in 1857 and fled elsewhere. Other transcontinental migrants—those who were tired of the heartache and backbreak of travel and who might be tempted to homestake in Wyoming—were daunted by the Indians. A few of the tribes had more or less gone over to the white man, but the Sioux—the wild-riding, relentless, implacable Sioux—were still on the warpath.

The climax of Indian fighting in the Northwest came in 1876, with the Battle of the Little Big Horn and the names that once had the sound of silver trumpets to little boys—Custer, Crook, Mackenzie, Sitting Bull, Dull Knife, Red Cloud. Their biggest victory, the Battle of the Little Big Horn, was also the Indians' biggest defeat;

after that descent into humiliation the white man would no longer be denied. By 1880 the Sioux had taken their last scalp; Wyoming enjoyed comparative security from then on.

In the relatively short time between then and now, a state twice the size of New York has had to get itself organized, settled, and built up. Some of the difficulties attendant upon those tasks, moreover, could not be remedied simply by the passage of time. Time could bring railroads, telegraph and telephone lines, paved roads, and all the other appurtenances of modern civilization. What it could not do was to change the basic character of the state. Wyoming has oil (including Teapot Dome); it has coal (the most extensive coal reserves in the United States); and it has a large number of different minerals (most of which are buried so far beneath the earth's surface that no way has been found of mining them in quantity). But even with its coal and oil and minerals, Wyoming is what it has always been—a grazing state pure and simple. The fact that there are nearly twenty times more domestic animals in the state than human beings pretty much sums up the story; it is simply not the sort of place that attracts people in large numbers.

Most of the people who live in Wyoming are native-born, although in the mining town of Rock Springs some fifty-odd nationalities are said to be represented—Greeks, Russians, Italians, Finns, Irish, Welsh, Chinese, and others. Rock Springs, however, is an exception.

Of the native-born, a considerable proportion are the sons and daughters, the grandsons and granddaughters, of the original settlers. There is a large strain of Texas ancestry in the state—brought up along the Texas Trail—and a similarly large strain of Midwest derivation. It strikes me that the Texas drawl is rapidly going down under the Midwestern twang; the speech of Wyoming appears to be getting closer and closer to the Ohio River and farther and farther away from the Rio Grande. But whatever its individual accent happens to be, it is a common language.

With a population of less than three individuals to the square mile, with the past so close to the present, with a network of personal associations crisscrossing the state, nearly everybody in Wyoming knows nearly everybody else. There are indeed times, as often has been said, when the place seems to come closer to being a secret society than a state.

Membership in the society, however, is fairly easy to come by— no initiation fees, no board of governors, no dues.

"All a man has to do," I was told by a rancher acquaintance, "is to move on in. The more the merrier. There's room for all. *Ain't* there room, though! Just look at all the room!"

"But what is there to do in Wyoming?" I have been frequently asked. "What is there to see?" The question has both a ready answer and one that is not so ready. The what-to-do part is simple—you can fish, you can ride, you can participate in the entertainment that is provided by any of the various dude ranches, or, if you are so minded, you can simply sit in the silence and invite your soul.

The what-to-see part is rather more complicated. First and foremost, of course, there is the scenery—all the scenery you can take in. But the state occupies such a lot of room that even its scenery is sometimes hard to come by. It is even possible to cross the southern part of Wyoming without being made to realize it has any. Geologically, Wyoming is a big, high mesa—the average altitude is 6000 feet. Its mountains—the Big Horns, the Tetons, the Wind Rivers, and the Absarokas—are simply the outthrusting peaks of the mesa. And they are all in the north and west, somewhat out of the beaten path. As Struthers Burt has said, in a highly readable book about Wyoming called *Powder River*, they go and hide themselves. And as an old-timer acquaintance of mine said more recently, "They ain't hankering after company."

To see Wyoming properly I would say that three things are necessary—an automobile, a willingness to make long hops, and a certain amount of interest in the American past. Given these—and time out for a few long horseback rides, to see the country close up—it is hard to imagine anyone's not finding it worth the while. What follows is one man's Baedeker; I know that I will be quarreled with for leaving this place or that place out. It should be said, too, that I have made no effort to arrange anything so ambitious as a "tour." What I have tried to do, instead, is to follow the itinerary of history—to begin at the beginning, before even the Indians came, and to trace the story of Wyoming up to the present.

The monuments left by primitive men are extremely few—the great slabs of Stonehenge, the huge statues on Easter Island, and the terraced pyramids found in some of the South Sea islands are those that come immediately to mind. Yet in the northern tip of the Big Horn Mountains in Wyoming—the Big Horns being in the north-central part of the state—there is one of the most arresting of them all. Everything we know about it (or rather everything that has been surmised about it) can be contained in a brief paragraph, but there is no question that it is one of the oldest works of man, if not the very oldest, on the North American continent. It is called the Medicine Wheel and outside the borders of Wyoming it is virtually unknown. Few visitors take the trouble to get to it, for it takes a certain amount of getting to, and I have been unable to find any reference to it in those books that deal with the prehistoric era in North America. In nearly every other country, the Medicine Wheel would be a national treasure; here we don't even know we have it.

Our family expedition started out for it early one morning from a ranch near Sheridan. The excellently paved road soon began the steep ascent of the Big Horns by means of switchbacks, more switchbacks, and a continuous series of hairpin curves—it is not a trip I would recommend to anyone troubled by high places. There is one place about thirty miles from Sheridan where on clear days it is possible to see the Black Hills, 200 miles to the east, and further along, still climbing, you come to a great jumble of huge boulders of all shapes and sizes that were deposited by a prehistoric glacier on the hill-like slope of one of the peaks. Known as "The Fallen City," the predominantly oblong blocks of stone do indeed suggest the scattered ruins—houses, temples, forums, villas—of an ancient, forgotten city leveled by some mysterious disaster. Then, a mile or so along, you reach a tremendous outcropping of rock, eight or ten stories high and having the shape of a V, that has been christened "Steamboat Rock." Though I grew up a Mississippi River man, I have never been able to find anything steamboaty about it. I am more reminded of the Winged Victory—the lofty spread of the V, massive though it is, strikes me as having the same kind of airy lightness, the same soaring quality, and the same feeling of momentarily arrested flight.

Shortly past "Steamboat Rock" the highway levels out and runs across a level plateau that is one of the saddles of the Big Horn range. You are now over 8000 feet high; the clean, high air, crisp and heady even in July, puts needles in your lungs. The road becomes a narrow passage through one of the heaviest stands of timber in Wyoming—pine, spruce, cedar, and fir—broken here and there by mountain meadows covered with wildflowers. We took time out to walk around in one; we found Indian paintbrush, gentians, harebells, touch-me-nots, lupines, and big tangles of wild rose. I have never seen such wildflowers anywhere.

But the real excitement of the trip to the Medicine Wheel comes after you leave the main highway and branch off on a state road. Immediately you start climbing again, and immediately the solitude swallows you up—except for three deer, a big hawk, and a grinning coyote that bounded out of nowhere, we passed not a living thing. Branching due west, the constantly twisting road rises to the summit of the Big Horn Range near a peak known as Bald Mountain (10,030 feet altitude) and then, some twenty-three miles from the highway, meets up with a dirt lane that is just barely wide enough for a car to travel on—the Medicine Wheel, it says on a sign, is three miles away.

It seemed more like three hundred—not in distance but in time. I thought I knew something about hazardous roads, but this one was the prize. Had I known what we were getting into—the foot-deep ruts, the slithery mud, the litter of rocks, the big patch of glassy ice (yes, ice in July) at a particularly abrupt curve where there is nothing between you and a sheer, precipitous drop of several hundred feet except some particularly thin air—had I known about all this, as I was about to say, we would have forsaken the advantages of the combustion engine and gone by foot. What would have happened had we met a car coming from the opposite direction I hate to think. It is not my habit to give advice, but I do believe that the Wyoming authorities in charge of such matters would be well advised to set aside certain hours for getting to the Medicine Wheel and certain other hours for getting back. That road just isn't a two-way street.

We got there, however. The road finally gave up the ghost and petered out and we had to walk the rest of the way. That mile-long climb is one of the things I will always remember. For when at last you gain the summit of the mountain, on which the Medicine Wheel lies, nearly 10,000 feet high, you have the feeling, in those pure, clean reaches of the upper air, that you have made your way to the moral top of the world. You understand why the Indians held this place in reverence as Big Medicine; some atavistic stirring tells you that it is Big Medicine still.

On top of the mountain, which levels off into a kind of small plateau and from which you can see for miles, there is an almost perfect circle made of rough, unhewed stones laid side by side. None of the stones is particularly large and no effort was made to fit them together. They were just laid there, one after the other, apparently as they came to hand. The circle, or wheel, is seventy feet in diameter and 245 feet in circumference. In its center is a mound of stones like a hub, three feet high, and twelve feet around, from which twenty-eight spokes radiate to the rim of the wheel. These spokes are also made of stones of varying shapes and sizes. Around the rim of the wheel, at irregular distances, are six stone mounds that are somewhat smaller than the one in the center. They now look like piles of rock that children at play might have heaped up, but when first discovered by the white man they were built up on three sides with the fourth side left open, after the fashion of an armchair. Five of them had the open side facing inward toward the center of the wheel, and the sixth, which is the one on the east point of the compass, faced outward toward the rising sun. The mound in the center for many years supported a bleached buffalo skull, the eye sockets of which also looked to the east, but it disappeared some years ago. The general suspicion is that some tourist made off with it.

All that is known for certain about the Medicine Wheel is that it is ages old—so old that even the Indians have no legends about it. The Crows say that the wheel was there when their people first came to the Big Horns. The old men of the tribe say they do not know who built it; they say that the wheel was there "before the light came" or "before the people had iron."

Archaeologists are no more help than the Indians. Some find a resemblance to the calendar stone of Mexico; others detect a link with Egypt and Babylon; still others surmise a kinship to Stonehenge. But all this is guess and speculation. Nothing has been proved. There is no question, however, that the wheel was used for some sacred purpose.

If few visitors to Wyoming ever get to the Medicine Wheel, practically everybody gets to Jackson Hole. And for good reason. Known as one of the scenic attractions of the United States, it is everything it is said to be—even more. Lying in the northwestern part of the state, not far from the Idaho line, it is in the Grand Teton country—some of the most wonderful country in the world.

A green, fertile valley watered by the Snake River and containing two indescribably beautiful lakes—Jackson and Jenny—Jackson Hole is some 400 square miles in area and is bounded by mountains on all sides. Naturally, the best way to see it is from one of these eminences. This involves a real climb, however, and those who haven't the time, wind, or energy can get a fine panoramic view by motoring to the top of nearby Signal Mountain. The towering sky line is dominated by ten major peaks. Grand Teton, the highest, is 13,766 feet; Mount St. John, the lowest, stops at 11,412 feet. All are part of the Teton Range, a massive barrier forty miles long. The range is tipped slightly toward the east, and the east face, exposed by uplift and erosion, is one of the steepest fault escarpments in the world —Grand Teton wasn't scaled until 1898. The name "The Tetons," bestowed by French trappers who penetrated the area in the early 1800's, was originally attached to but three mountains—Grand, Middle, and South Teton. The Frenchmen knew them as *les trois Tetons;* the blunt, forthright translation is "the three teats." An even earlier explorer, Wilson Price Hunt, called them the Pilot Knobs. An intrepid man, Hunt, but, in this instance at least, probably a little too genteel. *Les trois Tetons* won out over the Pilot Knobs.

They were first seen, however, by a fellow who didn't bother to do much christening, John Colter, the first white American to set foot in Wyoming. He got there in 1806.

An enlisted man under Lewis and Clark, he made his way with the expedition to the Pacific Coast, followed it back on the return journey to St. Louis as far as the mouth of the Yellowstone River, and then, meeting up with two trappers, he asked for and received his discharge. That was in August, 1806. Within a year, having tired of his partnership with the two other trappers and going it alone, he had rung up a long list of "firsts"—first explorer of the Big Horn River and the country of the Big Horns; the first white man to cross Union and Teton passes; the first white man to see the headwaters of the Wind, the Snake, and the Green rivers; the first white man to pass through what is now Yellowstone Park; and the first white American to see the Teton Mountains, the Teton Basin, and Jackson Hole.

Where Colter led, others followed. Jackson Hole, now a national monument, became a favorite rendezvous for the mountain men— it is named, incidentally, after one of them. So far as Colter's memory is concerned, there isn't a place in Wyoming that bears his name. And all he did was to discover it practically singlehanded.

After Colter and the other mountain men, history moved with the rush of a mountain river when the snows begin to melt. By 1840, the push to the West was on. By 1850, Wyoming was familiar territory to the restless thousands who made the long trek from Missouri to the Pacific Coast by way of the Oregon Trail.

More landmarks of the Oregon Trail are to be found in Wyoming than any place else along its two-thousand-mile route. Over in the Wind River mountain country in the western part of the state there is one spot where, in a ledge of soft limestone that lies flush with the surface of the ground, you can still see the deep ruts worn in the rock by the wagon wheels—seven pairs of ruts in all. And all along the way across the state, as you follow the course of the Sweetwater, you pass landmark after landmark noted in the diaries of the pioneers—Split Rock, Devil's Gate, Three Crossings, and many others.

But of all the names that are associated with our first transcontinental highway, the most famous are Fort Laramie and Independence Rock. Honesty compels me to say that I'm afraid that only the historical-minded will find them worth going out of the way for. Independence Rock is a rather unusual geological specimen, but the state is full of other geological specimens that can give it cards and spades. Actually, the Rock is a tremendous granite boulder; all in all, measured around its circumference, it covers an acre or more. It stands in the middle of nowhere, with sagebrush and buffalo grass stretching for miles, and unless you remember the things that it once stood for—a pause on the way; friends and fresh water; great distances conquered; a time of rest before another major effort—it is apt to strike you, prosaically, as nothing but a big old rock. Once known as the Register of the Desert, it used to be covered by thousands of names—50,000 is the figure usually given. You can still make out a number; some are chiseled in the stone.

The emigrants who followed the Oregon Trail got to Fort Laramie some two hundred miles before they got to Independence Rock. You drive to it, today, from the town of Torrington in the southeastern part of the state. And once there, after you have crossed the North Platte River, you are faced with some of the saddest, most melancholy ruins in the U.S.A.

Founded as an advanced outpost in 1834 by one of the fur companies, Fort Laramie was bought and garrisoned by the United States Government in 1849. It remained an active Army post until 1890, when it was sold. The state of Wyoming later obtained the property and transferred it to the National Park Service, which now looks after it as a national monument. It would be hard to think of any one place that bulks more dramatically in our history than Fort Laramie. Indians, fur trappers, the hell-for-leather boys of the Pony Express, stagecoach drivers, Forty-Niners, Brigham Young and his followers, gamblers, traders, prospectors, homeseekers, cowpunchers who brought in the first herds of cattle—Fort Laramie knew and sheltered them all.

But the fort today, like so many others, is rather a disappointment. Most of the old buildings have fallen into ruin and the ones still standing are in a bad state of disrepair. To me, however, the place had a kind of magic nonetheless—it was one of the places I had long wanted to see, and now I had. It was a warm, bright day when we were there and the grounds were completely deserted except for a little, fair-haired girl playing in the tall grass with an Indian doll dressed in the costume of the Sioux. There it was, I thought, the whole history of the American West—a blue-eyed child of the blue-eyed invaders, playing happily in unthinking possession, and those who were once among the fiercest enemies of her fathers reduced to nothing more dangerous than a toy.

A cowboy and a cow—here, I suppose, is the symbol of Wyoming in the average imagination. What has to be remembered is that it took the forces of history some time to whip the symbol into shape. The wealth that lies in the native grasses of Wyoming was discovered in 1864, when a Government trader with a string of cattle was caught on the plains in a December blizzard. There was nothing for him to do but turn the cattle loose and accept their loss. But in the spring, miles from where the animals had been set free, the trader came across his herd again—whole, fat, healthy, and in much better condition than when he saw it last.

That sort of news was bound to get around. By 1870 tales of the wonders of the Wyoming grasslands were general throughout the West. Up came the cows and cowboys on the long drive from Texas, heading for the open range—fifty million big unfenced acres of it. For more than a decade afterwards, the cattle barons were lords as far as they could see. They built their ranch houses, turned the Cheyenne Club in Cheyenne into one of the glittering social centers of the new world, incorporated their companies, turned loose their cattle on the open range, and organized the Wyoming Stock Growers Association, which, until very recent times, had something in the nature of a double nelson on the politics of the state.

They had it too good for it to last. The sheepmen wanted in, and so did the "nester," and finally, after something close to civil war broke out, and blizzard and drought and speculation took their toll, the free, spacious, untrammeled world of the big cattlemen went the way of the free, spacious, untrammeled world of the Indians they had dispossessed. Many of the early ranches, however, are still operating, although some have changed hands. Wyoming is not one of the big beef-producing states. But it does have, in the Wyoming Hereford Ranch just outside Cheyenne (visitors welcome), one of the most famous outfits in the West. Founded in the 1870's, it takes in 6000 acres that provide elbowroom for some 3000 head of whiteface cattle who can trace their distinguished lineage back to 500 ancestors brought over from Herefordshire, England, as breeding stock. The stock did its job so well that in 1945 the manager of the ranch turned down an offer of $100,000 for one of his bulls—a refusal that has already incorporated him in the folklore of the West.

But of all the ranches in Wyoming the most famous of all is one that has only incidentally to do with cattle. Known all over the U.S. simply as "Eaton's," it specializes in dudes. Sprawled out over some 7000 acres in and about the Big Horns, it has its own town, its own post office, its own telephone system, and its own mythology. It also has a place among the minor footnotes of American history in that the three Eaton brothers—Howard, Alden, and Willis—were the ones who started the whole dude-ranch business.

Howard, born, like his brothers, in Pittsburgh, headed west in 1880 and started the Custer Trail Ranch near Medora, North Dakota. Alden and Willis soon joined him. Their enthusiastic letters back East caused so many friends to come and visit them that the three brothers found themselves using up a substantial portion of their income for entertainment. One of their more perceptive guests, comprehending the situation, made a suggestion—why not charge something for board and lodging? The suggestion was adopted and that's how dude ranching was born. Looking through some old account books at Eaton's, I came across the name of their first paying guest—the first dude that ever was. He came from Buffalo, his name was Bert Ramsey, and he spent the summer of 1882 in the wilds of North Dakota. Two years later, in 1884, a less obscure dude went out to enjoy a few weeks with the Eatons—man by the name of Theodore Roosevelt.

The three brothers moved their seat of operations from Dakota to Wyoming in 1904 when they bought the property now occupied by the ranch. All three are now dead, but the ranch and the business are still in the family. With the old stone ranch house as its center, a whole community has grown up to take care of the requirements of the one hundred and twenty-five guests that the ranch can accommodate at one time.

To go to Wyoming and not visit Yellowstone Park is a little like going to New York City and not visiting Times Square. Be careful, though, that you are not trampled in the rush; over a million tourists now make their way to the park each year. That Yellowstone Park should be our Number One, four-star, seven-alarm tourist attraction is thoroughly in keeping with our national character. Here is the sort of thing we Americans seem to like best— one excitement popping loose after the other; a vast, 3472-square-mile Believe-It-Or-Not; Mother Nature putting on her biggest, best, most extravagant show. Consider some of the entertainments on the bill. Great travertine terraces. Spectacular waterfalls. The grand canyon of the Yellowstone River. Fossil forests. Mud volcanoes. A towering cliff of pure obsidian. Hot springs of all shapes, sizes, and colors. Yellowstone Lake, twenty miles long and nearly a mile and a half above sea level. More geysers, including one known as Old Faithful, than are to be found in all the rest of the world put together. Buffalo herds, elk, moose and deer. One of the nesting places of the rapidly vanishing trumpeter swan, and hundreds of lazy, shiftless, ingratiating panhandlers disguised as bears. With all that to choose from, you can hardly go wrong.

All the same, you can't help wishing that you'd been lucky enough to have been tagging after John Colter when he got to it for the first time. Not that Colter ever got any thanks for discovering it. All it did for him was to get him the reputation of being the biggest liar since Munchausen. His trouble, it seems, was that he played it straight; he came back and tried to give a factual report of what he had seen. Jim Bridger, another trapper who figures large in the early history of Wyoming and who also explored the Yellowstone Park area, fared much better. Beginning with the same batch of wonders as Colter, Bridger took the truth and then deliberately distorted it into a tall tale—consequently, instead of being put down as a chronic prevaricator, he is remembered as one of our great storytellers.

For instance: Bridger told how one day he sighted a magnificent elk, took aim, and fired. Instead of dropping, the elk seemed not even to have heard the report of the rifle. Drawing a second and more deliberate bead on the animal, Jim fired again—and still the elk went on grazing peacefully. Completely out of patience, Jim seized the rifle and rushed forward to club the elk into submission. Then, as he ran, he crashed into something hard and immovable that turned out to be a mountain of pure, transparent glass. But there was something stranger still. Not only was the mountain of glass, on the other side of which the elk continued to munch in peaceful security, but the glass had a telescopic effect—that elk was twenty-five miles away!

Then there was Jim's alarm-clock story. He said that across from one of his camping sites there was the bald, flat face of a mountain that had such a peculiar acoustical arrangement that any sound originating in camp was not echoed back for six hours. He said that upon retiring for the night he would call out "Time to get up! Time to get up!" and that six hours later the echo would wake him. And in telling of the fossil forests in the Yellowstone Park region Jim went on like this: "There was one place where petrified leaves and branches still clung to petrified trees and among them sat petrified birds singing petrified songs." All tall tales, of course. But in Yellowstone Park there *is* Obsidian Cliff, a huge outcropping of volcanic glass; there *are* places that take a moderately long time to return an echo; and there *are* petrified leaves, petrified branches and petrified trees.

It was not until 1870, when a full-fledged scientific expedition was sent by the Government into the wilds of the upper Yellowstone country, that the stories told by Colter and Bridger found sober, accurate corroboration. In 1872, Congress voted to set aside the area as a national park. One doesn't like to think of what would have happened to the place if it hadn't—hot-dog and hamburger stands everywhere, ten cents for a chip off Obsidian Cliff, a half dollar to see Old Faithful, a quarter to watch each of the other geysers, steam baths at the hot spring, beauty packs at the mud volcano, and who can say what else!

Here and there, as you travel about Wyoming, you come across places where people have gathered to live—the most important of these, in point of numbers, are Cheyenne, Casper, Laramie and Sheridan.

Sheridan (3737 altitude) is the largest town in Northern Wyoming. With the possible exception of Dubois, in the Wind River country, it has always struck me as being the most "western" of all

Wyoming's more sizable communities. The commercial establishments, in good cow-town fashion, are strung out along Main Street and there are always a few Crows and Cheyennes about. Along with the ranch hands, who now go in for cowboy garb that a sophisticated fifth-grader would look down upon as kindergarten stuff, the Indians have been brought up to date—instead of wearing buckskin and hand-tanned robes, they now go around in bright blankets of modern design milled in New England. The first building in Sheridan was erected in 1878 by a trapper named Jim Mason. The town itself was staked out on a forty-acre plot on May 10, 1882, and named in honor of the Civil War hero, General Philip H. Sheridan. Unlike Cheyenne, which had a way of blowing the roof off, Sheridan was always a rather sober community. It had a smithy and two general stores before it had a saloon—a state of affairs practically unheard of in the West—and only one person was arrested during its first two years. A case, I believe, of disturbing the peace.

Sheridan, however, has had its share of excitement. As late as 1939 a number of Sheridan residents, dissatisfied with Wyoming's political setup, called upon Northern Wyoming to secede from the rest of the state and form a separate, forty-ninth state of its own. The new state was to be called Absaroka and was to include Yellowstone Park and most of Wyoming north of the Platte. Sheridan's street commissioner appointed himself governor and named a small staff. The new state got no further than that, but residents of North Wyoming, when displeased with the action of the state government, appealed for redress to the "Governor of Absaroka." Interestingly enough, it worked—most of the matters in dispute were settled to the satisfaction of the "Absarokians."

Laramie (7145 altitude), the seat of the University of Wyoming, lies in the southeastern part of the state on the east bank of the Laramie River. One of Wyoming's oldest cities, it is also the state's intellectual center. Things were not always thus, however. Named for the French-Canadian trapper, Jack La Ramie, the town began as a tent settlement several weeks before the tracks of the Union Pacific Railroad reached it in the spring of 1868. A few months later 500 shacks had been built, and on May 9, 1868, the first train screeched and rattled into town.

That's when hell popped loose. A provisional government was formed, but by that time the outlaw element had taken over. The government was forced to resign and there then followed months of what can only be described as premeditated anarchy. In the established pattern of the American West, strict as a Hollywood scenario, civil war broke out. An army of 500 vigilantes laid plans for simultaneous raids on several outlaw hangouts on the night of October 29, 1868. Target Number One was a saloon and dance hall known as "Belle of the West." In the siege that followed, with most of the town pitching in, five men were killed, fifteen were wounded, and four outlaws were strung up on telegraph poles. Laramie, after that, began gradually to settle down—so much so that, by 1880, Edgar Wilson (Bill) Nye, one of this country's gentlest humorists, was able to be both its postmaster and justice of the peace at the same time. Nye left Laramie in 1883 to go to work for the *New York World*. In resigning his postmastership he wrote in part as follows:

> Post Office Divan
> Laramie City, W. T.
> Oct. 1, 1883.

To the President of the United States:

Sir: I beg leave at this time to officially tender my resignation as postmaster of this place, and in due form to deliver the great seal and key to the front door of this office. The safe combination is set on the number 33, 66, and 99, though I do not remember at this moment which comes first, or how many times you revolve the knob. . . .

You will find the postal cards that have not been used under the distributing table, and the coal down in the cellar. If the stove draws too hard, close the damper in the pipe and shut the general delivery window. . . .

You will find the key under the door-mat and you had better turn the cat out at night when you close the office. . . . If Deacon Hayford does not pay his box rent, you might as well put his mail in the general delivery, and when Bob Head gets drunk and insists on a letter from one of his wives every day in the week, you can salute him through the box delivery with an Old Queen Ann tomahawk, which you will find near the Etruscan water pail. . . .

Mr. President, as an official of this government, I now retire. . . .

> BILL NYE.

Casper (5123 altitude) is the second largest city in Wyoming. Situated in the central part of the state, it lies on the south side of the North Platte. The most industrialized community in Wyoming, specializing in oil, Casper's location at the crossroads of four national highways and two railroads has made it the distribution point for a wide trade area.

The Oregon Trail ran through the townsite of Casper some forty years before it was staked out in 1888. An estimated 300,000 people passed through before wagon traffic was rerouted in the 1860's to the more southerly Overland Trail.

Casper, like Laramie, was the child of a railroad—the Chicago and North Western. When the first passenger train arrived in June, 1888, nearly one hundred persons had located on the townsite. Since the Chicago and North Western was not then a main line, Casper's growth was considerably less rapid than that of the Union Pacific terminals. When the town was incorporated in 1899, the population was less than 400. An ordinance adopted at the first meeting of the city fathers made it unlawful to discharge firearms within the town's limits—which didn't keep the mayor from beating an enemy to the draw on Main Street a few months later—and another decree made it unlawful for any woman to "use any vile, profane, or indecent language . . . or to smoke any cigar, cigarette, or pipe" on the streets.

Casper had a brief attack of gold-rush fever in the early 1890's, which lasted until the "rich" veins turned out to be asbestos, and also went through a much more important boom when the first oil well in the neighborhood was brought in. The initial strike was made in 1889. By 1896 six wells were brought in and shortly thereafter the first pipe line was laid to the Casper refineries.

The boom transformed Casper from a crossroads settlement into a city larger than it is today. A local census in 1925 showed 32,000 people within the city and its neighboring refinery camps. The boom ended in the late 1920's. Several hundred miles of pipe line connected the fields with the Casper refineries, the rigs were dismantled, and the need for extensive field equipment was over. The big bust of 1929 completed the retrenchment and Casper's population fell to a little more than half its total during the boom years.

Cheyenne, pronounced *shy-ann* (6062 altitude), is Wyoming's capital and largest city. Founded in 1867 as another terminal of the Union Pacific, Cheyenne is old enough to have a few tenement dis-

tricts, but its new streets, new lawns, new hotels and new houses give
it the general appearance of having been settled not later than day
before yesterday.

Generally regarded as one of the roughest, toughest, six-shooting-
est communities of the West—second perhaps only to Tombstone—
Cheyenne's early reputation fitted it like a glove. The Union Pacific
rails came in on November 13, 1867, and by 1868 its noisy career was
in full blast. Cheyenne inherited all the lawlessness of those who
trailed along behind the Union Pacific rails, in addition to its own
flotsam and jetsam. Liquor was cheap, pay was good, ammunition
was plentiful and stakes were high.

By the middle 1870's, however, though still quick on the trigger,
Cheyenne was no longer so pronounced a wild-west cycle of Dante's
Inferno. By 1869 cattle were coming north from Texas, in 1870 the
first Wyoming-finished cattle were loaded at Cheyenne for the European market, and by 1877 the Cheyenne Plains were stocked. The
town then became the social and financial capital of a vast cattle-
ranching area, with the famous Cheyenne Club as its center. Population increased from 3456 in 1880 to approximately 10,000 in 1897,
and it has shown a steady, though moderate, increase ever since.
Cheyenne, with its cattle industry, three railroads, transcontinental
airline and highways, plus its state, county, and Federal offices, is
still the most important city in Wyoming.

One shouldn't be misled by those creameries, however—it still runs
more to redeye than butterfat. And once a year, just to prove that it
has kept its hand in, it stages a celebration called "Frontier Days"
that rocks the surrounding territory like an earthquake.

Cheyenne's Frontier Days is fairly indicative of Wyoming's basic
character. It's still cow country; in other words, still a place where a
man on a horse is regarded as being rather more important in the
scheme of things than a man on foot. I'm not so sure, however, that
the white man, on horse or on foot, isn't still in the position of being
an intruder. The notion keeps growing on me that in order to know
Wyoming—to know it as a New Yorker knows New York or a Parisian
knows Paris—you have to be an Indian. It may be the enormous silence, it may be the vast, unbroken emptiness, or it may be the
endless reaches of the sky—in any case, it seems to me that you have
to see it through the eyes of James Runningwater; you have to be
able to stand by a broken-down automobile and look at the grass

and see beyond the grass. Not being an Indian, that I cannot do. I can only fall back on what James Runningwater told me. "It is almost as it was," he said. "You can hear the land." That, to me, is Wyoming; it's where you can hear the land.

Nevada

by LUCIUS BEEBE

In the introduction to an anthology of Western folklore, the late Bernard De Voto, indisputably the ranking historian of the region, remarked that foremost among its blessings San Francisco counts the fact that it is West. "It is thinking accurately," says the Sage of Harvard Square. "For, stranger, San Francisco is West as all hell."

This signal favor of Providence is one which Nevada, and particularly the northwestern portion of the state lying just across the Sierra from California's most golden precincts, shares in generous measure. Indeed, in the days of the bonanzas, when the wealth of the Comstock was making almost every man in the Palace lobby a millionaire, San Francisco considered itself a sort of suburb of Virginia City, then the scene of the wealthiest tumults on earth. With the years things have changed, and it is more probable that San Francisco now considers Reno a suburb, just as Las Vegas is a winter resort for Los Angeles. But the bond between the cities of California and the Silver State is strong and enduring and it is founded on nothing so much as their joint participation in being, as Mr. De Voto put it, West as hell.

Nevada is still so very West, even in mid-20th Century, and so vast in its Westness that passengers on the Southern Pacific's overland trains crossing the seemingly illimitable desert between Salt Lake and Reno are sometimes terrified by its desolate prospect. For hundreds of miles at a stretch no habitation is visible save the occasional shacks of track gangs, and no life save the dust plume marking the distant passage of a lonely rancher's car through the alkali. On either side are gloomy mountain ranges, and the train crew will tell you that beyond these, both to the north and south, are other, apparently unending ranges, unimaginable desolations of desert over whose thousands of miles of dusty roads no vehicle may pass for months on end, and once-populous cities now crumbling and deserted. The informed trainman can recount that there are fewer than two and one half inhabitants for each of Nevada's 110,540 square miles.

The scenery of Nevada and its at times plutonian landscape—rivers that run to no sea, endless sage, geologic formations that would have interested Dante—are a far cry from the pretty pastorals of New England, the garden vistas of the Deep South or the conventional snow-capped peaks of the mountain states. To the first settlers who forged their way westward over uncharted trails toward California the Golden, Nevada was all a part of the "Great American Desert," implacably grim, hostile, a land of death and of legends of death.

To the Eastern city dweller, Nevada still may partake of these aspects on first sight, but automatic drive and the assurance of an air-cooled motor court, swimming pool and liberal Martinis at the day's end have robbed the desert of its terrors. Claustrophobia is an ailment unknown in the Nevada lexicon. There is space to swing a cat, to fall down in if one wishes. There is no fatigue implicit in driving 450 miles a day over its matchless highways. Its desert atmosphere makes it hang-over proof. The native Nevadan will tell you that the moon rises in more incredible fullness over the Great Salt Lake Desert or Toiyabe National Forest or the Washoe Hills, as the case may be, than anywhere else on earth. The sunset shadows creeping across the chocolate-ice-cream hills form shapes of history instantly discernible to the perceptive eye. The past is very close indeed in Nevada, and to the ear attuned to the vibrations of the Western continent the sound of stagecoaches on the night wind and the rattle of gunfire are reality and not illusion.

If there are fewer lyrics written about "Nevada the Beautiful," it is because the Nevada theme song has already been written. It is hard to improve on *Oh! Susanna* and *Oh, My Darling Clementine*.

Against the background of Archean geology and decay of empire it is possible to understand Nevada's tolerance of social nipups frowned upon by other states, the vehemence of its demands for booze-and-branch at all hours of day and night, its easy attitude toward divorce and its approval of legal gambling as one of the mainstays of the state's economic being.

Nevada is heir to the great tradition of the West and so far has escaped the density of industrial population which elsewhere beyond the wide Missouri has spelled the end of that tradition. It has never been an agricultural state with the usual inhibitions of sod busters. Its first settlement was based on mining, an occupation whose morals are known for tolerance. An important industry continues to be ranching—never conducive to a narrow philosophy of living—and its major source of revenue today, dwarfing all others almost to insignificance, is tourism.

Some of Nevada's allurements for visitors are shared by other states. Elsewhere there are fine weather, historic landmarks, hunting, fishing, winter sports, superb highways, luxury resorts and scenic vistas of lake and mountain. T-bone steaks are universal in the West. So are supermotels with swimming pools, valet service, room telephones, all-night coffee shops. Almost everywhere there are splendid bars—magnificent oases running the atmospheric gamut from frontier décor to the *moderne* of neon lighting and chrome. The visitor who follows the wagon tracks of the pioneers lives in upholstered ease, as the Union Pacific slogan has it, Everywhere West.

One thing he enjoys in Nevada alone—legally and in unabashed splendor—and that is gambling. The tourist trade comes to Nevada in search of fun and games and, again in the words of Mr. De Voto, the tourist trade is thinking accurately. Step right over yonder, stranger, to that long mahogany board where the gentlefolk are rejoicing, and the band is playing *Dixie!* Handy to the bar you will see gentlemen in green eye shades presiding over games of chance. You are welcome at either or both, twenty-four hours a day, and should you run out of the ready, an extension of credit may be arranged. Bartender, see to the stranger's pleasure!

The folklore, mores, economic and social backgrounds of Nevada originated in the mining of precious metals. Until the discovery late in 1858 of the surface bonanzas of the Comstock Lode at Virginia City the largest community in the Territory of Western Utah (as it was first designated) had been Mormon Station, a staging depot at the very base of the High Sierra. It had a population of 200.

The discovery of fantastic silver deposits in the Washoe Hills twenty-odd miles south of today's Reno started the greatest gold rush of history, backtracking across the Sierra from the already failing placers of the Mother Lode in California. At times the traffic eastward was so dense in Donner Pass and Echo Summit that westward-bound travel of any sort—even the valiant Pony Express—cooled its heels for days at a time in Carson Valley.

Overnight the world became Nevada-conscious through the silver riches of Virginia City. The surface diggings progressed downward into deep quartz operations to become the most famous silver mines in history. Virginia City flowered as the swaggering metropolis of the West. Its millionaires—James Flood, Jim Fair, Adolph Sutro, George Hearst and William Sharon—commenced altering the San Francisco sky line with vast rococo mansions. The wife of Nevada's richest man, John Mackay, popped the eyes of Paris and London with entertainments such as never before had been given by a private citizen. Marcus Daly departed the Comstock for Montana, there to make a few more fortunes in copper. Virginia City's date line ranked in the press of the world with that of Washington, Berlin, Rome and Boston. San Francisco went through a dementia of speculation in Comstock mining shares that enriched housemaids, beggared millionaires, finally wrecked the mighty Bank of California and drove its president, William Ralston, to probable suicide.

The name Virginia City was synonymous with unbelievable wealth. The discovery of the staggering deposit of silver and gold in the depths of the Consolidated Virginia mine, ever since capitalized as The Big Bonanza, caused Bismarck to order Germany off the silver standard. The Central Pacific Railroad, today the great Southern Pacific, was at first conceived as a feeder from Sacramento to tap the riches of the Comstock. Virginia City became the most important outpost of the powerful banking and express firm of Wells, Fargo & Co. The city had a railroad, opera house, oceans of champagne, balls with evening dress *de rigueur* and was the best theatrical road town in the entire United States. It also had violence as a commonplace and it had the *Territorial Enterprise*, prototype of frontier newspapers everywhere.

The consciousness of its Comstock beginnings has never entirely left Nevada. Other minor bonanzas followed at Austin, Eureka, Hamilton, Tonopah, Goldfield and Rhyolite—the last three after the turn of the 20th Century—and all served to keep alive faith in hard money and a mining economy, vestigial traces of which are Nevada's preference today for silver dollars and its scorn for "California cabbage." That the mining economy has disappeared (except in copper in the eastern part of the state) and been supplanted by tourism is not even now unanimously accepted. To doubt that gold and silver production will come back is regarded as a sort of breach of faith.

The fact that Nevada's yesterdays were not the yesterdays of Texas or Wyoming or New Mexico is not always understood by the rest of the United States. It never was a beef state. Even today, hair pants and bowed legs are indigenous only to Elko County in the center of Nevada. It was a place of urban life set down in the desert. Its horses were not tethered to the hitch rack in Main Street; they were harnessed to the shiny rigs of city dwellers. Its attire was the frock coat and top hat of banker, merchant, gambler or mine superintendent—or the garb of deep mine worker; rarely was it the florid attire of the cowpoke. There are probably more horses on dude ranches in Nevada today than there ever were in the bonanza years.

Reno and Las Vegas, Nevada's two principal cities, and almost the only date lines in the state known to the rest of the world today, both had their inception through the agency of the railroad—Reno as a division point on the Southern Pacific; and Las Vegas as a railroad land development conceived to sell lots in the southern desert by the acquisitive Sen. William A. Clark, of Montana's San Pedro, Los Angeles & Salt Lake Railroad, now the Union Pacific's Los Angeles Division.

The transition from a mining state to one dominated by tourism was practically painless to Reno where the substantial commerce of the state was already concentrated. But the mining communities simply fell apart at the seams, some, like Rhyolite, becoming ghost towns overnight; others, like Austin and Eureka, drawing out twilight existences based on motels and filling stations and memories of the glorious past. The eight short-line railroads, built for hauling ore and mining machinery, were torn up one by one. A certain amount of sporadic mine activity is centered at Tonopah, but this once populous boom city makes a living largely from the fact that it is just halfway between Reno and Vegas—a convenient overnight stopping spot. Virginia City saw that oblivion was at hand if it didn't do something about it, and quickly. Today it is one of the tourist meccas of the West, with as many as 10,000 people a day in summertime passing through its faded saloons and lingering in its once glittering mansions.

It may be pertinent to examine one more aspect of Nevada's social economy. Little of the great wealth produced by the Comstock remained in Nevada, in contrast with Colorado, where the great fortunes made from the mines of Leadville, Central City and Cripple Creek found their way to Denver and Colorado Springs, where they remain to the present time.

With the sole exception of John Mackay, the nabobs of Virginia City looted and left. Their monuments are mostly in San Francisco, where the Palace Hotel, the Hearst newspaper, the Fairmont, the Flood and Sharon buildings, Roos Brothers department store, the Wells Fargo Bank & Union Trust Company, all bear witness to the wealth removed from the deep mines of the Comstock.

Little stayed in Nevada save Mackay's endowments of St. Mary's in the Mountains Church in Virginia City, and the Mackay School of Mines which is a part of the University of Nevada at Reno.

No other single Nevada institution, no hospital, museum, historical society, school or public foundation is richly endowed with wealth originating in Nevada. The sole foundation of consequence for benefit of Nevada charities and public works, that of the late Major Max Fleischmann, is endowed with money made in yeast—elsewhere. Nevada sinks or swims on its own economy; it's root hog, or die, because no rich men have ever cared.

Throughout all the West of the Wells Fargo years, the properties of the frontier included—in addition to the thorough-braced Concord coach and Colt's Navy equalizer—the keno goose, the roulette wheel and the poker deck. A willingness to wager anything and everything on the turn of a card was the hallmark of life beyond the Missouri.

But with the taming of the frontier and the gradual decline of the old uninhibited West, professional and legalized gambling came into disrepute. It declined steadily, along with gun fighting, vigilante law and open prostitution, in the once-wild towns of Arizona and New Mexico, in the Black Hills, Colorado and Montana, although morality could hardly be said to have achieved any very drastic hold on these localities until around 1917.

Only in Nevada did gambling flourish with all the untrammeled hoorah, high stakes and picturesque characters of the bonanza years. All sorts of speculation and games of chance were given renewed vitality by the tremendous "excitements" in precious metals at Tonopah, Goldfield, Rawhide, Manhattan and Rhyolite. The presence of such financial notables as Charlie Schwab and a younger

Bernard Baruch in these tumultuous diggings did nothing to abate the gambling fever which overflowed from the mining exchanges to the saloons of Tex Rickard and Tom Kendall. In the Tonopah Club, George Wingfield, a cow hand from Oregon who later went on to own Reno's de luxe Riverside Hotel, made his first stake of $2200 from Frank Golden, later proprietor of Reno's Golden Hotel. Zeb Kendall, Tom's brother, made and lost seven substantial fortunes at the turn of the century; made them in mining properties and lost them at roulette, faro bank and the race track.

It can be said accurately that gambling in Nevada has enjoyed practically unbroken continuity from the state's earliest times until today, when Las Vegas is the world's most concentrated, not to say bedizened, capital of chance. In 1910, to be sure, a state law was passed outlawing roulette, dice and card games—with almost the same effect, locally, of national prohibition a decade later. Gambling, unabated and unregulated, went on with little attempt at concealment, and the familiar philosophy was that risking a dollar on an illegal card or throw of the dice was striking a blow for personal liberty.

By 1912 the farce of prohibited gambling was obvious, and Nevadans realistically modified the law to allow "social" games of chance, a regulation which, altered now and then, signified nothing until 1931, when the entire unworkable bundle of legislation passed into the limbo of noble experiments. The lifting of the ban on open gaming was celebrated with a statewide carnival which lasted nearly a fortnight.

Nevada's social and economic structure today might well be represented by an animated montage of craps, roulette, slot machines, twenty-one, keno and, in a few rare cases, by the now declining faro bank and big six wheel, all spinning, clicking, snapping, slapping and clattering twenty-four hours a day from Elko to Las Vegas and from Harolds Club in Reno to Honest Uncle Len Haffey's tables in the Delta in Virginia City. In such placid appearing crossroads as the tiny community of Beatty, whose country exterior masks Saturday night revelry of Babylonian proportions—in Minden, the state's dairy center—in Tonopah, Ely, Winnemucca, Carson City and Eureka—Nevada presents a solid front of ornate slot machines paying the customer approximately eighty cents of his every invested dollar. In larger communities there are attended games of craps, dice and roulette.

Obviously, the implications of an economy such as Nevada's are enormous. They range from such modest boons as all-night buffets embracing Maine lobster in aspic and truffled *foie gras* for an over-all dollar to the complete nonexistence of any state income, inheritance, or sales tax. Hotel apartments which elsewhere would be forty dollars a day for two are available in the upholstered magnificence of the Las Vegas "strip" for around eight dollars. A free one on the house is taken for granted in Nevada every third round. So are thousands of miles of magnificent state highways reaching from horizon to horizon. The house take of 12 per cent on twenty-one, 17 per cent on craps and their allied averages pays in Nevada for an uncommonly spacious and uninhibited way of life.

Nevadans themselves are entirely aware of the existence of such amiable desert-surrounded communities as Elko with its vast cattle ranges and dusty cowpokes shouldering their Saturday night way into the bar at Newt Crumley's remarkable urbane Stockman's Hotel; or of Carson City, the smallest state capital, where the chief executive may be seen reading his evening newspaper on the porch of the Governor's Mansion. They know the legend of Virginia City's great years when San Francisco's Montgomery Street was populated with Comstock millionaires in the same numbers as today crowd the lobby of the Shamrock in Houston. They recall the romantic youth of Austin, where the future Madame Emma Nevada sang for pennies outside the bar of the International Hotel. They know that the world's finest butter is produced amidst the lush meadows of Minden, where icy Carson Water flows in abundance from the adjacent Sierra.

But to the outer world, Nevada means just two places: Reno and Las Vegas. And these two communities in turn mean just one thing in the common awareness: de luxe gambling for practically unlimited stakes.

Nevada's two most notable communities fall into the social and economic pattern of the two California cities closest to them, and from which a major portion of their patronage derives. Reno, 235 railroad miles from San Francisco, reflects the character of that town as a mature, easygoing but conservative-minded metropolis in microcosm. Its architecture is more vertical than horizontal, its financial and professional life geared to the stable occupations of banking, insurance and lumber. The façade of Reno's gambling industry, as might be expected of a community so closely linked to San Francisco, is conservative, decorous, opulent and aware of the historic past. Ostentatious displays of wealth are infrequent and considered in bad taste.

Las Vegas, a free-wheeling luxury resort that suddenly blossomed in a desolation of sagebrush and alkali, mirrors the sports-coat and convertible-motor-car philosophy of life in Southern California. Its ranch-style architecture flows in terraced symmetry along U.S. 91 some 225 miles from Los Angeles. The guest lists of its super motels, which combine the functions of residence and casino, are generously recruited from top names in the film industry. Its night-club headliners playing to capacity audiences in sports shirts along the Las Vegas Strip are the same who please night-club audiences in hardly more formal attire along the County Strip in Hollywood. Las Vegas sprawls, both figuratively and literally, beside splendid swimming pools set amid landscapes planted to rare and exotic shrubs and flowers. It drinks tall, cool drinks of gin and lime rather than the Bourbon-and-branch of the old frontier, and it plays games of chance for vast sums tossed on the green-covered tables in ostentatious grandeur. Las Vegas is very young, very affluent, and sometimes very brash—as it will cheerfully admit.

Easily the capital of chance of the known universe, Las Vegas is a phenomenon that has to be seen, touched, tasted, smelled and heard to be believed, for the evidence of a single sense alone might be doubted. Its wonder and glory is The Strip, the glitter mile of de luxe resorts along U.S. 91 which rivals Hollywood in the dimensions of its publicization. Here is where the big names and big bankrolls assemble, where the sports cars are the gleamingest, the swimming pools the most photographed, the breakfasttime reports of losses and winnings the most fabulous. The big names on The Strip are the Desert Inn; El Rancho Vegas, pioneer of them all; the Last Frontier, which in addition to the conventional properties of a hotel-casino maintains a whole Western township complete with saloons, barber shops and a jail; the Thunderbird; the Flamingo; the Sands; and the Sahara.

While architecture differs—most of the exteriors are what is generally known as ranch-style-Californian with interior décors ranging from French Moroccan at the Sands to Texas-cattle-ranch at the Last Frontier—the basic pattern of The Strip is universal: rooms and meals at tariffs well below comparable accommodations elsewhere, living apartments handy to the gaming rooms, landscaped grounds with almost limitless resources of parking space, theater restaurants starring top Broadway and Hollywood names and round-the-clock operation of everything in sight.

Just to give you an idea of the implications of wealth involved in its operations and the hold on the public imagination it has achieved in recent years, it is interesting to note that during one month the manager of the Desert Inn received begging letters requesting that, for no visible reason, he shower down the sum of $950,000 upon importunate correspondents.

Life in Reno is characterized by less hysterical urgency around the gaming tables, but the city's yearly total of more than 4,000,000 out-of-town visitors, many of them conservatively well-to-do who shun Las Vegas' brassy flamboyance, assures it of something better than mere municipal solvency.

Reno's two luxury hotels, the Mapes and the Riverside (the latter the fourth of that name to stand on the banks of the Truckee) maintain floor shows only slightly less costly than those of the Vegas Strip, while its monstrous department stores of gambling—Harolds Club, the Golden-Bank, Nevada Club and Cal-Neva—almost always are in process of enlargement, usually a sign of economic health.

In the old days of less impetuous schedules, the Southern Pacific's Overland Limited, westbound, used to stop for as long as three-quarters of an hour to load mail and baggage in Reno at the convenient hour of ten in the evening, after having already dallied a half hour or so in Sparks on the outskirts of town to change engines. Informed transcontinental travelers, aware of the bonus of more than an hour's time in a city famed for fun, used to get off at Sparks and taxi to the Bank Club handily adjacent to the tracks in Reno. One could win or lose a tidy sum and hoist several nutritious drinks in an hour and, just before departing, the engineer was accustomed to give a long blast on his whistle and casino attendants shouted "Overland leaving" much as theater ushers call "curtain going up" at the end of intermission. Now, the train stops a bare three minutes in Reno, and the lagniappe of gaming enjoyed by travelers in the old days is just a memory.

Reno's dubious fame as a citadel of divorce and burial ground for broken hearts is so firmly established in the national credo that statistics are needed to combat it. For the record, Washoe County (in which Reno is located) yearly issues marriage licenses in a ratio of better than 4 to 1, as compared to the divorces granted. And that ratio has remained virtually constant for more than a decade.

Dude ranching—and all out-of-state residents here for divorce are classed as dudes—is undeniably a factor in the economy. The valley resorts south of Reno—Washoe Pines, Emmie Wood's Flying M-E Ranch and other de luxe dude ranches—charge more than $100 a week in summer and only slightly less out of season, and most of them are booked well in advance. Since a very large proportion of their clientele is patently well-to-do, this basic $100 per capita per week is by no means the entire financial story of the divorce picture.

Reno also has the University of Nevada. The university has better than 3,000 students, mostly native Nevadans, many of whom are supported by scholarships financed by Harolds Club, the Reno department store of gambling. Every year Harolds presents a scholarship to an outstanding student in each of the state's thirty-five high schools. The only requirement, aside from scholastic achievement, is that, during the four years in which he attends the university, he shall never enter the portals or play the devices of chance at Harolds Club.

Best known of the technical schools at N.U. is the Mackay School of Mines, endowed by the family of John Mackay, the silver king of Comstock times, for more than $3,000,000 at the turn of the century. It is one of the ranking institutions in its field in the country, the peer of those at Columbia, Missouri and the University of Colorado.

Another N.U. school that gets a lot of attention is its school of journalism. Whatever one's estimate of the worth of journalism schools, and the matter will get you an argument in any city room, N.U. has had a remarkable record for placement of graduates on Western newspapers.

Nevada life outside Reno and Las Vegas is less influenced by the economy of gambling and, with certain exceptions, more or less resembles small-town life elsewhere in the West. The old spacious violence characteristic of the frontier has, of course, largely disappeared, but now and then there is a reversion to type. Such was the case with the shooting outside the Senator Saloon directly across the street from the State Capitol in Carson City some years ago. Two cowpokes from Minden, meeting on the sidewalk, opened fire in the best Culver City tradition, scattering the citizenry and grievously ventilating each other. What fascinated Nevadans was not the shooting itself— to which they are acclimatized by tradition if not contemporary practice—but the fact that a number of stray slugs penetrated the contents of a delivery wagon full of laundry. The community rocked with merriment over what a local wit described as the first legitimate excuse for the condition in which laundries frequently return shirts to their customers.

The other communities of Nevada resemble nothing so much as rare and infrequent jewels strung along some of the finest highways in the world, where the natives consider eighty-five the normal cruising speed on their way to Lake Mead or Salt Lake. So splendid are Nevada's roads that the state is fast becoming a paradise for sports-car drivers, thousands of whom tool up from California every summer to make safari. The Nevada Horseless Carriage Club, largely sponsored by Harrah's Club of Reno, possesses one of the finest collections of antique and classic motorcars in the world.

Carson City, Nevada's tiny capital, is one of the few state capitals in the Union without a railroad, and save for its neon lights and cement sidewalks is a page right out of the Old West. The principal employers of its inhabitants are the state and Federal governments, whose ranking officers are available to callers to a degree that is unheard of in Washington or Albany. At noontime, when it is in session, the Nevada Senate rises for lunch in a body and occupies counter stools across the street, at the Senator Restaurant founded by State Senator Kenneth Johnson.

Nevada politics are a triumph of simplicity and democratic practice and, at election times, of almost intolerable bad feeling. Until the death, practically in harness, of that noble old war horse, Senator Pat McCarran, the state's politicians looked largely to him for guidance. Whatever other Americans may have felt about Mr. McCarran's foreign policies, Nevadans revered him as a personal senator and a deliverer of instant and effective service. The microscopic population of the state made it possible for him to give his personal attention to almost everyone.

In the days when the United States Senate was regarded as the world's most exclusive club, Nevada contributed a long succession of "silver senators" including the peerless William Morris Stewart, "father of American mining law"; John Percival Jones, hero of the great fire in Crown Point mine; William Sharon, satrap of the Bank of California on the Comstock; Francis G. Newlands, Sharon's son-in-law; and finally in our own generation, Key Pittman.

Nevada's towns extend north and south on the extreme Western edge of the state along the valleys and arable meadows which receive water from the Sierra: Reno, Carson City, Gardnerville and Minden; and east and west along the routes of the Southern Pacific and Western Pacific Railroads, where in the 19th Century came into being such communities as Wells, Elko, Palisade, Battle Mountain and Winnemucca, variously sustaining life as ranching centers, warehouses to remoter hamlets and as stopping places on U.S. Route 40.

If the traveler is amazed to discover such once flourishing communities as Eureka and Austin, he must remember that both of these towns once knew great mining activities and both formerly had railroads of their own connecting with the life-giving main line of the Southern Pacific.

The life of today's average Nevadan is uncomplicated by the urgency of existence in the East or elsewhere in an industrial age. He probably makes a living as proprietor of a motel, an ever-increasing industry everywhere in the state; as an employee of an eminently leisurely commonwealth; as a banker or insurance man in Reno, a city characterized by something less than the frenetic tensions of Wall Street; as a rancher in the agricultural communities of Yerington, Dayton, Fallon or Minden, or as a dealer or other employee in one of the many houses of chance.

One thing Nevadans share in common: when the fishing or deer hunting season opens, they will turn the locks on their places of business—barbershop or bar, bank or bagnio—for the duration. Other outdoor attractions, aimed at the evergrowing tourist trade, are increasingly occupying the Nevada mind. Lake Mead, for example, above Hoover Dam, has become perhaps the most improbably situated yachting center in the entire world. Reno Ski Bowl with its spectacular lifts is helping to make the town a year-'round instead of a seasonal resort. Desert explorers and rock collectors regard Nevada's southern deserts as a paradise of buttes productive of agate and other semiprecious stones.

Life in Virginia City, where the author makes his residence among the dusty but romantic souvenirs of the Comstock bonanzas, strives valiantly to maintain itself as a tattered page from the life of the authentic Old West. Since its only source of income is from tourists, it has to. It glories in its twenty saloons for 950-odd permanent residents, perhaps the greatest density of oases in the world; in Piper's Opera House where the mighty once assembled in claw-hammer coats to hear the celebrated of their generation perform *Hamlet* or

Mazeppa; and in the still functioning outrages of the *Territorial Enterprise.* Virginia City was delighted with the witticism attributed to Charlie Addis, C Street's foremost character and seventy-seven-year-old newsboy for the *Territorial Enterprise.*

Encountering another ancient who was carrying three loaves of bread under one arm and six bottles of Old Reprehensible under the other, Charlie incredulously asked, "What in hell are you going to do with all that bread?"

Perhaps the key to Nevada's feeling of superiority to and independence from the rest of the Union lies in the circumstance that it has more about it of the 19th Century and less of the 20th than any other part of the nation.

The one link with the immediate present, and the atomic future—the selection of Frenchman's Flat near Las Vegas as the proving ground for many tests of atomic armament—is viewed with distaste by Nevadans. Nor do they particularly admire the jet noises, the strange sights and sounds, the trailing vapors in the night skies that connote the jet age. Philosophically, however, they accept these things on the basis of the state's own highly explosive and pyrotechnic past. Any community, they reflect, that could survive the gunfire and the tumults of Nevada's pioneers can take the atomic age in its stride. A hydrogen bomb, did you say, stranger? You should have been in Carson City in the sixties when Senator William Morris Stewart tried cases before the Supreme Court with a Colt's Navy revolver in each hand! We're used to that sort of thing.

Utah

by SAMUEL W. TAYLOR

You get your suit pressed at a While-U-Wait shop, and when paying for it automatically slide a dime tip across the counter. The proprietor pushes the dime back. "I make a profit from my business," he says. "I don't want anything extra."

You pocket the dime, wondering if you've been away too long. You should have known better than to affront the dignity of a Mormon businessman.

You're on a tour of Utah, to see the state as a tourist might. You're talking with motel owners, gas-pump jockeys and hash slingers, and you're interested in what makes it Utah—things typical or peculiar, like the rainbow cliffs, the "hope" houses, and Salt Lake City during a Latter-day Saints Conference.

Often you'll carry away and remember the little things. You'll forget that, at Bingham, the biggest open-cut copper mine in North America has forty-two power shovels scooping up 200,000 tons a day, but you'll remember the hairbreadth approach to the mine through the town's single street, so narrow that the dogs proverbially wag their tails up and down. Everyone knows that a swimmer can't sink in the brine of Great Salt Lake, but what impresses you is that the granite boulders of the railroad embankment weigh so little in the dense water they literally float away during storms.

You are impressed with the primitive wildness of much of Utah, but what drives it home is the news that the only doctor of Blanding was drafted into the Army. Blanding, with 1178 people, is the largest city of San Juan County, into which could be dropped Delaware, Connecticut and Rhode Island. You ask a waitress if Blanding is a Mormon town. "Well, no, it isn't," she says. "There are six Gentiles here."

In any small town, the integration of Church affairs and daily life is complete; the Gentile either joins or cuts himself off from all social and recreational life. So he pitches in, and sometimes finds himself appointed to an office and a title in the Church.

You get to Blanding (from Salt Lake City, of course—everything begins and ends there) south and east on U. S. Highway 50. At Wellington, a few miles beyond Price, you stop for a snapshot of the tiny city hall and the "hope" house adjoining, and you have your only interview with a mayor. When he sees your camera, he breaks away from a customer and dashes across the street from his service station to tell you that Wellington is really going places, now that they've got water and a sewer system. The hope house, the mayor explains, is the Legion Hall, and he's a bit annoyed because the Legion doesn't clear away the weeds. Right here on the main drag too.

Nothing better illustrates the Mormon horror of going into debt than the hope house. It consists of a concrete basement roofed over and used for living quarters—or, as in this case, the Legion Hall. By largely doing the work himself, the canny native can get a roof over his head; and when he has saved the cash he'll build himself a house atop the basement—so he hopes, hence the name. You count hundreds of hope houses throughout the state, many with TV antennas sticking from the low roofs, or with brand-new cars alongside.

You continue southeast on U. S. 50 through big country, where nothing stops the eye and you can see forever, country so big it seems the rim of the world, but after you turn south at Crescent Junction you go over the rim and enter a new world. It's something from the moon. It's a stage set. It's fairyland. You accept it as you do Mickey Mouse, as fantasy.

You take the first branch road to the right, rough going over sand and slickrock, one-way road, thirty miles down and thirty back, and your destination has the enticing name of Dead Horse Point. But as you drink in the vista of the Colorado gorge, tier upon tier of rainbow cliffs to the end of vision, watching the living color of the stone bloom and fade and change with the time of day, you forget the name and the road and even that the natives unconsciously damn it with assertions it beats the Grand Canyon view. (Is a rose more beautiful than an Easter lily?) Now you're within gunshot range of Monument Canyon (not to be confused with Monument Valley), the Needles, Chesler Park, and other Technicolor fantasies, though you'll see them by Jeep, packhorse or airplane—not passenger car.

You think natural bridges are something, so you turn east to Arches National Monument. Here, at last count, were eighty-eight natural arches, or bridges—there is a technical difference between an arch and a bridge, though whatever it's called, Landscape Arch is the longest natural *span* in the world, at this writing. When you stand below this tremendous arch you wonder if it will be there tomorrow, for its time is running out and any day can be its last. It spans 291 feet and the enormous weight of this almost flat arch is supported by a ribbon of soft sandstone shaved by the cutting wind to barely six feet thick. Other spans have fallen in; you see their skeletons. Of those that remain there are double ones side by side and one atop the other, and twins that look like the ruins of an enormous pair of eyeglasses. The same erosive forces of wind and rain and frost that enlarge and eventually destroy an old arch are at work creating new ones. Natives watched the birth of the youngest arch here just fifteen years ago. Natural forces are one thing, vandalism another. The Goblet of Venus, down near Blanding, is now nothing but a picture on a post card. As a joke, a deer hunter shot its slender base away and it was a big laugh when it toppled.

You've thought of uranium as rare and exotic, a fearful thing from far reaches, and it seems a matter of course that in this fairyland uranium is the biggest industry. The towns of Moab, Monticello and Blanding are booming, mining uranium, trucking it, processing it, building roads to get it out. You watch the blasting at the painted cliffs high on the rim of a breathless canyon as a road is carved where no road could possibly be, except for uranium. There's oil down here, too, in country so wild they had to float sketchy drilling equipment down the deep gorge of the treacherous Colorado, and then cap off the oil because they had no equipment for getting it out. With roads going in they'll get the oil now, but eventually they'll dig more gold from the tourists, because of those roads, than from either oil or uranium.

There is no east-west road across Southern Utah, and by now nobody has to tell you why not. You leave the blacktop at Monticello, and from Blanding you continue south over slickrock and quicksand. You stop for a watermelon at Bluff, a ghost town of decaying sandstone mansions haunted by strangers; the Mormon founders moved on when the San Juan ate away their farmland and the Government gave their rangeland to the Indians. "Take your pick, four bits apiece, any size," says the old codger selling them. You ask if he's L.D.S. "No," he says, "you see, we raise melons; we don't have no time for religion." As you stagger to the car with the watermelon (the map says "Carry Water" doesn't it?) he calls, "Seen the Goosenecks? Well, you're seeing the sights, ain't you? Then, by God, see the Goosenecks!"

So you see the Goosenecks, the great convolutions of the San Juan, fifteen hundred feet below where you stand. And then, despite the big sign which warns against it, you fight the sand traps and the bottomless holes left by the last cloudburst and head south through Monument Valley, where the huge stone sentinels rise from the floor of the terrible plain one after another into the violet haze, impossible, unforgettable; you grow smaller and more puny by the mile.

Now you've crossed into Arizona, and you have to make a 250-mile triangle—west and north—to get back into Utah. You come north over the ridge in the Kaibab Forest on U. S. 89 and the trees fall away to the desert floor below, and ahead is the border of Utah. *Now, wait a minute,* you think, *this can't be.* For the boundary between Arizona and Utah is an arbitrary line ruled on the map by politicians in Washington. Yet ahead, running right along that accidental line, are tiers of the great painted cliffs.

You enter the cliffs and the state at Kanab, just a hop, skip and jump from the two best-known scenic attractions, Zion Park and Bryce Canyon. They're all you expected—Zion's Great White Throne rising a sheer 3000 feet out of the red cliffs, and the living kaleidoscope of Bryce's fiery city of stone. You can take in Cedar Breaks the same afternoon. This is your dish, if you want your scenery laid out for you on a platter. But if you want to fight for it a little, to see something not *every* tourist does, you detour from the main drag and head out State 24, southeast through Loa and Bicknell to the Wayne Wonderland, with its natural bridges, its weird sculpture and its Great Organ, a symphony of color. Here is Capitol Reef, with Chimney Rock rising blood red from the cream-plastic slopes. And from here, if you really want to earn your scenery, you make trips to the cream-and-yellow buttresses of Cathedral Valley or nature's gargoyles in the grotesque Valley of the Goblins.

You schedule your tour to be in Salt Lake City for the semi-annual Conference of the Church of Jesus Christ of Latter-day Saints, for then it is the city the Mormons themselves know and the city the average tourist never sees. Conference comes in April and October, not in the tourist season. During Conference week the faithful flood in from all over the world, coming "home"—whether you're born in Utah or not, it's home to all L.D.S.—back to Conference. Local residents stay at home during Conference week, turning their city over to the visitors. A tourist can still get a room at a hotel, for Conference visitors traditionally stay with friends.

A stream of 20,000 people flows into Temple Square for the afternoon session. At an eddy in the stream are two men wearing oilcloth vests lettered with anti-Mormon texts in two colors, passing out literature in the literal shadow of the wall. "Any converts?" you ask one. He just smiles, refusing to be baited, and hands you a tract, *How I Was Saved Out of Mormonism*.

Anyone can attend Conference. You don't have to show credentials or give any signs or passwords; there are no tickets; just walk in. But go early. Those who really want to sit down arrive hours before the morning session, with lunch in hand, prepared to homestead their seats all day long. "All seats taken!" newsboys shout at the south gate. "Get your paper here to sit on the grass!"

The front center section of the Tabernacle is reserved for those holding the office of bishop or better, and these officials can afford the luxury of arriving merely on time. They file in, well-fed, well-barbered, well-scrubbed, gregarious, alert and aggressive, and the double-breasted gray suit is almost a uniform. This is the amateur clergy—unsalaried, untrained, part-time officials who make their living as business and professional men—who run the Church at the local level. Above them, on the stand facing the audience, are the General Authorities, aloof in blue serge.

Everyone arises, and in the hush a man appears on the stand. He moves along the leather bench, his mane of silver hair gleaming in the TV lights. This is the Prophet, Seer and Revelator, David O. McKay, President of the Church. He takes his seat and the great audience sits, and in the air is a tangible feel of warmth and reverence. Conference is in session.

Practically all male Mormons hold the Priesthood and are eligible for office; there are enough offices in the Church to give a title and position to more than half the population, both men and women, from the age of twelve. You are, in effect, rubbing shoulders with an entire population of ministers.

In Utah, you have a curious feeling of isolation. This is a mountain island, and within its mental wall all is always officially well. In Utah bookcases you find on display the "approved" books—standard Church works and those written in the same style—*i.e.*, religious tracts. If Mormons read anything about Utah not "approved" they won't admit it. "When the Brodie book came out," you're told at the Salt Lake Library (reference is to *No Man Knows My History*, by Fawn M. Brodie, a biography of Joseph Smith, blacklisted in Utah), "people called for it with their own dust jackets, so that apparently they were carrying away *The Five Little Peppers*, or *Tom Swift and His Captive Gas-Filled Balloon*." You ask a Mormon his opinion of a new Utah book, just released, too new to have had the word passed. "I don't know whether I like it or not," he says. "I haven't been told yet."

A strange island, this Utah, populated by ministers who are passionately interested in their history—but only (to use their phrase regarding the Bible) as it is translated correctly.

During Conference the Hotel Utah is the place to eat, dance, hold a convention or meet somebody. Second choice is the Temple Square Hotel, also Church-owned. You're surprised to see smoking in the coffee shop of the Temple Square, and ask the cashier when the ban was lifted. "The 'No Smoking' signs are still up," she says. "But you've got to do business. So we leave up the signs and put out the ash trays." Officially, all Mormons are perfect; actually, some of them have a struggle. You're told the sale of chlorophyl tablets, presumably to kill tobacco breath, is sensational. The amazing thing is not that the stern demand of 100 per cent is broken, but that so few give up trying to meet it.

You will see more of Salt Lake City on a rubberneck bus than do many people who have lived there a lifetime. There are various tours offered, and the Grade AA Super DeLuxe model gives you the well-known city high spots, the canyons, the Tabernacle concert, Great Salt Lake and the Bingham mine in time for the blasting, in a one-day package.

The rubberneck tour makes you realize that Salt Lake City isn't all Mormon. It's only 60 per cent L.D.S., and the other 40 per cent is in there pitching. Competing churches have erected tremendous buildings to show there's somebody else on deck. You realize that everything in Utah is either Mormon or a reaction to it.

Then there's the small bungalow with red shutters which has, your driver announces, seven kitchens. After an intent silence a rubberneck asks, "Why?" and the driver says, "I don't know. I never asked Mr. Kitchen."

For some curious reason, outsiders cannot fathom the method of numbering streets, which is so simple that any native can walk into a strange town in Utah and go directly to any given address without asking directions. Your driver makes it all clear: "We are going west toward Sixth East on Ninth South. At the corner of Sixth East and Ninth South we will turn north on Sixth East. Then instead of going west on Ninth South toward Sixth East we will be going north on Sixth East from Ninth South."

This explains it perfectly.

A devout Saint, on his first visit to the Mormon Mecca, is startled at the way such words as Zion, Deseret, Mutual, L.D.S. and Temple are applied to business enterprises. He is appalled at the sign, "Temple Café, Drink Coca-Cola," for Coke is against the Word of Wisdom too. But what really curls his hair is the "Temple Wrecking Company."

As far back as you can remember, there have been oil booms, timed by coincidence to hit the papers at Conference. You have suspected promotion, but now they seem to be getting actual oil, so you decide to see what the boom looks like in the Uintah Basin, over in the northeastern corner of the state.

You go east along Daniels Canyon from Heber, on U. S. 40, and the aspen leaves shimmer butter-yellow against the deep green conifers. Daniels is just one of a dozen canyons that could be promoted as tourist attractions, except that Utah has so much scenery. Where the country opens up near Strawberry Reservoir a line of double-decked trucks comes barreling out of the mountains on a yellow dirt road. Here is the reason you've missed what used to be one of the characteristic features of Utah travel, the sheep herds trailing the highways. The trucks are packed with sheep, transporting an entire herd from mountain range onto winter range in the desert.

The trucks jam to a stop at a little café and the truckers swarm

out of the cabs. First they get the sheep up; a sheep that goes
down can smother within a few minutes. The truckers jab them
with hot shots—rods with sharp points and electric coils—and they
come up fast. Then the truckers stomp into the café and order coffee.
One gets a can of beer. None of them smokes. You notice such things
in Utah. The boss trucker tells you he hauls sheep spring and fall,
coal between times. "Hauled 70,000 sheep last spring off the desert
into the mountains, and only lost one head." He drains his coffee.
"Ready, boys? Let's top it."

You climb up through the "World's Largest Piñon and Cedar
Forest," the sign says, into the big country of the Uintah Basin, and
you wonder if you'll really get the courage someday to leave California for someplace like this, where you can have a hundred miles
of front yard. At Myton, you stop for honey, the best in the world,
because nothing blooms in the Basin that makes bad honey. There
are no fruit trees, not even much sage; it's clover honey.

When you stop for lunch there is watery imitation-maple sirup
for your waffles. You wonder why they don't serve local honey, why
you see French-fried shrimp, oysters and halibut steak featured on
this inland desert and rarely the beef, mutton, turkey and chicken
that Utah exports.

The Basin is another area where a few sketchy roads peter off into
nowhere. U. S. 40 runs along the north rim of the wild tangle of
plateaus and canyons and mesas that extends south the entire
length of the state and into Arizona, country so broken that just one
all-weather highway crosses its expanse (U. S. 50, which you traveled on the way to Blanding). This enormous wasteland, one quarter
of the entire state, is drained sterile by the deep gorges of the Green
and the Colorado.

To the north of U. S. 40 are the Uinta Mountains, claimed to be
the only range running east-and-west in the nation. Here are Utah's
highest mountains, rising from the immense desert, cradling dense
timber and a thousand lakes. This is the proverbial sportsmen's paradise; at least 100 of the lakes have never been fished. The high
Uintas have been preserved in their original state as a wilderness
area without roads or houses. Here is the great watershed of Utah,
the source of its best rivers. Ironically, much of the water of this
desert state is wasted, running from the slopes of the Uintas into the
sterile trap of the Green River gorge. Utah is 96 per cent scenery—
only 4 per cent of its land can be cultivated—yet so determined is

the state to keep the high Uintas primeval that the Central Utah Project, which would reclaim 200,000 acres from the desert by using some of the Uinta water, is opposed because it would injure the scenery.

At Roosevelt you find the Indians eating T-bones and the whites ordering hamburgers. The Utes not only nicked the Great White Father for thirty-two million bucks on an old land claim but they've got oil on the reservation besides. The whites gnaw their hamburgers and really pity those poor Utes, getting all this jack and not knowing how to spend it. They tell of Indians buying refrigerators and vacuum cleaners and washing machines without having electricity to run them, about big new cars. With a wink they point out squaws with permanents, walking down the street in evening dress at high noon. "The Government shouldn't give them money until they've been taught how to spend it," you're told. You hear of Indians driving blind drunk, and that they can't handle liquor, which is something the whites could give lessons on.

And you hear the oil stories, the ones you've heard about every oil field in the world. The one you like best is about the Watkins Man. He had a barren farm and a fertile wife and a battered car for selling his Watkins products, and then one day they struck oil on his farm. He took one look at the black stuff spurting from the ground and rushed into town for the one thing he always had yearned for, a gleaming new Lincoln. Soon the Watkins Man was rich, but unhappy. He had nothing to do. So he loaded up his Lincoln with Watkins products and returned to his route, selling the stuff at cost because he didn't need the money.

At Vernal, you find the town on the upbeat after a local recession, and you learn that an oil boom comes during drilling operations. Once wells are down and flowing, your drilling crews move away and the bottom drops out of your boom. Vernal is an isolated metropolis. In the old days the distance from markets made the going tough. You remember as a kid when relatives called from Vernal and your mother said what a blessing it would be when the railroad went through. "Blessing?" came the appalled reaction. "We never hope to live to see the day!" The old-timers had an unholy fear of Gentiles coming with the railroad. The railroad never did come, but oil and hardtop road brought Gentiles and strangers.

Dinosaur National Monument spraddles the Utah-Colorado line next door to Vernal, and after peering at a barren ledge containing vague outlines of what once were bones and now are rock like the rest of the ledge, you sympathize with the lady tourist alongside you. "Did we," she asks bleakly, "come 350 miles to see *this?*" For once Utah doesn't live up to its billing. But if it's scenery you want, Split Mountain, right next door, can make you forget the so-called bones. Split Mountain is exactly what its name implies. The gorge of the Green cuts through its middle from peak to base. And here you're in color again.

Vernal is like Blanding—the only surfaced road is back the way you came. But you can "earn" your scenery north on State 44 over the Uintas to Manila. Red Canyon and Horseshoe Canyon, on the way, make you feel it was effort well spent. And you wonder if the Utah genius for prosaic names for breath-taking scenes might have a sly system behind it. Perhaps Dinosaur Monument fell on its face for you because its name had fired your imagination. No amount of previous build-up can spoil a spectacle named Goosenecks, Dead Horse Point, or Horseshoe Canyon; these take you completely and delightfully by surprise.

At Manila, you're smack up against the Wyoming line, and you have to leave Utah again to get back into it, cutting across the southwest corner of Wyoming to Evanston. Here at a café the inevitable rack of picture post cards displays two scenes of native Wyoming, two dozen of Utah. There could be no greater tribute to Utah's scenic attractions.

There are two routes into Utah from Evanston. One takes you north alongside Crawford Mountain to Bear Lake, lying across the Utah-Idaho line. Bear Lake has the unreal, picture-post-card, blue-green intensity of Canada's famed Lake Louise, and from it you go over the hump and down Logan Canyon, a gem among the state's many canyons. (Incidentally, there is a Mormon Temple at Logan, one at Manti, in central Utah, and one down in the southwest corner of the state at St. George. Rumor has it that here, away from the tourist crush, interested Gentiles occasionally get a peek inside the doors, which doesn't happen at Salt Lake City.) The other route from Evanston is down Echo Canyon, with its red cliffs and weird erosions; and then, in the afternoon, you come into Weber Canyon and into another typical Utah scene—cars parked along the stream and fishermen casting across the waters. Most Utah men live minutes from a trout stream rippling among unsurpassed scenery, and to look at the number of fishermen, practically everybody takes advantage of it. But there are still fish for those who know how. And it goes deeper than that. "When things go wrong, when I get in a fight with the wife, when the kids are impossible and the world goes to hell," a fisherman tells you, "there's nothing an hour on the river can't cure."

As you travel the state you see everywhere the great new Church houses—ward chapels for local congregations, stake houses for groups of wards. This is the current passion in this land of high fevers. Throughout the tour you hear stories of wards overextending themselves, of faithful Saints mortgaging their homes in the furious competition to equal or better the neighboring ward chapel.

You stop one late afternoon for ice cream at a stand just across the street from a great new ward chapel. The lady at the counter tells you it has just been dedicated. That means paid for. The Mormons don't dedicate a debt to the Lord.

"Frankly, we didn't want to start it," the good sister says. "Some of us were bitterly opposed. But the stake presidency pushed it through. The ones who decide are the ones who can afford it. Once it was approved there was nothing to do but do it.

"The assessment for us was $1500. That's cash, and it wasn't easy to scrape it up. We also raised a ward calf; everybody raised something, a calf or a sheep or chickens or grain to sell for the building fund. Women took over extra duties so the men would be free to work on the ward house. The men went into the mountains and cut timber and sawed it, so the rough lumber didn't cost any cash. Everybody worked on the construction and finish and decoration. But even so, it cost $150,000. The Church puts up half of that. It was a struggle. We had our regular tithing on top of it all, and they're always dollaring you for something.

"Then came the big push, to finish it and be out of debt so it could be dedicated for Stake Conference." She sighs. "I don't know how we did it—somehow we did."

Then she smiles, and her face softens as she looks across the street. "Isn't it beautiful?" she whispers. "Isn't it lovely? I'm so fortunate, right here all day long where I can look at it. I just love that steeple, and the way the roof slants, and—oh, everything about it is just perfect! And now it's over with I'm so glad we made the sacrifice! Don't you think it's wonderful?"

Yes, you agree, you think it's wonderful, and you drive on in the twilight feeling warm from her warmth, knowing it is wonderful and she is wonderful and the other seventy-nine families of the ward are wonderful.

Utah is a rich field for research into the birth of new religions, and you spend an evening with each of four founders and prophets of new sects, as well as an entertaining afternoon with a gentleman who has his own private model which he figured out and proved strictly by mathematics. But you learn not to discuss this type of research at random. One of the great intellectual hobbies of Utah is research into the origins of Mormonism but this is a secret pursuit, discussed in strict confidence.

You find, on all levels, a blanket intolerance for contrary belief, peculiar among the people who have suffered so violent a history because of intolerance. "Let's not go to seed on tolerance," a university professor tells you. "Let's maintain a little healthy bigotry." This candor and lack of hypocrisy is refreshing, at least. Religion is based more on faith, after all, than on intellectual proof, and if you believe your brand is right, then that makes all the others wrong.

Mixed in with the co-operative tradition in Utah you find rugged individualism that really has knobs on. You can lead the Peculiar People, but don't try to shove them.

"The creamery penalized me ninety dollars a month because my milk was too rich," a Utah Valley man tells you. "Said people didn't want cream in their milk any more. Maybe they're afraid to let people get a taste of good Jersey milk." And, rather than reduce the quality of his milk, he sold out and got a job.

"Salt Lake is the worst city in the world to do business in," you're told by an individualist who moved to Ogden. "Rebates, kickbacks, discounts—my hell, practically everybody in Salt Lake can get it wholesale. Here I make twice the money for half the work."

You learn that Utah gained tremendously in population in the last few years as people poured into the Wasatch Oasis, the narrow strip of fertile land that runs down the center of the state from above Ogden to below Provo. Here in north-central Utah there's an industrial boom, and if you were born in Provo it's a shock to return to the country town of memory to find it such a bustling industrial city that there's a smog problem.

The old home, where your mother still lives, is now next door to an apartment house. Ernie Hansen's neighborhood grocery is gone and with it the houses of an entire block, to make room for the big

Sears store. The old Roylance orchard is a subdivision, the First Ward pasture a golf course, the city dump on East Center a city park.

Cities traditionally grow westward, the east sides degenerating into slums. Just to be different, all Utah cities grow eastward, and on the east foothills of Provo where there was nothing but sagebrush are now the showplaces of Snob Hill.

The mountains rise so abruptly into the morning sky that strangers in town tell you of an uneasy feeling that the peaks might topple over on them. And with autumn these overwhelming slopes are huge crazy quilts of raw color. Beyond the end of University Avenue to the north is Timpanogos, majestic and alone, 12,008 feet. Timp is a local institution, featured in publicity, held in deep reverence. There is a community hike up its slopes each summer, people swarming to its summit by the hundreds; and in July a ski meet is held on its high snows.

You make the fifty-mile Alpine Loop that circles Timp, seeing the convoluted cliffs of Provo Canyon, and Bridal Veil Falls, the prodigal autumn color of the woods and the power of sheer rock towering into the eternal snow above timberline. You walk into the viscera of the mountain at Timpanogos Cave National Monument, and find deep inside the cave the great heart-shaped stalactite, moist and blood-red. There are strict rules against touching any of the formations, and you wonder what would happen if you did; would the mountain tremble if you put out a hand to touch its heart? You go down American Fork Canyon to complete the Loop, and return to Provo.

When you feel a bit pensive about the passing of a country town you're told, "My hell, it's gone anyhow now; let's look ahead."

You find a curious rivalry between industry and education. Until the early 1940's Provo was The University City. Then with the arrival of Geneva Steel it became The Steel City, and the Brigham Young University was relegated to a seat far in the rear, behind a post. Then the brethren reached out and plucked a Mormon lawyer from Washington, D.C., to be president of the Church university, and things began happening. Ernest L. Wilkinson is an executive, a hard worker, a driver, a man who gets things done, rather than a lofty intellectual. He represented the Utes in putting the bite on the Great White Father for thirty-two million. Utah natives stand in awe of success like this; by now the story's grown, it was sixty-five million and his fee the largest in history. "When he wants a new building for the campus he just goes to Salt Lake and comes back with the money," you're told. "He knows where the bear sleeps."

You go up on the hill to see what is happening and are absolutely lost on the campus of your Alma Mater. The new buildings have dwarfed and misplaced the old ones. There are no landmarks left. The biggest and most prominent building on the campus in your day was the library, and now you can't find it; an undergrad (a mere boy; they sure go to college *young* these days) has to show you the way. The throb of jackhammers fills the academic air as workmen swarm over three and a quarter million dollars of additional construction.

When you attended these hallowed halls there were about 1500 students and a chilling rumor that the Church was going to turn the school over to the state or back to the Indians. Now they enroll a freshman class of about 3000. You pick up a campus paper and admire an ad for gals' underwear, featuring a photograph of a fetching young thing wearing a bra and Pantie Girdle P-17. Yes, things have changed at dear old BYU since your day.

The BYU admits students of all faiths, on condition they observe the Mormon moral code and take a two-hour class in religion each quarter. The base of religious instruction is broad, and a student can select courses in psychology of religion, religious philosophy, the Old Testament, history of religion and kindred subjects without being exposed to Mormon doctrine. Thus any Gentile may, at his own risk, enroll if he meets the academic standards. But the risk is real, for some 25 per cent of the Gentile students are baptized as converts before graduation, and there is the added hazard of marrying a Mormon gal met at school and joining the Church eventually. The Y is one of the most marryin' schools in the world. One year every member of the student body executive council got married—in fact they all married each other.

Along with the frank recognition that gals do wear bras and Pantie Girdle P-17's, you find more evidence of religious consciousness than there was back in the cynical 30's. The athletic teams now pray before each contest, a custom initiated by the players, not their elders. Students used to attend Church, if at all, in town. Now the school has two branches of religious services, and 1200 devout undergrads crowd into Campus Branch, their desire to bear testimony so great that the procedure has been put on an assembly-line basis. All those who feel impelled to tell of their personal conviction of the Gospel's

truth and the Divine agency of its Prophet are asked to stand, and
from the young army that arises are selected a lucky two dozen who
receive numbered cards. There are two traveling microphones, and
as holder of card No. 1 bears his testimony the holder of card No. 2
gets ready at the other mike, every moment being utilized, bearing
testimony by the numbers.

You leave the campus with one more evidence of size and change.
They now have campus police, who have given you a parking ticket.
And as you complete your tour of the state you notice that education
has vanquished industry. The new signs urge tourists to visit "Provo,
The University City."

You head west to leave the state, through Grantsville and past the
corner of stone wall sticking from the sagebrush that once was the
house where your mother grew up in a plural family during the brief
flowering of the Principle in Utah. You look back for a last glimpse
of the trade mark of the old Mormon towns, the Lombardy poplars,
and then you head west over the salt flats, the great and bitter barrier upon which for thousands of square miles there is no bush nor
twig nor weed nor blade of grass nor living thing (but have you seen
it bloom pink at the sunset and violet at the dawn?). The salt flats
isolate the state on the west as do the Uinta Mountains and Great
Salt Lake on the north, the broken canyon and mesa country on the
east, and the Grand Canyon on the south. You are leaving this physical island with its strange mental wall, in which a peculiar people
live their religion as a way of life.

You've put 5000 miles and four new tires on your car, you've been
to the end of every major road in Utah and several minor ones. You've
got enough material for a book, but what is the essence of it? What
story would you tell that would typify Utah?

Would it be about the rainmaker?

The irrigation ditches were running dry and the crops were burning up, so the county supervisors agreed to hire a rainmaker to end
the drought—for a fee reported at $100,000. The local Stake Presi-
dency became incensed. This was throwing money down a rathole.
Had people lost their faith? The way to get rain was to pray for it.
So some prayed, and some paid, and some to make sure both prayed
and paid. For three weeks nothing happened. Then one day some
clouds drifted over. The faithful put on a big burst of prayer and
the rainmaker put his machines into high gear. And down came the
glorious rain, and that delicious moist smell arose from the parched

earth. And then the rain quit. It had hardly dampened the surface. That was several years ago, but a violent argument is still raging in the county—what brought the rain, the machines or the prayer?

Or would it be about the Priesthood meeting?

A faithful Saint, a relative of yours, was coming to the end of a long and devout life, but was determined to climb out of his sickbed to go to Priesthood meeting. He hadn't missed Priesthood in forty years and he wasn't going to now—especially now. When the bishop phoned, as he did each day to find out how the good brother was, the wife said she didn't know what to do. "I don't think he should miss Priesthood meeting," the bishop said. "It means so much to him." And so as the good Saint lay upon his deathbed the Priesthood Quorum gathered at his house rather than in Church, and his bedroom became, for this once, a holy place of worship. He had gone to Church all his life; now the Church had come to him.

Maybe neither of these. Maybe it's impossible to roll Utah into a capsule. Why try?

On either side as you cross the salt flats you see the mirage of the floating mountains sailing on their peaks. At Bonneville, where the fastest things on wheels have sped, you turn onto the blinding surface and open your car up. It's rough up to fifty, then it begins smoothing out and then you're floating over the vast table of salt and it's just a question of time and nerve and gasoline. You head back to the highway dismayed that you couldn't crack ninety, and soon you're in Wendover, the state line, and spraddling the line is the biggest mannikin in the world, greeting your entrance into Nevada with the sign, "Where the West Begins."

At first this seems strange, but after you get into Nevada you realize how right it is. You haven't been in the West. In physical layout the villages of Utah are New England. You haven't found Western clothes, customs, language or mental attitude. You have been in an island fairyland of enormous beauty, peopled by a unique brand of tightly-knit Puritans.

HAWAII Remote Waipo Valley, an almost purely Polynesian pocket on the big island of Hawaii.

CALIFORNIA (*center spread*) Emerald Bay, a lovely forested cove on the shores of Lake Tahoe in the Sierra Nevadas.

OREGON A wild and colorful seascape at Cape Kiwanda, reached only by a one-mile walk on the beach from Pacific City.

UTAH The primitive rainbow trail, with a rider leading his pack through a sandstone gorge 2,000 feet deep.

IDAHO (*center spread*) A farm near Moscow, Idaho, radiates contentment from its nest of green, its fruitful work underway.

COLORADO Garden of the Gods: a wonderland of stone. In the distance rears much-loved, much-climbed Pikes Peak.

ARIZONA Desert saguaro blossoms open in tenuous glory amid the cactus of Organ Pipe National Monument.

TEXAS (*center spread*) A lone cowboy comes round one of the Monahans Sandhills. The shifting sands stretch for 100 miles in Texas and New Mexico.

LOUISIANA   Oak Alley, at Vacherie, is a pink Doric Temple with 28 columns matching in number the double row of 90-foot oaks which form the archway.

IOWA Abundance—here symbolized by Mrs. August Rettig, of Middle Amana, and a sampling of the soil's rich yield.

MISSOURI (*center spread*) A stretch of rich Missouri River bottom land, glowing with the glorious colors of fall.

NEBRASKA Scotts Bluff from the air, looking out over the high and exciting tablelands of Western Nebraska.

Colorado

by DEBS MYERS

In the old mining town of Fairplay, almost two miles high in the Colorado Rockies, stands a monument built to a burro named Prunes. Prunes, the townspeople say, was cussed and headstrong, but he was also a good-luck burro who brought fortune to every prospector who owned him.

When Prunes died, the people of Fairplay put a marker on his grave—"Prunes, a burro, 1867–1930"—and sent him off in style.

On the day I was at Fairplay an old man sat on a wooden box near the monument squinting through the sun at the mountains beyond the town. The old man said that his name was Frank Mayer, that he was 102 years old—"in this climate the only way for a man to die is for 'em to hang him"—and that he had been soldier, Indian scout and prospector. "Me and Prunes," he said, "belong to an ornery breed that's about gone. Maybe it's a good thing; we don't fit any more. But I don't worry about it because I've had fun and never in my whole life did I deliberately do one bad thing to any person." He sighed and added thoughtfully: "Except, of course, to a few rascals I had to kill."

The old man at the grave of the burro, living in the past in defiance of time, symbolizes an important transition in Colorado history—a transition that is certain to shape its future. The old-timers who built the state in their own image and wanted it to stay that way are about gone and their influence is dying. Colorado is no longer content to live in the shadow of its roaring legends.

There are still plenty of reminders of the past, but the typical Coloradan is too busy to tell you just how grandpop stood alone in the mine shaft, cut off and surrounded, with the claim jumpers charging across the gulch.

This does not mean that Colorado is losing its customary flamboyance. You are likely, as I did, to enter the office of a chamber-of-commerce manager and find seated behind the desk a young man wearing a ten-gallon hat, frontier pants and a purple shirt. Probably, if he could grow them, he would have purple whiskers.

And there are, inevitably, tourist traps aplenty, some of them ferociously picturesque and full of what Coloradans apologetically call atmosphere, but these are the natural hazards to be expected in a state that attracts more than 3,000,000 visitors a year.

No one has explained why Colorado needs phony atmosphere. It has the most awesome scenery in America: 600 mountain peaks more than 12,000 feet high, 300 peaks more than 13,000 feet high, and fifty-two mountains that stretch above 14,000 feet; it has brawling rivers racing across glacial canyons, lakes on the flat tops of mountains, tiny streams that make the kind of rippling noises that streams are supposed to make; it has uranium, oil and coal, silver and gold, and even a desert created from the sands of a long-vanished inland sea. When nature made Colorado, it was on a show-off bender.

Colorado isn't all mountainous. The eastern third of the state is as smooth as a tidal flat, which is what it was in the distant past. I had visited Colorado many times before (it is doubtful there's a better place anywhere for a summer vacation), but this trip was different; instead of settling down at a resort and taking it easy, I planned a leisurely trip by car across the state. Anyone who expects cool temperatures immediately upon crossing the state line is in for a disappointment. I came into Colorado by car at the eastern boundary on U. S. 40. The thermometer, in a gas station at Cheyenne Wells, just across the Colorado line from Kansas, recorded 102°.

The attendant in the gasoline station gave me two pieces of advice. "When you get up in the mountains," he said, "and your car starts knocking [which it did] just turn on the radio—loud. And don't worry about getting hurt falling into the canyons. You'd starve to death before you ever hit bottom."

Driving across this flat stretch of Colorado, I passed through Firstview, Kit Carson and Wildhorse—all prosaic farm communities. It's easy to guess how Firstview got its name; from here, on a clear day, you can see the Rocky Mountains, more than 150 miles away.

From far away the mountains are humped shadows; as you get closer, forty or fifty miles off, they have a theatrical, almost artificial, look, a little too dramatic to be authentic, like a cardboard television prop. Once you get to Denver you are close enough to know they're real; only twelve miles beyond Denver are the brown-and-green foothills and beyond the foothills towers the snow-capped Front Range.

In the old days Denver was a capering alley cat of a town. Today it understandably has quieted down. It isn't sedate or stuffy, you understand, far from it—merely mature enough to want to go to bed at night.

Denver is justifiably proud of its mountains and its climate. Residents insist that the sun, even during the winter, is strong enough to keep them tanned the year around, and that winter days often are mild enough for picnicking. And—as Coloradans are fond of pointing out—one of the nicest ways to start a day is to eat breakfast watching the sun strike a snow-capped mountain.

Denver has thirty-five parks within the city limits. The most elaborate, probably the finest owned by any city anywhere, is the Mountain Park System, which stretches over almost 25,000 acres of the Front Range. This area, within an hour's drive of Denver, includes lakes, trout streams, mountains, canyons, barbecue pits, picnic grounds and some of the world's most impressive scenery. It is doubtful if any other city has a back yard to match it.

This area also covers Red Rocks Park, where Denver residents sit in the summer to listen to their symphony play under the stars in an amphitheater made out of red sandstone; Lookout Mountain, where Buffalo Bill is buried, and 14,260-foot Mt. Evans, where some of the nation's leading physicists study cosmic rays in a laboratory jutting from the granite top of the mountain.

I left Denver and drove northwest; constantly, the peaks became clearer and sharper. By the time I reached Boulder, thirty miles from Denver, the mountains were rising from Boulder's back yard. Boulder is the home of the University of Colorado, and the only town in the United States that owns a glacier, from which it gets its water supply. This particular glacier is a mile long, nearly a mile wide and 500 feet deep, the largest in the Rocky Mountains.

The day I arrived in Boulder a group had just returned from a day-long climb to the glacier summit. The climbers included Jim Yeager, former University of Colorado football coach; this was his first venture at mountain climbing, and, he added, his last.

"I have two pieces of advice for mountain climbers," he said. "In the first place, don't go; if you must go, ride a horse."

It is relevant to point out here that in Colorado mountain climbing is more than a sport; it is a fetish. Local mountain climbers talk about the statistics of ridges, crevasses and peaks with the hot-eyed enthusiasm of a baseball fan discussing batting averages. This is likely to be a little startling to more sedentary visitors, who can't see the sense of risking their necks just to get to the top of a mountain, which probably would be uncomfortable once they got there.

Taking off from Boulder on the same northwest course, on a climbing road toward the mountain country, I stopped at Estes Park, only seventy miles from Denver. I came into the village of Estes late in the evening, when long shadows were slanting across the forested mountains rimming the town. Estes Park has only one industry—tourists. Townspeople say that during the summer a million and a quarter tourists travel along Elkhorn Avenue, the principal street. On a summer night, the village is a combination of Coney Island and a county fair. There are square dances, shooting galleries, hot-dog stands, a dozen kinds of games in which barkers challenge you to win an Indian blanket or a kewpie doll.

Estes Park has its quota of characters. One of these I met was a sixty-three-year-old painter named Dave Sterling, who has been painting the mountains, glaciers, lakes and trees of Colorado for more than thirty-five years. In his studio six miles west of Estes village, he delivers impromptu art lectures to prospective customers and other visitors who are merely curious.

On the day I entered the studio, Sterling was exhibiting picture after picture, and maintaining a running spiel before an audience of a dozen persons, several of them middle-aged women, who, it developed, were schoolteachers from Iowa. One of the teachers started to rise from her chair . . . "We better be going," she murmured. Sterling reached into his desk and confronted the schoolteacher with what appeared to be a .22 target pistol. "Hell's almighty, woman," he shouted, "I'm not through yet. If you're getting tired of this, just say shut up and see if I shut up." (The pistol later proved to be a toy reproduction.)

Now that his audience was quiet, not to mention spellbound, Sterling continued: "Art is winding up in the gutter and manure piles. The modern boys paint to scare you to death. I belong to the old school, me and Michelangelo. Any damn fool can dab paint on hard, but to handle paint, so that you see air instead of paint, you have to be the world's greatest artist, which conceivably I am. Though my worldly acquisitions are few, I am the richest man in the United States. Millionaires cry on my shoulder because I'm happy and they're not.

"Why is this? The answer is easy. If I had all the money in the world, where would I live, what would I do? Why, I would live right here, in this same cabin, and I would paint pictures of these dad-blamed mountains."

Estes Park is one of the entrances to Rocky Mountain National Park. I entered the park and drove to Grand Lake across Trail Ridge Road, which offers some of the most dramatic scenery in Colorado. The road, which partially follows an old trail used by the Utes and Arapahoes, rises from 7500 feet at Estes Park to a summit of 12,183 feet. High on the road the air has the tangy smell of a million Christmas trees; you can, if you're lucky, see deer, elk and perhaps mountain sheep; have your picture taken throwing a snowball; feed peanuts to chipmunks (by this time word must have spread among the chipmunks that all the chumps in the world pass along Trail Ridge Road); study the enduring imprint of glaciers, and overlook timbered canyons with lakes and rivers thousands of feet below.

High on Trail Ridge Road at Iceberg Lake, which is fed by melting snowbanks and is never entirely free from ice, someone overladen with civic spirit and red cells, or perhaps a headier stimulant, had crawled down a steep ledge and spelled out in the snow in huge letters, "Athol, Kansas." Later, I looked it up; there is such a town. It must breed a dedicated type of citizen.

There seems to be something about mountains that makes people want to leave the record of their passing, perhaps because the mountains seem so permanent. The inscription I liked best was scrawled on a rock on Trail Ridge Road overlooking Forest Canyon and the Gorge Lakes. It read: "This View Approved by Kilroy."

Grand Lake Village, at the western end of Trail Ridge Road, has a quiet, restful atmosphere that belies its gaudy past. More than seventy years ago, gold, silver and lead were discovered on the western slope of the Never Summer Mountains and Grand Lake became a mining town, filled with clamor and violence.

After five years of boom Grand Lake went bust and almost vanished when the gold gave out. The mining camps became ghost towns. Today Grand Lake is a thriving resort center, with hotels, lodges, cabins and dude ranches and even a yacht club, perhaps the only one in the world that holds annual regattas a mile and a half above sea level.

Some of the old-timers, like Jake Spitzmiller, have trouble realizing this is the same town they knew half a century ago. He made his first trip to Grand Lake in 1907 in a wagon across the mountain trails. He came to Grand Lake in those days to hunt, fish and prospect for gold. I asked him how he liked Grand Lake today, with all its tourists, boat races and modern gadgets. He contemplated; obviously he didn't want to make a snap judgment. "I think I'm going to like it," he said, "though I must admit the winters get very monotonous."

> *The ladies bow and the gents bow under,*
> *Hold your holts and swing like thunder.*

On the day I came across Rabbit Ears Pass—named because two rocks poke up high above the countryside—and into Steamboat Springs, the sidewalks were thronged and dozens of square dancers were cutting their fanciest didoes in the streets. The town seemed pleasantly daft and proud of it.

Steamboat Springs, a winding four-hour drive northwest of Grand Lake, is the most dance-happy town in the country. Two women named Portia Mansfield and Charlotte Perry are responsible for this. For more than thirty years, they have conducted a girls' camp and a coeducational theater-dance workshop for adults. Several years ago, to supplement an annual series of recitals, musicals and plays, they persuaded the town to sponsor a square-dance competition. Today this big summer festival is the world series of the square dance. Anyone who thinks he can "do-si-do and allemande left" is invited, regardless of how far away he lives, but he'd better be good. The competition is terrific.

As many as fifty square-dance sets dip and swirl at one time; the girls wear hoop skirts, pantalets and poke bonnets, the men fancy shirts, cowboy boots and frontier pants; judges prance from contestant to contestant, and the callers cry out, "When the birdie flies out and the crow hops in, that is the time for fun to begin." There is even a clinic for callers.

Steamboat Springs' reputation is not confined to the square dance. It is also one of the few towns where skiing is a regular part of the public-school curriculum. An instructor holds classes each afternoon for different grades of skiers, and children become adept at the simpler turns about the time they're in the second grade.

Perhaps you've wondered how a cow-and-farm town in the Rockies got the name of Steamboat Springs. Unlike some Colorado place names, this one makes sense. There used to be a spring in the vicinity; as it gushed from the ground it made a chugging noise like a side-wheeler steamboat.

Wherever I went in Colorado, people said, "You should go to Georgetown and see the Hotel de Paris," so I retraced my course across Rabbit Ears Pass, heading southeast, crossed Berthoud Pass, 11,314 feet high but comfortably wide for driving, past the tiny community of Empire into Georgetown. Georgetown was once the most important silver camp in Colorado; now it's a tired little town with little trace of its one-time opulence. The Hotel de Paris, fifty years ago the gathering place of celebrities like Sarah Bernhardt and Jay Gould, is shuttered and closed to customers, an ugly two-story brick building hemmed in by mountains.

The hotel became a landmark because its owner, a Frenchman named Louis Du Puy, was one of the most perverse, unpredictable and explosive characters ever to come to Colorado. After squandering his fortune, Du Puy deserted both the French and the American armies and wound up in Georgetown, where he was injured in a mine accident. Local citizens took up a collection and set him up in the hotel business.

Du Puy prided himself on his skill at sizing up a prospective boor; he ordered away those guests whose looks he didn't like. He hated women, and seldom permitted them in the hotel, even when his best friends tried to bring their wives to dinner. How much of this was temperament, and how much hard business sense, no one knows. At any rate, the Hotel de Paris attracted world celebrities, who would argue art, politics and romance with Du Puy, and eat the excellent food he cooked.

From Georgetown I set out for Central City, Colorado's most publicized mountain village. For some obscure whim, later regretted, I decided against the more conventional route through Idaho Springs in favor of a road leading across Virginia Canyon. There are people, it seems, who like to gape at the glories of nature while manipulating an automobile around hairpin turns on a narrow two-car road with nothing between them and the jagged rocks below but several thousand feet of invigorating mountain air. I'm not one of them. Nor was the man in the car immediately behind me. As soon as he arrived at Central City, he went into the Teller House, and gulped down a double bourbon. "That road," he said, "should be traveled only by Jeeps and jackasses."

Central City, known as the richest square mile on earth during its heyday as a mining town, is famous now for a summer festival which features opera and drama. The festival hires stars from the Metropolitan Opera and the Broadway stage, who like to come to Central City to combine a few weeks' pay with a mountain vacation. These celebrities, in turn, attract other celebrities, not to mention intellectuals, socialites and thousands of ordinary tourists who come to Central City merely to ogle and have a good time.

From the beginning Central City has done things with a flourish, even to building its houses, many of which dangle precariously from the side of a mountain. When President Grant visited the town in 1873, he walked from the stagecoach to the Teller House on a path of silver bricks. Today the Teller House, though ancient, is still ornate, a favorite gathering place for visitors who admire its Victorian ostentation. Many of them are impressed with the palpable antiquity of "the face on the barroom floor," a drawing which is preserved under glass on the wooden floor of the Teller House bar.

It's sad to spoil a good story, but the picture was drawn, not in the roistering old days but in 1936, by a Denver artist who did it on impulse before dawn one morning when the bar was deserted. At first the owners were indignant; it wasn't until some time later that they realized they had a good thing.

From Central City I headed west, back through Georgetown (carefully avoiding Virginia Canyon this time) over the Continental Divide on Loveland Pass (11,992 feet), and across Vail Pass (10,603 feet). (The Continental Divide is a giant ridgepole winding through the middle of Colorado, splitting it into two roughly equal sections, the eastern and the western slopes.) Heading west along an excellent highway merging U. S. 6 and U. S. 24, I came through Glenwood Canyon, where sheer walls rise 1000 feet above the foaming Colorado River as it gathers snows from the Continental Divide and cascades toward the Gulf of California. At the western edge of Glenwood Canyon is the town of Glenwood Springs, an attractive resort, mineral bath and ranch town. One of the show places of the town is the Colorado Hotel, which has kept intact through the years a suite formerly used by President Theodore Roosevelt when he came here on hunting trips. The suite is now occupied with equal comfort by both Democrats and Republicans.

An hour's drive southeast of Glenwood Springs is the town of Aspen. Imagine, if you can, a hard-bitten old sourdough, leathery and seamed with the years, who suddenly has taken to effete ways, hobnobbing with musicians, professors and other high domes, up to his hairy ears in good thoughts, good books and good deeds, wondering just what the hell has happened to him, and there you have a picture of Aspen.

Aspen is a mining town that has gone in for culture. Between 1879 and 1898 a silver boom made Aspen a town of more than 15,000 population, with two railroads and a sizable weekly payroll. Then the silver market collapsed and so did Aspen. Today it is booming again as a year-round resort and cultural center, with skiing, an opera group, summer study groups headed by leading educators, and a summer repertory theater.

Some of Aspen's unreconstructed old-timers take a jaundiced view of what they call Aspen's "culchaw." They long for the old days when mill and smelter smoke made a haze over Aspen's skies; and they insist that they'd walk a mile over broken glass to avoid hearing a symphony orchestra.

Most Aspen citizens, however, have learned to relax and like it. They realize that the old days are gone forever and are grateful that Aspen is a year-round resort, which means they can be soothed by the tourist dollar in December as well as in June. A lot of them even have developed a liking for the visitors, who, over all, are unpretentious people trying to have some quiet fun.

I met Frank Gimlet, a white-whiskered old man who used to be a hermit. Finally he gave it up. "Only one flaw to hermiting," he said, "too lonely, nobody to talk with." I encountered him sitting in a battered old automobile at the summit of Monarch Pass, more than two miles high in the Colorado Rockies. He motioned toward the cars traveling along the highway. "Look at the people in those cars," he said, "wearing skimpy clothes and burned as black as tobaccy, gadding about in their automobiles, thinking they're seeing Colorado. All they're seeing are the white and yellow lines on the highway. There's only one way to see Colorado, the way I used to do it. Just put a pick and provisions on the back of a jackass, go out into the hills and hunt for a glory hole."

Most Colorado visitors would agree with the old man on one point: there's an awful lot to see. This country is big, lavish, contradictory and sometimes frightening. The average visitor can see enough in a day to be overwhelmed; after traveling about Colorado for several weeks he learns he has just tapped the surface. To really see all the things in Colorado worth seeing—that's a lifetime job.

A few hours after I had driven into Grand Junction, the biggest town on the western slope, I overheard an old man say: "I still can't believe I'd ever see the day when that stuff meant money. Shucks, I've thrown a bushel of it away while I was hunting gold." He was talking about uranium.

To many people uranium is something precious and more than a little mysterious; to the miners of Western Colorado who have been mining it off-and-on for more than forty years, there isn't anything mysterious about it—it's just a yellow rock that has a pesky habit of petering out when you least expect it.

Uranium is mined on the red cliffs of the Colorado plateau, in the four-corners region of Colorado, New Mexico, Utah and Arizona. As almost everyone knows by now, uranium is the radioactive mineral that generates nuclear fission, and nuclear fission is the process by which atoms are split. It wasn't until the atom bomb that uranium took on a terrible, new significance. Up to that time, sometimes it was worth mining; sometimes it wasn't. Most miners tell you that mining uranium is a lot harder than mining gold. Whereas gold usually appears in veins, uranium appears in pods. The pods may be a foot long, or 100 feet long or longer, and it may be necessary to dig through fifty feet or more of worthless rock to reach a paying pod.

Even though a boom has developed in uranium, it would be wrong to believe that Grand Junction is a rowdy mining town. It is primarily a market and trade center. I was in Grand Junction on a Saturday night and there were more farmers than miners. The people still seem a little puzzled by what the uranium boom will do to their community; it's adding to the payrolls and increasing the population, that's sure, but to the people of Grand Junction it seems a tricky, undependable kind of metal. They can remember during the war when the uranium operations became secret, how the big trucks came lumbering up from the canyons carrying loads of the stuff, and then came Hiroshima. Some of the people in Grand Junction shake their heads and say they would just as soon that it were mined somewhere else.

Only thirty minutes by automobile from Grand Junction is the Colorado National Monument, 18,061 fantastic acres of odd-shaped monoliths, box canyons, precipitous cliffs, caves, petrified wood and prehistoric remains.

Dinosaur beds extend more than 100 miles along the banks of the Colorado River, and this has created in the Grand Junction area a group of amateur bone hunters who spend many of their week ends climbing over unsurveyed trails and bleak rock outcroppings in the hope of being able to sink a pick in the undug grave of an animal which died about 160 million years ago.

From Grand Junction, I headed southeast on U. S. 50, an excellent road, toward Gunnison. This is an easy half-a-day drive passing through the towns of Delta and Montrose. On the first part of the trip the scenery is reminiscent of those Western movies featuring wagon trains and Indian ambushes (the only danger these days is ambush by real-estate agents); gradually you enter the high-plateau country which has produced some of the best cattle in the world. Gunnison is an authentic Western town without much regard for the fripperies of the resort centers on the eastern slope. This isn't a place where people come to exhibit sun tans, play golf or lounge around in fancy sports clothes; the people who come to Gunnison come to fish.

It's the conversation you hear at breakfast, lunch and dinner, in hotels, lodges and on the street corners: Craig Goodwin pulled out a five-pounder yesterday while fishing from horseback; Pete Eastman's boy got four dandies yesterday just above 10-Mile Bridge; did you know that Bob Hope, the radio fellow, went fishing on the Gunnison River in a kayak and got dunked in four feet of water?

I went fishing with the Gunnison navy, known also as the sage-brush sailors. Because there are in the Gunnison River many in-viting spots beyond the reach of the most expert fly-caster or wader, some of the citizens fish while floating down the river in kayaks, which combine the features of the Eskimo's covered kayak and the duck hunter's flat-bottomed skiff.

About sixty miles west of Gunnison just off U. S. 50 is the Black Canyon of the Gunnison, the deepest gorge in Colorado, with walls rising almost vertically above the narrow bed of the river. It is what the name implies, a black canyon.

I took a good long look and headed southwest to Ouray, which with justification calls itself the Gem City of the Rockies. The town nestles in a pear-shaped valley at the very edge of three towering mountains, White House Mountain (13,493 feet) on the west, Hayden Mountain (13,100 feet) on the south, and Cascade Mountain (12,100 feet) to the northwest. To the east is a huge natural amphitheater which is part of a game refuge.

I left Ouray in a lashing rain and started the sharp ascent up Uncompahgre Canyon. This road, which directly overlooks Ouray at the outset, is twisting and narrow in places and it didn't help my morale to recall a story about a truck which had lost a wheel here, plunging down the mountainside and crashing through the roof of an Ouray home. About this time the windshield wipers quit working, and I was high up the climbing highway, into the clouds and swirling vapor, with the rain still falling. I saw a sign nailed to a tree and wanting to be certain I was on the right road I got out of the car and walked through the rain to the sign. It stated: "Vote for Jack Evans for Congress."

I know nothing about Jack Evans or his qualifications; I do know that at the precise moment I would not have voted for him. As it turned out, I was on the right road—U. S. 550, otherwise known as the Million-Dollar Highway. One story has it that it cost $1,000,000 to build the road; another that the road was so named because of the gold-bearing gravels with which it is surfaced. This much is certain: it furnishes a view of the most awesome scenery in Colorado. Here on Red Mountain Pass, words like "beautiful" and "magnificent" don't apply; this scenery is raw, elemental. The Red Mountains are saw-toothed masses of stone, colored an orange-red by iron pyrites in the rock, and they seem to split the sky.

In tortuous turns, the road leads sharply upward past mine shafts, old mills and tumbled houses, past curiously colored rock outcroppings once melted by volcanic fire, and great glacial chasms where creeping masses of ice gouged into the granite of the mountains. From the summit (11,018 feet) the highway leads downward through the San Juan National Forest to the town of Silverton, which, according to legend, got its name from the remark of a miner: "We may not have gold here, but we have silver by the ton." In the old days, Silverton had a population of 2153 people, 35 saloons, two breweries and a gaudy reputation. Today it is a pleasant, quiet town with only a few reminders of its lush and skittish days.

The people of Silverton claim a strange distinction; they say that in San Juan County, of which Silverton is the county seat, there is not an acre of tilled ground. When I asked an old man what the people did, he looked at me as though I were a little touched. "Why," he said, "we do a little mining, we look at the scenery and go fishing. What the hell else would anybody want to do?"

Two hours from Durango by automobile, in a corner of Colorado overlooking Arizona, New Mexico and Utah, is a forested, flat-topped mountain known as Mesa Verde—the green tableland. Here, amidst 50,275 acres of canyons and mesa lands, are the excavated ruins and cliff dwellings of ancient Indians who built a culture long since vanished.

Archaeologists have pieced together a partial history of these people—who they were, where they came from, where they went; yet much of it is still a mystery and probably will remain so. That, perhaps, is a basic reason why it exerts so powerful an attraction for tourists; approximately 100,000 of them come each summer to this out-of-the-way corner of Colorado, to inspect the ruins and conjecture among themselves about the riddles of the cliff dwellers' existence.

About 800 years ago the cliff dwellers deserted their homes and vanished. There have been varied theories as to why this happened: plague, superstition, or a surprise attack that resulted in annihilation. The archaeologists shake their heads to this; they attribute this mass exodus to a great drought which they believe afflicted the Southwest from 1276 to 1299; year after year the crops withered until the cliff dwellers lost heart and moved out of Mesa Verde.

Before they left, probably heading deeper into the west, they built on the mesa top a curious walled structure known as the Sun Temple. The accepted theory is that this ancient temple, built around intricate passageways and kivas (underground ceremonial rooms) was intended to placate the Sun God and to bring a merciful end to the drought. The temple was never completed. Why? No one knows, of course; perhaps because the people lost faith in the promises of their medicine men.

That is only one of the riddles. Where did the cliff dwellers finally find refuge when they made the long journey in search of water, what is the significance of the peculiar structure of the Sun Temple, what strange rituals took place in the underground ceremonial chambers? The answers—well, one guess is as good as another.

Leaving Mesa Verde, heading toward the town of Salida, I left the main highway to drive through an eerie desert of twisting sand known as the Great Sand Dunes National Monument. Here in South-Central Colorado close to the town of Alamosa, nature has played one of its most paradoxical tricks; in the middle of a state that is noted for its mountains and lakes is a vast expanse of barren sand, stretching to the edge of the Sangre de Cristo Range.

These shifting dunes, rising 100 feet and higher, are believed to have been formed from the bed of a huge inland sea that dried up ages ago. The color of the dunes changes with the light. In the glare of the sun, they are dazzling white; late in the afternoon, the sun tinges them with purple and red, and by moonlight the ridges are pale and bleak, making a plaintive whispering noise as the wind riffles through the sand.

This is a place of legends. There are stories of men and women found mysteriously dead, families which have disappeared, sheep-herders and their flocks who have gone into the wastes and never come back. There is a legend, also, of horses seen on the horizon at sunrise racing across the sand with webbed feet.

From Salida I made a side trip to the Royal Gorge, the Grand Canyon of the Arkansas, a walled gash in the mountains, 1000 feet deep, from rim to river bed. In addition to the Gorge itself, there are two chief items of interest: the 45-degree-angle railroad by which you can descend to the bottom of the canyon, and the 1260-foot-long suspension bridge across the chasm, the highest automobile bridge in the world.

I drove out on the slightly swaying bridge, looked straight down into the gorge and came back to Salida. From there I headed for Colorado Springs. Colorado Springs is a town where a lot of people come planning to spend a day before they push on deeper into the mountains; once they arrive and look over the place they're likely not to budge for the remainder of their vacations. How, they inquire, can any place be better than this?

There is some merit to this reasoning. This is a city more than a mile high, located where the plains end and the Rockies begin; it has broad streets, handsome homes, good hotels and restaurants, plenty of trees and shrubbery, a fine climate and a sprawling forested landscape that includes Pikes Peak. It also has numerous other scenic attractions including Garden of the Gods, Seven Falls and Cave of the Winds.

The townspeople take pride in their history, which is understandable; matter of fact, it's easier to understand Colorado Springs once you know how it got that way.

From the beginning it was inevitable that a city should be built where Colorado Springs now stands. It is at the foot of Ute Pass, which is one of the convenient ways in and out of the mountains, and, further, it was the center of mineral springs which purportedly had healing qualities. (It may be that all mineral springs everywhere in the world are purported to have healing qualities, just as all chorus girls are supposedly beautiful, all fat men jolly, all itchy old loafers on park benches wise.)

The two show places of Colorado Springs are, of course, Pikes Peak and the Broadmoor Hotel, both of which are large and almost equally scenic. The Broadmoor was conceived by an implausible character named Spencer (Spec) Penrose, who came west as a young fellow out of Harvard, tried his luck in the Cripple Creek gold field, found it was good, not to mention incredible, and wound up with a large number of fancy suits, the pockets of which were stashed with gold.

Penrose was a prodigious builder. He built a road up 9200-foot Cheyenne Mountain, just back of the hotel, and climaxed this by building a highway up Pikes Peak.

There are thousands of visitors who wouldn't think of coming to Colorado Springs without taking a trip up Pikes Peak. I went up, not on the highway built by Penrose but on the cog railway. The conductor kept up a stream of comment as we moved upward, and this is a capsuled version of what he said: "There never has been a passenger accident on any of these trains through the years, so sit back and enjoy yourselves. . . . The railroad is eight and nine-tenths miles long; it climbs from an initial elevation of 6571 feet to 14,110 feet above sea level at the summit. . . . The maximum grade is 25 per cent. . . . The black spot you see on the plains to your left is the Black Forest, a crest of Yellow Pine, sixteen miles northeast of Colorado Springs and more than forty air miles from here. . . . On clear days it is possible to see the wheat fields of Kansas more than 200 miles away. . . . We have now reached Windy Point, more than 12,000 feet high; the flowers you see are the same you would find approaching the North Pole. . . . On the left where you see the light-colored spots on the mountain is Cripple Creek. . . . Eight thousand feet below and more than sixteen miles away you see the city of Colorado Springs. . . . Before us is the Summit House, built on a foundation of ice. The top of Pikes Peak is a mass of small boulders filled with ice which thaws in the summer to a depth of five or six feet, but below this depth is a perpetual mass of rock and ice."

Sitting on the train in front of me were an old man and woman. The man obviously liked it all, the precipitous cliffs, the far look across the mountains, the thin air. When he pointed out the sights to his wife, she nervously shrugged him away, keeping her eyes trained on the floor of the railway car, away from the chasms. Once at the summit, she straightened her shoulders, grabbed the old man by the arm, and assumed command.

"All right, pa," she said grimly, "you've seen your passel of rock. Time's come to go home and put some corn in the bin."

My last stop in Colorado was Pueblo, an hour's drive south of Colorado Springs. Pueblo is Colorado's second largest city. Though it is a gateway and departure point for the tourist country, Pueblo, save for the week when the state fair is in operation, is too busy to fool around with frontier atmosphere. In Pueblo, the workingman wears overalls, not ranch clothes.

In contrast with most Colorado cities, Pueblo has an atmosphere of bustle and urgency; it is an industrial island in the midst of the plains country, with steel as its prime industry. At night, the red glare from the furnaces of the Colorado Fuel and Iron Corporation can be seen far across the countryside, a reminder that this is the largest steel mill west of the Mississippi.

That day driving back through the flatlands of eastern Colorado the brassy sun was baking the ground and the hot winds came across the fields with a whimpering noise. In the bludgeoning heat the countryside seemed lifeless, parched for water. Inevitably, the traveler contrasts this with the mountains, with the sprawling lakes on the flat mesa tops and the streams racing along the sides of canyons.

I thought back on Frank Mayer, the old man sitting at the grave of Prunes, the burro, in the little town of Fairplay and remembered what he had said about mountains.

"I reckon," he said, "there isn't a man in the whole world who, in his own heart, isn't a little humbled by a mountain. In my younger days, I used to climb on top of an old mountain called Silverheels, named after a dance-hall girl, and I used to wish they could bring all the big statesmen and the diplomats and the nabobs in the world right there to the summit of old Silverheels and say to 'em: 'You're kind of little and not very important, aren't you, compared to what you see on every side, so quit your fussing and act like gentlemen.'"

I recalled, too, an inscription on the walls of the Statehouse at Denver, and wondered if this was a prophecy of Colorado's future:

And men shall fashion glaciers into greenness
And harvest April rivers in the autumn.

PART IV *The Southwest*

Arizona

by DEBS MYERS

Arizona considers its winter climate to be among the most rewarding blessings the Almighty has seen fit to bestow upon man— not as important as breathing but a passably close second. This viewpoint has merit. When I boarded the train at New York City in midwinter, bound for Arizona, the sky was the color of warmed-over gravy and a bitter wind pounded the skyscrapers. At Chicago, rain had turned to sleet and the temperature was two below zero. Thirty-five hours later, 1887 miles beyond Chicago, when the train reached Phoenix, the temperature was 72 and a brilliant sun made it seem late spring.

Men on the street were in shirt sleeves, and girls wore summer dresses. The car that took me from the station to the hotel was a convertible, with the top down. The streets were lined with orange and palm trees; at the city's edges were orange, grapefruit, lemon and lime groves bearing fruit. In the hotel restaurant a man was drinking a rum collins while his wife sipped iced tea. The man unfolded a copy of the *Milwaukee Journal* and showed his wife the headline: "Sub-zero Blizzard Hits." "Really going through hell back home," he said, with snug satisfaction.

It wasn't many years ago that the word Arizona conjured up visions of Geronimo, Wyatt Earp, Billy the Kid and an implausibly stacked rancher's daughter, all galloping hell-bent for nowhere, like the jacket on a Zane Grey novel. Today millions of Americans have found out what Arizona is really like. In few places has so much happened so fast. In the lifetime of men and women who made their own laws and built Arizona into a state, cities with gleaming buildings and sprawling green lawns have grown where there were only sand, cacti and mesquite.

The desert itself—once a wasteland where only the tough or lucky could survive—is now a winter playground, occupied by travelers from October to May. Those who can afford it keep coming back. Thousands of others, fed up with snow, furnaces and virus cures that won't work, find or create a job and settle down to stay. (This isn't always easy. Typical of resort areas, prices aren't low, salaries aren't high, and jobs are often hard to find. In other words, living is simple, but it isn't always simple to make a living.)

Arizona claims to have more sun—more mellow, pleasant sun—than any other place in the world. Somehow, the sun seems to set the hormones of the visitors vibrating. Quiet, mild-appearing men emerge in gaudy cowboy clothes which afford equal freedom to their shirttails and inhibitions. Many women, following the same pattern, take on the appearance of Calamity Jane as processed by Elizabeth Arden; others, scorning Western styles, become antiseptically tweedy, as though they expected a fashion photographer to pop out of the mesquite and snap them with their favorite water spaniel.

A Phoenix newspaper columnist named Bert Fireman told me: "There are more cowboy clothes worn in Arizona now than during the peak of the cowboy days. In the old days when a cowboy came to town, he usually dressed in a blue serge suit from Sears Roebuck." It isn't easy, except for the experts, to distinguish the visitors from the genuine Westerners. Not all cowboys, alas, are bowlegged, or squint their eyes like William S. Hart.

When Arizonans talk about their climate—which, understandably, is a prime conversation piece—it is best to inquire which climate, because Arizona has a sumptuous variety. In midwinter, you can play golf in a T-shirt in the afternoon, but you'll need a jacket once the sun sets behind the mountains. There isn't much twilight in Arizona, just a soft blue sky overhead, then a sunset so incredible it appears painted by a daft surrealist. You can swim in Phoenix and a little more than an hour later, traveling by airplane, you can ski at Flagstaff. One day at the Grand Canyon, during a driving snow storm, I inquired about the weather at Phoenix and Tucson.

"Sun's out," I was told. "Temperature about 70." Further, while Phoenix and Tucson are sweltering during the summer, the people in the mountainous northern part of the state are likely to be sleeping under blankets. As an illustration, a ski meet is held at Flagstaff every Fourth of July.

To understand Arizona's climate, you need to know that this is a land of distance and geographical contrast. Arizona is spread over 113,956 square miles, which means, according to those statisticians who get excited about such things, that Arizona is as big as Illinois and Wisconsin put together, with room enough left over to graze a few hundred head of broad-beamed Hereford cattle. Arizona is far from flat; it has plenty of mountains, many of them in the midst of the desert. Nor does the desert itself fit the popular misconception of a bleak and tortured expanse of yellow-white sand, lifeless except for rattlesnakes, Gila monsters and itchy old prospectors willing to share the last swig out of their canteens with their faithful burros. (In Arizona, I saw only one prospector; he was methodically kicking his burro in the hindquarters in an effort to make the animal move.) Actually, the desert is full of life, both plant and animal; the year around there are cacti and green shrubbery, and in the spring when the flowers bloom it is a tapestry in Technicolor.

At first many visitors dislike the desert; intuitively, they feel it isn't to be trusted. But the desert has a way of creeping inside you. First thing you know, you're falling in love with the place, not wanting to live anywhere else. It happens to a lot of people, though few of them ever really get to know the desert. The desert is a place of moods, with the whims and guile of a range mustang. It is usually cozening, always contrary, and sometimes cruel.

In the mornings, the desert earth has the clean, fresh smell of herbs and shrubbery, and the wind makes a whispering noise like a random lullaby. During the full sun there is a hush over the land, the rocks glisten with fool's gold, and the mountains in the distance are silent reminders that this was once a brooding emptiness. At night, the desert comes into its own; from beyond the steel and stone of the cities it seems to move forward swiftly with the dusk. The towering pillars of saguaro cactus take on gnarled, primitive shapes, like crouching sentries left forever at their posts; the black silence breaks with the night cries of animals seeking food, and you know that the desert, for all its appearance of lulling peace, is a muted battleground where the struggle for survival goes on always.

A trip to the desert botanical garden outside Phoenix is rewarding for those interested in desert plant life. Most desert lore is based on whoppers grown respectable with the years. For instance, the purple sage celebrated in a book written by Zane Grey is gray; from a distance, it looks purple. The century plant blooms at intervals not greater than twenty-two years, then dies. The fluid in the barrel cactus, which reputedly has saved the lives of countless prospectors dying of thirst, isn't drinkable and if anyone is fool enough to try it, the fluid will coagulate in his stomach with agonizing results.

The bane of the desert is neither the summer heat nor the lack of rain, but the horde of jack rabbits which raid the gardens. Tomcats and gopher snakes are kept to kill the rabbits. However, a tomcat has to be unusually big and ornery to tackle a full-grown jack rabbit; the rabbit is likely to haul off, mule fashion, and kick the tomcat from here to there.

The gopher snakes hide behind plants and ambush the rabbits, in the style of miniature pythons, squeezing them to death.

Probably the desert has affected Arizona's character as a state; certainly, both are contradictory. Arizona is both frontier and metropolitan, ghost town and plush resort, cowboy and Indian, dowager and business big shot; it is a king-sized colorful Kansas with cactus and climate, and a fledgling Texas with less horn-tooting. The essential reason for these contradictions can be traced to the state's booming population. In 1920, Arizona had 334,162 people; in 1960 more than a million. This means the population more than tripled in forty years. It means also, inevitably, that Arizona's tempers, moods, whims and inclinations are changing almost as fast. The typical Arizonan—if there is one—is casual, not much given to guff or gabble, hard to hurry, harder to stampede; independent as a yearling bull in knee-high clover and just as fidgety if someone tries to shove him. (This independence applies to everything from politics to poker; he likes to play both by ear.) He's inclined to place a high premium on comfort—the climate isn't calculated to make a fellow want to get himself into a swivet—but, despite this he's willing to go along with the tourists and act picturesque, though there are times when he feels like a fool doing it. If he has lived in Arizona as long as five years, he considers himself something of an old-timer and feels qualified to cuss the summers authoritatively, though you would have to prod him with a blowtorch to get him to move anywhere else.

Contributing to the complexity of the Arizona character is the state's sizable Indian population. There are about 60,000 Indians in fifteen separate nations living on seventeen reservations. Like Indians in other states, many of them seem confused, apprehensive over the future, often resentful of the white man's careless way with promises and weary of his pretensions.

In Flagstaff, while talking with a young Navaho named Virgil Tiyo, I noticed an Indian and his wife, both blanketed, walking along the street with a portable radio, listening to Arthur Godfrey. A portly Eastern visitor, wearing boots, tight-fitting cowboy pants, purple shirt and big white hat, motioned for the Indians to halt, and took their picture. The visitor was laughing so hard he had trouble focusing the camera.

Tiyo turned to me, shaking his head. "I wish I had the money," he said, "to take the pictures of some of these people who consider us so comical. It would make an interesting album. At nights before I went to sleep I would get out the album and look at it. It might be that other Indians also would consider the pictures of these white men amusing. It might help us to sleep better."

A capsuled index to Arizona's character can be found in the city of Phoenix, which reflects much of the best in the state and probably a little of the worst. As befits the capital city of a state proud of its scenery, Phoenix is a lush green oasis rising dramatically from the treeless desert. Rimming the city on every side are gaunt mountains —Camelback, the Superstition, the Four Peaks—silently emphasizing that this was a barren nothingness before men created a farm empire by means of canals carved through the desert.

Some of these irrigation ditches follow the pattern established hundreds of years ago by Indians who built a primitive civilization, then vanished. According to legend, Phoenix was named by an early-day canal builder, Darrell Duppa—variously considered a scholar or stewbum, take your choice—who was impressed with the idea of a town rising on the ruins of a departed civilization.

Today Phoenix is in the heart of the Salt River Valley, an oval bowl twenty miles wide and forty miles long, where farmers raise lettuce, cotton and other crops the year around. The Salt River, in the Phoenix area, incidentally, has all the requisites of a river save one: no water. Except in unusual flood time, it's as dry as Carry Nation's cupboard.

The mountain snow water which rolls in the upper stretches of the Salt River is impounded by a series of dams forty to ninety miles away. This water, routed to the arid soil of the valley through canals, is the reason Phoenix has grown so rapidly.

Phoenix civic leaders predict a Phoenix population of a million by the year 2000, which illustrates how the buoyant desert air enables a man to look over the mesquite clumps to the mountaintops. "All you have to do," one said, "is to spit on the desert and something will grow. It isn't the old families, though, who have built this city. It's the newcomers. They see two things they like: climate and opportunity. If the old families had their way, this would still be a one-horse town."

In Phoenix the visitor soon learns to adjust himself to surprise. When I first walked into the high-ceilinged lobby of the Adams Hotel, a city landmark and rendezvous for cattlemen and politicians, I blinked and looked again. I had been conditioned to many types of wildlife in hotels, but this was the first time I ever had seen a bull in a hotel lobby, not a large bull, perhaps, by Arizona standards, but large enough to look moderately odd amidst the leather furnishings. It developed the bull was an ad for a livestock show.

From atop the Adams, where there is a swimming pool on the sun patio, or the fourteen-story Westward Ho, another excellent hotel, it is possible to see, stretching around the perimeter of the valley, the luxurious resorts and the lush private estates of such gentry as P. K. Wrigley and Fowler McCormick. Much of the capital that built these establishments comes from Midwestern and Eastern businessmen who came to Arizona to soak up the winter sunshine and decided to take partial root in the desert soil.

George Borg, a Midwestern industrialist, arrived in Phoenix in 1944 to negotiate for a research plant. He reserved rooms at Jokake Inn for four days. The deal failed to materialize but four months later Borg was still there. To his business associates who pressed him to return home, he wired, "If you want to see me, you'll have to come here." For a while, he reserved accommodations for the visiting executives at a guest ranch. Two years later he built Casa Blanca, one of the outstanding resorts of the countryside.

There are accommodations in and around Phoenix for every kind of visitor, from pleasant quarters in a motel, to the gold-plated resorts. The more noteworthy of these resorts include the Arizona Biltmore, one of the truly magnificent resort hotels of the country, the Castle Hot Springs Hotel, the San Marcos, El Chorro, the Wigwam, the Arizona Ambassador, the Arizona Manor, Camelback Inn, Jokake Inn, Paradise Inn, the Royal Palms and the Casa Blanca at Scottsdale.

Scottsdale is a little community which calls itself the West's most Western town and prides itself on being picturesque. With its store fronts of knotty pine, peeled pine porticoes and hitching rails, Scottsdale resembles a Western movie set in which the director decided to replace horses with station wagons. The town is the post-office address of many artists, writers and craftsmen.

Wickenburg, fifty miles northwest of Phoenix, is the capital of the dude-ranch country, proclaiming that it has every kind of ranch for every kind of dude. One of the best-known is the Remuda, started in 1925 by Jack Burden and Bob White, a couple of young fellows from the East. Burden and White were in Wickenburg on a week end discussing the idea of starting a dude ranch when a young woman named Sophie Fletcher asked them to recommend a place where she and a party of friends could relax and ride horses. They told her they knew the exact place, signed up the party, rented a ranch and horses the same afternoon and called their place the Remuda. Today the Remuda is operated by Mrs. Sophie Burden, who married her host, now dead, shortly thereafter.

"There's an extra man here. Is there an extra woman in the house?" A woman stepped into the group of square dancers. The caller clapped his hands to the boisterous rhythm of the phonograph music and set the dancers capering with:

> *Duck for an oyster, dive for a clam.*
> *Dive for your home in the happy land.*

The scene was a square dance at the Triple H resort ranch, eight miles east of Tucson. The caller was a rangy man in his shirt sleeves, an oversize Western tie loose at his neck. The dancers spun about the ranch-house floor, the people on the side lines tapped their feet in time with the music and the caller jigged a little as he cried out his commands:

> *When you meet your partner, what do you do?*
> *You swing your partner and she swings you.*

Square dances are common across the country, and this one was nothing unusual except for one thing: the caller was United States Supreme Court Justice William O. Douglas. If, by chance, you had last seen the Justice in his black robes grouped austerely with his colleagues in the marble Supreme Court building in Washington, the effect was—well, it was a little startling.

The people at the dance took it casually; Justice Douglas, it seems, comes to Arizona whenever he can and, if possible, attends a square dance. Earlier in the evening, when he had first entered the ranch house, several of the dancers greeted him as an old acquaintance.

"Doggone it, Judge," a man said, "for years I've been wanting to see you get off the bench and back into politics, but you've been ducking it."

The judge chuckled. "I'm still ducking," he said.

"Do you think, Judge," a woman inquired, "that you'll fall off a horse this trip?"

"I guess a man has to do a thing only once," Douglas said, "and he gets a reputation for it."

Later, leaving while the dance was still going on, I saw the swirling figures of the dancers outlined against the window and heard a man's voice—a little hoarse now—shouting:

> *I got a gal at the head of the holler.*
> *She won't lead and I won't foller.*

"That Judge Douglas," said an elderly man, standing in the doorway with his wife, "he's a pistol."

Matter of fact, it takes more than a Supreme Court Justice calling a square dance to surprise Tucson. For a sprightly city still suffering from growing pains, Tucson is curiously reminiscent of a wise old man who has seen too much to get into a dither about anything. Few cities combine so much of the old and new. Tucson has been under the flags of three countries: Spain, Mexico, America. During the Civil War, the town changed hands twice, both times without a battle. In 1861, the Union garrison abandoned the settlement and six months later the Confederates moved in. Later the Confederates retreated before the California volunteers, and on May 20, 1862, Tucson became Union territory again. In the old days it was a walled garrison town defending itself against raiding Apaches. In those days it was as tough a town as could be found in the West.

An early-day historian summarized the situation thus: "If the world were searched over I suppose there could not be found so degraded a set of villains as then formed the principal society of Tucson."

Today it is one of the fastest-growing, most vital and most colorful cities to be found anywhere. It isn't preciously Western, mind you, but naturally colorful. A street scene on a typical day is likely to include ranchers, cowboys, Indians from the nearby Papago Reservation, Mexicans, artists, writers, sculptors, soldiers from the Davis-Monthan Air Force Base, Eastern dudes, convalescents fleeing Eastern winters, university professors and students, and perhaps a professor with Geiger counter and burro, though the professor is likely to have sold his burro and bought a Jeep by this time.

A lot of visitors coming into Arizona by train stop first at Tucson, 121 miles southeast of Phoenix, and having stopped there, see no use in going farther. What, they ask, can be better than this? Tucson, like Phoenix, is a winter resort that lives up to the name: sunshine during eighty-four out of every hundred daylight hours during the year, an average humidity of 34 per cent and an altitude of 2400 feet. This adds up to a climate that is warm, sunny and dry.

In the past two decades Tucson has had a tremendous growth. Many of the newcomers have come because the climate is good for what ails them, whether it is rheumatism, asthma, arthritis or a plain dislike of cold weather.

The Tucson area receives an average of only 12.5 inches of rain a year and the city pumps its water out of deep wells which tap both the basic water table and the dry Santa Cruz River. This is causing a disturbing decline in the underground water level, but Tucson does not engage in public lamentation; it is too busy counting up its assets which include—in addition to its climate and the acquisition of new industry—copper, cattle, cotton and culture. Much of the culture is concentrated at the University of Arizona, which is located in the middle of the city on an attractive forty-acre tract (presented to the city in the 1890's by three public-spirited gamblers who evidently had a penchant for higher education).

The university represents a major victory over rival Phoenix. Many years ago, so the story goes, there were two pieces of political pie to be awarded, a state university and a state hospital. Phoenix, being the capital, had first choice and took the hospital, which appeared a more rewarding proposition than an infant college. Today the university has around 10,000 students and a good academic rating. Phoenix wryly wonders how it could have been so wrong.

Ultimately, though, Tucson's well-being rests on its climate. It has been only during recent years—since the organization of a promotional group known as the Sunshine Climate Club—that Tucson really has bragged about its advantages. Now thousands of persons are finding out every year that Tucson is not merely a place with a pleasant climate, but a place where they can live as relaxed, casual and carefree as they want, dependent only upon their ambitions and the state of their pocketbooks.

Like Phoenix, Tucson has tourist facilities designed to meet varying budgets—motels, ornate lodges, and hotels like the Santa Rita, the Pioneer and the Westerner. The elaborate resorts outside the city include El Conquistador, the Arizona Inn, Caravan Inn, El Dorado Lodge, Hacienda del Sol, Pepper Tree Inn, Sierra Vista Lodge and The Lodge on the Desert.

An illustration of what can happen to people who pull up stakes and move to Tucson is furnished by a young man named H. W. (Bill) Taylor and his wife, Susan. He originally lived in Detroit, where he owned an insurance brokerage business; she lived in Cincinnati. During the war they met while he was recovering from wounds suffered when a Jeep hit a mine, promptly fell in love and got married. Somehow, the brokerage business wasn't fun any more, so they sold out and headed for the West, hoping they would find a place they would like.

A couple of weeks later, they drove into Tucson, lounged in their convertible in the bright sunshine, breathed deeply of the clean desert air, looked at the distant mountains, wreathed in purple, and looked at each other.

"Honey," he said, "what do you think?"

"Uh-huh," she said.

They took the money from the sale of the brokerage firm and bought a 60-acre tract with 6000 trees bearing grapefruit, limes, lemons, oranges, dates and figs. The grove was beautiful, so was the house that went with it; there was, however, one trivial handicap. Neither knew anything about raising fruit.

The deal became effective on December 31, 1945. They spent New Year's eve in their new home, in the midst of the grove. The next morning Bill awakened first. "Susan," he said, "I'll pull up the blind so we can look out at all those oranges and grapefruit." He pulled up the blind. They looked and neither said anything. The impossible had happened—there was half an inch of snow on the ground.

Understandably, they didn't have it too good at first. It was mostly work and learning, with little money coming in. They experimented with new products. They canned dates, spiced dates, coated dates with brandy; they pickled figs, distilled an amber liquid called Passion Fruit Juice, candied citrus peel and made pecans into patties. Finally it began to pay off.

They were over the financial hump. They could relax at night, sit on their front lawn, watch the spread of stars overhead, and listen to the night noises of the desert—the deep hoot of the horned owl, the high-pitched bark of the fox, the howl of the coyote singing to the moon or perhaps to his missus.

The pretty girl, dressed in a bright sweater and slacks, stepped on the running board of her automobile, shielded the sun from her face with a road map and said, exasperated, "Will someone *please* tell me how to get to the Petrified Forest?"

A Forest Ranger, standing nearby, grinned. "Lady," he said, "you're smack-dab in it right now."

I had come up from Tucson and Phoenix across the Apache trail and through some of the most impressive scenery to be found anywhere. Now I was in the upper part of Arizona. The girl, on the running board, had expected—in common with many people—to find trees turned to stone and standing upright. Actually, the Petrified Forest is a 92,000-acre National Monument including five so-called forests of petrified logs.

It is doubtful, according to naturalists, that many of the trees even grew in this particular vicinity. They were probably swept into the area by flood waters and buried in the semitropical marshes which covered this land millions of years ago.

A few miles beyond the Petrified Forest is the Painted Desert, a 300-mile stretch of desert badlands tinted fantastic shades of orange, blue, red, yellow and brown by iron and other minerals in the soil.

Following Highway 66, to the west, I came to the Barringer Meteorite Crater, located between Winslow and Flagstaff, six miles off the main highway. The crater itself is a gaping hole in the mesa land; it is the story behind the crater which makes it fascinating.

About 50,000 years ago, a tremendous cluster of meteorites, believed to weigh between a million and ten million tons, plunged from outer space at a speed of many miles a second and gouged out a crater which today, after thousands of years of erosion, is nearly a mile in diameter and, measured from the tip of its elevated rim, 570 feet deep.

Within a few miles of the crater is the American Meteorite Museum, presided over when I was last there by a small, wiry man named Dr. Harvey H. Nininger who had spent more than twenty-five years studying and collecting meteorites. He had in his museum workshop more than 5000 stones and lumps of iron, which plunged from the sky and landed on the earth's surface. He shopped for meteorites like a housewife for a good loin of pork, paying a dollar a pound and up for any meteorite that struck his fancy. One of the meteorites, when found by Nininger, was being used as an anvil by a Mexican blacksmith. Another was being used as a weight on a sauerkraut barrel.

What happened when the cluster of meteorites smashed into what is now Arizona? "A scene of violence impossible to re-create," says Nininger. "A column of fire pierced the atmosphere. The earth quivered and rocked. Rock fragments fell in a mighty shower. The land throbbed again and again as though struck with a mighty hammer."

Flagstaff is a town with a genuine frontier flavor. It never had a boom, never had a bust, believes in comfortable living and is content with its lot. During the winter, the snow is likely to get a couple of feet deep, and for a long time the civic leaders seemed ashamed of it, what with Phoenix and Tucson frolicking in the sun. Then along came a man named Al Grasmoen and his wife, Ven, and demonstrated that the snow was really an asset. On a mountain fourteen miles north of Flagstaff, the Grasmoens opened a ski resort called the Snow Bowl. The first customers showed up wearing cowboy boots and hats. Today, on a week end, the slopes are thronged by hundreds of skiers. The senior classes of high schools in southern Arizona sometimes are given a trip to the Snow Bowl as a graduation present; for many it is their first experience with snow.

A two hours' drive north from Flagstaff—and the road is open throughout the winter—is the Grand Canyon, one of the great sights of the world. People many times have tried to describe it or paint it and few have succeeded; it has too many moods, too many shifting colors. Upon first looking at this chasm, a mile deep and ten miles across, most people are awed, overtaken with what—for lack of a better expression—I'll call cosmic intimidation.

Most visitors arriving at the Canyon ask two questions: "What caused it?" and "When did it happen?" The answers to the questions are: The brawling Colorado River; over a period of millions of years.

The Canyon isn't easy to visualize. You look at this massive cleft in the earth stretching for miles on every side and the thread of river down below. (At close range, you can see this isn't a thread of river but a giant with tremendous power.) It's hard enough for your imagination to bridge 10,000 years or even 1000 years; as for bridging millions of years—well, let's say that Nature has been doing nip-ups on this planet a lot longer than man; it isn't reassuring to contemplate, but it could be that man is overmatched.

There are numerous stories, some of them true, about the first comments of visitors looking into the Canyon. There was the little boy who wrote in his diary, "Today I spit a mile"; the Vassar co-ed who cooed, "Gee, isn't it cute"; the movie director who observed, "O.K., we've seen it, let's get on to L.A."

A favorite story of the Rangers deals with the Englishman who came all the way from London to see the Canyon. While looking through the binoculars at the Yavapai observation point, he was interrupted again and again by a loud-mouthed man who was determined to share his enthusiasm for the Canyon not only with his wife but with the Englishman as well.

Finally, the man slapped his wife and the Englishman on the shoulders simultaneously and boomed:

"By golly, folks, it sure does beat hell, doesn't it?"

For the first time the Englishman removed his attention from the binoculars. "My word," he said, "you've been everywhere, haven't you?"

The Canyon, from top to bottom, is filled with animal and plant life. Deer walk along the highways, and if a car stops, they're likely to stick their heads through an open window to beg for food. There are mountain lions who prey on the deer. It has the smack of a tall story, but Rangers insist that a few years ago two elderly sisters from Philadelphia saw a mountain lion sitting alongside a canyon road, figured it was tame like the deer, got out of the car and offered the lion titbits. The lion, understandably startled, backed away. The sisters moved closer. The lion retreated again, and when the sisters approached for the third time, he bounded off into the timber. The sisters, curiously, weren't in much danger—a mountain lion, the Rangers say, won't attack a human unless it is wounded or suffering from rabies. (This story is not guaranteed to convince a mountain lion.)

In the Canyon there also are mules. Except in the worst weather, visitors ride mules down the Canyon walls, a sixteen-mile round trip. (The south rim of the Canyon is open the year around, with excellent accommodations at El Tovar Hotel.) The mules are especially trained for the Canyon trip. Kickers and buckers get special attention. Trainers hitch an automobile tire to the hind leg of a kicker; no matter how hard he kicks, the tire comes back and whacks him. If he is a bucker, the tire is attached to his saddle; when the mule bucks, the tire jounces around, slapping him just about everyplace a mule can be slapped. Unless he is a fool—and most mules are wise when their own comfort is involved—he gives up in disgust.

At the Canyon I met one of the world's most profound students of mule psychology. He was a stubby man with white whiskers and he bore the improbable name of Colonel Custer Yarberry. He was about eighty, give or take a few years, and since the age of ten he had been currying mules, coaxing mules, cussing mules. He had been a mule trainer and handler at the Canyon for more than thirty years. His views on mules were pointed. "The only gentle mule," he observed, "is the one whose ornery bones have been bleaching in the sun for a quarter of a century."

I left the Canyon remembering Yarberry's final counsel: "A mule is a good deal like a woman. You can be scratching her between the ears and she can be nuzzling you and the next thing you know she's likely to kick you clean over Gabriel's left shoulder."

Heading back toward southern Arizona, I passed through the domed, brilliantly colored rocks of Oak Cliff Canyon and stopped in the little town of Sedona, the home of Max Ernst, dean of American surrealist painters. With his wife, Dorothea Tanning, also an artist, Ernst moved in 1947 from Paris to Sedona, where he set about building his own house by hand. (He decorated the walls, incidentally, before he got around to roofing the living room.) When I asked why he had come to Sedona, he gestured toward the red cliffs towering above his home. "That's the reason," he said.

After the arrival of Ernst and his wife other artists moved in and the sleepy trading center of Sedona is showing signs of becoming an art colony. This influx of arty newcomers is looked upon with skepticism by some of the old-timers. I spoke with an old man named Bill Fredericks, who had lived in Arizona, and the Arizona territory, for more than sixty years, trapping wild horses, now and then doing a little prospecting. For thirty years he had lived in a cabin, deep in the Canyon country outside Sedona, alone except for his dogs, the jack rabbits and an occasional mountain lion.

The day I saw him he tugged at the one suspender holding up his droopy pants, spat carefully over the front stoop of his cabin and said: "I liked it better in the old days when a man could be left alone. Arizona is changing too fast—too many dudes and gadgets." The old man snorted grumpily and looked at the surrounding cliffs. "Time's finally come when this country ain't safe. A few years back I decided to take a trip; I was out on my horse, minding my own business, thinking hard the way a man can on horseback, when all of a sudden there was an awful screeching and yowling and the next thing I knew I woke up in a hospital with a broken leg and a nurse standing beside my bed.

"'What happened?' I asked her, and she peers at me like maybe I'm a mite touched and says, 'Man, you got hit by a train,' and sure enough I had."

He hitched a thumb in his suspender and sighed. "Yep, Arizona's changing so fast, old-timers like me can't keep up with her. Reckon the time's coming when I'll have to clear out of here. Just too blamed much traffic."

New Mexico

by OLIVER LA FARGE

Not so long ago a merchant in the town of Española, New Mexico—which lies some twenty-five miles north of Santa Fe at the junction of U. S. Routes 64, 84, and 285—requested an Eastern manufacturer for an estimate on a sizable order of his product. The manufacturer sent back an estimate in pesos, with instructions as to the type of international bank draft he would require. The Española man had a lot of fun answering that letter.

A New Mexican never ceases to be surprised to hear visitors—standing within sight of a Chevron filling station, a clearly labeled United States post office, and a Coke-advertising drugstore, with a movie theater right down the street—ask the tariff on a purchase they are contemplating "when we take it back to the States." Often the tourists are distinctly sorry to be disillusioned, and offer considerable resistance.

Nevertheless, New Mexico belongs to the United States family, species *Western*, subspecies *Southwestern*; it's un-American only in its thoroughly American insistence on being its own kind of place. If you ask a New Mexican what constitutes the Southwest, he will name New Mexico and Arizona; after hesitation, he may add the adjacent portions of Colorado, Utah and Nevada. California, Texas, and Oklahoma he rejects, for reasons which will appear later.

The state partakes of the nature of all its species. It is large, the fifth largest in the Union, 122,634 square miles—but we don't think of ourselves as being so big, it's just that so many of the other states are smaller. The population is increasing fairly rapidly, but by Eastern standards it remains sparse. Its lowest portion, in the southeast, dips below 3000 feet—which to a New Mexican is virtually sea level—is intolerably hot in summer, and achieves subtropical flora and fauna where there is sufficient moisture. In the north, its mountains climb high; two of its highest peaks, Truchas and Wheeler, reach above 13,000 feet. There we have ski runs, and at the highest levels you might encounter even white ptarmigan, if you are very lucky and your lungs hold out.

Between those extremes the variety is great. You can be camping up in the northern mountains, and in the morning break up your camp under blue spruce and fir, wrangling your horses out of the lush grass and the columbines in the meadow where you caught your breakfast trout. By noon you can take your break under cottonwoods in an irrigated section of orchards and corn and chili fields, and camp that night in desert where you are lucky, and distinctly relieved, when you find the water hole. You could, alternatively, stay in the mountains until the heavy winter snows close you in.

The state has flat, drab, repulsive, strangely fascinating desert by the mile, dramatic, colorful canyon country, and vast spaces of open, sparse, yet productive range land. It has little Spanish villages of adobe houses, as close-clustered as medieval towns around their miniature plazas and churches.

You can fish for trout in clear streams and mountain lakes, and you can camp by arroyos which, if you dig down a few feet under their dry sands, may or may not yield up that seep of water which will sustain life—and down which the roaring waters of a cloudburst that happened fifty miles away can come at sixty miles an hour in a wall ten feet high, with a haze of dust hovering over the rushing wall and whole trees revolving in its mass.

We have certain conventional expectations of beauty, in mountains, in combinations of green land and water, in gaily painted cliffs or bright desert, but the perceptive eye learns to see beauty in less obvious forms. Much of New Mexico's real estate seems barren and monotonous on first sight; with a little time, as with the sea, those who live with it before their eyes learn to follow the constantly shifting moods, the delicate and incessant changes of light from day to day and from hour to hour, which give that empty-seeming country a life of its own.

Like most Western states, to a usually beautiful landscape New Mexico adds qualities of spaciousness, grandeur and drama. It also achieves softness. Its mountains, very old, lying at the southern end of the chain of the Rockies, do not rise to the line of eternal snow; relatively few peaks reach above timber line. They are not jagged but worn round by aeons of time. One might say that, like so much in this new-old state, they are older and mellower than the mountains of its neighbors.

Most Western states have, and exploit, Indians. New Mexico, next to Arizona, has by far the largest proportion of full bloods and of Indians living a basically Indian life. The presence of this picturesque element is one of the reasons why it is a great tourist state, to the profit of the Indians and of the community as a whole.

The Indians can be listed among the state's natural resources. Others are oil, gas, potash, pumice, and a scattering of other metals and minerals, to the list of which vanadium is the latest addition. These assets, and the lumber of its forests, have made wealth here and there, but they are not enough to make New Mexico rich. It is a ranching state, with cattle predominant in the center, south and east, sheep more to the north and west. Although your self-respecting cowpuncher still hates a lamb, the old, deadly sheep-and-cattle wars are over; the choice of which to run on a given range is made according to the nature of the feed and the terrain.

The average visitor, who wonders how animals can live on its sparse grazing lands, finds it hard to believe that New Mexico is also agricultural. Where there is water, it is.

Where there is water—that's the point. So seldom is there water, never is there enough water. In the richest parts of the mountains rainfall reaches thirty inches a year, but along the Rio Grande Valley the *average* is ten inches, which means that one dry year means hardship, several dry years in succession mean privation and ruin for men, crops and beasts. Of those few inches, much falls in storms so violent, in such masses, that the ground cannot absorb it and it runs off in flash floods. The dryest, most desert country is seamed, scarred and excavated by the violence of floodwaters. These waters are caught in the main rivers, but bring with them tons of silt, raising the river beds, so that another paradox of this hard land is the loss of tons of water and miles of good land through the development of marshes.

The life of the state, of the crops, of the grass which feeds the cattle and sheep, depends upon the winter snows and the chancy advent of gentle rains, what the Indians call she-rains, in July. A good snowfall in the highlands means steady water in the little creeks, which means in turn a flow in the irrigation ditches all through the growing season. Then the ribbons of fertile land above the watercourses will be richly green, there will be corn, wheat, apples, apricots, and alfalfa, the horses will be sleek, and in the fall fat lambs and calves will go to market and the drying strings of chili will make masses of scarlet against the warm brown walls of the adobe farmhouses.

Water is life, and the theft of water may be punished, extralegally, as one would punish the taking of life—which is one of the reasons why men are meticulous about closing their water gates the moment their time for irrigation is up. The last fight I know of occurred in one of the mountain villages in the dark. Epifanio Tal, as we may call him (the case did not come to court, so I don't want to use real names), had the water from midnight till two, Amadeo Fulano got it at two. Their watches did not agree. Epifanio still had the water running on his place when Amadeo went to open his gate, so he came storming across the field with his lantern in his hand. Both men were irritable from lack of sleep. Finally, Amadeo reached to turn off his neighbor's water, and Epifanio poked him in the stomach with his hoe handle, knocking him down. Epifanio picked up a stone and threw it, knocking Amadeo out cold. No one was seriously hurt and, both men being devout members of the cult known as *Penitentes*, the Elder Brother who was head of that order in their village stepped in and got them to patch up their quarrel.

Men may take the law in their own hands; there is also a special body of law dealing with water. As English common law never embraced irrigation, this body is based upon the ancient water laws of Spain.

The importance of water is personified in the famous Rio Grande. Take a look at it; it is a poor-seeming body of water, often no more than a muddy trickle, sometimes only a dry river bed, hardly worthy, anyone would say, of its high-sounding name or its place in the American mind. This meager stream is the subject of interstate disputes, of hearings in Congress, the occupation of special boards and committees. It is the subject of compacts between states and of treaties between the United States and Mexico; the construction of a dam near its headwaters may be a subject of international concern. The prosperity or reversion to desert of thousands of miles of land in both republics, from Colorado to the Gulf of Mexico, depends upon the vagaries of this unpromising-looking stream, and upon man's use and abuse of it and its tributaries.

The volume of water that moves in it is, in fact, considerable, but at every point along its length most of the constant flow is drawn off into the ditches, which is why it, and many other New Mexico rivers, seem so pitifully inadequate. The water may be flowing miles from the river bed, used to the last drop, and even so there is never enough.

In an acute form, then, New Mexico has the Western characteristic of too little water, which is one of the standard Western gripes. Another is that it is economically a colony, a producer of raw materials, much of the profits from which, including a considerable part of the profits of the cattle industry, are siphoned off to the East and West Coasts. The ultimate development of the state is to an alarming degree dependent upon the decisions of people to whom it is not home, is not essential, but merely an investment to be held only so long as it yields a good return.

In all of these things I have been describing a typical Western state with a few local peculiarities; New Mexico differs from all of her forty-nine sisters in far more than those. We are, for instance, a state which has the East on both sides of it, and much of the West to the east of it. The presence of California on the other side, with only our close sister, Arizona, between, is what puts us in the position of having the East on both sides; for Californians, in outlook, speech, habits, and in their less effulgent forms of raiment, are definitely Easterners. They form one of the two largest bodies of our tourists, and on the whole they are intelligent, appreciative visitors, even though it must be admitted that they do drive like madmen.

As to a large part of the West being to the east of us, I have reference to the sovereign (and don't forget it) state of Texas, and what seems to be its colony, Oklahoma. Texas claims above all to be The West, yet a New Mexican thinks of a Texan as being from, if not of, the East, and a New Mexican, Indian or non-Indian, will automatically speak of members of such Oklahoma tribes as Kiowas, Cheyennes or Osages as "eastern Indians."

Texas bulks large in our consciousness. For years, being a claiming sort of state, it claimed half of New Mexico, clear to the Rio Grande. It once even launched an invasion to annex the area. Latterly, the Texans have gone in for more peaceful conquest. Towards the Mexican border, in the area of the big cattle ranches, a large portion of the population derives from our neighbor to the south, while the eastern part of New Mexico, where it marches with the Lone Star State, is known as "the Texas Strip," because of the Texan dominance.

New Mexicans look down upon their great neighbor. Why shouldn't they? If they looked levelly towards the east, all they would see is sky. Any New Mexican can, and if given the opportunity will, tell you that New Mexico could be bigger than Texas if she chose to spread herself thin and flat, as her neighbor does. Texans, who comprise the other principal group of our tourists, condescend right back at us with vigor and often with charm.

An amiable sort of running feud goes on between the people of the two states, keeping both on their toes. When a Texan told me one time that he was a *real* old-timer, and that he personally had dug out the bed of the Pecos River, the Lord gave it to me to answer that, while he was doing that, I was up in the Sangre de Cristos melting snow to run in his ditch.

This exchange left us both happy and led to an agreeable acquaintance.

The Texan settlers form one of the elements in the endless diversity that is New Mexico. If they give the tone to the east and south, the north and west are colored and dominated by the Spanish-Americans.

The ancestors of these Spanish-Americans settled this country before Virginia or the Bay Colony existed, and have lived here ever since. They have been citizens of the United States for over a century, fought in the Civil War and in every major war since; they are devotedly patriotic, and as a regular thing send more than their share of men into the nation's battles.

New Mexico is the one place where the question of the hyphen is approached logically, although the logic leads to a beautiful illogic. All Americans except Indians are considered hyphenated; we are divided into two groups, Spanish-Americans and Anglo-Americans, and, just as in Salt Lake City even Jews are Gentiles, so here all but the Spanish are Anglo-American regardless of national origins.

One of the leading "Anglos" of Santa Fe is Chinese. About fifty years ago the *New Mexican,* the Santa Fe paper, mentioned that "a Chinaman" had arrived in town to open a laundry. He did. He brought his family. From the laundry he graduated to a restaurant which became, and remains, the most popular simple eating place in town.

The waitresses, Anglos and Spanish, work under the supervision of his wife, whom they address as "mother." I remember when his son, who later served with distinction in the Army Air Force, won the soap-box derby. The reception he gave at the leading hotel in town after his daughter's marriage, and the housewarming when the family, extended by marriages and grandchildren, moved into the houses they now occupy, are considered as among the largest and most chic Santa Fe has ever known. For some years he was chairman of the local Restaurateurs' Association. In this town, there is nothing surprising in all this, to him or to anyone else.

The Spanish settlers and conquerors, bringing with them old Spanish ways and an ancient faith, came from distant Mexico over deserts fiercer than any ocean, to conquer and convert a yet more ancient land. The Pueblo Indians had been planting their corn for centuries, and for centuries evolving their elaborate religion, the public manifestations of which, the great summer dances, are one of America's finest spectacles. For at least 2000 years men had farmed the little valleys; the art of irrigation was old and well established. Two dry-country farming peoples met. The native ones were conquered, revolted and drove out the conquerors; the Spaniards came back. In the end Indian and Spaniard settled down together to a harmonious pattern of social and cultural exchange and no little intermarriage, a pattern into which the Anglo-American newcomers are steadily merging.

These Spaniards were cut off from the world. A trip to the viceregal capital in Mexico was an adventure not to be lightly undertaken until, in recent days, the railroad and later the motor roads spanned the wastes, and the wild tribes that haunted them had been broken. North and east the mountains and prairies offered little attraction to the settler, and they, too, were thronged by wild tribes; to the west, the worst deserts of all cut the colony off from the West Coast. In speech and in customs the people kept and still keep much of 17th and 18th Century Spain, although in the last generation the language has decayed rapidly, soaking up English words and losing structure.

In the rural districts, old ways hold fast. The *velorio,* the lamenting wake for the dead, the wedding receptions with their great formality, vast eating and drinking, their dances led off by the bride in her wedding dress—and occasionally their fights—go on as they did 300 years ago. The people are still, by preference, wine drinkers, sweetish, heady wines, after the manner of Spain, and *cabrito,* a three-month-old kid roasted whole, remains, deservedly, a prime delicacy.

In some of the villages the *Penitentes,* a lay order with special ritual centering around Good Friday and Easter, maintain their practices. Because of excessive flagellation their rites were banned by the Catholic Church for a time, but the people refused to give them up. The present archbishop has wisely brought them under control by removing the ban and bringing the organization under the Church and into the open. Even in Santa Fe the religious processions are still maintained and the *alabados,* the traditional hymns, many of which were brought from Spain, are still sung.

West, north, and south of the Pueblo country, which was and is the main farming area, lay the various tribes of Apaches, the warriors, the raiders. They still hold to sections of their ancient range. On the Colorado border are the Jicarilla Apaches; in the southeastern part of the state, the Mescalero Apaches occupy the green, rich mountains which were once their ancient stronghold. In the northwestern corner some of the greatest of all the Apache tribes, the Navajos, are to this day trying to make a success of sheep ranching in a desert.

The Mescaleros and Jicarillas live in good grazing and timber country. They are prosperous, hard-working, and progressive. From the tourist point of view they don't offer much, as their old culture is almost gone. Some of the older Jicarilla men still wear their hair in braids, and a fair number of the women keep to the full-skirted, calico costume which became established among many tribes in the latter part of the last century. The Mescaleros offer less to the eye than that, but on the Fourth of July, if you can take hours of driving through very hot, bleak range country and rugged camping conditions, it is worth going to their celebration to see their renowned Crown Dance, a masked dance unlike any other, portraying the mountain spirits. The Jicarillas also have a masked ceremony, in which I have been allowed to participate in a very small way, but one should not try to attend uninvited.

Most people who know Apaches like them enormously and are enthusiastic about them. They are good friends and delightful companions. In the Southwest, at least, it is the common observation that Indians have a delightful sense of humor, and of all the tribes, the Apaches have the keenest and quickest. People sometimes ask me for examples, and then I am stumped, for it is not a humor of the formal joke; the things that made me laugh so hard became merely flat when repeated out of context. It is a sense of the ridiculous, kidding which is never malicious, a constant, pleased awareness that the funny side of life is also always with us and a readiness to indicate it by a quick, unexpected phrase. A form of it is in the roar of laughter that shook the medicine lodge when old Maipi, showing the young men how a certain song should be sung, lifted his voice so well that his upper plate jumped out and fell on the drum—and above all in the fact that he laughed as hard as the rest. It is in a thousand lesser, less obvious moments.

Apaches, including Navajos, are something else again when they are angry; you want to stay away from them. I remember when an Apache leader decided to put me off the reservation. Things were really sticky for a while, but fortunately there was a division of opinion, and he dropped the project. Later we became friends. When the women get angry, you want to get clear out of the country. I have seen Navajo women, in their velveteen blouses and their full, calico skirts and their jewelry, rising up one by one from where they sat behind their men in council and shouting at them to start fighting, and have watched the men's uneasy response and mounting tension. It was then that I understood why Navajo women are given such names as War Encircling, War in the Mountains, Followed to War, and Dancing for War. It was a profound relief when some influential leaders talked them down. I wasn't involved in what had made them so angry, but once they got going, I thought they might include me on principle.

By comparison with the tribes now known as Apache, the Navajos live in deep poverty on their ash heap of a desert, ever vainly presenting to the Great White Stepfather a dreadful bill of broken promises. Nonetheless, they have kept their old spirit and many of their old ways. Their big ceremonies are dances lasting all night for several nights, and most of them are held late in the fall. Attending them means driving over bad roads, rough camping, and sitting in the cold night on hard, cold ground. For those hardy enough, it is worth while. The dances, masked or unmasked, seen by the light of bonfires, the gatherings in themselves, the strange, hypnotic music— all these add up to a genuinely moving experience.

It is the Pueblos whom the tourists visit most, and with reason. Their villages are on or within easy reach of the paved highways; most conveniently, many of their dances occur annually on fixed dates. The villages, of warm, earth-colored adobe houses, are charming in themselves. The people are friendly by habit, and from long experience know how to deal with strangers. Almost all of them engage in some form of craftwork. The variety of their dances is bewildering. It is almost impossible to judge between them, but the most famous, and among the finest, are the Corn Dances of San Felipe, Cochití and Santo Domingo, in May, July and August. These are performed by lines of fifty or more men and women accompanied by drums and a powerful chorus.

When you attend one, you will be at first a trifle bewildered by the sheer mass, then fascinated by the costumes, the color, the music. Shortly after this you will find the performance monotonous, the sun hot, the ground hard, the dust annoying. This is the point at which many people leave. If you stay on, *and if you keep quiet,* the rhythms of drum, song and dance, the endlessly changing formations of the lines of dancers, the very heat and dust, unite and take hold. You will realize slowly that what looked simple is complex, disciplined, sophisticated. You will forget yourself. The chances are then that you will go away with that same odd, empty, satisfied feeling which comes after absorbing any great work of art.

Simply to complete the list of the assorted elements that make up the population of the state, we should note that its northwest corner touches the southeast corner of Utah. That point is inside the Navajo Reservation, but the Mormons have filtered down into the San Juan River Valley just to the east of it. To New Mexicans, Mormons are a variety of Anglo, however they may classify themselves. Their settlements are characterized by the planting of poplars and roses; the people by industry, temperance, hospitality, and great kindness towards strangers.

The most famous and most visited part of New Mexico is the central valley, the strip along the Rio Grande from Albuquerque north past Santa Fe to Taos, guarded on the south by the Sandia, on the west by the Jémez, on the east by the Sangre de Cristo Mountains. It is an area about a hundred and fifty miles long by about sixty miles wide, possessing a special magic. Here for thousands of years people have been drawn and have stayed in the slow, sunlit peace between the mountains.

Here, as many thousands of years ago as your imagination desires, men hunted, and here they acquired the art of planting corn, squash, and beans. Other men, other tribes, joined them in one millennium or another, from the north, the east, and the west, to form the chain of settled, semicivilized villages and towns, some of them almost cities, which the Spaniards found here.

In this same area the Spaniards settled and stayed. They, too, like the Pueblos, were isolated from the ever-changing, corroding, restless currents of time. The Mountain Men, dropping down into Taos for a spree, married, built houses, became one with the country. Currents from the main stream of the Anglos' westward migration flowed in between the mountains. The valley absorbed them all.

Latterly, in the last thirty years or so, there has occurred a curious, mixed immigration of artists and anthropologists who, like so many others, came to exploit and stayed to participate. Their influence has been profound. Art and science formed a firm alliance and the two made the earlier comers aware of the riches that lay in these many times and cultures, not superimposed, but existing and interchanging side by side. It was they who stopped and reversed the existing trend to replace the native adobe architecture as rapidly as possible with commonplace brick and frame houses.

The old Mountain Men dressed in a mixture of Indian and Spanish styles because that was the kind of clothing available. The artists and their surrounding group are likely to turn up in Indian moccasins, sombreros from Old Mexico, and any combination one can imagine in between. Out of an original, Western informality they have developed an atmosphere in which everyone, of either sex, dresses as he pleases, while adaptations of Spanish and Navajo women's dresses have ceased to be merely local and have spread throughout the country.

They are a picturesque group, these latecomers, ranging from what, since Dorothy Thomas' story on the subject, is known as the "fainting robin," the starveling poet without paper or typewriter, to the—shall I call her "expatriate"?—of wealth who may become the fainting robin's patron. They include artists and scientists of national and international standing. They will join a party, go to Mexico, or take off for the Navajo country at the drop of a sombrero, are active in local politics, have fifth columns in most of the newspapers, and by and large are steady, respectable workers. The kick which they, and the Indians, get out of observing the appearance and antics of the tourists is no greater than the kick the tourists get, legitimately, out of them.

I remember, in particular, John Sloan. Since the 1920's he had been the dean of Santa Fe painters, an indestructible man, everyone thought, and a leader in every imaginable interest from renovating the annual fiesta, which had become a shabby affair, to winning the Indians their rights. The news of his death came as many of his associates, painters such as Randall Davey, Josef Bakos, and Will Shuster, were on their way to a musicale given by a woman who had been one of his good friends and patrons. The musicale went off all right, but around the drinks afterward there was a sort of silent wake, remembering the landmarks of his old, faded velveteen Navajo shirt and his silver concho belt, remembering the unconventional stunts he used to start, sometimes in that very house, and looking at his magnificent portrait of the owner. There will never be anyone else like him, but the young ones keep coming up; new movements, new art centers, new rebellions are organized annually. The art colony that stretches loosely from Albuquerque to Taos is made up of extreme individualists, but its strength is collective, and it is continuously self-renewing.

To this rich mélange the last war brought the strangest addition of all, the atomic complex. On the eastern slope of the Jémez Mountains, where the adolescents of Los Alamos Ranch School used to study their books and ride their ponies, the great center of Los Alamos was established. It has brought into the valley an increment of people, mostly young and energetic, of far higher than average intelligence, education, and artistic sensitivity.

Just outside Albuquerque are Kirtland Air Force Base and Sandia Army Base, both concerned with the new weapons. In these installations is to be found one of the highest concentrations of intellectual commissioned officers anywhere in our armed services; Army colonels and Navy commanders with Ph.D. degrees are commonplace there. Considerably farther south, in the arid, open-range cattle country, are the White Sands Proving Grounds, where they shoot off the big rockets.

It gives us a queer feeling to have these activities in New Mexico, and to have their nerve center nestled cozily in the soft grandeur of the Jémez, overlooking the heart of our timeless valley. One has a feeling of some sort of violation, yet that feeling is based upon a dream, for out of this valley, as I have said, the young men keep going to war. There has been no greater violation than that a whole regiment of New Mexico men, out of the Spanish-speaking hill villages, from the country of the drawling cowhands, from the deserts and mountains of the Indians, a whole regiment of them, should have been lost on Bataan.

All of these elements give the state its character and give it, also, its quality of being at once rawly new and richly old, the home of peaceful farmers and craftsmen when Europe was at the bottom of the Dark Ages . . . and one of the newest states, full of hope and vinegar.

It is unfortunate that an honest description cannot stop at this point. It should be enough that on a Sunday a Pueblo Indian, having spent the preceding week cultivating his red, blue, and yellow corn in his ancestral field, will put on his Indian clothes to sing in the chorus of a dance in which his daughter, who during the week works at Los Alamos, will take the part of the Buffalo Maiden, that during the performance Spanish-American neighbors will kneel in the bower at one side of the pueblo's plaza to sing *alabados* before the image of its patron saint, while artists, scientists (both anthropologists and nuclear physicists), tourists and plain businessmen watch the performance with appreciation and respect. It should be enough, but it is not.

As in old melodramas, the lovely maiden, the happy home, are threatened by villains, of which here there are two principal ones. The first of these is a dwindling land base. In arid country, unirrigable land is used generally for grazing, and if the grazing is not carefully controlled, the grasses are eaten up, what shoots appear are consumed before seed can form, and the grass dies away. Then the hard rains carry off the soil, until the fertility has literally been mined out of the ground. This is happening over altogether too much of New Mexico.

The second villain is race hatred. In a community such as New Mexico the opportunity to demonstrate a real melting pot is priceless, and there are sections where that demonstration is being made. There are also sections, large ones, where the reverse is true. This is particularly the case where the Texas influence is strong, but it is not confined to those areas. An Indian may or may not be Jim Crowed, according to where he happens to land, regardless of whether or not that particular town makes a big noise about its Indians for the tourist trade.

The Spanish-Americans are politically powerful and sophisticated; nonetheless they, too, encounter race hatred. In parts of the state they are truly equals, and Spanish-Anglo marriages are common; in others, notably in the south and east, they, too, encounter a frank Jim Crow system.

Neither of these villains has as yet actually obtained a mortgage on the old homestead or tied the heroine across the railroad track. They are still more threat than imminent danger; and powerful groups in the state are working to defeat them.

What is New Mexico, then? How sum it up? It is a vast, harsh, poverty-stricken, varied, and beautiful land, a breeder of artists and warriors. It is the home, by birth or by passionate adoption, of a wildly assorted population which has shown itself capable of achieving homogeneity without sacrificing its diversity. It is primitive, undeveloped, overused, new, raw, rich with tradition, old and mellow. It is a land full of the essence of peace, although its history is one of invasions and conflicts. It is itself, an entity, at times infuriating, at times utterly delightful to its lovers, a land that draws and holds men and women with ties that cannot be explained or submitted to reason.

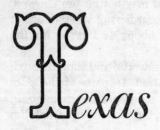

Texas

by SEAN O'FAOLAIN

What does the average traveler expect of Texas? Not much in the way of joys and pleasures, if I may judge by the slightly astonished headline I once achieved in a Waco newspaper. It said: IRISHMAN HERE FOR PLEASURE! All I can say is that if tourists, native or foreign, do often visit Texas for any other reason than pleasure, it is very foolish of them.

Still, I find it hard to blame them. Texas, in one way and another, has had a poor press, chiefly along the lines of:

> My grandfather lived in Texas,
> He couldn't write his name.
> He signed his checks with x's
> But they were worth a helluvalot just the same.

And we all know that Texans boast and brag from dawn to dark. I prefer to call it the Texan Flourish. Every yarn about Texas has to be taller than the last. Only yesterday a friend assured me on his Bible Belt oath that he once bought a bottle of whisky in Laredo marked *Guaranteed Not More Than 6 Weeks Old.*

If the average stranger expects anything at all of Texas he expects little more than emptiness, fat cattle, lean men, flat-chested women, oil derricks as thickly sown as pine plantations, and oil millionaires with more money than taste. He probably comes into the state from the east, from Shreveport, along Route 80. He plans a quick look at Dallas, chiefly because his wife wants to see the Neiman-Marcus store, and then drives as rapidly as he can through Amarillo for an ungratefully rapid exit to Santa Fe. And we have to admit that as he races northwestward from Dallas and Fort Worth, over that level-to-barely-rolling treeless, birdless, sun-scorched, wind-torn, dusty land called the Panhandle, he is not likely to find in nature a great deal to satisfy his eye or mind, unless he happens to be a man who loves expansive spaces of earth and air, stars at eye level and endless processions of little cloudlets which are not worth a damn to farmers longing for rain; or unless he is interested in such earthy treasures as fat stock, or green belts of wheat or oil or natural gas. No, this is not an exciting route; and those long, level, empty roads lure one on and on—out of Texas altogether. I am afraid most of us who have gone this way cheer with relief at the sight of the first New Mexican mesa. I confess that this was the sum of my own experience the first time I came here many years ago.

It is not the best way (nor the right frame of mind) for an entry into Texas, or an exit out of it. I think we should come in from the extreme southeast, through the shadowy pines and rice fields behind the Gulf—come in, perhaps, across Town Bluff Lake, under the longleaf, the shortleaf and the loblolly pines, beside the Alabama-Coushatta Indian reservation and that weird region called the Big Thicket, where wild grape and vines have made an almost impassable jungle, and so on down into Houston through the Sam Houston National Forest. Or we could take Route 87 by the woods and salt-marsh grasses of the coastal prairies of Jefferson and Chambers counties. Or, and this may be the best entry of all, we could drive due south for 350 miles through Dallas, Waco, Austin and San Antonio, more or less following the old Shawnee cattle trail.

Then, at San Antone, as they call it (some say S'Antone), we might take a wide sweep through Corpus Christi on the Gulf, to see the great cattle ranches of the southern tip—the King Ranch is down here, a million acres of it. Then north and west up the Rio Grande, with its citrus orchards and green farmlands, and, higher up, its isolated, poorer, brush-covered Spanish-speaking regions like Zapata County, until the country begins to be cut by gorge and canyon and covered with mesquite, stunted oak, huisache, chaparral, and that pretty, silvery-gray shrub called cenizo, and scores more that I cannot name; until at last the land grows quite wild and mountainous beyond Big Bend National Park; and from there we go on to El Paso and out to the inevitable Santa Fe.

Here we become aware of one of the main frustrations of Texas— its size. For if we have followed this last route we shall have left out Houston, missed two thirds of the coast, ignored the whole east, and the whole of the vast region northwest of the *balcones* or balconies, as they call the great semicircular escarpment west of Waco, Austin and San Antonio. Yet immediately behind the *balcones* lies one of the most picturesque parts in the whole state, all of it simply crawling with the ghosts of cowboy tradition and early ranch history. I remember how poignantly this hill country came to haunt Frank Dobie when he was teaching American history at Cambridge University during the war. As he looked out over the fens at evening, and watched the Lincolnshires being herded into their stalls, he saw again the mirages, as it were, of tens of thousands of Longhorns striding out of the south, every spring, on their way up the long, long trail to Kansas and Montana, their spurred and jingling riders screwing up their already sun-buttoned eyes to peer through the dusted glare at far horizons.

What *can* any traveler hope to do with a state of such ridiculously dropsical proportions? The place is bigger than France. It is nearly three times the size of Scotland, Wales and England put together. It has the supreme impertinence to be eight times the size of Ireland. Indeed, I wonder whether it isn't, after all, something of a frustration for Texans themselves to live cooped up inside 170,000,000 acres of state; a prison composed of 254 counties, of which nobody can ever hope to know intimately more than half a dozen? For vastness, also, can be a prison.

A mayor of Dallas once said to me, "This isn't a state—it's an empire," and the flourish of it was magnificently Texan; but I gathered that it must be very bothersome to feel that you are living in an empire when you are actually living in one-fiftieth part of a nation—and when, damn it, nothing would satisfy the nation but to add as the forty-ninth state a chunk of land even bigger than Texas. People sometimes say, irritably, that Texans are too big for their boots; perhaps the truth is that they are? I swear that this alleged Texan bragging—in so far as it has any real existence outside of joke books—is nothing but a sob for the lost lone star, a psychological compensation for lost national glory. As a member of a race which is not incapable of an occasional flourish, I know the disease very well.

Still, vastness is not without its virtues, such as widespread variety, dramatic contrasts, strange contradictions. In climate, for instance. Within thirty-six hours one could fly to Dallas from the hot sun of Los Angeles to find that bitter sleet, snow and rain, driving before a savage northwester, have shrouded the city in whiteness, covered every twig with hoarfrost, bent every birch into a grounded hoop; and then go on to find Waco wrapped in a low-lying fog from the Gulf; then come down through drizzling rain into a shivering Houston, and there, the next morning, have to fling open the windows and switch on the Oriental *punkah* in the ceiling to kill the exhausting heat crawling in from the sea at a humid 70°. Brownsville, at the mouth of the Rio Grande, can be subtropical; El Paso, dry as a bone; and I remember Lev Aronson, that excellent first cellist of the Dallas Symphony, telling me that the orchestra once had to play with their jackets off in Beaumont, east of Houston, in the merry month of March. The ideal months to travel here are April and May, and again in October and November.

Do Texans realize this vast variety of their state? I have a suspicion that they do not. I recall that impressive little chat I had one dull morning at Waco airport:

Me: (*With Old World pessimism*) That ceiling looks pretty low. Think we'll take off on time?

He: (*With New World optimism*) Of course we'll take off on time!

Me: You never know. Planes don't always.

He: Planes *always* take off on time from Waco. This is one of the safest and surest airports in the state of Texas.

What impressed me about this brief snatch was that it never occurred to this good citizen that before a plane can take off from one part of Texas it has to come in from some other part. In fact we had to wait an hour for our connection. It is a common jibe at Texans that they do not recognize the rest of the Union; in my observation Texans often don't recognize the rest of Texas. It is just too big.

So big, indeed, that changes in its landscape seem to occur insidiously. When, for instance, we drive west across the state we hardly notice the flatness beginning to acquire a faint roll like a swelling sea; that what was the green of the corn is now the green of ricefields (Texas and Louisiana are the two greatest rice states in the United States); that the tall trees are now not pines but oaks; that the oaks grow more small and stunted as the tall gums and the myrtles fade behind. Bit by bit we become aware of mesquite or cactus. Then that pallid grass, so affectingly pensive in the evening light of summer, or when winter mists it lightly, blends into coffee-colored, into sun-browned, into hard, black knobbly land where the little trees look like tethered black ponies. There is less cotton and more cattle—from the university tower at Austin one can see cotton to the east and cattle to the west. There are fewer fans, goatees, Negroes in old straw hats, louvered doors, fewer hotels with marble floors, fewer cloves in the hams or lobsters on the menu, more high-heeled boots, more white hats, more dust, more rodeos.

West of San Antone we are in game country among accumulating hills, all cedar-darkened and laurel-sheened. The creeks grow dry. White stones glare. The sky grows more merciless as the land grows more arid. But now we can bear it better because we breathe more easily as the land rises. Whereas at Austin we were only 650 feet above sea level, we find at Amarillo that we are 3600 feet up. Guadalupe Peak, if we should go that way, soars 8000 feet above the waters of the Gulf. All these changes develop slowly in an 800-mile drive.

Nature here is endlessly inventive. Even if one has no special interest in farming or folklore, bird life or plant life, Texas instan-taneously evokes one's curiosity about such things and keeps it on the alert: as when we discover, for example, that the political, social and even military history of Texas has grown with the very grass—the food of the bison on whose flesh the original nomad Comanches and Apaches lived—and that in the end the Indians were beaten out of their sheltering plains and hills not by rifles turned against them but against the wandering buffalo. It was with the decimation of the buffalo that the Indian menace began to wilt and old strong points like Fort Griffin became ghost towns, their work done. But empires fade and grass still grows. It went on nourishing those later ruminants of the prairies, the Longhorns of the great ranches.

Underground in Texas there is great wealth; underfoot there is also great wealth. The Agricultural and Mechanical College of Texas has estimated that the state's grasslands carry some 7,500,000 range cattle, 6,500,000 sheep and 2,500,000 goats.

I am a complete dilettante in plant lore, but in Texas I found myself fascinated by the subject, especially by the cacti. They are at their best across the Pecos River—its crescent encloses the rough country between Big Bend and El Paso. Some of the plants rise to six feet; some, the so-called globose type, spread three feet. All blossom tenderly—a rare sight for us Europeans—though some briefly and pathetically, dying, after so hard a life, so long a labor, within three short hours. I was delighted to lay eyes at last on the maguey. I could have drawn the maguey for you (and so could many inhabitants of northern Europe) at the age of seven: you find it all over our seaside parks—in green-painted cast iron! It is a sort of agave, something like the aloe, and of remarkable beauty. But, as for color, there must be several thousands of native flowers in this state whose dun soil, in its proper seasons, blossoms in acres upon acres of radiant hues. So much for the travelers who suppose Texas to be just one vast, blank, gray, dusty, monotonous state of uniformity.

The human surprises are just as varied. I recall my visit to Waco, where I had gone to look at Paul Baker's brilliant experimental theater (is there another like it in the United States, or even in Europe outside of Paris?). Within two hours on the campus I was informed that this daring venture is part of a Baptist-controlled university so conservative that it conferred an honorary degree on Harry Truman *in absentia* because he was known to take a drink occasionally; that no alcoholic drink could be bought openly in the town, other than watery beer; that to get hard liquor all one has to do is to drive a couple of miles into the next county; that any doctor could, in any case, prescribe a half dozen highballs for me if I really wanted them; that gambling is outlawed, as everywhere else in Texas, but that about twenty miles away first-class cockfights are held regularly, and I am sure that nobody imagines that nobody bets at cockfighting; that up to a little time ago, girl students on the University campus were not allowed to smoke or use make-up; and that I could buy the most sexy magazines at any drugstore. I may add that in this same Waco one may find 122 churches representing twenty-two different sects—a higher proportion between pastors and population than in Roman Catholic Ireland.

How can any place be so liberal in some things (most Baptist clergymen are against segregation) and so narrow-minded in others? I asked this question a score of times in Texas, and the nearest to a sensible answer came to me one night in talk with a wealthy oilman from San Patricio county—he was of Irish descent and a Roman Catholic. He said, "It all depends on the way you look at the world. In the Bible Belt the great idea is to prove to the good Lord by your strict behavior in this wicked world that you are worthy of enjoying the next. But this is God's good world. After all, He made it! Why can't we go ahead and enjoy the fruits of it? Within reason, of course. Another glass?" I am happy to say that distilled spirits are legal in Saint Patrick's county.

In Texas I find that it is wiser to measure matters by years rather than by miles. To give a simple instance, Fort Worth and Dallas are only thirty-two miles apart; each has its own meed of modernity, but essentially Dallas is much more modern, and far less traditional in the Texan sense, chiefly because it is a big mercantile and banking center, whereas Fort Worth is essentially the headquarters for the West Texas cattle industy. The one is as self-consciously culture-minded as the other is proudly cattle-minded—famous for the splendid Holsteins and Jerseys that have made Tarrant county one of the best dairy counties in Texas. If these two cities were not divided by many generations in their outlook, one would not find in Dallas one of the best symphonies west of the Mississippi; one of the best newspapers, the Dallas *News;* a lively theater; a fine periodical, *The Southwest Review;* first-rate bookshops; and, most surprising and welcome of all, a wonderful restaurant, La Vieille Varsovie, which truly ranks among the best in the United States; and every woman in America knows that one corner of Dallas, Neiman-Marcus's famous store, is forever Fifth Avenue.

The distance between Houston and San Antonio divides them by a bare two hundred miles; there is an age of difference between them in temperament. San Antonio *is* far older, of course—it was first visited by the Spanish in 1691—but it is also the nearest large city to the Mexican border, and hence more cosmopolitan, with a soothing Latin tempo. My own first impression of this charming city was that it was too good to be true; which meant that I feared I was being delighted by charms that, as they were the more familiar to me as a European, were thereby the less Texan—and after all I was in search of Texas. My lasting impression of San Antonio is a blend of envy and happy recollection; I leave it to Texans to decide how Texan they consider a city which offered me Italian grand opera, a symphony, affecting and sometimes lovely 18th-Century

Spanish missions; and another welcome restaurant, La Louisiane, allegedly French but more inclined, I thought, to serve Creole and Mexican food.

I still feel the general *ambiance* of San Antonio's picturesque Southern detail; see the rotting, green, sunshot, semitranslucent banana leaves, the light, delicate greenery trailing over old ironwork balconies, the tall palms, the large, cool, dim lobbies with marble floors like Italian houses, the magnolia, redbud, persimmon, *lluvia d' oro*. I respond again to their colors, their scent, their tropical suggestion. I feel the dark skins, hear the foreign words, taste the foreign food, remember the blend of Southern feeling and Northern conscience, as evident in the Church festivals, as in the double feature I saw at a neighborhood cinema in the Latin Quarter— *The Blood of Jesus* and *The Last of the Desperadoes*. I relax in the memory of the slow, sleepy, sun-drowsed tempo broken suddenly by noisy fiesta gaiety. I could go on and on, nostalgically. This is, to me, the most affecting town in Texas.

Drive on from there to Houston. What a leap in time! Houston is now the second-ranking port in the United States in point of movement of tonnage, rich in industries of every kind; busy, noisy, grinding away down by the ship channel and the turnabout like some dockside corner of Marseilles; inhabited by a great many people of wealth ("The residential part of Houston," says a folder, "now has over *One Thousand* millionaires"); and inhabited also by many people of taste. It possesses one of the most gracious residential suburbs in America; it has an excellent symphony; fine bookshops; a lavishly endowed Museum of Fine Arts; a passable restaurant or two; good clubs—the Petroleum, the Coronado, the Tejas.

Yet Houston is so very raw and recent, and in such a hurry, that while most of it has outrun its own past, much of it has not yet caught up with its own future. Its taxis are musty. Its hotels are unadmirable. Its press is away back. Its business center looks as if some superbillionaire had mail-ordered a dozen blocks of Manhattan C.O.D., to be dumped down among the old tin cans and slithering water rats of what once was Buffalo Bayou and now is the ship channel—where one sees masts and funnels teeming day and night. To say, then, that San Antonio and Houston are two hundred miles apart is to say nothing. They are two hundred years divided, at the very least.

Not, I hasten to say, that Houston is not an enormously exciting town with its own bizarre beauty. I remember vividly its brief streets of skyscrapers, so often crowned by clouds, ending as abruptly as if cut off by an ax. They gave me the sensation that this is a rapidly built and still unfinished city, and therefore a city gambling with time. I watched the evening skies from one of those high rooftops—the Gulf's gay sunset pink, ebbing faster and faster into a deeper blush and then into a sullen, sultry, stormy, dusky sea that suddenly vanishes completely, and one's eyes are drawn to the Manhattan lights of the city twinkling at one's feet. I remember those dramatic skies because they seemed to me to match this drama of the city's growth, and even of the growth of the whole state.

Houston is the natural dynamo and powerhouse of Texas. One cannot miss, immediately one arrives here, a sense of drive and competition that one gets nowhere else in the state. People move faster. You get a feeling that everybody is at least vicariously involved in the breakneck speed of the city's success, getting a kick by proxy out of the pervasive atmosphere of a gold-rush gamble.

I remember how entertained I was by the old taxi driver who acted as my native guide down to Galveston. He rolled out names to me as if they were dice, not men, assuming that every stranger must know all about the Cullens and the Joneses. I would say, "Do you mean Jesse Jones?" Or, "What was the history of this Cullen you are speaking about?" In his wonderful Texas drawl, like an expiring concertina with a hole in it, my driver would merely say, "Jesse Jones started working for eight bucks a month and made six hundred million"; or, "Cullen signed a check for fifty million for the University of Texas," just as if he were saying, "And then Aladdin got hold of an old magic lamp and——" Or he would point to some store, or factory and say, "Schlumberger's! That's a big outfit! What do they do? I dunno! But, hell, ain't it *big*?" And so on to more true fairy tales about this last get-rich-quick corner of America outside the uranium fields of Utah.

The things that gave me most pleasure here were to find that from as near as Eagle Lake, sixty-five miles away, you can bring into the streets of Houston quails, pheasants, pigeons, ducks; or to hear a youth of about twenty saying, as we looked at a dirty, built-around bit of bayou not three minutes from my hotel, "I used to swim here when I was a kid," as if he were an ancient-of-days remembering woodland ponds fifty miles out of town some seventy years ago; or, driving out past wonderful homes—pillared, snow-white, old Spanish, colonial style or *modernissimo*—set among mossed trees and well-watered lawns, hearing a friend driver saying, "So-and-so lives there; so-and-so lives here," just as in Beverly Hills one is shown the *palazzi* of movie stars. The whole place is as intimate as a country town crackling and sputtering with the latest gossip, though built to the proportions and with the amenities of a metropolis.

I recall the chat I had one evening about this with an elderly gentleman smoking a cigarillo in the lobby of my hotel; and especially his reply when I asked, "Austin, San Antone, Dallas, Houston—which would you live in if you had to choose?"

"Here—if I could make a couple of little changes."

"Such as?"

"Well, I'd put Houston where San Antone is, for the sake of the climate. I think I'd move the capital down from Austin. I'd like to see the Neiman-Marcus store transferred from Dallas, and there's a mighty good restaurant up there that I'd like to have near at hand. I'd install a good theater, a livelier newspaper, a few first-class hotels, a bigger airport, more public parks, a race track and a couple of drinking night clubs with gals. Otherwise Houston's perfect."

I still do not know if he meant it. Texas humor is as dry as most of Texas.

No stereotyped Texan, then. No monolithic Texas. Rather, a Texas full of variety, contradictions, idiosyncrasies. But we also find ourselves aware of change inside tradition. There are plenty of Texans who fear that their state is developing too fast, outrunning itself, losing touch more and more every year with its own traditional values. To those Texans, represented by long-memoried men like Bill Kittrell of Dallas or Dobie of Austin, the symbol of the old true Texan tradition is the remote cowboy and *vaquero* with his lonely, passionate, arrogant rejection of the ways of the busy world. The frontier, the ranches, the prairies, the dusty trails, the wide spaces under the lofty stars, the unending struggle between man and nature have here bred a stubborn individualism, an admiration for every kind of personal skill, self-reliance, independence and unconventionality—bred their own tempo, their own humor, their own heroism. They have bred a real culture in T. S. Eliot's definition of the word—i.e., a complete life mode; not something to be hung on the wall like a picture or an antique, but life as it is lived, fully and skillfully.

Within that old frontier way of life men could enjoy the luxury of

being persons; they could be different; they did not have to be
buttons out of a button mold. They were sometimes interesting, sometimes what we call colorful, sometimes gaudy, and on special occasions they could perform gestures splendid enough for an old saga.
To return to this old matter of the Texan Flourish, I should like to
recall my favorite instance. During the wartime landings in Sicily a
rangy Texan stood in the prow of a landing craft watching his first
European beach come nearer and nearer. As the boat grounded he
lifted his fist and flung out on the beach a lump of earth he had
brought with him all the way from America, shouting, "Come on,
boys! That's a fistful of Texas!" It takes a hundred years of frontier
tradition to produce that kind of heroic gesture.

The main enemy of the old ways is urbanization and industrialization. For over a generation now, the big ranches have been
disintegrating. There must be many reasons for this, but one all-too-
obvious reason is the old lure of the city's lights. Few of the famous
big ranches of the northwest now remain intact. The Pitchfork, the
Waggoner, and the 6666 are still there, but it is characteristic that
in 1951 the Matador, originally founded in 1878, was sold by its
Scottish owners and has since been broken up. Old Bob Thornton,
as traditional a figure as one could hope to find, ranch-born in 1884,
once said it all to me in two sentences: "The country around here has
now lost twenty-five per cent of its population to the city"; and he
groaned, almost in the same breath: "My boyhood is *fiction* to my
boys!" He was saying, in effect, that the more American Texas becomes, the less Texan it remains.

But Texas isn't just an old clock crunching away on a log-cabin
wall. It is a living organism. It has to grow and develop and adapt
itself. Unhappily, adaptability is not one of the strong points of
Texans. They look on innovations with a highly suspicious eye. A
slight illustration of this appeared not long ago in the Dallas *News*,
anent a meeting of the Confrérie des Chevaliers du Tastevin in Stan
Slawik's Vieille Varsovie restaurant. The writer sadly recalled the
time when such foreign whimsies as wine tasters and chevaliers and
Caviar de Beluga would have frightened the lives out of the brave
boys who rode the caboose to Kansas City with the cattle cars, for
whom beef was beef and food just something that stuck to a man's
ribs. It was all said in good fun, but there was, between the lines,
a hint that Texas was going to hell hand over fist and that if people
did not take care, cowboys would soon be starting every meal with

caviar and ending it with vintage port; together with a little suggestion, too, that all this wine-tasting stuff was an un-Texan, not to say
an un-American, activity.

A more serious illustration of Texan conservatism is the way in
which the liquor laws are handled. The state is dry or wet by local
option. Most of it, by area, is bone dry. But most of its population
lives in wet or anyway in damp areas. There is neither rhyme, reason,
system nor understanding about this wet-and-dry map of Texas.

The basic thing behind this peculiar behavior is, no doubt, the
tussle between the churches and liberal opinion. We are in the
Bible Belt down here. I have mentioned the town of Waco and its
high proportion between pastors and population. This can only mean
that practically all its people—including women, children, babies
and the infirm—go regularly to church and are well attended to by
churchmen between Sunday and Sunday. This is why, in this same
Waco, in one of those cafés where one may have a beer with food,
I noticed that my beer always came in the glass; and why, on looking around one night, I saw that every other client drinking beer
had his drink brought without the bottle. A trivial detail? It is a
tribute to the power of the dominant church in Texas. It means that
it pays economically as well as spiritually to be orthodox in Texas.
As a lawyer in Austin said to me, "One is easily corrupted into
conformity."

But surely the old frontier-pioneer values were not shaped in this
way? They were humane and humanist values, fashioned by men
and women giving simple, perhaps even crude, but always positive
answers to the positive challenges of the frontier way of life. No
church can replace positive responses by negative interdictions.
What bids fair to replace the old ways, in practice, is what one can
only call civic spirit. So, not too long ago, I noted that 152 churches
of the Baptist Association were organizing to work with the law-
enforcement agencies on the problem of juvenile delinquency. The
Baptist Church can be dynamic in other ways, too—creating a liberal
atmosphere of opinion on the Negro problem, or sending young
missioners off to places like Burma and Africa to work for God, or
organizing charities on a big scale, or, as we saw in Waco, founding
great educational institutions. All this strikes home as a more creative
approach to goodness than the old-fashioned hot-gospeling, drum-
beating, squeezebox-and-banjo-playing, nostrum-selling revivalist
campaigns (*From Dixieland to Canaan's Land*) that one still sees

marching across the state, offering noisily to "deliver all from sin, sickness, disease, poverty, doubt and fear." As Josephine Pinckney drily said—and we have to admit that she said it quite a while ago now—"Victorian ways have survived somewhat beyond their appointed time in the Bible Belt."

The future of Texas is with the larger cities. How strange and difficult and exciting their role is struck me forcibly one night in Dallas. I was at the symphony, for the *Magic Flute* overture, a *Scherzo* by Mendelssohn and Schubert's *Fifth Symphony*. It was a bitter night, wet, sleety, uncomfortable, so that the auditorium was half empty. The conductor, Walter Hendl, sensing that the atmosphere was more intimate than usual, dropped all formality and chatted with us from the podium after each item, reminiscing about his student days in Vienna and that city's close associations with Mozart and Mendelssohn. He was so informal that after the lively *Scherzo* he said: "Let's do it again for fun in double-quick time!"

It was a charming idea but as I relaxed, like everybody else, to enjoy the lovely, skittering music, I could not help thinking of the wind blowing across the Panhandle, down the cold, high, treeless plains, the drying creeks, the deep canyons, down over the rolling prairies. Every wire fence, I thought, would be netted with icicles in the morning, and if there were cattle out, their rumps would be to the wind and their fur blown rough. Certainly Mendelssohn never dreamed of so sophisticated a setting for his *Scherzo* as this auditorium. I wondered if there had been anything like it since Sarah Bernhardt played in *L'Aiglon* in a Texan tent for far-riding cowboys.

But when I came out from the symphony I found I could not buy me a hot toddy in the bars of proper Dallas, where the customer must provide his own liquor, and in the bar where I consoled myself with beer there was a young man blind drunk—from, I presumed, raw whisky. He was one of those lean young men, beautifully without hips, not a waste shred of flesh on his bones, in jeans, high-heeled boots, a cowboy hat on his poll—there was a rodeo at Fort Worth that week. For a boring while he kept appealing amorously to the girl behind the bar. Then—and I know it sounds too hackneyed to be true, but it is what happened—he began to part croon, part groan, in a rather fine tenor voice, the cowboy ballad that all the world knows, *Home on the Range:*

Where the graceful white swan
Goes gliding along
Like a maid in a heavenly dream. . . .

Outside, the rain went skittering against the windows, like the Mendelssohn *Scherzo*. The wind from the prairies blew it down the street.

"So?" I said to myself, as I got up and walked out, head down against the wind. "So *this* is Texas."

I might have had more sense. What snap judgment is ever worth its own breath? This tussle between past and present, tradition and innovation, the old and the new, is not confined to Texas. I know now that "this" is not Texas. But it is America. Has Texas at last joined the Union?

klahoma

by DEBS MYERS

Oklahoma is cattle and crops, oil and politics. It is the Pioneer Woman and a woman bandit named Belle Starr; prohibition and rambunctious individualism; Jacksonian democracy and Jim Crow; land rushes, rattlesnake roundups, cities born out of the red clay overnight, a writer named Marquis James, an artist named Acee Blue Eagle, a baseball pitcher named Carl Hubbell.

It is the sprawling plains, with flat heat over the flat land; it is also mountains, in the Kiamichi country, where at night the wind makes a grieving noise as though it were trying to say something that no one can understand. It is a farmer looking at the brassy sun, well-off now with money in the bank, but a little fearful always that the day will come again when his acres yield only bitterness and dust.

It is an illiterate Cherokee artist named Sequoyah who invented an Indian alphabet; Geronimo, proud and unconquered, in the stockade at Fort Sill; Jim Thorpe, warming up before a football game by standing on the 50-yard line and casually kicking goals at both ends of the field.

It is an Indian death march known as the Trail of Tears, and the biggest cowpath in history, the Chisholm Trail.

It is palomino horses prancing in a show ring, marcelled bulls selling for a fortune and, deep in the hills, razorback hogs not worth butchering.

It is Alfalfa Bill Murray, a governor with an iron whim, using the state militia as a police force and defying the legislature to impeach him: "Don't try to tell me what's in the state constitution—hell, I wrote it."

It is an oilman named Frank Phillips paying off the debt of every church in the city of Bartlesville; a town marshal named Oscar Morgan killing a bandit in a gun fight and declaring: "I'm alive because the good Lord was at my side, but for a minute we was both in an awful fix," or Will Rogers capsuling the truth in easy doses and packaging it with a rope.

Oklahoma is also a Choctaw Indian named Joe Oklahombi whom I met in the Kiamichi Mountains. He is known to his neighbors as a mild, agreeable man who likes to hunt and fish and be left alone. As far as anyone knows, he never let his temper get the best of him but once in his life; that was more than thirty years ago and it is still the talk of the countryside. It goes back to the time when he was an infantryman in France during World War I; he awakened one morning feeling mean-tempered and miserable, not like himself at all, and before the day was over he had captured 171 Germans and killed more than he wanted to count. For this he received a flock of medals, a couple of generals made a fuss over him, and he was promoted to private first class.

Now, well-padded and comfortable, Joe Oklahombi likes to sit with a fishing pole on the banks of Horsehead Creek outside his home at Wright City. When I asked him about the time he became a hero, he scratched his head and said he didn't know for sure what got into him. "I reckon for once in my life," he said, "I got the itch to be a bear. And, growing up in Oklahoma, a man learns fast that anytime he wants to be a bear, he better be a grizzly."

Oklahoma was born with a strain of grizzly; in the early days it knew drought, flood, tornadoes, guerrilla warfare and Indian rebellion. During the territorial days, before statehood, it was a stamping ground of gamblers and gunmen. Violence became so common that the nearest Federal judge, Isaac C. Parker, of Fort Smith, Arkansas —known as the "hanging judge"—installed a specially built gallows so that he could drop prisoners through the trap in simultaneous batches.

Today Oklahoma is prosperous, though not nearly so rich as it hopes to be, and respectable, though still a little seamy at the edges. Understandably, the people take pride in the state's colorful beginning, but they learned a long time ago that they can't live on legends. They are not much interested in how Grandpa and Uncle Clem shot it out with the Cheyennes; they prefer to talk about the new Turner Turnpike, a stretch of highway linking Oklahoma City and Tulsa; the new industry coming to the state; or the bull that a rancher named W. H. Delaney sold for $51,000.

Perhaps because Oklahoma underwent such a turbulent period of gestation and has taken such lusty strides in so short a time—statehood was not granted until 1907—it has been from the beginning a breeding ground of legends, misconceptions and exaggerations. One of these deals with the Indians; according to this stereotyped nonsense, most of them are rich, they drive about in hearses for pleasure cars and have console radios in their tepees. There are rich Indians (the Osages at one time were probably the wealthiest single group of people in the world), but, unhappily, most Indians aren't rich. There have been Indians who spent their money foolishly, which seems to be largely their own business, but I never have seen one driving a hearse or living in barbaric splendor in a radio-equipped tepee.

There are in Oklahoma approximately 110,000 persons of Indian descent, most of them half-bloods or over; this is almost one third of all the Indians in the United States. In most cases, of course, they're no different from any other Oklahomans. Many of them play important roles in state and civic affairs.

Another misconception deals with Oklahoma's climate, topography and people. There has been considerable writing to the effect that Oklahoma is flat, bleak and arid, tortured by heat, cold and its own inhibitions. In some of this, there is a little truth—not much. The summers usually are hot, the winters moderate. Spring comes early; autumn is a mellow season that starts in September and lasts through Christmas.

The topography includes almost everything: long stretches of prairie, hills, mountains, gulches, timbered valleys, game preserves, meandering streams and, surprisingly, almost half a million acres of land devoted to man-made lakes.

The people—well, they're contradictory, hard to peg. For years they voted dry, but bought bootleg whisky in prodigious amounts. They pride themselves on being defiantly independent—primed to haul off and kick the moon clean over the Red River—but reflect in a hundred ways a wistful desire for outside approval.

At their worst, they are astringently narrow-minded, prejudiced and reactionary; at their best they are spontaneously generous, progressive in a horse-sense prairie way and willing to experiment for the future good—a throwback probably to their restless fore-bears who were always looking for a better route over the ridge.

One of the best ways to get an insight into Oklahoma is to travel in the southern section of the state, amidst the rolling pasture land known as Hereford Heaven. This, as you can guess, is grazing country for those broad-beamed, white-faced cattle called Herefords. (It is pronounced either "hur-ferd" or "her-i-ford.") One of the better-known ranches in Hereford Heaven is owned by a former Oklahoma governor named Roy Turner. The ranch, near the town of Sulphur, sprawls over 10,000 acres of bluestem pasture grass, which by midspring is belly high to a Hereford bull. These cattle have it good; their barns are equipped with shower baths and fans, they are bathed once a week and curried, combed and curled. When Turner's most famous bull, "Old 81," was put to death in his rheu-matic old age, he was buried on the ranch in a tile-lined vault with a concrete-and-stone marker at the head of his grave. Turner's sorrow was understandable; the bull had sired more than a million dollars' worth of sons and daughters.

Turner himself reflects a big slice of Oklahoma life. He has combined oil, ranching and politics into one career and made him-self one of the dominant figures of the state. Like a lot of Okla-homans, he was born in Oklahoma and born poor. As a boy he worked in his father's livery stable in the little town of Kendrick. One day a stranger rented a rig and a team of horses and later, coming back from the ride, gave Turner a silver dollar for unhitching the horses.

Awed by this display of wealth, the boy asked his father if he knew the stranger's name. "Yep, young fellow trying to get ahead in the oil business," the elder Turner said, "name of Tom Slick." That was the last Roy Turner ever saw of Tom Slick—later to become one of the fabulous figures of the oil industry—but, then and there, amid the straw and red dirt of the livery stable, Turner decided to become an oilman.

Many years later, after working as a bookkeeper and salesman, he went into oil, branched into ranching as a sideline and ultimately ran for governor and was elected. The governorship of Oklahoma usually is a springboard to nowhere; in Oklahoma's short history two of its governors have been impeached and many of the others threatened with it. But Turner's record as governor was so impressive that President Truman offered him a Cabinet job as Secretary of Agriculture. Turner turned it down. He takes more pride in breeding livestock than in producing votes; his cattle have won a roomful of trophies and ribbons. There is a saying in Oklahoma that if Turner ever really put his mind to it he could breed a billy goat to a secondhand cultivator and come up with a mare that would win the Kentucky Derby.

With Turner and his general manager, Jim McClellan, I made a tour of the ranch. It wasn't hard to tell that Turner had got his start as an oilman. Discarded oil casing and oil pipe had been converted into stalls, and old storage tanks had been made into grain bins. The ranch represents an investment of $250,000 in land alone; including cattle, its value is said to be more than $1,000,000.

Turner and McClellan demonstrated for me how a bull is beautified before appearing in a show ring. First, the animal is soaped and lathered, his coat is combed and curried to bring out the natural curl, his tail is brushed to make it fluffy and his horns are scraped and polished. Then he is shoved into a wooden stand and strapped tightly while his hooves are filed and chiseled until they shine.

The bull represents a big investment and he couldn't be more coddled if he were a sultan, which, after all, is about what he is. It seems, however, that not even the experts can always tell about a bull. An animal that Turner once sold for $35,000 proved to be impotent and Turner refunded the money and took back the bull. Hormone shots were tried without success, and finally the bull was carved into steaks; reportedly fine steaks, too, which seems not unlikely at those prices.

We paused before a fence enclosing a bull named TP Zato Heir, the current pride of the Turner ranch. Turner specified the points that make this bull a champion: "short legs, deep body, which is uniformly well developed, with the top line and the bottom line of his body comparatively straight; a broad, placid face and a wide beam packed with solid meat." Without the horns he would have been reminiscent of one of the more intelligent-looking wrestlers you see on television. I asked McClellan how much the bull would bring if the ranch ever decided to sell him. "Maybe as much as a hundred thousand dollars," McClellan said. "How much on the butcher's block?" I asked. McClellan, pained by the thought, shrugged and said, "Not much—a few hundred dollars."

On the way back to the ranchhouse McClellan pointed to a cow with two calves grazing in the pasture. "She strutted in from the range a while back with a new calf, acting real proud," McClellan said. "But one of the boys got an idea she was up to something and followed her. Sure enough, she had hidden a twin calf in the tall grass and was sneaking back now and then to feed it." I asked why she did this. McClellan spat thoughtfully. "Just plain contrary," he said, "an Oklahoma cow."

From the Turner ranch I traveled south and east past Lake Murray, which is becoming a resort center of several states, and into Durant, at the edge of 93,000-acre Lake Texoma. So many artificial lakes have been established in such a few years in Oklahoma—where they used to say that even the frogs couldn't swim—it is little wonder that certain confusions have developed. As evidence of this, Bennett Story, editor of the Durant newspaper, told me of an incident which —well, make up your own mind. It seems that with the construction of the lake, gulls swarmed into the area for the first time. The countless crows, which had been making a lean living pestering farmers, watched the gulls swoop across the water, dive down and come up with fish; before long the crows were doing it too. It worked both ways, though: now the gulls follow behind the farmers as they plow their fields, battling with the crows for the worms.

From Durant I went deep into the southeastern part of the state to the town of Broken Bow, at the gateway to the Kiamichi Mountains. This is the country Will Rogers was talking about when he said: "There are old guys down there who have an old squirrel rifle laying up over the door on some deer horns and if they shoot at you and don't hit you in the eye—why, they call it a miss."

This is a rugged country of forested mountains, hidden meadows, and creeks flowing across rocky beds. The towns are small, built on lumbering, and the farm houses are mostly log cabins, surrounded by fences of hand-split palings. Lean cattle and razorback hogs run in the woods; farmers say there is only one way to tell whether a razorback hog is ready to butcher—hold him up by the ears, and if the body overbalances the snout, get out the knife. In the woods there are also squirrel, wild turkey and deer. I asked an old man who lives far back in the mountains if he shot many deer during season. "Hell, no," he said, "that's the only time I don't shoot 'em—too blamed many city fools around likely to kill you."

In Broken Bow I stayed at the Charles Wesley Hotel. Meals were served family style, with the guests sitting at long tables passing the food back and forth. Usually, there were two kinds of meats, four kinds of vegetables, cornbread, biscuits, plain bread, stacks of fresh butter, pickles, preserves, jelly and dessert. Second and third helpings were not only permissible—you were urged to take them. The price for all this was as implausible as the variety of the food: 85¢ weekdays, a dollar on Sunday.

After dinner the guests sat in rocking chairs on the front porch, smoking and making small talk. There is a story of the Kiamichis you've heard; whether it ever happened is doubtful, but it's the lore of the countryside.

It concerns an eighteen-year-old mountain boy who showed exceptional promise as a pitcher. A big-league baseball scout found the boy sitting on a fence rail and together they went for a walk in the woods. Suddenly the boy reached down with his left hand, picked up a rock and knocked down a squirrel perched in a tree 150 feet away. "Hey," the scout said, "I thought you were right-handed." "What the heck, mister," the boy answered. "You want I should squash him?"

This mountain country is steeped in Indian tradition; the Choctaws long ago built a civilization here, with their own capital, their own courts, their own laws; a primitive wilderness dominion that finally yielded to the white man's inroads. It goes back more than a hundred years to the grim migration which the Indians called the Trail of Tears, when the Federal Government uprooted the Five Civilized Tribes—the Cherokees, Choctaws, Chickasaws, Creeks and Seminoles—from their homes in the Southeastern states and forced them into the then-unoccupied lands of Oklahoma. Thousands died on the way. These Indians had lived in close contact with the whites for many years; among the Indians were farmers, stockmen, teachers and plantation owners, who had large estates and Negro slaves. In Oklahoma, each tribe established its own government, with tight hold over the lands allotted it by Federal authorities.

Many Choctaws still live in the Kiamichi country. In the community of Eagletown, I talked with an old Indian named John Tonekai, who likes to lean against the buildings on the main street, puff reflectively at a pipe and piece together from memory and legend an account of the old days when Choctaw word was law.

He tells of days when eagles roosted in the Kiamichi forests; of hunts through the snow for wolves, bear and panthers; of tribal ceremonies around flaming campfires; of fiery denunciations of the white men delivered by Choctaw statesmen in the council house at Tuskahoma; of funeral rites in the wilderness where friends would meet on an appointed day, long after the person they mourned had been buried, and wail and feast for days.

"In those times there were no prisons," John Tonekai says. "When a man did something wrong and the judge fined him or sentenced him to be whipped or executed he would go home until the day the judge told him to appear for punishment. If he was to be whipped, he would take off his shirt, put his arms around a tree and hold tight while a Choctaw official used the lash.

"If the man was sentenced to death, he bared his chest, a mark was drawn over his heart and he sat on a blanket facing the executioner. A man on each side would hold the prisoner's arms apart, and the prisoner would look straight into the gun while the shot was fired."

John Tonekai shakes his head. "Finally, though," he says, "we had to build jails. That was after the white men came."

Through the years the Indians and their white neighbors in the Kiamichi country have learned to get along together. There is one rule which visitors learn quickly: the Indians, understandably, resent being patronized. A state forester named W. H. (Bill) Mitchell, who has lived and worked in the mountains for more than twenty-five years, found this out when he first came to the Kiamichis. He got lost one night while fighting a fire deep in the woods and couldn't find his way back to his car, which he had left by a railroad track. Finally he came to a cabin in a clearing and was met at the door by an Indian man about his own age.

Mitchell, by sign language and mimicry, punctuated with "ugh, find 'em car, railroad track, choo-choo," tried to make clear that he was lost. The Indian listened impassively, saying nothing. Mitchell, getting desperate, churned around the clearing, pumping his arms and legs like pistons, occasionally throwing back his head to make a noise like a train whistle. The Indian watched with interest for a few minutes, then spoke for the first time. "If you're looking for the railroad track, it's a mile to your left."

Mitchell gasped. "You speak English?"

"I should," the Indian said. "I went to Cornell for four years."

Oklahoma is a great deal more than cattle and ranches, Indians and mountains. It is also towns and cities; the cities are dominated, of course, by Oklahoma City and Tulsa. It seems curious they both came out of the same pod, pretty much the same environment, for they look different, act differently and, much of the time, think differently. Oklahoma City is as convivial, casual and bouncy as a wet Airedale. Tulsa is more sophisticated, a little reminiscent of an oil field roughneck turned businessman, mature now, with a touch of gray at the temples, and less inclined toward skylarking.

Tulsa is a city built by oil. Oil butters Tulsa's bread, buys its groceries, pays its rent and builds the glistening office buildings that give Tulsa a dramatic sky line. Few cities have come so far so fast. In 1905, it was a roistering frontier settlement known as Tulsey Town, with a population of about 5000 including the customary quota of scalawags. Hogs, cows and goats roamed the streets; there were no sidewalks, no sewers or street lights.

In 1906 came the break that shaped Tulsa's future. The Glenn Oil Pool was discovered near Tulsa—the greatest high-grade petroleum strike up to that time. Realizing that the pool ultimately would play out, and that production would move elsewhere, Tulsa underwent a quick face-lifting with the idea of selling itself to the oilmen as their permanent home.

"You can't constantly move your families across the country, following oil discoveries," Tulsa told the oilmen; "you need a base of operations. This is it." The oilmen liked the idea; before long Tulsa was calling itself the oil capital of the world and it has been living up to the title ever since.

Today Tulsa is the headquarters of more than 700 companies dealing in oil directly or indirectly, a business that supports close to seventy per cent of the city's population.

Perhaps all cities which grow fast and get rich fast acquire a variety of wealthy screwballs dedicated to finding new ways to squander their money. Tulsa has had a few odd characters, but most of its wealthy men have devoted a substantial chunk of their time and money to improving the town. Foremost among the men responsible for Tulsa's growth and affluence is a former mule-skinner named W. G. (Bill) Skelly, president of the Skelly Oil Company. The newspapers frequently refer to him as Mr. Tulsa.

He learned the fundamentals of the oil business in Pennsylvania, came to Tulsa in 1913, organized his own company six years later and is now one of the most respected figures in the industry. He owns a radio station, is president of the International Petroleum Exposition and put up the money for the construction of the football stadium at the University of Tulsa.

Skelly is a blunt, aggressive man, with a robust sense of humor, and it was inevitable that stories and legends would be built about him; curiously in his case, most of them seem to be true. The story most Tulsans appear to like best—perhaps because of a deep-rooted skepticism concerning eastern financiers—concerns a time years ago when Skelly applied to a New York banker for a loan. The banker engaged in a pompous analysis of economic conditions, winding up: "I am convinced the future of the oil business is bleak."

"Tell me," Skelly said, "on your way to work this morning did you see any evidence that horses had been grazing on Fifth Avenue?"

"No, of course not," said the banker, startled.

"O.K.," Skelly said, "anytime you see horses pasturing on Fifth Avenue—you'll know the oil industry has gone to hell. Not until then."

Skelly got the loan.

Tulsa's pride is not limited to its business achievements; it goes in big for culture. Most cities the size of Tulsa are lucky to have one art museum—often the result of years of civic scrounging. Tulsa has two, both of them excellent—the Philbrook Art Center and the Gilcrease Foundation. Each was handed to the city on a silver platter.

Philbrook, located in one of the city's plushiest residential sections, was formerly the home of an oilman named Waite Phillips and his wife. They turned Philbrook over to the city, first providing funds for remodeling and endowment.

The Gilcrease Foundation, located three miles north of the city, is unique among art galleries; it houses what is probably the world's finest collection of modern Indian paintings. In addition to many of the better works of contemporary Indian artists, the collection includes the art of forty-five Indian tribes, dating back to 300 A.D., along with 62,000 letters, books and manuscripts. One of the letters, written by General George Custer, ends: "You will next hear from me . . . not from the plains of Philippi . . . but from those of Dakota, the home of S.B." The initials referred to Sitting Bull, the Sioux chief who later was Custer's conqueror.

Thomas Gilcrease, who established the foundation, is of Indian heritage; his grandmother was a Creek and he grew up in Indian territory. He got rich—you guessed it—in oil. For forty years he has been hoarding books and pictures that deal with Indian life, many of which he picked up during his travels in France and Italy. Hundreds of the pictures were done by white artists like Charles M. Russell and Frederic Remington, who painted Indians as part of the scene in their studies of the American West, but the solid core of the gallery is built around the work of Indian artists, who painted their own tribal ceremonies and customs. In establishing the gallery, Gilcrease made his intentions clear: "I just want to present the facts about the conquest of the West and the way the Indian was treated —maybe that will help people to think about it and draw their own conclusions."

Tulsa's cultural assets are not confined to art; there is the Tulsa Little Theater, which has the longest continuous history of any similar movement in Oklahoma. It was started in 1922, was located at intervals in a tent, a storeroom and a beer parlor and is now a vital force in the community with a professional director and draws excellent crowds.

Incidentally, it was the Tulsa Little Theater which first recognized the talent of a young fellow named Lynn Riggs, who used to come to Tulsa from the nearby town of Claremore and watch rehearsals of his play *Big Lake*, dealing with the days of the Indian Territory. It was during this time that he received word of the Guggenheim Fellowship award sending him to France, where he wrote *Green Grow the Lilacs*. As you may recall, this was something of a success on Broadway—especially after they made it into a musical and changed the title to *Oklahoma!*

Also, lest it be forgot, Tulsa is the birthplace of no less an organization than the SPEBSQSA, which, in the event you want to know, is the Society for the Preservation and Encouragement of Barber Shop Quartet Singing in America. It must have been a popular idea, albeit an uproarious one, for the organization now has over 300 chapters in the United States and foreign countries. And—hang on gamely— the women of Tulsa have now formed a national organization of Sweet Adelines.

For all its suave and elegant appearance, with its towering, compact business district, its gleaming stores and handsome homes, Tulsa isn't much of a night-club town. The upper crust centers much of its social activity around the city's night clubs. Other Tulsans rely on

their own initiative for entertainment, and much of it goes on in
their own homes. As a result, most of the catnips are on the quiet
side, the way a town like Tulsa wants it.

It is inevitable that a town so long dominated by a small group
of rich men would be staid and conservative and Tulsa is both. As
evidence of this, the building on the University of Tulsa campus that
ordinarily would be called the Student Union Building is known as
the Student Activities Building. It seems that some of the downtown
oilmen who make contributions to the university get a little queasy
at the mention of the word union.

Probably Tulsa, at its best, reflects most of the qualities Oklahoma
has tried to acquire; Oklahoma City reflects the qualities, good and
bad, which are instinctive with the state. Oklahoma City is restless,
beset with mighty longings; it is contrary, a maverick that refuses to
fit a pattern; it is typically Oklahoman in that if it likes something,
it likes it. If it doesn't, duck!

Almost everyone knows by now that Oklahoma City has the only
state capitol that sits on top of an oil field, with oil derricks towering
over the domeless statehouse; that it was created overnight during
a land rush; that during the years it has had a ringside seat at some
of the most incredible political shenanigans ever foisted upon a community, with knives and guns flourished in the legislative halls. To
a large part of Oklahoma it is known as "The City," and people from
outlying areas travel back and forth in their cars, almost like metropolitan commuters.

An Oklahoma City product whom the people watch from afar
with interest is Perle Skirvin Mesta, former United States minister
to Luxembourg. She is considered twice as lucky as even the luckier
Oklahomans; she inherited not one fortune but two—one from her
father, William B. Skirvin, an oilman who built the Skirvin Hotel,
and the other from her late husband, who was the president of a
tool company in Pittsburgh. On a visit to Oklahoma City in 1951
Mrs. Mesta, one of the most prolific party-givers of our time, found
the tables turned, she was given the full treatment with gifts, receptions and speeches.

Dan James, owner of the Skirvin Hotel and Skirvin Tower, put her
in what used to be the family suite at the hotel and put a bronze
nameplate on the door. "For sentiment's sake," he explained. The
townspeople seemed to like her fine. An old man who once had been

a crony of her father's summed her up this way: "She inherited a hell of a lot of money and she's kept it. That's the kind of diplomat we need—someone who knows how to keep from losing their shirt."

In every section of Oklahoma, from Oklahoma City and Tulsa to the smallest village, the oil companies have wielded a powerful influence on the people, their livelihood and progress. An example of this is the Phillips Petroleum Company of Bartlesville, founded by a one-time barber named Frank Phillips. He started with nothing much but an idea and upon his death in 1950 he had built a 660-million-dollar oil empire reaching into more than half of the states of the nation. It is a story that probably couldn't have happened anywhere but in Oklahoma and then only to a bet-the-sky character like Frank Phillips.

It is illustrative of Phillips' character that he never quit being proud of his days as a barber. A reporter once approached him in a hotel lobby and asked, apologetically: "Is it true, Mr. Phillips, that you used to be a barber?"

"You're damned right," said Phillips, "and if you can latch onto a pair of shears and come up to my room, I'll give you a better haircut than you got right now."

Phillips was born in Nebraska and became a barber in the town of Creston, Iowa; this decision to make a living as a barber was prompted by the fact that as a boy he had seen a barber wearing a pair of striped pants and wanted a pair like them. From a Methodist missionary he heard about oil fortunes being made in Oklahoma. He saved his money—including some commissions he had picked up as a spare-time salesman—talked his brother L.E. into going with him and went to Oklahoma, settling in Bartlesville. This was in 1904. "I think people are going to buy quite a passel of these gasoline buggies," Frank Phillips told his brother, "and they need gasoline to make 'em go. It may be this thing has a future."

Three months later the first Phillips well spouted oil on the grounds of what once had been an outlaw hideout on the banks of Caney Creek. Then they drilled three dry holes in a row. Their money was almost exhausted, and the brothers contemplated quitting. Instead they pinched pennies, moved the rig onto unproved ground, and struck a producer. During the next five years, when another dry hole wouldn't have caused undue worry, they struck eighty producers without a miss.

When the Phillips brothers learned that Bartlesville banks would lend money on horses, mules, farm lands and crops, but not on oil production, they started a bank of their own. One of their first customers was a quiet young man who wanted to borrow $500. Frank Phillips asked the young man his name.

"Henry Starr."

"What do you do?"

"I operate a little, here and there."

"Do you have any collateral?"

"Never heard of it."

Phillips advanced the young man the money. Later, he learned that Henry Starr was one of the most notorious bank robbers in the Southwest. Starr paid the note on the day it was due. This was during an era when an average of one bank robbery occurred each day in that part of the country. The Phillips bank was never robbed. There was a saying that the bandits held up other banks and put their money in the vaults of Frank Phillips.

Frank and L. E. Phillips then summoned a third brother, Waite—the same man who later gave the Philbrook Art Center to Tulsa—and the three decided to open a chain of banks. "Hell, men," said Frank Phillips, "we're not oilmen, we're bankers." They sold most of their properties. Then, as the First World War swept Europe, the price of oil rose to four dollars a barrel. Frank Phillips surveyed the situation. "Hell, men," he said to his brothers, "we're not bankers, we're oilmen."

With the remnants of their oil property they went back into the oil business and once more built up their holdings. They were producers of crude oil and had no intention of going into retail operations. "We're back in the oil business," Frank Phillips said, "but we'll never run a filling station."

Then the oil business underwent an important change. Refiners became big producers, the market became saturated and the Phillips Company couldn't go on as a producer only. Frank Phillips called his executive committee into session. "Gentlemen," he said, "I move that we build the damnedest string of filling stations anybody ever saw. I move further, if it's all right with you, that we make it unanimous." The committee agreed.

Today the Phillips Company sells its products at nearly 16,000 retail stations in twenty-eight states; it has pioneered in petroleum research and its activities reach into more than a dozen allied fields.

In Bartlesville the company even owns a luxurious apartment hotel.

The company emphasizes employee recreation, from bowling to basketball. The Phillips "66" basketball team has won so many championships it is likened to the Yankees.

Fourteen miles southwest of Bartlesville in the Osage Hills, Phillips built an elaborate ranch and museum which he called Woolaroc (a contraction of the words woods, lakes and rocks). At first the ranch was a personal plaything for Phillips; later he made it into one of the authentic show places of Oklahoma.

Phillips built dams and pumped water upstream. "I'm the only man in the world fool enough to pump water uphill, just so I can watch it flow back," he said. He stocked his ranch with an implausible variety of wild animals—llamas, yaks, gnus, buffalo, long-horned steers, red deer, peacock—just about every animal he thought anybody might want to see. Today, except for a few of the ornerier beasts, these animals graze wild in the preserve.

The museum emphasizes Southwestern history and includes one of the finest Western art collections in existence. There is also a frontier buckboard, the saddle of Buffalo Bill, guns, rugs, hides, knives, ancient Indian pottery and the single-engine airplane *Woolaroc I,* which Arthur Goebel, a Hollywood stunt flier, hired by Phillips to promote the sale of gasoline, flew to victory in a race to Honolulu in 1927.

Essentially, Oklahoma is a state of small cities and towns. One of these is Lawton, located in the picturesque Wichita Mountains at the edge of Fort Sill, one of the country's best-known Army posts. The annual Lawton Easter Pageant draws crowds estimated as high as 200,000. There is a story that an early-day marshal, Heck Thomas, once arrested a photographer named Lon Chaney for speeding—on horseback. The same Lon Chaney later turned out to be quite an actor. Other towns include Enid, increasingly important as a wheat-growing, processing and marketing center; Ponca City, which produced two of Oklahoma's most fabulous oil figures, Lew Wentz and E. W. Marland; Ardmore, which calls itself the capital of South Central Oklahoma; Muskogee, a quiet business town at the gateway to much of historic Indian Oklahoma; Okmulgee, former capital of the Creek Indian Nation and the home town of the late General Hugh (Iron Pants) Johnson; and Shawnee, which has suffered more than its share during the years from violent phenomena, such as flood and storm, but manages to remain one of the most prosperous of the smaller cities.

Oklahomans have a built-in genius for letting off steam, and this is particularly true of the town of Norman, home of the University of Oklahoma.

The University of Oklahoma isn't by any means exclusively an assembly line for producing muscular young men. For instance, its schools of geology and petroleum engineering are internationally known. In addition, the university has produced a number of artists and writers; and the University of Oklahoma Press, under the direction of Savoie Lottinville, a former Rhodes scholar, exerts a stimulating influence that extends beyond the state. George Lynn Cross, president, once jokingly observed that his was a university of which the football team could be proud.

Oklahoma's athletic and scholastic laurels aren't confined to the University of Oklahoma. The Agricultural and Mechanical College at Stillwater has not only had a powerful effect on the state's agricultural and livestock progress but has played an important role in cultural activities. Proudly, an A. and M. official showed me a copy of a Paris magazine of art criticism discussing the work of six American artists with reproductions of their paintings. Two of these six artists were from the A. and M. faculty, J. Jay McVicker and Dwight E. Stevens.

Probably the most important man in Oklahoma, year after year, isn't an oilman, a rancher, a politician or a big shot of any kind. It is the farmer, for farming—although oil pays almost half the state taxes —is still the backbone of Oklahoma's economy. Perhaps there never was nor could be a typical farmer, because farmers are individuals right to the bone marrow, but Ray Anderson, who, when I was there, lived near the town of Slapout, deep in Western Oklahoma, is a good example of what can happen to a man with a liking for a particular plot of ground.

During the dust storms of the early thirties, he saw his crops wither and creep back into the ground. He saw his horses die in the fields, their lungs clogged with dust, and he herded his cattle into a corner of the barnyard and shot them, one by one.

While a sizable chunk of the country was blowing away, and one third of the county's people were moving on, bound from nowhere to nowhere, he stayed on the land, managing somehow to feed his wife and family. For one thing, he didn't have any place to go—but, more than that, he liked the land. He always counted on next year.

In 1953, with the dust storms only a nagging memory, Anderson owned a 3900-acre farm worth a lot of money. He had cash in the bank. He had three trucks, a comfortable eight-room house, 300 head of Hereford cattle, 150 Hampshire hogs, a home freezer filled with beef, chickens, peas, roasting ears, peaches and strawberries. He was even thinking of buying an airplane.

Sometimes, in the evening, he liked to stand on his land, look out toward Kiowa Creek, listen to the lonely night sounds, and wonder about the crops still in the ground. "That's part of living on the prairies," he said, "you're always thinking of next year, never looking back; it's always next year's crop."

Arkansas

by CLYDE BRION DAVIS

To a good many Americans the state of Arkansas is merely an irregular rectangle on the United States map, just west of the Mississippi River, supported at the bottom by the state of Louisiana and
held down at the top by the state of Missouri; a sort of backwater
from the rushing stream of national traffic, quietly growing quaint
characters and more fantastically quaint legends. Or at least that is
its reputation.

To other Americans Arkansas is simply a vast, calm sea of growing
cotton—swelling white-crested bolls from horizon to horizon; or the
acrid sting of powder smoke in the misty dawn while swift-winging
mallards swoop in over the Grand Prairie rice fields; or the scream of
a tortured reel when a ten-pound bass pounces upon the lure in a
mountain lake; or the sad cry of night birds where ghostly cypress
knees lift above melancholy swamp waters. Or the intoxicating
aroma of lush, lush spring with honeysuckles embracing rail fences
and the dogwoods abloom and the flames of redbud trees quivering
with urgency and the fragrance of honey-locust trees humming with
the wings of a million wild bees, and the wooded hills echoing the
extravagant ecstasy of redbird, thrush and warbler.

Arkansas could be a barefoot farmer plowing his reluctant pink
acres with one ribby mule. Or a chorus of Negro voices singing at
twilight. Or mountains of bauxite tailings from mines that produce

practically all of the nation's aluminum ore. Or a vista of the wide, gray Father of Waters and a sturdy, squat tugboat, gnomelike descendant of the rococo old side-wheelers, wrestling its string of barges against the Mississippi current. Or hundreds of monuments honoring the Arkansas men and boys who died fighting the men and boys of Illinois, Pennsylvania and New Hampshire in the dreadful years of the Civil War.

In my boyhood I knew numerous elderly men who had taken part personally in that cataclysmic conflict, lending emphasis to the fact that in Arkansas the romantic past was not at all remote.

Even today in parts of the Delta region life goes on much as it must have before 1861. And in parts of the Ozark Mountains the march of years has changed conditions but little since the first moccasined frontiersmen moved west along the ridges from Kentucky and Tennessee and built their cabins beside sweet springs.

True, there is a growing awareness throughout the state that calendar leaves have been fluttering down and that the clock is ticking on. Preachers of progress are winning converts in the sleepiest of backwoods communities. But even today, if you get off the excellent main highways, you will find much the same atmosphere as when General Albert Pike wrote his stirring lines to the tune of *Dixie:*

> *Strong as lions, swift as eagles,*
> *Back to their kennels hunt these beagles!*
> *To arms! To arms! To arms in Dixie!*

The beagles, of course, were those blue-clad invaders from the North, many of whose bones went to dust in Arkansas soil. Of the earlier times, before Arkansas gained statehood in 1836, of the times of exploration and settlement, there are but a few relics surviving.

At the site of Arkansas Post (Poste Aux Arcansas), named by de Tonty for the Arcansas Indians, first colonized by the French and by Germans sent in the 18th Century by John Law, evil genius of the "Mississippi Bubble," all that remains is an ancient well. The "Petit Roche" of the Sieur Bernard de la Harpe, who in 1722 was seeking a legendary huge rock of pure emerald on the Arkansas River, still rests as a monument to his disappointment on the south shore of the river at Little Rock, almost as sacred to Arkansans as is Plymouth Rock to Massachusetts.

Then there is the Arkansas razorback. We can ignore the literal-minded Arkansans who scornfully deny his existence. Of course there are razorbacks. Otherwise, why are the University of Arkansas football teams called the Razorbacks?

The razorback is a sort of Arkansas symbol which might be likened to the British unicorn. He can lick many times his weight in wolves and run faster than a deer. While tall at the withers for a hog—say about ten hands—he is so thin, stories say, that he can squeeze through cracks in the Ozark lime rocks only three inches wide.

When a razorback wishes to travel he takes to the air like a flying squirrel, only better. He doesn't climb a tree to take off; he merely runs into the wind until he hits 60 mph, then flips on his side and soars like a glider. Utilizing hillside thermal updrafts, the Arkansas razorback climbs to 5000 feet. Ground observers undoubtedly have sighted him and reported a flying saucer in the neighborhood. I suppose it's possible that *all* flying saucers reported are merely Arkansas razorbacks on tour.

I have never seen a razorback. But neither have I seen a unicorn or a flying saucer. And I have little patience with those who sneer at the razorback as a fictional character. I think that question is highly irrelevant and immaterial. Are Hamlet and Huckleberry Finn less important just because they happen to be fictional characters?

The state of Arkansas is cut into two broad divisions—the hill country and the alluvial plains. The hill country lies roughly in the form of a crescent, with the high plateau of the Ozark Mountains running east and west along the Missouri border. The Boston Mountains, an extension of the Ozarks, drop south of the Arkansas River to join the Ouachita (pronounced Wash-i-tah) Mountains, which roll on east to Hot Springs National Park. The remainder of the state is delta country, sometimes as level as a billiard table.

Today's Arkansas traveler, if he arrives by air, will land at Little Rock, the capital and metropolis; if he comes by automobile or train, he inevitably will be drawn there. It is so near the center of the state that it might have been placed there with calipers.

Across the Arkansas River is North Little Rock, a chauvinistic community of about 50,000 which refuses to be absorbed by its bigger sister. Its original name was Argenta, because of a hole in the ground alleged to be a silver mine. But when it developed that the mine had no silver they dropped the name in disgust.

In the section along the river called "Little Dixie," or "Black Bottom," is the town's largest concentration of Negroes. The unofficial name of Washington Avenue is "Saturday Street" because Saturday brings happy throngs to the stores, hot catfish cafés and honky-tonks.

Park Hill rises sharply on the north limits of North Little Rock, one of the finest residential districts in either city. In Park Hill some genius discovered a method of making concrete look like weathered wood festooned with vines, and there are not only rustic vine-clad foot bridges but gigantic concrete toadstools that serve as bus stations. Another piece of studied quaintness is a replica of an old grist mill, complete with water wheel, which grinds no grist and serves no useful purpose except maybe as a trysting place for young people in the coolth of the evening.

North Little Rock used to have a reputation as a very tough town. But I was told that the police have cleaned up the place.

Little Rock itself is one of the most attractive small cities in America, with broad, clean streets, excellent hotels and shops, fine public buildings and parks and friendly people. Clerks and cashiers in stores and restaurants smile at a customer and say, "You all hurry back," or "Come back soon," and automobile drivers, believe it or not, are courteous even to pedestrians.

Little Rock, like most of the mid-South, takes religion seriously. Most faiths advertise with electric signs and some imposing neon crosses flame out against the smokeless sky. The sky is smokeless because all Little Rock uses natural gas.

Out on the Pine Bluff road there's a church obviously named for the motel trade; it is *The Dewdrop Pentecostal Church.*

Little Rock, of course, is in the midst of a region where people put some thought to names, particularly for their children. They often do quite well by the boys, but Arkansans love their little girls especially and adorn them with lovely and original names like Miladeen, Carutha, Florentine, Charlene, Loucrecia.

Speaking of names, I remember a girl reporter's interviewing an Ozark woman who, from the salubrious mountain air and water, was hale and hearty on her 105th birthday. The girl asked the old lady how to spell her Christian name, which she pronounced "Pishie," and the old lady said, "Well, I don't rightly know, but I got a picture with my name printed on it." So a great-granddaughter brought a lithograph from the bedroom and it was *Psyche at the Spring.*

Progressive Arkansans, who would be willing to trade the state's distinctiveness for more prosperity, do not like that kind of story. They also profess a distaste for folklore.

Curiously, however, they do not mind the original folklore tale of the Arkansas Traveler. The traveling gentleman, you may recall, pulled up his horse at the cabin of a surly squatter who couldn't repair his leaking roof when it was raining and the roof didn't need repairing when the weather was clear.

In Little Rock, one of the first things a visitor hears mentioned is the Territorial Capitol Restoration, which covers half a block on the edge of the downtown retail district.

I was escorted through the dozen or so buildings of handmade brick or hewn logs, including the territorial capitol, the first Little Rock office of the *Arkansas Gazette* and the home of Lieutenant C. F. M. Noland, who rode horseback to Washington with the Arkansas Constitution in 1835.

The restoration is realization of a dream of a native Little Rock woman, Mrs. James Fairfax Loughborough, who in 1939 persuaded the State Legislature to establish a commission with herself as chairman to engineer the project. At that time the historic buildings were in a sad state of disrepair. Some were Negro houses of prostitution and the block had been condemned as a fire hazard. Mrs. Loughborough restored and furnished the buildings with period pieces.

While 1835 does not seem particularly ancient when compared with many landmarks in the East, these buildings definitely hold an aura of romance. Thousands of visitors from all over the United States go through the Restoration each year and express their delight.

I was particularly interested in the fact that Sam Houston, following his strange resignation as Governor of Tennessee after the split with his bride of a week, had come to Little Rock on one of the most Gargantuan drunks in American history and no doubt roared along this ancient brick sidewalk stark naked after consigning his sombrero, boots and every stitch of clothing to the flames of his campfire.

Here Davy Crockett was entertained before and after his famous Little Rock shooting match, won, he later confessed, by surreptitiously poking a bullet in the hole made by his adversary's shot in the very center of the bull's-eye.

Here, also, must have walked fabulous General Albert Pike, who used to go goose hunting with a cannon loaded with BB shot and who gained wide fame as a lawyer, not only through his remarkable skill, but because he paraded to county courthouses behind a uniformed brass band.

Little Rock is proud of being the only state capital with three capitols—the Territorial Restoration, the "Greek Doric Temple" at Markham and Center Streets and the present capitol. The "Temple" housed the first state government and saw wild disorders during carpetbag days when, at one time, Arkansas had two governors, each with his own army.

Of course most Arkansas travelers go to Hot Springs. It's the oldest and one of the most famous spas in the Western Hemisphere, glittering right in the middle of the verdant Ouachita Mountains. Here is one region of great natural beauty which actually has been improved by the white man. The chain of lakes in Hot Springs National Park—Lake Catherine, Lake Hamilton and Lake Ouachita—were formed by dams. They range in length from twelve to fifty miles, enhancing the mountain scenery and providing year-round game fishing, bathing beaches and aquatic sports.

It's about sixty miles from Little Rock to Hot Springs by the old road. It's a scenic drive, but I sensed there was something wrong. Miles passed before I figured out what it was; there was nothing to look at but scenery—no patent-medicine signs, no cigarette billboards, no shaving-cream poetry. A state law prohibits roadside signs in Arkansas, practically repudiating our American civilization. What possible pleasure can a motorist gain from a view of a green lake sparkling in the lap of a pine-clad mountain unless it is seen framed between billboards advertising miracle detergent?

Several times our road crossed the new four-lane superhighway, which cuts the time between Little Rock and Hot Springs and eliminates most of the head-on collisions between tourists anxious to get to the horse races and tourists anxious to get away from the horse races.

Hot Springs is a focal point in Arkansas, but I really don't believe it is *of* Arkansas. It's a resort city. If I were set suddenly down in Hot Springs and told I was in California or Florida, I would not question it. Well, there are few places as green in California and there are no mountains in Florida, but you get the idea. The buildings and streets look scrubbed with soap and water and the sunshine is intense upon them.

Hot Springs boasts 300 hotels, apartments, rooming houses and motor courts; forty-seven hot springs flowing a million gallons daily, at temperatures from 102 to 147 degrees Fahrenheit, running mostly into eighteen bathhouses which each year give better than half a million baths.

Bath House Row is quite impressive, glistening behind lush greenery. Mostly the buildings tend toward the temple type of architecture, ranging from the Greek through the Moorish and almost but not quite to the Frank Lloyd Wright.

The hillsides of Hot Springs hold many fine residences with broad, landscaped lawns. Some of these, I was informed, belong to notorious Chicago and New York characters who have found sanctuary there. A couple of mansions reputedly built by Frank Costello and Owney Madden were pointed out to me.

We were late arriving at the Oaklawn track and the great grandstand was jampacked and already the concrete area before the parimutuel windows was littered with the discarded tickets of unrealized hopes.

We had only general-admission tickets and I spoke to an usher. He looked at me narrowly and then said, "Cap'n, if you all wants seats, go on down three aisles and see a boy name of Louey. Call 'im Louey like you know him and slip him a little. You know. Then y'all ask 'im about that block of four seats he's got."

So we went down three aisles and I grinned at the usher and said, "Hi, Louey. How you doin'?" and put out my hand. He gave me his hand doubtfully, but brightened when he felt the transfer of material goods and I asked about that block of four seats.

"Well, Colonel," he said—the transfer had promoted me several grades—"I guess you all know about those four seats, don't you?"

"How do you mean?"

He shrugged. "Well, they belongs to a party that ain't been here for three, four days. I dunno. Sure enough looks like they ain't coming today, but if they shows up you all have to get out."

We took a risk, and the owners did not appear.

It was a beautiful day with just a few shreds of white clouds drifting across a brilliant sky, and I don't know how any track could have a more beautiful setting than Oaklawn's mile ellipse snuggling between the high, green Ouachitas.

I am not a horse-race addict, but it must be admitted there is something to the pageantry and excitement of a race meet. One of my companions had a couple of lists of selections and apparently knew what she was about. When the two handicappers picked the same horse, she conservatively split a two-dollar ticket to place or show, and she was more than breaking even.

But when the bugle blipped out assembly for the sixth race and eight four-year-olds minced out in parade, my eye fell upon No. 7, a beautiful, long-legged beast named Andros, the best-looking horse I had seen all afternoon. There's a Greek island named Andros with a temple dedicated to Bacchus, and Bacchus was an interesting god. What more could I want? I plunged two bucks right on the nose of Andros. Andros ran last.

A couple weeks later Andros vindicated my faith by winning one of the big features of the season at greatly lengthened odds. However, I did not see that one.

About as far southeast of Little Rock as Hot Springs is southwest, is the town of Stuttgart, nationally famous as the duck capital of America. Stuttgart is in the Grand Prairie, as flat as the flattest of western plains and mostly treeless. For nearly a century this was cotton country—gigantic plantations operating both before and after the Civil War on a system of virtual feudalism. But at last cotton and nothing but cotton, year after year, exhausted the once rich alluvial soil and most of the land reverted to pasture.

Early in the 20th Century, however, a farmer discovered that the Grand Prairie subsoil held water on the surface and he experimented successfully with rice. Since then rice has become the second most important crop in Arkansas with an annual cash value of more than $50,000,000. Rice brought prosperity back to the blighted Grand Prairie. And it also brought wild ducks—by the million.

Ducks have become such an important byproduct of rice that the fame of Stuttgart rests on the former instead of the latter. The call letters of the local radio station are KWAK.

Each fall Stuttgart is invaded by duck hunters from all over the United States. They come by car, with or without trailer, train and plane, bearing prized fowling pieces of every description, decoys and often dogs. They fill every hotel, motel and tourist home; they camp out in tents and they live in their trailers. A goodly number of the hunters, of course, are Yankees, but Stuttgart doesn't mind *this* invasion, and as a matter of fact, turns the occasion into a festival, even roping off Main Street for outdoor dances.

When not blasting away from the duck blinds in early morning (some blinds are actually steam-heated), most duck hunters would rather talk than anything. Like golfers, they love to replay each shot.

Wearing their colorful garb, they congregate everywhere, recounting their adventures and misadventures, and arguing the merits of various shotguns—the pump gun, the autoloader and so on. If the truth be known, however, an occasional native grandpappy will go out at dawn with an old-fashioned hammer gun and get as many ducks as the engraved thousand-dollar pieces.

The climax of the Stuttgart duck festival is the annual duck-calling contest with a three-day barbecue, everything free to all comers. It is held in November for the so-called world's championship. Aspirants come from afar, the imperious callers who employ only hands and vocal organs and those who use store-bought aids. As the visiting Anatidaean virtuosos practice the conversational nuances of mallard, canvasback and teal, the jingle of Stuttgart cash registers helps to soothe native nerves.

About 40 per cent of the land under cultivation is now devoted to cotton and of that most is in the Delta region. Blytheville, up in the northeast corner of the state in Mississippi County, is the cotton capital. And Blytheville is one of the fastest-growing communities in Arkansas, especially busy on Saturday when the streets are filled with plantation people, black and white, buying and selling and pleasuring around the hot catfish stands and barbecue pits. The real carnival time comes in October, when the annual cotton-picking contests are held.

Historically, the Negro and cotton have been associated together, and the Negro population of Arkansas still runs approximately 25 per cent, heavily concentrated in the Delta country. In the north and west through the Ozarks and Boston Mountains there are so few Negroes that you might drive for a hundred miles without seeing one. On the other hand some cotton communities are entirely Negro.

In recent years Arkansas has lost nearly 10 per cent of its Negro population through the attraction of high wages in the North and West, and the desire to escape racial discrimination. Yet many a poor Arkansas sharecropper comes back disillusioned and bitter.

There was Remmie Dunlap who lived with his wife and children in a sharecropper cabin on a bayou in the lower Arkansas River valley. Remmie was back in Arkansas after several years of working in a Detroit auto factory, and he was glad to be back. His cabin was unpainted, he had no plumbing or electricity. But he had a garden and chickens and pigs and there were plenty of fish in the bayou.

He sat down on the tongue of his dish-wheeled wagon, took off his hat and rubbed his bald pate. "No, sir," he said, "I didn't like Dee-troit at all. Them Dee-troit colored folks is mighty biggety, they got no use for Southern niggers. Calls me Lynch Bait on account I come from Arkansas.

"All I does in this big factory is hold a nut while a white man, he screws in a bolt a million times a day and come night I stand up in a bus far as to Pine Bluff maybe, where we live in a great big brick house and climb up steps and steps to where Magnolia's got washing hanging all over the place and no fresh vegetables on the table and no dandelion greens and no fresh catfish and no fresh air even."

The last time I had ridden on a cross-country bus in Arkansas it was definitely Jim Crow with a painted line separating the rear or Negro section from the front. But the bus which I rode this time from Fort Smith to Little Rock had no such line or sign. It's true that the eight or ten Negro passengers automatically gravitated to the rear, and I don't know whether the driver would have said anything otherwise. He certainly said nothing to the young white men who moved to the rear with a couple of Negro soldiers and chatted with them.

About halfway to Little Rock there was a thirty-minute meal stop. In the restaurant an arrow pointed to the rear with a sign, "Colored waiting room and lunch this way."

The Negro passengers, men and women, started back but were stopped by a white waitress who said, "That isn't very clean back there right now. Why don't you people just eat up here?"

From the town of Crossett (home of the gigantic Crossett Lumber Co.) in Ashley County near the Louisiana line, swing westward through the magnificent shortleaf pine forests to what is known as the Coastal Plain of Arkansas. This country is devoted to general farming and livestock, but it also includes the rich oil and gas fields around El Dorado and Smackover (producing some 30,000,000 barrels of oil annually) and the great and happy watermelon region.

Watermelons grow big and sweet here. They market approximately 3,000,000 a year and they tell about a heavyweight champion that tipped the scales at 198 pounds and was shipped to a movie actor in Hollywood. Asked why, for goodness' sake, they hadn't sent it to one Elwin Charles Roe, the leading citizen of Ash Flat, Ark., who used to throw a baseball for the Brooklyn Dodgers, or even to General Douglas MacArthur, who was born in Little Rock, the answer was, "If Preacher Roe wants a watermelon he can raise it his-self and General MacArthur is a Republican."

When I think of Arkansas watermelons I always think of my brother's experience with a sterling character of the Ozarks. Passing a ten-acre patch of magnificent melons, my brother stopped and asked the farmer how about getting one.

The farmer said sure and plugged half a dozen until he found one he judged had reached the exquisite perfection of ripeness.

When my brother asked the price the farmer stared at him and said, "My God, mister, you don't think I'm *selling* watermelons, do you?"

Then the farmer explained that watermelons to him were *social* fruit. His ten acres were devoted to sociables, parties and good will.

"It's this way," he said. "I'm right proud of that melon you got. But do I sell it to you for money it's no different to you than sending to Montgomery Ward for a pair of gum boots. But do I give it to you and you're welcome and you eat it and you say, 'Dad burn, I never see such a scrumptious melon,' you'll feel friendly to-wards me even if you never see me again and I'll feel friendly to-wards you because I know you feel friendly to-wards me."

Speaking of pleasant Arkansas crops, mistletoe grows pretty much over the state. It's a parasite, of course, and appears in clumps high in hardwood trees. And it is regarded largely as the property of small boys who harvest it for Christmas money. The method of harvest is probably more fun than any other known to man. The boys shoot it down with .22 rifles.

Up above the Coastal Plain in Pike County, just where the Ouachita Mountains peter out, is the belly of an ancient volcano, the only igneous rock in the state. Here, in 1906, a poor farmer named John Huddleston was out fixing to plant his turnip greens when his eye fell on a crystal glittering in the sun.

"Well," said John Huddleston, "there's a nice diamond; it's about time something was turning up."

He took the crystal to a banker in Murfreesboro and the banker laughed. "Diamonds don't grow like that, John," he said, "but it's kind of pretty and I'll give you four bits for it."

John scorned the offer. He scratched around the turnip patch and found several more of the crystals and, although it's a "fur piece" from Murfreesboro to Little Rock, John Huddleston took his crystals to a jeweler in the capital. The jeweler examined the crystals and then exclaimed excitedly, "Man, do you realize what you've got here?"

"Sure enough," said John Huddleston. "They're diamonds, ain't they?" And they were—sure enough.

John Huddleston sold his scrubby eighty acres for what he considered a fortune—$36,000. And in the next twenty years mining operations took about 50,000 white, yellow and brown diamonds from that stony hollow. Most of the diamonds were industrial grade, but some were of fine jewel quality. One of more than forty carats is valued at $75,000, according to the Howard Millars family, which now maintains the diamond crater as a tourist attraction.

The Millars charge visitors $1.25 admission to the area and allow them to keep any diamonds they find. Such visitors are said to have found more than 800 diamonds, some of them of jewel quality.

As an Arkansas friend remarked: "One tourist is better than two bales of cotton—and he's easier to pick."

Arkansas has produced pearls of great price as well as diamonds. There are several factories on the lower White River that cut pearl buttons from fresh-water mussel shells, and, in the course of years, numerous pearls have been found in the river mussels at the Pearl Ann button plant at Clarendon where my father used to have a sawmill. Some of these pearls are worth several thousand dollars.

Arkansas people are much interested in a neighbor named Winthrop Rockefeller. Mr. Rockefeller, the tall, athletic son of John D. Rockefeller, Jr., has established residence at Petit Jean (pronounced Pettet Gene) where he has purchased some 800 mountain-top acres for the avowed purpose of raising Santa Gertrudis beef cattle.

Winding west and north from Petit Jean, one comes finally to Dardanelle, the southern terminus of the Dardanelle & Russellville Railroad, which has two and a half wonderful steam locomotives of the 1880 vintage. They used to have four but a wandering Hollywood property man hauled one out to the West Coast for use in historical movies. They committed cannibalism on the third to get parts to keep the other two running. These last have been slightly modernized—the original diamond smokestacks have been replaced by plain, unromantic-looking stovepipes.

One lean, overalled engineer was out working on his charge with a huge monkey wrench. He drawled sadly, "They been wonderful old engines in their day, but now you got to be a blacksmith and a steamfitter and a regular genius to keep 'em running."

On up into the picturesque Ozark country are the two great man-made lakes—Norfork and Bull Shoals. Norfork was raised by the dam on the north fork of the White River. It is fifty-four miles long and is populated by the biggest bass, large- and small-mouth, that I ever heard of.

Naturally, fishing is mighty popular in both Norfork and Bull Shoals Lakes, to say nothing of the summer float trips on the White River where one may drift lazily with the current in boat or barge on anything from one-day trips to a week or more.

You see a lot of the Ozarks running west to Eureka Springs, and you see a lot of the Ozarks right in Eureka Springs. There are towering peaks heavy with hardwoods and pine. In the spring there is the mingled fragrance of dogwoods, wild plum, crab apple and honeysuckle.

Eureka Springs is a town that never has had a circus, because there's not a level spot big enough to pitch a tent on. Spring Street climbs up the valley in a series of sharp S-turns. There aren't many cross streets, but climb sharply up one of them and you may find the book store of genial and erudite Otto Ernest Rayburn, who writes books and articles about Ozark folklore. He holds that the real Ozark hillbilly, like the mountaineer of North Carolina and Tennessee, speaks a pure Elizabethan English.

I am not entirely convinced. I never heard any Ozark citizen say "God's bodykin," or speak anything like a Shakespearean character. True, a good many words of Saxon origin and onomatopoeian nature are used casually in the Ozarks, especially by the ungodly. But so are they in Montana, Texas and on Third Avenue, New York.

Jesse and Frank James and Cole Younger used to hibernate occasionally in the Arkansas Ozarks, and there are stories of their unfailing courtesy toward the fair sex and their reverence toward preachers. Mr. Rayburn has a story about Jesse's marksmanship. At a party (maybe a church sociable) Jesse pasted an inch square of paper on a tree, strode away twenty paces, whirled suddenly and blazed away with a six-shooter in each hand. He fired eight times and every bullet was in that inch-square paper. Inasmuch as a .45 bullet is practically half an inch in diameter, there couldn't have been much left of that target after the first four or five shots.

Well, Eureka Springs is a strange town in a strange country. Near the top of the mountain is a Catholic Church which one enters through the belfry. Down the canyon is the Basin Park Hotel with the mountain rising so steeply in the rear that each of the seven floors has a ground entrance.

Eureka Springs is a health resort with sixty-three springs gurgling out water alleged to restore youth, vigor and ambition—which one needs if he's to walk those steep streets.

Beyond Eureka Springs, Route U. S. 62 covers some very rugged country, and there's the inevitable Inspiration Point with its inspiring view.

The highway passes close to Pea Ridge, scene of the Civil War's greatest battle west of the Mississippi. Even today histories vary as to who won the battle, but on both sides there were about 26,000 men engaged on March 8, 1862, and approximately 2500 casualties, including three Confederate generals killed. It was here that the great General Albert Pike brought in his brigade of Cherokee Indians recruited from Indian Territory on promise of plenty of Yankee scalps. But the Cherokees never had heard artillery before, and when the big guns opened up the Indians remembered that the fishing season was on and went back home.

Of course fried chicken is an Arkansas institution, and just outside Springdale, at the A. Q. Chicken House, I had fried chicken that was the answer to a fried-chicken fan's prayer. I know it isn't scientific, but I have a theory that it takes a native of Arkansas or Missouri (preferably a Negro) to achieve the heavenly, succulent, golden, crusty-sweet tenderness that makes fried chicken a food for the gods.

Fayetteville is a thriving city, the seat of the University of Arkansas. It's an old town and had rough times during the Civil War, changing hands several times. But it's not typical of the popular conception of Arkansas. As a matter of fact, Washington County usually votes Republican except when Fayetteville's favorite son U. S. Senator J. William Fulbright is running.

I visited the beautiful Fine Arts Center and saw an exhibition of paintings by faculty members and some of the work being done by students. All of it, strangely, was decidedly *avant-garde*. I was puzzled at first that these frank abstractions and nonobjective canvases should be in Arkansas. I wondered whether trouble might be in the offing if some legislative committee visits the Fine Arts Center and sees the taxpayers' money going to teach Arkansas boys and girls how to produce polychromatic doodles. But I don't know. Art is comparatively new to Arkansas. Perhaps it is natural, then, that they should turn to new forms.

Yes, Arkansas is changing. Even the various accents from the Ozark "thar" to the Delta "theah" are leveling off, especially among the young people, to plain "there." Radio, television, the movies, the wars and easy travel are having their effect.

But today's Arkansas traveler will find Arkansas *fundamentally* unchanged. Despite this age of standardization, he will find there a delightful distinctiveness. And, so far, happily, it is not the studied quaintness of some Western dude ranches or New England resort spots.

Arkansas automobile tags are inscribed "The Land of Opportunity." Well, there are opportunities, and aplenty. But I believe a more apt characterization might be simply "The Friendly State."

Louisiana

by JAMES STREET

She's the strange sister of the family, this state of Louisiana—the Frenchy one, never quite accepted in the household of the South and yet never denied, because she is so rich and so different, and so much fun.

She was named for France's fourteenth Louis, a genius and a rake; she's an archipelago of races, languages and religions, vociferously American, pugnaciously Southern and working hard to brew her potpourri into a democratic gumbo.

Most American states are two or three states, geographically and culturally; this dominion of pine and palm, red hills and black bottoms is a dozen.

Therefore, generalizations are dangerous. But we will gamble a few, this being a land where gambling is a man's heritage and Lady Luck is an old courtesan behind a carnival mask, choosing her lovers without regard to race, creed or future condition of servitude.

Louisiana is the Quebec of the United States, split across the middle by Arkansas fundamentalism and bursting with Texas big talk.

The Old South keeps his right eye on Louisiana in envy and contrition, winks at her with his left, and never can bring himself to believe that she, too, is one of his daughters. Yet she is the original Dixie, named for the *dix* bills which, like picayunes, were legal tender in the incubative days and called dixies by the helling Kentucky flatboatmen who really made the first Louisiana purchase with blood, brawn and raw whisky.

The nation thinks she's Catholic, but actually she's Protestant. The nation remembers her Huey Long who wanted to be President and forgets her Zachary Taylor who was. She's the Pelican State although possibly half of her people never have seen a pelican. She's the Creole State although many Louisianans never have seen a Creole and one good brother in the hill country defined a Creole as a Catholic albino.

She's a cuisine mecca for gourmets, but most of her folks eat corn bread. She's the Mississippi River, but the Red River is her backbone. She's New Orleans. That's as silly as saying that California is Los Angeles or that Pennsylvania is Philadelphia.

She's Mardi Gras and a hang-over, but the Sabine Valley rancher in cowboy boots and ten-gallon hat prefers the Texas State Fair at Dallas. She's a lazy Cajun drowsing by a lazier bayou while 80,000 hysterical partisans scream at a football game, for Louisiana takes her football as seriously as Columbus, Ohio—well, almost, anyhow, and that's saying a heap.

She's a cypress swamp, a lurking place for alligators and snakes, brooding in the foreboding shadows of parasitic Spanish moss. Now wait a minute, stranger. Those are oak trees. Cypress is rather rare these days because it is so valuable. There hasn't been a recorded death from snake bite within the memory of most men, and the alligators now are shoes and pocketbooks, much to the disgust of trappers who used to catch them barehanded and kill them with knives.

And that gray cowl on those trees is neither moss nor parasite. The Choctaw Indians called it falling hair. The Spaniards called it Frenchman's wig and the French called it Spaniard's beard. Somewhere along the line it was misnamed Spanish moss. It is an air plant (*Tillandsia usneoides*) and a cousin to the pineapple. Shred one of the strands and you will find a tiny, tough thread. The threads are used to stuff mattresses.

Spanish moss also is good for poems, ghosts and myths, ranging from Evangeline to John Henry to Huey 'ygod Pierce Long who, like Hitler, refuses to stay put, but comes back when the moon is dark and stalks the swamps and tall timber, shouting his battle cry: "Share the wealth! Every man a king!"

One visitor will say Louisiana is a mansion. Bless his romantic heart! Another will say she is a shanty. Bless his sociologic soul! They both are right—to a measure. Nevertheless, the average Louisianan, if there is such a thing, lives in a small town or on a small farm. His house is comfortable, his stomach full. He prefers beefsteak to frog legs.

His teen-age daughter wears jeans and his little son totes a brace of cap pistols, just like kids the country over. He pays very heavy state taxes, except on his land, so his children can have free lunches at school and he can ride on paved roads and retire, maybe, on Louisiana's old-age pension.

If a typical Louisianan (again a generalization) lives north of the Red River, which bisects the state from northwest to southeast, we will call him Lee Johnson. He is a Baptist or Methodist and boastful that he is Anglo-Saxon. He traces his ancestry to the Eastern seaboard, the southern part of course, thence to Tennessee or Mississippi. Grandpa was a Confederate veteran. Hero, naturally. As a Southerner, I wonder if none of the Confederate deserters ever had young'uns.

Anyway, Lee wears khaki on the farm or in the factory because it is comfortable and easy to wash. And before any interlopers—down here they are called the bleeding hearts, bluenoses, yellow-bellies and a few ungracious epithets—get any funny ideas, let me hasten to report that Lee Johnson has been to school. He has Sunday clothes, shoes and maybe an automobile. He dresses up for church, funerals and to go to town on Saturday. His parish may be dry by local option, so if he wants a drink he buys from a bootlegger.

The collar of Lee's shirt usually is open and the sun has reddened his neck. Hence, the sobriquet of redneck. It can be an endearing term when applied endearingly by friends, but strangers are cautioned to avoid it. For, as a rule, Lee Johnson resents being called a "redneck" because his skin is red just as much as his Negro friend resents the word "nigger" because his skin is black.

He is the Southerner of a thousand stories and a thousand legends; friendly, hospitable, his inherent shyness hidden behind his taciturn reserve or disguised completely by his exaggerated big talk and unbecoming boastfulness. He is not as quick to anger as the myth makers say, but don't push him, brother. Just don't push him.

However, if a typical Louisianan lives below the Red River—except in Lake Charles' southwest section or New Orleans' southeast section, which are separate provinces—we will call him René Le-Blanc.

He is a Roman Catholic and speaks a French patois that baffles linguists. His ancestors came from France via Acadia, now Nova Scotia, or directly from the mother country during the French Revolution. René and his kith are lumped together under the colloquial term of "Cajuns" (Acadians) and have leavened into one of the largest and most exciting ethnologic families ever to come from the American melting pot.

René LeBlanc, the bayou man, must not be confused with the Creole. (We will meet him later in New Orleans and environs.) René is the counterpart to Lee Johnson, up in the piney hills. He is volatile, prolific—repeat prolific—as thrifty as a squirrel, as eager as a chipmunk. He farms, traps, works the swamps, and fishes.

He and Lee are not cronies although their children mingle in college. Lee is inclined to look askance at René, and René probably feels sorry for Lee. It is a matter of conscience and pride, for Lee's pride is a bit stiff while René's is an asset to be used only when needed.

If Lee gets drunk, he hangs his head the next day. If René gets plastered, he brags about it and maybe throws in a few Gallic fibs about his amorous triumphs. Lee is a Nordic, in the broad sense, and René is a Latin, yet they live together under one government, in peace and usually in harmony.

Also, they both are Democrats by heritage and rebels by choice on all things except one: the constant and baffling Negro question. For Louisiana is roughly one third black, or shades thereof, and René and Lee, miles apart in so many ways, melt together instantly on this issue.

They believe firmly, belligerently firmly, in segregation and what is loosely called white supremacy. It is more than tradition. It is a faith, the substance of things accepted, the evidence of things long seen.

Here, as elsewhere in the South, the Negro story is snarled in mores and fears and social taboos. If you want to squabble about it, they will squabble and swap platitudes with you while a Negro brings strong black coffee and rich white milk, and somehow they blend.

Uncle Remus and John Henry are gone, and Simon Legree never lived, but the legends linger on.

Surely no state is more myth-ridden than Louisiana and she has quit trying to dispel the legends. Now she sells them to tourists. Her folks collect a pretty high tariff on romantic fantasies and use the take to buy tractors, combines and historical novels about their moon-dipped past.

For every year, hordes visit her fabulous New Orleans and quaint Cajun country (see guidebooks) to laugh and love or carp and whine, then to go back to their cornfields and city shops, a little wiser, a little poorer, but either confirmed Louisiana addicts or Louisiana critics, in any case connoisseurs, after a week, of a culture that baffled Mark Twain and fascinated Audubon and Lafcadio Hearn.

And this old state, like the rivers that green her mantle and muddy her feet, just keeps rolling along, producing most of the nation's domestic furs, sugar, rice and tetraethyl, and a lot of our oil, salt, timber, paper, sweet potatoes, strawberries, sulphur, cattle, cotton, fish and fun—and Hadacol, a patented elixir which, when I was there, was spending several millions a year to advertise "A Better Tomorrow" by drinking a tonic of 12 per cent alcohol seasoned with vitamins.

The Indians started it all and didn't have a chance. Many of them belonged to the Muskhogean nations and often settled their wars by playing a ball game or a sort of bowling contest called "chunky." We can remember them by the word "chunk," meaning to throw out, which is exactly what we did.

Spaniards were the first tourists. One legend says Alvarez de Pineda found the Mississippi River in 1519, and it's a fair bet that Hernando de Soto really did visit the country in 1541 or '42. After de Soto, a few more Spaniards piddled around here awhile, but didn't like the setup. And for more than a hundred years Louisiana was left to herself, her alligators, her pelicans, and her Indians who played ball games.

The French were smarter than the Spaniards, and in 1682 La Salle and fifty men came all the way down the Mississippi from Canada and claimed the whole valley as Louisiana, from mountains to mountains. To René Robert Cavelier, Sieur de La Salle, it was as plain as the cross hilt of his sword: whoever controlled the mouth of the Mississippi could control a continent. Great day in the morning! Fifty-one *voyageurs* and the richest empire of all times. Where are your monuments, dead men? Where are your struck coins?

La Salle, the first Louisianan, was assassinated in Texas. Oh, well. At least Huey Long was assassinated at home.

England, already on the Atlantic seaboard, and Spain in Florida finally got hep that the Mississippi was the key to the whole she-bang and began reaching. But France sent out the brothers Iberville and Bienville and on March 2, 1699, Frenchmen sailed into the mouth of the river—to stay.

The next day was Shrove Tuesday and they found a little bayou and named it Mardi Gras, which means Fat Tuesday. They got the name bayou from the Indians and it means a sluggish stream, any-thing from a creek to a small river.

That fall the English showed up in two ships; Bienville met them at a bend in the river and convinced them the French had a large force upstream. The English turned back, a strange thing for Eng-lishmen to do, and on that day at that place the bayou country was sealed off as a Gallic land. The bend still is called English Turn.

It may not look good in print, but Louisiana really got going in a gigantic promotional scheme of land speculation. John Law was the brains behind it. Mr. Law was a Scotsman who proved that several million Frenchmen could be wrong. He organized the *Compagnie d'Occident,* sometimes called the Mississippi Company or just plain John Company. The French government nodded approval while the company convinced gullible Frenchmen Louisiana was a paradise.

They sent out settlers and sold stock back home and soon the whole thing blew up, and France almost did, in that incredible fraud known as the Mississippi Bubble. However, the settlers were in Loui-siana and it was a matter of root, hog, or die. They rooted.

Survival was the first problem, and then women. There were not enough women. Governor Jean Baptiste Lemoyne, Sieur de Bien-ville, wrote the John Company that his men must have wives. "They are running in the woods after Indian girls," he reported. Some were caught and the Louisiana potpourri began stewing.

First came the delinquent girls, direct from a house of correction in Paris. Some took husbands. The others never got around to it. Next came the casket girls, *filles à la cassette,* so called because their possessions were in small chests shaped like caskets. The casket girls were ladies, in a sense. The correction girls were just females. So the potpourri stewed a little more, and the folks multiplied.

The French crown took the colony back from the John Company, and Louisiana had her feet on solid ground. The land was rich and she poured produce back to France—cotton, sugar sirup and rum.

Things were humming when England and France squared off for the French and Indian War. England won, France transferred Louisiana to Spain and the dons took over after trickery and bloodshed.

Now here came the Creoles, one of the most misused names in the American language. The word is the French form of *criollo*, a West-Indian Spanish corruption and kin to the English word "create." It came into use in Louisiana with union of the French settlers and the Spanish newcomers, and meant anything, including humans, born in the New World of Old World stock.

It started as an adjective. Hence, there were creole whites, the native-born descendants of original French and Spanish families, and creole Negroes, native-born descendants of the first Negro families.

Gradually, however, the troublesome word became a noun and was capitalized and here the white and Negro Creoles parted. To the white Creoles, the capitalized noun referred only to themselves. But to Negroes the word applied to their light-skinned kinsmen, mostly octoroons.

This is still the situation. So unless you know your way through the Louisiana labyrinth of color, caste and custom it is best to duck it except as an adjective, i.e., Creole cooking, Creole ways, and so forth. This does not apply, incidentally, if you like to argue and fight.

Actually there are few real Creoles in Louisiana today. They live mostly in and around New Orleans in clannish family groups, very close and quite conservative.

They often are called aristocrats and that's all right, if the word fits an American vocabulary. But their aristocracy stems from local prestige and tradition and not, as a rule, from Old World aristocracy.

The Creole melting pot was simmering when down came the Cajuns, first in trickles as exiles from Acadia where England had taken over, then in substantial groups until about 4000 came in. They were French rural stock and headed for the open lands of Bayou Teche, big enough to be a river in most states and approximately 100 miles west of New Orleans. The city Creoles accepted them as peasants and were happy to have them settle the bayous and swamps, near enough to be useful, yet far enough away never to be troublesome.

The Cajuns dug in like crawfish, learned more from the Indians than from the Creoles and claimed the bogs as their place to breathe and breed in their own way. They built skiffs called bateaux to navigate the bayous and chipped their canoelike pirogues—light enough to float on a fall of dew—from cypress logs to travel the swamps.

Soon after the United States was established, Spain buttered up the little seaboard republic by recognizing the Mississippi River as the western boundary of the United States, and to top it off, gave us the right to export through New Orleans, duty free.

That did it. Americans, feeling their oats and sowing them in a new freedom, poured into the Mississippi valley, loaded a few jugs of Monongahela whisky aboard their flatboats and started drifting way down yonder to New Orleans.

Buckskins and Kentucky rifle-guns. Long knives and tall men and taller tales. "I was raised with alligators and weaned on panthers' milk. Git out'n my way!"

The Creoles blanched and hid their daughters. Spain tried to slam the door, but it was too late. Americans were on the levees and they dug in, rightly aiming to stay a spell. They did.

> *I came from Alabama, wid my banjo on my knee,*
> *I'm gwyne to Louisiana, my true love for to see——*
> *O! Susanna. O! Don't you cry for me——*

Napoleon was hacking his swath across Europe and Spain ceded Louisiana back to France and the Louisiana Purchase was set up. The greatest buy in all history, $27,267,622 for a fan-shaped area extending from New Orleans to the Rocky Mountains and Canada. It cost about four cents an acre!

The United States took over on December 20, 1803. The Creoles mumbled in their pointed beards. The Americans whooped it up, and the Cajuns didn't give a whoop. English was made the official language.

On April 30, 1812, the territory of Orleans became the State of Louisiana and that same year the first steamboat came down the Mississippi to New Orleans.

The War of 1812 plunged Louisiana back into strife and settled her American status once and for all. The state's seacoast in those days was a haven for pirates, including Jean Lafitte and one Dominique You, a legend-covered gent who had been a cannoneer in Napoleon's army. Yes, these Frenchmen and the Creoles were critical of America in the way of so many Americans until the shooting starts.

Great Britain reasoned then as many Europeans have reasoned since: that the United States was filled with bickering factions and would collapse within if the proper peg were pulled. New Orleans was the peg. England tried to pull it. It didn't work.

A British army that had defeated Napoleon was landed south of New Orleans and a glorious thing happened, a national miracle. They got together—the Creole planters and the Barataria pirates, the Indians and the Negroes. Andrew Jackson and his Long Rifles were welcomed by the same men who, a few years before, had scorned the American flag and American ways.

The English were routed on January 8, 1815. Legend long since has draped the Battle of New Orleans in tinsel—the glamour of Jean Lafitte, the vengeance of Dominique You. The fact is that a large but confused invading army was defeated by a small, smart American army, well entrenched and beautifully handled by General Andrew Jackson.

Some romanticists insist the golden age of Louisiana then set in to last for forty-five years. This, however, is a matter of values. Her cane and cotton lands were so rich that field slavery was profitable. The traffic soared and slaves poured in, many of them down the Mississippi, sold down the river to the sugar plantations, to the salt mines of the Cajun country. The Cajuns themselves did not own many slaves. They were peasants and asked only to be left alone to tend their little farms and rear their broods under the eyes of their priests.

Manor houses bloomed and folks who were not so much back on the seaboard suddenly became somebody out here, their linen immaculate, their dueling pistols primed, their honor an intangible thing—trigger-happy and deadly. Each new nabob tried to outdo the others while slavery and foolish husbandry exhausted the earth.

During this era of silver doorknobs and sillabub, two unrelated events took place that affected Louisiana, in the long run, far more than all the promenades and minuets put together.

Down in New Orleans, around 1830, a group of bored students, fresh home from Paris, got together for a little binge. It was Shrove Tuesday and tomorrow was Ash Wednesday, the beginning of Lent. So they went out on the town. One legend says (and this one sounds plausible) that they rounded up a few courtesans, painted or masked their faces and they all went out on a hooray, parading the streets. It was a Fat Tuesday all right and this was the beginning of Mardi Gras, Louisiana edition. Street masking for Mardi Gras began about 1835 and the celebration sort of evolved, picking this from that and that from something else, until today it is one of the world's most famous hoedowns.

About the same time, Captain Henry Miller Shreve, a Yankee riverman, built the first steam snag boat and chugged up the Red River to remove the famous raft, an obstruction of logs and debris that had blocked the river for hundreds of years. He opened the Red River to commerce. The city of Shreveport is his monument and so, in a way, is the Red River Valley.

Audubon came down and tutored children and painted the birds. Sam'l Clemens came steamboating and sounding the river. "Mark ti-re-e-e! Mark twain!" He wrote a piece for a New Orleans paper and signed it "Mark Twain."

Lincoln came down and didn't like some of the things he saw. Sherman came down to be superintendent of the state university.

There also came a Yankee reporter-propagandist who really fired up a rumpus. Some sources insist he was one of the Beecher brothers who had a sister named Harriet Beecher Stowe. The legend that he was Henry Ward Beecher, a reporter in his youth, is pretty flimsy, but he could have been Charles Beecher, who came South, or even Edward, a writing fellow. Anyway, he went up the Red River, then back home and began pecking at slavery. Now, Harriet Beecher Stowe had never been South, but she read and listened, and she had a flair. Uncle Tom's cabin was in the Red River Valley. At least, that's what Mrs. Stowe said.

Louisiana has no monument to Harriet Beecher Stowe. However, at Natchitoches, in the Uncle Tom country, is a monument to a Negro. His shoulders are bent, his neck bowed and his hat doffed. The inscription reads, "Erected by the City of Natchitoches in Grateful Recognition of the Arduous and Faithful Service of the Good Darkies of Louisiana."

Many Negroes naturally resent the monument. Others sort of smile. Some get drunk and ask him the way to go home, and he always shows them. It seems a long ways from the Good Darkey monument in Red River Valley to Dillard University for Negroes in New Orleans.

By 1860, New Orleans was one of the country's great cities and the second largest port. Then one of her Creoles, General Pierre Gustave Toutant Beauregard, gave the command that opened fire on Fort Sumter, and the nation began her spasm.

The Civil War bled Louisiana white and left her with her throat cut and her back broken. After Farragut, an adopted son, ran the forts below New Orleans, the state was subdued inch by inch. General Ben Butler was in command of the Union army. They still call him "Beast" Butler around here.

Butler was succeeded by General N. P. Banks. There came a few second-class battles and a lot of first-rate cotton stealing and Louisiana was through.

Reconstruction, radical Republicans and riots stretched the state on the rack and then, twelve years after Appomattox, the occupation was over and Louisiana was dropped to the ground, limp and bloody. By the turn of the century, Louisiana was breathing again, or rather gasping in that torpor that gripped the conquered and colonized South.

The Louisiana revival came out of the eroded red hills of Winn Parish, the dreary pine stumps, the wasted land of turnip greens and fatback. He was Huey Pierce Long, salesman and lawyer, glib as a shell-game operator, sharp as a meat ax. And no governor of this era, excepting Franklin D. Roosevelt, shook the foundations so hard or was the object of so much affection, the target of so much hate.

A fair-to-middling library already has been written about Huey Long. Louisianans who knew him read the books and shrug and smile. They know it is easier to sell a legend than to kill it, and Huey has become a legend since a young doctor shot him down in 1935.

He was in power only eight years, the absolute boss of a Deep South state, and yet this is the genius John Gunther says might have brought fascism to the United States.

Louisianans who knew the Kingfish, as Long styled himself, tell me that Robert Penn Warren's *All the King's Men* is the novel that comes nearest to catching the dictator's personality and character.

He attempted a dictatorship in the rebellious South and died under the same code he espoused; for he dared impugn the racial honor of an opponent's family, and one of the boys cut him down. The tall stacks may belch smoke and write new laws in the sky. A million looms may hum and tractors snort where mules once mired, but this is still the South, still "white man's country." Huey Long, the master, made the most simple mistake. He led with his right. He charged "Tar brush!" And forgot to duck. And yet the Kingfish never used racism as a club. Only as a dagger.

Huey Long the demagogue was a cause. Huey Long the dictator was a result. It was inevitable that he should come roaring out of the red hills, himself a product of a beaten land, a bewildered people. He knew a frightening thing about democracy: that some citizens are willing to swap a peck of freedom for a pint of scarcity.

Huey Long learned about people by selling shortening, store-to-store. Loud. Vulgar. Flashy. He studied law at Tulane University and completed the course in less than a year. Brilliant. Shrewd. Witty.

Then he began piddling in politics, got beat once, and came swaggering out of the hills, bellowing his political gospel like a bull alligator: Take from the rich and give to the poor. Share the wealth. Every man a king!

The conservatives and some of the liberals, the money interests and some of the intellectuals rose up to meet him. The poor fell in behind him, the Rednecks and the Cajuns. The meek were to inherit the earth and here was their Pied Piper. Huey swung from the floor and Louisiana never knew what hit her.

He was elected governor in 1928. Build roads! Span the rivers! Free textbooks for all children. Make 'em go to school. Build a great university. A new capitol. Abolish the poll tax!

"Who is paying for it?" the businessman asked.

"You are," said Huey Pierce Long.

So he bonded his state to the hilt and began levying taxes. Of course, as always, the poor paid, too, but they got something to show for it; the roads, the schools, the textbooks.

His enemies tried to impeach him and he slapped them flat. The New Orleans machine arched its back, and he broke its back. He reorganized Louisiana until he controlled every thread in the political loom and could dictate elections from dogcatcher to governor. Then he had himself elected to the United States Senate, but did not take office until 1932.

It is hard to believe that he was governor only for four years, that he was senator only for three. He fought Franklin D. Roosevelt and was a serious threat for a Third Party. There is no judging what the man might have done.

He was back home, hand-running his legislature, when a brooding young doctor entered the Kingfish's skyscraper capitol and wounded him fatally with a small, foreign-made pistol as he came down a corridor, striding ahead of his bodyguard. The assassin was shot to a pulp; Long wheeled down some steps, and died thirty hours later of internal bleeding from one small wound. His hierarchy fell apart because some of his henchmen got too greedy and too careless, and a few of them wound up in jail. A reform movement swept the state and outsiders assumed the influence of the Kingfish was dead.

In many ways the state of Louisiana is a temple to Huey Pierce Long; the roads, the schools, the debt, the taxes. Raymond Swing summed him best when he wrote, in effect, that to understand the danger of Long you must understand his good works.

Well, Doctor Jekyll was a good doctor too.

So much for Huey Pierce Long. If you also are interested in Louisiana people and byways, in Cajun coffee and fish fries, then come with me. It won't cost much money if you duck the gambling joints and the slot machines that spin and clatter in so many of the roadside eateries. We will learn first that a parish is a county, that gumbo is a Negro-French word meaning a kind of soup, that *café noir* is black coffee, that *café au lait* is hot milk and hotter coffee, and that a conscience can be a nuisance. Gumbo ya-ya is a gabfest for women. Praline is a kind of candy and a Poor Boy is a foot-long sandwich made of French bread.

We came in the middle way, across Mississippi and the Pearl River and knew at once that we were in Louisiana—the swishing moss, the brooding swamps. A quaint little French village? Nope, but there was Bogalusa, a bustling little industrial city. The stuffed crabs were hot and peppery and the coffee was already getting good. The waitress chewed gum and came from the Midwest.

"Café noir," I said.

"Huh?"

"Black coffee."

"Oh."

She was the first person I asked: "What is Louisiana?"

"This is. And whatcha getting at, mister?" It was a dry, harsh tone, much harsher than the moss outside, than the warm February sky. "I just work around here. So whatcha getting at?"

Skip it, sister.

My first hitchhiker was standing on a corner in Covington, where the live oaks seemed to brush the top of my car. He had a shotgun in a leather case and was a big fellow about twenty-two.

He settled beside me and I said, "It doesn't take a shotgun to get a hitch around here, does it?"

"No, sir. Just taking my gun back to Baton Rouge. I like to hunt and might get in a little over there. My name's James Sanford and I go to L.S.U."

"You are big enough to play football, Jim."

"I do. Married too. Married when I was seventeen. Said I wanted my girl for my seventeenth birthday present, and I got her."

We were passing acres of tung trees, whence comes the valuable oil, and Jim said, "Used to call this Bloody Tangipahoa parish. Strawberry capital of the world. Lots of Yankees came down. Then Italians and Hungarians moved in, and the feudin' and fussin' started. Everybody gets along pretty good, though, now."

"What is Louisiana, Jim?"

"It's home," he said quickly, and then he thought about it. "I'm studying horticulture over at L.S.U. I like to make things grow. I suppose, in a way, you can say that I'm Louisiana. That's as good as any."

It was night, and flames spurted from a weird bevy of plants at Baton Rouge, lighting the Mississippi that makes this city a seaport 229 miles from the Gulf of Mexico. The woman behind the tobacco counter explained the flames. "Oil and ethyl," she said. "This is the ethyl capital of the world."

By now I realized that almost every place in Louisiana is a capital of something. The flame lights touched the skyscraper state house and the statue of Huey Long in a park where camellias bloomed, the seagoing tankers and Mississippi towboats. This is the capital of government for about 2,500,000 Louisianans, from the Slavonians and Dalmatians down near The Jump, where the river meets the sea, to the Scotch-Irish of Bastrop, up near the Arkansas line.

Tourists mingled with politicians and oilmen in the hotel lobby, the women chattering in a gumbo ya-ya and the men scowling. They wanted a drink, but it was Sunday and Louisiana's capital is a blue Sunday city by local option.

The visitors had been old-homing, visiting, for a fee, the hallowed plantation homes up the river between here and Natchez, the Audubon country. Some had been south, down the river road, and one couple had been to Carville and the leprosarium where Uncle Sam is trying to conquer a disease that is not half as contagious or as deadly as most people think. This couple was amazed at their discovery that the world's supply of perique tobacco is grown on 500 acres, more or less, down in St. James Parish.

Being an old-home hand myself, having lived in Natchez just long enough to catch the bug, I went down the river road to a twenty-two-room mansion whimsically called The Cottage and where, so long ago, folks sat on the upstairs gallery and watched the steamboat race between the *City of Natchez* and the *Robert E. Lee.*

The Cottage is owned by Frances Parkinson Keyes. She wasn't at home, so we sought Belle Grove, one of the most fabulous of all plantation homes and one of the most foolish, a deserted, decaying testimonial to vanity. Belle Grove was hard to find, but yonder she stood, a sagging barbed-wire fence, old trees and weeds, and a pink stucco palace of eighty rooms, give or take a few.

There was the levee where Negro children played and cattle grazed, and here was the manor rotting away, for this was death in the afternoon of the South's plantation era. Lizards scurried. Bees droned. No other sign of life except, high up the side of the monstrosity, was the proclamation: "Kilroy was here!"

Mary Evelyn Dickerson provided an answer to the wearisome myth of the swooning Southern lady and smelling salts. Miss Dickerson is pretty enough for a dance, soft enough for moonlight, an unscarred gladiator in one of the roughest, toughest political arenas in the world.

What is Louisiana? Why, it's progress and prosperity. She wasn't sure of the amount of the bonded debt. That's not her department.

The sun glistened on the bronze memorial to Huey Long, but there was another statue in Baton Rouge and surely more whimsical; a statue to Hebe erected by the W.C.T.U. Maybe the ladies forgot that Hebe was cupbearer to the gods.

Alexandria is the capital, here we go again, of Central Louisiana, called Cenla by a promotional group that hopes to make the land an oil-rich area and a haven for industry and tourists. And there is no doubt about it, Cenla is one of the best fishing sections in the country. It is a place where rice, cotton and cane grow in adjoining fields, where salt and oil come out of the ground and trees grow fast. Here in the steaming Red River Valley hickory skis are started on their journey to the snow hills, and roe of the paddlefish is sold as caviar.

Here, too, is the spacious Hotel Bentley, built by rich old Joe Bentley because another hotel wouldn't let him keep his dog in his room and insisted on his wearing a coat.

Alexandria is the hub of Louisiana, one spoke going northeast to Monroe, the natural-gas capital, an industrial beehive that feels of Arkansas. Another spoke goes northwest to Shreveport, the state's second city, architecturally modern and an oil-gushing Midas that feels of Texas. A third spoke leads southwest to Lake Charles, a shipping and oil center, and a nugget in the Gold Coast that sweeps around from Brownsville, Texas, to the Cajun country.

Across the Red River from Alexandria and in another world is Winnfield, birthplace of Huey Long, Mecca for his followers and a happy hunting ground for lawyers ever since the parish records were destroyed by fire. The issue in Winnfield the day I was there was the little town's new gymnasium for Negroes. It was better than the one for whites and some folks didn't like it.

The community, built around a square, would fit in Mississippi or Georgia—a Saturday marketplace where woodsmen and farmers shared coffee and conversation while their women shopped in an air-conditioned super market called Jitney Jungle and their children licked ice-cream cones.

"What is Louisiana?" I asked the first man I met.

"Well, around here the big 'uns are getting bigger and the little 'uns are getting littler. Louisiana is like any other place, brother. You work and live and do the best you can."

Then I met Thomas Jefferson Wilder. I would have known him anywhere, the Southerner of long furrows and hot suns, his neck red-burned; proud, friendly and religious. He and his wife had come to town to bring buttermilk and eggs.

"Me and Huey Long were boys together back in the country. Huey was sharp as a brier." He cut his eyes over at me in the humor and wisdom of a hunting man. "No, thanks. I don't smoke. Don't drink, neither. I'm a church man. Testify for the Lord twice a week."

We went out to the farm where he lived in a little white house. Hounds and hogs and flowers were in the yard and electricity pulled his pump.

It was a typical Southern hill farm, once exhausted but greening again through conservation and tender care.

"Look at it," said Brother Wilder. "My pine trees are coming back fast and the topsoil is building up. The Lord's been rightly good to me. Come on, let's go see Aunt Tishy Lowry. She was raised with Huey too."

Aunt Tishy had a framed picture of Huey in her hallway and when we left she said, "You all come," meaning, "Come again."

I didn't ask them what Louisiana is. That was obvious. Louisiana is a turnip patch and a cotton field, cool buttermilk on the gallery and hound dogs scratching in the shade.

From the hills of Winn Parish to the Red River bayous of Avoyelles Parish is a short trip, and yet they are poles apart because Avoyelles has a French heritage and Gallic appreciation of gay living, a swishing skirt, a heady drink and a quick-flip of the cards.

"We live and let live around here," said Alton R. deNux, who was mayor of Marksville and a dentist with a sense of humor. His Honor grew camellias and lived well, a friendly host who, like so many Southerners, used his tongue for three purposes: talk, taste and in cheek.

The parish is a network of navigable waterways where fish and ducks abound. We went down a long bayou in Edgar Coco's fishing boat, laughing and whooping, scaring turtles, wild hogs and a moccasin or so.

It was a wilderness of water and trees, and brooding silence. But all along the way were little yellow flags tied to the limbs that shadowed the water—seismograph markers for oil prospecting. The silence won't be long, now, boys: the Texans are coming!

Far, far down the bayou we met two lonely swampers in bright woolen shirts. A coffeepot, a gun and a few fish were in their boat. They spoke no English, but drank Scotch whisky.

Then to a fish fry where a gaunt Negro woman cooked fresh fish in deep boiling fat. She spoke a strange accent and wore a gay bandanna around her head. The fish was smoking hot, the salad stout, and there were no hush puppies, for most Louisianans, unlike other coastal Southerners, do not eat hush puppies, but prefer French bread.

The black land south, where stock roamed at large, was as flat as one of Aunt Tishy's batter cakes, through the town of Bunkie, which was named for its founder's pet monkey, and into the real

Cajun country. I was on watch for "quaint Cajuns" and "old quaint buggies."

There were Cajuns, all right, some of them dressed in their best. The men could have been straight from Madison Avenue, the women from Fifth. I was too busy dodging big automobiles to see many buggies. Amish buggies are more common in Pennsylvania than Cajun buggies in Louisiana.

Opelousas is the sweet-potato capital, where they have learned that the once lowly Southern 'tater is worth more per bushel than corn. Incidentally, sweet potatoes are those juicy red tubers erroneously called yams in the North. The error has taken hold down here and each year Opelousas celebrates a festival called the Yambilee, a sort of small-town Mardi Gras and maybe more fun.

Come to think of it, Louisiana must be the festival capital of the nation, for almost every city and town has some kind of to-do to celebrate something. These include New Orleans' Carnival, of course, and Hammond's Strawberry Festival, Shreveport's "Holiday in Dixie," Opelousas' Yambilee, Crowley's Rice Carnival, New Iberia's Sugar Festival, Grand Isle's Tarpon Rodeo, and the Cotton Carnival at Tallulah.

The moist, rich rice lands spread wide and over there was Crowley, the rice capital, and here was LaFayette, the Cajun capital where afternoon coffee still is called a *collation*.

The crawfish are running in the first stir of spring and the Cajuns catch them in shallow water, grind the flesh of their tails and steep the tasty concoction in herbs and peppers. The mixture then is stuffed into the hollowed-out chests of the crawfish and cooked into a soup called crawfish bisque. It is too good for a king, good enough only for peasants who know how to turn simple things into good food.

Iberia is the ancient name for Spain, but New Iberia is French and my first host here was A. J. Bowab, a Syrian. He talked of Brahma-Angus cattle, industrial surveys and oil barges on Bayou Teche.

This is the pepper capital and the big spoon of Louisiana's sugar bowl. The only "hills" around here are salt domes, miles wide and 5 to 6 miles deep, and the salt, as mined, is too pure for table use. Oil wells rim the domes, one of which is Avery Island. The island was the property of the Avery family for generations. Then years ago a McIlhenny married an Avery. That McIlhenny invented Tabasco Sauce and his son made it famous.

Today the island is owned by a joint family corporation. The McIlhennys lease land from the corporation to grow their tabasco peppers and on which is located the sauce factory. They also lease land for their famous Jungle Gardens. Exotic plants of all the world thrive on the gardens' 200 acres, which are sanctuary for thousands of birds, including egrets. Visitors come to see the soap trees from India, the Egyptian lotus, and daisies from the Mountains of the Moon and remain to gasp at the 50,000 azaleas and camellias.

Here also lived two friends who represented the extreme ends of the Louisiana index. One is Matt Vernon, a newspaper editor who went North to study and came back to tell his people about the good things he had learned, and to warn them about the bad things.

In another age, Matt Vernon would have ridden away with Nathan Bedford Forrest without asking why. Now he questions everything and has worked his shoulders stooped trying to mesh the Cajuns' agrarian traditions into the industrial revolution. The bigger the sacred cow the harder he hits; needling politicians and lashing Yankee reformers and Southern jingoes. Mr. Vernon since has sold his New Iberia paper and has moved his battleground to Eunice.

Being Southerners, we quickly got to the Negro question. "Emotional or rational?" he asked. "I can talk it either way."

"Me, too," I said. "But let's try it rational."

"O.K." He slouched back into the ease of a man on his own ground. "The big noise over the Negro question down here is getting behind the parade, pitifully. More progress toward acceptance of the Negro's rights has taken place in the last ten years than in the previous fifty. Just don't weep for us, brother. And don't yell at us."

It was his way of saying to all who cared to listen: "Don't point your finger at us as long as your own fingernails are dirty."

The other friend is Weeks Hall, a bachelor educated in New Orleans and Paris, and a painter until his right arm was mangled in an accident. Mr. Hall, the last of his line, lives in "The Shadows," the most photographed plantation home in the world and an architectural antique.

"What is Louisiana?" Weeks Hall poured bayou coffee into silver demitasses, sweetened it with rock sugar imported from New York and laced it with rum. "She is a romantic yesterday and a rich tomorrow. Texas is taking us."

Mr. Hall, a recluse to the point of phobia, amazed even the amazing Henry Miller, who spent several days at "The Shadows" while writing *The Air-Conditioned Nightmare.* Mr. Hall's apparel usually consists of blue denim trousers and easy shoes, but for special occasions he adds a blue denim shirt. It is most intriguing to hear him, surrounded by cut glass decanters, silver services and priceless antiques, call to his valet, "Lay out my blues." One expects to see him in evening clothes and cummerbund. One sees him in blue denim.

Tourists invade his yard at all hours, and in a futile attempt to offset their depredations he has instructed his yardmen to collect a small fee. However, in the confusion that attends Mr. Hall, he seldom pockets any tourist's tariff, but usually winds up lecturing them on Cajun cooking, French art and the unfathomable ignorance of Yankees.

Now whereas his friend, Matt Vernon, is a Southern realist, Weeks Hall is a romanticist, although, down deep, he is far more aware of political and social problems than he ever lets on. He is a passing breed in the South: Don Quixote in the trappings of Sir Walter Scott, yet versed in Voltaire and Thomas Jefferson.

Mr. Hall did me many honors. The two I prize most are his family's recipe for bayou coffee and an introduction to Dr. Thad St. Martin of Houma. Here is the recipe:

Parch green coffee beans in a skillet over a charcoal fire. Stir a bit of butter and a smidgen of sugar into the parched beans, then store the beans in airtight cans to be used as needed. Grind, and pour boiling water over the grounds in a French drip coffeepot.

Weeks Hall also gave an explanation of the difference between Creoles and Cajuns: "A Creole was an urban emigré, a Cajun was a rural refugee."

And now down to Houma, over the long, flat road where drivers seldom dim their lights, past Morgan City—a shrimp capital—and into the Terrebonne country, which means "good land." However, there is a lot of water.

Louisiana, incidentally, has the fourth longest coastline in the country. The marshes and water make this bright little city a fur-and-fish capital, and, of course, there is oil. Houma is pronounced

"Homer" and this is rather confusing because there is another Louisiana town named Homer.

Dr. Thad St. Martin is a Creole who put aside his medicine kit long enough to write *Madame Toussaint's Wedding Day*. He also is another contradiction in the Louisiana story, for Dr. St. Martin is a non-Catholic Creole who lives in a Cape Cod house on the bank of a bayou.

Mrs. St. Martin has all the charm, elegance and beauty that the song attributes to "Creole ladies with dancing eyes"—or however it goes. The only catch is that Mrs. St. Martin is not a Creole.

It was a lush February night and the St. Martins, and their foster daughter, Miss Cecele Edsberg, sat on their porch and discussed Louisiana. They had been shopping that day in New Orleans, sixty miles away, and Dr. St. Martin, a native, talked dispassionately about "the city," while Miss Edsberg talked impassionately. "It is the most glamorous city in America," she said. "Food, fun, politics —anyway you look at it." Miss Edsberg moved down from Illinois.

Dr. St. Martin smiled, perhaps remembering that, year in and year out, the biggest political issue in New Orleans is not the Long machine, graft or gambling, but everyday garbage collection. The garbage can is the political symbol of the housewife's wrath and the powers fear her retribution far more than ward heelers, Frankie Costello, reformers and smoke-filled rooms.

"New Orleans is a good-time city," Dr. St. Martin said. "It always has been. It has the best cooking in the country. The people work hard, but always find time for fun. Drink and food, opera, carnival dancing, horse racing, fishing, baseball, football—you name it and New Orleans will furnish it if it is practical, possible or profitable.

"First of all, it is a city in every sense of the word; cosmopolitan and blasé, wicked and righteous, mansions and slums. However, there is one side to New Orleans that we seldom read about. It is one of the nation's best medical centers."

So it is. Charity Hospital is one of the largest in the world and the medical schools include Tulane, Louisiana State University, Dillard's Flint-Goodridge Hospital for Negroes, and Loyola's School of Dentistry.

The St. Martins visit New Orleans as a well-to-do Connecticut family might visit New York. So where do they eat in the cuisine capital? On this day they had eaten at Galatoire's because they have known a waiter there for a long time. They had oysters *brochette*, broiled trout and broiled sheepshead, and water-cress salad.

Reluctantly I left the St. Martins' porch and headed for the "City of Sin," which actually is one of the most churchgoing communities in the country and home of the influential Baptist Bible Institute.

The Huey Long highway and railroad bridge over the Mississippi and the marshes is awesome, a steel string that is testimony to man's engineering conquest of the seemingly impossible.

Then there is New Orleans, her head cradled in a bend of the river, her feet in Lake Pontchartrain and her backbone along Canal Street. Call her what you will. I prefer the City of Courage, for no city has overcome more handicaps than this one.

Lyle Saxon called her "fabulous." Mark Twain spoke of her food as being as "delicious as the less criminal forms of sin." One of her politicians said of her wine-women-and-song philosophy that "you can make it illegal, but you can't make it unpopular." And this is the place where the first white women threatened to leave unless the food improved.

A thousand books have tried to explain New Orleans, but she continues to speak for herself; in the jazz music that she gave the world, in the roar of the Sugar Bowl crowd, in the rivets that make her a shipyard and the cranes that make her a port, in the looms that make her a garment center and Mardi Gras that makes her a painted lady for one night and a penitent mother the next morning.

More than half a million people live in the city proper, and this does not include the thickly settled environs. She is a Bohemian refuge for writers and artists and yet she sells fewer books than Dallas.

Now this is a matter of personal taste, but New Orleans is the only city I know anything about where you can drop in at almost any restaurant and get a good meal. The most famous eating places are Galatoire's, Antoine's, Arnaud's and Broussard's.

There is no mystery about Creole cooking. It is the natural consequence of geography and people. The Gulf of Mexico gives New Orleans an incredible variety of fish. So do the bayous and rivers. The land gives rice, used as Irish potatoes down here, herbs, peppers, okra, cushaws, a vegetable pear called *mirliton*, and just about anything else you need. Mix these with an Indian-French-Spanish-Negro taste and there it is.

However, the drinking is something else, for New Orleans, Gallic as she is, really is a hard-liquor city. This is the home of three of America's distinctive drinks: the Ramos Gin Fizz (gin, egg white, sugar, lemon and lime juice, orange flower water, sweet cream and soda water), the Roffignac (whisky, Hembarig, grenadine and seltzer), and the Sazerac, which is whisky, bitters and sugar served in a glass rinsed with absinthe.

Take with caution!

The Vieux Carré, called the French Quarter or simply the Quarter, is the original Nouvelle Orleans and is only a speck in the sprawling city and has become something of a bazaar and side show in this age of the fast tourist dollar. If you enjoy history, relics and romance, the best way to see the Quarter is to walk, provided you can duck the night clubs, the saloons and the girlie shows. However, if time is pressing, rent a carriage for a reasonable fee, listen to the guide and ask him questions, then take a short excursion on the river.

South Rampart is the Negro Broadway and voodoo no longer is prevalent but still is practiced secretly. Basin Street is a business thoroughfare and not a meeting place. Picayune, once a coin, now is a newspaper and the Storyville of jazz and brothels just ain't.

The famous and the infamous have been coming to New Orleans for a long time, and the city has sent out her share of personalities. From here came the galaxy of great jazz players, including Louis Armstrong and Jelly Roll Morton.

The Crescent City is a community of clubs and the most exclusive is the Boston Club, a political and business sanctum of a chosen few. It got its name from a card game called "Boston" and not from the Massachusetts city.

To the average American, New Orleans is known as the home of Mardi Gras and jazz music.

This distinctive music was born of the blues and the blues are of Negro origin. Perhaps it began at funerals, the plaintive wailing of trombones and other loud instruments so often used at burials around here. Anyway, somehow was started that four-beat time that mingled with the hot notes of ragtime, and jazz was born.

The early ragtime bands were "spasm" bands, nondescript units that improvised music in honky-tonks and the red-light district. These included such colorful musicians as "Stale Bread" Lacoume and his cohorts—"Warm Gravy," "Family Haircut," "Whisky" and "Seven Colors." Their instruments were a bass fiddle made of half a barrel, a cheese-box banjo, a soapbox guitar and a few other assorted doodads.

This crazy music, unique, stirring, Afro-American, stuck to its native hearth until about 1914, when talent scouts took Dixieland to Chicago.

Visitors here always want to see a jazz band and are disappointed to learn that the great jazz players now are in the North, for this city, like her Southern sisters, exports talent in droves. Here in everyday living you hear expressions and melodies that become famous up North in a few years.

The tapestry of New Orleans has a rich color, a feeling of hot reds and deep blues. But the tapestry is dirty in spots and frayed around the edges. Nevertheless, this city is one of the nation's original tapestries and you have not seen your homeland until you have seen New Orleans.

She is the Southern jewel, deep in a Louisiana setting and shining bright and proud. Although there are specks of dime-store tawdriness on the gem, she makes no attempt to hide them.

Sooner or later most American travelers come here. They whisper in St. Louis Cathedral, murmur in the Cabildo and shout in the hot spots. They soon fall into the slow tempo of Canal Street and eat and drink more than they should. On every side is dead history and live fun, and yet the most famous product of New Orleans is neither carnival nor coffee, but an eighty-two-year-old woman—the late Mrs. Meriwether Gilmer, known to the world as Dorothy Dix.

PART V *The West Central States*

Dakota

by JACK SCHAEFER

On old maps, not so old that men living cannot recall studying them in school, it was Dakota Territory, one piece, one area. On present maps it is split by an arbitrary line into two states with the colorless, unimaginative designations: North and South. There are differences between the two parts, man-made, results of years of double statehood and a more or less deliberate fostering of differences. There are people in both states who emphasize differences, people who become huffy if called simply Dakotans and insist upon the North-South distinction. But differences fade in the face of physical fact. Geography predominates. The old maps were right. Dakota is one piece, one place, one area. The very name, common to both states, defies the split. "Dakotah" is a Sioux word meaning "united."

But it *is* two states.

Like stiff-necked members of the same family going their own ways, they have little to do with each other—except when rows develop like the one over the bones of Sitting Bull. It is even difficult to get from one to the other except by automobile—and the surfaced line-crossing highways are few and far apart. Most of the railroads and bus lines and air routes run east-west across the states, not north-south from one to the other.

They are both wild-eyed and individualistic and they are both conservative—in opposite ways.

North, a constant hotbed of agrarian reform, is radical, progressive, upsetting in politics with a habit of electing opinionated men whom sober folk elsewhere often regard as sons of the wild jackass. South has had its political eccentrics, but nowadays is politically settled and conservative. North is restrained and sedate about such things as business and the daily duty of earning a living. South has the booster, the promotional, the sky's-the-limit spirit. It saw nothing blue-sky in its attempt to win the United Nations headquarters. It prepared a flossy brochure boosting its Black Hills for the site. Neighbors Wyoming and Nebraska lent mild support. Practical North remained aloof.

South has the larger population and more cities, yet its general impression is more rural. Its capital, Pierre (pronounced Pier), looks like an overgrown country town. Its capitol is an old-fashioned domed period piece, full of waste space, with rotunda and wide stairways and wide galleries and small Dickensian offices tucked away in odd corners. North is more rural by most standards, yet it gives a more settled, staid, businesslike impression. Its capital, Bismarck, looks like any small-scale, square-blocked city. Its capitol is a tall-towered, streamlined structure, very modern and quite functional.

South enjoys the colorful gesture. North thinks more of its dignity. South has a publicity department. North does not. South goes actively after the tourist trade. North sits back and lets what comes come. South's license plates are large, adding to the numbers a picture—in color—of a state boast, the Mount Rushmore heads. North's are small, narrow, completely practical, carrying only the identifying numbers.

This publicity difference is not necessarily the result of any special virtue (or vice) of either state. Nature endowed South with more tourist attractions and thus South has had a stronger taste of the money the tourist trade brings.

No. There is more to it than that. It is rooted in the people themselves. South's are apt to say: "Want to see our state? Wonderful! Come along and we'll show it to you." North's are more likely to put it: "Looking the state over? Fine. Go ahead and enjoy yourself."

Oh . . . Sitting Bull's bones?
He was killed by Indian police during the Ghost Dance troubles

of 1890 at his camp on Grand River in South's portion of the Standing
Rock Reservation which straddles the common state line.

His body, with those of the police killed in the fracas, was taken
into North's part of the reservation and buried at Fort Yates. When
the fort was abandoned in 1895 and all military graves removed, his
was left untouched. North liked the notion of having him there.

But South wanted him too. There were arguments through the
years, all futile. North had possession. Then came the Missouri Valley
flood-control program. The Oahe Dam reservoir, when completed,
would cover the grave. South swung into action.

Legal action first. Early in 1953, armed with powers of attorney
from some of Sitting Bull's living relatives, South asked North's
Health Department to approve a removal application. North's officials were shocked. Indignant telegrams flew about, some all the way
to Washington. Then one night a group of South's stalwarts (names
officially unknown) slipped north over the line and opened the grave.

What exactly they found, after 60-some years following a quick
unceremonial burial, is their secret. Whatever it was, they took it
southward over the line to a site already prepared—a good site, overlooking the union of the Grand and Missouri rivers close by the
obelisk in memory of Sacajawea, Indian woman guide of the Lewis
and Clark expedition. They buried it again and over the new grave
they poured twenty tons of concrete to offset any North reclamation
project.

There, for all practical and pointing-with-pride purposes, now lie
the bones of Sitting Bull. They rest under not only the tons of concrete but also under a six-ton splendid bust of the old medicine man
done by South's blue-sky sculptor, Korczak Ziolkowski.

After the kidnaping there were more indignant telegrams. Finally,
Mary Louise Defender of Fort Yates, Miss Indian America, acting
as North's special representative, smoked a pipe of peace with
South's Governor Anderson and the battle of the bones was over.

So much for North and South. This is about Dakota. One man's
view of Dakota; an amateur student of Western history who went
West to Dakota and found it all he had thought—and more.

Look at the outline on a map: two rectangular blocks aligned precisely east and west, one above the other. There are straight lines
three fourths of the way around. On the north, the Canadian border,
the famous 49th parallel. On the west, Montana and the upper part of

Wyoming. On the south, Nebraska, straight most of the way then hitting the Missouri River and following the curves downriver to the junction with the Big Sioux. On the east, up the Big Sioux bordering Iowa, then another straight stretch along Minnesota to pick up Big Stone Lake and above it Lake Traverse and on up the Red River of the North to the 49th parallel again.

The area enclosed is Dakota: 148,000-plus square miles of prairie and plain and Badlands and a shading of hills called mountains and a patch of mountains called hills; a huge chunk of territory averaging more than 350 miles in width and more than 400 miles in height on the map, bigger even than the great bull-shaped expanse of Montana, topped in extent only by Texas and California. By size and, more important, by topography, Dakota is the biggest batch of wide-open spaces in the United States. Only Texas could dispute that—and the wide-open spaces of Texas are of a different, less impressive caliber.

Look now along the North-South division line. Almost exactly in the middle the Missouri, the Big Muddy, cuts across. That is the center of Dakota. It is also the approximate center of North America.

Southward, near Pierre, is a small monument which claims to mark the geographic center of the continent. Diagonals from corner to corner of a standard map will intersect there. Northward, above Bismarck, near the town of Rugby, is a stone cairn also claiming to mark the geographic center of the continent.

But the precise spot is unimportant. Any spot in Central Dakota will do, can be shown to be approximately 1500 miles from the Atlantic, the Pacific, the Gulf of Mexico and the lower reaches of the Arctic Ocean. Dakota, neatly framed around that central area, is the heartland of North America.

"Dakota?" said the man at the airport. "What d'you want to go there for? Nothing but droughts and blizzards and fields of wheat. Probably can't even rent a car to get around in."

He was wrong. At Pierre, where the little plane out from Minneapolis landed, there were two rental cars.

Dakota's history, beginning late, moved slowly in terms of modern development. A whole century—from 1750 to 1850—can be taken in one gulp.

The Sioux, still bow-and-arrow, were unable to stand against the

Chippewa—who had some French guns—and were driven westward and spread into Dakota. The fur trappers, the mountain men penetrated all through the territory, taking out a rich plunder in pelts—and leaving no real impression.

In 1775, in the southeast corner where Yankton now stands, one Pierre Dorion married a Yankton Sioux woman and built a cabin and became Dakota's first permanent white resident. Up in the northeast corner, where rival fur companies out of Canada were having almost pitched battles, the North West Fur Company founded Pembina, Dakota's first permanent settlement.

The 1850's started things moving with a relative rush.

This was the period of freehand carving of territories and states by Congress. Dakota did not yet have its name, but settlers already were trickling into the eastern fringe along the Big Sioux. Land companies were starting townsites in the Sioux Falls area.

The settlers were few in number, perhaps no more than 200, but large in ambition, and they started yipping for territorial status. Congress was unimpressed.

Then, early in 1861, Congress suddenly yielded and gave Dakota its name and territorial status. Scattered over hundreds of thousands of square miles there were exactly 2402 white inhabitants.

That was Dakota in 1861. Within twenty-eight years it was ready to become two states.

"I came out here better than 40 years ago," said the man in the old swivel chair in the little false-fronted office building. "From Wisconsin. Thought I had t.b. and needed this higher and dryer climate. Turned out to be tight belt instead. After a time I went back to Wisconsin and couldn't stand it. Too many trees. Too many people and not my kind any more. Just had to get back to this plains country."

Territorial days—those were wild and woolly in Dakota and in basic ways established the modern character of the region.

The 60's were years of beginnings and troubles, Indian and otherwise. Gold had been found in Montana, and the National Government started a survey for a road northward and built forts along the way. Red Cloud, chief of the Oglala Sioux, perhaps the ablest leader of all the seven tribes, rallied them to resist the invasion. In a series of swift campaigns he forced acceptance of a treaty on his terms: abandonment of the forts and a pledge that all of the land between the Big Horn Mountains on the west, the Platte River on the south, the Missouri on the east and north would be left forever as a permanent Indian hunting ground. That included all of Dakota west of the Missouri River.

And all the while the settlers, the sodbusters, the homesteaders were trickling into Dakota.

The 70's were the years of the railroads and wheat—and gold.

The railroads were first. At last people could get to and into Dakota by rail. But why should they come?

The first answer was wheat.

Oliver Dalrymple is the key name. He had partners but he was the active manager, the man who proved what the black-soil region, the Red River Valley and the adjoining prairie could do. Buying big chunks of cheap railroad-grant land, he launched the original "bonanza farm," 12,000 acres at the one sweep, all in wheat. Investment money poured in. Huge farms transformed the virgin land into a rolling sea of wheat. Fifty to 100 sections in one piece was not unusual and a section is a mile square. Those were the days a man could pack food, sling a rifle over his shoulder, plow a furrow straight out till noon, eat lunch, and plow back in time, if he was lucky, to reach home for supper.

The second answer was gold—gold in the Black Hills!

The Indians knew it was there. They knew, too, what would happen if the white men knew. As early as the 30's white men had penetrated the Hills and found gold. They did not get out with it. A small piece of sandstone found near the town of Spearfish and now in a museum at Deadwood had the following crude inscription scratched on it: *came to these Hills in 1833 seven of us All ded but me Ezra Kind Killed by Ind Got all our gold 1834.* The Indians got him too.

The Hills were part of the area set aside by the treaty with Red Cloud to be forever Sioux hunting ground. In 1874, just six years after the signing, that highly controversial military glamour boy, General George Custer, led an expedition into the Hills. Maybe it had military purposes, scientific too. There were geologists along.

But why were prospectors permitted to go too? And why, when they hit gold near the present town of Custer, were messengers immediately dispatched at speed to make the word public outside?

The inevitable stampede started. A new strike, the big one, was made in Deadwood Gulch. In a matter of months 25,000 people were crowding into that narrow twisting gulley with its mushroom tent town, and other thousands were swarming through the Hills. Names like Wild Bill Hickok, Calamity Jane, Preacher Smith, Deadwood Dick, were adding flavor to the tales running through the country.

With a flamboyant gesture Dakota, the land of golden wheat and gold, was on the maps and on the national consciousness.

The 80's were the years of the cattle boom. Ranching in those days was not only profitable, it was fashionable. Investment money poured in; amateur ranchers too. Young Theodore Roosevelt was one of them. He went west to Dakota for a sample of the robust life and stayed the better part of four years. But easily the most remarkable was a handsome French nobleman from Paris named Antoine-Amedee-Marie-Vincent Manca de Vallambrosa, the Marquis de Mores.

The de Mores enterprises made many marks on Dakota. One was, and is, the little town of Medora, named for his American wife, in the heart of the northern Badlands. This was the site of his most ambitious project. He planned to raise cattle and sheep and ship the meat east. He built a big meat-packing plant at Medora. But he was a poor businessman, and the professional ranchers unloaded poor stock on him. At last he closed the plant and departed for Paris. Only the tall chimney of his Medora plant still stands. And nearby, the chateau he built is now a local museum.

Note that chateau. This de Mores, unlike most of the cattle-boom investors, lived in Dakota. He took part in local politics and cattle associations. He started stage and freight lines. He helped finance newspapers. He hunted with the best, with men like Granville Stuart. He tangled with a grizzly and killed it with a knife. He was straight out of a romantic storybook and he was real.

Then, with the terrible winter of 1886–87, the cattle boom collapsed.

At the time, Bismarck, the new territorial capital, was less than ten years old, but full of bounce. It laid the new capitol cornerstone with a flourish. General Grant was there, and Sitting Bull, and James Bryce, author of *The American Commonwealth*. What particularly impressed this visiting Englishman was a speech in which "it was proved that as Bismarck was the centre of Dakota, Dakota the centre of the United States, and the United States the centre of the world, Bismarck was destined to be the metropolitan hearth of the world's civilization." North, too, had its blue-sky tinge in those days.

And all the while the settlers, the sodbusters and the small independent ranchers, were coming into Dakota, spreading out over the far open spaces.

They came . . . the fiddle-footed and the restless always settling and never settled who would move on or back, leaving shacks to weather away in the endless wind . . . the land-grabbers who would pre-empt and homestead only long enough to prove title and sell out . . . the real-estate operators who would lay out townships and draw pretty pictures of buildings never to be built . . . and the solid whipcord men who would stand stubbornly through the hard years, and their women who would often, in the lean, long years, irrigate the dry land with their tears—and stay and make homes seemingly lost yet held in the immensity of the land.

They came, the land-hungry, from the Midwest and the East and Canada, and as many and more direct from the old countries; primarily nordics: Finns with their constant coffeepots and their "Finlander hells" or steam baths; Russian-Germans, many of them Mennonites, who had emigrated from Germany into Russia early in the century; Scandinavians with their insistence upon homeland cooking, Norwegians most numerous among them; a sturdy sampling of Dutch and Irish and English; even a colony of Icelanders in the Pembina area.

They came—and Dakota wanted them and welcomed them and urged them to come. They came as word spread that in Dakota the land was level with no trees or brush to clear away. During one sample week 9000 immigrants traveled by train through Chicago and more than 8000 were ticketed for Dakota.

Then, beginning in '86, there were several years of continued droughts. The Dakota land boom dwindled and collapsed. And reversed. The fiddle-footed, the quickly dissatisfied, the sell-out homesteaders, the weak willed, began to leave. It was a healthy winnowing process. For the stubborn whipcord men and their women— eccentric and independent and individualistic and stubborn—remained.

Year after year they had been petitioning Congress for statehood and the demand for division had been growing. In 1888 the Republican National Convention wrote a double-state plank into its platform. In 1889, after the new Republican Congress had acted, the new president, Benjamin Harrison, signed the official proclamations. The two documents were shuffled and placed on his desk with the texts covered, only the signature lines showing. Officially at least, no one knows which state was admitted first.

That was Dakota. That *is* Dakota, the real, the enduring Dakota. Dakota today remains, in modern terms, what it became in the territorial days. The past is close and often beckoning there.

"Stand over there and look down," said the man in worn overalls and ancient farmer's straw hat. "See those darker streaks in the grass running on around that ridge? Look like wagon tracks, don't they? Well, they are. That's where one of the old freight routes to Deadwood ran. You can't make out a thing down close by them. From up here they still show darker where the wheel ruts were. Sometimes looking down there you can get the notion it wasn't seventy-five years ago but only last week those wagons were moving along."

That North-South division was made by a political institution, the United States Congress. The real, the sensible, the logical division of Dakota is far more ancient—and is east-west. It was made by the Missouri River.

> *Ah-hah, I'm bound away*
> *'Cross the wide Mizzoura.*

That is not just a refrain from a song. It is a living slogan out of the past, still strong in the present. East of the Missouri is east; west of the Missouri is west.

East-river, west-river: Dakotans constantly use those labels. East-river country is chiefly farmland. West-river country is chiefly rangeland. East-river is shotgun country; west-river is rifle country.

No generalizations are absolute nowadays, but the cleavage cut by the Big Muddy is still distinct. A few old-timers claim they can tell which side they are on just by sniffing the air. A simpler test for visitors is a costume check. East-river has plenty of cowboy boots and wide-brimmed hats always in evidence. The majority are the drugstore variety, the mass-produced-for-the-tourist-trade relatively cheap type. West-river they are everywhere and the majority are forty dollars-plus boots and twenty dollars-plus hats, the true articles, usually battered and weary from years of weather and work. East-river they are worn for show, a form of regional fashion. West-river they are worn as practical working equipment.

Fort Pierre proves the point. Pierre, on the east bank, becomes ever more neat and respectable as more state-capital buildings and modern homes and motels are built. It is reminiscent of many another small city back east. You cross the long narrow bridge to the west bank and definitely there is a different feel in the air. You swing south a short distance, to where the Bad River comes in from the west, and the little town of Fort Pierre drowses during the day, looking much as it did when freighters outfitted there for the long haul to the Black Hills. At night Fort Pierre comes alive as cowboys from the west-river rangeland gather in the surprising number of taverns, and state employees from Pierre cross the river to join them. No doubt Fort Pierre gets a nightlife boost from the convenient fact that the river marks the time line, the shift from Central to Mountain Time, and its taverns can stay open an hour longer than those in Pierre. But it does not need the boost. It has the atmosphere, the tradition. An outlander, visiting those taverns, needs to be wary. He may find himself trapped by the west-river cowboy custom of setting up drinks for the crowd.

Northward at Bismarck it is the same. Bismarck itself, on the east bank, is a neat and respectable small city. You cross the river westward and are in Mandan. The names speak the difference. Bismarck was named by men looking eastward across the Atlantic, in the hope that the honor paid the German Iron Chancellor would attract German immigrants. Mandan was named for the Mandan Indians who once had villages there.

Mandan may fool you for a brief time, what you see of it just passing through. Much of it is of recent growth and has an eastern look. The Northern Pacific built a depot there which is a copy of George Washington's Mount Vernon. But the moment you wander off the main street, the western imprint is clear. Anywhere out toward the outskirts, the land opens and engulfs you with meaning and you suddenly realize this is it—this is the land of the high plains of the west. And just a short drop downriver, again on the west bank, is the site of old Fort Lincoln from which, one day in 1876, with banners flying and band playing, General Custer and his 7th Cavalry rode westward toward a rendezvous on the Little Big Horn.

It is the same almost anywhere along the Missouri. East of the river is east. West of the river is west.

Dakota is where, more distinctly and on a longer frontier than anywhere else in the United States, the west begins.

"I didn't use to believe those old stories about the blizzards," said the woman who ran the little six-room hotel. "But in '49 we had a whole month of them, one right on top the other. I'll have you know that was something. You could walk right up on the roof of this place from the drifts. It was ten days at one stretch before the road was open along here and I got mighty sick of canned pineapple too. But I'll have you know everybody pitched in and helped everybody else and those with airplanes dropped supplies around and we didn't lose a life at all. That's human life I mean. Maybe some Federal aid did come in—but we paid back every cent of it."

As geologists can point out, Dakota actually is divided into four quite distinct sections, neatly balanced: two east-river, two west-river. Starting from the east, the first is the Red River Valley.

This is a long narrow (in Dakota distance terms) strip running down the edge of North Dakota and fading out in the Lake Traverse and Big Stone Lake area of South Dakota. It is the last strip of rich, welcoming, never-failing farmland along the northern tier of American states before the beginning of the real prairies and plains—and it is a magnificent strip. It is one of the finest stretches of almost table-top farmland on the continent.

Tucked into the northeast corner is the sleepy little border town of Pembina which was not only the first permanent settlement in Dakota but the first in the entire American Northwest. A century ago it was the rallying center for the famous annual Pembina buffalo hunts. Now it is a quiet farmers' village, notable chiefly for its quaint old-fashioned gingerbready architecture.

This Red River Valley was the original home of the bonanza farms and of hard wheat when Dakota was winning the title of breadbasket of the world. It is still great wheat country, golden in harvesttime. But the huge farms have been broken up into merely big farms and diversified farming dominates, settled and reasonably sober and sedate.

It is farmland de luxe, almost untroubled even in the bad years by droughts and grasshopper plagues. But the Red River Valley is not distinctively Dakotan. It is shared the full length with Minnesota. Crossing this river brings no perceptible change. Dakota's half of the Red River Valley could be simply Minnesota lapping over.

The second section, all the vast remaining expanse of the east-river country from the Red River Valley over to the wide Missouri, is the Dakota prairie—that great glacial drift, rolling, treeless sea of soil left in ages past by the recurrent sheets of ice that crept down out of the north and leveled off the high places and filled in the low and, melting in defeat along the edges, created the Missouri Trench for the modern river.

That is Dakota. That is a good half of Dakota and most of it is distinctively Dakotan. It is not all pure prairie, only a mere ninety per cent.

In northeast South Dakota with Watertown, appropriately named, as the local capital is the southern lake region. Dozens of lakes and ponds and stretches of marshland speckle the nearly level surface. On up in North Dakota, a jump westward from Grand Forks, is the northern lake region. And on up further, between and above the towns of Bottineau and Rolla, pushing on over the Canadian border, are the Turtle Mountains. North Dakota calls them mountains. To anyone acquainted with the real mountains of the west, they are hills—a pleasant break in the prairie offering scenery and excellent hunting, but hills.

And it is not wholly treeless; almost every watercourse has its fringing of brushes and shrub growth and often genuine trees. But these are far between in the vastness of open spaces and usually dip below the general ground level so that they are lost in the far view. The effect for nearly countless miles is true treelessness. In fact, a real stand of trees, even along a watercourse, is such a rarity that most of the early prairie homes were sod-walled or built of rammed-earth blocks. Even today a city like Aberdeen, in the heart of the prairie, will boast of the trees, all planted by hand, which line its streets.

The prairie is natural grassland. Buffalo into the millions once roamed there; now the only buffalo east-river are on a state game farm close to the Canadian border. The prairie has been settled, tamed, plowed, broken to harness. That is sometimes hard to believe on the long lonely stretches of the graveled roads off the few good highways where the clusters of farm buildings dwindle to a mile or more apart and unbroken distances pull vision beyond grasp of the mind. But signs of the plow are rarely out of sight and those reminders of the taming—the fence lines—are constant companions.

As you push out into this prairie along any of the main east-west routes that slice across it, a sense of the land creeps in and grows until it dominates all else. The few farm buildings merge into their surroundings, natural objects in a natural world, and there is only the land, apparently limitless, serene, indifferent, enduring the surface scratchings of man, under the great rounded bowl of the sky. You begin to understand the quiet unhurried manner that marks so many Dakotans. The day wanes and ahead the sun drops to the horizon and an unbelievable glory of color claims the sky. The people of wooded or hilly or mountainous country do not know what sunsets are.

This is the section which, with some help from west-river, is now the breadbasket of the world—well, in this cold-war era, of half the world. Wheat is the major crop. Dairying is on the upgrade, but beef is still the real cattle business. The old longhorns which followed the buffalo are long since gone. It is Hereford country with a spotting of Angus and Durhams and mixed breeds.

A recent phenomenon is the annual parade of big combines moving north with the ripening grain. Once it was an annual wave of itinerant farmhands following the harvest; now it is a parade of machines, big and ungainly and flamboyant in red paint and almost frighteningly efficient, cutting and threshing and loading in the single operation. They come north out of Nebraska and Kansas and Oklahoma and Texas, crawling northward with the advancing season. In early August they are moving through South Dakota. By late August they are well up into North Dakota, heading into Canada.

This area, too, this prairie, is the bird-hunter's dream come true. From the beginning it abounded in game birds, waterfowl in the lake regions, grouse and prairie chicken everywhere. By time of statehood it was already well known to shotgun sportsmen. Expeditions in what were called "chicken wagons" roamed the seemingly endless acres. Frederic Remington described one such expedition in 1894, in pictures and text, for *Harper's* magazine. The text was ecstatic. And he knew only the beginning.

For the Dakotans have not been content with their natural bird endowment. Partridges and wild turkeys have been introduced and have thrived. So too have ring-necked pheasants. Emphatically so. In 1898 a Doctor Zitlitz brought two male and four female into South Dakota. There were some later stocking releases, never in quantity. There was no need. The pheasants had taken over. By the 1940's, despite constant slaughter called hunting, they had multiplied past counting. A mathematician in South Dakota recently calculated that during a good season there 15,000 birds are killed every hour. The hunter who fails to get his birds in Dakota is a hopeless dub.

About midway along the main east-west prairie routes are the small farm-center cities: Mitchell with its Corn Palace, built for the annual six-day harvest festival, and decorated anew each year inside and out with scenes and designs actually done in corn and other grains . . . Huron, boyhood home of Chic Sale, which holds the annual State Fair and is the undisputed pheasant-hunting headquarters . . . Aberdeen, quite a railroad and wholesale distribution as well as retail center, once the home of Hamlin Garland and of Frank L. Baum, the Oz-books man . . . Jamestown, where Maxwell Anderson went to school, home of North's oldest and only private college (there are plenty of state institutions) which offers a structure definitely worth seeing, the Voorhees Chapel . . . Minot, which started as a tent town when the Great Northern had to hesitate there in its push westward to build a bridge, then mushroomed so fast it was called the Magic City.

You move on along the east-west routes and distance engulfs you again and ahead is the Missouri River. All of them strike almost straight to it.

"Yep," said the man on the next stool at the little café. "Wheat didn't do so good this year. But I put me in sixty acres of soybeans too. First anywhere around these parts. Don't know how I'll make out on price, but the damn things sure grew. I'll lease me some more land next year and put in a section of them."

And so westward—across the wide Missouri. For simple talking purposes this next section begins with the river and covers all the rest of Dakota except the roughly oval island of the Black Hills in the southwest corner.

This is the Dakota plain. This is Dakota's slice of the great Missouri Plateau; Dakota's slice of the high plains of which the Missouri Plateau is only a part. Most of this section is semi-arid. That may seem strange if you consult a map, for the whole area is laced with rivers, tributaries of the Missouri. They strike across at almost regular intervals through the plains with names that are resonant of history: the White, the Bad, the Cheyenne, the Moreau, the Grand, the Cannonball, the Heart, the Knife, the Little Missouri, dwarfed only by its big brother, the Big Muddy itself.

When the rare local rains hit (they are apt to be sudden and brief and torrential in their briefness) the water sluices off the dry ground and the rivers rise in flash flood and the floodwaters sweep downstream and in a day or two, sometimes in a few hours, the rivers are low and lazy again. You stand on the bank of one, say the Bad, and make a superior comment to a native about such a grim name for such a mild stream. He merely chuckles and points to a tree, likely a northern willow, behind you. High up, well above your head, are mud marks on the bark. "It was up there for a while last week," he says.

This west-river plain is as treeless as the east-river prairie. It is deeply rolling country and broken country with areas marked by lonely buttes rising sharply in strange shapes. Everything is large scale, stretching the muscles of the mind. You drop to a low level and huge rolling shoulders of land seem to hem you in. You climb to a high level and vision races out a hundred miles and more in every direction and falters in the attempt to find a true horizon. Distances constantly deceive. The eastern mind fumbles them. Driving along, you tag behind a slow car waiting to top a rise ahead and see the road clear before passing—and suddenly realize the summit of that rise is still a mile or more away. . . . Those tiny objects far ahead are a water tower and a grain elevator, symbols of a town. Half an hour later with the speedometer still at seventy, they are still there, slightly larger but still there, far off, marking a town lost in the immensity of the land.

This was horse country and still is (a roundup of wild horses in the Medora area brought in more than 200 a few years ago) and the ability to sit a saddle, Western style, is taken for granted. But the horse is being reduced to certain specialties. Many a rancher and farmer has a small plane, not just for getting places in the Dakota distances, but for routine inspection of his acres and crops and herds. Normal work around a ranch is apt to be done in a jeep. It is a common sight to see a modern cowboy skittering in one along the inside of a fenceline checking the wire or heading straight across country in search of wandering stock. In the really tough areas, however, the horse holds its own—and no jeep has yet learned to ease into a herd and cut out the right animals or the difficult art of carrying a rider with hands free for roping a wayward steer in branding time.

"Ranching?" said the man at the first gasoline station in thirty-seven miles. "Old-style, eh? Nothing dudey and no jeeps. There's some around. Friend of mine has one about the same as it was when his pop was a pup. We'll just let bub here watch the station while I run you out. No. Not your car. Mine. Think I'm stingy with my gas?" That ranch was forty-five miles away.

When rains do hit and before the following sun and the endless wind have done their drying work, the west-river plain sets two traps for those unwary enough to wander off the surfaced or graveled roads even on foot. One is what can be called the ordinary mud, the common mud in the low places where the fine silt of ages of erosion has collected. It is not quicksand; it is mud, unbelievably gooey and often unbelievably deep. The story is still told of the passing stranger who saw a cowboy hat lying in a mudhole and carefully reached to pick it up. Underneath was a man's head. The stranger leaned down and took hold of the man under the armpits and hauled him out. "Thanks," said the mud-dripping cowboy. "Now help me pull up my horse."

The other trap is the gumbo. This has given its name to a whole desolate region north of the Black Hills. Gumbo is a black clayey soil that, when dry, bakes hard with endless cracked wrinkles, and, when wet, becomes an expanse of Gargantuan, gummy flypaper.

And of course, emphatically of course, the Dakota plain has the Badlands.

These are true parts of the plain. They do not rise above its general level; they drop below. They are not upthrusts of the earth's surface weathered into the present formations. They are the results of ages of erosion cutting down into the plain.

South's are out some from the Black Hills, below the town of Wall, the main tourist entering point. North's are along the Little Missouri. Of the two, the southern are the real Badlands, what should be called the Worselands, barren of mostly everything but beauty. The northern are more hospitable, wide spaced, with scattered rich grass-plots between the twisted buttes. But in both, the essential formations are the same type.

They cannot be described, those freakish, unearthly jumbles of ridges and hummocks and sharp cliffs and buttes, of domes and pyramids and cones and weirdly lovely shapes out of an artist's nightmare, striped in the browns and reds and grays and yellows

and black of the pressed sand and clay and lignite of which they
are formed . . . colors shifting in shade and tint with the shifting
light and the play of the shadows. They cannot be described. Many
people have tried—and the words limp behind the reality. They
cannot even truly be held in mind. No matter how often seen, there
are areas that always strain belief, are more weird and wonderful
than remembered. Hell with the fires burnt out, General Sully described them long ago. That—or a drunken surrealist's dream of
paradise.

*"No more coffee?" said the waitress in the little combination bar
and restaurant, coming back with the pot the third time. "You don't
come from around here. Folks out here like three or four cups with
a meal, so we just give it to them."*

So at last to the last section, the Black Hills.

They are not hills but mountains, not soaring in grandeur like the
Rockies and Sierras but solid and honest mountains nonetheless, seen
dark-topped with their superb pine and spruce forests in the distance
from far off on the plain all around. Geologists say they are the
world's oldest mountains. Certainly they are among the world's most
beautiful. And they are one of America's newest playgrounds. They
are Dakota's chief tourist attraction and they have been publicized
and exploited with unashamed exuberance.

Every town has its museum and special baits. Rapid City has its
Hangman's Hill and its Dinosaur Park with life-sized models in
cement of the prehistoric reptiles which roamed the region some
40,000,000 years ago. It also has (not tourist bait) a major Air
Force base. Belle Fourche (pronounced Bell Foosh) has its Black
Hills Round-Up. Sturgis has its Jack Pine Gypsy Tour and Key City
Rodeo. Spearfish has the Passion Play, brought to this country by
Josef Meier. This is technically the world's oldest; its previous
history in Germany traces back to 1242. It is presented in a fine
natural amphitheater by a huge cast, including a flock of sheep. It
is very impressive, and it is also somewhat ironic; the white man's
sacred drama has been deliberately transplanted to a site in the
once-sacred hills of the Indians.

Hot Springs has its Evans Plunge, largest natural warm-water
indoor swimming pool. Custer has its Gold Discovery Days. Deadwood has its annual Days of '76 jamboree and several nights a week

during the season retries Jack McCall for the shooting of Wild Bill
Hickok. This is one of the most enjoyable regional or folk plays
perpetrated anywhere for the tourist trade. It bursts out of No. 10
saloon to begin with a street chase, then adjourns into a nearby
building where, after the ticket-buying stampede subsides, McCall's
actual trial is re-enacted with surprising fidelity to fact and a
judicious attention to hilarious incident. Alibi Ike usually steals the
show.

Natural wonders are given full play: Spearfish Canyon, many a
person's earnest entry for the longest stretch of sheer winding
cliff-lined loveliness in the West; Custer State Park with its buffalo
herd and antelope preserve; Sylvan Lake; Wind Cave National Park;
Harney Peak; the Needles.

And, of course, all tourist trips lead eventually to Mount Rushmore.
But some lead on, not many miles away, to where that magnificently
mad sculptor, Korczak Ziolkowski, is gnawing away at a project
which outdoes even Mount Rushmore in planned scope and which,
if ever finished, might even outdraw it. He is carving a whole
mountain into a memorial to the great Sioux leader, Crazy Horse.

To see the Black Hills as a whole, climb to the ranger tower on
either of the two peaks, the southern Harney or the northern Terry.
You look out and all around are these mountains called hills, dark-
topped with their forests, reaching, tier on tier, into the distance.

And then, looking northeastward from this far southwest corner of
Dakota, vision gradually focuses beyond the hills themselves. There,
lighter in color, limitless into the horizon, is the plain and you
know that it sweeps on to the wide Missouri and that beyond,
farther beyond, is the great expanse of the prairie dropping imperceptibly across the seemingly endless miles to the Red River Valley.

That is Dakota. It is the least-known section of the United States.
It was one of the last frontiers and retains many frontier aspects.
It is still thinly populated in modern terms—not like the desert and
mountain states with concentrations of people in between raw
rough unused regions, but fairly well spread out and thinning
gradually from east to west. There is only one city in the 50,000
bracket, Sioux Falls; only three in the 25,000, Fargo, Grand Forks
and Rapid City; only a dozen in the entire territory which edge
past 10,000. There were no surfaced roads clear across until the
1930's. There are towns today which have declined with the coming
of the automobile, enabling people to live out more easily on the

land. There are ghost towns in which only a few lonely people still keep vigil. There are areas in which the population has dwindled with reversion of farmland to grassland and only a few relics of what were once homes remain. There are still big tracts set aside as Indian reservations. Except in the Black Hills there are no streams of tourists along the highways. Those who do come are easily absorbed into the wide-open accessible spaces.

And all this is an asset. Dakota as a whole still has an uncluttered, unsoiled air, a simple freshness, untainted by the stale weariness of most older overrun regions. The land, not what man has done with it, still predominates.

It is a rare and rewarding place for those interested in Western history. No other section offers the story of Western development with quite the same rounded completeness. Dakota has had every aspect and in abundance: the fur trade, the buffalo, the river traffic, the wagons westward, border trouble with the British, Indian wars, freighting and stage lines, the cattle empire, the open range giving way to fencing, the cattle and sheep wars, homesteading, town settlement, countyseat fights, capital rivalries, railroad surveys and rail-building races and station-site troubles, gold rushes, mining camps, the impact of new land and independence upon immigrants, the transition from territory to state. Its history is recent, close, the markings still plain. Historic sites, well preserved, dot the whole expanse.

Its people have an invincible friendliness, not pushing and back-slapping but honest; not the standardized "friendliness" calculated to bring patrons to dude ranches and sell drugstore-cowboy outfits and tourist curios, but the friendliness of people still stubborn and independent, still accustomed to relying upon their own resources, still sociable and neighborly, still able to be gullible, to have faith in their fellow men. It is sincere first-name country from the first handshake.

Dakotans still look at the land about them and at the sky over-head. They have absorbed the feeling of the open spaces, that there is room enough and there is time enough.

Nebraska

by MARI SANDOZ

Nebraska has been known as the Tree Planters' State, the Bug Eater, Flower, and Cornhusker State, and now finally, by legislative action, it has been named the Beef State. But long before any of these were coined it was called Quivira, the land that is yet to be found.

Back in my childhood in Nebraska, when our father shot a soaring eagle out of the sky, he liked to stroke the handsome shining head and talk grandly of Coronado.

"That Spaniard was right," Old Jules would tell us. "Here's another of the golden eagles he was looking for."

Father always laughed aloud at his joke about the early gold seeker and his land of Quivira, with a river six miles wide, fishes big as horses, and great canoes with golden eagles at their prows —a place where even common people supped from jugs and bowls of gold.

Yet perhaps none of it was too far from the truth, not even the six-mile-wide river. The old Missouri could spread out mightily in those days, and certainly more fabulous canoes than any Coronado had hoped to find churned their fiery way up the current and down, carrying more tangible wealth than even he dared dream of.

But it was a long time from Coronado to the Beef State's prize steaks on the platter, whether golden or plain. For a while the region was known as part of the Great American Desert and then as a very broad and dangerous stretch that must be crossed by the strings of emigrants hurrying West like ants before the winter.

By the time I was old enough to know these things I had spent a lot of time with the rolls of maps my father kept handy for the homeseekers he located at twenty-five dollars apiece, including the necessary surveying for the section of free land. Even before I could read I liked to spread them out on the floor while I let my baby brother cry and the bread dough sour. Nebraska really did look like a large section of a hackberry leaf, as an old Indian once showed me—a giant tilted leaf whose midrib was the bordering Missouri River. The veins of the leaf were the long streams flowing through the state toward the Big Muddy: the broad, flat-watered Platte, the Republican of such deceptively moderate and stable appearance, and the deep-canyoned, crystal-clear Niobrara that ran so swiftly past our home southwest of Rushville, in northwest Nebraska. Once, when father was in a good mood, he elevated the west end of the map to show us how tilted the state really was, rising from 800 feet above sea level in the southeast corner up past us to the Pine Ridge and the Wildcat Range of the western border, a climb to 5400 feet in around 450 miles.

It was this gradual climb toward the Continental Divide, with water and grass all the way westward—the direction the white man seems to move over the globe—that made the state the world's great path of empire. Sometimes my father and the old frontiersmen talked into morning light about those days that gave Nebraska more miles of migration on and along its waters than on any comparable stretch of earth. If I kept very quiet in the woodbox I could stay up to listen until I fell asleep.

This was how I learned that, when the first white men came to Nebraska, all its Indians lived in round houses of earth or skin, round because all the great things were round: the moon, the sun and the dwelling place of the Great Powers around the earth's horizon. Therefore the villages must be round, and their dwellings. When the Indians were put on reservations and sickened from tuberculosis, they believed it was because the houses were square, unholy. I recall one of the old Sioux who used to pick potatoes before mechanization came in. All his family had died of the coughing sickness because, he said, they had slept in a cornered log shack. He would never cross our doorstep but often sat outside on the woodblock for hours, visiting over his pipe.

The first pale-skinned men who came riding were drawn by a scent stronger than roasting buffalo ribs to a starving Indian—the rich, heady musk of the gold rumored in Quivira. Others came through the region following the secondhand stink of gold in furs and hides, and later the lure of the actual metal. But most of the emigrants who cut the deep trails through Nebraska, dropping their broken wagons, burying their dead, were drawn by a sweeter, a more enticing fragrance—free land for the homeless, and the independence that land can give.

"You can't think what the words 'free land' meant to a poor European," a man my father located back in 1888 told me. "Me and my brothers had lost our jobs in the hard times and were fighting with street gangs over the village cats for soup. Then we found a letter in a newspaper from a Herr Sandoz in America, telling of the free land in Nebraska, and perhaps a tourist pass on the railroad from New York. An uncle offered to borrow the money to send me to see. I wrote and the answer came." The old man looked at me quizzically. "It told about the land, and the need in the new country for wives. Old Jules was having wife trouble."

"No complaint about mail service?" I asked.

"That came later, all the years my brothers and I knew your father. He ran me off his place with a gun once because he thought I did not help get the mail service. But he had run me off before that because I would not join his mob that hung a troublemaker who was burning out the settlers and shooting into their houses."

I was silent. I had often thought of that, and of the time when father, a crack shot, had fired at a neighbor not fifty feet away. The bullet went over the man's head because I had struck the stock of the .30-.30 down as I saw father's finger tighten on the trigger.

"He was a violent man," the old settler added, "but he was the first in the wilderness, with no sheriff, no law except his gun. He settled over a thousand homesteaders on good land. Many who stayed got rich. He gave us trees to plant, plums and berries to content the women. Even after our fight, when the cowboys turned cattle into my corn and scared my young wife, Old Jules came to visit with his rifle, and shot target at tin cans nailed on posts. They were there twenty years, old and rusty, but nobody came to make me more trouble."

I nodded, thinking of all the men and women who went out to the world's wildernesses, seeking homes, land.

The people of Nebraska have grown conservative, some even reactionary, perhaps through the loss of young blood to the East. Lincoln, the capital, was long supposed to have the greatest concentration of DAR's for its size. Yet we fostered William Jennings Bryan, Populism and Senator George Norris, and no politician who has made a speech against the northwest wind of the Nebraska Panhandle, and faced the squinted, cynical eyes of the natives, can ever feel too sure which way we may jump next. Nebraska was long included in the Bible Belt, yet we calmly put a bayonet into Crazy Horse, the most modest and ascetic Sioux leader, this after he had surrendered all his weapons for the promise of peace and safety for his people. People from Nebraska occupy positions high and far. General Alfred M. Gruenther, Platte Center, was Supreme Allied Commander in Europe; the former Lincolnite, John M. Allison, was Ambassador to Japan. Some Nebraskans sit alone in Dannemora and Alcatraz. We have had a few pretty cool murderers, reaching from old Chief Blackbird to the recent killing of teen-age girls by young hoodlums, as elsewhere now. On the other hand we grew a most noted jurist, Dean Roscoe Pound, formerly of Harvard Law School.

Even now there are schools with one pupil, movable schools on skids, and pupils too far from any school at all, and yet Nebraska developed the nation's finest prose stylist, Willa Cather.

And if you are a man and want to live to be as old as possible, settle on a farm or in some small Nebraska town—where the average life span is the longest in the nation.

Much of this prairie state was long-grass country, "lightning country," the Indians called it, from the fierceness of the lightning-set prairie fires that sometimes burned for weeks, until they ran into the broad Missouri or were put out by rain, or by wind that turned them to feed upon their own ashes. Nebraska lies in the heart of the largest single piece of arable-grazable land in the world and contains, as one might expect, much fine corn ground and great stretches of wheat land. It also has several oil-rich regions, a 250-mile stretch of well-grassed sandhills geologically unmatched anywhere, a Toadstool Park of select badlands, and some rocky, craggy ridges that are higher and more montane than most of the mountains of the East. In much of the state you find yourself reaching for a blanket toward morning.

There are thousands of lakes here, the larger man-made, one 105 miles around, with fishing, boating and regattas, and the lovely deep blue of the far Nebraska sky in their depths. And there are handsome parks in all parts of the state, and forest and game reserves. Nowhere are the songs of the meadowlarks finer, the wild flowers and the sunsets more magnificent, than on the higher reaches of the state, and in the winter blizzard nothing stands between you and the North Pole save a barbed-wire fence with the posts all down.

"There is no place like Nebraska!" the University rooters sing lustily. Yet for some reason most of the first hundred thousand emigrants marched right through the region, up past Chimney Rock and on westward, until it seemed that nobody would ever stay. Our first white-man highway was the spreading Missouri, but the Platte, flowing the length of the state from west to east, became the real path of empire across our prairie. Its course was followed by the fur men, then by the various Overlanders seeking homes and safety and gold; by the Pony Express for a few profitless months, and by the telegraph and the first transcontinental railroad, until the broad river valley lay worn and bald, bare, it seemed, of every living root.

The first coast-to-coast auto road, the Lincoln Highway, followed the old ruts along the Platte, and the first transcontinental air mail. Today fine trains, high-speed buses and the planes that overtake the sun carry the ambitious up the Platte, though now they are headed for Hollywood, Reno, Yucca Flats or the uranium fields. Those going by car found a straight uncrowded free throughway here long before the East thought of one, and with the hypnotic menace of straight white pavement for hundreds of miles.

When the first heat of the Overlanders had cooled a little, weary emigrants began to spill off like golden grain sifting from a creaking wagon, leaving little settlements to sprout up all along from the Missouri westward, their main drags always headed into the sunset, even today.

Beyond the reach of a handful of troops at Fort Kearney there was no law except that of the fast draw, the belly knife or the ambush. With the danger from animals, Indians and finally outlaws, the most peaceful went armed, particularly the youths who had hit for the frontier for one reason or another and ended up choring for the horses around the stagecoach stations. Usually they were no better fitted to carry guns than the young malcontents today.

From the ranks of such young horse tenders at Nebraska stations rose both Wild Bill Hickok and Buffalo Bill Cody, the two most glamorized figures of the old Wild West. Both are still widely advertised as killers—Hickok of white men, Cody of Indians.

The two Bills went West beyond the law as youths now dream of getting beyond gravity. James Butler Hickok, called Duck Bill around the stage station until he grew the flowing mustaches that covered his long upper lip and made him handsome, went West because a man he knocked into a canal wasn't coming up. At Rock Creek station, he did a real piece of killing. He shot McCanles, the former station owner, for whom he had worked as a stock tender, and was the first man tried for murder in the new county. But this was only shooting a Carolinian, surely a Reb in July, 1861, not horse stealing, and so all Hickok got was the name of Wild Bill, from his wild account of how he killed his victim. But by 1866 he was ready material for the nation's postwar appetite for violence, and in Eastern print the name Wild Bill became a steppingstone to the title "Prince of Pistoleers." Yet Hickok still had to shoot buffalo along the Republican River to pay his gambling debts and buy the fancy dikings of the frontier dude. Today small boys and girls know a Wild Bill very unlike the man who was headed for oblivion and blindness until Jack McCall, also a former trail employee in Nebraska, salvaged him for the hero worshipers with one foolish bullet.

Bill Cody worked westward on the Overland trail and became a meat contractor for the railroad through north Kansas. He had an efficient crew to kill buffalo while he cut a handsome and picturesque figure around the frontier saloons. With his long shining hair, his big hat and his fringed buckskin he looked the romantic hero of the Wild West that the East was building up as an escape from its own drabness. A Broadway publicity man saw Cody, and made him the showiest showman of all time. But Bill was broke much of his forty years in the business and had to return West periodically to his ranch at North Platte.

Because violence and murder were the true golden coin after the Civil War, as they are in any postwar time, Cody was advertised as a killer, but only of buffalo and that other creature marked for extermination—the Indian. Yet no Western contemporary believed he killed even one Indian. As Luther North, of the Pawnee Scouts and a former partner of Cody's, once told me, "Cody wasn't reckless. He'd never hired Indians for his show if he had killed their relations."

Although Buffalo Bill was buried in 1917 he is still very much alive, not only around North Platte and up at Cody, Wyoming, but in the movies, on radio and TV, and in print. No real biography has appeared so far, perhaps because his is the story not of a man but of a dream, a wish fulfillment.

Although Nebraska has no gold mines, it has many stories of buried treasure; say around Nebraska City, at Maguire's Slough, in Knox County, and, my favorite, in Fly Speck Bill's cave. The Speck, nicknamed for the thick scattering of tiny dark freckles across his boyish face, was quietly hanged, but not until he had supposedly buried $300,000 in bullion stolen from the Sidney-Deadwood Gold Trail. Seems he stole this not too far from the spot where the Sioux were forced to sell the whole clutch of the Black Hills for a temporary meal ticket. The sale included the world's richest gold mine, the Homestake, from which the stolen bullion apparently came. One site given for Fly Speck's cave was across the Niobrara from our house, and I can recall many diggings around there. Once when some new treasure seekers came, Old Jules went over, his usual rifle across his arm. The men sprang out of their hole, hands on guns at the approach of what seemed an old mountain man, ragged beard, muskrat cap and all.

"What name you travelin' under?" father asked mildly, as was customary in a region where many had left their names behind with their pasts.

The men holstered their guns at Old Jules' combination of French accent and old-West etiquette. Later he brought them home to supper, as he did everyone. They thanked father for his generosity about the diggings.

"Hell, it ain't on my land!" he replied, laughing.

The gold seekers looked around our poor shacky house, at our bare feet, our patched clothing, and mother's gnarled and workworn hands and tried to pay for the good meal of grouse and homegrown trimmings. They were coldly refused. We were never poor enough to dig for gold on other people's land, or to accept pay for a meal.

It has been said that if you see one Nebraskan alone he will be squinting at the sky. See two and they will be talking about the weather, particularly its unhappy extremes: the deadly winter blizzards, summer scorchers, great floods of the Republican and Missouri regions, the sudden gully washers and hailstorms, the occasional dust storms and killing droughts. One October day can be so lovely it stops the heart, and the next the wind will drive the tumbleweeds like great herds of dark awkward sheep running before the wolf. A May day that is mellow and heavy with the sweetness of wild-plum and chokecherry blooms can bring you a blizzard to ruin the eastern apple crop and clean you out of cattle, or cost you an eye through snowblindness, as a May blizzard did me, back in my child-hood.

Question a Nebraskan and you may be told that swift and unpre-dictable weather changes are what keep a man watching his trail or even that they help him see the interdependence of all things, unconsciously expressing the rudiments of Indian religion as it matured on these Plains.

On the obvious and practical level, every Nebraska tribe had weather men and women and special ceremonials to bring rain, the sun, and so on, long before the white man stuck his bearded face over the horizon. In dry times we try a little rain making ourselves, from prayers to cloud seeding, but it may be years before we are as successful as one old Pawnee rain maker my father knew in the drought of the 1890's. For ten dollars he would bring an inch of rain to the surrounding fields; for twenty he made stronger medicine and guaranteed a soaker. Money was hard to come by, but one group of settlers in east Nebraska finally got twenty dollars together and threw in a jug of whisky. The rain maker went into his ritual and dances with genuine fervor. The sky darkened and the crowd cheered as the rain began to fall. But it turned to hail, enough hail to pound the whole country into the ground.

Nebraska, in a migratory flyway, has set up several sanctuaries for waterfowl, a large one north of Oshkosh, and another of 70,000 acres in Cherry County. The entire lake region is dark with flocks in the fall, the winding traceries of black that are thousands of sand hill cranes going south, the V's of geese, the clouds of ducks added to all the mallards hatched in the region. Father made expert hunters of his sons, and my sisters are good too. Even I learned to take a sound lead on mallards coming in fast on the north wind, although my lot was mostly the plucking and the cooking. I do remember pulling my first Canada goose out of a flock along the last pink rim of the west. The soft warm neck falling over my arm as I ran home with it made me want to cry.

Sound conservation has increased Nebraska's small game and

brought back the deer and the antelope and even varmints, the coyote and the bobcat, but never the buffalo. Anyone who grew up around the Sioux and the old hide hunters must be convinced that Nebraska was once the richest of buffalo ranges, with its excellent waterways, the thick seedy June grasses and the later bluestems that stood more than man-high and could always be tromped out of the deepest snow. The great herds moved like vast dark shadows over the prairie, deer bounding away at their approach, antelope fleeing in droves, while plovers, curlews, prairie chickens and the great black ravens rose everywhere before the thunder and shake of the earth as the buffalo neared. Wild turkeys kept out of their way and flew in heavy whirring clouds through the golden sun of evening to their roosting groves in the breaks that the heavy-shouldered buffalo liked to avoid. The elk and moose usually kept to broken timbered slopes too. The bighorn sheep was all through Pine Ridge and the Wildcat range of the Panhandle and eastward, his great head dark against the clouds as he looked over the swift waters of the Niobrara striking the roiling flank of the Missouri like an arrow from the west.

No gun roared anywhere then, and no stink of powder offended the nose. True, wolves and sometimes mountain lions pulled down any straggling buffalo, and half-naked brown men crept up on the herds, stampeding them over the sheer bluffs of the upper White River country and along the Niobrara. With the women and children to help, they drove the buffalo into pits or into gully or canyon surrounds.

The white man's lead and powder worked faster, and when the herds were only white bones on the prairie or piled in ricks like tardy snowdrifts along the railroad tracks, the longhorns came trailing out of Texas, climbing from one stream to another to the Union Pacific railhead. Angry men stood at their homestead lines, rifles or old muzzle-loaders across their forearms, but the new outfits spread over the public domain, laying verbal claim to the waterways and reinforcing their claim with armed range "protectors" to keep the settlers out.

The next move was into the real long-grass country, the sand hills of Nebraska, a vast egg-shaped region 250 miles long, with the deep Niobrara River canyon cutting around their northern boundary. Inside a low, choppy, windtorn border the hills rise in long, blue-hazed ridges that look like those of a sand bar when seen from a plane high up—sand ridges blown in upon an old lake bed that is black, heavy and generally water-impervious. Long valleys lie between these hills, one reaching over 200 miles.

The hills have many fine stretches of meadow, the wetter in wild hay and timothy, otherwise in alfalfa and bluegrass or even rye and corn to be hogged down by cattle. Strips of buckbrush lie along the foot of the ridges, or long sweeps of blue or yellow wild flowers and mats of bull-tongue cactus with great satiny yellow-green blossoms. Higher up are the fine waxy spikes of yucca bloom and the slender white gillyflowers, with nests of prairie roses that are as large as your palm to sweeten the air as you ride by.

The ridges are generally covered with range grasses, all except the highest, most exposed tops where the wind scoops blowouts for itself. Children were taught that these were always cupped out from the northwest—knowledge that could help them find their directions even in a blizzard. I once reached home that way, a long time ago.

These sand hills are the finest natural reservoir in the world—a great greenish-dun sponge that soaks up every drop of moisture from rain or snow and holds it in water tables and in the two thousand lakes. In most of the region the water works slowly southeastward until, with the lowering altitude, springs begin to ooze and flow as if a giant foot pressed on the great sponge, starting a dozen clear, constant streams that furnish water and power and delight to all those along their paths.

Once the Spade outfit claimed a bear-shaped region 150 miles long through the sand hills, mostly free land, but few settlers dared file within their fences. President Theodore Roosevelt, himself an old rancher, ordered the illegal fences down and sent troops to carry out his orders when the cattlemen defied him. I recall something of the long trials that followed. My father, the locater, the old hunter who knew every section corner, was the star witness. I recall a strange man, plainly not a homeseeker, at our place a long time during those tense days. Once when he was shaving in our kitchen I saw a holster under his arm, not worn openly over goat-hair chaps like the cowboys riding through.

"Secret Service man," father said shortly when I dared ask about this.

I recall mother's worried face, and then father's picture in the Omaha papers when the Spade owner went to the penitentiary for land fraud.

"Whole country be run over by homeseekers now, come spring," father said, bringing home a new surveying outfit. He was gone day and night for the next few years, locating the land-hungry.

Yet the sand hills are still sparsely settled. Cherry County alone is the size of Rhode Island and Connecticut together, with a total population of around 10,000. There are around 300,000 head of cattle, which makes it the world's leading county in beef population. It was in Valentine, the county seat, in 1884, that my father saw his first man killed, with at least fifty men standing around, and no hand was lifted against the murderer. To Jules, the young medical student come west from the orderly little republic of Switzerland, this was a shocking occurrence, to be told and retold many times.

But the people of the sand hills are still the independent and co-operative sort who survive in new regions. Most of the men have leathery faces and wind-scabbed lips, their eyes sun-squinted, foreheads white under the big hats—the tall, lean-hipped men of the cow country everywhere.

"They growed 'em long as potato sprouts in the cellar, reachin' fer the sun," an old cowman said when we talked about Pat Hooper, all the Hoopers. The family had come into the hills before the last Sioux alarm. Pat is well over sixty now, slouch-shouldered in the saddle, with the long face, the lined cheeks and bleached eyes of the years he was one of the head punchers of the region. But he can still send a loop with what seems the speed and precision of a bullet. His kind still top off the outlaw bronc that has never heard of the ten-second limit in rodeo contests. Men like Pat have squeeze chutes now for the branding and dehorning, and perhaps planes to cover the range, with every alfalfa patch a landing field, the windmill tails the windsocks.

Fleeing criminals still hit for the broken sand hills. The ranches are often five, even ten miles apart but there are radios everywhere now, and telephones to rally swift turnouts against a bad man as for the first iridescent smoke sign of a prairie fire on the horizon. The outlaw is hunted by Winchester-armed men in cars and jeeps and from the air. The sandhillers have no locks on their doors and they intend to keep them so.

There are, however, some who remember less peaceful days, the days of the cattleman-settler troubles. D. J. Cole was a boy when his father was shot down between the plow handles on his homestead.

"But my mother was not the woman to be run out, not even by murderers," he told me, his voice quiet.

Mrs. Cole stayed and her son grew up a typical native of the hills, pleasant and soft-spoken, his eyes grave in their nest of sun wrinkles —a man as much at home in the saddle as in the halls of the state capitol.

Although about fortieth in the country by population, Omaha, by geographic and financial position, is a big city, second only to Denver in the whole region between Chicago and the West Coast. It wields a commensurate influence—a one-newspaper town, but a moneyed town, the center of the cattle business, packing more beef than any other place on earth. Omaha long had a cowboy mayor, the old trail driver who traveled under the name of Jim Dahlman, his own, Murray, left behind in Texas.

Omaha has spread to take in the old Mormon Winter Quarters and its monument to their pioneers who wintered there in 1846–7, many in holes in the frozen ground, and to the 600 who died. And it was early Nebraska ranch owners like Swan, Paxton and Creighton who organized the Union Stock Yards, which now handle over two million dollars of livestock each market day.

Their Stock Yards 400 Club is a take-off on the more pretentious goings-on uptown. The club meets in the office building that stands like an upended tall red shoe box in the middle of the vast acreage of stock pens and baled hay. But many members have a prominent part in the flossier doings, too, particularly in Ak-sar-ben, Omaha's big social and publicity circus of the year, with a king in satin knee breeches, a middle-aged king, as is inevitable in a man of importance. His queen, however, is selected for more pertinent qualifications: youth and beauty.

Omaha has its detractors, naturally. The state's one race disturbance occurred here, one that left the courthouse with great slabs of pavement torn up all around, and there have been charges of gangsterism and corruption, particularly political. But thanks to its location and hotels, it remains very popular for conventions and celebrations. The city took the lead in the Golden Spike Days, commemorating the transcontinental railroad, complete with Lucius Beebe and what was rumored as a prearranged bit of local color— a shot from Beebe's Colt in the Fontenelle bar. Like much of the shooting of the old days, it left no corpse, but, I hope, a nice realistic stench of genuine black powder.

Although one mayor banned *Idiot's Delight* for a while, the Omaha Community Playhouse has given many stars their start. On Sundays packing-house workers mingle with the local Bohemians and the mink-coaters inside the rosy marble walls of the Joslyn Memorial for music and art. I recall seeing a couple there once, stocky, middle-aged, whispering together in their own tongue. They were plainly in their awkward best attire, and looked very scrubbed yet with a hint of the fertilizer vats of South Omaha about them. But they stood transfixed before Grant Wood's *Stone City*, their broad faces alight with wonder and that glow that deep recognition brings. Perhaps they had been very homesick for a little white church somewhere back in Lithuania.

Come to think of it, for all the booming industry and the making and breaking of senators, there is a kind of innocence about Omaha. Approached from almost any direction in the spring, the residence streets and many in the business sections, too, have a kind of village air, the buildings set back on neat terraces, fronted by tumbles of bridal wreath. It spills white and foamy down slope after slope of the hilly city, and makes a kind of pale mistiness along the side streets in both directions, while from far away somewhere there is a hint of the purple and the fragrance of lilacs.

Kansans have something of the righteous self-assurance of the Abolitionists who came West; South Dakotans figuratively push their big hats back with the dash of old Deadwood. Nebraskans often seem a little uncertain, a little apologetic, perhaps because they are less one thing than many. There are still traces of the old French traders and river men along the Missouri River towns—faces with the roguishness of the old *voyageur* and the strong dark hair of the Indian. And sometimes only a warmth of nature and an oblique sense of humor will reveal the Indian, with the hair perhaps blond and the eye as blue as a Niobrara harebell.

Many of our towns were started by companies of settlers from the East and from Europe too; Germans, Irish, Swiss and so on, and many Scandinavians. In Nebraska the Johnsons far outnumber the Smiths, and a candidate with a Swedish name is almost a shoo-in at election time. But it's only in the name now, for the characteristic faces, the general build and coloring that set these stocks apart until recently are disappearing, even from the so-called clannish Czechs in towns like Wilber, Loma, or sections of Crete.

The Bohemians have been recognized as a tough, hardy lot from the first one to settle in Nebraska Territory, who apparently walked clear to St. Joseph, Missouri, for his groceries. One young woman drove the cattle of a relative all the way from Wisconsin to Nebraska, afoot, and in my childhood I knew a man and wife, immigrants from Prague, who had pushed a wheelbarrow with their few household goods clear across Nebraska to our region for a homestead.

I recall many fine strong faces among these people, some with the red-brown eye that I've seen only among Czechs, a few northern Italians and an occasional Yorkshireman. The eyes are unchanged, of course, but they look different now. When I stopped off at our Czech centers to ask about the old-timers, I discovered that they are either dead, moved away, or somehow look like the usual older people on television quiz shows. I asked for one fine salty old character who had never learned passable English. He was pointed out to me, getting into a convertible with golf clubs.

"Oh, it's him, all right," I was told.

"Looks like he's been to California," I remarked.

"No, he's slicked up some since we got TV out here. Watches it all the time, evenings."

I remember the fine gray handle-bar mustaches, a neat side part to the whitening hair, an underslung pipe with a metal lid, and bib overalls big enough to turn around in. Now he was clean-shaven, in a loud shirt, maroon slacks and sandals, his hair in a thin white crew cut. All the proportions of the man seemed changed, his face and his figure.

But I was certain I knew two Czechs who would never change. Old Anna Pavelka wouldn't. She had worked as a girl in the Red Cloud home of Willa Cather and was the original of her Antonia. Anna had the earnest face, the sweep of cheekbone, the deep-socketed eye, the husky upper arm. But Anna Pavelka was eighty-six and died the week I was to hunt her up. That left me with the most typical Czech of all, the complex mixture of intellect, temperament and practicality, of the volcanic and the charmingly witty and placid that is the essence of our Czech settlers. This was Professor Orin Stepanek, of the state university. Born in Crete, Nebraska, on, as he always insisted, the wrong side of the tracks, he had the sturdiness of many of his people, with tawny skin, the breadth of planed cheekbone, a fine intensity of eye under coal-black brows, the expressive shoulders and hands, the fine incisive vocabulary, the rich imagination. Although a dynamic teacher of Slavic languages, Continental literature and the cultural approach to life, the carpenter that his father was could not be entirely denied. In his basement he upholstered furniture, and at his table one ate the finest of Czech liver dumplings and roast pork with sweet cabbage.

Yet there are still a few naturals for Willa Cather's Farmer Rosicky left. The spiritual daughters of her Antonia are still there, too, but in slacks and lipstick, perhaps with prize-winning 4-H beeves.

Lincoln always impresses me with its shining cleanness. New buildings, new fronts or at least new sandblasts make the wide streets, overlooked by the white capitol tower, seem even more open to the sun.

The German-Russians brought their onion-top churches to this city of colonial descendants. Often, too, you see Mennonites from a nearby settlement on the streets, the people who brought secret palmfuls of winter wheat to America. Crosses of that wheat are the parents of the fields from mid-Nebraska out through the Panhandle, where the wind runs in bright waves over the golden tablelands and around the black oil derricks.

Although Lincoln treated bank robbers to a $2,000,000 bond and currency haul, it has often been called the Holy City for its many churches and its former ban on saloons and Sunday movies. But war and new industry have changed many things. Every year around a quarter million visitors to the state fair can see the $10,000,000 capitol, built pay-as-you-go into the depression years, and the museums of the Historical Society and the University. The latter has perhaps the world's largest mammoth, standing some fourteen feet high, and many similar exhibits, mostly from the vast fossil beds of the Panhandle and Lincoln County.

There is a natural division across the state at the 100th meridian, where the altitude goes up and the rainfall down—the old arbitrary boundary between corn and cattle culture, the walking plow and the lariat, the old Bible Belt and the land of the gamblers. To be sure, the gambling was less often at poker and roulette than a staking of time, property and life against the violences of nature, the Indians, Western bad men and the range wars.

Now there is more security west of the 100th. Most of the water for the reservoir-fed portion of our million and a half acres under irrigation comes from there. The spreading agro-industrial region is richest along the North Platte. Scotts Bluff, the high country's last rampart against the river that cut this wide valley through the table-land, looks benignly over a lush checkering of irrigated fields and the booming town that is its namesake. Scottsbluff is not only a booming city but a good city. I saw young Japanese, Sioux, Mexican and mill-run young Americans laughing together at the hamburger joints and along the streets. I mentioned this to a mother of teen-agers.

"Oh, we don't have to worry much about our young people here," she said. "Everybody keeps a friendly eye on them—all like good relatives together." She was from the East and could not know that this was very much like the attitude toward young people in the Sioux villages camped in the shadow of the Bluff a hundred years ago.

Up north, off the old Black Hills trail, lies Wild Horse table, named for the herds that once dotted the western reaches of the state and ran like swift shadows over the prairie, their manes and tails a dense cloudiness about them in the wind. They had increased to fabulous numbers since they first came with the Spaniards, here where their prehistoric ancestors, beginning with the fourteen-inch Dawn Horse, once roamed before the Ice Age. I remember our last mustang from these parts—a fox mare so wily she remained in no corral if she could get her nose to the top. Not even the broncobusters breaking Powder River outlaws ever got their ropes on this one. I was still a small girl when she died, but I knew that an era passed with her.

In our northwestern section lies the heart of the state's unpubli-cized scenery. Here is the heading of the Niobrara Valley that cuts clear across northern Nebraska, deep and timbered, moodily golden in the October sun. Beyond are the sheer bluffs and buttes of the White River country, and then Pine Ridge standing dark against the sky.

This is the region of the Sioux and Cheyenne last stands. Wounded Knee is just over the Dakota line. At Fort Robinson, Crazy Horse was bayoneted, and two years later the Dull Knife Cheyennes preferred to die fighting on the January snow rather than return to the hated

Indian Territory. They were pursued over the bluffs for thirteen sub-zero days, until not even one woman was left to run with a child on her back.

And here Dr. Walter Reed, later to conquer yellow fever, was post surgeon and had Old Jules under his care for eight months after he crushed an ankle in a well accident and lay on the prairie for days.

Trade with the Sioux reservations over in South Dakota helped build up the Nebraska border towns from Chadron to Valentine, and the Indians added picturesqueness to their streets. But now, with the Government's withdrawal from the reservations and the accelerated unlanding of the Indians, these towns are swamped by Sioux seeking a livelihood, housing, schools, relief. Signs saying "No INDIANS ALLOWED" have gone up everywhere, the first discrimination in openhearted western Nebraska.

I saw one of the old Sioux on a bus last spring. He looked at me in the quiet way they have and after a while he overcame his reticence and sat down beside me.

"You Sandoz? Straight Eye daughter?" he asked, unfolding a little clipping about my taking a turn around the state.

"Yes," I said, and then I knew who he was, an old friend of my father's, one who had been in the Wounded Knee troubles.

"Me"—poking his thumb toward himself—"me been Lincoln," he said in his awkward English. "Show nephew how do medicine dance."

"How are you people making it?" I asked him, falling into the old local words.

The old man's thin braids stirred a little over his dusty calico shirt. "Bad, very bad," he said.

After a while we talked of old White Eye and Ghost Bear and other friends of my father's. Dead or gone down into sadness, he said, as he looked out over the green alfalfa and winter-wheat fields, the big barns and farmsteads and the ribbon of white highway running where his father had chased buffalo such a short while ago.

With good Sioux manners and even some exuberance, the old man looked into my face. "Indian buy drink now, all over. Drink beer."

"Yes, I know," I said, as I dug out my cigarettes. He took the package, his hand shaking a little in eagerness, and together we smoked in silence, in the good Sioux silence of friends, and when I got off to change buses, I held out my hand. "Don't let the young people forget the old ways of honor," I wanted to say, but I couldn't.

He took my hand, and then the other with his left, the left that is nearest the heart. As the bus started away, I looked after the old man in his mended shirt, sitting, face straight ahead, the thin gray hair hanging down under the old black hat.

I must not forget Mirage Flats, where my father filed the first claim, sank the first well. The Flats is now a fruitful irrigated region, and Walgren's Lake, the reputed home of Nebraska's most persistent sea monster, is a playground. But here on Mirage Flats was the country school where two of my brothers and I learned to speak the tongue of our native land. Here, at ten, I wrote my first short story under the direction of a young teacher who regretted the isolation that our foreignness and our father's feuds and tempers thrust upon us. The story was published in the junior page of a newspaper. I showed it to father and he locked me in the cellar. A Sandoz did not even read fiction, father told me, and she certainly did not write it.

As always, Old Jules' temper soon cooled and he took me quail hunting, but it was understood that the gate to writing was permanently closed. I was, however, already a fence jumper. Years later, the hour he was dying, Old Jules forgot his long opposition.

"Why don't you write my life sometime?" he said. And I did.

New regions seldom applaud the worker in the creative fields. For years Nebraska's interest in art was largely confined to the excellent Indian work displayed in the museums in Lincoln and more recently out at Scottsbluff and in the Hastings House of Yesterday, the latter with the largest collection of High Plains historical material under one roof. But the last twenty years have seen a sprouting of painters out over the state, as though rain had suddenly come to a desert.

Perhaps, among outdoor men, the urge to paint is stimulated by the swift, subtle flow of blue hazes against the Nebraska hills, the yellow-greens, the tans, russets and mauves of the rolling prairie, the patterns of the contoured fields, and the unsurpassed sunrises and sunsets over it all.

Whatever the reason, from Wyoming to the Joslyn, ranchers, farmers, truck drivers, bankers, a café owner, an office worker in South Omaha, a hog breeder—and the professionals, of course—all paint and often achieve shows.

"It's paint rags 'stead a pliers in my old ditty box now," a gnarled cowman replied when I wondered about the easel beside him in the jeep out on the range. "My boy down to the university drug me to look at some pictures Fair time. I seen right away I could do better."

This is my Nebraska, this and the brooding times of evening, when one can sense the recent passing of the buffalo and the Indian, and of all those footsore hopefuls who toiled up the Platte and onward to build the Western empire. And of all the hopefuls who did not go that far.

Once, over twenty years ago, I took Carl Sandburg through the new state capitol. Slowly, silently he saw it all, from the magnificent rotunda to the parapet high up under the crowning statue of the Sower. A long time he gazed out beyond the town, to the spreading horizon in every direction. And when we were down and outside again, Sandburg looked up at the tall white spire a long time too.

Finally he spoke: "You know, this building growing out of the Nebraska corn lands, that's an American tall tale."

Kansas

by DEBS MYERS

The state of Kansas was born of conflict and came of age with a Bible in one hand and a rifle in the other. During its seven years' existence as a territory and a hundred years as a state, it has known guerrilla war, drought, flood, dust, blizzards and grasshopper plagues, has taken these calamities defiantly in stride, put their bitter lessons to everyday use, and has built a sprawling farm empire that sends beef and bread across the world.

For many years Kansas was a spawning ground of gaudy characters and a venturesome kind of progress; few states have produced as many saints and scoundrels, hypocrites and heroes. A country editor named William Allen White once wrote: "When anything is going to happen in this country, it happens first in Kansas. . . . Sooner or later, other states take up these things, and then Kansas goes on breeding other troubles."

Today, with the lean years only a prodding memory, Kansas has become staid and prosperous—a symbol of orthodoxy and starched respectability.

In view of the state's colorful past and sizable achievements, Kansans often wonder why they are regarded in so unflattering a light by so many people. Most Kansans wouldn't willingly live anywhere else; yet they realize that to much of the nation Kansas is viewed almost as an island unto itself, strong in quiet, neighborly virtue, but increasingly barren of the ferment that produces challenge and conflict of ideas.

In this threadbare conception, Kansas is considered as 82,158 square miles of flat and cheerless prairie, producing little except wheat and tedium. And the more than 2,000,000 people of Kansas (if you would accept this same misconception) are uniformly austere and melancholy, tortured by heat, dust, cold, tornadoes and their own consciences.

How much of this is true? Fortunately, very little. The landscape is varied and so are the people. Far from being a flat and monotonous plain, Kansas rises nearly 3000 feet from east to west. The eastern part of the state is rich in hills, trees and water; the ground is lush and rolling. It is an area of small towns, farms, orchards and valleys. The western section of the state (closer physically to the public conception) is a vast, almost treeless land. The farms are large, and the population is spread thinly over prairies which stretch as far as a man can see. Yet to the people who live in Western Kansas the land is good; the brooding immensity of the plains offers expansion and opportunity.

There are fundamental differences between the people of Eastern and Western Kansas. In Eastern Kansas, many of the people are spiritual descendants of the New England Puritans. They are cautious and frugal. Their farms are small and their crops diversified. A farmer outside Topeka said: "My grandfather gave me the best advice I ever got. 'Don't let your farm get so big you don't know every cow and clod on it. And every time you make a quarter, squirrel away a nickel.'"

In Western Kansas the farms and the stakes are bigger. Wheat is the crop that counts and the fortunes of the countryside ride with the abundance of the harvest. The people are used to boom-and-bust. This is a land for taking a chance, riding a hunch or a piece of ground into a fortune or a prat fall.

This too was once the stomping ground of Wild Bill Hickok and Bat Masterson; a region noted for its cattle drives, garish pleasures and sudden death. Today the people in Western Kansas have outgrown their wild-and-woolly past; like other Kansans, they trust in the Bible and in their own horse sense. But deep inside is a strain of maverick, hard to fence in.

To understand Kansas you must understand its violent beginning. In 1855 it was a territory fighting a preview of the Civil War, a struggle to determine whether Kansas would enter the Union slave or free.

In this same year, at North Elba, New York, a slavery-hating fanatic named John Brown received a letter from five of his sons who the year before had emigrated to Kansas. In this letter the sons told Brown of the wrongs done them by the proslavery border ruffians.

That night, after hours of prayer, Brown opened his Bible and read: "And the Lord said unto Saul, go out and slay the Philistines."

"I then saw the light," Brown later said, "and while my wife and I were kneeling in prayer, I heard the voice of the Lord saying— 'John Brown, go to Kansas and slay the border ruffians.'

"The next morning, in obedience to the command of Almighty God, I started out to save Kansas."

Just what Brown saved in Kansas is still a matter of controversy. Some Kansans regard him as a murderer and horse thief; others think him an idealist, patriot and martyr. Perhaps he was something of all these things; certainly he was a symbol.

In leading a war of retribution against the proslavers, Brown fanned a flame that swept Kansas. Farm homes were burned and families driven into the fields. Towns were attacked and looted. From New England, following John Brown, came hundreds of fighting abolitionists, determined to shape the new state in the image of their own zealous conscience. When President James Buchanan offered a reward of $250 for the capture of Brown, the fiery old abolitionist countered with an offer of $2.50 for the person of Buchanan. When the proslavers from Missouri continued to raid across the border, Brown said: "To make them permanent settlers, I will have to drive them into the ground, like fence posts."

Kansas became known as Bleeding Kansas.

In 1859 Brown left Kansas to set off a slave insurrection in the South, was captured at Harper's Ferry, Virginia and hanged for treason, a lonely, unrepentant old man. ("I hold myself accountable to God.") But he planted his bootprints deep in Kansas history.

In 1861 Kansas went into the Union as a free state, and three months later its people answered Lincoln's call for volunteers to defend the Union.

Many of the New England abolitionists settled in Kansas. They were men and women of stern religious conviction and a passionate insistence on personal morality. The heritage which they left Kansas resulted sometimes in a narrowing of personal freedom; during the 1920's, for example, there was a legal ban in Kansas on Sunday movies and the sale of cigarettes.

Meanwhile, other Kansans of less astringent piety turned to political and social reform, a prairie brand of protest which had repercussions across the land. The combination of the two made Kansas for many years an incubator of ideas, symptoms and portent.

Abolition, Prohibition, Populism (an early-day brand of political radicalism), the Bull Moose (when insurgents led by Theodore Roosevelt split from the Republican Party), the guarantee of bank deposits, the blue-sky law regulating investment companies—these were some of the ideas which came whanging out of Kansas and had their effect on millions of people. But many of the beliefs which long dominated the state have gone. Kansas has lost its zeal for political, economic and moral reform. Even the state prohibition law, in effect since 1881, was repealed in 1948 by a majority of 60,000 votes. (This invalidated William Allen White's prediction that Kansans would "vote dry as long as they can stagger to the polls.")

Today most Kansans are fundamentally orthodox and proud of it. This orthodoxy applies to their religion, politics and living habits. The rambunctious human juices which flavored John Brown, William Allen White and other vital, picturesque figures have been distilled into a less exciting amber that produces people with a great deal of solid character, but very few characters. William Allen White commented on this when he wondered what had happened to Kansas' "rugged Shakespearean characters."

Part of the answer to that question lies in the state's current prosperity. As a breeding place of ideas and curious personalities, Kansas was poor and sometimes hungry; a state with a patch on the seat of its pants, driven by short rations and pride into a restless quest for better living. In those days complacency was akin to shiftlessness; to get ahead a man needed imagination as well as drive and patience.

Today full stomachs have appeased much of the old hunger for experimentation. Well-fed and well-to-do, Kansas is still building and still acquiring, but, mostly, it is interested in defending what it already has. The spirit of challenge in many parts of the state has given way to a searching for conformity. There are thoughtful men and women, born and bred in Kansas, who fear this is leading the state into a creative rut. Most Kansans aren't worried over this; they look at their thriving farms and cities and feel that if this is a rut—well, it certainly is a pleasant one.

And, after all, Kansans are inclined to say, there can't be much wrong with the creative processes of a state that has produced so many distinguished citizens who have made their imprint on the times. But when Kansas boasts of these notables, the skeptics nod wryly and ask: "Uh-huh, but how many of 'em stayed in Kansas?" There is a feeling on the part of some Kansans that the state's itch for conformity has chased many of its young men and women to greener, less-confining pastures, where the challenging in mind and spirit could find elbow room and compatibility.

Kansans themselves are to blame for many of the public misconceptions about Kansas. From the beginning, perhaps from an overflowing of Puritanical zeal, they have taken a curious pride in muffling their virtues and preaching their shortcomings: Their summer winds were the hottest, their winter winds the coldest, their droughts the driest and their grasshoppers the hungriest. Today, for the first time, Kansas is taking off its hair shirt and beginning to brag a little. As more and more Kansans see other parts of the world, they realize there are plenty of blessings which begin at home.

Actually, the Kansas climate is like the climate in most plains states. There are stifling hot summers and pleasant summers, there are cold winters and mild winters. The yearly mean temperature is 54°. As far as tornadoes are concerned—well, Kansas has its share, and often they are rip-roarers, but there are many thousands of Kansans who never have seen a tornado. To most visitors, and to a lot of Kansans, the biggest irritant in the Kansas climate is the nagging wind. Some people cuss and rail at the wind, and others accept it calmly; either way it is an inevitable part of their lives. With a degree of candor rare in the attitude of newspapers concerning the weather in their own communities, the *Wichita Eagle,* on April 15, 1880, commented on the Kansas wind in what conceivably may be the most forthright weather story ever written:

"It may as well be asserted here and now that Kansas as a paradise has her failings, not the least of which is her everlasting spring winds. If there is a man, woman or child in Sedgwick County whose eyes are not filled with dust, and their minds with disgust, he, she or it must be an idiot or awful pious. From everlasting to everlasting this wind for a week has howled and screeched and snorted until you couldn't tell your grandfather from a jackass rabbit."

In Kansas, every man is his own weather prophet and the moods of the people are governed by the turning seasons. In the summer, when Kansas has the appearance of a grandmother's quilt patched with gold and green, there is an urgency about men and women as they watch the sky; for the harvest and their hopes are hitched to the wind, the sun and the rain. In the autumn, if the harvest has been good, a festive confident feeling is apparent in the people; they seem to reflect the strength that has come from the bone marrow of the land. This quiet rejoicing finds an outlet in the dozens of farm expositions held across the state.

I visited the fair and festival held each fall in the town of Norwich. Here the people of the countryside come, togged in their Sunday best, and the glut of the land is visible on every side.

There are rows of potatoes, watermelons, pumpkins, squash, carrots and roasting ears; showcases filled with cakes, pies, candy, biscuits and cheese; there are displays of dahlias, marigolds, zinnias and woolflower; exhibits of needlepoint, spinning, lacemaking and wood carving—all part of the productive energy of a people proud of their craftsmanship. There is the din and warmth of carnival: the pied-piper wheeze of a merry-go-round, the shrill excitement at the bingo booth, the muted conversation of farm boys and girls walking the streets together.

The talk is the talk of the countryside:

"The missus just can't pass up a rummage sale; this time she buys a pan, a lampshade and a corset, and she was mad as all get-out when I says, 'Honey, why don't you wear 'em all at once?' "

"The old man insisted on them bringing the body of his boy back from the soldier cemetery in France; he said if there was rain falling on that grave, he wanted it to be Kansas rain."

A parade, led by the Norwich American Legion Post, comes down the street. There is a float decorated in green and covered with red-tissue poppies; it bears a sign: "We must not forget." Next comes a long line of riders on horseback, then more floats. On one float there is a boy with a telescope peering at a placard which reads: "Christian homes, honesty and truth." There are bands with bare-legged majorettes, and boys on decorated bicycles.

At the horse show, held at the high-school football field, are riders and riding clubs from the towns of the region: Wichita, Anthony, Kingman, Belle Plaine, Zenda, Rago, Harper and Cheney. The names of the contestants reflect an ancestry which stretches across the ocean: Stuchal, Dunkelburger, Lichlider and Helmburger.

The master of ceremonies sits on a chair atop a truck and twangs his words through a microphone. He mingles advice to the riders with homespun humor: "Why don't you give that ornery horse an aspirin? Maybe he's got a headache"; "Take that horse down and bring him back fast—if you need to, step on his carbureter"; or "Let's give the younger riders a hand, folks; doggonit, this younger generation can't mess things up worse than us old folks."

There are contests on the horses' gait and training, and relay races; and there is a square dance, in which the riders solemnly wheel their horses to the hillbilly music of a phonograph record entitled *Hell Among the Yearlings.* A man calls the dance for the riders:

> All to your places, straight up your faces,
> Let out your bellyband, stretch your traces,
> Circle eight, hands around.
> Line up your pardner and line up eight,
> Hook those rowels in that old crow bait.
> Riding Old Paint and Leading Old Ball,
> Get home this summer and not next fall.
> Grab your pardner by the craw
> And swing her clear to Arkansas.

The horse show ends and slowly the people drift back to the town of Norwich and to their homes across the countryside; the carnival banners are being taken down and the exhibits hauled away. In the autumn sun the town seems comfortable and secure, sure of itself and sure of the land. It is late afternoon now, the carnival din is hushed and the sun is slanting long shadows toward Sand Creek back of town aways; on the prairie the sun is a long time setting.

Traditionally, the farms and small towns like Norwich have been the backbone of the Kansas economy, but with the flow of new industry into the state during the past decades the bigger towns have broadened their trade areas and their influence. The biggest, richest, fastest-growing town in Kansas is Wichita. Wichita is located in the Low Plains of South Central Kansas, the blending ground between the rolling hills of Eastern Kansas and the flat treeless plains of Western Kansas. It grew up as a cowtown and collapsed with the shifting westward of the Chisholm cattle trail, became prosperous again as a farm town and went into a tailspin when the bottom fell out of farm and real-estate values. Today it makes its money not only from farm products and livestock but from varied industrial production, from the manufacture and maintenance of airplanes and from oil.

In Wichita, as elsewhere in Kansas, the churches play an important role in community life. There are citizens who devote from three to five nights a week to church functions: prayer meetings, pie suppers, Bible study, choir practice, missionary meetings, youth assemblies.

A businessman told me: "I've been attending the same church for about fifty years. I was baptized in this church; I met a lot of my closest friends there; I courted my wife in the church when we both sang in the choir; I've raised my children in the Sunday school and one of my sons grew up in the Sunday school with the girl he later married. Now they're starting their children over the same route."

One hundred and seventy miles northeast of Wichita is Topeka, the capital of Kansas since statehood, and a city which never has lost its leisurely small-town flavor. People here are rarely in such a hurry they lack time to stop on a street corner and visit. From surface impressions, Topeka is a town that doesn't know the meaning of jangled nerves, yet it is the home of the Menninger Foundation built by Drs. William Menninger and Karl Menninger into the largest training center for psychiatrists in the world. (Dr. Karl recently psychoanalyzed Kansas and found it suffering from a "feeling of inferiority . . . an apologetic manner . . . a tendency to join in a bantering ridicule. . . .")

Topeka was once a ferry point on the Kaw River for the thousands of '49ers heading for the California gold fields; today the Kaw bisects the city. In the bottomland, adjacent to the river, are meat-packing plants, flour mills, wholesale houses and small industries. In the northern part of town are the Santa Fe shops, covering 565 acres. In the western part of the city is Washburn Municipal University and close to the university is the Menninger Foundation.

As political center of Kansas, Topeka has produced public figures who have made their mark on the state. Men like the late Charles Curtis, part Indian and one-time jockey who was vice-president under Herbert Hoover; Arthur Capper, former governor and former

United States senator; and Alfred M. Landon, former governor who was the Republican presidential nominee in 1936.

In addition to Topeka and Wichita, there are numerous other important towns in the state: Kansas City, second-largest town in the state, a meat-packing, hay-market and grain-storage center which zealously defends its separate identity though there is no discernible dividing line between it and Kansas City, Missouri; Hutchinson, fourth largest town in Kansas, a salt-mining and milling center; Coffeyville, a farm and industrial town, where eight persons were shot to death in 1892 during a raid by the notorious Dalton gang; Arkansas City, an oil shipping and refining center, where oil-rich Indians from Oklahoma used to splurge and play; Dodge City, once the most famous cowtown in the West and sometimes called the "buckle on the Kansas wheat belt"; and Abilene, also renowned years ago for its frontier wildness and known now as the boyhood home of President Dwight D. Eisenhower.

And there is also, in the south central part of Kansas, close to the Oklahoma border, a rustic little town named Medicine Lodge. In appearance and behavior the town is typical of the countryside—quiet, peaceful, knowing its place in the sun and satisfied with it; but in the 1890's Medicine Lodge kicked up a squall that echoed through the nation. At that time it was the home of two of the most remarkable of all Kansas figures: Sockless Jerry Simpson, the spokesman of a rag, tag and bobtail creed of political prairie-shakers known as the Populists, and Carry Nation, the hatchet-wielding saloon-smasher. Simpson was a political radical and religious skeptic; Carry Nation distrusted all politicians and was a religious fanatic. There is no record that these two ever came to grips; if they had, the smiting and bellowing would have been awful to behold.

Today Simpson is almost forgotten; Medicine Lodge is conservative, predominantly Republican, but there are many persons who remember Carry Nation, most of them with affection. Mrs. Riley MacGregor, the wife of a Medicine Lodge lawyer and legislator, recalls Carry Nation. "I lived next door to her as a little girl. She was good to me and good to other children. I think she was a kindly, misunderstood lady."

Medicine Lodge had its first glimpse of Carry Nation in 1889 when her husband, David Nation, became minister of the Christian Church. At the time Carry Nation was forty-three years old, a chunkily built woman with a determined jaw, who sat in the front pew of the church while her husband preached, giving him brusque instructions on when to raise or lower his voice and when to gesture: "Louder, husband," or "Husband, point your finger at the congregation."

When she thought that the Reverend Nation had talked enough, or when she felt that he was giving a dull performance, she would step into the aisle and say: "That's enough for today." On those occasions when the Reverend Nation ignored her and continued speaking, she would stride to the pulpit, bang shut the Bible, give him his hat and point toward the door.

As a child Carry Nation had been sickly and subject to visions, and at an early age she decided she was a confidante of the Almighty. Her first husband had died of alcoholism.

As she grew older, she grew more emotional, domineering and meddlesome. If she saw a young man smoking a cigarette, she was likely to snatch the cigarette from his mouth and slap his face. When she found a boy with his arms around a girl, she flew into a frenzy, warning the girl that this is a sinful world overrun with vultures. If she noticed a girl exposing a few inches of ankle, she delivered a lecture on morality. But all this was only a warmup; the hatchet-wielding, the wrecked saloons, jail, headlines and vaudeville were still ahead.

Within a few years Carry Nation was the leader of the temperance forces in Medicine Lodge. She frequently arose in prayer meeting at the church, listed the names of the saloonkeepers in town, and demanded to know why officials permitted them to operate in violation of the state law. When she met on the street a man who was known to operate a saloon, she made it a custom to bar his pathway, point a finger and say: "How do you do, maker of drunkards and widows?"

One Saturday afternoon in 1899, Carry Nation and her little band of temperance workers marched down Main Street and dropped to their knees in prayer in front of a saloon owned by a man named Mart Strong. Then, while an assistant manipulated a creaking hand organ, Carry Nation flourished her umbrella high above her poke bonnet, and led the singing of her favorite temperance song:

> *They who tarry at the wine cup,*
> *They who tarry at the wine cup,*
> *They who tarry at the wine cup,*
> *They have sorrow, they have woe.*

This was the beginning. Within a few months, she closed every saloon in Medicine Lodge. She next moved on the saloons in nearby Kiowa, then on her third raid, she made a shambles of a saloon in Wichita, destroying in the process a voluptuous oil painting entitled *Cleopatra at the Bath*, the work of a young Wichita artist named John Noble, who later made an international reputation.

Carry Nation became a national and then a world figure. In 1911, feeble and broke, she died in a hospital at Leavenworth, Kansas. During her life she had instigated scores of riots, been arrested more than twenty-five times, been beaten up a dozen times, scandalized both her enemies and friends, appeared as a temperance lecturer on theatrical platforms, including burlesque, and had helped to bring about national prohibition. Today there is a liquor store only one block from the yellow-brick house in which she lived in Medicine Lodge; and in 1948 her home town went resoundingly wet.

Not long ago a crowd of followers made a sober pilgrimage to her home and dedicated it as a W.C.T.U. memorial. The furnishings include her original bar-smashing hatchet, her old rocking chair and desk and the satchel in which she carried bricks to shatter saloon mirrors.

Jerry Simpson, Medicine Lodge's other famous product, was of a different cut of jib. He was a Great Lakes sailor who had come to Kansas in 1878 at the age of thirty-six and acquired a farm outside Medicine Lodge. His cattle died in a blizzard and he was forced to sell his farm. He then became town marshal of Medicine Lodge at a salary of twenty-five dollars a month. He was a spare, wiry man with a drooping mustache, who borrowed books on history and theology from the Medicine Lodge ministers and then buttonholed them on the street corners to argue about what he had read. In 1890, partly as a joke and partly because it was hard to find anyone to accept the nomination, the Populists persuaded Simpson to run for Congress in the seventh Kansas district. The Populists were not believed to have a chance, and Simpson took the nomination with the wry observation: "Wouldn't it be a hell of a joke if I got elected."

In his campaign Jerry Simpson became the symbol of the unrest sweeping Kansas, of a contagious, singing, foot-stamping crusade that singled out Wall Street as a money-grabbing Old Nick to be overthrown, and called on the people to raise less corn and more hell.

Simpson proved to be a curious, compelling figure on the hustings; to his enemies he was a rube and demagogue and to his followers he was a folk hero who spoke their minds and hopes. "The price of corn is so low that our farmers burn their corn," he told the crowds, "and by the light of that burning corn they read the history of their long injustices." "My opponent wears fine soft silk hosiery. I have no money with which to buy silk hosiery. The facts of the business are I have no socks at all save the natural buff my mother gave me." He illustrated this point by hitching up his pants legs and showing his bare shanks.

Admirers sent socks to Simpson by the hundreds, including a knitted sock four feet long, which Simpson's followers mounted on a pole and carried in their parades. Simpson's opponents called him uncultured and cited as proof a letter in his own handwriting in which he had misspelled the name of Medicine Lodge. "Again I plead guilty," Sockless Jerry said, "and I tell you further I wouldn't give a tinker's dern for a man who can't spell a word more than one way."

Simpson was elected to Congress and served three terms. He became known throughout the nation as an odd, incorruptible figure challenging and disturbing the people's conscience. He wanted a better deal for the prairie farmers and he said so in words that made headlines. Kansas was the seedbed of the Populist movement and Sockless Jerry was the prophet.

With the return of good times, the Populist party disintegrated and the Populists disappeared from public life. Sockless Jerry made his last political race in 1898 when he ran again for Congress and was defeated. Seven years later he died, refusing religious ministration and comforting himself on his deathbed by telling friends: "Populism never will die—it is a cumulative indignation which shall come again and again."

The Populist decline was accelerated by William Allen White, a young, obscure country editor in Emporia, Kansas. In 1896 White wrote an editorial entitled "What's the Matter with Kansas," which had repercussions across the land. In those days, when Kansas was a ragged shadow of its present prosperous self, White concluded there was only one thing wrong with Kansas: the Populists. Drive the Populists from public life, he urged; put an end to the careers of "old human hoop skirts" like Jerry Simpson and give Kansas a chance to win back its self-respect.

Under the Populists, White said, Kansas had become "poorer and ornrier and meaner than a spavined, distempered mule." With flailing sarcasm, White wrote: "Whoop it up for the ragged trousers; put the lazy greasy frizzle, who can't pay his debts, on the altar, and bow down and worship him. Let the state ideal be high. What we need is not the respect of our fellow men, but the chance to get something for nothing."

This editorial projected White for the first time into national attention and into the receptive arms of the Republican Old Guard. In later years, however, White became a Republican liberal—on occasion even a political heretic of sorts, who lambasted his party between elections and returned to the fold on election day. As time mellowed his memories, White revised his opinion of the Populists. He considered them "probably sowers of seeds, but a mighty un-promising looking band of sowers." He later wrote: "The rumps of seedy farmers sticking out of the courthouse windows, as the Farm-ers' Alliance met, cast the shadow of a great twilight . . . Being what I was, a child of the governing classes, I was blinded by my birthright."

White was born in Kansas and, in the minds of many persons, was the most typical Kansan who ever lived. He was kindly, neigh-borly, practical, idealistic. He had wisdom, warmth and an instinctive feeling for what was in the minds of people. He made the Emporia *Gazette* a spokesman for the small-town conscience. White was a friend of many of the important men of his generation, he exerted a wide influence on the issues of his time; yet as an editor he insisted, first and last, that the *Gazette* be a local newspaper, con-cerned primarily with the affairs of Emporia.

In directing the *Gazette,* White never forgot the advice given him as a student at the University of Kansas by a poet-professor named William Herbert Carruth: "You know it's vastly more impor-tant than many pious prayers and tons of highfalutin aspirations to get a street in a country town made wide enough so that two loads of hay going in opposite directions still leave it possible for a woman to drive a horse between them without getting hay wisps on her buggy top."

This interest in intimate, day-to-day events of his own town helped shape White's character. He knew his town better than any man, and knowing Emporia, he knew a lot about America.

White has been dead since 1944, yet his memory has a vital, unifying effect on Emporia. In street-corner controversies, in meet-ings of the city officials, wherever men and women gather in Emporia to pool the community wisdom, his words are recalled and used to settle issues. Today in Peter Pan Park, donated by Mr. and Mrs. White to Emporia in memory of their daughter, Mary, there is a bronze bust of White—a memorial to the man who made Emporia famous.

Emporia is a quiet, friendly town, as much a part of the prairies as the bluestem pasture grass in the Flint Hills beyond the city's edge. It has two colleges and twenty-eight churches.

In appearance Emporia is pretty much what you would expect the home town of America's most famous country editor to be—a place of comfortable, middle-class homes set back on streets, lined with elm and maple trees, of men sitting on their front porches with slippered feet propped on the porch rail, neighbors trading small talk over the back fence, of parks thronged with children.

The *Gazette,* owned by White's son, is operated by veteran staff members who learned the business under White's direction. White's office, just off the news room, is unchanged from the day he left it. There are autographed pictures on the walls from men who have helped to shape the events of the times: Theodore Roosevelt, Mark Hanna, Herbert Hoover, Robert M. LaFollette, William Jennings Bryan and Alfred Landon. Also on the wall is a note White received on his seventy-fifth birthday from Franklin Roosevelt: "Congratulations on reaching the three-quarter mark. I hope that during the next 25 years you will be for me all the time instead of only three and one half years out of every four. I think that in a quarter of a century the firm of White and Roosevelt might be able to bring the four freedoms to at least this nation of ours."

Of the many things written about White, many townspeople think he unintentionally summed up his own life best when he wrote an editorial years ago describing the life of a typical country editor: "He has given all his life to his town; he has spent thousands of dollars to promote its growth; he has watched every house on the townsite rise and has made an item in the paper about it; he has written up the weddings of many of the grandmothers and grandfathers of the town; he has chronicled the birth of their children and their children's children. The old scrapbooks are filled with kind things he has written. Old men and old women scan these pages with eyes that have lost their luster, and on the rusty clippings there fall many tears. In this book many a woman reads the little verse below the name of a child whom only she and God remember. In some other scrapbook a man long since out of the current of life reads the story of his little triumphs in the world; in the family Bible is a clipping—yellow and crisp with years—that tells of a daughter's wedding and the social glory that descended upon the house that one great day."

During the years Kansas has put up with much: grasshoppers, chinch bugs, border ruffians, windstorms, drought, floods, rascals and fanatics.

In the 1930's the dust came; stifling winds of forty-five to sixty miles an hour rooted the crops from the ground and blew them away, leaving a grayish blanket on the fields. The crops which escaped the wind crept back into the ground. Clouds of dirt blotted the sun and airport radios sent out the laconic warning: "no visibility, no ceiling." People wore dust masks to protect their noses and throats and made wry jokes about gophers digging their homes in the air. During the middle of a dust storm, Kansans said, Lady Godiva could have ridden her horse down the main street of some Kansas towns without even the horse seeing her. An old man walked the roads wearing on his back a sign which read: "Beware. The Lord is wrathful."

In parts of western Kansas dunes of gray dirt piled up where there were once plowed fields; farmers lost crop after crop and some of them said to hell with it and moved away. Most of them stayed with the land; they had a grim patience and, besides, there was no place to go.

Today Kansas once more is covered with grass and grain; the old miseries are only nagging memories now. Across the Kansas prairie at harvesttime, great combines clank through the knee-high wheat and into the bins of the combines pours a stream of yellow kernels that means bread for the world's bellyache.

Outside Wichita, a farmer named Sam Barner shielded his face from the sun with a big hand and watched the flailing reels of a combine chew the wheat into spears of rubble. Barner had worked on his farm most of his life; he had known good times and despair.

"We've seen about everything there is to see," Barner said, "and still we're alive and full of beans. I guess a lot of folks think we're mighty set in our ways, and I guess we are. But we insist on working out things for ourselves in our own individual way, and with all this talk about individualism going on in the world, Kansas may come up one of these days with some ideas, agitation and answers that will make a powerful lot of sense."

Barner sifted a handful of grain through his hands and looked at the long rows of wheat glistening and bending in the sun. "When that day comes," he said, "people are going to forget all this stuff about Kansas being stodgy and conservative and cautious because things in Kansas are going to be popping hotter than hog grease on a griddle."

Minnesota

by GRACE FLANDRAU

The train, smooth and fast and filled with the chill of the air-conditioning, rushed northward toward Minnesota. I had asked, as usual, to be told the exact moment we crossed the border, although the much-bored conductor insisted it would look the same on either side. But there *was* a difference, and I felt it, when we did cross.

The scene outside the car windows, however, needed none of the sentimentality of the native's return to make it beautiful. This was southeastern Minnesota, a flawless farming country, silvery under the spring sky and touched with the delicate expectancy of spring. The greens brighter for the blackness of the rich plowed earth, the willows a mist of yellow, the wide, grandfatherly old oaks foolish with tasseled buds. A place of gently rolling hills and groves and wild fruit trees tumbling down the slopes; of well-painted farm buildings and serene cattle, 4-H to a cow, standing dreamily at the barnyard gates. Where such names as Blooming Prairie, Belle Plaine, Elysian, Harmony and the tender Sleepy Eye speak for the feeling of the early settlers.

Although this is the oldest part of the state in point of settlement, it is still wonderfully free, just here, from the untidiness of advancing urbanism. But as we traveled north, more towns appeared. Soon we were near the one-time village Will and Charlie Mayo put on the map of the world. Rochester—where the Mayo boys worked

in their father's dispensary, drove him on his rounds, learned their
first anatomy from the skeleton of an old Sioux. Gradually, too, the
country became more chasmed, more picturesque. Gradually we
approached the Mississippi.

It came into view, not magnificently as seen from across the
valley, but glimpsed, lying quiet and swollen with spring floods over
the lowlands. Then it made its turn below St. Paul, a modest group
of skyscrapers appeared and we bumbled across the trestle into the
city.

At first, levees and river seemed strangely quiet to me. Then I
remembered it was still too early for much water-borne traffic. But
there was something wrong about that too. No Minnesota spring
could produce an evening as warm and humid as this. Where were
the invigorating airs the early travelers wrote about? The astringent
cold that cured your sore throat? I'll tell you where. They were just
around the corner and by morning they had turned it, bringing a
blizzard with them. A "good old Minnesota blizzard" is the loving
local term. And that, too, was as it should be. I was glad to be home
again.

When, as sometimes happens, Minnesota is spoken of as Midwestern, Minnesotans are likely to remark rather firmly, that it is
not a Middle Western, but a Northwestern state. It is a big state—
larger than all of New England, with Maryland and New Jersey
thrown in. Of mountains there are none, and the tall bluffs along the
rivers give to the country above an exhilarating sense of height.
Worth noting, too, is the fact that because of its great length from
north to south, it lies in two distinct "Life" zones so-called, the
Canadian and the Transitional. A fact which accounts in part for
the immense variety of plant and animal life, and of birds.

All in all, it is appropriate that *minne,* the Siouan word for water,
should be included in our name. (The suffix *sota* means, not the
sky-blue of the advertisements, but turgid or whitish.) On three
sides we are mostly bounded by water. On the east by the Mississippi
and its tributary from the north, the beautiful St. Croix. And farther
north and east, for 150 spectacular miles, by Lake Superior, no less.
On the west, is the Red River of the North, almost the only river
of importance in the United States to flow due north.

The most remarkable boundary is the chain of wilderness lakes
and rivers, streams and portages along the Canadian border, in

many parts accessible only by canoe, on foot, in motorboat or hydroplane. Yet at a time when the Pilgrims had hardly ventured far enough inland to lose the sound of the sea, it was a fairly well traveled route along which Frenchmen carried on their dramatic, wicked, venerable fur trade. Today, for sportsmen, poets, naturalists, wildlifers and just anybody who wants to get away from it all, it is the most favored region in Minnesota.

There are also, in good round numbers so dear to Chambers of Commerce, our ten thousand lakes, plus the largest number of marshes, swamps, sloughs, fens, muskegs and bogs (lovely words) of any state in the Union. And finally, there is the three-way divide from which our waters rush off—some north to Hudson's Bay, others east to the Atlantic, the rest south to the Gulf of Mexico.

There is also the weather—to which the more vigorous aspects of our personality are attributed. Minnesota's melodrama in four acts.

There are the blue, arctic Minnesota winters: snow, light, and dry and deep on roofs and lawns, slipping in a dazzle of white mist from the suddenly released branch of the evergreen that grows in every yard. Snow falling in soft, big flakes, or fine and hard, driven before terrible winds to blot out the world in days-long blizzards.

(There are the tales heard as a child, of men and women lost and frozen a few feet from their doors. Of the great-uncle who, snowbound in a deserted cabin, made a saw out of a piece of barrel hoop, sharpened a clasp knife and hacked off a piece of each of his frozen feet. And on the fine-drawn face of the man who so often told the story, a shadow whose meaning the child in some way understood: the question, whether he would have had the courage to do the same, and the fear, indeed the certainty, that he would not.)

Winters with everyone on skates, and on toboggans; curling, ice boating, playing hockey. Skiing, which is now the leading winter sport, was at first popular only among the Scandinavians.

The brief and boisterous period which follows is known as the Minnesota spring. It's a time, too—and somehow it makes them the more touching—for the gentle woods flowers, the crocuses and snowdrops, the blood root, anemone and violets. For the full white bloom of the wild plums and crab apples; for the lilacs and jonquils and for the lovely wild orchid which is Minnesota's flower—the pink lady's-slipper, or its sturdier cousin, the green-brown jack-in-the-pulpit.

Then the yards gay with bridal wreath and syringa and Minnesota's summer comes in with a bang. Of this season it must be said at once that while there are a great many "sparkling, winelike" days, there are not a few dog days, of which the less said the better. Nor can we, I'm afraid, ignore the Minnesota storms; on a single night in a single county where I once visited, there took place, in one corner, a cloudburst, in another a cyclone, and in between a thunderstorm in which seven cows were killed.

> *From the half*
> *of the sky*
> *that which lives there*
> *is coming and makes a noise.*

So sang the ancient Chippewa poet. And how right he was.

With the final act comes the redemption—the Indian summer, Minnesota's matchless fall when all its violence is distilled into color. Skies wildly blue, air crisp and ozone-scented. The thinning brilliant underbrush alive with ruffed grouse and quail and pheasant. Deer step the highways, wild ducks in unequaled numbers and varieties rock on all the waters. The beaver, mink, otter, muskrat and all our countless fur-bearing animals thicken their coats, and up in the northern swamps the squaws bend the wild rice over their birch-bark canoes and beat out the grain.

Also, throughout the state, the weather doesn't differ greatly except that in some places it is colder. Caprice, too, plays a part. For all the time-worn quip, "the coldest winter I ever knew was the summer I spent in Duluth," the day I recently spent there would make the third circle of the Inferno pleasantly cool. And almost anywhere it can be sixty in the morning, eighty at noon, near freezing in the evening.

Which brings us to a gray-eyed young Norwegian farmer beside whom, on a broiling day in Montevideo, Minnesota, I watched a parade. "Yes," he said, "I guess it gets hotter and gets colder here than most places. But it don't get monotonous. My brother out on the Coast says the weather there is always the same. He says it gets monotonous and he's coming home." Monotony is not, in fact, regarded favorably in Minnesota, nor is it, as we shall see, a condition that generally obtains.

A river beside which one's childhood is spent, even if it is the Mississippi, is likely to be taken pretty much for granted. Certainly it meant little to me until the day I stood, a small, scared pupil before a violin master of the Paris Conservatory. He was a sensitive, irascible man, cloistered in his own country as only a Frenchman of that time could be, and had endured me with pain till he learned where I was from. The effect was startling. *"Le Mee-see-see-pee!"* Never, but never, as a boy studying his geography, had he expected even to *see* a native from those shores, much less that one should be his pupil! Jean Jacques Rousseau was in his head, Paul and Virginia and all the virgin rivers, the exotic forests of the world. Next day his delicate little son was permitted a glimpse of me, but cautioned, I am sure, not to come too close.

The Mississippi was the highway that brought the modern world to the Northwest, from the day in 1823, when the first small steamboat staggered upstream to dock at the brand-new military post across from where St. Paul now stands. Soon an excited river traffic began, which by mid-century had built up a kind of climax, not only in numbers but in the nearly lunatic enthusiasm of the travelers. The beauties of woods, waterfalls, gardens of wild flowers; of the "sparkling, winelike" days; the sight of the buffalo and, in St. Paul, of the Chippewa lounging picturesquely about the streets, sent a rush of indescribably purple prose to tongue and pen. Settlers poured in from more easterly states and in countless thousands from overseas: from Ireland first, then Germany and soon from all the Scandinavian countries—workers and peasants who were glad to pay any price in toil and privation for independence and the right to own their own land.

As late as 1930, Norwegian was heard in parts of Southern Minnesota as often as English. In the town of Northfield, the Norwegian college of St. Olaf was founded, now famous for its magnificent *a cappella* choir. And where one of its professors, Ole Rölvaag, wrote his great novel *Giants in the Earth*. In the farming village of Scandia, some thirty miles north of St. Paul, on a certain summer day each year, throngs of handsome, well-dressed people from all over the state come back to celebrate an anniversary—the founding, in 1850, of one of the very first Swedish settlements in Minnesota. The Danes were fewer, but their dairying skills have had far-reaching economic effects. As has the Scandinavian predilection for co-operative enterprise.

In my childhood, Anglo-Saxon Minnesotans tended to regard the foreign-born and their progeny, especially those on the farms, as beings from a different planet. And indeed, there was some difference in dress and appearance. Now all that is changed. Everybody wears the same kind of clothes and looks the same in them. Along the leafy streets of the old river towns are handsome houses occupied for generations by the same families, persons quite as distinguished as, and indistinguishable from, any in the cities.

Everywhere, too, even in the big cities, one is still relatively near the wilderness, the almost unchanged wilderness the early settlers knew. Near the duck pass, the trout or small-mouth-bass stream, the camp in the deep woods, where on a path springy with fallen pine needles the young and as yet fearless deer love to stand and stare into your face as long as you stare into theirs: or, at your approach, a half dozen balls of feathers ricochet out of the brush, and the mother grouse scolds and drags her pretended broken wing to fool you. And where at night, on the shining lakes, the loons make those sounds literary people love, so inadequately, to describe.

To see Minnesota at its most moving and when it is most itself is, to me at least, to see it in the growing time of high midsummer. And to set out, as I did one year, up the beautiful valley of the Minnesota, a river which flows across Southern Minnesota from the west and empties into the Mississippi. This is a rich and beautiful farming country and the Germans who settled here gave nostalgic German names to their towns. In their part of the valley, German was spoken for many years, German ways predominated. However, aside from occasional polka dancing in the streets, to the music of German brass bands, this is no longer true.

(Indeed, the idea that the various racial groups in Minnesota retain the customs of their forebears is an illusion. It is true that for a national festival they may put on the old costumes, dance the old dances to the old tunes. But it is not a part of their daily living. When the girls, for instance, are being themselves, it is in their smart ready-made dresses, with their beauty-parlor hairdos. In the blue jeans in which they lead their 4-H calves or panda-faced lambs into the judging ring. When they preside over their classrooms or dance in their strapless evening gowns at their university or high-school proms. Americans, and in a hundred ways, making the most of it.)

It was hot that day, in the valley, especially so in the pleasant town of Le Seuer, of which I remember only a superlative corn- and pea-canning factory which featured such surprising items as field thermometers perpetually taking the soil's temperature, and radio-telephone conversations between the head office and, for all I know, the peas themselves. And, too, the presence in this Minnesota town of large groups of Bahamians and West Indians, who would later move on to harvest other crops.

My objective was the town of New Ulm to which I had once been taken as a child. Of that occasion, however, I remember nothing but the sound of a cannon, fired not in war but at a cere- mony in honor of Charles Eugene Flandrau and the winning of a battle many years before.

This lovely valley was once a part of the Sioux lands, and one often wonders what these primitive Americans understood of the treaties by which they bartered away their homes and hunting grounds. At any rate, when a summer came in which they found themselves not only without land, but without the food, money or goods promised them, they rose and savagely murdered over a thousand white men and women and children.

Flandrau had been Associate Justice of the Supreme Court of the territory, and later of the state. He was living in the valley when the massacre began, and was elected commander-in-chief of the defenders at New Ulm, where about 1500 women and children had taken refuge. The gallantry and brilliance with which he won the three-day battle make it one of the most moving episodes of our frontier history.

Modern New Ulm is a solid, prosperous town, with pleasant, shady streets and yards bright with flowers. Here is a Flandrau State Park and a commemorative monument. But it was a small bronze plaque, identifying the building where the women and children awaited the outcome of the siege, that moved me most. That and an incident which occurred when Flandrau was evacuating a village to the advancing Sioux. The departing settlers had poisoned a barrelful of whisky and left it in the square. It was one way of fighting Indians; but Flandrau, the last to leave, pulled the plug and drained away the poisoned liquor.

I married into his family long after he died, and I wish I could remember, of that one day I saw him, more than the sound of a cannon.

Farther up in the valley is the gay and friendly town of Montevideo, which we found in the throes of its annual fiesta, the streets
crowded with tall, well-boned men and women, and hordes of
sturdy, bare-armed children. This celebration, in the weird American way, is dedicated to Uruguay, and Uruguay responds by sending an official representative. The hotel swarmed with pretty queens,
girls mostly from other farming communities and named, like the
goddesses of old, for the products of the earth—corn, flax, soybeans
and all the rest. Although less poetically, there were also a Boxcar
and an Overall queen. Less poetic, too, was the booming voice heard
above the bands and the singing in the streets, of the radio loud-
speaker, talking endlessly of prices, crops, livestock, and of remedies
for all kinds of livestock ailments.

There was also a reception, given by the widow of one of Minnesota's thirteen Scandinavian governors—fourteen, if you count Harold
Stassen who is half Scandinavian—Mrs. Theodore Christianson, at her
farm some miles distant. On one side the pleasant, reconstructed
farmhouse overlooks the bluff above the river, on the other it faces
an endless, sunlit sweep of land, carpeted now with growing grain.
And the look of the country, or perhaps the purity of the air—the
ethereal lightness of air without dust and without humidity—seemed
suddenly to reveal a quality of my state I had vaguely felt but never
before defined.

The quality of newness. Of skies that had not had to look down
through all the ages upon human suffering; of an air not yet heavy
with human sighs. A newness which is not felt in the actual wilderness but only, by contrast, in those places to which human beings
have recently, and in not too great numbers, come.

It seemed to me that unconsciously, it was felt by the people who
were there that day, and of whom there was hardly one who did
not point to an island in the river, or a spot along the shore, or upon
the bright country above, as the place where his forebears had
"taken up" land, and where he or one of his parents had been born.

One of these, a vigorous man with keen, friendly gray eyes,
invited me to breakfast. "Will eight o'clock suit you?"—the hour set
late, I felt sure, on my account.

He is a farmer and a power in the agricultural affairs of the
region—a man who is extraordinarily well informed but who is also
quite impassioned. So that such phrases as "those fellows in the

cities," "Wall Street," "those bankers"—men who, he believed, had no relation to droughts, floods, frosts, but did have too high prices for what you bought, low prices for what you sold—had a way of erupting violently. "I've only got two men now, maybe in a couple of years I won't have any. If they don't want collectivized farms"— this on a note of the horror felt, I suppose, by most land-owning men —"they better take care of the farmers."

But there is in him, too, still another man. The one who belongs to the soil. We drove slowly past his fields, stopping to look at the barley, the tufted bright-green rows of soybeans, striped in between with the black, black earth—the perfect pattern of a fashionable modern fabric. And, crowning it all, there was his flax—the deep blue of flax in bloom. A lake of color more like a mirage than a lake. A blue that eludes you, as if the massed green stems had only been breathed upon by color. A blue like no other in the world and that reaches less into your eyes than deep into your heart.

Now, as you continue westward, you begin to be aware of something different. There are times when, over a hill or through an opening in the vista, you see too far. You see nothing but light. You are in the midst of nowhere, a shining emptiness, a vast floor, flat and wide as the sea, spreading away to and beyond the whole circle of the horizon. And no sound but the hum of wind along the telegraph wires, the liquid call of a bird or a human voice at once loud and nearly extinguished by the immensity into which it falls. The West, the Prairie, the great valley of the Red River of the North.

You must see the prairies where they are perfect, or you will not see them at all. There must not be the tiniest rise or fall of the earth, or your new sense of dimension will be lost. It must also be away from the centers of activity—out where the great farms are, and where the occasional groups of grain elevators, the straight march of the telegraph poles, the rare, thin lines of planted trees are merely perpendicular lines that accentuate the total flatness.

The low, wooded course of the Red River of the North is scarcely noticeable in these wide vistas. Here, in summers long past, the wild grass grew tall as a man, and the hooves of the buffalo were stained red with the juice of the wild berries. And yet even after Jim Hill brought in his railroad, the soil was considered valueless by everybody but him. Possibly, too, fear of the winter with nothing to stop the sweep of the winds, or to mitigate the heat of summer, may have held back the pioneers. Perhaps it is still only a place for the strong. But from those who are not, something also may be learned.

So there was the delicate-looking man who stood so long beside his weedy flax field, under some compulsion to talk. Sometimes it was about his pioneer grandparents. How their money had run out back on the Mississippi, so they had walked the remaining 300 miles, his mother, then twelve, barefoot and driving the cows. When they did arrive, nothing here but empty prairie, the sod hut, the meager hand tools. "I couldn't have done it," he would repeat, accusing himself.

Or else it was his own hard life he dwelt upon. Six hundred acres to farm and he couldn't get help or pay for it if he could. He had suffered a back injury, too, from which he could not recover. Lightning had recently burned his barns. You needed sons on a farm, and he had none. "I don't know, maybe they had it better then than we do."

Sometimes he didn't talk at all. His tractor chugged softly in the potato patch, in the grove of trembling, silver aspens a meadow lark repeated a clear melodious phrase. And I felt that his thoughts were not really on what he said, but were concerned with what a human being wants; what he needs to be happy; why he lives at all. He, too, a Norwegian, with the something they have that is a little remote and dreamlike in their pale eyes.

It seemed strange, now, to turn eastward—as if one had come to feel that any movement should still be toward the west. Strange to see hills again, and shady towns, and normal-sized farms; to motor hour after hour between undefaced green walls—the second growth now replacing the virgin forests which once covered most of the state.

Blue lakes were everywhere in wild profusion, and wherever a dirt road leads back from the highway, there would be signs bearing such names as K'Mon Inn, Nip Inn, Step Inn and similar whimsies. I was relieved to see them there, having got the impression from one of those most dedicated of pessimists, a Conservation officer, that our Minnesota lakes were beginning to dry up.

Throughout this northerly half of the state are the great state and national parks and forests, the experimental stations for the study and preservation of wild life, the reforestation projects in which Government and lumber companies collaborate in planting new trees.

Here, too, are the reservations where the Chippewa, once the lords of it all, mostly live. And where, in the town of Walker, we paid a visit to one of the state's most distinguished citizens—Ed Rogers, county attorney, and a three-fourths Chippewa Indian. And it was gratifying to hear Indians discussed sympathetically, but without sentimentality. They must be assimilated into American life as other races and peoples have been, but this cannot happen, he believes, while they remain on reservations. As long as they are together, "they'll just be Indians." I should have liked to ask what that is. But one answer is to be found in the translations of their songs by a Minnesota woman who is one of the nation's great authorities on Indian music and poetry, Miss Frances Densmore. And how like any girl was the young Chippewa who sang:

> *What are you saying to me?*
> *I am arrayed like the rose*
> *And as beautiful as they. . . .*

In this region, too, you will get a notion of Minnesota's summer hysteria: in the motor launches, whose interiors are a forest of fine-stemmed rods held tenderly between the owners' knees; at the camps where nothing but fishing is thought of, and on the lakes where nothing else is done.

Strange, too, that here, where such delicious fish as trout of all kinds, wall-eyed and northern pike, and a dozen others abound, the local menus should be largely given over to lobster tails from South Africa, shrimp from Japan and other embalmed delicacies from remote parts of the world.

Often, in Northeastern Minnesota, beside the remote beauty of green forest and blue water, of small, pine-ringed fields ripening on lonely-seeming farms, and quiet ponds where water lilies lie open in full bloom and the wicked pitcher plants wait with their traps set for unwary flies—beside all this organic, surface life, you are aware of something else. You see how the roots even of the tall trees clutch only the surface of bare rock, and you walk on what you learn, with a kind of dreamy satisfaction, is the oldest of all granites. And near the town of Ely, you come upon a softly jade-colored stone known as Ely Green, perhaps the very oldest substance known to man. Two and a half billion years, estimates the latest authority.

Nor is this all. For in this region is Minnesota's greatest geologic spectacle, the open-pit mines of the Mesabi Iron Range. Vast sunken amphitheaters, huge gaping earth wounds bleeding strange and subtle tones of red—rust red, blue or brown or purple reds, and the violent orange of water sometimes lying in the pits. And looking down into them from the observation platforms, you seem to see no men at all, only cranes that whirl, great steel jaws that bite into the red earth, trucks that seem to be self-propelled along roads that spiral around the walls of the pits, and small grublike vehicles which rise nimbly up the steep runways to the trains which, night and day, rumble down to the great docks at Superior and Duluth.

Duluth I remember from childhood with a kind of enchantment. A perpendicular city, a toy town, built straight up and down like a city in a fairy tale. Its air heady with the freshness of the gigantic lake beside which it seemed so precariously to be perched.

Well, it is anything but a toy city now. And yet something of that wry magic remains. It still climbs its steep escarpment and for twenty-four miles along the top looks out over a breath-taking blue void of sky and water. The sense, too, of excitement and urgency still exists, and by some is attributed to the climate: "Nine months of winter and three of poor sledding." A libel.

I'd like to touch upon another subject of which Duluthians are very, very tired. Namely, bears. In Duluth, one hears, bears occasionally stroll into restaurants or are found by startled homecomers in the back yard playing with the children. Even more fascinating is an event reported in the publication *North Country*.

Two men, it seems, went out one morning in their motorboat to take a turn around the harbor. There was also present a large bear, out for a swim.

When the boat loitered too near him, he, deciding he preferred to ride, promptly climbed in and the two gentlemen promptly climbed out. The boat, unguided, tore wildly around the harbor with the bear calmly seated in the stern.

Apparently a boat captained by a bear is news even in Duluth, and brought the citizens flocking to the water front. Finally the bear, bored by it all, resumed his swim. I think I should like to live in Duluth.

Little Falls is a town on the Mississippi, in the center of the state—a farming and a vacation region that was once the richest part of our pinelands; a place that has always had—for me, at least

—an air of incompleteness, as if the forests ought still to be there. It is also a part of Minnesota greatly loved by one of her most celebrated sons—Charles Lindbergh.

Just outside Little Falls is a park dedicated to Lindbergh's father, the Minnesota Congressman Charles A. Lindbergh. There is also the small house where Lindbergh spent the first seventeen and most formative years of his life. In his book, *The Spirit of St. Louis*, he writes with simple and moving artistry about his childhood here, of the tales he heard from his parents and his Swedish grandparents.

He writes about being trapped in a Minnesota blizzard, and about the time his barnstorming plane was forced down in a Minnesota swamp. You recognize the fields he plowed, learn how often, in Washington, father and son talked of the summer when they would return to the Minnesota farm.

In the Lindbergh house are a few mementoes of a boy's childhood: toys, agates, the claw of an eagle and the jawbone of a large pike. But what is of most interest to us, I think, is that this man, who is a symbol of the modern world of flight, should have seen and heard Minnesota's early settlers.

Seventy miles south, also on the Mississippi, we come to Minnesota's urban phenomenon—the Siamese but *not* identical twin cities of St. Paul and Minneapolis.

St. Paul, which had a few years' start, grew steeply up and down her hills and bluffs along the Mississippi. Minneapolis was born on the high, level plateau across the river with all the vast, empty West as her front yard. At her back were the falls which stopped navigation, a geographic circumstance that made St. Paul a great transportation center but gave the power of the river to Minneapolis. The nucleus of population in both cities came from the eastern seaboard. But soon Germans in large numbers settled in St. Paul, as did the gifted, generous, always intensely human and therefore incalculable Irish, while an influx of able, hard-working, hardheaded, forward-looking Swedes made Minneapolis one of the largest Swedish cities in the world.

There is a much-quoted pronouncement to the effect that St. Paul is the last city of the East, Minneapolis the first city of the West. And perhaps it has, or did have, an element of truth. Anyhow, St. Paul was delighted to accept it as a tribute to what she liked to consider her superior gentility, while Minneapolis was quite as satisfied to be the first city of the West, or more accurately, the Northwest. In many ways she still is.

Both are interesting and distinguished cities. Minneapolis, the expansive extrovert, is bigger, more luxurious, has more amusements, stays up later at night, and possesses, perhaps, a more youthful and venturesome spirit. St. Paul is the more cautious and reflective introvert, but one who has known how to make her caution pay.

The Minneapolis names most widely known have for generations been connected with the city's great flour-milling industry. Indeed, it is said that ambitious explorers who like to think themselves first in some remote jungle are not a little annoyed to find the sarongs worn by native women made of flour sacks stamped with the simple legend Pillsbury's Best.

One of the town's cultural delights, incidentally, is a superb Chinese bronze and jade collection—assembled by Alfred Pillsbury and given to the Institute of Art. Another remarkable collection in the Institute, acquired by another Pillsbury, consists entirely of gold objects of great beauty and antiquity. This collection is also Chinese and is one of the very few of its kind in the world.

I suppose a state university—no matter what city it is in—belongs less to the city than to the whole state. In this way, the extraordinary university in Minneapolis *is* Minnesota. I felt this especially when I returned, with the memory fresh in my mind, of so many far-off towns and farms and lonely lakes, and all that variety of peoples whose sons and daughters are, in this university, unified in more ways than in the learning they receive.

It is particularly appropriate that the Mayo Foundation should be a part of the university. No story is more essentially Minnesotan than that of the Mayo brothers. Their diagnostic and surgical genius and organizing ability brought them world-wide fame and yet, with a kind of ingrained unpretentiousness and also a stubborn wisdom, they refused to leave their Minnesota village, but brought the world to them. And now, a great medical building on the campus of the university is called in their honor the Mayo Memorial. A far cry indeed from the skeleton of an old Sioux.

I have left St. Paul to the last because, for reasons not always clear even to me, I think it is the best. On a late August afternoon, just touched by a portent of Indian summer, I walked about the city. I went up onto "the Hill," and along Summit Avenue, once the city's finest street. The shadows were blue under the immense overarching trees; the sunlight yellow as honey on the broad asphalt. And between the mansions once built and now abandoned by the town's plutocracy, there lies spread before you the whole wide, shining valley of the Mississippi.

I stopped to look at the narrow brownstone house in which Scott Fitzgerald lived as a boy, and recalled the pale, handsome and somehow haunted face of the young man I knew only before his explosion into fame. A writer who died just as his vision was reaching the stature of his enormous talent.

I passed the house where Sinclair Lewis spent some of the many restless years after he left his native Sauk Centre. (Incidentally, when I visited Sauk Centre shortly before, I found no one who could point out the place where Lewis was born.) I recalled a visit Lewis paid in St. Paul, some time after *Main Street*, to my brother-in-law, Charles Macomb Flandrau, for whose *Viva Mexico* Lewis had unbounded enthusiasm. He had turned up, unexpectedly, at Flandrau's house in St. Paul, and that night they dined with me. Afterward, Lewis embarked on an interminable monologue made up of imaginary conversations in the American idiom. Flandrau, high-strung, easily bored and not unaccustomed to the center of the stage himself protested angrily, "If you don't stop *talking* I shall leave this house." Lewis, smiling indulgently, went right on. Whereupon Flandrau flung out of the room and into the quiet street. Next morning, pale and shaken, he appeared at our door. "He found me. He talked *all night*. I'm locking myself in here until he is out of Minnesota." Some months later, when *Babbitt* appeared, much of the dialogue had a strangely familiar ring.

It was a relief to leave an avenue so full of echoes and go down into the older town, where the narrow streets have kept something of the old flavor, even though the buildings which flank them have undergone alarming face liftings. Here the former residence streets are mostly a jumble of rooming houses or houses made over into shops and warehouses. On one such street, however, the chaos resolves into a broad, well-tended lawn surrounded by a beautiful wrought-iron fence, and the sturdy, gray-stone mansion is a historic residence. It was built by Alexander Ramsey, who came out in 1849 to be first governor of the Territory of Minnesota.

One of the handsomest of St. Paul's more modern buildings is the courthouse, where a magnificent Carl Milles statue—believed by many to be his finest work—is to be seen. The remarkable setting in

which it is placed is a loggia of blue-black marble, three stories high
and relieved by touches of bronze and a dim, gilt and mirrored ceiling. At the far end stands the colossal statue of an Indian, carved
in veined, cream-white onyx and holding in his hand a pipe of peace.
The tall, proud figure is imbued with a nobility which, you are made
to feel—by I do not know what magic—is not his alone, but is or must
become a part of all men. A summons, stern as it may be prophetic,
to a future of which no man need be afraid.

This sense of the future brought to my mind the motto inscribed
on the first Great Seal of Minnesota—*I wish to look beyond.* Many
Minnesotans, I believe, would feel that it sums up the history and
very spirit of their state.

Whether it is truer here than of any other part of America is less
important, I think, than that they should feel it to be. That there
should be a place, loved in childhood, where, as the Hindu poet wrote
of his native valley, the fragrances are sweeter, the moonlight softer
than in any other.

> *Blessed am I that am born to this land*
> *And that her best gift to me*
> *Is that I love her. . . .*

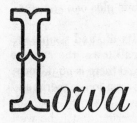

Iowa

by PAUL ENGLE

Iowa is the heart of the Heartland.

Its greatest single force is dirt—fat dirt; out of its soil each year more wealth is produced than in all the gold mines of the world. Gently the land rises and falls, not flat, not broken into steep hills, but always tilting its fertile face to the sun.

When a military highway was needed from Dubuque to the Missouri border in the early days of the mounted dragoons, a farmer was hired. He yoked up ten oxen to a long sod-breaking plow and headed south. Day after day they moved, ahead of them the untouched grass and grove, behind them a lengthening furrow of black dirt. No sound but the man's yell to his animals, and the silken, tearing rip of the plow splitting that sod for the first time ever. It was natural for Iowa to use for its military road only the peaceful oxen and the plow. For this is an abundant land.

And when a few years ago the Soviet Union sent the first group of agricultural experts to America to find out what free men working on their own land could raise, it was natural that the Russians should come first to Iowa. And when the Red farmers arrived they were given, in once "isolationist" Iowa, a wealthy welcome, told everything they wanted to know, shown all the methods and secrets of production. They went to the First Presbyterian Church in Jefferson and held hymnbooks, probably for the first time in their lives, watched 4-H boys demonstrate how to kill corn borers, and 4-H girls bake sweet rolls. They lifted their arms at the right time in the Iowa song for the line "That's where the tall corn grows," and they saw their first real drugstore with a soda fountain and ate "Tummy Busters. Eat Two and Get a Free One—49 cents plus one cent tax." For this is an abundant land.

Iowa is the middlest of the Middle West. Its life and people are balanced and solid. It is a country of the small town, the average comfortable life. There are no great fortunes and there is no poverty. But it has the highest standard of living for its area in the world and it has a quarter of all the best land in America.

Look at the map of Iowa, the Missouri wavering down the west side and the Mississippi down the east. Jutting eastward is a fine round pot belly, the broad Mississippi bending around it like a belt. For this is an abundant land.

Iowa carries nothing to excess save its virtues and its weather. It has always been the place of the sensible medium, and of the peace that goes with it. The only Quaker President, Herbert Hoover, came from a little Iowa town. There has never been a war on Iowa soil, or a battle of any consequence. One massacre by the Sioux of a few white settlers. John Brown trained his men at a Quaker settlement, where they did strange calisthenics and drilled with wooden swords. One of his men was censured for hugging girls, which was as violent an act as any of the group committed in Iowa. When the time for fighting came, Brown left his peaceful settlement, where the Quakers had assisted him without knowing his wicked purpose, and went off to bloody Harpers Ferry. Iowa men marched off to Vicksburg, but the Civil War never came to their state.

When my grandfather rode with the Fifth Iowa Cavalry in the 60's, he chased the Sioux in Dakota Territory but never caught up with him. Inkpadutah, the leader of the Sioux who massacred thirty-two men, women and children at Spirit Lake, realized that Iowa was too peaceful for such wild goings-on, and fled west.

Kentucky was the Dark and Bloody Ground, but Iowa has always been the Bright and Bloodless Ground.

Of the Missouri River the old saying is: too thick to drink, too thin to plow. But Iowa is just right to plow, no waste land, no swamps, no mountains, no large forests. Glaciers scoured off the soil from other states and dumped it on this lucky land, giving Iowa its long reaches of loam. After grass had grown and died for centuries, sinking its roots so deep that prairie fires couldn't burn them out, the soil became as rich as the side of a fat hog.

Then the settlers came, and the sod-breaking plows, with their great oak beams to hold the point of the plow down against the tough buck of the roots, and the great crops began to spring up. France had its Field of the Cloth of Gold, but Iowa still has its Fields of the Cloth of Green.

The common shape of Iowa landscape is the little valley, with tiny streams everywhere like veins meshing a marvelous body. And along all of the streams, wooded slopes with willow, elm, maple, hickory, black walnut. The streams are everywhere, the dark rivers with the silt of fields: Raccoon, Coon, Wolf, Catfish, Mosquito, Polecat, Opossum, Pike, Turkey, Skunk, Cedar, Crab-apple, Squaw, and Five Barrel Creek, so called because dragoons found five barrels of whisky buried near it. And most lyrical of all, in the high hills of northeastern Iowa, the Tête de Mort (call it Teddymore), proof that the French once were here, and that a band of Dakotahs was killed by Sac Indians and scalped and thrown over a cliff.

There is no soft nonsense about the seasons in Iowa. Winter is a savage season; blizzards out of the west rattle the teeth in your skull. Frost goes deep in the fallow ground; snow piles up and when the ice comes, impenetrable, squirrels scamper over it hungrily. But then will come the incredible May morning when the sun drips a gold life on the land, seeds jump in delight under the plowed fields, the sprouted corn turns the countryside into tufted quilts, and the pigs squirm out into the light of day ("Sows opened weak on the Chicago market" says the radio report) and calves jump stiff legged around the barn. The air itself has the quality of food and breathing is nourishment. The pastures glitter with green.

Then summer overwhelms us. We can hear the crops growing, the corn up an inch a day, the pigs grunting their growth as they crunch their food—more elaborately planned and mixed than that of any child (buttermilk, yeast, fish, soybeans, sugar, corn, limestone, cobalt, acetate, zinc carbonate, linseed oil, rolled oats, fish liver, manganese sulphate, vitamins, antibiotics, riboflavin, and many others). The porkers have had their "one-shot wormer" and are busy hanging bacon on their slick sides. The whole state turns into a skillet, frying human, animal and plant life. Midnight differs a few degrees from intense noon. Corn grows tall and men grow limp. People droop by night and drop by day. But everything flourishes.

Autumn is the Iowa season. All of the winter's frozen rest, the spring plowing, the summer cultivating, move toward the final act of harvest. The land browns, oats ripen, corn begins to dent, hay is cut, the alfalfa for the third time. As the long corn leaves turn brittle the air itself turns crisp and tree leaves burn the branches for a while before falling. It is a season truly called "the fall." Things come to earth, the crops to barn, the kids to school. The delirious activity of summer slows down, as the urgency of jobs to get done before it's too late falls away.

Between summer and autumn come the county fairs, with their rows of Jerseys, Guernseys (with the highest butter-fat content in their milk), of Holsteins (the largest producers of milk in bulk), the mouse-colored Brown Swiss with their calves looking like heavy-boned fawns, the glistening flanks of Black Angus beef steers, polished and combed, or the ruddy Herefords with their white faces. And there is usually a single hog litter totaling a ton. The wildly carved running horses on the merry-go-round carry children to the same sweet and brassy tunes. The exhibits of farm machinery are fantastic, the prize squash, pumpkin, corn, startle the eye with their size. And of course there are the formidable yet delicate and fluffy cakes with blue and red prize ribbons on them, the prize pickles, canned beans, enough to shatter the stablest stomach. Along the race track where the horses are jogging with their light sulkies and the old-time horsemen with their legs straddling the shafts, families are engaged in that most typical, most delightful Iowa activity—consuming food.

What people come? Farmers with their families, faces tanned but a sharp white line around the neck where the shirt collar kept off the sun, with the deliberate walk of men accustomed to plowed fields and bumpy pastures. They watch the fat-steer judging and the heavy draft-horse judging, look at the machinery, take a suspicious glance at the Kewpie doll stands and the jaded girlie shows, but mostly they talk, talk to other farmers they haven't seen in a coon's age. (What's the age of a coon?) Everywhere clusters of men arguing weather, crops, prices (today's prices are mentioned in the tone of voice one uses coming home from a funeral), politics, the Government (in the tone one uses for a difficult uncle you don't really want around but whose wealth might be needed later on).

The women are here, too, and the kids; it's a family affair, something for everybody, the home-convenience exhibits for the ladies and the Ferris wheel for the screaming kids. But town people are here too, especially the ones who grew up on farms and moved away. They've changed some, they walk a little faster and gesture more abruptly, but they still like the smells of the barns and the bawl of the calves and the leathery tang of harness being soaped for the afternoon's first trotting heat. You can take the boy out of the farm but you can't take the farm out of the boy.

Across the top of the Great Seal of Iowa is the motto: Our Liberties We Prize and Our Rights We Will Maintain. And to prove that those rights will be maintained, a soldier with rifle stands in the foreground, a plow and a great swirling flag behind him. To a surprising extent, they are maintained, although now and then there is a little uncertainty as to just whose rights are meant. A few years ago the body of a GI was refused burial at a Sioux City cemetery, although he had died protecting his country's liberties, because he was too much a 100 per cent American, a real Indian. But this is rare. It is a matter of pride that the first case to come before the Supreme Court of Iowa Territory gave freedom to a Negro slave. And this same regard for human liberty came up a century later when a Negro Army officer stationed at a radar base near Waverly could not find housing for his family, although an apartment was available. When the other tenants heard about it, they petitioned to have him as a neighbor and welcomed his family with a celebration.

There has always been a sense of the just in Iowa. More than a hundred years ago when the defiant Sac Chief Black Hawk was presented to Andy Jackson in Washington he looked him in the eye and said simply, "I am a man and you are another."

Even obscenity gets a fair hearing. A few years ago the ladies of Dubuque were frightened by the appearance of comics, reprints, pocket books near schools. Hearings were held and the naughty evidence was introduced, such fiction as that of Erskine Caldwell, Richard Bissell (Dubuque's own, author of *A Stretch on the River* and *The Pajama Game*), and the usual popular novels, along with some gruesome comics and a history of art which charmingly proved that the female nude had interested more artists than had bowls of fruit or happy children. But in the end, the decision taken was the moderate, middle one to be expected of Iowa people: the chance of censorship was worse than the chance of indiscriminate novels being read. One argument of real power in a state essentially rural-minded was that the corset sections of mail-order catalogs contained more photographs of undressed models than any of the books being questioned.

When the Russians came to Iowa they expected to find the fields full of people. As they were driven along the roads between the luxuriant corn and oats and alfalfa, with the yards and pastures full of hogs and cattle, they kept asking, "But where are the workers?" Usually they were told that a man and his wife and children, with an occasional hired man, farmed the place. One of them exclaimed, "By you one man—by us a hundred!" What he did not realize was that this staggering production of food by a few people was done by the same class of farmers the Soviet had murdered in the early 30's. They had never seen a husking hook fastened to a glove. They kept asking at the agricultural college at Ames who was their *boss* in Washington, and could not believe that the college operated independently of the Federal Government. When they asked Guy Stover, Jr., a farmer near Reinbeck, who told him what to plant, he replied: "Nobody tells me what to plant. Nobody. I can let the whole farm grow up in weeds if I want to and nobody can say a thing."

They ate meals of roast beef, vegetables, ice cream, angel-food cake, salad, milk, all of which came from the same farm. They discovered that small-town newspapers in Iowa were thicker than Russia's national dailies. They had their first experience of motels, a dime store, golf, a country club. They discovered, as the Charles City *Press* put it, every reason under the sun why the Iowa farmer produced twenty times as much food as the Russian farmer, except the main one, the freedom under which the Iowa farmer operates.

The Russians came in the hope of learning how to feed their people. That was natural, for men and women have always come to Iowa with hope. In the 1850's came a group of Germans calling itself The Community of True Inspiration, who believed that God still spoke directly to man. They settled between Iowa City and Grinnell and built seven little Amana villages in the medieval manner, the families living close together in the communities and going out to work in the fields. They had the wisdom to realize that the Lord could best be served with good land rather than poor, and took up 26,000 acres of rich bottom soil and wooded hills along the Iowa River. They ate in communal houses (five times a day, in leisure and abundance, with excellent grape and dandelion wine brought out to those working in the fields at noon). All property save clothing and furniture was held in common. Each adult received a tiny sum known as "year-money" for odd expenses, the least-skilled worker in the hog house receiving the same housing and maintenance as the most responsible farm head. God was worshiped not in churches but in houses without cross or decoration and no music save the unaccompanied human voice grandly ringing out the hymns written by their own brilliant prophet Christian Metz.

They flourished in their isolated, abundant and devout life until the wicked world came to them by newspaper, paved road, car, radio, and the young people began to yearn for the things they saw others having, like bicycles and Sunday baseball. They voted to dissolve the old communal-property idea and to form a corporation in which everyone worked for a salary. Each adult was given one share of Class A voting stock; when issued in 1932 a share was worth fifty-four dollars—today it is worth many times that. Houses are painted, cars are everywhere, television aerials rise as high as the native hickory and oak trees.

Again Iowa released the energies of people who came to her. Working with odd items from local shops, George Foerstner and others created a little freezer. And now in the cornfields at Middle Amana, where oxen loafed not long ago and daily prayers out of the early 18th Century were uttered in praise of God and in disparagement of weak man, there is a bright new factory from which more home freezers are sold than from any other plant in the world.

Iowa has always believed in bringing together the holy and the useful. Dutch who would not conform to the established church in Holland came in 1847 to found the town of Pella, where every May the old Dutch clothes and the wooden shoes come out, and there is dancing in the street. Why shouldn't they dance? They're in Iowa raising tulips, and raising the hem of their long dresses, oh so slightly.

And the French came to start their own idealistic community at Icaria on the Nodaway. Property was held in common, but alas, not the zeal for work. A dance hall was built, however, with plenty of zeal and native wood, but soon there were only individual men and women working their own lives.

The Hungarians came after the failure of the 1848 revolt against Austria. But they were aristocrats full of zeal to build a New Buda in northwestern Iowa, and what the land needed was a sharp plow, not an edged sword.

The Norwegians came to northeastern Iowa, in the handsome hill

country, to settle the town of Decorah and found Luther College.
Some crossed the frozen Mississippi in the depth of winter, proving
the stern devotion of a faith that could build log cabins in a wilderness and a hundred years later produce blond, unbeaten football
teams with Viking names.

Naturally, the Mennonites came here to build their fine farms, with
that same combination of hard work and solid faith. Around Kalona
they wrestled with some hard questions: Was it right to drive an
automobile? (Most drive buggies; a few, cars with the chrome
painted out.) Was it proper to use a tractor with metal tires but not
with rubber tires? Would pickles tied to the feet cure a child of con-
vulsions? Should the preachers forbid turkey roasts, ice-cream suppers, imposing weddings, laces, corsets, Christmas trees? The men in
their beards, the women and children in their black bonnets and
high shoes, come into Iowa City to shop, and to peer quietly at the
naughty world. And then go home to work their rich farms with their
old simplicity.

The Czechs came to Spillville in the northeastern country, where
Anton Dvorak came to write his music in the peaceful valley where
his native language was still spoken. And signs across part of Cedar
Rapids today are in Czech, and the Sokols do their fine gymnastics
and the kolaches are made with prunes or poppy seeds. Once a
Czech girl named Jaroslava Holobulova graduated from Coe College
at the top of her class.

But most amusing of all the peoples who came to Iowa were the
English younger sons who settled in Le Mars in the northwest to
learn farming in the 1880's. They brought to Iowa their own sporting
ways; cricket practice was held on Broken Kettle Creek, and the
Le Mars cricket team beat St. Paul. Polo was played against Cherokee and Council Bluffs. But the polo ball proved more attractive than
the humble pumpkin, and the younger sons left the plow in the furrow and rode into town to "paint the place a rip, staring red."

But the purpose of these gay British boys, since the place was
Iowa, was to learn how to raise food. A visiting newspaperman wrote
about them: "The young men who make up this community are . . .
graduates of Oxford or Cambridge. On one farm I met two tall and
handsome young farmers whose uncle had been a distinguished
member of Parliament. The last time I had seen them was in a
London drawing room. This time they tramped me through the mud
and manure of the barnyard to show me some newly bought stock.

They were boarding with a Dutch farmer at three dollars a week in order to learn practical farming. . . . Another young farmer had been connected with a Shanghai bank. There was a brother to Lord Ducie, not to speak of future baronets, viscounts, and honorables . . ."

But real liberty had its price. One of the Englishmen wrote that he could no longer stand the Iowa attitude: "The other evening on the closing of the House of Lords (as they had named a saloon), I was standing with four or five friends talking when the deputy marshal comes up and requests me in his usually suave manner to 'cheese this racket.' Liberty is constantly jammed down your throat here, but it seems to me an exploded theory, when an officer can do what he likes with your right of speech." Discouraged by equal parts of being told to cheese it and of hard work, the younger sons gave up their western ghosts and left.

The English were the gayest of all the Iowa settlers. More solid were the "Hook-and-Eye Dutch," who refused to put up the tops of their buggies because the sun was no harder on them than on the horse.

But no matter what their origins, Iowa people believed in education. With the lowest rate of illiteracy in the United States, it is natural that one of the country's largest manufacturers of fountain pens should be the W. A. Sheaffer Pen plant, at Fort Madison, and that one of the finest state-wide newspapers should be the Des Moines *Register*, unique today in having an editorial page with generous convictions and the courage to express them. Iowa believes, with the mixture of idealism and practicality which has always distinguished the people of Iowa, that personal freedom is nothing but old-fashioned right, and every man's due.

The Cowles family is a solid example of what human character can mean to a state, through its many gifts to colleges, the foundation it has endowed, and through dramatizing in the pages of the *Register* the fact that a nation's security lies as much in its ideals as in its bombs, and that liberties must be prized, even at the risk of offending subscribers.

Even in liquor, Iowa has chosen the medium way. Knowing the strong temperance feeling among the people, and yet suspecting that, since it was mentioned in the Old Testament, drinking might be here to stay, the state compromised. Under the fancy that a man would remain soberer if he took a bottle home, where there was no one to observe but the kiddies, all bars (save for beer) were outlawed. State liquor stores were set up without advertising or decoration. Some dramatic things have happened as a result.

Because of a fear that liquor purchases might be criticized by their neighbors, many people in the first year drove to the next town to buy where they might be unrecognized. On the way, they would pass the cars of those from the next town hurrying over to *their* liquor store to buy in secret. One enterprising newspaper, the Eagle Grove *Eagle*, discovered that, on the basis of gross liquor sales, Eagle Grove and nearby Clarion had exchanged populations. Any action connected with the naughty word "liquor" is news.

The demon rum even lurks behind innocent beef cattle, and caused one governor embarrassment. At an Iowa State Fair, the governor accepted the grand-champion baby beef, only to discover that it was owned by the Storz Brewing Company of Omaha. He gave it away for charity. And at the Waterloo Cattle Congress he agreed to pose with the grand-champion bull, a colossal animal, and then found that it belonged to a Milwaukee brewer named Pabst. It's a delicate thing when the governor of the state producing the finest fat cattle can't be photographed with a baby beef or giant bull without first sniffing them for fumes of alcohol.

But in the long run, Iowa's system works out for the average best. It returns an annual profit to the state of several million dollars, so that drinking might be called patriotic. At the same time that those who loathe the spectacle of public bars are spared that hideous sight, their neighbors who like a nip are allowed to buy all they wish.

Realizing that the surest way to produce a balanced people was to educate them, the first General Assembly to meet in Iowa founded a university. Later came the first law school west of the Mississippi. And since the state believes that fertility in the arts should try to equal fertility in the soil, it was only natural that the University of Iowa should have been the first in America to bring all the creative arts to the campus, boldly and with honor to the artist. Students were encouraged to write plays, novels, poetry, short stories, compose a string quartet or a symphony, to paint in oil or gouache or water colors, to carve in wood or stone or metal, or to act in plays.

At Iowa, the creative artist is equal to the scholar: Philip Bezanson of the University Music Department composed a piano concerto which was conducted by Dimitri Mitropoulos with the New York Philharmonic Orchestra, and the soloist was John Sims of the Music Department; and in the same field house where the Iowa basketball team won the Big Ten championship two years running, Mitropoulos conducted the Berlioz *Requiem*. University of Iowa painters and sculptors exhibit in the finest shows in the country; more poets from the University of Iowa were represented in the *New Campus Writing* one year than from any other institution. Tennessee Williams wrote some of his first plays at the superb University theater. Some thirty novels have been published out of the Fiction Workshop.

Iowa's congenial attitude toward the arts has had some remarkable effects on the personality of the state. In Des Moines the state capitol is so extreme an example of ornate decoration that it has the complex beauty of the grotesque (the people, however, seem to love it). Across town, out Grand Avenue with its 19th-Century big houses covered with gingerbread, is the new municipal Art Center, designed by Eliel Saarinen, the 20th-Century architect from Finland. On the walls may be an exhibit of modern art; its variety and abundance will amaze you.

Go to one of the most congenial cities for art in America, Cedar Rapids. At Coe College there has been a long-term exhibit of the most advanced art from the Solomon R. Guggenheim Museum in New York. For fifty years Cedar Rapids has had its own art association and for many years its own symphony orchestra. It was not chance that Grant Wood painted his first oils here; dozens were bought locally long before he became famous. (I remember the time he painted on a canvas—for a startled eighth-grade art class I belonged to—the sound of a piece of music, following the sound over the curves and whirls with his brush.) It was in the country around Cedar Rapids that he found the neat and formal landscape for his paintings. Here were the artificial-looking trees, which he had seen first on his mother's china, trees rounded by the steady wind before Wood rounded them on his own imagined hills. Here he saw the patterned corn, the young sprouts lined across the fields like knots tied on a quilt. Wood painted the birthplace of Herbert Hoover at nearby West Branch (settled by the same Quakers who had befriended John Brown in the bloody days). With his instinct for order, which he found in the cultivated and controlled Iowa landscape, he cleaned up the field beyond the little white house. When a resident of West Branch saw the painting, he remarked gratefully, "Well,

Grant, that's the house all right, and we sure thank you for mowing them weeds."

So it is natural that in Cedar Rapids there should live Marvin Cone, the country's leading painter of all the shapes and richness and variety of wooden barns, and all the intricate, many-doored interiors of haunted houses. For he, too, has found in the Iowa scene a pattern and a pride.

Every summer at the county fairs one sees the letters "4-H" everywhere. They stand for Head, Heart, Hands, Health, and are an effort not only to make better farmers out of the young people but to give them better lives, to improve the style of clothes worn by the girls and the style of public speaking used by the boys. Some of the finest baby-beef steers in the world are owned by 4-H boys and girls, who feed them, brush them, keep records of costs and diet, tend them like pets, and then compete at the fairs, selling them for the fanciest prices, often over a thousand dollars for one animal. Girls compete in the same ring with boys and sometimes beat them. It's a fine sight to see a young girl leading a Black Angus curried to glossy brilliance or a Hereford to a glowing ruddiness; and at times a tearful sight when a creature which has been pampered and worked over for a year is sold for slaughter.

When the 4-H members take part in a contest, there is no public posturing in bathing suits. The *healthiest* boy and girl from each county are chosen, and compete in a state-wide and then a national contest. For the girls, there is no mere beauty contest, but one for the best groomed—in clothes each has made—but many of these girls would brighten a bathing suit too.

The Iowa farmer has come a long way since the frontier grace at meals:

> *Mush is rough,*
> *Mush is tough,*
> *Thank Thee, Lord,*
> *We've got enough.*

His problem is no longer getting enough mush, but producing too much beef, pork, corn, wheat. When nearly everybody else in America has been increasing his income, the farmer's has dropped by 30 per cent. He was urged to raise as much food as possible, and the wars exaggerated this. But suddenly, just when the farmer had bought more machines to produce more food, there is too much food. Corn is sealed in round metal bins outside every town in Iowa. Too many hogs go to market (you can't let a hog wait, and you can't tell it to stop eating; when it's ready for market it's got to go), and the price is down to half what it was not long ago.

Now the farmer is traditionally "agin the Guvment," but of late years he has turned, kicking and screaming most of the time, to that same Government which he has cussed out with such pleasure. He doesn't want controls. The old phrase "independent as a hog on ice" is a wonderfully and miserably accurate description of the farmer's position. A fat hog sliding across the ice is the least independent thing in the world. The farmer wants to be his own boss, he doesn't want anyone telling *him* what to do, but he finds the market a mighty slippery place. He looks at his corn-fattened beef cattle, or his hogs, and knows he will get barely his cost back, and maybe not that. So he looks toward that suspicious and remote city called Washington. He wants to remain individualistic, but he doesn't want to go bankrupt. When the same situation rose in the early thirties, the farmers overturned milk trucks, brought guns to auctions and forced the sale of foreclosed farms for a dollar. These people were called "sons of wild jackasses."

The result is a mild schizophrenia on the farms. Leave me alone but help me. The younger farmers accept the curious combination of the individual going his own way (my father, born on a farm, used to say that a real country was one where a man could go to hell the way he wanted to) and the Government stretching out a long, helping arm from Washington.

The state grows with the times, too, for recently industrial production surpassed agricultural. New factories are coming in, many small and specialized ones to the smaller towns. The big cereal plants, the agricultural machinery factories, the Quaker Oats in Cedar Rapids where entire boxcars of grain are picked up and rolled over on their sides, an aluminum factory on the Mississippi, all expand the state's income and alter its rural character.

Even in fighting, Iowa men have struck a balance. In 1870 two men fought until they were, as the old account says, a mangled mass. Both were arrested, whereupon each said that it had all been for fun, just to see whether a man from Kentucky could beat a man from Maine. The loser even argued that the winner should not be fined because, after all, he had won.

The famous Iowa 34th Division of World War II fought from North Africa to Sicily to Italy to Germany, still looking after those plain rights. Yet Buffalo Bill, born down at Le Claire on the Mississippi, had to leave Iowa for a more violent life.

Iowa balances a furious physical climate with a congenial human climate, for the hearts of the people are as abundant as the land around them. Graced from the beginning with a fullness of food, they have made abundance and creativeness an integral part of their rights and liberties. If there is hope anywhere in this wicked world or in these many states, it is certainly here, exploding like popcorn in a pan. (Of course Iowa raises more popcorn than any other state). When a farmer falls sick at harvesttime, neighbors move in with fifteen corn pickers and gather his crop in a day. When the young writers, musicians, painters, sculptors of the United States want a sympathetic community as an alternative to New York, here is a university welcoming them not merely as students but as artists. When Marvin Cone needed a year away from teaching so that he could paint without distraction, businessmen (those same maligned businessmen of whose stony hearts we read) put together a purse of money and told him to spend it anywhere he wished. And he painted more in one year than in any other five.

Suddenly, those outrageous seasons no longer matter in the face of the life, the people, the hope. They become rather a source of pride that one survives them, a source of that very abundant fertility which hard work meets halfway, between heaven and earth, between the two great rivers.

Missouri

by PHIL STONG

"I'm from Missouri" is a phrase heard not only in every one of the other forty-nine states—but also in London and Rome and Vienna and Timbuktu. Even before the rise of Harry Truman, Missourians got around.

When "You'll have to show me" follows the first phrase, do not be fooled by the humorous quotation marks in the Missourian voice. And do not—repeat not—believe that it is a request for information. It is a demand for supporting evidence on whatever you are saying or trying to sell. If you can't produce it, God help you.

If you have heard the dubious legend about the origin of the phrase—that Missouri miners, arriving late at the silver rush in Colorado, had to be shown how to dig silver—forget it. Missourians never arrived late anywhere where diggings were good, or asked any questions when they got there.

The only thing riskier than trying to show a Missourian something is to confuse his home state with another. Kansas Citians are especially dangerous—I'm married to one, and I shudder when someone assumes that Kansas City is in Kansas, and then says, "Well, there *is* a Kansas City, Kansas." The answer will be a languid question, "Is there?" Certainly it's disingenuous, but it states the Missouri faith —that there is nothing like Missouri, that Missouri is a body of land

completely surrounded by inferior, benighted, pitiable, unimportant
territory.

It was in St. Louis that Johnny done Frankie wrong, and W. C.
Handy dreamed up the bluest of all blues; and it was no rhyme-
dictated accident of Tin Pan Alley that the cowboy in *Oklahoma!*
sings "Ev'rythin's up to date in Kansas City," for Kansas City has
always been Oklahoma's shopping and good-time town.

From the days of the freighters and the Santa Fe and Oregon
Trails and the Pony Express, Missouri is still "home" and "back East"
to large sections of the West and Southwest. Indeed, it is only in
Missouri, say the Missourians, that "Texans don't dare to brag." Too
many of them started out from here without a longhorn or an oil
well to their names.

As the oldest state completely west of the Mississippi, Missouri
views all of western America with the eyes of a worldly-wise
grandmother, amused, uncritical, faintly patronizing—and above
all, well satisfied with her own racy past—the memories of lovers
—of dashing fellows from France and Spain; Virginia cavaliers,
Bostonians not too godly to hurry to a land boom; earnest, idealistic
Germans fleeing a Germany already, in 1830, hostile to democratic
ideals; roistering boatmen from New Orleans and Cincinnati; woodsmen in coonskin caps, trappers and miners and priests and outlaws
—good, bad, but very few indifferent, among these men who poured
across the last great river into Missouri in the surge of America
across the continent.

For many, Missouri was the jumping-off place to the wilder
West. For others of the merchant's temperament, it was rich enough
and wild enough and far enough west to be a stopping place—there
was more money to be made in outfitting the wagon trains of the
gold-and-silver seekers than in going with them. The rich Black
Prairie of north Missouri appealed to the Southern planters, the
Ozarks looked like home to the Kentucky mountaineers, and the
rivers—not only the giant Mississippi and the Missouri, but the wonderful web of smaller streams, attracted everybody.

Many a westward traveler, approaching the dusty plains and
deserts between him and the Pacific, looked at this wealth of water
and unpacked his wagon. Shovels meant for mining went into the
rich black dirt of north Missouri farms. Trees cut from the thick
woods along the rivers made a snugger home than huts of sod or
adobe. This was a new land fresh and wild as anything farther

west—but pleasant and hospitable to human beings. It caught and held its lovers, as it still does—especially in October.

Wherever they are, Missourians get homesick in October. At our house in Connecticut, it is not the calendar, or the starting of the furnace, that heralds the month, but my Missouri wife looking wistful, staring out the window at the first color in the trees. "I wish we could get some black walnuts," says Virginia, "or run out to Grandview for some apples—Ben Davis apples, not these big vulgar Baldwins they have here—and some cider, real old-fashioned cider from Independence, no Yankee water added."

"No real old-fashioned worms taken out, either," I usually say, though it never gets me anywhere. Everybody knows that Missouri worms are harmless—they only add protein to the cider.

But there comes a time when you have to go to Missouri in October and see for yourself.

Missouri is larger than all New England, I found—by 3000 square miles. It is also younger, warmer (though sometimes colder in the winter), richer, brighter (especially in October), racially far more complex, lazier, friendlier, more shiftless and more gracious. It is less raw, less righteous, less ambitious than most of the other Midwest states. In its 132 years it has reached a mood like its autumnal weather, a golden leisure of the spirit, a readiness to laugh but not to disapprove. I saw no frantic struggle for a future here, but no fear, either. "Ev'rythin's up to date in Kansas City," as the song says, and everything's booming in St. Louis, growing in the northern prairie, resting in the Ozarks.

A good place to start is at Jefferson City, the capital, and a good time is the one we picked—early twilight of the first day in October. The lights were coming on and there were two bridges over the Missouri River, the one we were driving on and the one below, traced by golden blobs of lamplight on the water.

This is a proper entrance to the Missouri scene, over a river and into a town, for settlement followed the many-fingered rivers in this state and the townspeople everywhere are not so much train meeters as river watchers. Up the Missouri, past Jefferson City, have come many strange craft: French pirogues and Creole flatboats, gaudy passenger steamers—flaunting their gilt and mahogany and New Orleans-French cuisine by day, meekly tying up by night because the Missouri is even more capricious, dangerous, and violent than the Mississippi—barges and tugboats and latter-day excursion steamers, now, alas, vanished from the inhospitable waters of the Missouri—rather, from its shoals and snags, for water in depth is what the Missouri has always lacked.

In Jefferson City and all other river towns, we learned, jet planes score the heavens with their vapor trails, and few Missourians will gawk skyward. But let a tiny feather of wake show in the river or someone yell, "Boat coming!" and people will come running to the riverbank.

Over the river and into Jefferson City we came, and turning left, saw the State Capitol on its lighted hill, with Ceres from Roman myth on top, four hundred feet above the river, looking down at the American Titan, Thomas Jefferson, on his rostrum in the center of the great stairs leading to the portico. The elegant structural lines of the building derive from Renaissance Italy, the columns from Corinth, Greece, and the building material, a luminous off-white marble, from Carthage, Missouri.

The famous murals of one of Missouri's most gifted sons, of a famous Democratic family—that stormy petrel of the art world, Thomas Hart Benton—may be seen in the Capitol's House Lounge, perhaps the most fiercely attacked and fiercely championed paintings in 20th-Century America. They dare to show Missouri through the clear, cool, sardonic, but affectionate eyes of the native-born artist.

No pioneer mothers show their muscles here; no pie-faced airborne angels lead the prairie schooners westward; there are no scrolls or scales of justice or flaming swords or smoking cannon. This is Missouri "social history," with plenty of wild Missouri action. In one panel Frankie is shooting Johnny—in the seat of his pants. In others, slaves are auctioned, Holy Rollers are baptized in a river, politicians shout, women roll pastry and change diapers, a judge dozes on the bench of a courtroom complete with cuspidor—at which many have fired and some have missed.

Fine black plumes of smoke go up from paddle steamers and chunky 19th-Century locomotives, from tar-and-feathering bonfires and factory chimneys, rolling from panel to panel like a Wagnerian motif. But smoke is strangely absent from one object—the fat cigar jutting like a small, sinister torpedo from between the fat fingers of Boss Tom Pendergast of Kansas City.

This dormant cigar and the large, sleepy face of its owner brought down the heavens on the head of Mr. Benton. Democrats cried that he had cruelly libeled Mr. Pendergast, and Republicans objected to the preservation of the Pendergast features in any light at all. "Paint 'em out," went the cry. "Run Benton out of the state." But the pay-off was a victory, not only for the artist but for the wry, realistic humor of Missourians. After sixteen years, the murals are still there, and will be till the Renaissance palace enclosing them falls off its bluff into the Missouri River.

Columbia is, in its own unabashed phrase, "the Athens of Missouri." It has not only the oldest state university west of the Mississippi but Christian College for women, founded in 1851 by a stubborn Missourian because the state university, of which he was then president, would not admit his female offspring. Here also is Stephens College, five years younger than Christian but possibly more famous because it has had Joan Crawford as a student and the late Maude Adams as professor of the drama, and operates its own riding stables, a country club with chauffeur service to shuttle the girls to and from the campus, and a flying field for pupil pilots. It also offers charm courses and jaunts to Florida in aid of "social graces."

Columbia is the heart of "Little Dixie." Jefferson City, across the Missouri, was held by Union forces throughout the Civil War; but Columbia was, by and large, a Johnny Reb town. The largest of its old homes have the true pillared porticoes of the South. The waitress is likely to call you Mistuh Man or you-all, and the food she brings will be either fried chicken or ham and beans, with corn bread—or, if you squawk for it, beef; but it is better not to squawk. This is not beef country—Missouri cooks almost invariably overcook it. But if you say so, the waitress' eyes will fill with tears and all the Missouri diners within earshot will give you an icy stare.

Columbia on an autumn afternoon is a charming town to drive through slowly, as we did, down quiet residential streets under a golden rain of falling leaves, out Boon's Lick Trail, past the women's colleges, then south around the stadium and back to the sunlit campus of Missouri U.

You will want to explore the School of Journalism, oldest in the world (founded in 1908). The daily *Missourian* is published here, with an overpowering staff of several hundred students and with its own presses, linotypes, photographic laboratories, press services and engraving rooms.

Floyd Shoemaker, secretary of the State Historical Society of Missouri sat at his desk in the M. U. Library Building.

"The first appearance of 'Show me' in print," he explained to us, "was in a song published in 1898, *I'm From Missouri and You've Got to Show Me*. But in the colloquial speech it runs much farther back. Maybe one of your Connecticut Yankee peddlers ran into it in trying to sell his wooden nutmegs. I'm willing to bet with you that some outsider coined it, some high-binder, shellgame, crooked foreigner who met his match here in Missouri.

"Not that we wouldn't have used it first if we'd thought of it. We don't mince words about anything, not even ourselves, here in Missouri. You know about the Boone County man, not so very long dead, who spent years writing a biographical dictionary called *The S.O.B.'s of Boone County*? He always said, 'I'll never finish it. Every time I go into Boonville or Columbia, I get new material.' And yet —I knew him—let an out-of-stater make cracks about Missouri or Boone County, and he rolled his sleeves up fast."

Mules seemed at this point a more pacific topic.

"Mules?" Mr. Shoemaker's voice softened. "Those marvelous creatures. The best little, smartest little, toughest little beasts in these United States. Go over to the School of Agriculture experimental farm and hear about them from experts."

At the school on the edge of town, we heard the voice of the tractor loud upon the land, and saw the glitter of every modern machine that man has invented to do his farming for him. The prospect for the mule looked bleak. But soon we found that his little candle still burnt in this heartless, mechanistic world. Professor L. A. Weaver, chairman of the Department of Animal Husbandry, and his assistant, John M. Kays, looked at each other, smiled, sighed, and told us about the Missouri mule.

"He's strong," said Mr. Weaver, "and smart. *Too* smart for many human beings. He is easy to take care of, healthier than the horse, and he feeds himself. He won't drink when he's too hot, and in a barnful of oats he'll eat just as much as he needs, where a horse would founder."

"Horses are dumb?" I asked.

"At least nervous. The mule is a great relaxer. You can see that when he rolls—and he rolls every chance he gets. He is happily at home in the universe—or at least in Missouri; and the horse, like man—non-Missourian man—is an anxious, ambitious, miserable fellow."

"Some non-Missourians appreciate him," said Mr. Kays. "Carolina tobacco planters buy him, and the Greek and Spanish governments. But there aren't enough of him left. Here in Little Dixie we used to raise mules by the thousand."

I said with a feeling that I was hitting below the belt, "Have you any at the School of Agriculture farm?"

They both said quickly, "We always keep a pair."

"For old times' sake?" I asked.

"No," said Mr. Kays. "For mud and ice. Here in Missouri we have every kind of weather there is—and for some of it nothing is any good except the Missouri mule."

This is Daniel Boone—or rather, Boon—country. Except for Boone County, named at a later, more educated time, the *e* is missing. You follow Boon's Lick Trail (now U. S. 40) from Columbia to Boonville, an Old South town with Classic-Revival mansions and a sunny cobbled street leading to the river wharf which was once the heart of Boonville business.

Here is Kemper Military School and its formal red-brick campus —the oldest military academy west of the Mississippi, founded in 1844. It is distinguished also by its good nature in answering questions about its worst pupil, Will Rogers, who hit the campus in 1897 out of Indian Territory in a ten-gallon hat and high-heeled red-top boots with spurs, coiled ropes draping his luggage. Colonel H. C. Johnston says, "Will Rogers was here for a year and a half, doing second- and third-year high-school work. His version of his stay here —that he spent one year in the guardhouse and the other in fourth grade—was wrong on both counts. He was an erratic student, but an indefatigable prankster." Of himself in the elegant Kemper uniform, Will later said, "One of my kids saw a picture of me and said, 'Mamma, I knew Daddy had been everything, but I never knew he was a bellhop.'"

The first land battle of the Civil War was fought four miles from Boonville on June 17, 1861, the Virginians of Little Dixie being even quicker on the trigger than the Virginians back in Virginia. It is said that there are only two Republican families today in all of Howard County, and none in Boonville. Some Republicans landed here from the river but they went south into the Ozarks or west into the Great Plains. Occasionally a good Democrat went West too. In the Boonville law office of Judge Roy D. Williams you can see the notice posted in 1826 by a Howard County saddle maker, offering a reward of one cent for the capture of his missing apprentice, Kit Carson. This was not an evaluation of young Kit's abilities but a kindly effort to help a young Southern gentleman without capital find richer hunting grounds out West.

Driving east from Howard and Boone counties, you traverse the last of Little Dixie, Callaway County. It has been known as the Kingdom of Callaway since 1861, when four hundred old men and boys, armed with one log painted to resemble a cannon, bludgeoned a promise from the leader of the invading Union militia to stay out of the Kingdom if they in turn would disperse their "forces." The agreement was kept and all was quiet in the Kingdom for the rest of the 19th Century.

In the twentieth, however, two earth-shaking events have taken place. Native-born Henry Bellaman wrote the best-seller *King's Row* about Callaway County, with too much candor to please his neighbors—and Winston Churchill appeared with President Truman in Fulton in 1946 to accept a degree from Westminster College (enrollment that year, 233) and to make his "Iron Curtain" speech, whose rumblings are still heard on world seismographs.

From the lilies and languors of Little Dixie you roll suddenly into a brave fresh old world—Missouri's Rhineland, settled by German intellectuals in the 1830's. The road to Hermann runs south from U. S. 40 through the woods, walnuts and oaks and hickories, to the Missouri-Rhine, then over the bridge and into a fairy-tale German town, swept, scrubbed and dusted from its gabled roofs and medieval balconies to the cozy cobblestones in the steep streets. Here German is often spoken. Hermann predates both World Wars, and during the Civil War its people supplied the extra liberal pressure needed to keep Missouri officially in the Union.

They paid for their abolitionism—but not too much, as you can see when you pass the courthouse. For there is the famous "artillery" of Hermann, which saved the town from the army of Confederate General Marmaduke—one cannon. Six old men were left in town when the young men departed to join the Union Army, and they dragged their one cannon from hill to hill, firing one shot from each, till General Marmaduke thought he was surrounded. He caught up with it in time, however, and rolled it into the Missouri River, but the townsfolk fished it out and put it in its present place of honor.

In firing a salute to Hermann's fiftieth anniversary, in 1886, this venerable blunderbuss outdid itself and slightly burst asunder. "It's looking sort of frail," said a Hermannite standing near us as we looked at it, "but that's all right. We shan't be needing it again." German Hermann, Missouri, is still a morning town—full of sunny faith in the future of Missouri and America.

Out of old Germany you follow a long, gently curling road southwest toward another province of old America, the Ozark Highlands, the world of the hound-dog, the hilltop cabin and fiddle music at moonrise. Presently we were rolling along a peaceful road that climbed over wave after wave of hills, each one higher than the last. The sun at our right was going down, and only the ledges at our left burned with autumn color. From the last high shelf, in the warm dusk, our road turned right and downward, to the shores of Lake Taneycomo and the pillared front of old Hotel Rockaway.

Here the fishermen come in, with catches of jack salmon and bass and yellow cat and with the ambling stride of luxuriously tired sportsmen. Here you can eat your good dinner in peace and quiet, or by cocking an ear you can listen to Ozark conversation. It is slow and mild, as by this time you will expect in Missouri.

"You ever think that li'l ol' houn'-dog of Jim Bacon's would take the prize?" (There was a spur-of-the-moment hound show hereabouts today.)

"I want to get some water-ground meal at Kissee Mills before I leave."

"Can't. The water's over it, and old John Hires has gone to Colorado."

"I don't care how many damn dams and new lakes they make, give me old Taneycomo." Then sadly, "Wonder what will happen to Taney when the new lake fills up?"

Lately through the Ozark Hills, one of the last redoubts of natural man, with their sweep of wild and carefree uplands and their 19th-Century calm, their coonhounds and foxhounds and leaning cabins and tarantellas to fiddle music, there is heard the swelling roll of thunder on the left—a warning of the end that is coming to this way of life. It is the thunder of water, not gushing in its age-old mountain chasms but dammed and released by man, guided into valleys and over the roofs of towns, stocked with fish and outboard motors, and calling in the outside world.

Look at Forsyth, or rather, look *for* it. Not long ago it was a little

Ozark town sleeping in the sun since 1837, apparently world without end. Now its streets and homes are under water and the hallways of its ancient courthouse are filled with mud. It is part of the bed of Bull Shoals Lake and nothing can save it. There is a new town of Forsyth on higher ground, with a "modern"-style courthouse, paved streets, sewers, a $75,000 golf course, boat docks and stone bathhouses.

There will be more ducks, they say, when the big lake rises, and more fish. My guess is that there will be fewer ducks because there will be more hunters; perhaps fewer fish, too, per fisherman. The new sportsmen will be a different breed, the kind who will like the glittering new eight-story "Fishermen's Apartment Hotel" (*sic*).

But the old spirit is not dead yet. We stopped at a group of tourist cabins and found a note tacked on the open office door: "Cabins 1, 5 and 8 ready. No. 9 will be to fix. Look around, take one, and we will be back about four o'clock." That's the authentic voice of Ozark hospitality.

The trip from the Anglo-Saxon world of the Ozarks to Old France in eastern Missouri is like interplanetary travel, and also like a short cruise between centuries, made not by rocket ship or time machine but by a day's drive from Taneycomo to the Mississippi River. No rocket would do. For the full flavor of this part of the state, you need a good slow automobile, a bright October day, and the kind of soul that takes easily to transmigration.

Two hundred miles of the Ozark uplands lie before you like a Persian rug flung carelessly over the top of the world, here rucked up into gleaming ridges and there smoldering in the shadow of the valleys. It is also, my wife kept saying, like a giant spice chest spilled under the sun, cinnamon and nutmeg and cloves and cayenne. The truth is that it is like nothing I have seen anywhere, not even October in New England. There are red and black oak, hickory and maple and yellow pine, hawthorn and sumac and the rare smoke tree. The hillsides are so steep that plants on the north and northeast exposures are of the Appalachian family, while those on the south and southwest belong to Texas and Oklahoma and New Mexico. For Missouri is a meeting point not only of human history but also of East and West, botanically speaking. We made the two hundred miles last as long as possible.

Under all this fire lies water, rumbling through the earth, gushing, swirling and bursting in spray, through cracks in the mountain porphyry and granite to form the "sinks" and pools and rushing rivers of this Big Spring Country. Among hundreds of giants, Big Spring, near Van Buren, is largest of all; its average flow of 252,000,000 gallons a day would supply water for the city of St. Louis. It must be dazzling at midday, but in twilight, as we saw it, it is pure magic. Deep in its own state park, at the end of a lonely, twisting road, one comes upon it, a smooth wide torrent of unearthly blue sliding out of a ledge of rock at the foot of a high, darkling cliff.

We drove on to Poplar Bluff, where the Ozark upland ends on the rim of the alluvial plains of the Missouri delta. Here, in the delta, the cotton blossom doesn't blow in October, but the fields are dotted with the last white fluffs of cotton bolls clinging to the stem. Up and down the sunny aisles go the gleaners of all ages from six to sixty, for when the machines have finished, the human hand and eye take over. There are flashes along the ground of white goose wings, and in the air a strong exultant honking. The geese's work was done last spring, and pleasant enough it was too—the eating of delicious bugs and weeds between the cotton plants. Now the birds are honking at the autumn sun. If cotton is "a lazy man's crop," it is a lazy goose's too.

From the Delta we proceeded to New Madrid (pronounced *Mad*rid) in the southeastern corner of Missouri, where we took El Camino Real, the much-traveled road to St. Louis, and found ourselves in a new kind of country, and in another century. The life of this 200-mile road, since the Spaniards hacked it out of forest and swamp in 1789, has been a procession of violence: invaders invaded, butchers butchered, Indian heroes and Indian villains, the tramp of early miners toward Missouri silver—and lead and other minerals— the scuffle of Spaniard against Frenchman, and Frenchman against Englishman, and in the end, the footbeats of a brand-new breed, the Americans, who came to stay.

Four flags have been carried along this road, and the priests of many faiths have walked here: Catholics in dusty cassocks, German Lutherans, Anglican vicars of George III, Defender of the Faith, Wesleyans and Baptists and Scottish Covenanters. There was witchcraft here and religious frenzy, martyrdom and atheism.

On this Royal Road—now U. S. 61—you arrive at Cape Girardeau, where the Cherokees crossed the Mississippi on their "Trail of Tears" from Georgia and Tennessee to exile in the Indian Territory now called Oklahoma. Not far from here is the hilltop grave of Major Louis Lorimier, the French-Canadian adventurer who worked first for Spain, then for Britain, then stirred up the Indians against the new republic, but finally yielded to the accomplished fact of the Louisiana Purchase and became a good American. Beside him lies his "consort," Charlotte Pemanpieh Bougainville, under her epitaph, "noblest matron of the Shawnee race."

Missouri cemeteries, like Missouri homes, often sit high over the rivers—"to watch the boats come in."

From Cape Girardeau north, the road runs for ten miles between walls of roses, then it bends northeast through uplands toward the river, skirting an astonishing intruder on Missouri soil, the 18th-Century Illinois-French town of Kaskaskia. Its twenty-odd square miles were suddenly cut off from Illinois by the capricious Mississippi, and the Illinois town now sits on the Missouri shore like a pearl in an oyster, or like a cinder in the eye—depending on which state is doing the talking.

Four or five miles ahead, El Camino Real comes to another kind of island in Missouri—the ancient and beautiful 18th-Century town of Ste. Genevieve, awash in the 20th Century, quiet in its place and perfect in its time like a Pompeii where the lava only burned the calendars and stopped the clocks. Ste. Genevieve, dating from 1735, is the oldest permanent settlement in Missouri west of the Mississippi. (Kaskaskia is older, but it was east of the river when founded.)

In many of the oldest houses of Ste. Genevieve, the original families still live today among their exquisite possessions—inlaid furniture from old-time Paris, harps and Pleyel pianos and music boxes still tinkling with schottisches and waltzes popular in France a century or more ago.

This town lives by the Angelus, ringing out from the parish church in Du Bourg Place at six A.M. and noon and six P.M. There are processions on all holy days, and on New Years' Eve masked celebrants go singing *La Guignolée* and stopping at every house for wine. We saw a procession ourselves, that October afternoon, of very small children with bent heads and prayerful hands winding into the very large church—an incredibly large church for a town of about 3000 people.

Du Bourg Place is bordered by the old houses and pink-walled gardens of the first families of Ste. Genevieve, each one a temptation to the curious visitor. And best of all, if your face is clean and you have a civil tongue in your head, you will be freely welcomed to these houses. There is no French *hauteur* in French Missouri—only French *politesse*, heightened and warmed by pioneer hospitality.

In the famous Philipson-Vallé house the Henry Rozier family still lives, descendants of Ferdinand Rozier who arrived here in 1811 with a young man named John James Audubon and set up a mercantile business. But as a businessman M. Audubon turned out to be a fine bird painter, and the partnership dissolved. From the walls of this house the Rozier and Vallé ancestors look down on the same chairs they used to sit in, and *grand'mère* Odile Vallé, of blessed memory for her charities, can smile on the unchipped, untarnished fittings of her tea table, on the old brandy in her fine French glasses, and, best of all, on her young descendant, Hank Rozier. In the houses of Ste. Genevieve, life has a golden continuity such as I have seen nowhere else in the nation. "It's cozy," said my wife, and the word did not sound condescending.

Against the walls of these old gardens we saw beds of coppery chrysanthemums, always a French favorite, and here and there the last fall blossoms of an almost vanished beauty, the old General Jacqueminot Rose.

Up the hill again one goes to the Old Cemetery, the last home of all the Vallés and Roziers and other fathers of the town—and of an unnumbered group of nameless passengers who died in a steamboat explosion just off the Ste. Genevieve shore, who sleep together in a sunny hollow, aliens and of unknown faith, but welcome here among the angels and the crucifixes.

St. Louis is the largest city on the Mississippi, almost twice as big in population as New Orleans. But many of its citizens seldom see the river to which the city owes its birth. Although St. Louis stretches for miles along the crescent-shaped shore, its 20th-Century growth has been inland, a steady fan-wise expansion toward the west.

One of its monuments, Carl Milles' sculptural group, *The Meeting of the Waters*, has misled more people than perhaps any other symbolic art in America. Facing the Union Station, it is the only bit of St. Louis remembered by millions of travelers who spend an hour or two between trains in this great railroad center. But the Missouri and Mississippi Rivers meet about twenty miles northeast of this statuary, as the crow flies, in a no man's land of swamp and tangled willows beyond the city limits.

Although named for a saint, St. Louis early became a center for free-thinking French intellectuals, followers of Voltaire and Rousseau and Diderot, and admirers even of Thomas Paine and Thomas Jefferson, regarded by the devout as infidels. (They were devout Deists.) Of the huge library of Auguste Chouteau, the celebrated fur trader and early pillar of the city, one fourth of the titles had been proscribed on the Catholic Index of that day.

In the spring of 1804, with the threat of Puritan rigor approaching from American rule (the Louisiana Purchase had been signed in Paris the year before), there was a sad day when the Spanish flag was lowered in the Place d'Armes, and the French flag was raised for one night before the alien Stars and Stripes should be run up. And that night, among other noises in the rebellious city, rang the cry, "God shall never cross the Mississippi!" There are persons in Iowa and Kansas who say He never has, so far as Missouri is concerned.

At any rate, the state has never had a Blue Law on its books, in spite of the influx of *les Bostonnais,* as the French St. Louisans scornfully called all Americans. Far more welcome were the "good" Germans who poured in after the German Revolution of 1848, bringing their arts and crafts, their cobblers, beer and music, and above all their zeal for freedom.

St. Louis, to the eye of the visitor, is old and new, beautiful and ugly, with formal parks and monuments, rows of "town houses" fashionable in the 1870's, and sudden vistas down short private streets barred by private gates, under the shoulders of the roaring business district. Here the ten-story Wainwright Building, though dwarfed now by others, still claims prestige as America's first and model skyscraper. Here is the courthouse of the long-drawn-out miserable trials of the Dred Scott case. There is the Art Museum, left over from the World's Fair of 1904. And yonder is Washington University, founded by the grandfather of T. S. Eliot, who somewhere in the waste land of his pre-British past harbors a memory of St. Louis, Missouri.

One of these streets is the *Back Street* of St. Louisan Fannie Hurst; there on South Broadway Eugene Field was born and played with his gingham dog and calico cat; those iron "galeries" stem from the French West Indies; that planter's punch you have drunk from Jamaica to Bermuda and back originated here, in the old Planter's

Hotel; in one of these houses the American Winston Churchill was born, to write *Richard Carvel* and *The Crisis,* and in due time to reply to his British namesake, who was worrying about the duplication of names, "You, sir, had better insert your middle initial, since I, having been born in 1871, owned our name unchallenged for three years." That's how the "S" (for Spencer) was introduced into the most celebrated by-line of our times.

The American Churchill's attitude befits a St. Louisan—proud, dignified and reasonable. These are friendly people, kindly toward newcomers who do not offend by acting either brash or stuffy. Though St. Louis is a city of successful businessmen, there is little shop talk after hours, and anybody who throws his wealth around had better go back where he came from—which will certainly not be St. Louis. In spite of its 20th-Century sedate elegance, this city has not forgotten where *it* came from—its youth as a hard-living, hard-fighting river town.

At night, when the theaters and hotel supper clubs are full, there are still St. Louisans who drive down through the dark, deserted streets for a glimpse of the quiet river. The levees are still there. We saw them, sloping up from the water's edge, their cobblestones moon-pricked and cut by shadows from the empty, leaning warehouses which once held all the water-borne riches of this midcontinental river valley. On a night in late October, the levees hold in their very silence the ghosts and echoes of the past; of rafts and pirogues and stern-wheelers, and boatmen and river pirates and black men straining at bales of furs and cotton, and at crated china and pianos for the city's overlords.

In the last century three Missourians have emerged to world-wide fame. The first, in time as well as in genius, was Mark Twain of Hannibal.

No lions whelped in the streets of Florida, Missouri, on the November night in 1835 when Samuel Clemens was born; but Halley's comet flashed over it, not to be seen again until the April night in 1910, when he lay dying. Now the 200-odd inhabitants of Florida are content with the single claim to fame that, for the first four years of his life, Sam Clemens lived in their town.

Hannibal, on the river, thirty-five miles northeast of Florida, considers itself, rightfully, the wellspring of his legend. Here is his world, the "little white town drowsing in the sunlight," from which he drew the rich strands of his Missouri novels, from which he embarked for

Life on the Mississippi, and which sent him into the world as a not-so-Innocent Abroad.

That white frame house beside the stone museum on Hill Street is the Clemens home—or, if you like, Tom Sawyer's home. The fence beside it is marked "Tom Sawyer's fence," but whether Sam ever painted it himself cannot be proved. It is a neat respectable house, in which Jane Clemens brought up her family after the neat respectable way of her Tennessee and Virginia forebears, only once bursting forth at Sam, when he was brought home half drowned from swimming in forbidden Bear Creek: "I guess there wasn't much danger. People born to be hanged are safe in water."

Across the street is the "Becky Thatcher House," the home of Becky's prototype, Laura Hawkins. It houses now one of the finest bookshops in Missouri, and upstairs, the restored rooms of the Hawkins family. To the young Sam, this house stood for all that was elegant. It is much more richly furnished than his own. The mirrors and polished-mahogany candlesticks and prism-hung table lamps gave him his first inkling that beauty as well as usefulness could be considered in setting a domestic scene. In the bedroom of the child, Laura, lingers a breath of Becky Thatcher's charm for Tom. Her blue silk dress, her cambric nightgown and her petticoat are laid across her small four-poster, and her long stockings on the chair are of the softest white lisle.

Up the Hill we drove—it is called Holliday's Hill now, but of course its true name is Cardiff—and sat on the warm stones near the Memorial Lighthouse, where once stood the house of Mrs. Holliday. In *Tom Sawyer* she was the Widow Douglas, who kept a lamp burning at night in her window to guide the paddle steamers. From here you can see the bluffs where Tom and Huck climbed, and Jackson's Island, where Huck and Nigger Jim hid out before starting their long trip down the Mississippi on a raft.

There have been changes in the river, some made by its own whims, and others, like the Mark Twain Bridge, by man. But down there at the water's edge a few small white grasshopper figures were diving in the warm fall weather, and any two of them might have been naked young Sam Clemens and that other river rat, Tom Blankenship, better known as Huckleberry Finn.

No boats came along while we were there, but they still do sometimes—a tugboat with its string of barges, or occasionally the last of the stern-wheelers, the *Gordon C. Greene* of Cincinnati. When this happens, the cry goes out through Hannibal, "Stee-eee-eeeamboat a-comin'," just as it did in Mark Twain's day, and the people all go hurrying, not seeing his ghost among them.

Westward from Hannibal and the river, you drive through a rich and smiling country, the farmlands chosen by the canny Southern planters, where the Black Angus cattle grow fat, the houses and barns are freshly painted, and the towns rest complacent in the shadow of huge trees.

You drive toward another shadow, at first no bigger than a man's hand with a pistol in it, but spreading darkly out of history over the whole countryside, into legend and ballad, and a world celebrity that surpasses Mark Twain's own. For this is the country of Jesse James, that dark figure which sprang from the dragons' teeth of the Civil War and grew, even during his thirty-five years on earth, larger than life and only half as natural. The gallant guerrilla, the avenger of the attempted hanging of his stepfather by Union Kansas raiders, the Robin Hood defending the poor, the handsome, brave and chivalrous hero—that is what the world by short memory has made of the outlaw Jesse James.

Here in Northwest Missouri, he was born, and robbed the trains and banks, and finally hid and died, shot down for the $10,000 price on his head by a man who posed as his friend. Through this countryside he was hunted, and saved by respectable citizens from justice. He actually slept in more houses than George Washington allegedly slept in, says Homer Croy, his biographer, and the fact is a matter of pride to descendants of the householders—the otherwise decent men who lied for him.

The Robin Hood aspect of the legend rests, so far as I can find out, on one incident supposed to have happened in the Ozarks. The story is that Jesse and his brother Frank and Cole Younger, having lunched at a widow's home, learned that she expected the mortgage holder on her house to arrive that day and set about foreclosing. The James brothers gave her the $800 she needed, then rode away and ambushed the mortgage holder and took the money back at gun point. This proves (to some) that they were not only philanthropists but humorists.

Chivalry? The James boys never gave their victims an even break, and Jesse often finished off a wounded and helpless trainman or bank employee out of sheer ill temper.

Then what can you do about this monstrous evil legend? When the oldest inhabitant in one place has told you, "The James boys weren't so bad. Lots of people sympathized with them," you can go, as we did, from one crime scene to another, to Otterville and Osceola, Savannah and Lexington and Liberty—only a partial list of towns in Missouri that drew their attention between forays into many other states. And you can visit the house where Jesse James was born and the house where he was killed. Between the two there is not so much as a hair's breadth in comfort or culture or pleasantness.

The birthplace at Kearny, near Excelsior Springs, is a weather-beaten log house clinging to the frame ell added in 1893. The door into the original kitchen is only five feet high. The fireplace, damaged in the bombing that killed Jesse's half-brother and tore off their mother's arm, has now fallen in. In the front wing you can see the sampler worked by this strange, hysterical woman in her girl-hood, before she met and married the Baptist minister, Robert James, who fathered Frank and Jesse and then sensibly went away and died in California before his sons set off on their blazing orbit.

There is nothing here of Home Sweet Home.

The other house sat for years after Jesse's death on a high terraced street inside St. Joseph, hoodooed perhaps more by its decrepitude than by its history. It rented in those days for eight dollars a month. Finally someone bought it and hauled it out to Highway 71, where it now stands near a Jesse James Tourist Court, a filling station and a hot-dog stand. Signs beside the road say, "Stop! This is the Jesse James House. See the Bullet Hole." For a price, of course.

The bullet hole is there, all right, in the wall of the mean front room, though it looks as if it had been made by an atomic weapon. The loving hands of tourists picked and chipped off souvenirs till the management covered the gap with glass.

There is a "blood" stain on the floor which, the guide explains, must be periodiocally renewed, so many pilgrims walk over it. The bed is said to be the original on which Jesse's bleeding body was laid; it does not look comfortable. Neither does anything else in the house, and the cramped proportions of the rooms preclude any possibility that Jesse and his family ever enjoyed domestic luxury from his many robberies.

You can see a picture of Jesse here, taken as he lay dead on a wooden plank, and it will dispose of the fable of his beauty. He had black hair and a lightish beard, a pug nose and high, flat cheekbones.

Even so, the picture is probably less forbidding than his face in life, for the lids are down over his cold, terrible blue eyes.

The James legend aside, St. Joseph is now Missouri's third largest town and a place so relaxed and with so little boosterism that its city limits have not changed since 1909. Its most interesting antiquity is the Pony Express stables on Penn Street (rebuilt in the 1880's), which St. Joseph hopes to turn into a museum.

The St. Joseph *Gazette* once employed Eugene Field, whose conversation probably paid him better than his verse. Both here and in Kansas City later, he had unlimited credit and drinks on the house at all the best saloons, for as long as Gene Field sat talking in a bar, the place was crowded.

If you want to see where he courted his bride, you may still drive "in those leafy aisles, where Cupid smiles, in Lover's Lane, Saint Jo."

Missouri's third world celebrity is Harry S. Truman, of Independence and Kansas City.

Sue Gentry, of the Independence *Examiner*, said, "The most emotion I have ever seen the town show was on the night the Trumans came home 'for good.' The town was glad to have them home. But it also meant that the shooting was over. The newspapermen, who swarmed here for nearly eight years—'like the locusts of 1856,' as some old-timers said—have gone to greener pastures."

So have the cordons of Secret Service men—the city police do what little guarding is necessary, mostly against autograph seekers—to the delight of a certain newsboy. For one whole summer he had tried to collect for his papers at the Truman house, but "Those men would never let me in." He got a check by mail, of course, as soon as Mrs. Truman learned about it.

The former Summer White House in Independence is the family home of Mrs. Truman, a large, comfortable Victorian house with gables and jigsaw work and several porches. "Of course he had to have a porch at the White House," said a passing policeman to us. "They *lived* on those porches here, and Washington's just as hot as Independence in the summer."

Mrs. Truman is a member of the esteemed Wallace and Gates families in Independence. Her people made Queen of the Pantry flour, a favorite of Missouri cake bakers, who are famous in their own right. "Mrs. Truman and her mother have never been the 'running-in' kind of neighbors," we were told, "but they could always be counted on in time of trouble." The former First Lady goes to the same grocery store and the same hairdresser she has always patronized.

As for the former President, he drives regularly to his office in Kansas City. Once in a rare while he walks on a downtown street alone, and someone will stop and turn around and say, "Why, I believe that's Harry Truman." That's how easy it is to retire from the floodlights of the world theater into the shadowy wings of one's own Missouri town.

If you have planned well for October in Missouri, you will be in Kansas City toward the end of the month. That is when you can visit the American Royal Livestock and Horse Show, greatest spectacle in the state, and see this "Gateway to the West" at its glittering finest. There will be cowmen in the best hotels and night clubs, and their wives and daughters will be buying smart clothes in the shops, side by side with oil heiresses from Kansas and Oklahoma. For just as St. Louis faces the East Coast and Europe, this town looks squarely westward. And do not believe those British novelists who put a silly, dowdy American woman in their books and say she comes from Kansas City. There are more handsome and distinguished-looking women here, on Petticoat Lane, than on any other street I have seen, including Park Avenue and the Waldorf's Peacock Alley.

Over the foundations of its rough-and-ready past, and the morass of Pendergast politics and corruption, Kansas City has held up a crest of high-style urban civilization. Where St. Louis is sedately luxurious, this town is rich but cheerful. In the Hotel Muehlebach, in the magnificent Kansas City Club, in the exclusive River Club—built in 1950 on the summit of Quality Hill overlooking the Missouri and the Kaw rivers—you see people paying for their fun, but *having* it. There is more talk between tables here than in St. Louis, livelier dancing, better eating; and fewer signs of that common malady of the successful—guilty conscience.

Listen to the trenchant voice of Thomas Hart Benton, in *An Artist in America,* written some years after he fled from Paris and New York to make his home in Kansas City: "There is a difference between the precious gentility of the West and that of the East. Your western people are very friendly even when the desire to be of a superior quality runs them into affectation and pose. . . . The better part of the male gentility of the western cities seem to be secretly aware that the antics of a pink coat are not exactly in harmony with the substance of western life. . . . This basic uneasiness keeps them quite human and I must say that, so far, I have not met a really complete ass among them."

This from Mr. Benton is a staggering hyperbole of praise.

The American Royal Livestock and Horse Show, which draws exhibitors and spectators from all over the United States, has its own immense pavilions—six acres of floor space—clinging to the bluff at Twenty-third Street.

In spite of Mr. Benton's aversion to pink coats, there are hunters and steeplechasers shown here that probably cannot be matched in England, and the jodhpurs and hard hats and gentlemanly stocks worn by both sexes, are overwhelming. There are splendid Western saddles, too, and five-gaited horses—out here riders believe that the horse himself should do part of the work—and every other kind from the brewers' big brown Clydesdales to midget ponies.

The cattle and sheep and hog shows take place in the daytime, and draw the working farmer, the livestock broker and the packer. They also draw me, a onetime farmer. For this is the biggest and best livestock show in America—maybe in the whole world.

Also there, in the flesh, are the Missouri mules, the clean-boned "pulling machines" with the trim, pointed ears. And they are never alone in their stalls. These mules are pets—working pets, of course, but closer to the human race than any horse. Ed D. Frazier, veteran mule breeder of Drexel, Missouri, explained it this way: "If we don't stay around here, our mules droop, they don't show well. So mother and the kids and I spell each other. Sure, we sell them, but we sort of hate to. You know, the Rhode Island Democrats wanted me to *give* them a mascot, free for nothing. But I wa'n't that good a Democrat. Besides, you don't just give a Missouri mule away. He's a character and you want to know who's going to handle him. I just told those Yankees they'd have to show me cash and proof they'd treat him right. He's still right here in Missouri where he belongs."